THE COMPLETE WORKS OF SAINT JOHN OF THE CROSS IN THREE VOLUMES: VOLUME III

Uniform with this volume

VOLUME I

GENERAL INTRODUCTION

ASCENT OF MOUNT CARMEL

DARK NIGHT OF THE SOUL

VOLUME II

SPIRITUAL CANTICLE

POEMS

THE COMPLETE WORKS OF SAINT JOHN OF THE CROSS

DOCTOR OF THE CHURCH

Translated and edited by
E. ALLISON PEERS
from the critical edition of
P. SILVERIO DE SANTA TERESA, C.D.

III

LIVING FLAME OF LOVE
CAUTIONS AND COUNSELS
SPIRITUAL SENTENCES AND MAXIMS
LETTERS AND DOCUMENTS
INDICES

THE NEWMAN PRESS
WESTMINSTER, MARYLAND

NIHIL OBSTAT : GEORGIVS SMITH, S.T.D., PH.D.

CENSOR DEPVTATVS

IMPRIMATVR : E. MORROGH BERNARD

VICARIVS GENERALIS

WESTMONASTERII : DIE XXIV SEPTEMBRIS MCMLII

New Edition, revised 1953

Made and printed in Great Britain by
William Clowes and Sons, Limited, London and Beccles

CONTENTS

LIVING FLAME OF LOVE

LIVING FLAME OF LOVE: SECOND REDACTION

CAUTIONS

COUNSELS TO A RELIGIOUS FOR THE ATTAINMENT OF PERFECTION

SPIRITUAL SENTENCES AND MAXIMS

LETTERS AND DOCUMENTS

LETTERS OF SAINT JOHN OF THE CROSS

TRANSLATOR'S APPENDIX TO THE LETTERS

SUNDRY DOCUMENTS

WRITTEN OR SIGNED BY ST. JOHN OF THE CROSS

INDICES

THE COMPLETE WORKS OF SAINT JOHN OF THE CROSS

LIVING FLAME OF LOVE

INTRODUCTION

ONE of the Carmelite followers of St. John of the Cross whose depositions at the Segovian process of 1627 are still extant remarks that the teaching of the Saint so far transcends that of other mystical writers that where they leave off, there it may be said to begin. The reader of the *Spiritual Canticle*, which occupies the preceding volume of the present edition, may well subscribe to this statement. Beyond such sublimity of description, one would suppose, there can only lie the ineffable. Yet it must be agreed that in the *Living Flame of Love*—the shortest of his four great treatises—St. John of the Cross takes us still farther into the mysteries of which he is so rare an exponent and presents us with a work, less tenderly appealing, no doubt, than the *Spiritual Canticle*, but written with greater eloquence and ardour, impetuosity and lyrical fervour, telling of a love more completely refined and of a soul nearer than ever to God.

The poem expounded in the treatise consists of but four stanzas and the preface describes the author's attitude to his own exposition of them.

I have felt some unwillingness . . . to expound these four stanzas . . . for they relate to things so interior and spiritual that words commonly fail to describe them, since spirit transcends sense and it is with difficulty that anything can be said of the substance thereof. For it is hard to speak of that which passes in the depths of the spirit if one have not deep spirituality; wherefore, having little thereof myself, I have delayed writing until now. But now that the Lord appears to have opened knowledge somewhat to me and given me some fervour . . . I have taken courage, knowing for certain that out of my own resources I can say naught that is of any value, especially in things of such sublimity and substance.[1]

[1] [Cf. p. 13, below.]

I

These words indicate that a special preparation has been undergone by one whose writing was habitually of exceptional sublimity, and who, furthermore, was unusually reticent about anything which might redound to his own praise. From the outset of the treatise, therefore, we should be prepared to find that the Saint had reached a point as near as possible to perfection. Although 'in the stanzas which we expounded above' (i.e. the *Spiritual Canticle*), he tells us, in fact, 'we spoke of the most perfect degree of perfection to which a man may attain in this life, which is transformation in God, nevertheless these stanzas treat of a love which is even more completed and perfected within this same state of transformation.' 'There is no reason for marvelling,' he remarks, meeting an objection which might easily be raised by a reader, 'that God should grant such high and rare favours to those souls on whom He bestows consolations. . . . For God said that the Father, the Son and the Holy Spirit would come to him that loved Him and make Their abode in him, and this would come to pass by His making him live and dwell in the Father, the Son and the Holy Spirit, in the life of God.'[1]

In the first stanza, the soul is already transformed in God, and is 'adorned with such a marvellous wealth of gifts and virtues,' and so near to eternal bliss, that it is separated from such bliss only by a frail and delicate web which it entreats God to sunder so that its glorification may be completed.[2] Fit theme for the pen of one who, like St. John of the Cross, could rejoice in what he happily terms 'exercises of love.' Within the soul thus transformed there is held, as it were, a 'feast of the Holy Spirit'; and, now that purgation is past, the soul's intimacy is so 'secure, substantial and delectable' that the devil cannot enter and impede its joy.[3]

Having expressed its desire to be united with God in glory, the soul passes, in the second stanza, to a consideration of the perfections of the Most Holy Trinity, dwelling upon its ineffable happiness as it is cauterized, wounded and touched by that gentle hand. So exquisite is the 'savour of eternal life' which this experience produces that the soul desires to escape, by means of death, that it may know that life in its fullness. 'I die,' it exclaims in the words of St. John of the Cross's own poem, 'because I do not die.'[4]

'May God be pleased to grant me His favour here!' exclaims the Saint before entering upon the commentary to his third stanza, for he

---

[1] Cf. p. 14, below.   [2] [Cf. p. 17, below.]
[3] [Cf. p. 21, below.]   [4] Cf. Vol. II, p. 428.

felt its 'profound meaning' to be as difficult to convey as to understand. The soul now 'gives deepest thanks to its Spouse for the great
favours which it receives from union with Him, for by means of this
union He has given it great and abundant knowledge of Himself
wherewith the faculties and senses . . . have been enlightened and enkindled with love, and can now be illumined, as indeed they are, and
through the heat of love can give light and love to Him Who enkindled
and enamoured them and infused into them such Divine gifts.' This is
so for many reasons—among others because 'the true lover is content
only when all that he is, and all that he is worth and can be worth, and
all that he has and can have, are employed in the Beloved; and the more
of this there is, the greater is the pleasure that he receives in giving it.'[1]
Sublime and profound indeed is the application which follows of the
similitude of the lamp, which, with its double office of giving light
and burning, represents the wonderful effects of the love of God within
purified souls—that is, where the terrible purgations of sense and spirit
have formed the 'deep caverns of sense.'

When St. John of the Cross reaches this point, his ardour abates
for a time, and he follows, rather sadly, a line of thought suggested by
an abuse of too frequent occurrence in the world of the spirit—the
unskilled direction of souls that have reached the highest stages of
Christian perfection. So greatly was he oppressed by this impediment
to sanctity that he allows himself to discuss it in a long digression
which fills no less than one-fifth of his entire treatise[2]. Concurrently
with his exposure of the harm caused by unskilful direction—a theme
which is also treated by St. Teresa—he makes a rapid synthesis, on the
lines laid down in the *Ascent* and the *Dark Night*, of the progress of
the soul from the moment of its initiation into the spiritual life to its
transformation in God through love.

The commentary on the fourth stanza finds the author once more
immersed in the theme of Divine love. With ineffable tenderness the
soul describes to the Beloved His awakening within it and His secret
indwelling. After developing at some length the various manners of
this awakening, the Saint passes to the delectable aspiration of God
within the soul, but here at length words fail him and he breaks the
strings of his lyre, leaving the last lines of the poem practically without
commentary.

[1] Cf. p. 53, below.
[2] For the reader's convenience, the *editio princeps* divided this commentary into seventeen paragraphs, which, however, we do not observe, as in this edition the whole treatise
is divided into numbered paragraphs.

The period at which the *Living Flame of Love* was written can be fixed within narrow limits—i.e. between May 1585 and April 1587, a period during which the Saint was Vicar-Provincial of the Order in Andalusia.[1] This we know from P. Juan Evangelista, who tells us that the author composed the treatise in a fortnight, without abandoning any of his obligations or duties as Vicar-Provincial. There seems no reason to doubt the exactness of this statement. Difficulty has been found in the fact that the *Canticle* contains a reference to the *Living Flame*,[2] while the *Living Flame* mentions the *Canticle*.[3] But, if we admit the authenticity of both redactions of the *Canticle*, this is easily explained, for it is in the second redaction of that commentary that we find the former of the two quotations. The first redaction, as we have said, was written in 1584, some months before the *Living Flame* could possibly have been begun, while the second redaction must have been completed by August 1586, a date which not only falls well within the limits for the composition of the *Living Flame*, but gives us the likelier of the two possible years in which it might have been composed, since during the second year of his vicariate the Saint travelled much more widely than during the first, which saw him in Granada almost continuously.

Both the stanzas known as the *Living Flame* and the commentary upon them were composed, as we learn from the Prologue, at the repeated entreaty of the Saint's spiritual daughter, Doña Ana de Peñalosa, a Segovian widow living in Granada with her brother and a generous benefactress of the Discalced Reform in her native city.[4] Not unnaturally, considering the scanty leisure which he had had for writing it, St. John of the Cross revised it some time after it was written and thus gave us the second redaction which is included in this edition with the first. There is ample external evidence for the authenticity of this second redaction, which was made during the last months of his life at La Peñuela.[5] Here he lived for about six weeks before illness overtook him, and for some two months altogether. Both P. Jerónimo de San José[6] and P. José de Jesús María[7] refer to the Saint's being occupied there with the revision of 'the last of his mystical treatises,' and Francisco de San Hilarión, who lived with him at this time,

[1] Cf. Vol. I, p. xxviii.
[2] Stanza XXXI, Second Redaction [Vol. II, p. 342].
[3] Prologue [p. 14, below].
[4] Cf. Letters XXIV, XXVIII [pp. 272, 275, below], which are addressed to Doña Ana del Mercado y Peñalosa.
[5] Cf. Vol. I, p. xxviii.
[6] *Historia*, etc., Bk. VII, chap. iii, p. 709.   [7] *Vida*, Bk. III, chap. xiv.

describes how he would go out daily to pray in the garden before sunrise, then come in to say Mass and finally return to his cell for prayer or 'the writing of some small books (*libricos*) which he left upon certain stanzas.'[1] Although the name of this commentary is not given, the use of the diminutive termination and the fact that the Saint's other commentaries are earlier in date makes it probable that the *Living Flame* is referred to. Nor does the evidence end here. The existence of some very early copies of this treatise, which we shall describe later, enables us to judge, from internal as well as from external testimony, the genuineness of the second redaction, the probability of which, in our view, is so great as to amount practically to certainty.

The revision is chiefly concerned with the commentary upon the first three stanzas, which varies considerably in the two versions; the commentaries on the fourth stanza are almost identical until near the end. In the original Spanish, the second version is almost exactly one-seventh longer than the first. The doctrinal content of the book is unaffected; the additions are chiefly designed to amplify or clarify; of omissions there are very few. Occasionally a new paragraph (such as the fifteenth of the commentary on the first stanza) seems to have been inserted to meet some particular difficulty caused by the sublimity of the Saint's instruction. No new stanzas are introduced, nor is the order of the stanzas changed as in the *Spiritual Canticle*.

The principal critic to combat the genuineness of the second redaction of the *Living Flame* is M. Baruzi,[2] who holds that 'certains affadissements d'ordre littéraire sont assez troublants,' and then proceeds to discuss what he considers graver objections. He cites, for example, the phrase '(endeavouring to persuade love to set it free) from the knot of this life,' which in the second redaction becomes 'from mortal flesh.'[3] In the first phrase he finds 'energy,' which disappears in the second. We do not ourselves see any great improvement in the alteration, but we certainly fail to find any great *affadissement* in it. In any case, M. Baruzi has been unfortunate in his example, for the 'energetic' words 'from the knot of this life' are an addition of the *editio princeps* to the reading of the manuscripts, and only two manuscripts have 'from mortal flesh.' Furthermore, it may be added that the Saint did, to our certain knowledge, make numerous corrections as insignificant as this in his own manuscripts. So much is proved by

[1] N.L.M., MS. 12,738, fol. 17.
[2] *Saint Jean de la Croix*, Paris, 1924, pp. 35–42; 1931 (2nd edition), pp. 33–40.
[3] Stanza I, § 2 [pp. 18, 107, below].

the Sanlúcar codex of the *Spiritual Canticle*, where we find frequent marginal emendations made in what is beyond all doubt St. John of the Cross's own hand.

A more serious objection made by M. Baruzi to the genuineness of the second redaction is what he alleges to be its weakening of the thought and expression of the first. Before the objection could be considered valid it would be necessary to show that the changes made are not in conformity either with his thought or with the form which he gives to his writings, and this we believe to be impossible. To our own mind the majority of the changes strengthen the original rather than weaken it, as, for example, with the two passages beginning 'For in this preparatory state of purgation . . .'[1] which the reader can compare for himself. In the original text the Saint had explained only why the flame was 'not sweet, but grievous'; in the revised text he enlarges upon other of its qualities. There are many similar examples of this type of treatment.

M. Baruzi considers, further, that in the second redaction he finds 'le souci de diminuer en quelque sorte l'ardeur mystique et de rappeler le plus souvent possible que les états humains, même les plus hauts, ne sont qu'une très imparfaite image de la vie de gloire.' He cites two examples of this, both taken from the commentary on the line: 'That tenderly woundest my soul in its deepest centre.'

'The centre of the soul,' says the first redaction, 'is God; and, when the soul has attained to Him according to the whole capacity of its being. . . .'[2] The second redaction omits the word 'whole,' which, according to M. Baruzi, disfigures the passage. Once again, his example is not happily chosen, for both Codex 17,950 (S), which we normally follow, and Codex 8,795 (Bz) have the word 'whole,' which will be found in our edition.[3] The other MSS. omit the word, and P. Gerardo, whose edition is used by M. Baruzi, follows them. In any case, no part of the sense is strictly lost in Spanish by the omission of the word: 'the capacity of its being' means 'the whole capacity of its being'; the adjective simply gives emphasis.

No better founded is the objection that the second redaction continually insists that even the highest human states are only an imperfect image of the life of bliss. We reproduce the passages chosen by M. Baruzi from Stanza I, §§ 12–13, in illustration of this thesis.

---

[1] [Cf. pp. 25, 115, below.]
[2] [P. 22, below.]
[3] [P. 111, below.]

First Redaction

The centre of the soul is God; and, when the soul has attained to Him according to the whole capacity of its being, and according to the force of its operation, it will have reached the last and the deep centre of the soul, which will be when with all its powers it loves and understands and enjoys God; and so long as it attains not as far as this, although it be in God, Who is its centre by grace and by His own communication, still, if it has the power of movement to go farther and strength to do more, and is not satisfied, then, although it is in the centre, it is not in the deepest centre, since it is capable of going still farther.[1]

Second Redaction

The centre of the soul is God; and, when the soul has attained to Him according to the whole capacity of its being, and according to the force of its operation and inclination, it will have reached its last and deepest centre in God, which will be when with all its powers it understands and loves and enjoys God; and, so long as it has not attained as far as this, *as is the case in this mortal life, wherein the soul cannot attain to God with all its powers*, then, although it be in this its centre, which is God, by grace and by His own communication which He has with it, still, inasmuch as it has the power of movement and strength to go farther, and is not satisfied, then, although it may be in the centre, it is nevertheless not in the deepest centre, since it is capable of going to the deepest centre of God.[2]

M. Baruzi's second example, taken from the same commentary (§ 13), runs thus:

First Redaction

And thus, when the soul says that the flame wounds it in its deepest centre, it means that it wounds it in the farthest point attained by its own substance and virtue and power. This it says to indicate the copiousness and abundance of its glory and delight, which is the greater and the more tender when the soul is the more fervently and substantially transformed and centred in God. This is something much greater than comes to pass in the ordinary union of love. . . . For this soul, which is now in such sweetness and glory, and the soul that enjoys only the ordinary union of love, are in a certain way comparable respectively to the fire of God, which, says Isaias, is in Sion, and which signifies the Church Militant, and to the furnace of God which was in Jerusalem and which signifies the vision of peace.[3]

---

[1] § 12, p. 22, below.
[2] P. 111, below. The italics are M. Baruzi's.
[3] Pp. 23–24, below

SECOND REDACTION

And thus, when the soul says here that the flame *of love* wounds it in its deepest centre, it means that the Holy Spirit wounds and assails it in the farthest point attained by its own substance, virtue and power. *This it says, not because it desires to indicate here that this flame wounds it as substantially and completely as it will do*[1] *in the beatific vision of God in the life to come.* . . . And thus these two kinds (of union)—that is, of union alone, and of love and union with enkindling of love—are in a certain way comparable respectively to the fire of God, which, says Isaias, is in Sion, and to the furnace of God which is in Jerusalem. The one signifies the Church Militant . . . and the other signifies the vision of peace, *which is the (Church) Triumphant.*[2]

We can see no such fundamental divergence as M. Baruzi finds in these passages. The author of the additions and emendations does no more than adapt the commentary to the aim set down in the exposition to the stanza, in order to make it clearer and more definite, possibly with the less instructed of his readers in view who would otherwise find it obscure. In the Exposition the Saint describes, so clearly that he who runs may read, how the soul that sees itself 'adorned with . . . a marvellous wealth of gifts and virtues' longs to achieve union with God in glory, the only obstacle to which is its earthly life; to which end it entreats 'this flame, which is the Holy Spirit,' to 'break the web of this sweet encounter.'[3] This is the theme of the whole of the *Living Flame*: it is only natural that, in revising his own work, the Saint should try to bring it out more clearly.

Finally, M. Baruzi remarks upon a few modifications of detail, which, taken together with the fundamental changes already noted, he considers of cumulative significance. The figure of fire and flame, he says, in itself so natural and simple, is of frequent occurrence in the first redaction, but to the author of the second seemed insufficiently clear. So we find in the first (Stanza I, § 15) 'for it must be known that this flame,'[4] which the second amplifies to read, 'for it must be known that this flame, which is God.'[5] In the next paragraph, again, the second redaction reminds the reader that 'this flame' of the first redaction 'is the Holy Spirit.'[6] Once more, in the second of the longer passages cited above, the Holy Spirit is quite unnecessarily introduced into the later redaction.

---

[1] [*Lit.*, 'that this is as substantial and complete as'.]
[2] Pp. 112–113, below. The italics are M. Baruzi's.
[3] P. 17, below.   [4] P. 25, below.
[5] [*Lit.*, 'this flame of God.' P. 114, below.]   [6] [Pp. 25, 114, below.]

But if, in the first redaction, and at the very beginning of his commentary, St. John of the Cross had made this formal comparison between the flame and the Holy Spirit, why should it be considered unnatural that, in revising his work, he should repeat it for the better understanding of his doctrine? Such modifications appear to us to be an argument in favour of the authenticity of the second redaction rather than against it.

But why, it may be asked (as M. Baruzi has asked), was the *Living Flame* published according to the first redaction rather than according to the second? It is undeniable, as the most superficial comparison of the second redaction with the *editio princeps* will suffice to show, that there is no kind of relation between these. But the answer casts no reflection on the authenticity of the second redaction—it is simply that it was unknown until P. Andrés de la Encarnación discovered it in collating the various copies of the commentary with a view to preparing his own projected edition. P. Andrés himself held it to be genuine and would certainly have published it had his edition ever been completed.[1]

It will be relevant here to quote a few lines copied by P. Andrés on a blank sheet at the end of MS. P of the second redaction:

This manuscript has revealed the fact that our father St. John of the Cross wrote a second time, or revised, the book of the *Flame of Love*, for there are found in it many things which are not to be seen either in the work as printed or in many old manuscripts which agree with it, and also many additions and things set down at greater length and more clearly, which it is evident cannot be the work of any other hand than that of the glorious father. . . .[2]

From this note it is clear that nothing was previously known about the second redaction of the *Living Flame*, and also that the examination of it made by P. Andrés, who, as we have seen, was no mean critic, led him to think very highly of it. The editors who followed immediately upon P. Salablanca were content to reproduce his edition, for the most part quite uncritically. If the second redaction of the *Spiritual Canticle* escaped attention for so long, despite its additional stanza, its annotations and additional passages of commentary, it is easy to understand how that of the *Living Flame* should have been overlooked, its additions and modifications being, relatively speaking, so few. There are fewer copies extant of the second redaction of the *Living Flame* than of

[1] [Cf. Vol I, pp. lxvii, ff.]
[2] [The remainder of the note, which is not relevant to the discussion, will be found in P Silverio, Vol. IV, pp. xxii–xxiii.]

the *Spiritual Canticle*, nor are these copies as satisfactory. We now describe the manuscripts of each redaction.

MANUSCRIPTS OF THE FIRST REDACTION

Toledo. The Codex belonging to the Discalced Carmelite nuns of Toledo which contains the *Dark Night* [cf. Vol. I, p. 321] also contains a copy of the *Living Flame*. It is written in several hands and probably dates from the end of the sixteenth century.

Sacro Monte. At the end of the *Canticle* as it appears in this manuscript [Vol. II, p. 10] is a copy of the *Living Flame* with the title 'Exposition of the stanzas which treat of the very intimate and perfected union and transformation of the soul in God, (made) at the request of Sra. Doña Ana de Peñalosa by him who composed them.' With few and unimportant exceptions, this copy, which was made at the same time as that of the *Canticle* in the same Codex, agrees with the foregoing, even in the infrequent phrases which it omits.

Córdoba. This fine copy, which belongs to the Discalced Carmelite nuns of Córdoba, is entitled 'Exposition of the stanzas which treat of the very intimate and perfected union of the soul with God, composed and expounded by the holy father Fray John of the Cross, religious of the Order of Our Lady of Carmel, the first man to assume the Discalced habit.' The copy dates from the Saint's own time, and is in a large, clear hand; there are a good many copyist's slips but few variants of importance.

MS. 18,160. An early copy in a legible hand, containing also the *Ascent* and the *Dark Night* [cf. Vol. I, pp. 7, 323]. The Prologue is missing from this copy, as are also the note referring to Boscán [p. 16, below] and III, § 53, together with various shorter passages. The copy also has numerous variants.

MS. 6,624. This MS., dated 1755, we have described in Vol. I, pp. 6, 321. The copy of the *Living Flame* agrees almost exactly with that of the Toledo MS.

Alba de Tormes. Described in Vol. I, pp. 5–6, 321. The copy of the *Living Flame* follows that of the *Spiritual Canticle* and is prefaced only by the words 'Via illuminativa.' It is in a much more unsatisfactory condition than that of any of the other three treatises which with it comprise the Codex. Long passages of the commentary on each stanza are omitted, and only the first and the last paragraphs are copied of the seventeen into which the editions divide the commentary on the line 'The deep caverns of sense.' The impression which the copy gives is that the amanuensis was anxious to complete his work at the first possible moment.

Pamplona. Described in Vol. I, pp. 7, 323. On p. 230 of this Codex, under the title 'Of how the soul must behave which God sets in the dark night of the spirit,' we read: 'The same holy father, Fray John of the Cross, explaining certain stanzas which he composed on the intimate union of the soul with God which begin "O, living flame of love,"' says as follows in his explanation of the third stanza on that line 'The deep caverns of sense.' The copy then begins at III, § 27 of our edition, and continues, with slight variants and numerous long omissions, as far as III, § 58. It thus has no critical value.

Manuscripts of the Second Redaction

MS. 17,950 (N.L.M.). The copy of the *Living Flame* begins: 'I.H.S. Exposition of the Stanzas which treat of the very intimate and perfected union and transformation of the soul in God, by the father Fray John of the Cross, Discalced Carmelite, at the request of Doña Ana de Peñalosa, composed in prayer in the same year 1584.' The copy is in a woman's hand and has no corrections. P. Andrés tells us that it belonged to the Discalced Carmelite nuns of Seville; no doubt the copyist (certainly an Andalusian) was one of the nuns. A peculiarity of this MS. is that the Prologue is signed by St. John of the Cross. The transcription, which dates from the time of the Saint, is well done; there are practically no omissions; and the copyist's errors are easily rectified. On the whole, the copy is a very satisfactory one and may well serve as basis for the edition of this second redaction.

Cordoba. A fine copy in a man's hand and of the same period as MS. 17,950. It originally belonged to a Discalced Carmelite *desierto* in the Sierra of Córdoba and in the eighteenth century came into the possession of the Discalced Carmelite nuns of Córdoba. Besides having a title similar to that of MS. 17,950, but rather shorter, it has a sub-title of contemporary date: 'Stanzas made by the soul in the last union in God.' The copy agrees closely with that of Seville and has scarcely any serious errors.

MS. 8,795. Described in Vol. I, p. 321. The *Living Flame* is reproduced substantially as in the two preceding MSS., under the title 'Stanzas made by the soul in the last union with God, made and commented by the father Fray John of the Cross.' The first eighteen folios are in a small and bad hand and the remainder in a much better hand. In the commentary on the third stanza are added some late corrections.

This is one of the MSS. recommended by P. Andrés for his edition of the *Living Flame*.

Palencia. A well-written copy in an excellent state of preservation, but unsatisfactory from the critical standpoint, as P. Andrés noted. It is contemporary with, or perhaps rather later than, the last years of the Saint's life.

Burgos. A generally correct MS. dating from the late eighteenth century. The version of the *Living Flame* follows the Palencia MS., from which it seems to be copied. The title is identical with that of the Sacro Monte MS. (first redaction) save that there are added the words 'namely the father Fray John of the Cross, Discalced Carmelite.'

A note may be added on the principal editions of the *Living Flame*. The *editio princeps* introduces many variants, and occasionally omits passages, and even whole paragraphs, though normally short ones. It also regularly omits the Latin texts of the Scriptural quotations. But many of the changes it makes aim at clarifying the Saint's exposition and the editions which follow it depart from it very little.

P. Gerardo's edition (1912) gave precedence to the second redaction over the first, which it printed as an appendix. Our own proceeding is to give both redactions their full weight; as a basis for the first we have used the Toledo MS., and, for the second, that of Seville.

The following abbreviations are used in the footnotes:

First Redaction

A=MS. of the Discalced Carmelite Friars of Alba de Tormes.
B=MS. 6,624 (N.L.M.).
C=MS. of the Discalced Carmelite Nuns of Córdoba.
G=MS. 18,160 (N.L.M.).
Gr=MS. Sacro Monte, Granada.
P=MS. of the Discalced Carmelite Nuns of Pamplona.
T=MS. of the Discalced Carmelite Nuns of Toledo.

Second Redaction

Bg=MS. of the Discalced Carmelite Friars of Burgos.
Bz=MS. 8,795 (N.L.M.).
C=MS. of the Discalced Carmelite Nuns of Córdoba.
P=MS. of the Discalced Carmelite Nuns of Palencia.
S=MS. 17,950 (N.L.M.).

The *editio princeps* (Alcalá, 1618) is referred to throughout as e.p.

LIVING FLAME OF LOVE

Exposition of the stanzas which treat of the most intimate and perfected union and transformation of the soul in God, written at the request of Doña Ana de Peñalosa by the author of the stanzas themselves.[1]

PROLOGUE[2]

I HAVE felt some unwillingness, most noble and devout lady,[3] to expound these four stanzas which you have[4] requested me to explain, for they relate to things so interior and spiritual that words commonly fail to describe them, since spirit transcends sense and it is with difficulty that anything can be said of the substance thereof. For it is hard to speak of that which passes in the depths of the spirit[5] if one have not deep spirituality; wherefore, having little thereof myself, I have delayed writing until now. But now that the Lord appears to have opened knowledge somewhat to me and given me some fervour[6] (which must arise from your devout desire, for perhaps, as these words have been written for you, His Majesty desires them to be expounded for you)[7] I have taken courage, knowing for certain that out of my own resources I can say naught that is of any value, especially in things of such sublimity and substance. Wherefore my part herein will be limited to the defects and errors that this book may contain, for which reason I submit it all to the better judgment and understanding

---

[1] The MSS. vary greatly here. We follow Gr. B and T have neither title nor sub-title. A has only the words: 'Unitive Way.' The same is true of the MSS. of the second redaction (cf. p. 103, below). E.p. reads: 'Living Flame of Love and Exposition of the stanzas which treat of the most intimate union and transformation of the soul with God, by the venerable Father Fray John of the Cross, first discalced friar of the Reform of our Lady of Carmel and coadjutor of the blessed Mother St. Teresa of Jesus, foundress of the same Reform.'

[2] G omits the prologue.

[3] E.p. omits: 'most noble and devout lady.'

[4] E.p. substitutes 'they' for 'you.'

[5] E.p. abbreviates: 'since spirit transcends sense and it is hard to speak of the depths of the spirit.'

[6] E.p.: 'some fervour of spirit.' [Cf. the 'certain degree of fervour' of *Spiritual Canticle*, Prologue (Vol. II, p. 23, of this edition).]

[7] E.p. omits the parenthesis.

13

of our Mother[1] the Roman Catholic Church, under whose guidance no man goes astray. And, with this preamble, relying upon Divine Scripture, and making clear that all which is said herein is as far removed from all that there is to say as is a picture from a living person, I shall make bold to say that which I know.[2]

2. And there is no reason for marvelling that God should grant such high and rare favours[3] to those souls on whom He bestows consolations. For if we consider that He is God, and that He bestows them as God, with infinite love and goodness, it will not seem to us unreasonable. For God said that the Father, the Son and the Holy Spirit would come to him that loved Him and make Their abode in him,[4] and this would come to pass by His making him live[5] and dwell in the Father, the Son and the Holy Spirit, in the life of God, as the soul explains in these stanzas.

3. For although in the stanzas which we expounded above[6] we spoke of the most perfect degree of perfection to which a man may attain in this life, which is transformation in God, nevertheless these stanzas treat of a love which is even more completed[7] and perfected within this same state of transformation. For, although it is true that both these stanzas and those speak of a state of transformation beyond which, as such, a soul cannot pass, yet none the less, with time and practice, as I say, the soul may become more completely perfected and grounded in love. Even so, when a log of wood has been set upon the fire, it is transformed into fire and united with it; yet, as the fire grows hotter and the wood remains upon it for a longer time, it glows much more and becomes more completely enkindled, until it gives out sparks of fire and flame.

4. And it is of [8] this degree of enkindled love that the soul must be understood as speaking when it is at last transformed and perfected interiorly in the fire of love; not only is it united with this fire[9] but it has now become one living flame within it. Such the soul feels itself to be, and as such it speaks in these stanzas, with an intimate and delicate

---

[1] E.p.: 'our holy Mother.'
[2] E.p. modifies thus: 'relying upon Divine Scripture, and observing that all which is said herein is much less than that which happens in that intimate union with God, I shall make bold to say that which I know.'
[3] Gr: 'such high and great and rare favours.'
[4] St. John xiv, 23.
[5] A: 'making him come.'
[6] [i.e., in the 'Spiritual Canticle.']
[7] C: 'treat of that which is greater and more completed.'
[8] [Lit., 'in.']
[9] [Lit., 'in this fire.'] E.p.: 'with this Divine fire.'

sweetness of love, burning in the flame thereof, and extolling in these stanzas certain effects thereof which are wrought in itself.[1] These I shall expound in the same order as with the other stanzas, setting them down first all together, then setting down each stanza and expounding it briefly, and finally setting down each line and expounding it by itself alone.

[1] E.p.: 'burning in the flame thereof and considering here certain marvellous effects thereof which are wrought in itself.'

END OF THE PROLOGUE

STANZAS OF THE SOUL

IN THE INTIMATE COMMUNICATION OF UNION OF THE LOVE OF GOD

1. Oh, living flame of love   That tenderly woundest my soul in its deepest centre,
    Since thou art no longer oppressive, perfect me now if it be thy will,   Break the web of this sweet encounter.

2. Oh, sweet burn!   Oh, delectable wound!   Oh, soft hand! Oh, delicate touch
    That savours of eternal life and pays every debt!   In slaying, thou hast changed death into life.

3. Oh, lamps of fire,   In whose splendours[1] the deep caverns of sense which were dark and blind
    With strange brightness   Give heat and light together to their Beloved!

4. How gently and lovingly thou awakenest in my bosom,
    Where thou dwellest secretly and alone!
    And in thy sweet breathing, full of blessing and glory,   How delicately thou inspirest my love![2]

---

[1] A, B, T: 'Of whose splendours.'

[2] The MSS., with the exception of G, here add the following note, which is omitted from e.p. [and from all later editions until that of 1912]: 'The arrangement of these *liras* resembles that of those which in Boscán are adapted in a divine [i.e., spiritual] sense [*vueltas a lo divino*], and which say:

> La soledad siguiendo,
> Llorando mi fortuna,
> Me voy por los caminos, que se ofrecen, etc.

In these there are six feet [i.e. lines], of which the fourth rhymes with the first, the fifth with the second, and the sixth with the third.'

[The reference is to an adaptation *a lo divino* made by Sebastián de Córdoba (*Las Obras de Boscán y Garcilaso trasladadas en materias cristianas y religiosas*, Granada, 1575) of the first lines of Garcilaso's 'Canción segunda.' On this, see J. Baruzi, *Saint Jean de la Croix*, etc., Paris, 1924, pp. 108–12, Dámaso Alonso, *La Poesía de San Juan de la Cruz*, Madrid, 1942, pp. 47–90, and Emeterio G. S. de Jesús María, O.C.D., *Las Raíces de la poesía sanjuanista y Dámaso Alonso*, Burgos, 1950, pp. 80–6. In his *Poesía española*, Madrid, 1950, Sr. Alonso returns to the subject (pp. 287–9), and also (pp. 229 ff.) makes some interesting remarks on these adaptations *a lo divino* in general.]

16

STANZA THE FIRST

**Oh, living flame of love   That tenderly woundest my soul in its deepest centre,
Since thou art no longer oppressive, perfect me now if it be thy will,   Break the web of this sweet encounter.**

EXPOSITION

THE soul feels itself to be at last wholly enkindled[1] in Divine union, its palate to be wholly bathed in glory and love, and from the very inmost part of its substance to be flowing veritable rivers of glory, abounding in delights, for it perceives[2] that from its belly are flowing the rivers of living water which the Son of God[3] said would flow from such souls.[4] It seems to this soul that, since it is transformed in God with such vehemence and is in so lofty a way possessed of Him, and is adorned with such a marvellous wealth of gifts and virtues, it is very near to bliss, from which it is divided only by a slender web.[5] And, seeing that that delicate flame of love that burns within it is, as it were, glorifying it with a glory both gentle and powerful[6] whensoever it assails it, to such a degree that, whensoever it is so absorbed and assailed, it believes that it is about to enter upon eternal life and that this web of mortal life will be broken, and that there remains but a very short space of time, yet during this space it cannot be perfectly glorified in its essence, the soul addresses[7] this flame, which is the Holy Spirit, with great yearning, begging Him now to break this its mortal life in that sweet encounter, so that of a truth He may communicate to it perfectly that which it believes Him to be about to give to it and to work in it whensoever He meets it[8]—namely, complete and perfect glory. And thus the soul says:

Oh, living flame of love

[1] A: 'transformed.'
[2] E.p. abbreviates: 'in Divine union and transformed through love in God, for it perceives.'
[3] E.p.: 'which Christ Our Lord.'   [4] St. John vii, 38.
[5] E.p.: 'slender and delicate web.' A: 'thin web.'
[6] E.p.: 'with gentle foretastes of glory.'
[7] E.p. abbreviates: 'will be broken, the soul addresses.'
[8] E.p. omits: 'and to work in it whensoever He meets it.'

17

2. In order to extol the fervour and delight wherewith it speaks in these four stanzas, the soul begins each of them with the word 'Oh' or 'How,' which words signify affectionate exultation. Each time that they are used they show that something is passing within the soul beyond that which can be expressed by the tongue. And the word 'Oh' serves also to express a deep yearning and earnest supplication with the aim of persuasion; for both these reasons the soul uses that word in this stanza, intimating and extolling its great desire, and endeavouring to persuade love to set it free.[1]

3. This flame of love is the Spirit of its Spouse—that is, the Holy Spirit. And this flame the soul feels within it, not only as a fire that has consumed and transformed it in sweet love, but also as a fire which burns within it and sends out flame, as I have said, and that flame bathes the soul in glory and refreshes it with the temper of Divine life.[2] And this is the operation of the Holy Spirit in the soul that is transformed in love, that the acts that He performs within it cause it to send out flames, which are the enkindling of love,[3] wherein the will of the soul is united, and it loves most deeply,[4] being made one with that flame in love.[5] And thus these acts of love of the soul are most precious, and even one of them is of greater merit and worth than all that the soul may have done in its life apart from this transformation, however much this may be.[6] Like to the difference that exists between a habit and an act is that which exists between transformation in love and the flame of love; it is the same difference as that between the log of wood that is enkindled and the flame which it sends forth, for the flame is the effect of the fire that burns there.

4. Wherefore the soul that is in a state of transformation of love may be said to be, in its ordinary habit, like to the log of wood that is continually assailed by the fire; and the acts of this soul are the flame that arises from the fire of love: the more intense is the fire of union,[7] the more vehemently does its flame issue forth. In the which flame the acts of the will are united and rise upward, being carried away and absorbed in the flame of the Holy Spirit, even as the angel rose upward

---

[1] E.p. adds: 'from the knot of this life.'
[2] E.p.: 'of eternal life.'
[3] [*Lit.*, 'enkindlings.'] C omits: 'which are the enkindling of love.'
[4] C: 'most sweetly.'
[5] [*Lit.*, 'being made one love.'] E.p.: 'being made one thing with that flame through love.'
[6] [The Spanish adds: 'etc.'] E.p. abbreviates: 'is of greater merit than many more that the soul may have done.'
[7] C: 'the fire of the love of union.'

to God in the flame of the sacrifice of Manue.[1] In this state, therefore, the soul can perform no acts, but it is the Holy Spirit that moves it to perform them; wherefore all its acts are Divine, since it is impelled and moved to them by God.[2] Hence it seems to the soul that whensoever this flame breaks forth, causing it to love with the Divine temper and sweetness, it is granting it eternal life, since it raises it to the operation of God in God.[3]

5. This is the language[4] used and employed by God when He speaks to souls that are purified and clean: these words are wholly enkindled, even as David said: 'Thy word is vehemently enkindled.'[5] And the Prophet asked: 'Are not my words as a fire?'[6] These words, as God Himself says through Saint John, are spirit and life,[7] and are felt to be such by souls[8] that have ears to hear them, who, as I say, are souls that are pure and enkindled with love. But those that have not a healthy palate, and desire other things, cannot relish the spirit and life that these words contain; for which reason, the loftier were the words spoken by the Son of God, the more they displeased certain persons because of those persons' impurity,[9] as when the Lord preached that sweet and loving doctrine of the Holy Eucharist, and many of His hearers turned back.[10]

6. Because such persons are not attracted by this language of God, which He speaks inwardly, they must not think that others will not be attracted by it. On the occasion here mentioned it greatly attracted Saint Peter, so that he said to Christ: 'Lord, whither shall we go, for Thou hast the words of eternal life?'[11] And the Samaritan woman forgot her water and her pitcher, because of the sweetness of the words of God. And thus, when this soul is so near to God that it is transformed in the flame of love, wherein Father, Son and Holy Spirit communicate Themselves to it, how is it a thing incredible that it should be said to enjoy a foretaste of eternal life,[12] though this cannot be perfectly so, since that is not permitted by the conditions of this life?

---

[1] [Judges xiii, 20.]

[2] G: 'since they are impelled and moved by God.' E.p.: 'In this present state, therefore, the soul cannot perform these acts save if the Holy Spirit move it very specially thereto; wherefore all its acts are Divine, inasmuch as it is moved in this special way by God.'

[3] E.p.: 'to a Divine operation in God.'

[4] [Lit., 'the language and the words.']

[5] [Psalm cxviii, 140: Ignitum eloquium tuum vehementer.]

[6] Jeremias xxiii, 29.   [7] [St. John vi, 64.]

[8] E.p.: 'and their virtue and efficacy are felt by souls.'

[9] E.p.: 'the more insipid did certain persons find them because of the impurity of those who heard them.'

[10] St. John vi, 67.   [11] St. John vi, 69.

[12] G: 'commune with it, it can certainly be said that it enjoys eternal life.'

But the delight caused in the soul by that flaming of the Holy Spirit is so sublime that it teaches the soul what is the savour of eternal life. For that reason it speaks of the flame as living[1]; not that it is not always living, but because its effect is to make the soul live spiritually in God, and experience the life of God, even as David says: 'My heart and my flesh have rejoiced in the living God.'[2] There was no necessity for him to use the word 'living,' since God is ever living; he uses it to show that spirit and sense had a living experience of God, being wrought in God—which is to have experience[3] of the living God, that is to say, the life of God and life eternal. David spoke in that passage of the living God because he had had experience of Him in a living manner, albeit not perfectly, but he had had as it were a foretaste of eternal life.[4] And thus in this flame the soul has so living a perception of God and experiences Him with such great sweetness and delight that it says: 'Oh, living flame of love!'

That tenderly woundest

7. That is, that touchest me tenderly with Thy love. For, inasmuch as this flame is a flame of Divine life, it wounds the soul with the tenderness of the life of God; and so deeply and profoundly does it wound it and fill it with tenderness that it causes it to melt in love, so that there may be fulfilled in it that which came to pass to the Bride in the Song of Songs. She conceived such great tenderness that she melted away, wherefore she says in that place: 'When the Spouse spake, my soul melted.'[5] For this is the effect that the speaking of God causes in the soul.

8. But how can we say that this flame wounds the soul, when there is nothing in the soul to be wounded, since it is wholly consumed by the fire of love? It is a marvellous thing: for, as love is never idle, but is continually in motion, it is ever throwing out sparks, like a flame, in every direction; and, as the office[6] of love is to wound, that it may enkindle with love and cause delight, so, when it is as it were a living

---

[1] E.p. abbreviates: 'how is it a thing incredible to say that in this flaming of the Holy Spirit it enjoys a foretaste of eternal life, though this cannot be perfectly, since that is not permitted by the conditions of this life? For this reason it speaks of this flame as living.'

[2] Psalm lxxxiii, 3 [A.V., lxxxiv, 2].

[3] [The word translated 'have experience of' is that rendered 'be attracted by' at the beginning of this paragraph, and 'relish' near the end of the preceding one.]

[4] E.p. gives the Scriptural text in Latin only; then continues with only the slightest variation as far as 'experience of God'; and finally, substitutes for 'being wrought in God' 'and this is to rejoice in the living God.' C has: 'experience of God, which is to have experience of [see last note] the living God—that is, the life of God and eternal life.'

Canticles v, 6.   [6] G: 'the effect.'

flame, within the soul, it is ever sending forth its arrow-wounds, like
most tender sparks of delicate love, joyfully and happily exercising the
arts and playings[1] of love. Even so, in his palace, at his marriage, did
Assuerus show forth his graces to Esther his bride, revealing to her
there his riches[2] and the glory of his greatness.[3] Thus that which the
Wise Man said in the Proverbs is now fulfilled in this soul, namely: 'I
was delighted every day as I played before him at all times,[4] playing
over the whole earth, and my delight is to be with the children of men,
namely, by giving myself to them.'[5] Wherefore these wounds, which
are the playings of God,[6] are the sparks of these tender touches of flame
which touch the soul intermittently and proceed from the fire of love,
which is not idle, but whose flames, says the stanza, strike and wound

My soul in its deepest centre,

9. For this feast of the Holy Spirit takes place in the substance of the
soul, where neither the devil nor the world nor sense can enter;[7] and
therefore the more interior it is, the more is it secure, substantial and
delectable; for the more interior it is the purer is it, and the more of
purity there is in it, the more abundantly and frequently and widely
does God communicate Himself. And thus the delight and rejoicing of
the soul and the spirit is the greater herein because it is God that
works all this and the soul of its own power does naught therein;[8] for
the soul can do naught of itself,[9] save through the bodily senses and by
their help, from which in this case the soul is very free and very far
removed, its only business being the reception of God, Who alone
can work in the depth of the soul, without the aid of the senses, and
can move the soul in that which it does.[10] And thus all the movements
of such a soul are Divine; and, although they come from Him, they
belong to the soul likewise, for God works them in the soul, with its
own aid, since it gives its will and consent thereto.[11] And, since to say

---

[1] E.p.: 'the arts and devices.'
[2] G abbreviates: 'show forth his riches to Esther his bride.' E.p.: 'show forth his riches
to the fair Esther.'
[3] [Esther ii, 17–18.]   [4] G, T, e.p. omit: 'as I played before him at all times.'
[5] [Proverbs viii, 30–1.]   [6] E.p.: 'of Divine knowledge.'
[7] Thus e.p.: The MSS. [and P. Silverio] read: 'where neither the centre of sense nor
the devil can enter.'
[8] E.p. adds: 'in the sense that we shall presently describe.'
[9] E.p.: 'can do naught naturally and by its own industry.'
[10] [Lit., 'in itself in the work.'] G: 'He alone can make the soul work, and can move, etc.'
A, B, omit 'in itself.' C has: 'in itself and in the work.'
[11] E.p.: 'He alone, without the aid of the senses, can work and move the soul and work
within it, in its own depth; and thus all the movements of such a soul are Divine; and,
although they come from God, they belong likewise to the soul.'

that He wounds the soul in its deepest centre is to imply that the soul has other centres which are less deep, it is necessary to explain in what way this is so.

10. In the first place, it must be known that the soul, inasmuch as it is spirit, has not height and depth, nor greater or lesser degrees of profundity in its own being, as have bodies that can be measured.[1] For, since there are no parts in the soul, there is no difference between its inward and its outward being; it is all the same, and it has no depths of greater or lesser profundity in a way that can be measured[2]; for it cannot be more enlightened in one part than in another, as is the case with physical bodies, but the whole of it is enlightened in one manner, either to a greater or to a lesser degree, in the same way as the air is enlightened or unenlightened to a greater or a lesser degree.[3]

11. We term[4] the deepest centre of a thing the farthest point to which its being and virtue and the force of its operation and movement can attain, and beyond which they cannot pass. Thus fire or a stone has natural movement and power, and strength to reach the centre of its sphere, and cannot pass beyond it, neither can help remaining in it, save by reason of some contrary impediment. Accordingly, we shall say that a stone, when it is within the earth, is in[5] its centre, because it is within the sphere of its activity and movement, which is the element of earth; but it is not in the deepest part of that element, which is the middle of the earth, because it still has power and force to descend and to attain thither if that which impedes it be taken away; and when it attains to its centre and there remains to it no more power of its own to move farther, we shall say that it is in the deepest centre.

12. The centre of the soul is God; and, when the soul has attained to Him according to the whole capacity of its being,[6] and according to the force of its operation, it will have reached the last and the deep centre of the soul, which will be when with all its powers it loves and understands and enjoys God; and so long as it attains not as far as this, although it be in God, Who is its centre by grace and by His own communication, still, if it has the power of movement to go farther and strength to do more, and is not satisfied, then, although it is in the centre, it is not in the deepest centre, since it is capable of going still

---

[1] [*Lit.*, 'quantitative bodies,' i.e. bodies that contain matter, have bulk.]

[2] E.p. omits: 'in a way that can be measured.'

[3] G omits: 'and it has no depths . . . measured' and from 'but the whole' to the end of the paragraph. A omits from 'and it has no depths' to the end of the paragraph.

[4] E.p.: 'in the same way as the air. But, setting aside this acceptation of the measurable [*cuantitativa*] and material depth and centre, we term.'

[5] E.p.: 'is, as it were, in.'   [6] E.p.: 'according to its being.'

farther. Love[1] unites the soul with God, and, the more degrees of love
the soul has, the more profoundly does it enter into God and the more
is it centred in Him[2]; and thus[3] we can say that, as are the degrees of
love of God, so are the centres, each one deeper than another,[4] which
the soul has in God; these are the many mansions which, He said, were
in His Father's house.[5] And thus the soul which has one degree of love
is already in its centre in God,[6] since one degree of love suffices for a
soul to abide in Him through grace. If it have two degrees of love, it
will have entered into[7] another and a more interior centre with God;
and, if it attain to three, it will have entered into the third. If it attain to
the last degree, the love of God will succeed in wounding the soul
even in its deepest centre—that is, in transforming and enlightening
it as regards all the being and power and virtue of the soul, such as it is
capable of receiving, until it be brought into such a state that it appears
to be God.[8] In this state the soul is like the crystal that is clear and pure;
the more degrees of light it receives, the greater concentration of light
there is in it, and this enlightenment continues to such a degree that at
last it attains a point at which the light is centred in it with such copiousness that it comes to appear to be wholly light, and cannot be distinguished from the light, for it is enlightened to the greatest possible
extent and thus appears to be light itself.

13. And thus, when the soul says that the flame wounds it in its
deepest centre, it means that it wounds it in the farthest point attained
by its own substance[9] and virtue and power. This it says to indicate
the copiousness and[10] abundance of its glory and delight, which is the
greater and the more tender when the soul is the more fervently and
substantially transformed and centred in God. This is something
much greater than comes to pass in the ordinary union of love, because
of the greater fervency of the fire, which here, as we say, gives forth
living flame. For this soul, which is now in such sweetness and glory,

[1] C adds: 'which is the strength and virtue of the soul.'
[2] G: 'and finds itself with Him.'
[3] E.p.: 'and thus, according to this way of speaking which we are following.'
[4] [Lit., 'one more than another.'] G: 'some more interior than others.'
[5] [St. John xiv, 2.]
[6] E.p.: 'is already in God, Who is its centre.'
[7] [Lit., 'will have centred itself in,' and similarly in the following clause.]
[8] E.p.: 'into the third. And if it attain to a very profound degree of love, the love of
God will succeed in wounding that which we call the deepest [or "profoundest"] centre
of the soul, and the soul will be transformed and enlightened in a very lofty degree,
according to its being, power and virtue, until it be brought into such a state that it is very
like to God.'
[9] E.p.: 'that it wounds it by touching most deeply its own substance.'
[10] E.p.: omits 'copiousness and.'

and the soul that enjoys only the ordinary union of love, are in a certain way comparable respectively to the fire of God[1] which, says Isaias, is in Sion, and which signifies the Church Militant, and to the furnace of God which was in Jerusalem and which signifies the vision of peace.[2] For the soul in this state is like a furnace enkindled, the vision whereof is, as we say, the more peaceful and glorious and tender in proportion as the flame of this furnace is more vehemently enkindled than common fire. And thus, when the soul feels that this living flame is communicating all blessings to it after a living manner, because this Divine love brings everything with it, it says: 'Oh, living flame of love, that tenderly woundest.' This is as though it were to say: Oh, love enkindled, that art tenderly glorifying me with thy loving movements in the greatest capacity and power of my soul, that is to say, art giving me Divine intelligence according to the entire capacity of my understanding, and communicating love to me according to the utmost power of my will, and delighting me in the substance of the soul with the affluence and copiousness of the sweetness of Thy Divine contact and substantial union, according to its utmost purity and the capacity of my memory.[3] This comes to pass in a greater degree than it is possible for the soul to describe at the time when this flame uprises in it.

14. Now, inasmuch as the soul has been purged with respect to its faculties and to its substance,[4] and has been made most pure, Wisdom absorbs it, in a profound and subtle and sublime manner, by means of its flame; the which Wisdom reacheth from one end even to another by reason of her purity.[5] And in that absorption of wisdom the Holy Spirit brings to pass the glorious vibrations of His flame, of which we have spoken; wherefore, since it is so sweet, the soul then says:

Since thou art no longer oppressive,[6]

[1] G abbreviates: 'This is something much greater than in the communion of love, and thus these souls are comparable [respectively] to the fire of God.'

[2] [Isaias xxxi, 9.]

[3] B, Gr, T: 'of my memory and freedom' [anchura: lit., 'breadth']. E.p.: 'according to the utmost freedom of my will: that is, by raising to the greatest height, through the Divine intelligence, the capacity of my understanding, in the most intense fervour of my will, and in a substantial union, as has already been described.'

[4] E.p.: 'Now, inasmuch as the soul has been wholly purged.'

[5] [Wisdom vii, 24.]

[6] [The word esquiva cannot be rendered by a single word. Its commonest meanings fall into two categories: (1) shy, reserved, disdainful; (2) harsh, unsociable, rough-mannered. Apart from the difficulties in the metaphorical use of the second group of these words, however, the definition at the beginning of § 15 suggests the employment of an adjective corresponding to one of the three verbs given which are similar in sense.]

15. That is to say, since thou dost no longer afflict or oppress or weary as thou didst aforetime. For it must be known that this flame, when the soul was in the state of spiritual purgation[1]—that is, when it was entering upon contemplation—was not as friendly[2] and sweet to it as it now is in this state of union. And we must tarry here a little in order to explain how this comes to pass.[3]

16. Here it must be known that, before this Divine fire of love is introduced into the substance of the soul, and is united with it, by means of a purity and purgation which is perfect and complete,[4] this flame is wounding the soul, and destroying and consuming in it the imperfections of its evil habits; and this is the operation of the Holy Spirit, wherein He prepares it for Divine union and the transformation of its substance[5] in God through love. For the same fire of love which afterwards is united with the soul and glorifies it[6] is that which aforetime assailed it in order to purge it; even as the fire that penetrates the log of wood is the same that first of all attacked and wounded it with its flame, cleansing and stripping it of its accidents of ugliness,[7] until, by means of its heat, it had prepared it to such a degree that it could enter it and transform it into itself. In this operation the soul endures great suffering and experiences grievous afflictions in its spirit, which at times overflow into the senses, at which times this flame is very oppressive. For in this preparatory state of purgation the flame is not bright to it, but dark. Neither is it sweet to it, but grievous; for, although at times it kindles within it the heat of love, this is accompanied by torment and affliction. And it is not delectable to it, but arid; it brings it neither refreshment nor peace, but consumes and proves it; neither is it glorious to it, but rather it makes it miserable and bitter, by means of the spiritual light of self-knowledge which it sheds upon it, for God sends fire, as Jeremias says, into its bones,[8] and tries it by fire, as David says likewise.

17. And thus at this time the soul also suffers great darkness in the understanding, many aridities and afflictions in the will and grievous knowledge of its miseries in the memory, for the eye of its spiritual

---

[1] C: 'spiritual perfection.'
[2] E.p.: 'as peaceful.' A reads: 'entering upon contemplation, did not deal with it sweetly as now it does in this state of union.'
[3] E.p. omits this last sentence.
[4] E.p.: 'into the inmost depth of the soul, and is united with it, by means of a perfect purity and purgation.'
[5] E.p.: 'for Divine union and transformation.'
[6] E.p.: 'is united with the soul in this glory of love.'
[7] [*Lit.*, 'its ugly accidents.'] E.p.: 'its cold accidents[*frios* for *feos*].'
[8] [Lamentations i, 13.]

self-knowledge is very bright. And in its substance the soul suffers profoundly from its poverty and abandonment. Dry and cold, and at times hot, it finds relief in naught, nor is there any thought that can console it, nor can it raise its heart to God, since this flame has become so oppressive to it. Even so, says Job, did God treat him in this operation, where he says: 'Thou art changed to be cruel to me.'[1] For, when the soul suffers all these things together, they become like purgatory to it and any description of this falls short of the reality. At times it is indeed very little less terrible than purgatory and I can think now of no way to describe this state of oppression, and that which the soul feels and suffers in it, save by using these words of Jeremias which refer to it: 'I am the man that see my poverty by the rod of His indignation; He hath threatened me and brought me into darkness and not into light; so greatly is He turned against me and turneth His hand. My skin and my flesh He hath made old: He hath broken my bones. He hath builded a wall round about me and hath compassed me with gall and labour. He hath set me in dark places as those that are dead for ever. He hath builded against me round about, that I may not get out. He hath made my imprisonment heavy; yea, and when I have lifted up my voice and cried, He hath shut out my prayer. He hath surrounded my ways with square stones and hath turned my steps and paths upside down.'[2]

18. All this says Jeremias; and he continues at much greater length. Now, since this is the remedy and medicine which God gives to the soul for its many infirmities, that He may bring it health, the soul must needs suffer in the purgation and remedy, according to the nature of its sickness. For here its heart is laid upon the coals, so that every kind of evil spirit is driven away from it;[3] and here its infirmities are continually brought to light and are laid bare before its eyes that it may feel them, and then they are cured. And that which aforetime was hidden and set deep within the soul is now seen and felt by it, in the light and heat of the fire, whereas aforetime it saw nothing. Even so, in the water and smoke that the fire drives out of the wood, are seen the humidity and the frigidity which it had aforetime, though this was realized by none. But now, being brought near to this flame, the soul clearly sees and feels its miseries, for—oh, wondrous thing!—there arise within it contraries against contraries, some of which, as the philosophers[4] say,

---

[1] Job xxx, 21.   [2] Lamentations iii, 1-9.
[3] G: 'so that every kind of torment is wrought within it.'
[4] G: 'the physicists.'

become visible in reacting to others; and they make war in the soul, striving to expel each other in order that they may reign within it. For, as this flame is of brightest light, and assails the soul, its light shines in the darkness of the soul, which is as dark as the light is bright; and then the soul is conscious of its natural darkness, which opposes itself to the supernatural light, and it is not conscious of the supernatural light, because the darkness comprehends it not. And thus it will be conscious of this its natural darkness for so long as the light beats upon it, for souls can have no perception of their darkness until they come near to the Divine light, and only when the darkness has been driven out is the soul illumined and able to see the light, its eye having been cleansed and strengthened. For, to sight that is weak and not clear, infinite light is total darkness and the faculty suffers deprivation through excess of sense.[1]

19. And thus this flame was oppressive to the soul in the sight of its understanding, for, being both loving and tender, the flame assails the will in a loving and a tender manner; and the hardness of the one is felt by comparison with the tenderness of the other and the aridity of the one by comparison with the love of the other. The will is conscious of its natural hardness and aridity with respect to God and is not conscious of love and tenderness; for hardness and aridity cannot comprehend these other contrary things until they are driven out by them and love and tenderness of God reign in the will, for two contraries cannot co-exist in one subject. And in the same way, since this flame is very extensive, the will is conscious of its littleness by comparison with it, and thus it suffers great affliction until it acts upon it and dilates it and gives it greater capacity. And in this way the flame has been oppressive to it according to the will, since the sweet food of love is insipid to a palate that is not weaned from other affections. And finally, since this flame is of vast wealth and goodness and delight, the soul, which of itself has great poverty and has no good thing of its own, nor can give any satisfaction, is clearly conscious of its poverty and misery and wickedness by contrast with this wealth and goodness and delight of the flame (for wickedness comprehends not goodness, and so forth) until this flame succeeds in purifying the soul, and together with transformation gives it riches, glories and delights. In this way the flame was at first oppressive to it, and in this way the soul has ordinarily

---

[1] [The phrase *el excelente sensible* is difficult, and P. Gurdon suggests to me an emendation *excedente*. That this is the sense of the phrase I have little doubt, but the *eminente* of the second redaction hardly justifies a change in the original text.]

to endure the worst possible suffering in its substance and faculties, experiencing great anguish and affliction from the battle which is being waged by the contrary forces within its suffering self. God, Who is all perfection, wars against all the imperfect habits of the soul, and, purifying the soul[1] with the heat of His flame, He uproots these habits from it, and prepares it, so that at last He may enter it and be united with it by His sweet, peaceful and glorious love, as is the fire when it has entered the wood.

20. This severe purgation comes to pass in few souls—in those alone whom He desires to raise to some degree of union by means of contemplation; and those who are to be raised to the highest degree of all are the most severely purged. This happens as follows. When God desires to bring the soul forth from its ordinary state—that is, from its natural way and operation—to a spiritual life, and to lead it from meditation to contemplation, which is a state rather heavenly than earthly, wherein He communicates Himself through union of love, He begins at once to communicate Himself to the spirit, which is still impure and imperfect, and has evil habits, so that each soul suffers according to the degree of its imperfection; and at times this purgation is in some ways as grievous to the soul whom it is preparing for the reception of perfect union here below as is that of purgatory, wherein we are purged in order to see God in the life to come.

21. As to the intensity of this purgation—when it is greater and when less, and when it is according to the will and when according to the understanding or the memory, and when and how it is according to the substance of the soul, and likewise when it affects the entire soul and when its sensual part only, and how it may be known when it is each of these—we have treated this in the *Dark Night* of the *Ascent of Mount Carmel* and it affects not our purpose here, wherefore I say no more of it.[2] It suffices here to know that God Himself,[3] Who desires to enter the soul by union and transformation of love, is He that aforetime was assailing it and purging it with the light and heat of His Divine flame, even as the fire that enters the wood is the same fire that has prepared it before entering it. And thus that very flame[4] that is here

---

[1] C: 'and, shedding Himself upon the soul.' [The word translated 'purifying' is normally applied to leather, and means 'tanning,' 'dressing.']

[2] E.p. omits the whole of § 20, the latter part of § 19, and this first sentence of § 21.

[3] A abbreviates: 'from meditation to contemplation, wherein He communicates Himself through union of love. And finally, abbreviating as much as is possible, it suffices that God Himself.'

[4] E.p. abbreviates: 'of His Divine flame. And thus that very flame.'

sweet to the soul was aforetime bitter[1] to it. It is therefore as if the soul were to say: Since not only art thou not dark to me as thou wert aforetime, but art the Divine light of my understanding,[2] wherewith I can look upon thee, and dost not only not cause my weakness to faint,[3] but art rather the strength of my will wherewith I can love thee and enjoy thee, now that it is wholly converted into Divine love, and since thou art not pain and affliction to the substance of my soul,[4] but art rather its glory and delights and boundless freedom, therefore may there be said of me that which is sung in the Divine Songs,[5] in these words: 'Who is this that cometh up from the desert, abounding in delights, leaning upon her Beloved and scattering love on every side?'[6]

Perfect me now if it be thy will,

22. That is to say: Perfect and consummate the spiritual marriage in me with the beatific vision of Thyself. For, although it is true that in this state that is so lofty, the more completely transformed is the soul the more conformed is it, for it knows nothing of itself, neither is able to ask anything for itself, but all is for its Beloved; for charity seeks nothing of its own, but only the things of the Beloved;[7] nevertheless, since it still lives in hope, and thus cannot fail to be conscious of something that is lacking, it sighs deeply, though with sweetness and joy,[8] in proportion as it still lacks complete possession of the adoption of God's sonship, wherein, when its glory is consummated, its desire will be at rest. This desire, although here below the soul may have closer union[9] with God, will never be satisfied until this glory shall appear,[10] especially if it has already tasted the sweetness and delight thereof,[11] which it has in this state. This sweetness is such that, had God not granted a favour to its flesh, and covered its natural being with His right hand (as He did to Moses in the rock, that he might see His glory and not die,[12] for from this right hand the natural being receives refreshment and delight rather than harm), it would have died at each touch

---

[1] [*esquiva*.]
[2] A omits 'of my understanding.'
[3] A, G omit 'my weakness.'
[4] A, e.p.: 'and affliction to my soul.'
[5] A, G: 'in the Songs.' E: 'which is said in the Songs.'
[6] [Canticles viii, 5. The quotation ends at the word 'Beloved.']
[7] 1 Corinthians xiii, 5. E.p.: 'for it knows nothing, neither seeks to ask anything, and it looks not for itself, but for its Beloved in everything, for charity seeks nothing save the good and glory of the Beloved.'
[8] A omits 'though with sweetness and joy.'
[9] G: 'may be more [closely] united.' E.p.: 'may be more [closely] joined.'
[10] Psalm xvi, 15 [A.V., xvii, 15].
[11] E.p.: 'the delight and the expectation thereof.'
[12] [Exodus xxxiii, 22.]

of this flame, and its natural being would have been corrupted, since its lower part would have no means of enduring so great and sublime a fire.[1]

23. Wherefore this desire and the soul's entreaty for it are not accompanied by pain, for the soul in this state is no longer capable of pain, but its entreaty is made with great sweetness and delight and conformity of the reason and the senses.[2] It is for this reason that it says: 'If it be Thy will.' For the will and desire are to such an extent united with God[3] that the soul regards it as its glory that it should fulfil the will of God in it. Such are the glimpses of glory and such is the love that filters through the crevices of the door, in order that it may enter, though it cannot do so because of the smallness of our earthly house,[4] that the soul would have little love if it entreated not to be allowed to enter into that perfection and consummation of love. Furthermore, the soul now sees that in the power of that delectable communication the Holy Spirit is impelling and inviting it, by wondrous ways and with sweet affections, to that boundless glory which He is setting before its eyes, saying that which is said to the Bride in the Songs, namely: 'See (she says) that which my Spouse is saying to me: "Arise[5] and make haste, my love, my dove, my fair one, and come; for winter is now past and the rain is over and gone and the flowers have appeared in our land. And the time of pruning has come and the voice of the turtle is heard in our land,[6] and the fig tree has put forth her figs and the vines in flower have yielded their fragrance. Arise, my love, my fair one, and come, my dove, into the holes of the rock, into the cavern of the wall; show me thy face; let thy voice sound in my ears; for thy voice is sweet, and thy face comely."'[7] All these things the soul most clearly[8] perceives that the Holy Spirit is saying to her in that sweet and tender flame.[9] Wherefore the soul here makes answer: 'Perfect me now if it be Thy will.' Herein she makes Him those two petitions which in Saint Matthew He[10] commanded us to make: *Adveniat regnum tuum. Fiat*

[1] E.p.: 'it seems that it would have died at each touch of this flame, since its lower part would not have the strength to endure so great and sublime a fire.'
[2] E.p.: 'Wherefore this desire is not accompanied by pain, for the soul in this state is no longer in a condition of pain, but its entreaty is made with great sweetness and delight and conformity.'
[3] E.p. adds: 'each in its own way.'
[4] E.p. omits: 'the crevices . . . earthly house.'
[5] E.p. abbreviates: 'in the Songs: Arise.'
[6] E.p. omits: 'And the time . . . in our land.'
[7] Canticles ii, 10–14.
[8] E.p. omits: 'most clearly.'
[9] [*Lit.*, 'flaming.'] E.p. has 'flame.'
[10] E.p.: 'which Christ our Saviour.'

voluntas tua.[1] This is as much as to say: Give me this kingdom perfectly, as is Thy will, and, that this may come to pass:

Break the web of this sweet encounter.

24. For it is this web which hinders so important a business as this, since it is easy to reach God once the separating obstacles and webs are taken away. These webs which must be broken if we are to possess God perfectly are reduced to three, namely: the temporal, which comprises every creature; the natural, which comprises the operations[2] and inclinations that are purely natural; and the sensual, which comprises only union of the soul in the body, which is sensual and animal life, whereof Saint Paul says: 'We know that if this our earthly house be dissolved we have a dwelling-place of God in the heavens.'[3] The first two webs must of necessity be broken in order that we may attain to this possession of the union of God through love,[4] wherein all things of the world are put aside and renounced,[5] and all the natural affections and appetites are mortified, and the operations of the soul become Divine. All this was broken by the encounters of the soul with this flame when it was oppressive to it; for, in spiritual purgation, as we have said above,[6] the soul succeeds in breaking these two webs and in being united, as it now is, and there remains to be broken only the third web of the life of sense. For this reason the soul here speaks of a web and not of webs; for there is now no other web than this, which, being already so delicate and fine and so greatly spiritualized by this union, is attacked[7] by the flame, not in a severe and oppressive way, as were the others, but sweetly and delectably. And thus the death of such souls is ever[8] sweeter and gentler than was their whole life; for they die amid the delectable encounters and impulses of love, like the swan, which sings most sweetly when it is about to die and is at the point of death.[9] For this reason David said: 'Precious is the death of the just'[10]; for at such a time the rivers of love of the soul are about to enter the sea,[11] and they are so broad and dense and motionless[12] that they seem to

---

[1] St. Matthew vi, 10.   [2] E.p.: 'which comprises all the operations.'
[3] [2 Corinthians v, 1.]
[4] E.p.: 'this possession of God through the union of love.'
[5] Gr: 'denounced.'   [6] E.p. omits: 'as we have said above.'
[7] E.p. abbreviates: 'no other web than this, which is attacked.'
[8] E.p. omits: 'ever.'
[9] E.p. omits: 'and is at the point of death.' [The phrase rendered 'is about to die' may also mean 'wishes to die.']
[10] Psalm cxv, 15 [A.V., cxvi, 15].   [11] E.p.: 'the sea of loving.'
[12] [The word translated 'dense and motionless' is *represados*, 'restrained,' 'dammed up.']

be seas already. The beginning and the end[1] unite together to accompany the just man as he departs and goes forth to his kingdom, and praises are heard from the ends of the earth, which are the glory of the just man.[2]

25. When, at that time, amid these glorious encounters, the soul feels itself very near to[3] going forth in abundance to the perfect possession of its kingdom, since it sees itself to be pure and rich[4] and prepared for this, God permits it in this state to see His beauty,[5] and entrusts it with the gifts and virtues that He has given it, and all this turns into love and praise, since there is no leaven to corrupt the mass. And when it sees that it has only now to break the frail web of this human condition of natural life wherein it feels itself to be enmeshed and imprisoned, and its liberty to be impeded, it desires to be loosed and to see itself with Christ,[6] and to burst these bonds of spirit and of flesh, which are of very different kinds, so that each may receive its deserts, the flesh remaining upon the earth and the spirit returning to God that gave it.[7] For the flesh[8] profiteth nothing, as Saint John says,[9] but has rather been a hindrance to this spiritual good; and the soul grieves that a life which is so high should be obstructed by another that is so low, and therefore begs that this web may be broken.[10]

26. This life is called a web for three reasons: first, because of the bond that exists between spirit and flesh; second, because it makes a division between God and the soul; third, because even as a web is not so opaque and dense but that the light can shine through it, even so in this state this bond appears to it to be a very fine web, since it is greatly spiritualized and enlightened and refined, so that the Divinity cannot but shine through it. And when the soul becomes conscious of the power of the life to come, it feels keenly the weakness of this other life, which appears to it as a very fine web—even as a spider's web, which is the name that David gives to it, saying: 'Our years shall be considered as a spider.'[11] And it is much less still in the eyes of a soul that is so greatly enlarged; for, since this soul has entered into the con-

---

[1] [P. Silverio's text has: 'the first and the last.' E.p. reads: 'the beginning and the end, the first and the last.']

[2] [Cf. Isaias xxiv, 16.]   [3] E.p.: 'and on the very point of.'

[4] E.p.: 'pure and rich, in so far as is in conformity with the faith and with the state of this life.'

[5] [Or, 'its (own) beauty.']   [6] Philippians i, 23.

[7] Ecclesiastes xii, 7.   [8] E.p.: 'For mortal flesh.'

[9] St. John vi, 64 [A.V., vi, 63].

[10] A omits from 'and entrusts it' to the end of the paragraph, and also the whole of the next paragraph.

[11] Psalm lxxxix, 9 [A.V., xc, 9]. E.p. omits this quotation.

sciousness of God, it is conscious of things in the way that God is; and in the sight of God, as David also says, a thousand years are as yesterday when it is past.[1] And according to Isaias all nations are as if they were not.[2] And they have the same importance to the soul—namely, all things are to it as nothing, and to its own eyes it is itself nothing: to it its God alone is all.

27. But here one point should be noticed. Why does the soul beg that the web may be broken, rather than be cut or allowed to wear itself out, since all these things would seem to have the same result? We may say that this is for four reasons. First, in order to use language of greater propriety, for in an encounter it is more proper to say that a thing is broken than that it is cut or wears away. Second, because love delights in the force of love and in forceful and impetuous contacts, and these are produced by breaking rather than by cutting or wearing away. Third, because love desires that the act should be very brief, since it will then be the more quickly concluded; the briefer and more spiritual is it, the greater is its power and worth. For virtue in union is stronger than virtue that is scattered; and love is introduced as form is introduced into matter, namely, in an instant, and until then there has been no act but only dispositions for an act; and thus spiritual acts which are done in an instant are for the most part dispositions of successive affections and desires, very few of which succeed in becoming acts. For this cause the Wise Man said: 'Better is the end of a prayer than the beginning.'[3] But those that so succeed instantly become acts in God, for which reason it is said that the short prayer penetrates the Heavens. Wherefore the soul that is prepared[4] can perform more acts, and acts of greater intensity, in a short time than the soul that is not prepared can perform in a long time; for the latter wastes its strength in the preparation of the spirit, and, even when this is done, the fire has not yet penetrated the wood. But into the soul that is prepared love enters continuously, for the spark seizes upon the dry fuel at its first contact; and thus the soul that is kindled in love prefers the short act

[1] Psalm lxxxix, 4 [A.V., xc, 4].   [2] Isaias xl, 17.   [3] [Ecclesiastes vii, 9.]
[4] E.p.: 'Second, because love delights in force and in forceful and impetuous contacts, and these are produced by breaking rather than by cutting or wearing away. Third, because the soul has so much love that it desires that this act of breaking the web should be very brief so that it may be quickly concluded; the briefer and more spiritual is it, the greater is its power and worth. For the virtue of love is here more united and stronger, and the perfection of transforming love is introduced [into the soul] as form is introduced into matter, namely, in an instant, and until then there has been no act of transformative informing, but only dispositions thereto of desires and affections successively repeated, which in very few attain to the perfect act of transformation. Wherefore the soul that is prepared, etc.'

of the breaking of the web to the duration of the act of cutting it or of waiting for it to wear away. The fourth reason is so that the web of life may the more quickly come to an end, for cutting a thing and allowing it to wear away are acts performed after greater deliberation when the thing is riper, and seem to require more time and a stage of greater maturity, whereas breaking needs not to wait for maturity or for anything else of the kind.

28. And this the soul desires—namely, that it may not have to wait until its life come naturally to an end[1] nor even to tarry until it be cut[2] —because the force of love, and the propensities which it feels, make it desire and entreat that its life may be broken[3] by some encounter and supernatural assault of love. For the soul in this state knows very well that it is the habit of God to take away such souls before their time in order to give them good things and to remove them from evil things, perfecting them in a short time by means of that love and giving them that which they might have gained gradually in a long time, even as the Wise Man says, in these words: 'He that is pleasing to God is made beloved, and living among sinners he was translated and taken away, lest wickedness should alter his understanding or deceit beguile his soul. Being made perfect in a short space, he fulfilled a long time; for his soul was pleasing to God, therefore hastened He to take him out of the midst'.[4] For this reason it is a great thing for the soul to exercise itself constantly in love, so that, when it is perfected here below, it may not stay long, either in this world or in the next, before seeing God face to face.

29. But let us now see why the soul calls this interior assault of the Holy Spirit an encounter rather than by any other name. It is because, as we have said, the soul in God is conscious of an infinite desire that its life may come to an end so that it may have the consummation thereof in glory; yet, because the time is not yet come, this is not accomplished[5]; and thus, so that the soul may be the more completely perfected and raised up above the flesh, God makes certain assaults upon it that are glorious and Divine and after the manner of encounters—indeed, they are encounters—wherewith He penetrates the

---

[1] A omits all the rest of the chapter except for the final lines ('and since my petitions . . . for ever').

[2] E.p. omits: 'nor even . . . cut.'

[3] E.p.: 'incline it with resignation to the breaking of its life.'

[4] Wisdom iv, 10–11, 13–14. E.p. has 'from the world' for 'out of the midst.'

[5] E.p. reads: '. . . of the Holy Spirit an encounter. The reason is that, although the soul is conscious of a great desire that its life may come to an end, yet, because the time is not yet come, this is not accomplished.'

soul continually, deifying its substance and making it Divine.[1] Herein He absorbs the soul, above all being, in the Being of God, for He has encountered it[2] and pierced it to the quick in the Holy Spirit, Whose communications are impetuous when they are full of fervour, as is this communication. This encounter, since it has a lively taste of God, the soul calls sweet; not that many other touches and encounters which it receives in this state are not also sweet and delectable, but rather that this is eminently so above all the rest; for God effects it, as we have said, in order to loose the soul and glorify it.[3] Wherefore the soul takes courage to say: 'Break the web of this sweet encounter.'

30. And thus this whole stanza is as though the soul were to say: Oh, flame of the Holy Spirit, that so intimately and tenderly[4] dost pierce the substance of my soul and cauterize it with Thy heat! Since Thou art now so loving as to show Thyself with the desire of giving Thyself to me in perfect and eternal life; if formerly my petitions did not reach Thine ears, when in their weakness my sense and spirit suffered with yearnings and fatigues of love by reason of the great weakness and impurity and the little strength of love that they had, I entreated Thee to loose me, for with desire did my soul desire Thee when my impatient love would not suffer me to be conformed with the condition of this life that Thou desiredst me to live, and the past assaults of love sufficed not in Thy sight, because they had not sufficient substance; now that I am so greatly strengthened in love that not alone do my sense and spirit[5] not fail before Thee, but rather my heart and my flesh are strengthened in Thy sight, they rejoice in the living God with a great conformity between their various parts. Therefore do I entreat that which Thou desirest me to entreat, and that which Thou desirest not, that desire I not, nor can I desire it,[6] nor does it pass through my mind to entreat it; and, since my petitions are now more effective and more reasonable in Thine eyes (for they go forth from Thee and Thou desirest them, and I pray to Thee with delight and rejoicing in the Holy Spirit, and my judgment comes forth from Thy countenance,[7] which comes to pass when Thou esteemest and hearest my prayers), do Thou break the slender web of this life, and let it not come to pass that age and years cut it after a natural manner,[8]

---

[1] E.p.: 'making it as it were Divine.'
[2] E.p.: 'Herein the soul absorbs the Being of God, for He has encountered it.'
[3] E.p. adds: 'perfectly.'
[4] C: 'so tenderly and intimately.' G: 'so tenderly.'
[5] E.p.: 'my spirit and sense.'
[6] E.p.: 'nor does it seem that I can desire it.'   [7] [Psalm xvi, 2.]
[8] E.p. omits: 'and let . . . manner.'

so that I may be able to love Thee with the fullness and satisfaction which my soul desires, without end, for ever.[1]

STANZA II

Oh, sweet burn! Oh, delectable wound! Oh, soft hand! Oh, delicate touch
That savours of eternal life and pays every debt! In slaying, thou hast changed death into life.

EXPOSITION

IN this stanza the soul explains how the three Persons of the Most Holy Trinity, Father, Son and Holy Spirit, are They that effect within it this Divine work of union. Thus the 'hand,' the 'burn' and the 'touch' are in substance one and the same thing; and the soul gives them these names, inasmuch as they describe the effect which is caused by each. The 'burn' is the Holy Spirit, the 'hand' is the Father and the 'touch' is the Son. And thus the soul here magnifies the Father, the Son and the Holy Spirit, dwelling upon[2] three great favours and blessings which They work within it, since They have changed its death into life, transforming it in Themselves. The first is the delectable wound, which the soul attributes to the Holy Spirit, wherefore it is called a burn. The second is the desire for eternal life, which it attributes to the Son, and therefore calls a delicate touch. The third is a gift wherewith the soul is right well pleased, and this it attributes to the Father, and therefore calls it a soft hand. And although the soul here names the three things,[3] because of the properties of their effects, it addresses only one of them, saying: 'Thou hast changed death into life.' For they all work in one, and the soul attributes the whole of their work to one, and the whole of it to all of them. There follows the line:

Oh, sweet burn!

2. In the Book of Deuteronomy Moses says that our Lord God is a consuming fire[4]—that is to say, a fire of love. This fire, as it is of infinite power, is able to consume to an extent which cannot be measured, and by burning with great vehemence to transform into itself that

---

[1] C adds: 'And here the first verse [copla] comes to an end.'
[2] G: 'magnifying.'
[3] G, e.p.: 'names the three Persons.' G adds: 'by reason of the effects which they cause.'   [4] Deuteronomy iv, 24.

which it touches. But it burns everything according to the degree of the preparation thereof; some things more and others less; and likewise according to its own pleasure, and after the manner and at the time which it pleases. And since God is an infinite fire of love, when therefore He is pleased to touch the soul with some severity, the heat of the soul rises to such a degree that the soul believes that it is being burned with a heat greater than any other in the world. For this reason it speaks of this touch as of a burn, for it is experienced where the fire is most intense[1] and most concentrated, and the effect of its heat is greater than that of other fires. And when this Divine fire has transformed the substance of [2] the soul into itself, not only is the soul conscious of the burn, but it has itself become one burn of vehement fire.

3. And it is a wondrous thing, worthy to be related,[3] that, though this fire of God is so vehement and so consuming that it would consume a thousand worlds more easily than natural fire[4] consumes a straw of flax,[5] it consumes not the spirits wherein it burns, neither destroys them; but rather, in proportion to its strength and heat, it brings them delight and deifies them, burning sweetly in them by reason of the purity of their spirits.[6] Thus did it come to pass, as we read in the Acts of the Apostles, when this fire descended with great vehemence and enkindled the disciples[7]; and, as Saint Gregory says, they burned inwardly with sweetness.[8] And it is this that the Church says, in these words: 'There came fire from Heaven, burning not but giving splendour; consuming not but enlightening.'[9] For, in these communications, since their object is to magnify the soul, this fire afflicts it not but rather enlarges it; it wearies it not, but delights it and makes it glorious and rich, for which cause the soul calls it sweet.

4.[10] And thus the happy soul that by great good fortune attains to this burning knows everything, tastes everything, does all that it desires, and prospers, and none prevails against it or touches it. For it is of this soul that the Apostle says: 'The spiritual man judgeth all things, and he himself is judged of no man.'[11] *Et iterum*: 'The spiritual man searcheth all things,[12] yea, the deep things of God.'[13]

---

[1] C: 'where the fire is brightest and most intense.'
[2] E.p. omits: 'the substance of.'   [3] E.p. omits: 'worthy to be related.'
[4] [*Lit.*, 'than fire.']   [5] G: 'a little flax.'
[6] E.p.: 'burning sweetly, according to the strength which He has given them.'
[7] [Acts ii, 3.]   [8] Hom. XXX, in Evang.
[9] In officio feriæ 2ª Pent.
[10] A omits § 4 and § 5 down to the words 'three manners.'
[11] 1 Corinthians ii, 15.
[12] E.p.: '... of no man, and, in another place, that he penetrateth all things.'
[13] 1 Corinthians ii, 10.

5. Oh, the great glory of you souls that are worthy to attain to this supreme fire, which, while it has infinite power to consume and annihilate you, consumes you not, but grants you a boundless consummation[1] in glory! Marvel not that God should bring certain souls to such a state; for in certain ways the sun[2] is conspicuous for the marvellous effects which it causes; as the Holy Spirit says, it burns the mountains of the just after three manners.[3] Since, then, this burn is so sweet, as we have here explained, how delectable, may we believe, will it not be in one that is touched by such fire? Of this the soul would fain speak, but speaks not, limiting itself to expressing its wonder and esteem in this word 'Oh,' saying:

Oh, delectable wound!

6. This wound is inflicted by the same burn that cures it,[4] and, as it is made, it is healed; for it is in some ways similar to a burn caused by natural fire, which, when it is applied to a wound, makes a greater wound, and causes the first, which has been produced by iron or in some other way, to be turned into a wound inflicted by fire; and the more it is subjected to the burning, the greater is the wound caused by the fire, until the whole of the matter is destroyed.[5] Even so this Divine burn of love heals the wound which has been inflicted in the soul by love, and with each application it becomes greater. For the healing of love is to hurt and wound once more that which has been hurt and wounded already, until the soul comes to be wholly dissolved in the wound of love. And in this way, when it is now completely turned into a wound of love, it regains its perfect health,[6] and is transformed in love and wounded in love. So in this case he that is most severely wounded is most healthy, and he that is altogether wounded is altogether healthy. Yet, even if this soul be altogether wounded and altogether healthy, the burning still performs its office, which is to wound with love; but then it has also to relieve[7] the wound which has been healed, after the manner aforementioned. Wherefore the soul says: 'Oh, delectable wound!' The loftier and the more sublime is the

---

1 [The play upon the words *consumir* ('consume') and *consumar* ('consummate,' 'perfect') cannot be exactly rendered in English.]
2 [*el sol.*] E.p. has 'He alone': *él solo.*
3 [Ecclus. xliii, 4.] E.p. omits: 'as . . . manners.'
4 E.p.: 'is cured by Him Who inflicts it.'
5 [*Lit.*, 'dissolved'—a word repeated below.]
6 A omits the rest of § 6 and § 7 down to the words: 'Oh, then, thou delectable wound!'
7 [The past participle of this verb (*regalar*) has also the meaning 'delectable,' and is so translated in the verse-line above, and elsewhere in the text.]

fire of love that has caused the wound, the more delectable is the wound. For, as the Holy Spirit inflicted the wound in order to relieve it, and as He has a great desire and will to relieve it, the wound, therefore, is great, in order that it[1] may be greatly relieved.

7. Oh, happy wound, inflicted by One Who cannot but heal![2] Oh, fortunate and most happy wound, inflicted only for the relief [3] and delight of the soul! Great is the wound, since great is He that has inflicted it; and great is the relief, since the fire of love is infinite and is measured according to its capacity.[4] Oh, then, thou delectable wound! So much the more sublimely delectable art thou in proportion as the burn of love has touched the inmost centre of the substance of the soul,[5] burning all that was capable of being burned, that it might relieve all that was capable of being relieved. This burn and this wound, in my opinion, represent the highest degree to which the soul can attain in this state. But there are many other ways[6] wherein the soul attains not so far as this, nor are they like this; for this is a touch of the Divinity in the soul, without any form or figure whether formal or imaginary.

8. But there is another and a most sublime way wherein the soul may be cauterized, which is after this manner. It will come to pass that, when the soul is enkindled in this love, although not so perfectly[7] as in the way of which we have spoken (though it is most meet that it should be so with a view to that which I am about to describe), the soul will be conscious of an assault upon it made by a seraph armed with a dart[8] of most enkindled love, which will pierce that enkindled coal of fire, the soul, or, to speak more exactly, that flame, and will cauterize it in a sublime manner; and, when it has pierced and cauterized it thus, the flame will rush forth and will rise suddenly and vehemently, even as comes to pass in a white-hot furnace or forge; when they stir and poke the fire,[9] the flame becomes hotter and the fire revives, and then the soul is conscious of this wound, with a delight which transcends all description. For, not only is it moved through and through by the stirring and the impetuous motion given to its fire,[10] wherein the heat

---

[1] E.p.: 'in order that the soul that receives it.'
[2] C: 'Who can do naught else than comfort.'   [3] [regalo.]
[4] E.p. omits: 'and is measured according to its capacity.'
[5] E.p.: 'touches the inmost centre of the soul.'
[6] C adds: 'in which God cauterizes the soul.'
[7] Gr: 'although it is not so much cauterized.'
[8] [dardo. The same word is used by St. Teresa in her description (Life, Chap. xxix) of the transverberation of her heart, though the pictorial representations of that event generally show the seraph armed with a long spear.]
[9] E.p.: 'when they disturb the fuel and turn it over.'
[10] E.p.: '. . . moved when they turn the fuel over and by the motion given to its fire.'

and melting of love are great, but the keen wound[1] and the healing
herb wherewith the effect of the dart was being greatly assuaged[2] are
felt by it in the substance of the spirit, even as in the heart of him whose
soul has been thus pierced.

9. Who can speak fittingly of this grain of mustard seed which
now seems to remain in the centre of the heart of the spirit, and which
is the point of the wound and the refinement of its delight[3]? For the
soul feels that there has remained within it, as it were, a grain of
mustard seed, most minute, highly enkindled and wondrous keen;[4]
keen also and enkindled even to the circumference to which its substance extends, and the virtue of that point of the wound. Thence the
substance and the virtue of the herb are subtly diffused through all the
spiritual and substantial[5] veins of the soul, according to its potentiality
and the strength of the heat.[6] And the soul feels its love to be increasing
and to be growing in strength and refinement to such a degree that it
seems to have within it seas of fire which reach to the farthest heights
and depths of the spheres, filling it wholly with love.[7]

10. And that whereof the soul now has fruition cannot be further
described, save by saying that the soul is now conscious of the fitness
of the comparison of the Kingdom of Heaven with the grain of mustard
seed made in the Gospel; which grain, because of its great heat, small
as it is, grows into a great tree.[8] For the soul sees that it has become
like a vast fire of love[9] and the point of its virtue is in the heart of the
spirit.

11. Few souls attain to this state, but some have done so, especially
those whose virtue and spirituality was to be transmitted to the succession of their children. For God bestows spiritual wealth and strength
upon the head of a house according as He means his descendants to
inherit the first-fruits of the Spirit.

12. Let us return, then, to the work done by that seraph, which in

---

1 E.p.: 'the keen and efficacious wound.'
2 [This seems the most probable of various interpretations. The literal translation
would read: 'the herb wherewith the iron was being intensely (or keenly) tempered.']
3 C: 'of this intimate point of the wound which seems to remain in the centre of the
heart of the spirit, which is where the refinement of its delight is felt?' E.p. (from the end
of § 8) has: 'are felt by the soul [which also feels] the depth of its spirit pierced and the
refinement of the delight [of this], whereof none can speak fittingly.'
4 E.p. adds here: 'in the inmost heart of the spirit, which is the point of the wound'
and continues: '[Here] is the substance and virtue, etc.'
5 E.p. omits: 'and substantial.' G: 'through all the spiritual veins, nerves and arteries
of the soul.'
6 A omits the rest of this paragraph and the whole of the two paragraphs following.
7 E.p.: 'seas of fire which fill it wholly with love.'
8 St. Matthew xiii, 31-2.   9 G and e.p. end the sentence here.

truth is to strike and to wound. If the effect of the wound should sometimes be permitted to pass outward to the bodily senses, to an extent
corresponding to the interior wound, the effect of the impact and the
wound will be felt without, as came to pass when the seraph wounded
the soul of Saint Francis with love, and in that way the effect of those
wounds became outwardly visible. For God bestows no favours upon
the body without bestowing them first and principally upon the soul.
And then, the greater is the delight and strength of love which causes
the wound within, the greater is the pain of that wound without,[1]
and if the one grows, the other grows likewise. This comes to pass
because, since these souls have been purged and made strong in God,
all that pertains to God and is strong and sweet is a delight[2] to them in
their spirits, which are strong and healthy; to their weak and corruptible flesh, however, it causes pain and torture; wherefore it is a wondrous thing to feel the pain growing with the pleasure. This wonder
Job perceived in his wounds, when he said to God: 'Turning to me,
Thou tormentest me wonderfully.'[3] For it is a great marvel and a
thing worthy of the abundance of God and of the sweetness which He
has laid up for them that fear Him,[4] that, the greater is the pain and
torment of which the soul is conscious, the greater is its pleasure and
delight.

13. Oh, immeasurable greatness, in all things showing thyself
omnipotent! Who but Thou, Lord, could cause sweetness in the midst
of bitterness and pleasure in torment? How delectable a wound, then,
art thou, since the deeper is thy mark, the greater delight dost thou
cause! But when the wound is within the soul, and is not communicated
without, it can be far more intense and sublime;[5] for, as the flesh is the
bridle of the spirit, so, when the blessings of the spirit are communicated to it, the flesh draws in the rein and curbs this fleet steed and
restrains its great energy;[6] for the body, being then corrupted, presses
down the soul, and the habits of life oppress the spiritual sense when
it muses upon many things.[7] Wherefore, he that will place great
reliance upon bodily sense will never become a very spiritual
person.

14. This I say for those who think that they can attain to the powers

---

[1] A omits the rest of this paragraph and the first two sentences of the paragraph
following.
[2] E.p.: '... strong in God, the strong and sweet Spirit of God is a delight.'
[3] Job x, 16.   [4] Psalm xxx, 20 [A.V., xxxi, 19].
[5] G: 'and solid.'   [6] C: 'its grace and energy.'
[7] Wisdom ix, 15.

and the height of the spirit by means of the power and operation of
sense alone, which is low. They cannot attain thereto save when
bodily sense is left without. It is quite different when the affection of
feeling overflows from spirit into sense, for herein, as Saint Paul says,
there may be much spirituality;[1] for, when the intensity of his realization of the sufferings of Christ was so great that it overflowed into his
body, he writes to the Galatians, saying: 'I bear in my body the marks
of my Lord Jesus.'[2] As the wound and the burn, therefore, are such as
this, what will be the hand that takes part therein, and what will be the
touch that causes it? This the soul describes, extolling it rather than
expounding it, in the following line,[3] saying:

Oh, soft hand! Oh, delicate touch

15. Oh, hand, as generous as thou art powerful and rich, richly and
powerfully dost thou give me thy gifts! Oh, soft hand, the softer for
this soul, and softly laid upon it, for if thou wert to lean hardly upon it
the whole world would perish; for at Thy glance alone the earth
shakes,[4] and the nations are undone,[5] and the mountains crumble to
pieces.[6] Once more, then,[7] I say: 'Oh, soft hand!' For whereas thou
wert harsh and severe to Job,[8] since thou didst touch him so very
heavily,[9] thou art laid very firmly but very lovingly and graciously
upon my soul, and art as soft and as gentle to me as thou wert hard to
him, touching me firmly with sweet love even as thou didst touch him
with severity. For Thou slayest and Thou givest life and there is none
that can flee from Thy hand. But Thou, oh, Life Divine, never slayest
save to give life, even as Thou never woundest save to heal. Thou
hast wounded me, oh, hand Divine, in order to heal me, and thou hast
slain in me that which would have slain me, but for the life of God
wherein now I see that I live. And this Thou didst with the liberality of
Thy habitual[10] grace, through the touch wherewith Thou didst touch
me—namely, the splendour of Thy glory and the image of Thy sub-

---

[1] G: 'I will not for this reason exclude the feeling which overflows from spirit into
sense, as is seen in Saint Paul.'
[2] Galatians vi, 17.
[3] E.p.: 'And thus, as are the wound and the burn, so will be the hand that takes part
therein, and as is the touch, so will be He that causes it. This the soul describes in the
following line.'
[4] Psalm ciii, 32 [A.V., civ, 32].   [5] E.p.: 'the nations tremble.'
[6] Habakkuk iii, 6.
[7] G abbreviates: 'softer still for this soul, as thou touchest me more firmly. Once more,
then, etc.'
[8] Job xix, 21.   [9] E.p.: 'since thou didst touch him so heavily.'
[10] [Lit., 'general.'] So A, B, C, G, Gr. E.p.: 'generous.' The MSS. of the second
redaction vary between 'generous' and 'gracious.' See p. 133, below.

stance, which is Thy only begotten Son;[1] in Whom, since He is Thy wisdom, Thou reachest from one end to another mightily through His purity.[2]

16. Oh, then, thou delicate touch, Thou Word, Son of God, Who, through the delicateness of Thy Divine Being, dost subtly penetrate the substance of my soul, and, touching it wholly and delicately, dost absorb it wholly in Thyself in Divine ways of sweetness which have never been heard of in the land of Chanaan, nor seen in Theman![3] Oh, delicate touch of the Word, delicate, yea, wondrously delicate, to me, which, having overthrown the mountains and broken the stones in Mount Horeb with the shadow of Thy power and strength that went before Thee, didst reveal Thyself to the Prophet with the whisper of gentle air.[4] Oh, gentle air, that art so delicate and gentle![5] Say, how dost Thou touch the soul so gently and delicately when Thou art so terrible and powerful? Oh, blessed, twice blessed, the soul whom Thou dost touch so gently[6] though Thou art so terrible and powerful! Tell it out to the world. But nay, tell it not to the world, for the world knows naught of air so gentle, and will not feel Thee, because it can neither receive Thee nor see Thee.[7]

17. Oh, my God and my life! They whom Thou refinest[8] shall know Thee and behold Thee when Thou touchest them, since purity corresponds with purity.[9] Thou dost touch them the more delicately because Thou art hidden in the substance of their souls, which have been beautified and made delicate,[10] and because they are withdrawn from all creatures and from all traces of creature, and Thou hidest them in the hiding-place of Thy presence,[11] which is Thy Divine Son, and dost conceal them from the disturbance of men.[12] Once again, then, oh, delicate touch, and again most delicate, that with the strength of Thy delicacy dost melt the soul and removest it from all other touches and makest it Thine own alone. So delicate an effect and impression dost Thou leave in the soul that every other touch, of everything

---

[1] Hebrews i, 3.   [2] Wisdom [vii, 24] viii, 1.
[3] Baruch iii, 22.   [4] 3 Kings [A.V., 1 Kings] xix, 11–12.
[5] A, G, e.p. omit: 'that art so delicate and gentle.' A also omits the rest of the paragraph.
[6] C: 'so delicately.' B: 'so happily and delicately.'
[7] E.p.: 'because it cannot receive these lofty things.' [St. John xiv, 17.]
[8] [*Lit.*, 'They who become delicate': the word 'delicate' is also used below, where I render 'purity,' but the sense is evidently 'refined,' 'purified.']
[9] [*Lit.*, 'delicacy . . . delicacy.']   [10] E.p.: 'in their souls, made delicate.'
[11] [*Lit.*, 'Thy face.' Cf. Psalm xxx, 21 (A.V., xxxi, 21).]
[12] E.p.: 'Thou hidest them in the hidden place of Thy presence, from the disturbance of men.' A omits the remainder of this paragraph and the first sentence of the paragraph following.

else, whether high or low, will seem to it rude and gross if it touches the soul, and even the sight of other things will offend it, and to have to do with them and touch them will cause it trouble and grievous torment.

18. The more delicate is a thing, the broader and more capacious it is; and the more delicate it is, the more it becomes diffusive and communicative. Oh, then, thou delicate touch, that dost infuse Thyself the more by reason of Thy delicacy, while the vessel of my soul, through this Thy touch, becomes the simpler, purer, more delicate and more capacious! Oh, then, thou delicate touch, so delicate that, when naught[1] is felt in the touch, Thou dost touch the soul the more, and, by penetrating deeply within it, Thou dost make it at Thy touch the more Divine, according as Thy Divine Being[2] wherewith Thou dost touch the soul is far removed from the way and manner thereof and free from all outward seeming[3] of form and figure! Oh, then, at last, Thou delicate, most delicate touch, that touchest not the soul save with Thy most pure and simple Being, which is infinite, and therefore infinitely delicate! Wherefore it is a touch

That savours of eternal life

19. Although this is not so in a perfect degree, there is indeed a certain savour herein of life eternal, as has been said above, which the soul tastes in this touch of God. And it is not incredible that this should be so if we believe, as we must believe, that this touch is substantial, that is to say, is a touch of the Substance of God in the substance of the soul;[4] and to this many holy men have attained in this life. Wherefore the delicacy of the delight which is felt in this touch is impossible of description; nor would I willingly speak thereof, lest it should be supposed that it is no more than that which I say; for there are no words to expound and enumerate such sublime things of God as come to pass in these souls; whereof the proper way to speak is for one that knows them to understand them inwardly and feel them and enjoy them and be silent concerning them. For the soul in this state sees that these things are in some measure like the white stone which Saint John says will be given to him that conquers, and on the stone a name shall

---

[1] [*Lit.*, 'when no bulk.']
[2] E.p.: 'while the vessel of my soul, through this Thy touch, is simple and pure and has capacity to receive Thee. Oh, then, Thou delicate touch, that feelest naught material within Thyself, yet dost touch the soul the more and the more deeply, changing it from the human into the Divine, according as Thy Divine Being.'
[3] [*Lit.*, 'from all husk.']
[4] E.p.: 'that this touch is most substantial and that the Substance of God touches the substance of the soul.'

be written, which no man knoweth saving he that receiveth it.[1] This alone can be said of it with truth, that it savours of eternal life.[2] For, although in this life we may not have perfect fruition of it, as in glory, yet nevertheless this touch, being of God, savours of eternal life. And in this way the soul in such a state tastes of all the things of God,[3] and there are communicated to it fortitude, wisdom, love, beauty, grace and goodness, and so forth. For as God is all these things, the soul tastes them in one single touch of God, and thus the soul has fruition of Him according to its faculties and its substance.

20. And of this good which comes to the soul a part sometimes overflows into the body through the union of the spirit, and this is enjoyed by all the substance of sense and all the members of the body and the very marrow and bones, not as feebly as is usually the case, but with a feeling of great delight and glory, which is felt even in the remotest joints of the feet and hands. And the body feels such glory in the glory of the soul that it magnifies God after its own manner, perceiving that He is in its very bones,[4] even as David said: 'All my bones shall say, "God, who is like to Thee?"'[5] And since all that can be said concerning this matter is less than the truth, it suffices to say of the bodily experience, as of the spiritual, that it savours of eternal life.[6]

And pays every debt!

21. Here it behoves us to explain what debts are these which the soul now recognizes as paid. It must be known that the souls which attain to this lofty kingdom have commonly passed through many trials and tribulations, since it behoves us to enter through many tribulations into the kingdom of the heavens;[7] which things have in this state already passed, for henceforth there is no more suffering.[8] That which has to be suffered by those who are about to attain to union with God is trials and temptations of many kinds in sense, and trials and tribulations and temptations and darknesses and perils in the spirit, so that both these parts may be purged together, as we said in

---

[1] Apocalypse ii, 17.
[2] A omits the rest of this paragraph and all of the paragraph following except the last sentence.
[3] E.p.: 'tastes in a wondrous manner, and by participation, of all the things of God.'
[4] E.p. abbreviates: 'in one single touch of God, in a certain eminent way. And of this good which comes to the soul some of the unction of the spirit sometimes overflows into the body, and it seems to penetrate to its very bones.'
[5] Psalm xxxiv, 10 [A.V., xxxv, 10].
[6] E.p. abbreviates: 'it suffices to say that it savours of eternal life.'
[7] Acts xiv, 21 [A.V., xiv, 22].
[8] E.p. omits: 'for . . . suffering.'

the exposition of the fourth line of the first stanza.[1] And the reason for these trials is that the delight and knowledge of God cannot well find a home in the soul if sense and spirit be not thoroughly purged and toughened and purified. And thus, since trials and penances purify and refine the soul and tribulations and temptations and darknesses and perils refine and prepare the spirit, it behoves the soul to pass through them to attain to transformation in God, even as those beyond the grave must do, by going through purgatory, some with greater intensity and others with less, some spending more time therein and others less, according to the degrees of union to which God is pleased to raise them and the degree of purgation which they have to undergo.

22. By means of these trials whereinto God leads the soul and the senses, the soul gradually acquires virtues and strength and perfection, together with bitterness, for virtue is made perfect in weakness,[2] and is wrought by the experience of sufferings. For iron cannot be subservient to the intelligence[3] of the artificer, unless he use fire and a hammer, which do harm to the iron if it be compared with what it was in its former state. Even so Jeremias says that God taught him, saying: 'He sent fire into my bones and taught me.'[4] And he likewise says of the hammer: 'Thou hast chastised me, Lord, and I was instructed and became wise.'[5] Even so the Preacher says: 'He that is not tried, what does he know and whereof has he knowledge?'[6]

23. And here it behoves us to note why it is that there are so few that attain to this lofty state. It must be known that this is not because God is pleased that there should be few raised to this high spiritual state—on the contrary, it would please Him if all were so raised—but rather because He finds few vessels in whom He can perform so high and lofty a work. For, when He proves them in small things and finds them weak and sees that they at once flee[7] from labour, and desire not to submit to the least discomfort or mortification, or to work with solid patience, He finds that they are not strong enough to bear the favour which He was granting them when He began to purge them,[8] and goes no farther with their purification, neither does He lift them up

---

[1] E.p.: 'as we said in the *Ascent of Mount Carmel* and in the *Dark Night.*'
[2] 2 Corinthians xii, 9.   [3] E.p.: 'to the plan.'
[4] Lamentations i, 13.   [5] Jeremias xxxi, 18.
[6] Ecclesiasticus xxxiv, 9. [The two verbs have different senses in the original. We might bring out this difference by paraphrasing: 'what wisdom has he and what thing can he recognize?']
[7] E.p. abbreviates: 'to this lofty state. The reason is that in this lofty and sublime work which God begins there are many weak souls; as these at once flee.'
[8] E.p.: 'began to carve (or 'form') them.'

from the dust of the earth, since for this they would need greater fortitude and constancy. To these, then, who would fain make progress,
yet cannot suffer the smallest things nor submit themselves to them,
can be made the reply which we find in Jeremias in these words: 'If
thou hast run with those who went on foot and hast laboured, how
canst thou contend with horses? And as thou hast had quietness in the
land of peace, how wilt thou do in the pride of Jordan?'[1] This is as
though he were to say: If in the trials which commonly and ordinarily
afflict all those who live this human life thy pace was so slow that thou
didst run and countedst all as labour, how wilt thou be able to keep
pace with the step of a horse—that is to say, to leave these ordinary
and common trials and pass from them to others of greater strength and
swiftness? And if thou hast been loth to make war against the peace
and pleasure of this land of thine, which is thy sensual nature, but
seekest to be quiet and to have comfort therein, what wilt thou do in
the pride of Jordan? That is, how wilt thou suffer the impetuous waters
of spiritual tribulation and trial, which are more interior?

24.[2] Oh, souls that seek to walk in security and comfort! If ye
did but know how necessary it is to suffer and endure in order to
reach this lofty state, and of what great benefit it is to suffer and be
mortified in order to reach such lofty blessings, ye would in no way
seek consolation, either from God or from the creatures,[3] but would
rather bear the cross, together with pure vinegar and gall, and would
count this a great happiness, for, being thus dead to the world and to
your own selves, ye would live to God in the delights of the spirit;
and, bearing outward things with patience, ye would become worthy
for God to set His eyes upon you to cleanse and purge you more inwardly by means of more interior spiritual trials.[4] For they to whom
God is to grant so notable a favour[5] as to tempt them more interiorly
must have rendered Him many services, and have had much patience
and constancy for His sake, and be very acceptable in their lives in His
sight. This we read of the holy man Tobias, to whom Raphael said
that, because he had been acceptable to God, He had granted him this
favour of sending him a temptation that should prove him more in
order that he might give him more.[6] And even so, says the Scripture,

[1] Jeremias xii, 5.   [2] A omits this and the two following paragraphs.
[3] E.p.: 'seek consolation in aught.'
[4] Gr: 'more inward spiritual trials, in order to give you more inward blessings.' B:
'more inward spiritual trials.' C: 'inward spiritual trials, in order to give you inward
blessings.'   [5] E.p.: 'such a favour.'
[6] Tobias xii, 13. E.p. begins the sentence: 'And thus the angel spake to the holy man
Tobias, saying that, etc.'

all that remained to him of life, after that time, caused him joy. In the same way we read of Job that, when God accepted him as His servant, as He did in the presence of the good and the evil spirits, He then granted him the favour of sending him those heavy trials, that He might afterwards exalt him, as indeed He did, both in spiritual and in temporal things, and much more so than before.[1]

25. Even so acts God to those whom He desires to exalt with the chiefest exaltation; He causes them to be tempted to the highest degree possible, that He may also deify them to the highest degree possible, by granting them union[2] in His wisdom, which is the highest state, and purging them first of all in this wisdom to the highest possible degree, even as David observes, where he says: 'The wisdom of the Lord is silver tried by the fire, proved in the earth of our flesh and purged seven times,'[3] which is the greatest purgation possible.[4] And there is no reason to tarry here any longer in order to show how each of the seven purgations leads us to this communion with God,[5] which here below is like silver, for, however high it be, it is not yet as gold.[6]

26. But it greatly behoves the soul to have much constancy and patience in these tribulations and trials, whether they come from without or from within, and are spiritual or corporeal, greater or lesser. It must take them all as from the hand of God for its healing and its good, and not flee from them, since they are health to the soul. This the Wise Man counsels, in these words: 'If the spirit of him that is powerful descend upon thee, leave not thy place' (that is, the place and abode of thy healing, by which is meant that trial); for the healing, he says, will cause great sins to cease.[7] That is, it will cut the thread of thy sins and imperfections, which is evil habit, that they go not farther. And thus interior perils and trials quench and purify the evil and imperfect habits of the soul. Wherefore we must count it a great favour when the Lord sends us interior trials, realizing that there are few who deserve to suffer that they may reach the goal of this lofty state of attainment to perfection through suffering.

27. As the soul now remembers that it has been very well recom-

---

[1] [Job i, 8; xlii, 12.]

[2] E.p.: 'to exalt with the chiefest betterment, allowing them to be tempted, afflicted, tormented and purified, interiorly and exteriorly, as far as is possible, that He may deify them, by granting them union.'

[3] Psalm xi, 7 [A.V., xii, 6].

[4] E.p.: 'seven times—that is, greatly purged.'

[5] [P. Silverio reads eloquio, an archaic word meaning literally 'speech.'] C has: 'this colloquy of God'; G: 'this union with God'; e.p.: 'this Divine wisdom.'

[6] E.p.: 'as precious gold, which is kept for [the life of] glory.'

[7] Ecclesiastes x, 4.

pensed for all its past trials, since now *sicut tenebræ ejus, ita et lumen ejus*,[1] and, as the soul aforetime shared in tribulations, it now shares in consolations; and as all its trials, within and without, have been amply rewarded by Divine blessings of soul and body,[2] there is none of its trials that has not a correspondingly great reward. And thus the soul confesses that it is now well satisfied, when it says in this line: 'And pays every debt.' Even so David said in his own case, in these words: 'Many and grievous are the tribulations that Thou hast shown me, and Thou didst deliver me from them all, and from the depths of the earth hast Thou brought me out again; Thou hast multiplied Thy magnificence, and, turning to me, hast comforted me.'[3] And thus this soul that aforetime was without, at the gates of the palace (like Mardochai weeping in the streets of Susan, because his life was in peril, and clothed in sackcloth, refusing to receive the garments from Queen Esther, and having received no favour or reward for the services that he had rendered the King, and his faithfulness in serving the honour and life of the King),[4] is recompensed in a single day for all its trials and services, for not only is it made to enter the palace and stand before the King, clad in regal vesture, but likewise it is crowned, and given a sceptre, and a royal seat, and possession of the King's ring, so that it may do all that it desires, and need do naught that it desires not to do in the kingdom of its Spouse;[5] for those that are in this state receive all that they desire. It is well recompensed indeed for the whole debt, since its enemies are now dead—namely, the desires that were going about seeking to take away its life—and it now lives in God. For this cause the soul next says:

In slaying, thou hast changed death into life.

28. Death is naught else than privation of life, for, when life comes, there remains no trace of death. With respect to the spirit, there are two kinds of life; one is beatific, which consists in seeing God,[6] and this will be attained by means of [7] the natural death of the body, as Saint Paul says in these words: 'We know that if this our house of clay be dissolved, we have a dwelling of God in the heavens.'[8] The other is perfect spiritual life, which is the possession of God through the

---

[1] Psalm cxxxviii, 12 [A.V., cxxxix, 12].   [2] E.p. omits: 'of soul and body.'
[3] Psalm lxx, 20 [A.V., lxxi, 20–1].   [4] Esther iv, 1–4.
[5] E.p.: 'but likewise a diadem is placed on its head and it is as another Esther in the possession of the kingdom, so that it may do all that it desires in the kingdom of its Spouse.'
[6] G adds: 'face to face.'   [7] E.p.: 'and this must be preceded by.'
[8] 2 Corinthians v, 1.

union of love, and this is attained through the complete mortification of all vices and desires and of the soul's entire nature.[1] And until this be done, the soul cannot attain to the perfection of this spiritual life of union with God, even as the Apostle says likewise in these words: 'If you live according to the flesh, you shall die; but if by the spirit you mortify the deeds of the flesh, you shall live.'[2]

29. It must be known, then, that that which the soul here calls death is all that is meant by the 'old man', namely, the employment of the faculties—memory, understanding and will—and the use and occupation of them in things of the world, and the occupation of the desires in the pleasure afforded by created things. All this is the exercise of the old life, which is the death of the new, or spiritual, life. Herein the soul will be unable to live perfectly if it die not perfectly likewise to the old man, as the Apostle warns us when he says that we should put off the old man, and put on the new man, who according to God is created in justice and holiness.[3] In this new life, when the soul has reached the perfection of union with God, as we are saying here, all the desires of the soul, and its faculties and their operations, which of themselves were the operations of death and the privation of spiritual life, are changed into Divine operations.[4]

30. And as each living creature lives by its operation, as the philosophers say, having its operations in God, through the union that they have with God, the soul lives the life of God and its death has been changed into life.[5] For the understanding, which before this union understood in a natural way[6] with the strength and vigour of its natural light, is now moved and informed by another principle, that of the supernatural light of God, and has been changed into the Divine, for its understanding and that of God are now both one. And the will, which aforetime loved after the manner of death, that is to say, meanly and with its natural affection, has now[7] been changed into the life of Divine love; for it loves after a lofty manner with Divine affection and is moved by the Holy Spirit in Whom it now lives, since its will and His will are now only one.[8] And the memory, which of itself perceived

---

[1] E.p. omits: 'and of the soul's entire nature.'
[2] Romans viii, 13.   [3] Ephesians iv, 22–4.
[4] E.p.: 'all the affections of the soul, its faculties and operations, of themselves imperfect and mean, become Divine.'
[5] A omits almost all the rest of the commentary on this line.
[6] E.p.: 'understood inadequately [cortamente].'
[7] E.p.: 'by another principle and a higher light of God. And the will, which aforetime loved lukewarmly, has now, etc.'
[8] E.p. omits: 'since . . . only one.'

only the forms and figures of created things, has become changed, so
that it has in its mind the eternal years. And the desire, which enjoyed
only creature food that wrought death, is now changed so that it
tastes and enjoys Divine food, being now moved by another and a
more living principle, which is the delight of God; so that it is now the
desire of God.[1] And finally, all the movements and operations which
the soul had aforetime, and which belonged to the principle of its
natural life, are now in this union changed into movements of God.
For the soul, like the true daughter of God that it now is, is moved
wholly by the Spirit of God, even as Saint Paul says: 'That they that
are moved by the Spirit of God are sons of God.'[2] So the understanding of the soul is now the understanding of God; and its will is the will
of God; and its memory is the memory of God; and its delight is the
delight of God;[3] and the substance of the soul, although it is not the
Substance of God, for into this it cannot be changed, is nevertheless
united in Him and absorbed in Him, and is thus God by participation
in God, which comes to pass in this perfect state of the spiritual life,
although not so perfectly as in the next life. And in this way[4] by
'slaying, thou hast changed death into life.' And for this reason the
soul may here say very truly with Saint Paul: 'I live, now not I, but
Christ liveth in me.'[5] And thus the death[6] of this soul is changed into
the life of God, and the soul becomes absorbed in life, since within it
there is likewise fulfilled the saying of the Apostle: 'Death is absorbed
in victory.'[7] And likewise the words of Osee, the prophet, who says:
'O death, I will be thy death, saith God.'[8]

31. In this way the soul is absorbed in life, being withdrawn from all
that is secular and temporal and freed from that which belongs to its
own unruly nature, so that it is brought into the cellars of the King,[9]
where it rejoices and is glad in its Beloved, and remembers His breasts
more than wine, saying: 'I am black but beautiful, daughters of Jerusalem';[10] for my natural blackness is changed into the beauty of the
heavenly King. Wherefore, oh burning of the fire that infinitely burnest
above all fires else, the more thou burnest me the sweeter art thou to

---

[1] E.p.: 'And the desire, which aforetime was inclined to the food of the creatures, now
tastes and enjoys Divine food, being now moved by another and a more living principle,
which is the sweetness of God.'

[2] Romans viii, 14.

[3] E.p. omits: 'So the understanding . . . delight of God.'

[4] E.p. adds: 'he well says.'   [5] Galatians ii, 20.

[6] E.p.: 'the death and coldness.'

[7] 1 Corinthians xv, 54.   [8] Osee xiii, 14.

[9] C: 'into the streets of the King.' G: 'into the royal chamber.'

[10] Canticles i, 4.

me! And oh, delectable wound, thou art to me most delectable health, more so than all other health and delights of the world! And oh, soft hand, that art infinitely soft above all softness,[1] the more thou art laid upon me and dost press upon me, the softer to me art thou! And oh, delicate touch, whose delicateness is more subtle and more curious than all the subtle beauties of the creatures, surpassing them infinitely, and sweeter and more delicious than honey and the honeycomb, since thou savourest of eternal life, the more intimately[2] thou dost touch me the greater is the delight that thou givest me; and infinitely more precious art thou than gold and precious stones, since thou payest debts which naught else could pay, turning death into life in a way most marvellous.

32. In this state of life, perfect as it is, the soul is, as it were, keeping festival, and has in its mouth[3] a great song of joy to God, and, as it were, a song new and ever new, turned into joy[4] and love, and having knowledge of its lofty state. At times it rejoices, saying within its spirit those words of Job, namely: 'My glory shall always be renewed and as a palm tree shall I multiply my days.'[5] Which is as much as to say: God Who, remaining within Himself unchangeably, makes all things new, as the Wise Man says, being united for ever in my glory, will make my glory ever new, that is to say, He will not suffer it to grow old as it was before; and I shall multiply my days—that is, my merits—unto Heaven, even as the palm tree multiplies its branches. And all that David says in the twenty-ninth Psalm the soul sings inwardly to God, particularly those last lines which say: 'Thou hast turned for me my mourning into joy, Thou hast cut my sackcloth, and hast compassed me with gladness, to the end that my glory may sing to Thee, and may not be ashamed (for here no pain reaches the soul). O Lord my God, I will praise Thee for ever.'[6] For the soul now feels God to be so solicitous in granting it favours and to be magnifying it with such precious and delicate and endearing words, and granting it favour upon favour, that it believes that there is no other soul in the world whom He thus favours, nor aught else wherewith He occupies Himself, but that He is wholly for itself alone. And, when it feels this, it confesses its feeling in the words of the Songs: 'My Beloved to me and I to Him.'[7]

---

[1] G: 'above all soft hands.' [2] G. T: 'infinitely.'
[3] [Lit., 'palate.'] [4] C: 'into grace.'
[5] [Job xxix, 18, 20.] [6] Psalm xxix, 12–13 [A.V., xxx, 11–12].
[7] Canticles ii, 16. E.p.: 'And it makes this confession in the Songs: "I wholly to my Beloved and my Beloved wholly to me."'

STANZA III

Oh, lamps of fire, In whose splendours the deep caverns of sense which were dark and blind
With strange brightness Give heat and light together to their Beloved!

EXPOSITION

MAY God be pleased to grant me His favour here, for in truth it is very needful if I am to explain[1] the profound meaning of this stanza; great attention, too, is necessary in him that reads it, for, if he have no experience of this, it will perhaps be somewhat obscure to him, though, if perchance he should have had such experience, it will be clear and pleasing.[2] In this stanza, the soul gives deepest thanks to its Spouse for the great favours which it receives[3] from union with Him, for by means of this union He has given it great and abundant knowledge[4] of Himself, wherewith the faculties and senses of the soul, which before this union were dark and blinded by other kinds of love,[5] have been enlightened and enkindled with love, and can now be illumined, as indeed they are, and through the heat of love can give light and love[6] to Him Who enkindled and enamoured them and infused into them such Divine gifts. For the true lover is content only when all that he is, and all that he is worth and can be worth, and all that he has and can have, are employed in the Beloved; and the more of this there is, the greater is the pleasure that he receives in giving it. In the first place, it must be known that lamps have two properties, which are to give light and to burn. There follows the line:

Oh, lamps of fire,

2. In order to understand this line, it must be known that God, in His one and simple Being, is all the virtues and grandeurs of His attributes;[7] for He is omnipotent, wise, good, merciful, just, strong

---

[1] E.p. begins: 'Great is the need here of the favour of God in order that I may explain.'
[2] E.p.: 'if he have no experience of this, that which is here treated will be very obscure, though, if perchance he should have had such experience, it will be clear and pleasing.'
[3] E.p.: 'which it has received.'
[4] E.p.: 'by means of this union abundant and most sublime knowledge.'
[5] E.p.: 'were dark and blind.'
[6] E.p.: 'and are illumined with the heat of love, in order that they may respond by offering that same light and love.'
[7] G: 'in His one and most simple Being, contains all the perfections and grandeurs of His attributes.'

and loving, and has other infinite[1] attributes and virtues whereof we have no knowledge here below; and, as He is all these things when He is united with the soul, at the time when He is pleased to reveal knowledge to it, it is able to see in Him all these virtues and grandeurs, clearly and distinctly—namely, omnipotence, goodness, wisdom, justice, mercy and so forth, all in one simple Being. And, as each of these things is the very Being of God in one sole reality, which is the Father or the Son or the Holy Spirit, each attribute being God Himself and God being infinite light and infinite Divine fire, as we have said above, it follows from this that in each of these attributes, which, as we say, are innumerable, and are His virtues, He gives light and burns as God.[2]

3. And thus according to these kinds of knowledge of God which the soul here possesses, actually distinct in one single act, God Himself is to the soul as many lamps, which give light to it each in a distinct way, for from each lamp[3] the soul has knowledge and by each is given the heat of love, in its own way and all in one simple being, as we say; and all these are one lamp,[4] which is the Word, which, as Saint Paul says, is the brightness of the glory of the Father. This lamp[5] is all these lamps, since it gives light and burns in all these ways; and this the soul is able to see—namely, that this one lamp is many lamps to it. For, as it is one, it can do all things, and has all virtues, and comprehends all spirits,[6] and thus in one act it gives light and burns according to all its grandeurs and virtues—in many ways, we may say, yet in one way.[7] For it gives light and burns as being omnipotent, and gives light and burns as being wise, and gives light and burns as being good, and gives light and burns as being strong, as being just, as being true, and as having each of the other Divine virtues and qualities which are in God, giving the soul intelligence and love concerning Him, both according to all these virtues distinctly and also according to each one. For when He communicates Himself, since He is all of them and each one of them, He gives the soul light and love Divine according to them all, and according to each one of them; for, wheresoever the fire is

---

[1] E.p. omits: 'infinite.'

[2] E.p. omits: 'which . . . His virtues' and reads: 'as Very God.'

[3] G: 'And thus according to these distinct kinds of knowledge of God which the soul here possesses, knowing all these perfections with one sole act, God Himself comes to be to the soul as many lamps, etc.' E.p.: 'here possesses, in unity, God Himself is to the soul as many lamps, for from each lamp.'

[4] A, C, Gr: 'and all one being and all one lamp.'

[5] E.p. abbreviates: 'and all these are one lamp, which lamp.'

[6] A omits the whole of what follows, down to the words 'well of living waters' in § 7.

[7] E.p.: 'and thus we may say that it gives light and burns in many ways, yet in one way.'

applied,[1] and whatever be the effect that it causes, it gives its heat and brightness; since this always happens in one manner.[2] For the brightness that this light gives inasmuch as it is omnipotence produces in the soul light and heat of the love of God inasmuch as He is omnipotent, and therefore God is now to the soul a lamp of omnipotence which gives it light and burns in it according to this attribute. And the brightness which this lamp gives inasmuch as it is wisdom produces the heat of the love of God in the soul inasmuch as He is wise and according to this God is to the soul a lamp of wisdom. And the brightness which this lamp of God gives inasmuch as it is goodness produces the heat of the love of God in the soul inasmuch as He is good, and accordingly God is then to the soul a lamp of goodness. In the same way He is a lamp of justice to it, and of fortitude, and of mercy, for the light[3] that He gives to the soul from each of these attributes and from all the rest produces in the soul the heat of the love of God inasmuch as He is such. And thus in this lofty communication and manifestation (which, as I think, is the greatest that can come to the soul in this life), God is to the soul as innumerable lamps which give it light and love.[4]

4. These lamps gave light to Moses[5] on Mount Sinai, where God passed before him and he quickly fell prostrate on the ground, and proclaimed some of the grandeurs which he saw in God; and, loving Him according to those things which he had seen, he proclaimed them each separately, saying: 'Emperor, Lord, God that art merciful, clement, patient, of much compassion, true, that keepest mercy for thousands, that takest away sins and evil deeds and faults, and art so righteous that there is no man who of himself is innocent before Thee.'[6] Herein it is clear that the majority of the attributes and virtues of God which Moses then learned and loved were those of God's omnipotence, dominion, deity, mercy, justice, truth and uprightness; which was a most profound knowledge and a most sublime delight of love.

5. From this it follows that the delight and rapture of love which the soul receives in the fire of the light of these lamps is wondrous, boundless and as vast as that of many lamps, each of which burns with love,

[1] G omits the rest of the paragraph except the final sentence and has many minor variations and omissions throughout the remainder of the chapter.

[2] E.p. abbreviates: 'giving the soul intelligence and love, and revealing itself to it, in a manner corresponding to its capacity, according to them all.'

[3] E.p. abbreviates: 'inasmuch as He is wise, and so of the remaining attributes, for the light.'

[4] G: 'as innumerable lamps which enkindle it and illumine it in love of God Himself so that it knows Him and loves Him most ardently according to all His attributes.'

[5] [Lit., 'gave light well to Moses.'] E.p.: 'allowed Moses to see Him.'

[6] Exodus xxxiv, 6–7.

the heat of one being added to the heat of another, and the flame of one to the flame of another, as the light of one gives light to another, and all of them become one light and fire, and each of them becomes one fire. The soul is completely absorbed in these delicate flames, and wounded subtly in each of them, and in all of them more deeply and subtly wounded in love of life, so that it can see quite clearly that that love belongs to life eternal, which is the union of all blessings. So that the soul in that state knows well the truth of those words of the Spouse in the Songs, where He says that the lamps of love were lamps of fire and flames. Beauteous art thou in thy footsteps and thy shoes, oh, prince's daughter! Who can recount the magnificence and rarity of thy delight in the love of thy lamps and thy wondrous splendour?[1] For if one single lamp of those that passed before Abraham caused him great and darksome[2] horror, when God passed by, giving him knowledge of the rigorous justice which He was about to work upon the Chanaanites,[3] shall not all these lamps of the knowledge of God which give thee a pleasant[4] and loving light cause thee more light and joy of love than that single lamp caused horror and darkness in Abraham? And how great and how excellent and how manifold shall be thy light and joy, since in it all and from it all thou perceivest that He is giving thee His fruition and love, loving thee according to His virtues and attributes and qualities!

6. For he that loves another and does him good loves him and does him good according to his own attributes and properties. And thus since thy Spouse, Who is within thee, is omnipotent, He gives thee omnipotence and loves thee therewith; and since He is wise, thou perceivest that He loves thee with wisdom; since He is good, thou perceivest that He loves thee with goodness; since He is holy, thou perceivest that He loves thee with holiness; since He is just, thou perceivest that He loves thee justly; since He is merciful, thou perceivest that He loves thee with mercy; since He is compassionate and clement, thou perceivest that He loves thee with meekness and clemency; since His Being is strong and sublime and delicate, thou perceivest that He loves thee with strength, sublimity and delicacy; and since He is clean and pure, thou perceivest that He loves thee with cleanness and purity; and since He is true, thou perceivest that He loves thee truly; and since He is liberal, thou perceivest likewise that He

---

[1] Canticles vii, 1. E.p. omits: 'Beauteous . . . splendour.'
[2] E.p. omits 'and darksome.' [3] [Genesis xv, 12–17.]
[4] [Lit., 'a friendly.']

loves thee with liberality, without self-interest, and only that He may do thee good; as He is the virtue of the greatest humility, He loves thee with the greatest humility, and with the greatest esteem, making Himself thine equal and making thee His equal, joyfully revealing to thee, in these ways, His countenance, full of graces,[1] and saying to thee: I am thine and for thee, and I delight to be such as I am that I may give Myself to thee and be thine.

7. Who, then, can describe that which thou perceivest, oh, blessed soul, when thou seest thyself to be thus loved and to be exalted with such esteem? Thy belly, which is thy will, we shall describe as the heap of wheat which is covered and set about with lilies.[2] For in these grains of the wheat of the bread of life[3] which thou art tasting all together, the lilies of the virtues that surround thee are giving thee delight. For these daughters of the King, which are these virtues, are delighting thee wondrously with the fragrance of their aromatic spices, which are the knowledge that He gives thee; and thou art so wholly engulfed and absorbed therein that thou art also the well of living waters that run with vehemence from Mount Libanus, which is God,[4] in the which stream thou art become marvellously glad with all the harmony of thy soul and even of thy body. Thus may the words of the Psalm be accomplished in thee, namely: 'The vehemence of the river makes glad the city of God.'[5]

8. Oh, wondrous thing! At this time the soul is overflowing with Divine waters, which flow from it as from an abundant source,[6] whose waters gush in all directions. For, although it is true that this communication is light and fire from these lamps of God, yet this fire, as we have said, is here so sweet that, vast as it is, it is like the waters of life which quench the thirst of the spirit with the vehemence that it desires.[7] Thus, though these are lamps of fire, they are living waters of the spirit, even as were those that came upon the Apostles, which, though they were lamps of fire,[8] were also pure and clear water, as the prophet Ezechiel called them when he prophesied that coming of the Holy Spirit, saying: 'I will pour out upon you, saith God, clean water,

---

[1] E.p., B abbreviate: 'that He loves thee with holiness, and so forth; and since He is liberal, thou perceivest likewise that He loves thee with liberality, without self-interest, and only that He may do thee good, joyfully revealing to thee this His countenance, full of graces.'

[2] Canticles vii, 2.

[3] [*Lit.*, 'grains of bread of life.']

[4] Canticles iv, 15.

[5] Psalm xlv, 5 [A.V., xlvi, 4].

[6] E.p. adds: 'that looks upon eternal life.'

[7] [Cf. here a poem attributed to St. John of the Cross, referred to in Vol. II, p. 413.]

[8] C: 'were tongues of fire.'

and will put My spirit in the midst of you.'[1] And thus this fire is likewise water, since it is prefigured in the fire that Jeremias hid, which
belonged to the sacrifice, which was water when it was hidden and fire
when it was brought forth and used for the sacrifice.[2] And thus this
spirit of God, while hidden in the veins of the soul, is like sweet and
delectable water quenching the thirst of the spirit in the substance of
the soul;[3] and, when the soul offers the sacrifice of love, it becomes
living flames of fire,[4] which are the lamps of the act of love described,
as we said, by the Spouse in the Songs, in these words: 'The lamps
thereof are lamps of fire and of flames';[5] which the soul calls them here
also. For not only does the soul taste them as waters of wisdom within
itself, but likewise as fire of love, in an act of love, saying: 'Oh, lamps
of fire.' And all that can be said of this matter is less than what there is
to be said. If we consider that the soul is transformed in God, it will be
understood in some wise how it is true that it has become a fountain of
living waters, boiling and burning in the fire of love, which is God.

In whose splendours

9. It has already been explained that these splendours are the communications of these Divine lamps, wherein the soul that is in union
shines forth in splendour with its faculties—memory, understanding
and will—which are now illumined and united in this loving knowledge. It must be understood that this enlightenment of splendour is
not like a material fire which, with its bursts of flame, enlightens and
heats things that are outside it, but is like one that heats things that[6]
are within it, as is the soul in this state. For this reason the soul says:
'In whose splendours': that is to say, it is 'within'—not 'near' but
'within'—its splendours, in the flames of the lamps, the soul being
transformed into flame. And so we shall say that it is like the air which
is within the flame and is enkindled and transformed into fire, for flame
is naught else but enkindled air; and the movements made by this
flame are not simply those of air nor simply those of fire, but of air and
fire together, and the fire causes the air that is enkindled within it to
burn.

10. And in this way we shall understand that the soul with its faculties is illumined within the splendours of God. And the movements of

---

[1] Ezechiel xxxvi, 25–6.
[2] 2 Machabees i, 20–2. [The reference in this passage is to Nehemias. No doubt there is
a scribal error here: a change of only two letters is involved.]
[3] E.p. omits: 'in the substance of the soul.'
[4] C: 'of fire of love.'   [5] [Canticles viii, 6.]
[6] So e.p. The other authorities [followed by P. Silverio] read: 'but is like those that.'

this flame, which are the flickerings and the flamings forth that we have described above, are not wrought only by the soul that is transformed in the flame of the Holy Spirit, neither are they wrought by Him alone; but by Him and by the soul together, the Spirit moving the soul, even as fire moves air that is enkindled. And thus these movements of God and the soul together are not only splendours, but also glorifications[1] which God works in the soul. For these movements or flickerings[2] are the fires[3] and the joyful festivals which we said, in the second line of the first stanza, the Holy Spirit brings to pass within the soul, wherein it seems that He is ever about to grant it eternal life. And thus those movements and bursts of flame are, as it were, provocations that the Spirit is causing the soul so that He may in the end remove it to His perfect glory and make it at last to enter truly within Himself. For all the blessings, both the early and the late, the great and the small, that God grants the soul He grants to it always with this motive, which pertains both to Him and to the soul, of bringing it to eternal life.[4] Just so is it when fire makes movements and motions in the enkindled air which it has within itself; the purpose of these is to bring it to the centre[5] of its sphere; and all these flickerings are attempts to bring it there, but, because the air is in its own sphere, this cannot be done. In the same way, although these movements of the Holy Spirit are most highly enkindled and are most effective in absorbing the soul into great glory, yet this is not accomplished perfectly until the time comes for the soul to leave the sphere of air—which is this life of the flesh— and to enter into the centre of its spirit, which is perfect life in Christ.

11. But it must be understood that these movements are movements of the soul rather than of God; for these glimpses of glory in God that are given to the soul are not stable, perfect and continuous, as they will be in the soul hereafter, without any change[6] between greater and lesser, and without any intervening movements; and then the soul will see clearly how, although here below it appeared that God was moving in it, God moves not in Himself, even as the fire moves not in its sphere. But these splendours are inestimable graces and favours

---

[1] E.p.: '. . . together are as it were glorifications.'

[2] E.p.: 'movements and bursts of flame or flickerings.'

[3] A, C: 'the playing(s)'—i.e. of the fire: the general sense is the same as in the text. [The reading of the text, however, does not agree so well with the following substantive.]

[4] E.p. omits the whole of this sentence.

[5] E.p.: 'to the summit.'

[6] E.p. abbreviates (from the beginning of the paragraph) thus: 'These glimpses of glory in God that are here given to the soul are now more continuous than they used to be, and more perfect and stable; but in the next life they will be most perfect, without change.'

that God grants to the soul, which by another name are called over-shadowings, and these, in my opinion, are among the highest favours that can be granted here on earth in this process of transformation.

12. To understand this it must be realized that 'overshadowing' means the casting of a shadow, and for a man to cast his shadow over another signifies that he protects him and grants him favours. When the shadow touches the person, this is a sign that he who overshadows him is now near to befriend and protect him. For this reason it was said to the Virgin, that the power of the Most High would overshadow her,[1] because the Holy Spirit was to approach her so nearly that He would come upon her. Herein it is to be noted that everything has and makes a shadow which corresponds to its nature and size. If the thing is dense and opaque, it will make a dark and dense shadow, and if it is clearer and lighter it will make a lighter shadow: this we see with a log of wood or with crystal; the one, being opaque, will make a dark shadow, and the other, being light, will make a light shadow.

13. Even so in spiritual matters. Death is the privation of all things. The shadow of death, then, will be darkness which in one sense de-prives us of all things. This name was given to it by the Psalmist, where he said: *Sedentes in tenebris et in umbra mortis*;[2] whether the darkness be spiritual, and relate to spiritual death, or bodily, and relate to bodily death. The shadow of life will be light: if Divine, Divine light; if human, natural light. What, then, will be the shadow of beauty? It will be other beauty, of the nature and proportions of that beauty. So the shadow of strength will be other strength, of the nature and quality of that strength. And the shadow of wisdom will be other wisdom; or, more correctly, it will be the same beauty and the same strength and the same wisdom in shadow, wherein will be recognized the nature and proportions of which the shadow is cast.[3]

14. What, then, will be the shadows that the Holy Spirit will cast upon the soul—namely, the shadows of all the grandeurs of His virtues and attributes? For He is so near to the soul that they not only touch it in shadow, but the soul is united with them in shadow, and experiences them in shadow,[4] and it understands and experiences the nature and proportions of God in the shadow of God—that is, by

---

[1] St. Luke i, 35.   [2] Psalm cvi, 10 [A.V., cvii, 10].
[3] E.p. continues (after the Latin quotation): 'and thus the shadow of beauty will be as other beauty, of the proportions and properties of that beauty of which it is the shadow; and the shadow of strength will be as other strength, of its proportions and qualities. And the shadow of wisdom, etc.'
[4] E.p. omits: 'and experiences them in shadow.'

understanding and experiencing the nature of Divine power in the shadow of omnipotence; and it understands and experiences Divine wisdom in the shadow of Divine wisdom; understands and experiences infinite goodness in the shadow of infinite goodness which surrounds it; understands and experiences the delight of God infused in the shadow of the delight of God; and, finally,[1] experiences the glory of God in the shadow of glory which causes it to know and experience the nature and proportions of the glory of God when all these pass by in bright and enkindled shadows. For the attributes of God and His virtues are lamps which, resplendent and enkindled as they are, will cast shadows that are resplendent and enkindled according to His nature and proportions, and will cast a multitude of them in one sole being.

15. Oh, what this will be for the soul, when it experiences the power of that figure which Ezechiel saw in that beast with four forms, and in that wheel with four wheels, when he saw that its appearance was as the appearance of kindled coals and as the appearance of lamps! The soul will see the wheel, which is wisdom, full of eyes within and without, which are wondrous manifestations of wisdom, and will hear the sound that they made as they passed, which was like the sound of a multitude and of great armies, signifying in one number many different things of God, which the soul[2] here understands[3] in one single sound of God's passing through it. Finally, it will experience that sound of the beating of wings, which Ezechiel says was as the sound of many waters and as the sound of the Most High God;[4] this indicates the vehemence of the Divine waters, which, at the beating of the wings of the Holy Spirit, overwhelm the soul and make it to rejoice in the flame of love,[5] so that it now enjoys the glory of God in His protection and the favour of His shadow, even as this prophet says in that place that that vision was the similitude of the glory of the Lord.[6] And to what a height may this happy soul now find itself raised! How greatly will it know itself to be exalted! How wondrous will it see itself to be in holy beauty! How far beyond all telling! For so copiously does it become immersed in the waters of these Divine splendours that it is able to see the Eternal Father with bounteous hand pouring

[1] E.p. abbreviates: 'of Divine wisdom; and finally.'
[2] E.p. abbreviates: 'which signifies many things in one, which the soul.'
[3] E.p.: 'here knows.'
[4] [Ezechiel i, 15–25.]
[5] E.p.: 'which, at the descent of the Holy Spirit, assails the soul in a flame of love.'
[6] [Ezechiel i, 28.]

forth the upper and the lower streams that water the earth,[1] even as the father of Axa gave these to her when she longed for them, for these irrigating waters penetrate both soul and body.[2]

16. Oh, wondrous thing, that all these lamps of the Divine attributes should be one simple being in which alone they are experienced, and yet that the distinction between them should be visible and perceptible,[3] the one being as completely enkindled as the other and the one being substantially the other! Oh, abyss of delights, the more abundant in proportion as thy riches are gathered together in infinite unity and simplicity, so that each one is known and experienced in such a way that the perfect knowledge and absorption of the other may not be impeded thereby, but rather each thing within thee is the light of the other, so that through thy purity, oh, Divine wisdom, many things are seen in thee when one thing is seen,[4] since thou art the store-house of the treasures of the Eternal Father. For in thy splendours are

The deep caverns of sense

17. These caverns are the faculties of the soul—memory, understanding and will—of which the depth is proportionate to their capacity for great blessings, for they can be filled with nothing less than the infinite.[5] By considering what they suffer when they are empty we can realize in some measure the greatness of their joy and delight when they are filled with their God, for one contrary can give light to another.[6] In the first place, it must be noted that these caverns of the faculties, when they are not empty and purged and cleansed from all creature affection, are not conscious of their great emptiness, which is due to their profound capacity; for in this life any trifle that remains within them suffices to keep them so cumbered and fascinated that they are neither conscious of their loss nor do they miss the immense blessings that might be theirs, nor are they aware of their own capacity. And it is a wondrous thing that, despite their capacity for infinite

[1] [Judges i, 15. If we follow the Vulgate we shall read 'watery ground' for 'springs,' but the application is less apt.]

[2] E.p.: 'Oh, to what a height is this happy soul now raised! Oh, how is it exalted! How greatly does it wonder at what it sees, even within the limits of faith! Who shall be able to say this, since it is so completely immersed in the waters of these Divine splendours, where with bounteous hand the Eternal Father pours forth the upper and the lower streams that water the earth, for these irrigating waters penetrate both soul and body.'

[3] E.p.: 'one simple being, and yet in it the distinction between them is conceived and understood.'

[4] E.p.: 'is a light which hinders not the other, and through thy purity, oh, Divine wisdom, many things are known in thee in one.'

[5] E.p.: 'for they cannot be filled save with the infinite.'

[6] [Cf. p. 27, l. 1, above.]

blessing, the least thing suffices to cumber them, so that they cannot receive these blessings[1] until they are completely empty, as we shall say hereafter. But, when they are empty and clean, the hunger and thirst and yearning of their spiritual sense become intolerable; for, as the capacities[2] of these caverns are deep, their pain is deep likewise; as is also the food that they lack, which, as I say, is God. And this great feeling of pain commonly occurs towards the close of the illumination and purification of the soul, ere it attain to union,[3] wherein it has satisfaction. For, when the spiritual appetite is empty and purged from every creature and from every creature affection, and its natural temper is lost, and it has become attempered to the Divine, and its emptiness is disposed to be filled, and the Divine communication of union with God has not yet reached it, then the suffering caused by this emptiness and thirst is worse than death, especially when the soul is vouchsafed some foresight or glimpse of the Divine ray and this is not communicated to it. It is souls in this condition that suffer with impatient love, so that they cannot remain long without either receiving or dying.[4]

18. With respect to the first cavern which we here describe—namely, the understanding—its emptiness is thirst for God, and this is so great that David compares it to that of the hart, finding no greater thirst wherewith to compare it, for the thirst of the hart is said to be most vehement. Even as the hart[5] (says David) desires the fountains of the waters, even so does my soul desire Thee, O God.[6] This thirst is for the waters of the wisdom of God which is the object of the understanding.

19. The second cavern is the will, and the emptiness thereof is hunger for God, so great that it causes the soul to swoon, even as David says, in these words: 'My soul desires and faints in the tabernacles of the Lord.[7]' And this hunger is for the perfection of love to which the soul aspires.

20. The third cavern is the memory, whereof the emptiness is the melting away and languishing of the soul for the possession of God, as Jeremias notes in these words: *Memoria memor ero et tabescet in me anima mea.*[8] That is: With remembrance I shall remember. *Id est:*

[1] E.p. adds: 'perfectly.'   [2] [*Lit.*, 'the stomachs.']
[3] E.p.: 'to perfect union.'
[4] A omits all the rest of the commentary on this stanza, except §§ 59, 60.
[5] E.p.: 'wherewith to compare it, when he says: Even as the hart, etc.'
[6] Psalm xli, 1 [A.V., xlii, 1].
[7] Psalm lxxxiii, 3 [A.V., lxxxiv, 2].
[8] Lamentations iii, 20–1. E.p. omits the Latin text.

I shall remember well and my soul shall melt away within me; turning over these things in my heart, I shall live in hope of God.

21. The capacity of these caverns, then, is deep; for that which they are capable of containing, which is God, is deep and infinite; and thus in a certain sense their capacity will be infinite, and likewise their thirst will be infinite, and their hunger also will be deep and infinite, and their languishing and pain are infinite death. For, although the soul suffers not so intensely as in the next life, it suffers nevertheless a vivid image of that infinite privation, since it is to a certain extent prepared to receive fullness; although this suffering is of another kind, for it dwells in the bosom of the love of the will, and this love does not alleviate the pain;[1] for the greater it is, the greater is the impatience of the soul for the possession of its God, for Whom it hopes continually with intense desire.

22. But, seeing it is certain that, when the soul desires God with entire truth, it already (as Saint Gregory says in writing of Saint John[2]) possesses Him Whom it loves, how comes it, O God, that it yearns for Him Whom it already possesses? For, in the desire which, as Saint Peter says,[3] the angels have to see the Son of God, there is neither pain nor yearning, since they possess Him already; so it seems that, if the soul possesses God more completely according as it desires Him more earnestly, the possession of God should give delight and satisfaction to the soul. Even so the angels have delight when they are fulfilling their desire in possession, and satisfying their spirit continually with desire, yet have none of the weariness that comes from satiety; wherefore, since they have no weariness, they continually desire, and because they have possession they have no pain. Thus, the greater is the desire of the soul in this state, the more satisfaction and desire it should experience, since it has the more of God and has not grief or pain.[4]

23. In this matter, however, it is well to note clearly the difference that exists between the possession of God through grace itself alone and the possession of Him through union; for the one consists in deep

---

[1] E.p.: 'and their languishing and pain are in a way infinite. And thus, when the soul suffers, although it suffers not so intensely as in the next life, yet [its suffering] seems to be a vivid image of that [suffering] yonder, since the soul is to a certain extent prepared to receive fullness, the privation of which is the greatest pain; although this pain is of another kind, for it dwells in the bosom of the love of the will, and here [on earth] love alleviates not pain.'

[2] Hom. XXX in Evang.   E.p. omits: 'in writing of St. John.'

[3] [1 St. Peter i, 12.]

[4] E.p. abbreviates: 'and satisfaction to the soul; and the greater is its desire, the more satisfaction and delight it should now feel in this desire, since it has the more of God; and thus it ought not to feel grief or pain.'

mutual love, but in the other there is also communication. There is as great a difference between these states as there is between betrothal and marriage. For in betrothal there is only a consent by agreement, and a unity of will between the two parties, and the jewels and the adornment of the bride-to-be, given her graciously by the bridegroom. But in marriage there is likewise communication between the persons, and union.[1] During the betrothal, although from time to time the bride-groom sees the bride and gives her gifts, as we have said, there is no union between them, for that is the end of betrothal. Even so, when the soul has attained to such purity in itself and in its faculties that the will is well purged of other strange tastes and desires, according to its lower and higher parts, and when it has given its consent to God with respect to all this, and the will of God and of the soul are as one in a consent that is ready and free, then it has attained to the possession of God through grace of will, in so far as can be by means of will and grace; and this signifies that God has given it, through its own consent, His true and entire consent, which comes through His grace.[2]

24. And this is the lofty state of spiritual betrothal of the soul with the Word, wherein the Spouse grants the soul great favours, and visits it most lovingly and frequently, wherein the soul receives great favours and delights. But these have nothing to do with those of marriage, for they are all preparations for the union of marriage; and, though it is true that they come to the soul[3] when it is completely purged from all creature affection (for spiritual betrothal, as we say, cannot take place until this happens), nevertheless[4] the soul has need of other and positive preparations on the part of God, of His visits and gifts whereby He purifies the soul ever more completely and beautifies and refines it so that it may be fitly prepared for such high union. In some souls more time is necessary than in others, for God works here according to the state of the soul.[5] This is prefigured in those maidens who were chosen for King Assuerus; although they had been taken

[1] E.p.: 'In this matter, however, we must note the difference that exists between the possession of God through grace alone and the possession of Him through union; for the one is a question of mutual love and the other argues a very special communication. This difference may be understood after the manner of that which exists between betrothal and marriage. For in betrothal there is an agreement and one will between the two parties, and the few jewels and ornaments of the bride-to-be given her graciously by the bride-groom. But in marriage there is likewise union and communication between the persons.'

[2] E.p. abbreviates: 'to the possession of God through grace, in the betrothal and con-formity of its will.'

[3] E.p.: 'But these have nothing to do with those of the spiritual marriage, for, though it is true that they all come to the soul.'

[4] E.p. adds: 'for union and marriage.'

[5] E.p. omits: 'for God . . . the soul.'

from their own countries and from their fathers' houses, yet, before they were sent to the king's bed, they were kept waiting for a year, albeit within the enclosure of the palace.[1] For one half of the year they were prepared with certain ointments[2] of myrrh and other spices, and for the other half of the year with other and choicer ointments, after which they went to the king's bed.

25. During the time, then, of this betrothal and expectation of marriage in the unctions of the Holy Spirit, when the ointments that prepare the soul for union with God are very choice, the yearnings of the caverns of the soul are wont to be extreme and delicate. For, as those ointments are a most proximate preparation for union with God, because they are nearest to God and for this cause make the soul more desirous of Him and inspire it with a more delicate affection for Him, the desire is more delicate and also deeper; for the desire for God is a preparation for union with God.

26. Oh, how good a place would this be to warn souls whom God is leading to these delicate anointings to take care what they are doing and into whose hands they commit themselves, lest they go backward, were not this beyond the limits of that whereof we are speaking! But such is the compassion and pity that fills my heart when I see souls[3] going backward, and not only failing to submit themselves to the anointing of the spirit so that they may make progress therein, but even losing the effects of that anointing which they have received, that I must not fail to warn them here as to what they should do in order to avoid such loss, even though this should cause us to delay the return to our subject a little. I shall return to it shortly, and indeed all this will help us to understand the properties of these caverns. And since it is very necessary, not only for these souls that prosper on this way but also for all the rest who seek their Beloved, I am anxious to describe it.

27.[4] First, it must be known that, if a soul is seeking God, its Beloved is seeking it much more; and, if it sends after Him its loving desires, which are as fragrant to Him as a pillar of smoke that issues from the aromatic spices of myrrh and incense, He likewise sends after it the fragrance of His ointments, wherewith He draws the soul and causes it to run after Him. These ointments are His Divine inspirations and touches, which, whenever they are His, are ordered and ruled with

---

[1] [Esther ii, 12.] [2] C: 'certain odours.'
[3] E.p.: 'certain souls.'
[4] P begins here and continues as far as § 59, with certain omissions.

respect to the perfection of the law of God and of faith, in which perfection the soul must ever draw nearer and nearer to God. And thus the soul must understand that the desire of God in all the favours that He bestows upon it in the unction and fragrance of His ointments is to prepare it for other choicer and more delicate ointments which are more after the temper of God, until it reaches such a delicate and pure state of preparation that it merits union with God and substantial transformation in all its faculties.

28. When, therefore, the soul reflects that God is the principal agent in this matter, and the guide of its blind self [1] Who will take it by the hand and lead it where it could not of itself go (namely, to the supernatural things which neither its understanding nor its will nor its memory could know as they are), then its chief care will be to see that it sets no obstacle in the way of the guide, who is the Holy Spirit, upon the road by which God is leading it, and which is ordained according to the law of God and faith, as we are saying. And this impediment may come to the soul if it allows itself to be led by another blind guide; and these blind guides that might lead it out of its way are three, namely, the spiritual director, the devil, and its own self.

29. With regard to the first of these, it is of great importance for the soul that desires to profit, and not to fall back, to consider[2] in whose hands it is placing itself; for as is the master, so will be the disciple, and as is the father, so will be the son. There is hardly anyone who in all respects will guide the soul perfectly along the highest stretch of the road, or even along the intermediate stretches, for it is needful that such a guide should be wise and discreet and experienced. The fundamental requirement of a guide in spiritual things is knowledge and discretion; yet, if a guide have no experience of the higher part of the road, he will be unable to direct the soul therein, when God leads it so far. A guide might even do the soul great harm if, not himself understanding the way of the spirit,[3] he should cause the soul, as often happens, to lose the unction of these delicate ointments, wherewith the Holy Spirit gradually prepares it for Himself, and if instead of this he should guide the soul by other and lower paths of which he has read here and there, and which are suitable only for beginners. Such guides know no more than how to deal with beginners—please God they may know even so

---

[1] [*Lit.*, 'and the blind man's boy.'] E.p. omits this phrase.
[2] C adds 'most diligently' and omits 'great' earlier in the sentence.
[3] E.p.: 'the roads of the spirit.'

much!—and refuse to allow souls to go beyond these rudimentary
acts of meditation and imagination, even though God is seeking to lead
them farther, so that they may never exceed or depart from their natural
capacity,[1] whereby they can achieve very little.

30. And in order that we may understand this the better, we must
know that the state of beginners comprises meditation and discursive
acts. In this state, it is necessary for the soul to be given material for
meditation, and to make interior acts on its own account, and to take
advantage of the spiritual heat and fire which come from sense; this is
necessary in order to accustom the senses and desires to good things,
so that, by being fed with this delight, they may become detached from
the world. But, when this has been to some extent effected, God
begins to bring the soul into the state of contemplation, which is wont
to happen very quickly, especially in religious, because these, having
renounced things of the world, quickly attune their senses and desires
to God; and then they have nothing to do save to pass from meditation to contemplation, which happens when the discursive acts and the
meditation of the soul itself cease, and the first fervours and sweetness
of sense cease likewise, so that the soul cannot meditate as before, or
find any help in the senses; for the senses remain in a state of aridity,
inasmuch as their treasure is transformed into spirit, and no longer
falls within the capacity of sense. And, as all the operations which the
soul can perform on its own account naturally depend upon sense
only, it follows that God is the agent in this state and the soul is the
recipient; for the soul behaves only as one that receives and as one in
whom these things are being wrought; and God as One that gives and
acts and as One that works these things in the soul, giving it spiritual
blessings in contemplation,[2] which is Divine love and knowledge in
one—that is, a loving knowledge, wherein the soul has not to use its
natural acts and meditations, for it can no longer enter into them as
before.

31. It follows that at this time the soul must be led in a way entirely
contrary to the way wherein it was led at first. If formerly it was given
material for meditation, and practised meditation, this material must
now be taken from it and it must not meditate; for, as I say, it will be
unable to do so even though it would, and it will become distracted.
And if formerly it sought sweetness and fervour, and found it, now

---

[1] E.p. omits: 'so that . . . capacity.'
[2] E.p.: 'that God in this state is in a special way the agent who infuses and teaches, and
the soul is one that receives, [to whom He is] giving very spiritual blessings in contemplation.'

it must neither seek it nor desire it, for not only will it be unable to find it through its own diligence, but it will rather find aridity, for it turns from the quiet and peaceful blessings which were secretly given to its spirit, to the work that it desires to do with sense; and thus it will lose the one and not obtain the other, since no blessings are now given to it by means of sense as they were formerly. Wherefore in this state the soul must never have meditation imposed upon it, nor must it make any acts, nor strive after sweetness or fervour;[1] for this would be to set an obstacle in the way of the principal agent, who, as I say, is God. For God secretly and quietly infuses into the soul loving knowledge and wisdom without any intervention of specific acts,[2] although sometimes He specifically produces them in the soul for some length of time. And the soul has then to walk with loving advertence to God, without making specific acts, but conducting itself, as we have said, passively,[3] and making no efforts of its own, but preserving this simple, pure and loving advertence, like one that opens his eyes with the advertence of love.

32. Since God, then, as giver, is communing with the soul by means of loving and simple knowledge, the soul must likewise commune with Him by receiving with a loving and simple knowledge or advertence, so that knowledge may be united with knowledge and love with love. For it is meet that he who receives should behave in conformity with that which he receives, and not otherwise, in order to be able to receive and retain it as it is given to him; for, as the philosophers say, anything that is received is in the recipient according to the manner of acting of the recipient.[4] Wherefore it is clear that if the soul at this time were not to abandon its natural procedure of active meditation, it would not receive this blessing in other than a natural way. It would not, in fact, receive it, but would retain its natural act alone, for the supernatural cannot be received in a natural way, nor can it have aught to do with it.[5] And thus,[6] if the soul at this time desires to work on its

---

[1] E.p.: 'any acts produced by means of reflection, nor strive knowingly after sweetness or fervour.'

[2] E.p.: 'without any great difference, expression or multiplication of acts.'

[3] E.p.: 'without performing any other specific acts than those to which it feels that He is inclining it, but conducting itself, as it were, passively.'

[4] E.p. omits: 'for . . . recipient.' G gives the phrase in Latin.

[5] G: 'for the supernatural cannot be contained in the soul that is occupied in natural operations and acts.'

[6] E.p.: 'were not to abandon its ordinary discursive procedure, it would not receive this blessing save in a scanty and imperfect way, and thus it would not receive it with that perfection wherewith it was bestowed; for, being so superior and infused a blessing, it cannot be contained in so scanty and imperfect a form. And thus, etc.'

own account, and to do aught else than remain, quite passively and tranquilly, in that passive and loving advertence whereof we have spoken, making no natural act, save if God should unite it with Himself in some act, it would set a total and effective impediment in the way of the blessings which God is communicating to it supernaturally in loving knowledge.[1] This comes to pass first of all in the exercise of purgation,[2] as we have said above, and afterwards in increased sweetness of love. If, as I say, and as in truth is the case, the soul continues to receive these blessings passively and after the supernatural manner of God, and not after the manner of the natural soul,[3] it follows that, in order to receive them, this soul must be quite disencumbered, at ease, peaceful, serene and adapted to the manner of God; like the air, which receives greater illumination and heat from the sun when it is pure and cleansed and at rest. And thus the soul must be attached to nothing—nay, not even to any kind of meditation or sweetness, whether of sense or of spirit. For the spirit needs to be so free and so completely annihilated that any thought[4] or meditation which the soul in this state might desire, or any pleasure to which it may conceive an attachment, would impede and disturb it and would introduce noise into the deep silence which it is meet that the soul should observe, according both to sense and to spirit, so that it may hear the deep and delicate voice of God which speaks to the heart in this secret place, as He said through Osee,[5] in the utmost peace and tranquillity, so that the soul may listen and hear, as David heard, the words of God, when He speaks this peace in the soul. When this comes to pass, and the soul is conscious of being led into silence, and hearkens, it must forget even that loving advertence of which I have spoken, so that it may remain free for that which is then desired of it; for it must practise that advertence only when it is not conscious of being brought into solitude or rest or forgetfulness or attentiveness of the spirit, which is always accompanied by a certain interior absorption.[6]

---

1 E.p. omits: 'whereof we have spoken' and continues 'reasoning [i.e. meditating] not as formerly, it would place an impediment in the way of the blessings which God is communicating to it in loving knowledge.'

2 C: 'in loving knowledge in the exercise of purgation.'

3 E.p.: 'after the manner of God and not after the manner of the soul.'

4 E.p.: 'any particular thought.'

5 Osee ii, 14.

6 E.p.: 'and hearkens, even the loving awareness of which I have spoken must be most pure, without any anxiety or reflection, so that the soul almost forgets it through being wholly occupied in hearing, in order that it may remain free for that which is then desired of it.'

33. Wherefore[1] at no time or season, when once the soul has begun to enter into this pure and restful state of contemplation, must it seek to gather to itself meditations, neither must it desire to find help in spiritual sweetness or delight,[2] but it must stand in complete detachment above all this and its spirit must be freed from it, as the prophet Habacuc said that he must needs do, in these words: 'I will stand upon my watch over my senses—that is, leaving them below—and I will fix my step upon the munition of my faculties—that is, not allowing them to advance a step in thought—and I will watch to see that which will be said to me—that is, I will receive that which is communicated to me.[3]' For we have already said that contemplation is receiving, and it is not possible that this loftiest wisdom and lineage of contemplation can be received save in a spirit that is silent and detached from[4] sweetness and knowledge. For this is that which is said by Isaias, in these words: 'Whom shall He teach knowledge and whom shall He make to hear[5] that which is heard?'[6] Them that are weaned from milk—that is, from sweetness and pleasures—and them that are drawn from the breasts—that is, from attachment to particular acts and knowledge. Take away the mist and the mote and the hairs, and cleanse thine eye, and the bright sun shall shine upon thee, and thou shalt see. Set the soul in the liberty of peace, and draw it away from the yoke and slavery of its operation, which is the captivity of Egypt; for all this is little more than gathering straw to make bricks; and lead it to the promised land flowing with milk and honey.

34. Oh, spiritual director, remember that it is to give the soul this freedom and holy rest which belongs to His sons that God calls it into the wilderness. There it journeys clad in festal robes, and with jewels of silver and of gold, having now despoiled Egypt[7] and taken away its riches. And not only so, but the Egyptians are drowned[8] in the sea of contemplation, where the Egyptian of sense finds no support or foothold, and sets free the child of God—that is, the spirit that has gone forth from the narrow limits and bounds of natural operation (which is to say from its lowly understanding, its crude perception,

---

[1] E.p.: 'This manner and [sic] forgetfulness is always accompanied by a certain interior absorption. Wherefore, etc.'

[2] E.p. adds: 'as is said at length in the tenth chapter of the first book of the *Dark Night*, and previously in the last chapter of the second book, and in the first chapter [*the second in our edition*] of the third book of the *Ascent of Mount Carmel*.'

[3] [Habacuc ii, 1.] E.p. adds: 'passively.'   [4] E.p.: 'from particular.'

[5] E.p.: 'to understand.'   [6] Isaias xxviii, 9.

[7] Gr, P add: 'which is the sensual part.'

[8] [*Lit.*, 'they are drowned.'] E.p.: 'but it drowns its enemies.' C: 'but it drowns the Egyptians.'

and its miserable liking)—so that God may give it the sweet manna; and, though the sweetness of this contains within itself all these sweetnesses and delights for which thou desirest to make the soul work, nevertheless, being so delicious that it melts in the mouth, the soul shall not taste of it if it desire to taste of any other delight or aught else, for it shall not receive it. Endeavour, then, to detach[1] the soul from all coveting of sweetness, pleasure and meditation, and disturb it not with care and solicitude of any kind for higher things, still less for lower things, but bring it into the greatest possible degree of solitude and withdrawal. For the more nearly the soul attains all this, and the sooner it reaches this restful tranquillity, the more abundantly does it become infused with the spirit of Divine wisdom, the loving, tranquil, lonely, peaceful, sweet ravisher of the spirit. At times the soul will feel itself to be tenderly and serenely ravished and wounded, knowing not by whom, nor whence, nor how, since the Spirit communicates Himself without any act on the part of the soul.[2]

35. And the smallest part of this that God brings to pass in the soul in holy rest and solitude is an inestimable blessing, greater than either the soul itself, or he that guides it, can imagine; and, if this be not realized at the time, it will in due course become manifest. But now, at least, the soul will be able to attain to a perception of estrangement and withdrawal from all things, sometimes more so than at others, together with a sweet aspiration of love and life in the spirit, and with an inclination to solitude and a sense of weariness with regard to creatures and the world. For, when the soul tastes of the spirit, it conceives a distaste for all that pertains to the flesh.

36. But the interior blessings that this silent contemplation leaves impressed upon the soul without its perception of them are, as I say, inestimable; for they are in fact the most secret and delicate anointings of the Holy Spirit, whereby He secretly fills the soul with riches and gifts and graces, for, after all, being God, He acts as God.[3] These blessings, then, and these great riches, these sublime and delicate anointings and touches of the Holy Spirit, which, on account of their delicate and subtle purity, can be understood neither by the soul nor by him that has to do with it, but only by Him Who infuses them in order to make the soul more pleasing to Himself: these blessings, with the greatest[4] facility, by even the very slightest of such acts as the soul

---

[1] E.p.: 'to uproot.'   [2] E.p. adds: 'in the sense aforementioned.'
[3] E.p. adds: 'and works as God.'
[4] C, G: 'the most welcome' [gratísima for grandísima].

may desire to make by applying its sense or desire to the attainment of some knowledge or sweetness or pleasure, are disturbed and hindered, which is a grave evil and a great shame and pity.

37. Oh, how grave a matter is this, and what cause it gives for wonder, that, while the harm done is inconspicuous, and the interference almost negligible, the harm should be more serious, and a matter for deeper sorrow and regret, than the disquieting and ruining of many souls of a more ordinary nature[1] which have not attained to this state of such supreme fineness and delicacy. It is as though a portrait of supreme beauty were touched by a clumsy hand, and were daubed with strange, crude colours. This would be a greater and a more crying shame than if many more ordinary portraits were besmeared in this way, and a matter of greater grief and pity. For, when the work of so delicate a hand has been so roughly treated, who will be able to restore its beauty?[2]

38. Although the gravity of this evil cannot be exaggerated, it is so common that there will hardly be found a single spiritual director who does not inflict it upon souls whom God is beginning, in this way, to draw nearer to Himself[3] in contemplation. For, whenever God is anointing the soul with some most delicate unction of loving knowledge—serene, peaceful, lonely and very far removed from sense and from all that has to do with thought— and when the soul cannot meditate or find pleasure in aught,[4] whether in higher things or in lower, or in any knowledge, since God is keeping it full of that lonely unction and inclined to solitude and rest, there will come some director who has no knowledge save of hammering and pounding like a blacksmith, and, because his only teaching is of that kind, he will say: 'Come now, leave all this, for you are only wasting time and living in idleness. Get to work, meditate and make interior acts, for it is right that you should do these things for yourself and be diligent about them, for these other things are the practices of Illuminists and fools.'

39. And thus, since such persons have no understanding of the degrees of prayer or of the ways of the spirit, they cannot see that those acts which they counsel the soul to perform, and that progress along the path of meditation, have been done already, for such a soul as we

[1] E.p.: 'than one which would appear much greater in ordinary souls.'

[2] E.p. omits this sentence. G has: 'For who will be able to amend and perfect that which was wrought by that Divine hand and which this [unskilful director] spoils with his lack of comprehension?'

[3] [The verb is *recoger*, from which is derived *recogimiento*, 'recollection.']

[4] E.p.: 'and when He is keeping it in such a state that it cannot find pleasure in aught, or meditate upon aught.'

have been describing has by this time attained to negation of sense; and, when the goal has been reached, and the road traversed, there is no need to set out on the road again, for to do this would only be to walk away[1] from the goal. And thus, not understanding that such a soul is already upon the way[2] of the spirit, where there is no meditation, that its meditation[3] is now coming to an end, that God is the agent,[4] and that He is secretly speaking to the solitary soul, while the soul keeps silence, such a director applies fresh ointments[5] to the soul, relating to cruder knowledge and sweetness, and, by imposing these things upon it, he takes away its solitude and recollection, and consequently spoils the wondrous work that God was painting in it. In this way the soul neither does one thing nor makes progress in another; it is just as if the director were merely striking an anvil.[6]

40. Let such as these take heed and remember that the Holy Spirit is the principal agent and mover of souls and never loses His care for them; and that they themselves are not agents, but only instruments to lead souls by the rule of faith and the law of God, according to the spirit that God is giving to each one. Let them not, therefore, merely aim at guiding a soul according to their own way and the manner suitable to themselves, but let them see if they know the way by which God is leading the soul, and, if they know it not, let them leave the soul in peace and not disturb it. And, in conformity with this, let them seek to lead the soul into greater solitude and liberty and tranquillity, and to give it a certain freedom so that the bodily and spiritual senses may not be bound to anything when God leads the soul in this way, and let them not worry or grieve, thinking that it is doing nothing. For when it is detached from all knowledge of its own, and from every desire and all affections of its sensual part, and dwells in the pure negation of poverty of spirit, wholly emptied of the mists of sweetness, wholly weaned from the breast and from milk (which is what the soul must be careful to do, as far as in it lies, and the director must aid the soul to deny itself in all these ways), it is impossible[7] that God will not perform His own part. It is more impossible than that the sun should fail to shine in a serene and unclouded sky; for as the sun, when it

---

[1] C: 'to descend.' [2] B, G, e.p.: 'is already in the life.'
[3] C, G, Gr, e.p.: 'its sense.' [4] E.p. adds: 'in a particular way.'
[5] G: 'such a soul, by making acts or meditating, does naught else than apply to itself fresh ointments.' [The word translated 'ointments,' both here and in the text, is generally rendered 'unctions' above.]
[6] P: 'were striking hard earth.' E.p. omits: 'it is . . . anvil.'
[7] E.p. adds: 'according to the method of procedure of the Divine goodness and mercy.'

rises in the morning and shines into your house, will enter if you open the shutter,[1] even so will God, Who keeps Israel and slumbers not, still less sleeps,[2] enter the soul that is empty and fill it with blessings.

41. God, like the sun, is above our souls and ready to enter them. Let spiritual directors, then, be content with preparing the soul according to evangelical perfection, which consists in the detachment and emptiness of sense and of spirit; and let them not seek to go beyond this in the building up of the soul, for that work belongs only to the Lord, from Whom comes down every perfect gift.[3] For, if the Lord build not the house, in vain does he labour that builds it;[4] and in every soul, in the manner that seems good to Him, He will build a supernatural building. Prepare, then, the nature of the soul by annihilating its operations, for these disturb rather than help. That is your office; and the office of God, as the Wise Man says,[5] is to direct the soul to supernatural blessings by ways and in manners whereof neither you nor the soul can know anything. Say not, again: 'Oh, he is making no progress, for he is doing nothing!' For if the understanding of the soul[6] at that time has no more pleasure in objects of the understanding than it had before, it is making progress in walking towards the supernatural. And say not: 'Oh, but he understands nothing distinctly.' For if the soul were to understand anything distinctly,[7] it would be making no progress, for God is incomprehensible and transcends the understanding; and thus the greater the progress it makes, the farther it must withdraw from itself, walking in faith, believing and not understanding;[8] and thus it approaches God more nearly by not understanding than by understanding. Grieve not, therefore, at this, for if the understanding goes not backward and desires not to occupy itself with distinct knowledge and other ideas pertaining to this world, it is making progress. For in this case not to go backward is to go forward; it is to progress in faith,[9] for, when the understanding knows not, neither can know, what God is, it is walking toward Him by not understanding; and thus what you are condemning in your penitent is fitting for his good, rather than that he should embarrass himself with distinct kinds of understanding.[10]

42. 'Oh,' you will say, 'but if the understanding understands not

---

[1] C, G: 'the window.' E.p.: 'if you open the door.'
[2] Psalm cxx, 4 [A.V., cxxi, 4].   [3] St. James i, 17.
[4] Psalm cxxvi, 1 [A.V., cxxvii, 1].   [5] [Proverbs xvi, 9.]
[6] E.p. omits: 'the understanding of.'
[7] E.p. adds: 'at that time.'   [8] E.p.: 'and not seeing.
[9] P, e.p.: 'For to go forward is to progress in faith.'
[10] E.p. adds: 'and not walk in perfect faith.'

distinctly, the will at least will be idle and will not love, for it is impossible to love that which one understands not.' There is truth in this, especially as regards the natural acts and operations of the soul, where the will loves only that of which the understanding has distinct knowledge. But in the contemplation[1] of which we are speaking, wherein God, as we have said, infuses into the soul, there is no necessity for distinct knowledge, nor for the soul to perform any acts, for God, in one act, is communicating[2] to the soul loving knowledge, which at one and the same time is like light giving heat without any distinction being perceptible between the two, and at that time as is understanding, even so is love in the will. As this knowledge is general and dark, and the understanding is unable to understand distinctly that which it understands, the will likewise loves in a general way without the making of any distinction. And, as God in this delicate communication is both light and love, He informs these two faculties equally, though at times He acts on the one more than on the other. At times, therefore, the soul is more conscious of understanding than of love, and at other times it is more conscious of love[3] than of understanding; and at times all is understanding, and there is hardly any love; while at other times all is love and there is no understanding. And thus, as far as the acts are concerned which the soul performs on its own account, there can be no love without understanding; but in the acts which God performs in the soul, it is different, for He can communicate Himself in the one faculty and not in the other. Thus He can enkindle the will by means of a touch of the heat of His love, although the understanding may have no understanding thereof, just as a person can receive heat from a fire without seeing that he is near the fire. And in this way the will may oftentimes feel itself to be enkindled or filled with tenderness and love without knowing or understanding anything more distinctly than before, since God is setting love in order in it, even as the Bride says in the Songs, in these words: 'The King introduced me into the cellar of wine, and set in order charity in me.'[4]

43. There is no reason, therefore, to fear that the will in this state will be idle; for, if it ceases to perform acts concerning particular kinds of knowledge, as far as its own efforts are concerned, God performs them within it, inebriating it in infused love, either by means of the

---

[1] E.p.: 'But in the period of contemplation.'
[2] E.p.: 'nor for the soul to engage in much reasoning, for at that time God is communicating.'
[3] E.p. has 'of more intense love,' and omits the rest of the paragraph.
[4] Canticles ii, 4.

knowledge of contemplation, or without such knowledge, as we have just said; and these acts are as much better than those made by the soul and as much more meritorious[1] and delectable, as the mover and infuser of this love[2]—namely, God—is better than the soul; and God establishes love in the soul because the will is near God and is detached from other pleasures. The soul, therefore, must see to it that the will is empty and stripped of its affections; for, if it is not going backward by desiring to experience some sweetness or pleasure, it is going forward, even though it have no particular perception of this in God, and it is soaring upward to God above all things, since it takes no pleasure in anything. It is going toward God, although it may be taking no particular and distinct delight in Him, nor may be loving Him with any distinct act, for it is taking greater pleasure in Him secretly, by means of that dark and general infusion of love, than it does in all things that are distinct,[3] for it sees clearly in this state that nothing gives it so much pleasure as that solitary quiet. And it is loving Him above all things that can be loved, since it has flung from itself all other kinds of sweetness and pleasure which have become distasteful to it. And there is thus no reason to be troubled, for, if the will can find no sweetness and pleasure in particular acts, it is going forward; seeing that to refrain from going backward and from embracing anything that belongs to sense is to go forward towards the inaccessible, which is God, and thus there is no wonder that the soul has no perception thereof.[4] Wherefore, in order to journey to God, the will has rather to be continually detaching itself from everything delectable and pleasant than to be conceiving an attachment to it. In this way it completely fulfils the precept of love, which is to love God above all things; and this cannot be unless it have spiritual emptiness and detachment[5] with regard to them all.[6]

44. Neither is there any cause for misgivings when the memory is voided of its forms and figures, for, since God has no form or figure,

---

[1] E.p.: 'And therefore there is no reason to fear that the soul in this state will be idle for, if it ceases to perform acts governed by particular kinds of knowledge, as far as its own efforts are concerned, He inebriates it, nevertheless, in infused love, by means of the knowledge of contemplation, as we have just said; and these acts which are performed through following infused contemplation are as much better and as much more meritorious.'

[2] E.p.: 'the mover who infuses this love.'

[3] E.p.: 'than if it were governed by distinct kinds of knowledge.'

[4] E.p. omits: 'and thus . . . thereof.'

[5] Thus B, C, G, Gr., P.   T, e.p.: 'special emptiness.'

[6] E.p.: 'and if this is to happen with all perfection, it must happen with this special emptiness and detachment as to them all.'

the memory is safe if it be voided of form or figure, and it is approaching God the more nearly; for, the more it leans upon the imagination, the farther it is going from God, and the greater is the peril wherein it walks, since God is incomprehensible and therefore cannot be apprehended by the imagination.

45. Such directors as we have been describing fail to understand souls that are now walking in this solitary and quiet contemplation,[1] because they themselves have not advanced beyond a very ordinary kind of meditation, or similar act, nor perhaps have arrived even so far; and they think, as I have said, that these souls are idle, because the animal man—that is, one that advances not beyond the animal feelings of the sensual part of the soul—perceives not, as Saint Paul says, the things that are of God.[2] Wherefore they disturb the peace of this quiet and hushed contemplation which God has been giving these souls by His own power, and they make their penitents meditate and reason and perform acts, not without causing them great displeasure, repugnance and distraction, since their souls would fain remain in their quiet and peaceful state of recollection; but their directors persuade them to strive after sweetness and fervour, though they ought rather to advise them the contrary. The penitents, however, are unable to do as they did previously, and can enter into none of these things, for the time for them has now passed and they belong no more to their proper path; and so they are doubly disturbed, and believe that they are going to perdition; and their directors encourage them in this belief, and parch their spirits, and take from them the precious unctions wherewith God was anointing them in solitude and tranquillity. This, as I have said, is a great evil; their directors are plunging them into mire and mourning,[3] for they are losing one thing and labouring without profit at the other.

46. Such persons have no knowledge of what spirituality is, and they offer a great insult and great irreverence to God, by laying their coarse hands where God is working. For it has cost Him dearly to bring these souls to this place and He greatly esteems having brought them to this solitude and emptiness of their faculties and operations, that He may speak to their heart, which is what He ever desires. He

---

[1] G continues, after 'wherein it walks': 'and the farther it withdraws itself from it [i.e. the imagination], the more surely it journeys. And those [directors] who are not experienced cannot properly understand these souls, nor do they know that the Lord is keeping them in this state of quiet contemplation.'

[2] 1 Corinthians ii, 14.

[3] [i.e. mourning for what they lose and the mire of their present unhappy state from which they strive to get free.]

has Himself taken them by the hand, and He Himself reigns in their souls in abundant peace and quietness, causing the natural acts[1] of their faculties to fail wherewith they toiled all night and wrought nothing. And He has brought peace to their spirits without the operation of sense, for neither sense nor any act thereof is capable of receiving spirit.

47. How precious in His sight is this tranquillity or slumbering or annihilation of sense can be clearly seen in that adjuration, so notable and effective, that He utters in the Songs, where He says: 'I adjure you, daughters of Jerusalem, by the goats and harts of the fields, that ye awaken not my beloved nor cause her to wake until she please.'[2] Herein, by introducing these solitary and retiring animals, He gives us to understand how much He loves that solitary forgetfulness and slumber. But these spiritual directors will not let the soul have repose or quiet, but demand that it shall continually labour and work, that it may leave no room for God to work, and that that which He is working may be undone and wiped out through the operation of the soul. They have become as the little foxes which tear down the flowering vine of the soul;[3] for which reason God complains through Isaias, saying: 'You have devoured[4] My vineyard.'[5]

48. But, it may possibly be said, these directors err with good intent, through insufficiency of knowledge. This, however, does not excuse them for the advice which they are rash enough to give without first learning to understand either the way that the soul is taking or its spirit. If they understand not this, they are laying their coarse hands upon things that they understand not, instead of leaving them for those who understand them better; for it is a thing of no small weight, and no slight crime, to cause the soul to lose inestimable blessings by counselling it to go out of its way and to leave it prostrate.[6] And thus one who rashly errs, being under an obligation to give reliable advice —as is every man, whatever his office—shall not go unpunished, by reason of the harm that he has done. For the business of God has to be undertaken with great circumspection, and with eyes wide open, most of all in matters so delicate and sublime as the conduct of these souls, where a man may bring them almost infinite gain if the advice that he gives be good and almost infinite loss if it be mistaken.

49. But if you will still maintain that such a director has some

---

[1] E.p.: 'the discursive acts.'   [2] Canticles iii, 5.
[3] Canticles ii, 15. E.p.: 'which destroy.'
[4] G, e.p.: 'You have destroyed.' C: 'You have eaten.'
[5] Isaias iii, 14.   [6] [Lit., 'right on the ground.']

excuse, though for myself I can see none, you will at least be unable to say that there is any excuse for one who, in his treatment of a soul, never allows it to go out of his jurisdiction, for certain vain reasons and intentions which he best knows. Such a person will not go unpunished, for it is certain that, if that soul is to make progress by going forward on the spiritual road, wherein God is ever aiding it, it will have to change the style and method of its prayer, and it will of necessity require instruction of a higher kind and a deeper spirituality than that of such a director. For not all directors have sufficient knowledge to meet all the possibilities and cases which they encounter on the spiritual road, neither is their spirituality so perfect that they know how a soul has to be guided and directed in every state of the spiritual life; at least no man should think that he knows everything concerning this, or that God will cease leading a given soul farther onward. Not everyone who can hew a block of wood is able to carve an image; nor is everyone who can carve it able to smooth and polish it; nor is he that can polish it able to paint it; nor can everyone that is able to paint it complete it with the final touches. Each one of these, in working upon an image, can do no more than that with which he himself is familiar, and, if he tries to do more, he will only ruin his work.

50. How, then, we may ask, if you are only a hewer of wood, and merely try to make a soul despise the world and mortify its desires; or, if at best you are a carver, which means that you can lead a soul to holy meditations, but can do no more: how, in such a case, will this soul attain to the final perfection of a delicate painting, the art of which consists neither in the hewing of wood, nor in the carving of it, nor even in the outlining of it, but in the work which God Himself must do in it? It is certain, then, that if your instruction is always of one kind, and you cause the soul to be continually bound to you, it will either go backward, or, at the least, will not go forward.[1] For what, I ask you, will the image be like, if you never do any work upon it save hewing and hammering, which in the language of the soul is exercising the faculties? When will this image be finished? When or how will it be left for God to paint it? Is it possible that you yourself can perform all these offices, and consider yourself so consummate a master that this soul shall never need any other?

51. And supposing that you have sufficient experience to direct some one soul, which perchance may have no ability to advance beyond your teaching, it is surely impossible for you to have sufficient experi-

---

[1] P omits the remainder of this paragraph, and the three paragraphs following.

ence for the direction of all those whom you refuse to allow to go out of your hands; for God leads each soul along different roads and there shall hardly be found a single spirit who can walk even half the way which is suitable for another. Who can be like Saint Paul and have the skill to make himself all things to all men, that he may gain them all?[1] You yourself tyrannize over souls, and take away their liberty, and arrogate to yourself the breadth and liberty of evangelical doctrine, so that you not only strive that they may not leave you, but, what is worse, if any one of them[2] should at some time go and ask the advice of another director, or discuss with him anything that he could not suitably discuss with you, or if God should lead him in order to teach him something which you teach him not, you behave to him (I say it not without shame) like a husband who is jealous of his wife; nor is your jealousy even due to a desire for the honour of God—it is due only to your own pride and presumption.[3] For how can you know that that soul has not the need to go to another? Great is the indignation of God with such directors, whom He promises punishment when He speaks through the prophet Ezechiel and says: 'Ye fed not My flock but clothed yourselves with their wool and drank their milk; I will require My flock at your hand.'[4]

52. Such persons, then, ought to give these souls freedom, for they have an obligation to allow them to go to others and to put a good face upon it, since they know not by what means God desires such souls to make progress, especially when they dislike the instruction that they are receiving, which is a sign that God is leading them on farther by another way and that they need another director. The director himself, in such a case, should advise a change, since any other advice springs from foolish pride and presumption.

53.[5] Let us now leave this question and speak of another pestilential habit of such directors as these, or of others even worse than they. For it may come to pass that God will be anointing certain souls with holy desires and impulses to leave the world, to change their life and condition, to serve Him and despise the world (it is a great thing in His eyes that they should have been brought thus far, for the things of the world are not according to the heart of God), and these directors, using human arguments or putting forward considerations quite

---

[1] [1 Corinthians ix, 22.]
[2] E.p.: 'if you know that any one of them.'
[3] G: 'you behave harshly to him, which is not due to your zeal (celo) for the honour and glory of God, but to jealousy (celos) coming from your own pride and presumption.'
[4] Ezechiel xxxiv, 2, 3, 10.   [5] G omits this paragraph.

contrary to the doctrine of Christ and His way of mortification and despising of all things, advise them to delay their decision, or place obstacles in their path, from motives of their own interest or their own pleasure, or because they fear where no fear is; or, what is still worse, they sometimes labour[1] to remove these desires from their penitents' hearts. Such directors show a wrong spirit, and are undevout, and clad, as it were, in very worldly garb, having little of the tenderness of Christ, since they neither enter themselves, nor allow others to enter. And our Saviour says: 'Woe unto you that have taken away the key of knowledge, and enter not in yourselves nor allow others to enter!'[2] For these persons in truth are placed like barriers and obstacles at the gate of Heaven, remembering not that God has placed them there that they may compel those whom God calls to enter in, as He has commanded;[3] whereas they, on the other hand, are compelling souls not to enter in by the narrow gate that leads to life; in this way such a man is a blind guide who can obstruct the guidance of the Holy Spirit in the soul. This comes to pass in many ways, as has here been said; some do it knowingly, others unconsciously; but neither class shall remain unpunished, since, having assumed their office, they are under an obligation to know and consider what they do.

54. The other blind guide of whom we have spoken, who can hinder the soul in this kind of recollection, is the devil, who, being himself blind, desires the soul to be blind also. When the soul is in these lofty and solitary places wherein are infused the delicate unctions of the Holy Spirit (at which he has great grief and envy, for he sees the soul flying beyond him, and can in no wise lay hold on it, though he sees that it is gaining great riches), the devil tries to cover this detachment and withdrawal, as it were, with cataracts of knowledge and mists of sensible sweetness, which are sometimes good, so that he may entice the soul more surely, and thus cause it to have commerce once more with sense, and to look at these things and embrace them, so that it may continue its journey to God in reliance upon this good knowledge and these delights. And herein he distracts it and very easily withdraws it from that solitude and recollection, wherein, as we have said, the Holy Spirit is working these great things secretly. And then the soul, being of itself inclined to sensible enjoyment, especially if these are the things which it is really desiring, is very easily led to cling to

---

[1] E.p.: 'set out.'   [2] St. Luke xi, 52.
[3] E.p. adds: 'in His Gospel.' C: 'saying through St. Luke: Insist, make them come in, that My house may be filled with guests.'

such kinds of knowledge and such delights, and withdraws itself from the solitude wherein God works. For (it says), as previously it was doing nothing, this other state seems better, for it is now doing something. It is a great pity that it cannot realize how, for the sake of one mouthful, it is preventing itself from feeding wholly upon God Himself, when He absorbs it in these solitary and spiritual unctions of His mouth.

55. In this way, with hardly any trouble, the devil works the greatest injuries, causing the soul to lose great riches, and dragging it forth like a fish, with the tiniest bait, from the depths of the pure waters of the spirit, where it had no support or foothold but was engulfed and immersed in God. And hereupon he drags it to the bank, giving it help and support, and showing it something whereon it may lean, so that it may walk upon its own feet with great labour instead of floating in the waters of Siloe, that go with silence,[1] bathed in the unctions of God. And this the devil does to such an extent[2] that it is a matter for great marvel; and, since a slight injury is more serious to a soul in this condition than is a serious injury to many other souls, as we have said,[3] there is hardly any soul walking on this road which does not meet with great injuries and suffer great losses. For the evil one takes his stand, with great cunning, on the road which leads from sense to spirit,[4] deceiving and luring the soul by means of sense, and giving it sensual things, as we have said, so that it may rest in them and not escape from him; and the soul is entrapped with the greatest ease,[5] for it knows of nothing better than this, and thinks not that anything is being lost by it, but rather considers it a great blessing, and receives it readily, thinking that God has come to visit it; and in this way it fails to enter into the innermost chamber of the Spouse, but stands at the door to see what is happening. The devil, as Job says, beholdeth every high thing—that is to say, concerning souls—that he may assault it.[6] And if perchance any soul enters into recollection, he labours to bring about its ruin by means of horrors, fears or pains of the body, or by outward sounds and noises, causing it to be distracted by sense,[7] in order to bring it out and distract it from the interior spirit, until he

---

[1] [Isaias viii, 6.]

[2] P: 'And to this the devil attaches such importance.'

[3] E.p.: 'and since a slight injury inflicted upon many souls in this condition is more serious.'

[4] C, Gr, P add: 'as is his invariable custom, so that it [the soul] shall not pass from sense to spirit.'

[5] T: 'with the greatest difficulty.'   [6] [Job xli, 25: A.V., xli, 34.]

[7] E.p.: 'by the sound.'

can do no more and so leaves it. And with such ease does he corrupt these precious souls, and squander their great riches, that, although he thinks this of greater importance than to bring about the fall of many others, he esteems it not highly because of the facility with which it is done and the little effort that it costs him. In this sense we may understand that which God said to Job concerning the devil, namely: 'He shall drink up a river and shall not marvel, and he trusteth that the Jordan may run into his mouth—by the Jordan being understood the summit of perfection. In his eyes as with a hook shall he take him, and with stakes shall he bore through his nostrils.'[1] That is, with the darts of the knowledge, wherewith he is piercing the soul, he will disperse its spirituality; for the breath which goes out through his nostrils, when they are pierced, is dispersed in many directions. And later he says: 'The beams of the sun shall be under him and they shall scatter gold under him as mire.'[2] For he causes souls that have been enlightened to lose the marvellous rays of Divine knowledge, and from souls that are rich he takes away and scatters the precious gold of Divine adornment.

56. Oh, souls! Since God is showing you such sovereign[3] mercies as to lead you through this state of solitude and recollection, withdrawing you from your labours of sense, return not to sense again. Lay aside your operations, for, though once, when you were beginners, they helped you to deny the world and yourselves, they will now be a great obstacle and hindrance to you, since God is granting you the grace of Himself working within you. If you are careful to set your faculties[4] upon naught soever, withdrawing them from everything and in no way hindering them, which is the proper part for you to play in this state, and if you only wait upon God with loving and pure attentiveness, as I said above, in the way which I there described (working no violence to the soul[5] save to detach it from everything and set it free,[6] lest you disturb and spoil its peace or tranquillity), God will feed[7] your soul for you with heavenly food,[8] since you are not hindering Him.[9]

---

[1] Job xl, 18-19 [A.V., xl, 23-4].   [2] Job xli, 21 [A.V., xli, 30].
[3] C, Gr: 'noted.' G: 'singular.'   [4] E.p.: 'your operations.'
[5] [P. Silverio's text has (for 'working no violence to the soul') 'which must be when you have no desire to be attentive, for you must work no violence to the soul.' This seems to be a corruption.] E.p. abbreviates: 'with loving and pure attentiveness, without working violence to the soul.'
[6] B, G, e.p.: 'and raise it.'   [7] B: 'will cure.'
[8] [Lit., 'celestial refection.'] C: 'spiritual perfection.'
[9] G: 'God will regale it for you and fill it with spiritual blessings if you hinder Him not by means of operations of sense.'

57. The third blind guide of the soul is the soul itself, which, not understanding itself, as we have said, becomes perturbed and does itself harm. For it knows not how to work save by means of sense, and thus, when God is pleased to bring it into that emptiness and solitude where it can neither use its faculties nor make any acts, it sees that it is doing nothing, and strives to do something:[1] in this way it becomes distracted and full of aridity and displeasure, whereas formerly it was rejoicing in the rest of the spiritual silence and peace wherein God was secretly giving it joy. And it may come to pass that God persists in keeping the soul in that silent tranquillity, while the soul persists in crying out with its imagination and walking with its understanding; even as children, whom their mothers carry in their arms so that they may not have to walk, keep crying and striking out with their feet because they are anxious to walk, and thus neither make any progress themselves nor allow their mothers to do so. Or it is as when a painter is painting a portrait and his subject will not allow him to do anything because he keeps moving.

58. The soul in this state must bear in mind that, although it is not conscious of making any progress, it is making much more than when it was walking on foot; for it is because God is bearing it in His arms that it is not conscious of such movement. And although it is doing[2] nothing, it is nevertheless accomplishing much more than if it were working, since God is working within it. And it is not remarkable that the soul should be unable to see this, for sense cannot perceive that which God works in the soul. Let the soul leave itself in the hands of God and have confidence in Him and entrust itself neither to the hands nor to the works of others; for, if it remains thus, it will make sure progress, since it is in no danger save when it desires to occupy its faculties in something.[3]

59. Let us now return to the matter of these deep caverns of the faculties wherein we said that the suffering of the soul is wont to be great when God is anointing and preparing it with these subtle[4] unctions in order that He may unite it with Himself. These unctions are sometimes so subtle and sublime that they penetrate the inmost substance of the depth of the soul,[5] preparing it and filling it with

---

¹ E.p. adds: 'more sensibly and expressly.'   ² E.p.: 'it seems to be doing.'
³ E.p.: 'and have confidence in Him; for, if it do this, it will make sure progress, for it is in no danger save when it desires, on its own account or in its own way, to work with its faculties.' P ends the treatise here and A recommences with the following paragraph.
⁴ E.p.: 'subtle and delicate.'
⁵ E.p.: 'the inmost part of the ground [i.e. bottom] of the soul.'

sweetness in such a way that its suffering and fainting with desire in the boundless emptiness of these caverns is likewise boundless. Here we must note this: if the unctions that were preparing these caverns for the union of the spiritual marriage are as sublime as we have said, what will the possession be which they afterwards attain? It is certain that, even as was the thirst and hunger and suffering of the caverns, so now will be the satisfaction and fullness and delight thereof; and, as was the delicacy of the preparations, even so will be the wonder of the possession and fruition of sense,[1] which is the vigour and virtue that belong to the substance of the soul that it may perceive and have fruition of the objects of the faculties.

60. These faculties the soul here calls caverns, and with great propriety,[2] for, as it perceives[3] that they are able to contain the deep intelligences and splendours of these lamps, the soul is able to see clearly that they have a depth as great as is that of the intelligence and the love; and that they have capacity and depth as great as are the various things[4] which they receive from the intelligences, the sweetnesses and the fruitions; all of which things are established and received in this cavern of the sense of the soul, which is the soul's virtue of capacity for possessing, perceiving and having pleasure in everything, as I say. Even as the common sense of the fancy is a receptacle for all objects of the outward senses, even so this ordinary sense of the soul is enlightened and made rich by a possession that is so lofty and glorious.

Which were dark and blind

61. There are two reasons for which the eye may be unable to see: either it may be in darkness or it may be blind. God is the light and the object[5] of the soul; when this light illumines it not, it is in darkness, even though its power of vision may be most excellent. When it is in sin, or when it employs its desires upon aught else, it is then blind; and even though the light of God then shines upon it,[6] it sees it not, being blind. The darkness of the soul is the ignorance of the soul;[7] before God enlightened it through this transformation, it was blind and ignorant concerning many good things of God, even as the Wise Man says that he was blind before Wisdom illumined him, using these words: 'He illumined my ignorance.'[8]

---

[1] E.p.: 'the fruition and possession of the feeling of the soul.'
[2] C: 'and very profoundly.'   [3] [*Lit.*, 'they perceive.' Cf. p. 179, below.]
[4] E.p.: 'the various causes.'   [5] E.p.: 'and the true object.'
[6] E.p.: 'even though it may not lack the light of God.'
[7] E.p.: 'By the darkness of the soul is [meant] its practical ignorance.'
[8] Ecclesiasticus li, 26.

62. Speaking spiritually, it is one thing to be in darkness and another to be in thick darkness; for to be in thick darkness is to be blind (that is, as we have said, in sin); but to be in darkness only is something that may happen when one is not in sin. This may be in two ways: in the natural sense, when the soul has no light from certain natural things; and in the supernatural sense, when it has no light from supernatural things; and, with regard to both these things, the soul here says that its understanding[1] was dark before this precious union.[2] For, until the Lord said: *Fiat lux*,[3] thick darkness was upon the face of the abyss of the cavern of sense; and the deeper is this abyss and the more profound are its caverns, when God, Who is light, enlightens it not, the more abysmal and profound is the thick darkness that is upon it. And thus it is impossible for the soul to raise its eyes to the Divine light, or even to think of such light, for it knows not of what manner is this light, since it has never seen it; wherefore it cannot desire it, but will rather desire thick darkness, knowing not what it is like; and it will go from one darkness to another, guided by that darkness, for darkness cannot lead to anything save to fresh darkness. Then, as David says: 'Day unto day uttereth speech, and night unto night showeth its night.'[4] And thus one abyss calls to another abyss; an abyss of thick darkness to another abyss of thick darkness and an abyss of light to another abyss of light; each like calls to its like and infuses it.[5] And thus the light of the grace that God had already given to this soul, wherewith He had opened the eye of its abyss to the Divine light, and so had made it pleasing to Himself, has called to another abyss of grace, which is this Divine transformation of the soul in God, whereby the eye of sense is so greatly enlightened and made pleasing to Him[6] that light and will are both one, the natural light is united to the supernatural and the supernatural light alone shines; even as the light created by God was united with that of the sun and the light of the sun alone now shines without the other failing.

63. And the soul was also blind inasmuch as it took pleasure in other things than God; for the blindness of the higher and rational sense is that desire which, like a cataract and a cloud, overlays and covers the eye of reason,[7] so that the soul shall not see the things that

---

[1] So Gr, T, e.p., A, B, C, G have: 'its sense.'
[2] E.p.: 'that its understanding was dark, without God.'
[3] Genesis i, 3.   [4] Psalm xviii, 2 [A.V., xix, 2].
[5] E.p. omits: 'and infuses it.'
[6] E.p. reads 'very greatly enlightened and made pleasing to Him' and omits the rest of the paragraph.
[7] E.p.: 'of the heart' [*corazón* for *razón*].

are in front of it. And thus, for as long as the soul took any pleasure in sense, it was blind and could not see the great riches and Divine beauties that were behind. For just as, if a man sets anything before his eyes, however small, this suffices to obstruct his sight so that he cannot see other things that may be in front of him, however large they be, just so any small desire or idle act in the soul suffices to obstruct its vision of all these great and Divine things, which come after the pleasures and desires for which the soul longs.

64. Oh, that one might describe here how impossible it is for the soul that has other desires to judge of the things of God as they are! For, in order to judge the things of God aright, the soul must cast out wholly from itself its own desire and pleasure and must not judge them together with Him; else it will infallibly[1] come to consider the things of God as though they were not of God and those that are not of God as though they were of God. For, when that cataract and cloud covers the eye of judgment, the soul sees nothing but the cataract[2]—sometimes of one colour, sometimes of another, just as it may happen to be; and the soul thinks that the cataract is God, for, as we have said, it can see nothing beyond the cataract, which covers the senses, and God cannot be apprehended by sense. And thus desire and the pleasures of the soul hinder it from a knowledge of lofty things, as the Wise Man says, in these words: 'The union of vanity obscureth good things, and the inconstancy of desire overturneth the sense, though there be no malice.'[3]

65. Wherefore those persons who are not spiritual enough to be purged of their desires and pleasures, and still to some extent follow their animal nature with respect to these, may think much of the base and vile things of the spirit, which are those that come nearest to the sensual condition wherein they still live, and they will consider them to be of great importance; while those things that are lofty and spiritual, which are those that are farthest withdrawn from sense, they will count of small importance and will not esteem them, and will even consider them to be folly, as Saint Paul says, in these words: 'The animal man perceiveth not the things of God; they are to him as foolishness and he cannot understand them.'[4] The animal man is he that still lives according to the desires and pleasures of his nature. For, although these may be derived from spirit and be born there, yet, if one desires to cling to them with his natural desire, they then become

---

[1] E.p. omits this word.
[2] Here and below, e.p. reads 'cloud' for 'cataract.'
[3] Wisdom iv, 12.
[4] 1 Corinthians ii, 14.

natural desires; for it is of small importance that the object of this desire should be supernatural if the desire proceeds from itself and has its root and strength in nature, for it has the same substance and nature as if it related to matter and a natural object.[1]

66. You will say to me: 'But when God is desired, is not this supernatural?' I reply that it is not always so, but only when God infuses this desire, and Himself gives it its strength,[2] and then it is a very different thing. When you, of your own accord, desire to possess Him, this is no more than natural;[3] nor will it ever be otherwise unless it be informed by God. And thus when you, of your own accord, desire to cling to spiritual pleasures, and exercise your own natural desire, you are spreading a cataract over the eye of the soul and you are an animal being and cannot therefore understand or judge that which is spiritual, which is higher than any natural desire and sense. And if you are still doubtful, I know not what to say to you save to bid you read these words again, and then perhaps you will cease to doubt, for what I have said is the substance of the truth, and I cannot possibly enlarge upon it here any further. This sense, then, which before was dark, without this Divine light of God, and was blind, because of its desires, is now in such a condition that its deep caverns, by means of this Divine union:

With strange brightness Give heat and light together to their Beloved!

67. For, now that these caverns of the faculties are so wonderfully and marvellously infused[4] with the wondrous splendours of those lamps, as we have said, which are burning within them, they are sending back to God in God, over and above the surrender which they are making to God, since they are illumined and enkindled in God, those same splendours which the soul has received with loving glory;[5] they turn to God in God, and become themselves lamps enkindled in the splendours of the Divine lamps, giving to the Beloved some of the

---

[1] E.p. abbreviates: 'and not esteem them. He is an animal man who still lives according to the desires of his nature, for although occasionally these may be connected with spiritual things, yet, if a man desires to cling to them with his natural desire, they then become natural desires; for it is of small importance that the object of this desire should be spiritual, etc.'

[2] E.p.: 'but only when the motive is supernatural and God gives such a desire its strength.'

[3] E.p. adds: 'in its manner,' and omits the rest of the sentence.

[4] E.p.: 'placed.' T: 'so greatly mortified and so marvellously infused.'

[5] E.p. alters the order of the clauses in this sentence, but makes no other change save the addition of 'of themselves' after 'the surrender.'

same light and heat of love that the soul receives; for in this state, after the same manner as they receive, they are giving to the Giver with the very brightness that He gives to them; even as does glass when the sun strikes it; although the former is after a nobler manner, because the exercise of the will intervenes.

68. 'With strange brightness' signifies that the brightness is strange in a way that is far remote from all common thought and all description and every way and manner.[1] For the brightness with which God visits the soul is like to the brightness wherewith the understanding receives Divine wisdom and is made one with the understanding of God; for one cannot give save in the way wherein is given to him. And like to the brightness[2] wherewith the will is united with goodness[3] is the brightness wherewith the soul gives to God in God the same goodness; for the soul receives it only to give it again. In the same way, according to the brightness wherewith the soul has knowledge of the greatness of God, being united therein, it shines and gives heat of love. According to the brightness of the other Divine attributes which are here communicated to the soul—fortitude, beauty, justice, etc.—are the manners of brightness wherewith the sense, having fruition, is giving to its Beloved, in its Beloved, that same light and heat that it is receiving from its Beloved; for, since in this state it has been made one and the same thing with Him, it is after a certain manner God by participation; for, although this is not so as perfectly as in the next life, the soul is, as we have said, as it were a shadow of God. And in this way, since the soul, by means of this substantial[4] transformation, is the shadow of God, it does in God and through God that which He does through Himself in the soul, in the same way as He does it.[5] For the will of these two is one;[6] and, even as God is giving Himself to the soul with free and gracious will, even so likewise the soul, having a will that is the freer and the more generous in proportion as it has a greater degree of union with God, is giving God in God to God Himself, and thus the gift of the soul to God is true and entire.[7] For in this state the soul truly sees that God belongs to it, and that it possesses Him with

---

[1] E.p. ends the sentence at 'description.'

[2] E.p. abbreviates: 'wherewith the understanding received Divine wisdom. And like to the brightness.'

[3] T: 'with the will.' E.p.: 'with the Divine will.'

[4] E.p. omits 'substantial.'   [5] E.p. omits: 'in . . . does it.'

[6] C, G, Gr add: 'and the operation of the soul and of God is one.'

[7] E.p.: 'a greater degree of union with God in God, is as it were giving to God God Himself, through that loving complacency which it has for the Divine Being and perfections, and this is a mystical and affective gift of the soul to God.'

hereditary possession, as an adopted child of God,[1] by rightful owner-ship, through the grace that God gave to it of Himself, and it sees that, since He belongs to it, it may give and communicate Him to whom-soever it desires; and thus it gives Him to its Beloved,[2] Who is the very God that gave Himself to it. And herein the soul pays all that it owes; for, of its own will, it gives as much as it has received with inestimable delight and joy, giving to the Holy Spirit that which is His in a voluntary surrender, that He may be loved as He deserves.

69. And herein is the inestimable delight of the soul: to see that it is giving to God that which is His own and which becomes Him according to His infinite Being. For, although it is true that the soul cannot give God Himself to Himself anew, since He in Himself is ever Himself, yet, in so far as the soul is itself concerned, it gives perfectly and truly,[3] giving all that He had given to it, to pay the debt of love. And this is to give as has been given to it, and God is repaid by that gift of the soul—yet with less than this He cannot be paid. And this He takes with gratitude, as something belonging to the soul that it gives to Him anew,[4] and because of this He loves the soul and sur-renders Himself to it anew, wherein the soul loves Him.[5] And so at this time there is a reciprocal love between God and the soul, in the agree-ment of the union and surrender of marriage, wherein the possessions of both, which are the Divine Being, are possessed by each one freely, and[6] are possessed likewise by both together in the voluntary surrender of each to the other, wherein each says to the other that which the Son of God said to the Father in Saint John, namely: *Omnia mea tua sunt, et tua mea sunt et clarificatus sum in eis.*[7] That is: All My things are Thine, and Thine are Mine, and I am glorified in them. In the next life this happens without any intermission in the fruition thereof. And in this state of union, when the communication between the soul and God takes place in the act and exercise of love, that gift can evidently be made by the soul,[8] although it is greater than its capacity and its being; for it is evident that one who possesses many kingdoms and peoples as his own, although they be much greater in importance than himself, can perfectly well give them to whom he desires.

---

[1] E.p. omits 'with hereditary possession.'
[2] E.p. abbreviates: 'gave to it of Himself. It gives Him, then, to its Beloved.'
[3] E.p.: 'and wisely.'
[4] E.p. has 'in the aforementioned sense' for 'anew.'
[5] [*Lit.*, 'He loves the soul'; probably a slip (*al* for *el*).]
[6] E.p. omits: 'are possessed by each one freely, and.'   [7] St. John xvii, 10.
[8] [P. Silverio's text has 'to' for 'by'; this is probably a slip (*al* for *el*) similar to that noted in n. 5, above.]

70. This is the great satisfaction and contentment of the soul, to see that it is giving to God more than it is itself worth, since it is giving to God Himself with such great liberality, as that which is its own, with that Divine light and that warmth of love which are given to it; in the next life this comes to pass through the light of glory,[1] and, in this life, through most enlightened faith.[2] And in this way, the deep caverns of sense, with strange brightness, give heat and light together to their Beloved. 'Together,' because the communication of the Father and of the Son and of the Holy Spirit in the soul are made together, and are the light and fire of love.

71. But here we must make a brief observation on the brightness wherewith the soul makes this surrender. Concerning this it must be noted that, in the act of this union, as the soul enjoys a certain image of fruition which is caused by the union of the understanding and the affection in God, being delighted thereby and constrained, it makes the surrender of God to God, and of itself in God, in wondrous manners. For, with respect to love, the soul presents itself to God with strange brightness; and equally so with respect to this shadow of fruition; and likewise with respect to praise, and, in the same way, with respect to gratitude.

72. With regard to the first of these, which is love, the soul has three principal kinds of love which may be called brightnesses. The first is that the soul now loves God, not through itself, but through God Himself; which is a wondrous brightness, since it loves through the Holy Spirit,[3] even as the Father loves the Son, as Saint John says: 'May the love wherewith Thou hast loved Me,' says the Son to the Father, 'be in them and I in them.'[4] The second kind of brightness is to love God in God; for in this vehement union the soul is absorbed in the love of God and God surrenders Himself to the soul with great vehemence. The third kind of love which is brightness is that the soul here loves Him for Who He is; it loves Him not only because He is bountiful, good, glorious,[5] and so forth, with respect to itself, but much more earnestly because He is all this in Himself essentially.

73. And with regard to this image of fruition there are also three other principal kinds of brightness, no less wonderful. The first is that the soul in this state has fruition of God through God Himself, for as

---

[1] E.p. adds: 'and of love.' [2] E.p. adds: 'and most enkindled love.'
[3] E.p.: 'since it loves enkindled by the Holy Spirit, and having in itself the Holy Spirit.'
[4] St. John xvii, 26.
[5] E.p.: 'bountiful, good, liberal.' T: 'bountiful, good [*used substantivally*], glory.'

the soul in this state unites understanding with wisdom and goodness and so forth,[1] albeit not so clearly as it will do in the next life, it delights greatly in all these things, understood distinctly, as we have said above. The second principal brightness belonging to this love is that the soul delights itself duly in God alone, without any intermingling of creatures. The third delight is that it enjoys Him for Who He is alone, without any other intermingling of its own pleasure.[2]

74. And with respect to the praise which the soul offers to God in this union, there are three kinds of brightness here also. First, the soul praises God as a duty, for it sees that He created it to offer Him praise, as He says through Isaias: 'I have formed this people for Myself; it shall sing My praises.'[3] The second kind of brightness of this praise comes from the blessings which the soul receives and the delight that it has in offering praise.[4] The third is that it praises God for that which He is in Himself; even if to do so caused the soul no delight at all, it would still praise Him for Who He is.

75. With respect to gratitude, again, there are three principal kinds of brightness. First, there is gratitude for the natural and spiritual blessings and the benefits which the soul has received. Secondly, there is the great delight which the soul has in praising God, because it is absorbed with great vehemence in this praise. Thirdly, the soul praises God only for that which He is, and this praise is much more profound and delectable.

STANZA IV

**How gently and lovingly thou awakenest in my bosom,
Where thou dwellest secretly and alone!
And in thy sweet breathing, full of blessing and glory, How
delicately thou inspirest my love!**

Exposition

HERE the soul turns to its Spouse with great love, extolling Him and giving Him thanks for two wondrous effects which He sometimes produces within it by means of this union, noting likewise in what way He produces each and also the effect upon itself which in each case is the result thereof.

---

[1] E.p. adds: 'which it knows with such enlightenment.' A, B, C, G, Gr read: 'in omnipotence, wisdom and goodness, and so forth.'

[2] E.p. adds: 'or of anything created.'

[3] Isaias xliii, 21. [4] E.p.: 'in praising this great Lord.'

2. The first effect is the awakening of God in the soul, and the means whereby this is produced are those of gentleness and love. The second effect is the breathing of God in the soul and the means thereof are in the blessing and glory that are communicated to the soul in this breathing. And that which is produced thereby in the soul is a delicate and tender inspiration of love.

3. The stanza, then, has this meaning: Thine awakening, O Word and Spouse, in the centre and depth of my soul, which is its pure and inmost substance,[1] wherein alone, secretly and in silence, Thou dwellest as its Lord, not only as in Thine own house, nor even as in Thine own bed, but intimately and closely united as in mine own bosom—how gentle and how loving is this! That is, it is exceedingly gentle and loving; and in this delectable breathing which in this Thine awakening Thou makest delectable for me, filled as it is with blessing and glory, with what delicacy dost Thou inspire me with love and affection for Thyself! Herein the soul uses a similitude of the breathing of one that awakens from his sleep; for in truth, the soul in this condition feels it to be so. There follows the line:

How gently and lovingly thou awakenest in my bosom,

4. There are many ways in which God awakens in the soul: so many that, if we had to enumerate them, we should never end. But this awakening of the Son of God which the soul here desires to describe, is, as I believe, one of the loftiest and one which brings the most good to the soul. For this awakening is a movement of the Word in the substance[2] of the soul, of such greatness and dominion and glory, and of such intimate sweetness, that it seems to the soul that all the balms and perfumed spices and flowers in the world are mingled and shaken and revolved together to give that sweetness; and that all the kingdoms and dominions of the world and all the powers and virtues of Heaven are moved.[3] And not only so, but all the virtues and substances and perfections and graces of all created things shine forth and make the same movement together and in unison. For, as Saint John says, all things in Him are life,[4] and in Him they live and are and move, as the Apostle says likewise.[5] Hence it comes to pass that, when this great Emperor moves in the soul, Whose kingdom, as Isaias

---

1 E.p. omits: 'which . . . substance.'
2 E.p.: 'in the depth.'
3 A, B, T: 'move it.'
4 St. John i, 3.
5 Acts xvii, 28.

says, is borne upon His shoulders[1] (namely, the three spheres, the celestial, the terrestrial and the infernal, and the things that are in them; and He sustains them all, as Saint Paul says, in the Word of His power),[2] then all the spheres seem to move together. Just as, when the earth moves, all material things that are upon it move likewise, as if they were nothing, even so,[3] when this Prince moves, He carries His court with Him, and the court carries not Him.

5. Yet this comparison is highly unsuitable, for in this latter case not only do all seem to be moving, but they also reveal the beauties of their being, virtue, loveliness and graces, and the root of their duration and life. For there the soul is able to see how all creatures, above and below,[4] have their life and duration in Him, and it sees clearly that which the Book of Wisdom expresses in these words: 'By Me kings reign, by Me princes rule and the powerful exercise justice and understand it.'[5] And although it is true that the soul is now able to see that these things are distinct from God, inasmuch as they have a created being, and it sees them in Him, with their force, root and strength, it knows equally that God, in His own Being, is all these things, in an infinite and pre-eminent way, to such a point that it understands them better in His Being[6] than in themselves. And this is the great delight of this awakening:[7] to know the creatures through God and not God through the creatures; to know the effects through their cause and not the cause through the effects; for the latter knowledge is secondary and this other is essential.[8]

6. And the manner of this knowledge[9] in the soul, since God is immovable, is a wondrous thing, for, although in reality God moves not,[10] it seems to the soul that He is indeed moving; for, as the soul is renewed and moved by God that it may behold this supernatural sight, and there is revealed to it in this great renewal that Divine life and the being and harmony of every creature in it which has its movements in

---

[1] Isaias ix, 6. E.p.: 'Hence it comes to pass that, when this great Emperor is pleased to reveal Himself to the soul, moving by means of this manner of enlightenment and yet not moving in the soul, Who bears His kingdom, as Isaias says, upon His shoulder.'

[2] Hebrews i, 3.

[3] E.p.: 'Just as, if the earth were to move, all natural things that are upon it would move likewise, even so.'

[4] E.p.: 'inferior and superior.'   [5] The quotation is from Proverbs viii, 15.

[6] E.p.: 'in this its beginning.'

[7] E.p. adds here: 'to know the effects through their cause' and omits the remainder of the paragraph.

[8] C omits this and the preceding clause.   [9] E.p.: 'of this movement.'

[10] E.p. omits 'in reality' and continues: 'the soul is renewed and moved by Him, and there is revealed to it in a wondrous renewal that Divine life and the being and harmony of every creature, so that the cause takes the name,' etc.

God, it seems to the soul that it is God that is moving, and thus the cause takes the name of the effect which it produces, according to which effect it may be said that God is moving, even as the Wise Man says: 'Wisdom is more movable than all movable things.'[1] And this is not because it moves itself, but because it is the beginning and root of all movement; remaining in itself stable, as the passage goes on to say, it renews all things. And thus what is here meant is that wisdom is more active than all active things. And thus we should say here that it is the soul that is moved in this motion, and is awakened from the sleep of its natural vision to a supernatural vision,[2] for which reason it is very properly given the name of an awakening.

7. But God, as the soul has been enabled to see, is always moving, ruling and giving being and virtue and grace and gifts to all creatures, containing them all in Himself, virtually, presentially and substantially;[3] so that in one single glance[4] the soul sees that which God is in Himself and that which He is in the creatures. Even so, when a palace is thrown open, a man may see at one and the same time the eminence of the person who is within the palace and also what he is doing. And it is this, as I understand, that happens upon this awakening and glance of the soul. Though the soul is substantially in God, as is every creature,[5] He draws back from before it some of the veils and curtains which are in front of it, so that it may see of what nature He is,[6] and then there is revealed to it, and it is able to see (though somewhat darkly, since not all the veils are drawn back)[7] that face of His[8] that is full of graces. And, since it is moving all things by its power, there appears together with it that which it is doing, and it appears to move in them, and they in it, with continual movement; and for this reason the soul believes that God has moved and awakened, whereas in reality that which has moved and awakened is itself.

8. For such is the lowly nature of this kind of life which we live that we believe others to be as we are ourselves; and we judge others as we are ourselves, so that our judgment begins with[9] ourselves and not outside ourselves. In this way the thief believes that others steal likewise; and he that lusts, that others are lustful like himself; and he that bears malice, that others bear malice, his judgment proceeding from his own malice; and the good man thinks well of others, his

---

[1] Wisdom vii, 24.   [2] E.p. omits: 'from the sleep . . . supernatural vision.'
[3] E.p.: 'and most eminently.'   [4] E.p. omits: 'in one single glance.'
[5] E.p. omits: 'Though the soul . . . creature.'   [6] E.p.: 'may see what He is.'
[7] E.p. adds: 'for there remains that of faith.'   [8] E.p.: 'that Divine face.'
[9] So T.   A, B, C, G, Gr: 'proceeds from and begins with.'

judgment proceeding from the goodness of his own thoughts; and so likewise he that is negligent and slothful[1] thinks that others are the same. And hence, when we are negligent and slothful in the sight of God, we think that it is God Who is slothful and negligent with us, as we read in the forty-third Psalm, where David says to God: 'Arise, Lord, why sleepest Thou?'[2] He attributes to God qualities that are in man; for though it is they that have fallen and are asleep, yet it is God Whom he bids arise and awaken, though He that keepeth Israel never sleeps.

9. But in truth, though every blessing that comes to man is from God,[3] and man, of his own power, can do naught that is good, it is true to say that our awakening is an awakening of God, and our up-rising is an uprising of God. And thus it is as though David had said: Raise us up and raise us up again[4] and awaken us, for we are asleep and we have fallen in two ways. Wherefore, since the soul had fallen into a sleep, whence of itself it could never awaken, and it is God alone that has been able to open its eyes and cause this awakening, it very pro-perly describes it as an awakening of God, in these words: 'Thou awakenest in my bosom.' Do Thou awaken us, then, and enlighten us, my Lord, that we may know and love the blessings that Thou hast ever set before us, and we shall know that Thou hast been moved to grant us favours, and that Thou hast been mindful of us.

10. That which the soul knows and feels in this awakening con-cerning the excellence of God is wholly indescribable,[5] for, since there is a communication of the excellence of God in the substance of the soul, which is that breast of the soul whereof the lines here speak, there is heard in the soul the immense power of the voice of a multitude of excellences, of thousands upon thousands of virtues.[6] In these the soul is entrenched and remains terribly and firmly arrayed among them like ranks of armies and made sweet and gracious in all the sweetnesses and graces of the creatures.[7]

---

[1] [Lit., 'asleep'; and so also below.]   [2] Psalm xliii, 23 [A.V., xliv, 23].

[3] E.p. abbreviates, from the end of § 7, thus: 'there appears together with it that which it is doing. And this is the awakening of the soul, although furthermore, in truth, though every blessing that comes to man is from God.'

[4] [Lit., 'Raise us up twice.']   [5] A, Bz, T, e.p.: 'invisible.'

[6] G, Gr, add: 'of God, which can never be numbered.'

[7] E.p.: 'concerning the excellence of God in the depth of the soul is wholly indescrib-able. This is the sleep of the soul whereof the lines here speak. There resounds in the soul an immense power, in the voice of a multitude of excellences, of thousands upon thou-sands of virtues. In these the soul halts and stops, and remains terribly and firmly arrayed like hosts of armies, and made sweet and gracious in that which comprises all the sweet-nesses and graces of the creatures.'

11. But this question will be raised: How can the soul bear so violent[1] a communication while in the flesh, when indeed there is no means and strength in it to suffer so greatly and not faint away, since the mere sight of King Assuerus on his throne, in royal apparel and adorned with gold and precious stones,[2] caused Queen Esther such great fear when she saw how terrible he was to behold that she fainted away, as she confesses in that place where she says she fainted away by reason of the fear caused by his great glory, since he seemed to her like an angel and his face was full of graces.[3] For glory oppresses him that looks upon it if it glorifies not. And how much more should the soul faint here, since it is no angel that it sees, but God, Whose face is full of graces[4] of all the creatures and of terrible power and glory and Whose voice is the multitude of His excellences? Concerning this Job enquires, when we have such difficulty in hearing a drop,[5] who shall be able to abide the greatness of His thunder.[6] And elsewhere he says: 'I will not that He contend and treat with me with much strength, lest perchance He oppress me with the weight of His greatness.'[7]

12. But the reason why the soul faints not away and fears not in this awakening which is so powerful and glorious is twofold. First, being, as it now is, in the state of perfection, wherein its lower part is throughly purged and conformed with the spirit, it has not the suffering and pain that are wont to be experienced in spiritual communications of spirit and sense when these are not purged and prepared to receive them; although this suffices not to prevent the soul from suffering when it is faced with such greatness and glory; since, although its nature be very pure, yet it will be corrupted because it exceeds nature, even as a physical faculty is corrupted by any sensible thing which exceeds its power,[8] in which sense must be taken that which we quoted from Job. The second reason is the more relevant: it is that which the soul gave in the first line—namely, that God shows Himself gentle and loving. For, just as God shows the soul this greatness and glory in order to comfort and magnify it, just so does He

---

[1] [Lit., 'so strong.']
[2] Gr, T: 'precious pearls.'
[3] Esther xv, 16.
[4] E.p.: 'since it is no angel that it knows, but God Himself, the Lord of the angels, Whose face is full of graces.'
[5] Several MSS. have 'particle' [cf. A.V., 'portion']. A reads: 'spark.' E.p. has: 'if we can scarcely hear a whisper thereof, how shall one be able,' etc.
[6] Job xxvi, 14.
[7] Job xxiii, 6.
[8] [This reading is obtained by substituting in the Spanish text *excedente* for *excelente*, a change suggested by P. Gurdon. No other reading seems to make sense of the passage.]

grant it grace so that it receives no suffering, and protect its nature,
showing the spirit His greatness, with tenderness and love, without
the natural senses perceiving this, so that the soul knows not if it is in
the body or out of the body.[1] This may easily be done by that God
Who protected Moses with His right hand that he might see His
glory.[2] And thus the soul feels the gentleness and lovingness of God
proportionately to His power and dominion and greatness, since in
God all these things are one and the same. And thus the delight of the
soul is strong, and the protection given to it is strong in gentleness
and love, so that it may be able to endure the strength of this delight;
and thus the soul, far from fainting away, becomes strong and powerful. For, when Esther swooned, this was because the King showed himself to her at first unfavourably; for, as we read in that place, he showed
her his burning[3] eyes and the fury of his breast. But when he looked
favourably upon her, stretching out his sceptre and touching her with
it and embracing her, she returned to herself, for he had said to her that
he was her brother and she was not to fear.

13. And thus, when the King of Heaven has shown Himself as a
friend to the soul, as its equal[4] and its brother, the soul is no longer
afraid. For when, in gentleness and not in wrath, He shows to it the
strength of His power and the love of His goodness, He communicates to it the strength and love of His breast, and comes out to it from
the throne (which is the soul[5]), even as a spouse from his bridal
chamber where he was hidden. He inclines to the soul, touches it with
the sceptre of His majesty and embraces it as a brother. The soul
beholds the royal apparel and perceives its fragrance—namely, the
wondrous virtues of God; it observes the splendour of gold, which is
charity; it sees the glittering of the precious stones, which are knowledge of created substances, both higher and lower;[6] it looks upon
the face of the Word, which is full of graces that strike this queen
(which is the soul) and likewise clothe her, so that she is transformed
in these virtues of the King of Heaven and sees herself a queen indeed,
and says of herself truly that which David says in the forty-fourth
Psalm, namely: 'The queen stood at Thy right hand in apparel of

---

[1] E.p. abbreviates: 'and prepared to receive them. The second and more important
reason is that which is given in the first line—namely, that God shows Himself gentle
and loving. For, just as He shows the soul this greatness and glory in order to comfort
and magnify it, just so does He grant it grace and strength, and protect its nature, showing His greatness to the spirit with tenderness and love.'

[2] Exodus xxxiii, 22.   [3] E.p.: 'burning and enkindled.'
[4] E.p.: 'as its Spouse.'   [5] E.p. omits: 'which is the soul.'
[6] E.p.: 'which are supernatural knowledge.'

gold and surrounded with variety.'[1] And, since all this comes to pass in the inmost substance of the soul, it adds next:

Where thou dwellest secretly and alone!

14. The soul says that He dwells secretly in its breast, because, as we have said, this sweet embrace is made in the depth of the substance of the soul.[2] That is to say that God dwells secretly in all souls[3] and is hidden in their substance; for, were this not so, they would be unable to exist. But there is a difference between these two manners of dwelling, and a great one. For in some He dwells alone, and in others He dwells not alone; in some He dwells contented[4] and in others He dwells displeased; in some He dwells as in His house, ordering it and ruling everything, while in others He dwells as a stranger in the house of another, where He is not allowed to do anything or to give any commands. Where He dwells with the greatest content and most completely alone is in the soul wherein dwell fewest desires and pleasures of its own; here He is in His own house and rules and governs it. And the more completely alone does He dwell in the soul, the more secretly He dwells; and thus in this soul wherein dwells no desire neither any other image or form of aught that is created, He dwells most secretly, with the more intimate, more interior and closer embrace, according as the soul, as we say, is the more purely and completely withdrawn from all save God. And thus He dwells secretly, since the devil cannot attain to this place and to this embrace, neither can any understanding attain[5] to a knowledge of the manner thereof. But He dwells not secretly with respect to the soul which is in this state of perfection, for it ever perceives that He is within it. Only when the Beloved causes these awakenings to take place does it seem to the soul that He Who aforetime was asleep in its bosom is awakening; and, although it felt and enjoyed His presence, it was as if the Beloved were asleep in its bosom;[6] and the understanding and love of two persons cannot be mutually communicated until both have awakened.[7]

15. Oh, how happy is this soul that is ever conscious of God reposing and resting within its breast! Oh, how well is it that it should withdraw from all things, flee from business and live in boundless

---

[1] Psalm xliv, 10 [A.V., xlv, 9].   [2] E.p. adds: 'and its faculties.'
[3] C adds: 'as absolute lord of them.'
[4] E.p. abbreviates: 'But there is a difference between these two manners of dwelling; for in some He dwells contented.'
    [5] E.p.: 'well attain.'   [6] E.p. ends the paragraph here.
    [7] C: 'for when one of two persons is asleep, the understanding of both cannot be mutually communicated until both are awake.'

tranquillity, lest anything, however small,[1] should disturb or move the
bosom[2] of the Beloved within it. He is there, habitually, as it were,
asleep in this embrace with the substance of the soul;[3] and of this the
soul is quite conscious, and habitually has full fruition,[4] for, if He were
forever awake within it, what would this state be like? Knowledge and
love would be forever communicated to the soul, and it would be
living in glory. For, if one single awakening of God within the soul,
and one glance from His eye, set it in such bliss, as we have said, what
would its condition be if He were habitually awake[5] within it?

16. In other souls, that have not attained to this union, He dwells
secretly likewise; and He is not displeased, because they are not yet
perfectly prepared for union. Such souls are not as a rule conscious of
His presence save when He effects certain delectable awakenings within
them, but these are not of the same kind as that other awakening, nor
have they aught to do with it. This awakening is not so secret from
the devil, or from the understanding, as that other, for something can
always be understood concerning it by means of the movements of
sense, inasmuch as sense is not completely annihilated until the soul
attains to union, but still preserves certain actions pertaining to the
spiritual element,[6] for it is not yet wholly spiritualized. But in this
awakening which the Spouse effects in this perfect soul, everything is
perfect; for it is He that is its sole cause.[7] Thus, in that inspiration and
awakening, which is as if a man awakened and breathed, the soul is
conscious of the breathing of God, wherefore it says:

**And in thy sweet breathing, full of blessing and glory,   How
delicately thou inspirest my love!**

17. Of that breathing of God I should not wish to speak, neither do
I desire now to speak; for I see clearly that I cannot say aught concerning it, and that, were I to speak of it, it would seem less[8] than it is.
For it is a breathing of God Himself,[9] wherein, in that awakening of
lofty knowledge of the Deity, the Holy Spirit breathes into the soul in
proportion to the knowledge[10] wherein He most profoundly absorbs

---

1 [*Lit.*, 'lest a speck.']
2 A: 'or renew the sleep' [*renueve el sueño* for *remueva el seno*].
3 E.p.: 'with the soul.'
4 C adds: 'of His awakenings, though not always.'
5 A, T: 'habitually disposed.'
6 E.p. omits: 'pertaining to the spiritual element.' C has 'sensual' for 'spiritual.'
7 E.p. adds: 'in the sense mentioned above.'
8 C: 'much less.'   9 E.p. adds: 'to the soul.'
10 C: 'to the intelligence and knowledge.'

it in the Holy Spirit, inspiring it with most delicate love for Himself according to that which it has seen; for, the soul being[1] full of blessing and glory, the Holy Spirit has filled it with goodness and glory, wherein He has inspired it with a love for Himself which transcends all description and all sense, in the deep things of God. And for that reason I leave speaking of it here.[2]

[1] Bz, C, Gr, e.p.: 'for, His breathing being.'
[2] E.p.: 'wherein He inspires it with a love for Himself which transcends all glory and all sense, and for that reason I leave speaking of it.'

LIVING FLAME OF LOVE

(SECOND REDACTION)

Exposition of the stanzas which treat of the most intimate and perfected union and transformation of the soul in God, written by P. Fray John of the Cross, Discalced Carmelite, at the request of Doña Ana de Peñalosa and composed in prayer by their author in the year 1584.[1]

PROLOGUE

I HAVE felt some unwillingness, most noble and devout lady, to expound these four stanzas which you have requested me to explain, for they relate to things so interior and spiritual that words commonly fail to describe them, since spirit transcends sense and it is with difficulty that anything can be said of the substance of the spirit[2] if one have not deep spirituality. Wherefore, having little thereof myself, I have delayed writing until now, when it appears that the Lord has opened knowledge somewhat to me and given me some fervour (which must arise from your devout desire, for perhaps, as these words have been written for you,[3] His Majesty desires them to be expounded for you). So I have taken courage, knowing for certain that out of my own resources I can say naught that is of any value, especially in things of such sublimity and substance. Wherefore my part herein will be limited to the defects and errors that this book may contain, for which reason I submit it all to the better judgment and understanding of our holy[4] Mother the Roman Catholic Church, with whose guidance no man goes astray. And, with this preamble, relying upon Divine Scripture, and making clear that all which is said herein is as far removed from all that there is to say as is a picture from a living person, I shall make bold to say that which I know.

2. And there is no reason for marvelling that God should grant

---

[1] So S, with which are practically identical Bg and P.   C omits the title, beginning with the word 'Prologue.' Bz begins: 'Stanzas made by the soul in the final union with God, made and commented by Father Fray John of the Cross.'

[2] Bg, P omit: 'of the spirit.' Bz, C read as in the first redaction.

[3] S: 'for your devotion.'　　　　　　　　　[4] Bz, S omit: 'holy.'

such high[1] and rare favours[2] to those souls on whom He bestows consolations. For if we consider that He is God, and that He bestows them as God, with infinite love and goodness, it will not seem to us unreasonable. For God said that the Father and the Son and the Holy Spirit would come to him that loved Him and make their abode in him,[3] and this would come to pass by His making him live and dwell in the Father and the Son and the Holy Spirit, in the life of God, as the soul explains in these stanzas.

3. For although in the stanzas which we expounded above we spoke of the most perfect degree of perfection[4] to which a man may attain in this life, which is transformation in God, nevertheless these stanzas treat of a love which is even more completed and perfected within this same state of transformation. For, although it is true that both those stanzas and these speak of a state of transformation beyond which, as such, a soul cannot pass, yet none the less, with time and practice, as I say, the soul may become more completely perfected and grounded in love. Even so, when a log of wood has been set upon the fire, it is transformed into fire and united with it;[5] yet, as the fire grows hotter and the wood remains upon it for a longer time, it glows much more and becomes more completely enkindled, until it gives out sparks of fire and flame.

4. And it is of this degree of enkindled love that the soul must be understood as speaking when it is at last so far transformed and perfected interiorly in the fire of love[6] that not only is it united with this fire but it has now become one living flame within it. Such the soul feels itself to be, and as such it speaks in these stanzas, with an intimate and delicate sweetness of love, burning in the flame thereof, and extolling in these stanzas certain effects thereof which are wrought in itself. These I shall expound in the same order as with the other stanzas, setting them down first all together, then setting down each stanza and expounding it briefly, and finally setting down each line and expounding it by itself alone.[7]

---

[1] Bg, P: 'such high and sublime.'
[2] Bz: 'such high and rare marvels and favours.'
[3] St. John xiv, 23.   [4] C: 'of prayer and perfection.'
[5] Bg, P: 'and consumed in it.'   [6] C: 'of Divine love.'
[7] C: 'and finally expounding each verse by itself alone.' S adds: 'Fray John of the Cross, Discalced Carmelite.' C adds: 'Fray John of the †. Soli Deo honor et gloria. Amen.'

END OF THE PROLOGUE

STANZAS MADE BY THE SOUL
IN THE INTIMATE UNION OF GOD[1]

1. Oh, living flame of love   That tenderly woundest my soul in
   its deepest centre,[2]
   Since thou art no longer oppressive, perfect me now if it be
   thy will,   Break the web of this sweet encounter.

2. Oh, sweet burn![3] Oh, delectable wound!   Oh, soft hand!
   Oh, delicate touch
   That savours of eternal life and pays every debt!   In slaying,
   thou hast changed death into life.

3. Oh, lamps of fire,   In whose splendours the deep caverns of
   sense which were dark and blind
   With strange brightness   Give heat and light together to their
   Beloved!

4. How gently and lovingly thou awakenest in my bosom,
   Where thou dwellest secretly and alone!
   And in thy sweet breathing, full of blessing and glory,   How
   delicately thou inspirest my love![4]

---

[1] S adds: 'its Beloved Spouse.'
[2] Bz, P: 'That tenderly woundest the deepest centre of my soul.'
[3] Bz: 'Oh, sweet captivity!' [*cautiverio* for *cauterio*].
[4] The MSS. here add the note which will be found above as note 2 on p. 16.

STANZA THE FIRST

**Oh, living flame of love   That tenderly woundest my soul in its deepest centre,[1]
Since thou art no longer oppressive, perfect me now if it be thy will,   Break the web of this sweet encounter.**

EXPOSITION

THE soul feels itself to be at last wholly enkindled in Divine union, and its palate to be wholly bathed in glory and love, and from the very inmost part[2] of its substance to be flowing veritable rivers of glory, abounding in delights, for it perceives that from its belly are flowing the rivers of living water which the Son of God said would flow from such souls.[3] It seems to this soul that, since it is transformed in God with such vehemence and is in so lofty a way possessed of Him, and is adorned with such a marvellous wealth of gifts and virtues, it is very near to bliss, from which it is divided only by a slender web. And, seeing that that delicate flame of love that burns within it is, as it were, glorifying it with a glory both gentle and powerful whensoever it assails it, to such a degree that, whensoever it is absorbed and assailed, it believes that it is about to enter upon eternal life[4] and that this web of mortal life will be broken, and that there remains but a very short space of time, yet during this space it cannot be perfectly glorified in its essence, the soul addresses this flame, which is the Holy Spirit, with great yearning, begging Him now to break this its mortal life in that sweet encounter, so that of a truth He may communicate to it perfectly that which it believes Him to be about to give to it whensoever He meets it—namely, complete and perfect glory. And thus the soul says:

Oh, living flame of love

2. In order to extol the fervour and delight wherewith it speaks in

---

[1] P: 'That tenderly woundest the deepest centre of my soul!'
[2] Bg, C, P: 'from the very last part.'
[3] St. John vii, 38.   [4] Bg, P: 'eternal life and glory.

these four stanzas, the soul begins each of them with the word 'Oh' or 'How,' which words signify affectionate exultation. Each time that they are used they show that something is passing within the soul beyond that which can be expressed by the tongue. And the word 'Oh' serves also to express a deep yearning and earnest supplication with the aim of persuasion; for both these reasons the soul uses that word in this stanza, intimating and extolling its great desire, and endeavouring to persuade love to set it free.[1]

3. This flame of love is the Spirit of its Spouse—that is, the Holy Spirit. And this flame the soul feels within it, not only as a fire that has consumed and transformed it in sweet love, but also as a fire which burns within it and sends out flame, as I have said, and that flame, each time that it breaks forth, bathes the soul in glory and refreshes it with the temper of Divine life. And this is the operation of the Holy Spirit in the soul that is transformed in love, that the acts that He performs within it cause it to send out flames, which are the enkindling of love, wherein the will of the soul is united, and it loves most deeply, being made one with that flame in love. And thus these acts of love of the soul are most precious,[2] and even one of them is of greater merit and worth than all that the soul has done in its life apart from this transformation, however much this may be. Like to the difference that exists between a habit and an act is that which exists between transformation in love and the flame of love; it is the same difference as that between the log of wood that is enkindled and the flame which it sends forth, for the flame is the effect of the fire that burns there.

4. Wherefore it may be said that the soul that is in this state of transformation of love is in its ordinary habit, and that it is like to the log of wood that is continually assailed by the fire; and the acts of this soul are the flame that arises from the fire of love: the more intense is the fire of union, the more vehemently does its flame issue forth. In this flame the acts of the will are united and rise upward, being carried away and absorbed in the flame of the Holy Spirit, even as the angel rose upward to God in the flame of the sacrifice of Manue.[3] In this state, therefore, the soul can perform no acts, but it is the Holy Spirit that performs them and moves it to perform them; wherefore all its acts are Divine, since it is impelled and moved to them by God. Hence it seems to the soul that whensoever this flame breaks forth, causing it to

[1] Bz: 'to desire it.' Bg, P read as in the text, but add: 'from mortal flesh.'
[2] Bg, P: 'most pure.'   [3] Judges xiii, 20.

love with the Divine temper and sweetness, it is granting it eternal life, since it raises it to the operation of God in God.

5. This is the language used by God when He speaks to souls that are purified and clean: words wholly enkindled,[1] even as David said: 'Thy word is vehemently enkindled.'[2] And the Prophet asked: 'Are not my words as a fire?'[3] These words, as God Himself says, through Saint John, are spirit and life,[4] and are felt to be such by souls that have ears to hear them, who, as I say, are souls that are pure and enkindled with love. But those that have not a healthy palate,[5] and desire other things, cannot relish the spirit and life that these words contain, but rather find insipidity in them. For this reason, the loftier were the words spoken by the Son of God, the more they displeased certain persons because of these persons' impurity, as when the Lord preached that sweet[6] and loving doctrine of the Holy Eucharist, and many of His hearers turned back.[7]

6. Because such persons are not attracted by this language of God, which He speaks inwardly, they must not think that others will not be attracted by it. On the occasion here mentioned it greatly attracted Saint Peter, so that he said to Christ: 'Lord, whither shall we go, for Thou hast the words of eternal life?'[8] And the Samaritan woman forgot her water and her pitcher, because of the sweetness of the words of God. And thus, when this soul is so near to God that it is transformed in the flame of love, wherein the Father and the Son and the Holy Spirit communicate Themselves to it, how is it a thing incredible that it should be said to enjoy a foretaste of eternal life, though this cannot be perfectly so, since that is not permitted by the conditions of this life? But the delight caused in the soul by that flaming of the Holy Spirit is so sublime that it teaches the soul what is the savour of eternal life. For that reason it speaks of the flame as living; not that it is not always living, but because its effect is to make the soul live spiritually in God, and experience[9] the life of God, even as David says: 'My heart and my flesh have rejoiced in the living God.'[10] There was no necessity for him to use the word 'living,'[11] since God is ever living; he uses it to show that spirit and sense had a living experience

[1] Bg, P: 'these words are wholly enkindled.'
[2] Psalm cxviii, 140. [*Ignitum eloquium tuum vehementer.*]
[3] Jeremias xxiii, 29.   [4] St. John vi, 64.
[5] Bg, P: 'that keep not their palate clean.'   [6] S: 'that sovereign.'
[7] [St. John vi, 67.]   [8] St. John vi, 69.
[9] Bg, P: 'and live.'
[10] Psalm lxxxiii, 3 [A.V., lxxxiv, 2].
[11] Bg, P: 'to use the words "living God."'

of God, being wrought in God[1]—which is to have experience[2] of the living God, that is to say, the life of God and life eternal. David spoke in that passage of the living God because he had had experience of Him in a living manner, albeit not perfectly, but he had had, as it were, a foretaste of eternal life. And thus in this flame the soul has so living[3] a perception of God and experiences Him with such great sweetness and delight that it says: 'Oh, living flame of love!'

That tenderly woundest

7. That is, that touchest me tenderly with Thy heat. For, inasmuch as this flame is a flame of Divine life, it wounds the soul with the tenderness of the life of God; and so deeply and profoundly does it wound it and fill it with tenderness that it causes it to melt in love, so that there may be fulfilled in it that which came to pass to the Bride in the Song of Songs. She conceived such great tenderness that she melted away, wherefore she says in that place: 'When the Spouse spake, my soul melted.'[4] For this is the effect that the speaking of God causes in the soul.

8. But how can we say that this flame wounds the soul, when there is nothing in the soul to be wounded, since it is wholly consumed[5] by the fire of love? It is a marvellous thing: for, as love is never idle, but is continually in movement, it is ever throwing out sparks, like a flame, in every direction; and, as the office of love is to wound, that it may enkindle with love and cause delight, so, when it is, as it were, a living flame within the soul, it is ever sending forth its arrow-wounds, like most tender sparks of delicate love, joyfully and happily exercising the arts and playings of love. Even so, in his palace,[6] at his marriage, did Assuerus show forth his graces to Esther his bride,[7] revealing to her there his riches and the glory of his greatness.[8] Thus that which the Wise Man said in the Proverbs is now fulfilled in this soul, namely: 'I was delighted every day as I played[9] before him at all times, playing over all lands, and my delight is to be with the children of men, namely, by giving myself to them.'[10] Wherefore these wounds, which are the playing[11] of God, are the sparks of these tender touches of flame which touch the soul intermittently and proceed from the fire of

---

[1] Bg, P: 'being made living in God.' [2] [Cf. p. 20, n. 3, above.]
[3] Bz: 'has so certain.' [4] Canticles v, 6.
[5] Bg, P: 'wholly captivated and consumed.'
[6] Bg, P: 'in the palace of his love.'
[7] C: 'his fairest bride.' [8] [Esther ii, 17–18.]
[9] Bz: 'We were delighted every day as we played.' [10] Proverbs viii, 30–1.
[11] Bg P: 'the fires' [*fuegos* for *juegos*].

love, which is not idle, but whose flames, says the stanza, strike and wound

My soul in its deepest centre,

9. For this feast of the Holy Spirit takes place in the substance of the soul, where neither the devil nor the world nor sense can enter;[1] and therefore the more interior[2] it is, the more is it secure, substantial and delectable; for the more interior it is, the purer is it, and the more of purity there is in it, the more abundantly and frequently and widely does God communicate Himself. And thus the delight and rejoicing of the soul and the spirit is the greater herein because it is God that works all this and the soul of its own power does naught therein; for the soul can do naught of itself, save through the bodily senses and by their help, from which in this case the soul is very free and very far removed, its only business being the reception of God, Who alone can work in the depth[3] of the soul, without the aid of the senses, and can move the soul therein. And thus all the movements of such a soul are Divine; and, although they come from Him, they belong to the soul likewise, for God works them in the soul, with its own aid, since it gives its will and consent thereto. And, since to say that He wounds the soul in its deepest centre is to imply that the soul has other centres which are less profound,[4] it is necessary to explain in what way this is so.

10. In the first place, it must be known that the soul, inasmuch as it is spirit, has neither height nor depth, neither greater nor lesser degrees of profundity in its own being, as have bodies that can be measured. For, since there are no parts in the soul, there is no difference between its inward and its outward being; it is all the same, and it has no depths of greater or lesser profundity of a kind that can be measured; for it cannot be more enlightened in one part than in another, as is the case with physical bodies, but the whole of it is enlightened in one manner, either to a greater or to a lesser degree, in the same way as the air is enlightened or unenlightened,[5] to a greater or a lesser degree.

11. We term the deepest centre of a thing the farthest point to which its being and virtue and the force of its operation and movement can attain, and beyond which they cannot pass. Thus fire and a stone have

---

[1] Bg, P: 'where neither sense enters nor can the devil attain.'
[2] Bg, P: 'the more delectable and interior.'
[3] Bg, P: 'in the depth and inmost part.'
[4] Bz, C, S: 'other and profounder centres.'
[5] Bz omits: 'or unenlightened.'

natural movement and power, and strength to reach the centre of their sphere, and cannot pass beyond it, neither can help reaching it and remaining in it, save by reason of some contrary and violent impediment. Accordingly, we shall say that a stone, when in some way it is within the earth, is in some way in its centre, and this although it be not in the deepest part of the earth, because it is within the sphere of its centre and activity and movement; but we shall not say that it is in its deepest centre, which is the middle of the earth, and therefore it still has power and force and inclination to descend and to attain to this farthest and deepest centre if that which impedes it be taken away; and when it attains to its centre and there remains to it no more power and inclination of its own to move farther, we shall say that it is in its deepest centre.

12. The centre of the soul is God; and, when the soul has attained to Him according to the whole capacity[1] of its being, and according to the force of its operation and inclination, it will have reached its last and deepest centre in God, which will be when with all its powers it understands and loves and enjoys God; and, so long as it has not attained as far as this, as is the case in this mortal life, wherein the soul cannot attain to God with all its powers,[2] then, although it be in this its centre, which is God, by grace and by His own communication which He has with it, still, inasmuch as it has the power of movement and strength to go farther, and is not satisfied, then, although it may be in the centre,[3] it is nevertheless not in the deepest centre, since it is capable of going to the deepest centre of God.[4]

13. It is to be observed, then, that love is the inclination of the soul and the strength and power which it has to go to God, for, by means of love, the soul is united with God; and thus, the more degrees of love the soul has, the more profoundly does it enter into God and the more is it centred in Him. Therefore we can say that, as are the degrees of the love of God of which the soul is capable, so are the centres of which it is capable in God, each one being more interior than another; for the strongest love is the most unitive love,[5] and in this sense we may understand the many mansions which, said the Son of God, were in His Father's house.[6] So that, for the soul to be in its centre, which is God, as we have said, it suffices for it to have one degree of love, since with one degree alone it may be united with Him through grace. If it

---

[1] P: 'according to the quality.'
[3] C: 'although it is satisfied.'
[5] C: 'the most vital love.'

[2] Bz omits: 'with all its powers.'
[4] S: 'the deepest centre in God.'
[6] St. John xiv, 2.

have two degrees of love, it will be united and have entered into another and a more interior centre[1] with God; and, if it attain to three, it will have entered into the third; and, if it attain to the last degree, the love of God will succeed in wounding the soul even in its remotest and deepest centre—that is, in transforming and enlightening it as regards all its being and power and virtue, such as it is capable of receiving, until it be brought into such a state that it appears to be God. In this state it is as when the crystal that is clear and pure is assailed by the light; the more degrees of light it receives, the greater concentration of light there is in it, and the greater is its enlightenment. And the copiousness of light may reach such a point that it comes to appear to be wholly light, and cannot be distinguished from the light; being enlightened to the greatest possible extent, it appears to be light itself.[2]

14. And thus, when the soul says here that the flame of love wounds it in its deepest centre, it means that the Holy Spirit wounds and assails it in the farthest point attained by its own substance, virtue and power. This it says, not because it desires to indicate here that this flame wounds it as substantially and completely as it will do in the beatific vision of God in the life to come, for, although in this mortal life the soul may reach as high a state of perfection as that whereof we are speaking, it reaches not the perfect state of glory, nor can it do so, although peradventure it may happen that God will grant it such a favour fleetingly. But it says this to indicate the copiousness and abundance of delight and glory of which it is conscious in this kind of communication in the Holy Spirit. This delight is the greater and the more tender when the soul is the more fervently and substantially transformed and centred in God; and this, being the maximum to which the soul can attain in this life (though, as we say, not as perfectly as in the life to come), is called the deepest centre. It is true that the habit of charity in the soul may be as perfect in this life as in the next, but neither its operation nor its fruit can be so, although the fruit and the operation of love grow in this state to such an extent that they become very much like those of the life to come; so much so that to the soul it appears that they are so and it ventures to use those words which one ventures to use only of the next life, namely: 'in the deepest centre of my soul.'

15. And since rare occurrences, of which few have had experience,[3]

[1] C: 'degree.'
[2] C abbreviates: 'to appear to be wholly light, and there is no kind of distinction between it and the light, but all appears to be light.'
[3] C: 'have had knowledge.'

are the more marvellous and the less credible, as is that which we are describing as happening to the soul in this state, I do not doubt that certain persons, who understand it not through their learning neither know it by experience,[1] will either disbelieve it or will consider it to be exaggerated, or will think that it is not in itself as great a thing as it is. But to all these I reply that the Father of lights, Whose hand is not shortened and Who, like the sun's ray, sheds His blessings abundantly without respect of persons, wheresoever there is cause, showing Himself likewise joyfully to men as they walk in the roads and paths, hesitates not, neither disdains, to have His delights in common[2] with the sons of men all over the round earth. And it must not be held incredible that in a faithful soul which has already been tried and proved and purged in the fire of tribulations and trials and various temptations, and found faithful in love, there should be fulfilled that which was promised by the Son of God—namely that, if any man loved Him, the Holy Spirit would come within him and would abide and dwell in him.[3] And this comes to pass when the understanding is divinely illumined in the wisdom of the Son, and the will is made glad in the Holy Spirit, and the Father, with His power and strength, absorbs the soul in the embrace and abyss of His sweetness.[4]

16. And if, as is truly the case, this habitually comes to pass in certain souls, it is credible that such a soul as that whereof we are speaking will not be backward in receiving these favours from God. For that which we are describing as coming to pass in it, through the operation of the Holy Spirit which He brings about in it, is much greater than that which comes to pass in the communication and transformation of love. For the one is like a burning coal; but the other, as we have said, is like a coal heated with such fervency[5] that it not only burns, but gives forth living flame. And thus these two kinds of union —that is, of union alone, and of love and union with enkindling of love—are in a certain way comparable respectively to the fire of God which, says Isaias, is in Sion, and to the furnace of God which is in Jerusalem.[6] The one signifies the Church Militant, wherein the fire of charity is enkindled to no extreme degree; and the other signifies the vision of peace, which is the Church Triumphant, where this fire is as in a furnace enkindled in perfection of love. Although, as we said, this

---

[1] S omits 'not' and has 'and' for 'neither.'   [2] Bz omits 'in common.'
[3] St. John xiv, 23.
[4] So C, S. Bz: 'in the delectable embrace of His sweetness.' Bg, P: 'in the embrace of His sweetness.'
[5] Bz: 'a coal which will absorb so much fire.'   [6] Isaias xxxi, 9.

soul has not attained to such perfection as this, yet, in comparison with the other and common union, it is like a furnace enkindled, and its vision is as much more peaceful and glorious and tender as the flame is brighter and more resplendent than that of a burning coal.

17. Therefore, when the soul feels that this living flame of love is communicating all blessings to it after a living manner, because this Divine love brings everything with it, it says: 'Oh, living flame of love, that tenderly woundest.' This is as though it were to say: Oh, love enkindled, that with thy loving movements art delectably glorifying me according to the capacity and power of my soul—that is to say, art giving me Divine intelligence according to the ability and capacity of my understanding, and communicating love to me according to the utmost power of my will, and delighting me in the substance of the soul with the torrent of thy delight, in thy Divine contact and substantial union, according to the greater purity of my substance and the capacity and freedom of my memory. This comes to pass, and in a greater degree than it is possible for the soul to describe, at the time when this flame of love uprises in it. Inasmuch as the soul has been well purged[1] with respect to its substance and to its faculties —memory, understanding and will—the Divine Substance,[2] which, as the Wise Man says, toucheth all things by reason of its purity,[3] absorbs it in a profound and subtle and sublime manner; and in that absorption of the soul in wisdom, the Holy Spirit brings to pass the glorious vibrations of His flame;[4] and, since it is so sweet, the soul then says:

Since thou art no longer oppressive,[5]

18. That is to say, since thou dost no longer afflict or oppress or weary as thou didst aforetime. For it must be known that this flame, which is God,[6] when the soul was in the state of spiritual purgation— that is, when it was entering upon contemplation—was not as friendly and sweet to it as it now is in this state of union. And we must tarry here for some time in order to explain how this comes to pass.

19. Here it must be known that, before this Divine fire of love is introduced into the substance of the soul, and is united with it, by means of a purity and purgation which is perfect and complete, this flame, which is the Holy Spirit, is wounding the soul, and destroying and consuming in it the imperfections of its evil habits; and this is the

---

[1] Bg, P add: 'and made pure.'
[2] Bg, P: 'the Divine Wisdom.'
[3] Wisdom vii, 24.
[4] C: 'of His soul' [alma for llama].
[5] [Cf. p. 24, n. 6, above.]
[6] Cf. p. 8, above.

operation of the Holy Spirit, wherein He prepares it for Divine union[1] and the transformation of love in God. For it must be known that the same fire of love which afterwards is united with the soul and glorifies it is that which aforetime assailed it in order to purge it; even as the fire that penetrates the log of wood is the same that first of all attacked and wounded it with its flame, cleansing and stripping it of its accidents of ugliness,[2] until, by means of its heat, it had prepared it to such a degree that it could enter it and transform it into itself, which is what spiritual persons call the Purgative Way. In this operation the soul endures great suffering and experiences grievous afflictions in its spirit, which habitually overflow into the senses, at which times this flame is very oppressive. For in this preparatory state of purgation the flame is not bright to it, but dark, and if it gives it any light at all, it is only that it may see and feel its own faults and miseries. Neither is it sweet to it, but grievous; for, although at times it kindles within it the heat of love, this is accompanied by torment and affliction. And it is not delectable to it, but arid; for, although at times, through its benignity, it gives the soul a certain amount of comfort which will strengthen and encourage it, yet, both before and after this happens, it compensates and recompenses it with further trials. Nor does it bring it either refreshment or peace, but consumes and proves it, making it to faint and grieve at its own self-knowledge. And thus it is not glorious to it; rather it makes it miserable and bitter, by means of the spiritual light of self-knowledge which it sheds upon it;[3] for God sends fire, as Jeremias says, into its bones, and instructs it, and, as David says likewise, tries it by fire.

20. And thus at this time the soul suffers great darkness with respect to the understanding, great aridities and afflictions with respect to the will, and grievous knowledge of its miseries in the memory, inasmuch as its spiritual eye is very bright with respect to self-knowledge. And in its substance the soul suffers from abandonment and the greatest[4] poverty. Dry and cold, and at times hot, it finds relief in naught, nor is there any thought[5] that can console it, nor can it even raise its heart to God, since this flame has become so oppressive to it. Even so, says Job, did God treat him in this operation, where he says: 'Thou art changed to be cruel to me.'[6] For, when the soul suffers all these things

---

[1] S: 'for due union.'
[2] [Lit., 'its ugly accidents.'] C: 'its cold accidents' [frios for feos].
[3] Bz omits: 'by means . . . sheds upon it.'
[4] Bg, P: 'the profoundest.'   [5] Bz, C: 'a thought.'
[6] Job xxx, 21.

together, it seems to it in truth that God has become cruel to it and bitter.[1]

21. The sufferings of the soul at this time are indescribable: they are, indeed, very little less than those of purgatory.[2] I can think now of no way to describe this state of oppression, to explain how great it is and to show what an extreme is reached by that which the soul feels and suffers in it, save by using these words of Jeremias which refer to it: 'I am the man that see my poverty by the rod of His indignation; He hath threatened me and brought me into darkness and not into light; so greatly is He turned against me and turneth His hand. My skin and my flesh He hath made old: He hath broken my bones. He hath surrounded me round about and hath compassed me with gall and labour. He hath set me in dark places as those that are dead for ever. He hath builded against me round about, that I may not get out. He hath made my imprisonment heavy; yea, and when I have lifted up my voice and cried, He hath shut out my prayer. He hath obstructed my ways with square stones and hath turned my steps and my paths upside down.'[3] All this says Jeremias; and he continues at much greater length. Now, inasmuch as in this way God is remedying and curing the soul in its many infirmities that He may bring it health, the soul must needs suffer in this purgation and remedy according to the nature of its sickness. For here, as it were, Tobias lays its heart upon the coals,[4] so that every kind of evil spirit is set free and driven away from it; and thus all its infirmities are here continually brought to light, and, being set before its eyes, are felt by it and cured.

22. And the weaknesses and miseries which the soul had afore-time hidden and set deep within it (which aforetime it neither saw nor felt) are now seen and felt by it, by means of the light and heat of the Divine fire, just as the humidity which was in the wood was not realized until the fire attacked it, and made it sweat and smoke and steam, as the imperfect soul does when it is brought near to this flame. For at this season—oh, wondrous thing!—there arise within the soul contraries against contraries, the things of the soul against the things of God, which assail the soul; and some of these, as the philosophers say, become visible in reacting to others, and they make war in the soul, striving to expel each other in order that they may reign within it. That is to say, the virtues and properties of God, which are perfect

---

[1] [Lit., 'and tasteless.']
[2] So Bz, C. The other authorities have 'of a purgatory.' Bg, P read: 'sometimes' for 'indeed.'
[3] Lamentations iii, 1–9.   [4] Tobias vi, 16.

in the extreme, war against the habits and properties of the soul, which
are imperfect in the extreme, so that the soul has to suffer the existence
of two contraries within it. For, as this flame is of brightest light, and
assails the soul, its light shines in the darkness of the soul, which is as
dark as the light is bright; and then the soul is conscious of its vicious,
natural darkness, which sets[1] itself against the supernatural light, and
it is not conscious of the supernatural light, because it has it not within
itself, as it has its own darkness, and the darkness comprehends not
the light. And thus it will be conscious of this its darkness for so long
as the light beats upon it, for souls can have no perception of their
darkness save when the Divine light beats upon them and only when
the Divine light drives out the darkness is the soul illumined and transformed and able to see the Divine light,[2] its spiritual eye having been
cleansed and strengthened by the Divine light. For infinite light will
produce total darkness in sight that is impure and weak and the faculty
will be subdued by excess of sense. And thus this flame was oppressive
to the soul in the sight of its understanding.

23. And since this flame is of itself extremely loving, it assails the
will in a loving and a tender manner; and since the will is of itself
extremely arid and hard, the hardness of the one is felt by comparison
with the tenderness of the other, and the aridity of the one by comparison with the love of the other, and the will becomes conscious of its
natural hardness and aridity with respect to God, when this flame
beats lovingly and tenderly upon it. And it is not conscious of the love
and tenderness of the flame (being prevented by its hardness and
aridity, wherein these other contraries, tenderness and love, can find
no place) until one group of the contraries is driven out by the other
and the love and tenderness of God reign in the will. And in this way
this flame has been oppressive to the will—in making it to feel and
suffer its hardness and aridity. And in the same way, since this flame is
most extensive and vast, and the will is restricted and narrow, the will
is conscious of its narrowness and restraint while the flame is beating
upon it, until the flame acts upon it and dilates and enlarges it and makes
it able to receive it. And likewise, since this flame is sweet and delectable, and the spiritual palate of the will was distempered by the
humours of inordinate[3] affections, it was insipid and bitter to it, and it
was unable to taste the sweet food of the love of God. And so, when

---

[1] Bg, P: 'opposes.'
[2] Bg, P: 'beats upon it, and the soul will be enlightened and transformed and will be
able to see the Divine light.'
[3] Bg, P: 'distempered.'

the will is brought near to this most extensive and most delectable flame, it is conscious also of its constraint and insipidity, and is not conscious of the savour of the flame because it feels[1] none within itself, but feels only that which it has in itself—namely, its own misery. And finally, since this flame is of vast wealth and goodness and delight, and the soul of itself has great poverty and has no good thing of its own, nor can give any satisfaction, it realizes and is clearly conscious of its miseries and poverty and wickedness by contrast with this wealth and goodness and delight, and realizes not the wealth and goodness and delight of the flame (for wickedness comprehends not goodness, nor poverty, riches, and so forth) until this flame succeeds in purifying the soul, and together with transformation gives it riches, glories and delights. In this way the flame was at first oppressive to the soul beyond all description, by reason of the battle which was being waged within it by the contrary forces. God, Who is all perfection, wars against all the imperfect habits of the soul, so that He may transform it in Himself and make it sweet, bright and peaceful, as does the fire when it has entered the wood.

24. This severe purgation comes to pass in few souls—in those alone whom the Lord desires to raise to a higher degree of union; for He prepares each one with a purgation of greater or less severity, according to the degree to which He desires to raise it, and also according to its impurity and imperfection. And so this pain is like that of purgatory; for, just as in purgatory spirits are purged in order that they may be able to see God through clear vision in the life to come, so, after their own manner, souls are purged in this state in order that they may be able to be transformed in Him through love in this life.[2]

25. As to the intensity of this purgation—when it is greater and when less, and when it is according to the understanding and when according to the will and how according to the memory, and when and how it comes according to the substance of the soul, and likewise when it purges the entire soul and when its sensual part only, and how it may be known when it is of one kind and when of another, and at what time and point and season of the spiritual way it begins—we have treated this in the *Dark Night of the Ascent of Mount Carmel* and it affects not our purpose here, wherefore I speak not of it. It suffices here to know that God Himself, Who desires to enter the soul by union and transformation of love, is He that aforetime has been assailing it and purging it with the light and heat of His Divine flame,

---

[1] Bg, P: 'it has.'   [2] Bz: 'in this union.'

even as the fire that enters the wood is the same fire that has prepared it,[1] as we have said. And thus that very flame that has played inwardly upon the soul and is now sweet to it was aforetime oppressive to it, when it was playing upon it without.[2]

26. And it is this that the soul desires to convey when it says in this line: 'Since thou art no longer oppressive.' This, briefly, is as though the soul were to say: Since not only art thou not dark to me as thou wert aforetime, but art the Divine light of my understanding, wherewith I can now look upon thee, and dost not only not cause my weakness to faint, but art rather the strength of my will wherewith I can love thee and enjoy thee, now that it is wholly converted into Divine love, and since thou art not pain and affliction to the substance of my soul, but art rather its glory and delight and boundless freedom, therefore may there be said of me that which is sung in the Divine Songs, in these words: 'Who is this that cometh up from the desert, abounding in delights, leaning upon her Beloved and scattering love on every side?'[3] Thus, then, it is.

Perfect me now if it be thy will,

27. That is to say: Perfect and consummate the spiritual marriage in me with the beatific vision of Thyself—for it is this that the soul beseeches. For, although it is true that in this state that is so lofty, the more completely transformed in love is the soul the more conformed is it, and that it knows nothing of itself, neither is able to ask anything for itself, but all is for its Beloved; since charity, as Saint Paul says, seeks nothing for itself, but only for the Beloved;[4] nevertheless, since it lives in hope, and thus cannot fail to be conscious of something that is lacking, it sighs deeply, though with sweetness and joy, in proportion as it still lacks complete possession of the adoption of the sons of God, wherein, when its glory is consummated, its desire will be at rest.[5] This desire, although here below the soul may have closer union with God, will never be satisfied or at rest until its glory shall appear, especially if it has already tasted the sweetness and delight thereof, which it has in this state. This sweetness is such that, had God not granted a favour to its flesh, and covered its natural being with His

---

[1] Bg, P add: 'before entering it.'
[2] S reads: 'Thus that very flame that aforetime was oppressive to it is now sweet to it.' Bz: 'And thus, having played upon it, it was aforetime oppressive to it, in playing upon it.'
[3] Canticles viii, 5. [The quotation ends at the word 'Beloved.']
[4] 1 Corinthians xiii, 5.
[5] Bz, C: 'will be removed.' S: 'will be ended.'

right hand (as He did to Moses in the rock, that he might see His glory and not die[1]) it would have died at each touch of this flame, and its natural being would have been destroyed, since its lower part would have no means of enduring so great and sublime a fire of glory.

28. Wherefore this desire and the soul's entreaty for it are not accompanied by pain, for the soul in this state is no longer capable of suffering pain, but its entreaty is made with delectable and sweet desire, and the soul entreats conformity between its spirit and its senses. It is for this reason that it says in this line: 'Perfect me now, if it be Thy will.' For the will and desire are to such an extent united with God that the soul regards it as its glory that it should fulfil the will of God in it. Such are the glimpses of glory and love that in these touches filter through the crevices of the door of the soul, in order to enter, though they cannot do so because of the smallness of our earthly house, that the soul would have little love if it entreated not to be allowed to enter into that perfection and consummation of love. Furthermore, the soul now sees that in that delectable power and communication with the Spouse, the Holy Spirit is impelling and inviting it, by means of that boundless glory which He is setting before its eyes, in wondrous ways and with sweet affections, saying to it in its spirit that which is said to the Bride in the Songs, which she relates in these words: 'See that which my Spouse is saying to me: "Arise and make haste, my love, my dove, my fair one, and come; for winter is now past and the rain is ended and gone far away, and the flowers have appeared in our land. And the time of pruning has come and the voice of the turtle is heard in our land; the fig tree has produced her fruits, the vines in flower have yielded their fragrance. Arise, my love, my fair one, and come, my dove, into the holes of the rock, into the cavern of the wall; show me thy sweet face, let thy voice sound in my ears, for thy voice is sweet, and thy countenance is comely."'[2] All these things the soul perceives, and she most clearly understands, in the sublime sense of glory, that the Holy Spirit is showing them to her in that tender and sweet flame,[3] desiring to bring her in to that glory. Wherefore the soul, being thus impelled, here makes answer: 'Perfect me now if it be Thy will.' Herein she makes the Spouse those two petitions which He taught us in the Gospel, namely: *Adveniat regnum tuum. Fiat voluntas tua.*[4] And thus it is as though she were to say: Give me this kingdom per-

---

[1] Exodus xxxiii, 22.   [2] Canticles ii, 10–14.
[3] [*Lit.*, 'flaming.']   [4] St. Matthew vi, 10.

fectly, if it be Thy will—that is, according to Thy will. And that this may come to pass:

Break the web of this sweet encounter.

29. It is this web which hinders so important a business as this, since it is easy to reach God once the obstacles which separate the soul from union with God are taken away and the webs are broken. The webs which can hinder this union and which must be broken if the soul is to approach God and possess Him perfectly may be said to be three, namely: the temporal, which comprises all creatures; the natural, which comprises the operations and inclinations that are purely natural; and the third, the sensual, which comprises only[1] union of the soul with the body, which is sensual and animal life, whereof Saint Paul says: 'We know that if this our earthly house be dissolved we have a dwelling-place of God in the heavens.'[2] The first two webs must of necessity be broken in order that we may attain to this possession of the union of God, wherein all things of the world shall be put aside and renounced, and all the natural affections and appetites be mortified, and the operations of the soul, from being natural, become Divine. All this was broken and effected in the soul by the oppressive encounters of this flame when it was oppressive to it; for, through spiritual purgation, as we have said above, the soul succeeds in breaking these two webs and thence in becoming united with God, as it now is, and there remains to be broken only the third web of this life of sense. For this reason the soul here speaks of a web and not of webs; for there is now no other web to be broken than this, which, being already so delicate and fine and so greatly spiritualized by this union with God, is not attacked by the flame severely, as were the two others, but sweetly and delectably. For this reason the soul speaks here and calls the encounter 'sweet,' for it is the sweeter and the more delectable inasmuch as the soul believes it to be about to break the web of life.

30. Therefore it must be known, with regard to the natural dying[3] of souls that reach this state, that, though the manner of their death, from the natural standpoint, is similar to that of others, yet in the cause and mode of their death there is a great difference. For while the deaths of others may be caused by infirmities or length of days, when these souls die, although it may be from some infirmity, or from old age, their

---

[1] Bg, P omit: 'only.' [2] 2 Corinthians v, 1.
[3] Several manuscripts read 'love' for 'dying.'

spirits are wrested away by nothing less than some loving impulse and encounter far loftier and of greater power and strength than any in the past, for it has succeeded in breaking the web and bearing away a jewel, which is the spirit. And thus the death of such souls is very sweet and gentle, more so than was their spiritual life all their life long, for they die amid the delectable encounters and sublimest impulses of love, being like to the swan, which sings most gently[1] when it is at the point of death. For this reason David said that the death of saints in the fear of God was precious[2], for at such a time all the riches of the soul come to unite together, and the rivers of love of the soul are about to enter the sea, and these are so broad and dense and motion-less[3] that they seem to be seas already. From the beginning to the end, their treasures unite together to accompany the just man as he departs and goes forth to his kingdom, and praises are heard from the ends of the earth,[4] which, as Isaias says, are the glories of the just man.

31. When, therefore, at the time of these glorious encounters, the soul feels itself very near to going forth[5] to possess its kingdom com-pletely and perfectly, in the abundance wherewith it sees itself en-riched (for it knows itself now to be pure and rich and full of virtues and prepared for this, since in this state God permits it to see His beauty[6] and entrusts it with the gifts and virtues that He has given it, and all this turns into love and praise, without a trace of presumption or vanity, since there is no leaven of imperfection to corrupt the mass), and when it sees that it has only now to break this frail web of natural life wherein it feels itself to be enmeshed and imprisoned, and its liberty to be impeded, together with its desire to behold itself loosed[7] and to see itself with Christ (for it grieves that a life which is so strong and high should be obstructed by another that is so weak and low), it begs that this web may be broken, saying: 'Break the web of this sweet encounter.'

32. This life is called a web for three reasons: first, because of the bond that exists between spirit and flesh; second, because it makes a division between God and the soul; third, because even as a web is not so thick[8] and dense but that the light can shine through it, even so in this state this bond appears to it to be a very fine web, since it is

---

[1] Bg, P: 'most sweetly.'   [2] Psalm cxv, 15 [A.V., cxvi, 15].
[3] [Cf. p. 31, n. 12, above.]
[4] C: 'praises of the blessings of the earth are heard.'
[5] Bg, P: 'very near to ascending.'   [6] [Or, 'its (own) beauty.']
[7] Bg, P: 'to be loosed.'   [8] Bg, C: 'so opaque.'

greatly spiritualized and enlightened and refined so that the Divinity cannot but shine through it. And when the soul becomes conscious of the power of the life to come, it feels keenly the weakness of this other life, which appears to it as a very fine web—even as a spider's web, which is the name that David gives to it, saying: 'Our years shall be considered as a spider.'[1] And it is much less still in the eyes of a soul that is so greatly enlarged; for, since this soul has entered into the consciousness of God, it is conscious of things in the way that God is; and in the sight of God, as David also says, a thousand years are as yesterday when it is past.[2] And according to Isaias all nations are as if they were not.[3] And they have the same importance to the soul, namely, all things are to it as nothing, and to its own eyes it is itself nothing: to it its God alone is all.

33. But here one point should be noticed. Why does the soul here beg that the web may be broken, rather than cut or allowed to wear itself out, since all these things would seem to have the same result? We may say that this is for four reasons. First, in order to use language of greater propriety, for in an encounter it is more proper to say that a thing is broken than that it is cut or wears away. Second, because love delights in the force of love and in forceful and impetuous contacts, and these are produced by breaking rather than by cutting or wearing away. Third, because love desires that the act should be very brief, so that it may then be the more quickly concluded; the quicker[4] and more spiritual is it, the greater is its power and worth. For virtue in union is stronger than virtue that is scattered; and love is introduced as form is introduced into matter, namely, in an instant, and until then there has been no act but only dispositions for an act; and thus spiritual acts are performed in the soul as in an instant, since they are infused by God, but the other acts, which are performed by the soul of its own accord, may more properly be called dispositions of successive affections and desires which never succeed in becoming perfect acts of love or contemplation, save occasionally when, as I say, God forms and perfects them with great rapidity in the spirit.[5] For this cause the Wise Man said that the end of a prayer is better than the beginning, and, as is commonly said, the short prayer penetrates the Heavens. Wherefore the soul that is already prepared can perform more acts and acts of greater intensity[6] in a short time than the soul that is not prepared can

---

[1] Psalm lxxxix, 9 [A.V., xc, 9].   [2] Psalm lxxxix, 4 [A.V., xc, 4].
[3] Isaias xl, 17. Bg, P add: 'before Him.'   [4] Bg, C, P: 'the briefer.'
[5] S: 'God forms them in the spirit.'
[6] Bg, P: 'more acts and more interior acts.'

perform in a long time; and merely because of its thorough preparation, it is wont to remain for a long time[1] in the act of love or contemplation. And the soul that is not prepared wastes its strength in the
preparation of the spirit, and even when this is done the fire has not yet
penetrated the wood, whether because of its great humidity, or because
of the scant heat generated in the preparation, or for both these causes.
But into the soul that is prepared the act of love enters continuously,
for the spark seizes upon the dry fuel at each contact; and thus the
soul that is kindled in love prefers the short act of breaking the web
to the duration of the act of cutting it or of its wearing away. The
fourth reason is that the web of life[2] may be more quickly destroyed,
for cutting a thing and allowing it to wear away are acts performed
after greater deliberation, as it is necessary to wait until the thing is
riper, or worn, or for some other condition, whereas breaking apparently needs not to wait for maturity or for anything else.

34. And this is the desire of the enamoured soul, which brooks not
the delay of waiting until its life come naturally to an end or until at
such a time it be cut, because the force of love and the propensities
which it feels make it desire and entreat that its life may be at once
broken by some encounter and supernatural assault of love. The soul
in this state knows very well that it is the habit of God to take away
before their time the souls that He greatly loves, perfecting in them in
a short time, by means of that love, that which in any event[3] they
might have gained gradually in their ordinary progress. It is this that
is said by the Wise Man[4]: 'He that is pleasing to God is made beloved,
and living among sinners he was translated and taken away, lest
wickedness should alter[5] his understanding or deceit beguile his soul.
Being made perfect in a short space, he fulfilled a long time. For his
soul was pleasing to God, therefore hastened He to take him out of the
midst,' etc.[6] Thus far we quote the words of the Wise Man, wherein it
will be seen with what propriety and reason the soul uses that word
'break'; for in these words the Holy Spirit uses the two terms 'take
away'[7] and 'haste,' which are far removed from the idea of any delay.[8]
In speaking of 'haste,' God indicates the speed wherewith He has

---

[1] Bz, C: 'for a sufficient time.'   [2] Bg, P: 'that life.'
[3] Bg, P: 'in a long time.'
[4] Bz abbreviates: 'perfecting them in a short time, for it is this that is said by the Wise
Man.'
[5] C: 'should take away.'   [6] Wisdom iv, 10–11, 13–14.
[7] [The word translated 'take away' has in the original Spanish the meaning of 'take
away violently,' 'snatch away.']
[8] S adds: 'in that which is done by God.'

caused the love of the just man to be perfected in a short time; and by the words 'take away' He indicates that He has borne him off before his natural time. For this reason it is a great thing for the soul to practise the acts of love in this life, so that, when a soul is perfected in a short time, it may not stay long, either in this world or the next, without seeing God.

35. But let us also now see why the soul calls this interior assault of the Holy Spirit an encounter rather than by any other name. The reason is because, as we have said, the soul in God is conscious of an infinite desire that its life may come to an end, yet, because the time of its perfecting is not yet come, this is not accomplished; and it sees that, to the end that it may be the more completely perfected and raised up[1] above the flesh, God makes these assaults upon it that are glorious and Divine and after the manner of encounters, which, as they have the object of purifying it and bringing it out of the flesh, are indeed encounters, wherewith He penetrates the soul continually, deifying its substance and making it Divine, wherein the Being of God absorbs the soul above all being. The reason for this is that God has encountered the soul and pierced it to the quick in the Holy Spirit, Whose communications are impetuous when they are full of fervour,[2] as is this encounter, which the soul, since it has a lively taste of God, calls sweet; not that many other touches and encounters which it receives in this state are not also sweet, but rather that this is eminently so above all the rest; for God effects it, as we have said,[3] in order to loose the soul and glorify it quickly. Wherefore the soul takes courage to say: 'Break the web of this sweet encounter.'

36. To sum up this whole stanza, then, it is as though the soul were to say: Oh, flame of the Holy Spirit, that so intimately and tenderly dost pierce the substance of my soul and cauterize it with Thy glorious heat! Since Thou art now so loving as to show Thyself with the desire of giving Thyself to me in eternal life; if before now my petitions did not reach Thine ears, when with yearnings and fatigues of love my sense and spirit suffered by reason of my great weakness and impurity and the little fortitude of love that I had, I entreated Thee to loose me, and to bear me away with Thee, for with desire did my soul desire Thee since my impatient love would not suffer me to be conformed with the condition of this life that Thou desiredst me still to live,[4] and

---

[1] Bg, Bz, P: 'and carried away.' [2] Bz: 'are favoured.'
[3] Bg, P have 'shines upon it' for 'effects it.' Bz omits: 'for God . . . said.'
[4] C: 'that Thou wouldst desire should come to me.'

the past assaults of love sufficed not, because they were not of sufficient quality for me to attain my desire; now that I am so greatly strengthened in love that not alone do my sense and spirit not fail before Thee, but rather my heart and my flesh are strengthened in Thy sight, they rejoice in the living God with a great conformity between their various parts. Therefore do I entreat that which Thou desirest me to entreat, and that which Thou desirest not, that desire I not, nor can I desire it,[1] nor does it pass through my mind to desire it; and, since my petitions are now more effective and more greatly esteemed in Thine eyes (for they go forth from Thee and Thou movest me to make them, and I pray to Thee with delight[2] and rejoicing in the Holy Spirit, and my judgment comes forth from Thy countenance, which comes to pass when Thou esteemest and hearest my prayers), do Thou break the slender web of this life, and let it not come to pass that age and years cut it after a natural manner, so that I may be able to love Thee with the fullness and satisfaction which my soul desires without end, for ever.

STANZA II

Oh, sweet burn! Oh, delectable wound![3]   Oh, soft hand! Oh, delicate touch
That savours of eternal life and pays every debt!   In slaying, thou hast changed death into life.

EXPOSITION

IN this stanza the soul explains how the three Persons of the Most Holy Trinity, Father, Son and Holy Spirit, are They that[4] effect within it this Divine work of union. Thus the 'hand,' the 'burn' and the 'touch' are in substance one and the same thing; and the soul gives them these names, inasmuch as they describe the effect which is caused by each. The 'burn' is the Holy Spirit, the 'hand' is the Father and the 'touch,' the Son. And thus the soul here magnifies the Father and the Son and the Holy Spirit, dwelling upon[5] three great favours[6] and blessings which They work within it, since They have changed its death into life, transforming it in Themselves. The first is the delectable wound, which the soul attributes to the Holy Spirit, wherefore it

---

1 S omits: 'nor can I desire it.'
3 S has 'flame' [*llama* for *llaga*].
5 Bg omits: 'dwelling upon.'

2 Bz: 'with fervour.'
4 Bg, P omit: 'are They that.'
6 P has 'walls' for 'favours.'

is called a sweet[1] burn. The second is the desire for eternal life, which it attributes to the Son, and therefore calls a delicate touch. The third is His having transformed the soul in Himself, which is a gift[2] wherewith it is well pleased; this is attributed to the Father, and therefore the soul calls it a soft hand. And although the soul here names the three things, because of the properties of their effects, it addresses only one of them, saying: 'Thou hast changed death into life.' For they all work in one, and thus the soul attributes the whole of their work to one, and the whole of it to all of them. There follows the line:

Oh, sweet burn!

2. This burn, as we said, here signifies the Holy Spirit, for, as Moses says in Deuteronomy, our Lord God is a consuming fire[3]—that is, a fire of love. This fire, as it is of infinite power, is able, to an extent which cannot be measured, to consume and transform into itself the soul that it touches. But it burns and absorbs everything according to the preparation thereof; one thing more and another less; and this according to its own pleasure, and after the manner and at the time which it pleases. And since God is an infinite fire of love, when therefore He is pleased to touch the soul with some severity, the heat of the soul rises to such a degree of love that the soul believes that it is being burned with a heat greater than any other in the world. For this reason, in this union it speaks of the Holy Spirit as of a burn; for, just as in a burn the fire is most intense and vehement, and its effect is greater than that of other fires, so the soul describes the act of this union as a burn with respect to other acts, since it is, more properly than any other, an enkindled fire of love. And inasmuch as this Divine fire, in this case, has transformed the soul into itself, not only is the soul conscious of the burn, but it has itself become one burn of vehement fire.

3. And it is a wondrous thing, worthy to be related, that, though this fire of God is so vehement and so consuming that it would consume a thousand worlds more easily than fire here on earth consumes a straw of flax, it consumes not the soul wherein it burns in this way, neither destroys it, still less causes it any affliction, but rather, in proportion to the strength of love, it brings it delight and deifies it, glowing and burning in it sweetly. And this is due to the purity and perfection of the spirit wherein it burns in the Holy Spirit.[4] Thus did it

[1] Only Bg, P have 'sweet.'   [2] So Bg, P. The other authorities have 'a debt.'
[3] Deuteronomy iv, 24.
[4] So S.   The other authorities omit: 'in the Holy Spirit.'

come to pass, as we read in the Acts of the Apostles, when this fire descended with great vehemence and enkindled the disciples;[1] and, as Saint Gregory says,[2] they burned inwardly and sweetly in love. And this is that which is intended by the Church, when she says to this same purpose: There came fire from Heaven, burning not but giving splendour; consuming not but enlightening.[3] For, in these communications, since the object of God is to magnify the soul, this fire wearies it not and afflicts it not but rather enlarges it and delights it; nor does it blacken it and cover it with ashes, as fire does to coal, but it makes it glorious and rich, for which cause the soul calls it a sweet burn.

4. And thus the happy soul that by great good fortune attains to this burning knows everything, tastes everything, does all that it desires, and prospers, and none prevails against it and nothing touches it. For it is of this soul that the Apostle says: 'The spiritual man judgeth all things, and he himself is judged of no man.'[4] *Et iterum*:[5] 'The spiritual man searcheth all things, yea, the depth of God.'[6] For this is the property of love, to seek out all the good things of the Beloved.

5. Oh, the great glory of you souls that are worthy to attain to this supreme fire,[7] for, while it has infinite power to consume and annihilate you, it is certain that it consumes you not, but grants you a boundless consummation in glory![8] Marvel not that God should bring certain souls to so high a state; for the sun is conspicuous for certain marvellous effects which it causes; as the Holy Spirit says, it burns the mountains of the saints after three manners.[9] Since, then, this burn is so sweet, as we have here explained, how delectable, may we believe, will it not be in one that is touched by it? Of this the soul would fain speak, yet speaks not, but keeps this esteem in its heart, and in its mouth the wonder implied in this word 'Oh,' saying: 'Oh, sweet burn!'

Oh, delectable wound![10]

6. Having addressed the burn, the soul now addresses the wound caused by the burn; and, as the burn was sweet, as has been said, the wound, according to reason, must be like to the burn. And thus the wound caused by a sweet burn will be a delectable wound, for, since

---

[1] Acts ii, 3.
[2] Hom. XXX, in Evang.
[3] [In officio feriæ 2ᵃᵉ Pent.]
[4] 1 Corinthians ii, 15.
[5] Bz: 'And again.'
[6] 1 Corinthians ii, 10.
[7] Bg, P: 'to this state of supreme fire.'
[8] [See p. 38, n. 1, above.]
[9] [Ecclesiasticus xliii, 4.]
[10] S has 'flame' [*llama* for *llaga*].

the burn is one of sweet love, the wound will be one of sweet love and thus will be sweetly delectable.

7. And for an explanation to be made of the nature of the wound here addressed by the soul, it must be known that a burn caused by material fire always leaves a wound on the part subjected to it. And fire has this property that, if it be applied to a wound that was not caused by fire, it is turned into a wound inflicted by fire. And this burn of love has the property that, when it touches a soul, whether this soul be wounded by other wounds, such as miseries and sins, or whether it be whole, it at once leaves it wounded with love. Thus wounds due to another cause have now become wounds of love.[1] But there is this difference between this loving burn and a burn caused by material fire, that the wound made by the latter can only be healed by the application of other medicines, whereas the wound made by the burn of love can be cured by no other medicine, but only by the same burn that has caused the wound. And the same burn that cures the wound inflicts a wound as it cures it; for each time that the burn of love touches the wound of love, it inflicts a greater wound of love, and thus it cures and heals the more inasmuch as it wounds the more; for when the lover is most wounded he is most whole and the cure wrought by love is the infliction of a hurt and a wound over and above the wound already inflicted, until the wound is so severe that the soul comes to be wholly dissolved in the wound of love. And in this way, when it is now completely cauterized and turned into a wound of love, it regains its perfect health in love, because it is transformed in love. In this way must be understood the wound of which the soul here speaks: it is altogether wounded and altogether healthy. Yet, though the soul is altogether wounded and altogether healthy, the burning of love still performs its office, which is to touch and to wound with love; and, inasmuch as this love is wholly delectable and wholly healthy, the effect which it produces is a relieving[2] of the wound, after the manner of a good physician. Wherefore the soul well says in this place: 'Oh, delectable wound!' Oh, then, wound the more delectable according as the fire of love that causes it is the loftier and the more sublime! For, as the Holy Spirit inflicted the wound only in order to relieve

[1] Bz abbreviates: 'wounded by other wounds, they have now become wounds of love.'

[2] [The past participle of this verb (*regalar*) has also the meaning 'delectable.' It is so translated in the verse-line above and elsewhere in this passage, and where the words 'relief,' 'relieve' occur, the play on the noun (or verb) and the adjective is to be understood.]

it, and as He has a great desire and will to relieve the soul, the wound will be great, for greatly will it be relieved.[1]

8. Oh, happy wound, inflicted by One Who cannot but heal! Oh, fortunate and most happy wound, for thou wert inflicted only for relief, and the quality of thy pain is the relief and delight of the wounded soul! Great art thou, oh, delectable wound, since great is He that has inflicted thee; and great is thy relief, because the fire of love is infinite and it relieves thee according to thy capacity and greatness. Oh, then, thou delectable wound! So much the more sublimely delectable[2] art thou in proportion as the burn has touched the infinite centre[3] of the substance of the soul, burning all that was capable of being burned, that it might relieve all that was capable of being relieved. We may represent this burn and this wound as being the highest degree to which the soul can attain in this state. There are many other ways wherein God cauterizes the soul which attain not so far as this, nor are they like this; for this is purely a touch of the Divinity in the soul, without any form or figure, whether intellectual or imaginary.

9. But there is another and a most sublime way wherein the soul may be cauterized, by means of an intellectual figure, which is after this manner. It will come to pass that, when the soul is enkindled in the love of God, although not to the high degree of which we have spoken (though it is most meet that it should be so for that which I am about to describe), the soul will be conscious of an assault upon it made by a seraph with an arrow or a dart[4] completely enkindled in fire of love, which will pierce the soul, now enkindled like a coal, or, to speak more truly, like a flame, and will cauterize it in a sublime manner; and when it has pierced and cauterized it thus with that arrow, the flame (that is, the soul) will rush forth and will rise suddenly and vehemently, even as comes to pass in a red-hot furnace or forge, when they stir or poke the fire,[5] and make the flame hotter. Then, upon being struck by this enkindled dart, the soul is conscious of the wound with a sovereign delight;[6] for, not only is it moved through and through in great sweetness,[7] by the stirring and the impetuous motion caused by that seraph, wherein it feels the great heat and melting of love, but the keen wound and the healing herb wherewith the

---

[1] Bg, P omit: 'for greatly will it be relieved.'

[2] Bg, P [intensify the play upon words by reading]: 'so much the more sublimely and delectably relieved' [*regaladamente regalada*].

[3] Bg, P: 'the last centre.'

[4] [Cf. p. 39, n. 8, above. The word 'arrow' (*flecha*) is not found in the first redaction.]

[5] Bz, C add: 'and the fire revives.'

[6] C, S: 'with a surpassing sovereign delight.'   [7] Bg: 'in great solitude.'

effect of the dart was being greatly assuaged[1] are felt by it like a keen point in the substance of the spirit, even as in the heart of him whose soul has been thus pierced.

10. Who can speak fittingly of this intimate point of the wound which seems to strike the very centre of the heart of the spirit, which is the point wherein is felt the refinement of its delight?[2] For the soul feels, as it were, a grain of mustard seed, most minute, highly enkindled and wondrous keen, which sends out from itself to its circumference[3] a keen and enkindled fire of love; which fire, arising from the substance and virtue of that keen point, wherein lies the substance and the virtue of the herb, is felt by the soul to be subtly diffused through all its spiritual and substantial veins, according to its potentiality and strength. Herein it feels its heat to be increasing and to be growing in strength and its love to be becoming so refined in this heat that it seems to have within it seas of loving fire which reach to the farthest heights and depths of the spheres, filling it wholly with love. Herein it seems to the soul that the whole universe is a sea of love wherein it is engulfed, and it can descry no term or goal at which this love can come to an end, but feels within itself, as we have said, the keen point and centre of love.

11. And that whereof the soul now has fruition cannot be further described, save by saying that the soul is now conscious of the aptness of the comparison made in the Gospel between the Kingdom of Heaven and the grain of mustard seed; which grain, because of its great heat, although small, grows into a great tree.[4] For the soul sees that it has become like a vast fire of love which arises from that enkindled point in the heart of the spirit.

12. Few souls attain to a state as high as this, but some have done so, especially those whose virtue and spirituality was to be transmitted to the succession of their children. For God bestows spiritual wealth and strength upon the head of a house, together with the first-fruits of the Spirit, according to the greater or lesser number of the descendants who are to inherit his doctrine and spirituality.

13. Let us return, then, to the work done by that seraph, which in truth is to strike and to wound the spirit interiorly. If God should sometimes permit the effect of the wound to pass outward to the bodily senses, to an extent corresponding to the interior wound, the effect of

---

[1] [Cf. p. 40, n. 2, above.]   [2] C omits this last clause.
[3] C: 'which sows in the circumference.' Bz has 'disseminates' for 'sows.'
[4] St. Matthew xiii, 31-2.

the impact and the wound will be felt without, as came to pass when the seraph wounded[1] the soul of Saint Francis with love, inflicting upon him five wounds, and in that way the effect of these wounds became visible in his body, and he was actually wounded, and received the imprint of the wounds in his body as he had also received them in his soul. For, as a rule, God bestows no favours upon the body without bestowing them first and principally upon the soul. And then, the greater is the delight and strength of love which causes the wound within the soul, the more of it is manifested outwardly in the bodily wound, and if the one grows, the other grows likewise. This comes to pass because, when these souls have been purified and made strong[2] in God, that which to their corruptible flesh causes pain and torture is sweet and delectable to their strong and healthy spirits; wherefore it is a wondrous thing to feel the pain growing in the pleasure. This wonder Job perceived in his wounds, when he said to God: 'Turning to me, Thou tormentest me wonderfully.'[3] For it is a great marvel, and a thing worthy of the abundance of the sweetness and delight which God has laid up for them that fear Him,[4] that, the greater is the pain and torment of which the soul is conscious, the greater is the pleasure and delight[5] which He causes it to enjoy. But when the wound is within the soul only, and is not communicated without, the delight can be far more intense and sublime; for, as the flesh has the spirit in check, so, when the blessings of the spirit are communicated to it, the flesh draws in the rein and bridles this fleet steed, which is the spirit, and restrains its great energy; for, if it makes use of its strength, the rein will break. But until it break, its freedom will be continually oppressed. For, as the Wise Man says: 'The corruptible body presseth down the soul and the earthly tabernacle weigheth down the spiritual sense which of itself museth upon many things.'[6]

14. This I say that it may be understood that he who will ever cling to natural reasoning and ability in his journey to God will not become a very spiritual person. For there are some who think that they can attain to the powers and the height of supernatural spirituality by means of the power and operation of sense alone, though this of itself is low and no more than natural. They cannot attain thereto save by setting aside and renouncing bodily sense and its operation. But it is quite different when a spiritual effect overflows from spirit into

[1] Bg, P: 'struck.'
[2] So Bg. The other authorities [and P. Silverio] read 'and set upon God.'
[3] Job x, 16.
[4] Psalm xxx, 20 [A.V., xxxi, 19].
[5] S: 'and sweetness.'
[6] Wisdom ix, 15.

sense, for, when this is the case, great spirituality may accrue,[1] as is clear from what we have said of the wounds, the outward manifestation of which corresponds to an inward power. This came to pass in Saint Paul, when the intensity of his soul's realization of the sufferings of Christ was so great that it overflowed into his body, as he writes to the Galatians, saying: 'I bear in my body the marks[2] of my Lord Jesus.'[3]

15. No more need be said about the burn and the wound, but if they are as we have here depicted them, what, do we believe, will be the hand that inflicts this burn, and what will be the touch? This the soul describes in the line following, lauding it rather than expounding it, and saying:

Oh, soft hand!   Oh, delicate touch

16. This hand, as we have said, is the merciful and omnipotent Father. Since it is as generous and liberal as it is powerful and rich, we must understand that it will give rich and powerful gifts to the soul when it is opened to grant it favours, and thus the soul calls it a 'soft' hand. This is as though the soul were to say: Oh, hand, the softer to this my soul as softly touching it and softly laid upon it, since if thou wert to lean hardly upon it the whole world would perish; for at Thy glance alone the earth shakes,[4] the nations faint and the mountains crumble to pieces. Once more, then, I say: Oh, soft hand! For whereas thou wert harsh and severe to Job, since thou didst touch him somewhat heavily,[5] to me thou art as loving[6] and gentle as thou wert hard to him, and art laid upon my soul very firmly, but very lovingly and graciously and softly. For Thou givest death and Thou givest life and there is none that can escape from Thy hand. But Thou, oh, Life Divine, never slayest save to give life, even as Thou never woundest save to heal. When Thou chastisest, Thou touchest lightly,[7] yet Thy touch suffices to consume the world; but, when Thou bringest joy, Thou art laid firmly upon the soul and thus the joys of Thy sweetness are without number. Thou hast wounded me, oh, hand Divine, in order to heal me, and thou hast slain in me that which would have slain me but for the life of God wherein now I see that I live. And this Thou didst with the liberality[8] of Thy generous[9] grace, which Thou

---

[1] Bg, P: 'is apt to accrue.'   [2] Bz: 'the pains.'
[3] Galatians vi, 17.   [4] Psalm ciii, 32 [A.V., civ, 32].
[5] So S.   Bz: 'so heavily.' Bg, C, P: 'so very heavily.'
[6] Bz: 'as pleasant.'   [7] S: 'sweetly.'
[8] C, S: 'liberty.'   [9] Bg, Bz, P: 'gracious.'

showedst me in the touch wherewith Thou didst touch me—namely, the splendour of Thy glory and the image of Thy substance, which is Thy only begotten Son;[1] in Whom, since He is Thy wisdom, Thou reachest from one end to another mightily.[2] And this Thy only begotten Son, oh, merciful hand of the Father, is the delicate touch wherewith in the power of Thy burn Thou didst touch me and wound me.

17. Oh, then, thou delicate touch, Thou Word, Son of God, Who, through the delicateness of Thy Divine Being, dost subtly penetrate the substance of my soul, and, touching it wholly and delicately, dost absorb it wholly in Thyself in Divine ways of delight and sweetness which have never been heard of in the land of Chanaan, nor seen in Theman![3] Oh, delicate touch of the Word, delicate, yea, wondrously delicate to me, which, having overthrown the mountains and broken the stones in Mount Horeb with the shadow of Thy power and strength that went before Thee, didst reveal Thyself more sweetly and powerfully to the Prophet with the whisper of gentle air.[4] Oh, gentle touch, that art so delicate and gentle! Say, Word, Son of God, how dost Thou touch the soul so gently and delicately when Thou art so terrible and powerful? Oh blessed, thrice blessed,[5] the soul whom Thou dost touch so delicately and gently though Thou art so terrible and powerful![6] Tell this out to the world. Nay, tell it not to the world, for the world knows naught of air so gentle, and will not feel[7] Thee, because it can neither receive Thee nor see Thee.[8] Only they who withdraw from the world and whom Thou refinest shall know Thee,[9] my God and my life, and behold Thee when Thou touchest them delicately, since purity corresponds with purity,[10] and thus they shall feel Thee and rejoice in Thee. Thou dost touch them the more delicately because the substance of their souls has been beautified and purified and made delicate, and has been withdrawn from every creature and from every trace and touch of creature, and Thou art dwelling secretly and surely within them. And thou hidest them in the hiding-place of Thy presence (which is the Word) from the disturbance of men.[11]

18. Once again, then, oh, delicate touch, and again most delicate, the stronger and more powerful for being more delicate, that with the strength of Thy delicacy dost melt and remove the soul from all other

---

[1] Hebrews i, 3.
[2] Wisdom viii, 1.
[3] Baruch iii, 22.
[4] [3 Kings xix, 11–12.]
[5] S omits: 'thrice blessed.'
[6] Bz omits this sentence.
[7] S: 'will not receive Thee.'
[8] St. John xiv, 17.
[9] [Cf. p. 43, n. 8, above.]
[10] [*Lit.*, 'delicacy . . . delicacy.']
[11] Psalm xxx, 21 [A.V., xxxi, 21].

touches of created things and makest it Thine own alone and unitest it
with Thyself. So gracious[1] an effect and impression dost Thou leave
in the soul that every other touch, of everything else, whether high or
low, seems to it rude and gross,[2] and even the sight of other things will
offend it, and to have to do with them[3] and touch them will cause it
trouble and grievous torment.

19. And it must be known that, the more delicate in itself is a thing,
the broader and more capacious it is; and the more subtle and delicate
it is, the more it becomes diffused[4] and communicative. The Word—
that is, the touch which touches the soul—is infinitely subtle and
delicate; and the soul is a vessel broad and capacious enough for the
great purification and delicacy which belongs to it in this state. Oh,
then, thou delicate touch, that dost infuse Thyself the more copiously
and abundantly into my soul by reason of Thy greater subtlety[5] and of
the greater purity of my soul!

20. And it must also be known that, the more subtle and delicate
is the touch, the greater is the delight and pleasure that it communicates where it touches; and the less so it is, the less weight and bulk
has the touch.[6] This Divine touch has neither bulk nor weight, for the
Word, Who effects it, is far removed from any kind of mode and
manner, and free from any kind of weight, of form, figure or accident,
such as is wont to restrict and limit substance. And thus this touch of
which the soul speaks here, being substantial (that is, of the Divine
Substance), is ineffable. Oh, then, at last, thou ineffably delicate
touch, that art the Word, that touchest not the soul save with Thy most
pure and simple Being,[7] which, being infinite, is infinitely delicate,
and therefore touches most subtly, lovingly, eminently and delicately!

That savours of eternal life

21. Although this is not so in a perfect degree, there is indeed a
certain savour herein of life eternal, as has been said above, which the
soul tastes in this touch of God. And it is not incredible that this
should be so if we believe, as we must believe, that this touch is substantial, that is to say, is a touch of the Substance of God in the substance of the soul; and to this many holy men have attained in this

[1] [*Delgado.*] Bg, P: 'delicate' [*delicado*].   [2] Bg adds: 'if it touches the soul.'
[3] Bg, P: 'to tolerate them.'   [4] Bg: 'diffusive.'
[5] Bz, C, S: 'substance.'
[6] [I suspect a corrupt reading here; the passage as it stands is a literal rendering of the
original.]
[7] Bg, P: 'with Thy most simple and sincere Being.' S: 'with Thy purest Substance and
Thy most simple Being.'

life. Wherefore the delicacy of the delight which is felt in this touch is impossible of description; nor would I willingly speak thereof, lest it should be supposed that it is no more than that which I say; for there are no words to expound[1] such sublime things of God as come to pass in these souls; whereof the proper way to speak is for one that knows them to understand them inwardly and to feel them inwardly and enjoy them and be silent concerning them. For the soul in this state sees that these things are in some measure like the white stone which Saint John says will be given to him that conquers, and on the stone a name shall be written, which no man knoweth saving he that receiveth it.[2] This alone can be said of it with truth, that it savours of eternal life. For, although in this life we may not have perfect fruition of it, as in glory, yet nevertheless this touch, being of God, savours of eternal life. And in this way the soul in such a state tastes of the things of God, and there are communicated to it fortitude, wisdom, love, beauty, grace and goodness, and so forth. For, as God is all these things, the soul tastes them in one single touch of God, and thus the soul has fruition of Him according to its faculties and its substance.

22. And in this good which comes to the soul the unction of the Holy Spirit sometimes overflows into the body, and this is enjoyed by all the substance of sense and all the members of the body and the very marrow and bones, not as feebly as is usually the case, but with a feeling of great delight and glory, which is felt even in the remotest joints of the feet and hands. And the body feels such glory in the glory of the soul that it magnifies God after its own manner, perceiving that He is in its very bones, even as David said: 'All my bones shall say, "God, who is like unto Thee?"'[3] And since all that can be said concerning this matter is less than the truth, it suffices to say of the bodily experience, as of the spiritual, that it savours of eternal life.

And pays every debt!

23. This the soul says because, in the savour of eternal life which it here experiences, it feels that it is being recompensed for the trials through which it has passed in order to come to this state. Herein it feels itself not only duly paid and satisfied, but excessively rewarded, so that it well understands the truth of the promise of the Spouse in the Gospel that He will reward the soul an hundredfold.[4] Thus there has been no tribulation, or temptation, or penance, or any other trial

---

[1] Bg, P add: 'and enumerate.'   [2] Apocalypse ii, 17.
[3] Psalm xxxiv, 10 [A.V., xxxv, 10].   [4] St. Matthew xix, 23.

through which the soul has passed on this road[1] to which there does not correspond an hundredfold of consolation and delight in this life, so that the soul may very well now say: 'And pays every debt.'

24. And, in order that we may know what debts are these which the soul now recognizes as paid, it must be known that in the ordinary way no soul can attain to this lofty state and kingdom of the betrothal without first having passed through many tribulations and trials, since, as is said in the Acts of the Apostles, it behoves us to enter through many tribulations into the kingdom of the heavens;[2] which things have in this state passed, for henceforth the soul, being purified, has no more suffering.

25. The trials which are suffered by those that are to come to this state are of three kinds, namely: trials and discomforts, fears and temptations which come from the world, and that in many ways; temptations and aridities and afflictions relating to sense; tribulations, darknesses, perils,[3] abandonments, temptations and other trials relating to the spirit, so that in this way the soul may be purged according both to its spiritual and to its sensual part, in the way that we described in the exposition of the fourth line of the first stanza. And the reason why these trials are necessary for the soul that is to reach this state is that, just as a liquor of great excellence is placed only in a strong vessel, which has been made ready and purified, so this most lofty union[4] cannot belong to a soul that has not been fortified by trials and temptations, and purified with tribulations, darknesses and perils, one of which classes, purifies and fortifies sense and the other refines and purifies and disposes the spirit.[5] For even as impure spirits, in order to be united with God in glory, pass through the pains of fire in the life to come, even so, in order to reach the union of perfection in this life, they must pass through the fire of these said pains, a fire which burns more violently in some and less so in others, and for longer in some than in others, according to the degree of union to which God is pleased to raise them and conformably with the degree of purgation which they have to undergo.

26. By means of these trials whereinto God leads the soul and the senses, the soul gradually acquires virtues, strength and perfection, together with bitterness, for virtue is made perfect in weakness,[6] and is

---

[1] S omits: 'on this road.'
[2] Acts xiv, 21 [A.V., xiv, 22].
[3] C: 'appetites.'
[4] Bg, P: 'unction.'
[5] Bg, P: 'refines and purges the spirit.'
[6] 2 Corinthians xii, 9.

wrought by the experience of sufferings. For iron cannot adapt itself
and be subservient to the intelligence of the artificer, unless he use fire
and a hammer, like the fire which Jeremias says that God put into his
understanding, saying: 'He sent fire into my bones and taught me.'[1]
And Jeremias likewise says of the hammer: 'Thou hast chastised me,
Lord, and I was instructed.'[2] Even so says the Preacher: 'He that is not
tried, what can he know? And he that hath no experience knoweth
little.'[3]

27. And here it behoves us to note the reason why there are so few
that attain to this lofty state of the perfection of union with God. It
must be known that it is not because God is pleased that there should
be few[4] raised to this high spiritual state, for it would rather please
Him that all souls should be perfect, but it is rather that He finds few
vessels which can bear so high and lofty a work. For, when He proves
them in small things and finds them weak and sees that they at once
flee from labour, and desire not to submit to the least discomfort or
mortification,[5] He finds that they are not strong and faithful in the
little things wherein He has granted them the favour of beginning to
purge and fashion them, and sees that they will be much less so in
great things; so He goes no farther with their purification, neither
lifts them up from the dust of the earth, through the labour of mortification, since for this they would need greater constancy and fortitude
than they exhibit. And thus there are many who desire to make
progress and constantly entreat God to bring them and let them pass
to this state of perfection, and when it pleases God to begin to bring
them through[6] the first trials and mortifications, as is necessary, they
are unwilling to pass through them, and flee away, to escape from the
narrow road of life and seek the broad road of their own consolation,
which is that of their perdition, and thus they give God no opportunity,
refusing to receive what they have asked when He begins to give it to
them. And so they are like useless vessels: they would fain arrive at
the state of perfection but are unwilling to be led thither by the road
of trials which leads to it, nor will they hardly set foot upon that road
by submitting to the smallest trials which are those that souls are wont
to suffer. To these may be made the reply which we find in Jeremias, in
these words: 'If thou hast run with those who went on foot, and hast
laboured, how canst thou contend with horses? And as thou hast had

---

[1] Lamentations i, 13.   [2] Jeremias xxxi, 18.
[3] Ecclesiasticus xxxiv, 9–10 [cf. p. 46, n. 6, above].
[4] Bg, P: 'is not pleased that there should be many.'
[5] Bg adds: 'or to work with solid patience.'   [6] Bz: 'to fashion them with.'

quietness in the land of peace, how wilt thou do in the pride of Jordan?'[1] This is as though he were to say: If in the trials which commonly and ordinarily afflict all those who live this human life thou countedst all as labour, and thoughtest thyself to be running, because thy pace was so slow, how wilt thou be able to keep pace with the step of a horse— that is to say, with trials that are more than ordinary and common, for which is required more than human strength and swiftness? And if thou hast been loth to break away from the peace and pleasure[2] of this land of thine, which is thy sensual nature, and hast not desired to make war against it or to oppose it in any way, I know not how thou wilt desire to enter the impetuous waters of spiritual tribulation and trial, which are more interior.

28. Oh, souls that seek to walk in security and comfort in spiritual things! If ye did but know how necessary it is to suffer and endure in order to reach this security and consolation, and how without this[3] ye cannot attain to that which the soul desires, but will rather go backward, ye would in no way seek consolation, either from God or from the creatures, but would rather bear the cross, and, having embraced it, would desire to drink pure vinegar and gall, and would count this a great happiness, for, being thus dead to the world and to your own selves, ye would live to God in the delights of the spirit; and, bearing a few outward things with patience and faithfulness, ye would become worthy for God to set His eyes upon you, to purge and cleanse you more inwardly by means of more interior spiritual trials, and to give you more interior blessings. For they to whom God is to grant so notable a favour as to tempt them more interiorly, and thus to advance them in gifts and deservings, must have rendered Him many services, and have had much patience and constancy for His sake, and have been very acceptable in His sight in their lives and works. This was true of the holy man Tobias, to whom Saint Raphael said that, because he had been acceptable to God, He had granted him this favour of sending him a temptation that should prove him the more in order that he might exalt him the more.[4] And all that remained to him of life after that temptation caused him joy, as says the Divine Scripture. In the same way we read of holy Job that, when God accepted him as His servant, as He did in the presence of the good and the evil spirits, He then granted him the favour of sending him those great[5] trials, that he

---

[1] Jeremias xii, 5.   [2] Bg, P omit: 'and pleasure.'
[3] Bg, P: 'and if ye did but understand that.'
[4] Tobias xii, 13.   [5] Bg, Bz, C, P: 'heavy.'

might afterwards exalt him, as indeed He did, by multiplying blessings to him, both spiritual and temporal.[1]

29. In the same way does God act to those whom He desires to exalt with the most important exaltation; He makes and causes them to be tempted in order that He may raise them as far as is possible—that is, that He may bring them to union with Divine wisdom, which, as David says, is silver tried by the fire and proved in the earth[2] (that is, that of our flesh) and purged seven times, which is the greatest purgation possible. And there is no reason to tarry here any longer in order to describe these seven purgations and to show how each of them leads us to this wisdom, and how there correspond to them seven degrees of love in this wisdom,[3] which in this life is to the soul like that silver spoken of by David, but in the life to come will be to it like gold.

30. It greatly behoves the soul, then, to have much patience and constancy in all the tribulations and trials[4] which God sends it, whether they come from without or from within, and are spiritual or corporeal, greater or lesser. It must take them all as from His hand for its healing and its good, and not flee from them, since they are health[5] to it, but follow the counsel of the Wise Man, who says: 'If the spirit of him that has the power descend upon thee, abandon not thy place'[6] (that is, the place and abode of thy probation, by which is meant that trial that He sends thee); for the healing, he says, will cause great[7] sins to cease. That is, it will cut the roots of thy sins and imperfections, which are evil habits; for battling with trials, perils and temptations quenches the evil and imperfect habits of the soul and purifies and strengthens it. Wherefore the soul must count it a great favour when God sends it interior and exterior trials,[8] realizing that there are very few who deserve to be perfected by suffering, and to suffer that they may come to this lofty state.

31. We return to our exposition. The soul is now aware that all has turned out very well for it, since now *sicut tenebræ ejus, ita et lumen ejus*;[9] and, as the soul aforetime shared in tribulations, it now shares in consolations and in the kingdom; and as all its trials, within and with-

---

[1] [Job i, 8; xlii, 12.]   [2] Psalm xi, 7 [A.V., xii, 6].
[3] Bz omits this clause.
[4] Bz abbreviates: 'which in this life consists in the soul's great constancy and patience in all the tribulations and trials.'
[5] Bz: 'sanctity' [*santidad* for *sanidad*].   [6] Ecclesiastes x, 4.
[7] Bg, P: 'very great.'
[8] Bg, P: 'sends it trials and temptations.'
[9] Psalm cxxxviii, 12 [A.V., cxxxix, 12].

out, have been amply rewarded by Divine blessings of soul and body,
there is none of its trials that has not a correspondingly great reward.
And thus the soul confesses that it is now well satisfied, when it says:
'And pays every debt.' In this line it gives thanks to God, even as
David gave Him thanks for having delivered him from trials, in that
verse where he says: 'Many and grievous are the tribulations that Thou
hast shown me, and Thou didst deliver me from them all, and from the
depths of the earth hast Thou brought me out again; Thou hast
multiplied Thy magnificence, and, turning to me, hast comforted
me.'[1] And thus this soul that before reaching this state was without,
at the gates of the palace (like Mardochai, sitting weeping in the streets
of Susan, because his life was in peril, and clothed in sackcloth,
refusing to receive the garments from Queen Esther, and having received no reward for services rendered the King, and his faithfulness
in defending his honour and life[2]), is recompensed, like Mardochai, in a
single day for all its trials and services, for not only is it made to enter
the palace and stand before the King, clad in regal vesture, but likewise it is crowned, and given a sceptre, and a royal seat, and possession
of the royal ring, so that it may do all that it desires, and need do naught
that it desires not to do in the kingdom of its Spouse; for those that
are in this state receive all that they desire. Herein not only is it recompensed, but the Jews, its enemies, are now dead—namely, the imperfect desires that were taking away its spiritual life, wherein it now
lives according to its faculties and desires. For this cause the soul next
says:

In slaying, thou hast changed death into life.

32. For death is naught else than privation of life: when life comes,
there remains no trace of death. With respect to the spirit, there are
two kinds of life; one is beatific, which consists in seeing God, and
this will be attained by means of the natural death of the body, as
Saint Paul says in these words: 'We know that if this our house of
clay be dissolved, we have a dwelling of God in the heavens.'[3] The
other is perfect spiritual life, which is the possession of God through
the union of love, and this is attained through the complete mortification of all vices and desires[4] and of the soul's entire nature. And
until this be done, the soul cannot attain to the perfection of this
spiritual life of union with God, even as the Apostle says likewise in

[1] Psalm lxx, 20 [A.V., lxxi, 20–1].   [2] Esther iv, 1–4.
[3] 2 Corinthians v, 1.   [4] Bz: 'of all its members and desires.'

these words: 'If you live according to the flesh, you shall die; but if by the spirit you mortify the deeds of the flesh, you shall live.'[1]

33. It must be known, then, that that which the soul here calls death is all that is meant by the 'old man': namely, the employment of the faculties—memory, understanding and will—and the use and occupation of them in things of the world, and in the desires and pleasures taken in created things. All this is the exercise of the old life, which is the death of the new, or spiritual, life. Herein the soul will be unable to live perfectly if the old man die not perfectly likewise, as the Apostle warns us when he says that we should put off the old man, and put on the new man, who according to the omnipotent God is created in justice and holiness.[2] In this new life, which begins when the soul has reached this perfection of union with God, as we are saying here, all the desires of the soul and its faculties according to its inclinations and operations, which of themselves were the operation of death and the privation of spiritual life, are changed into Divine operations.

34. And as each living creature lives by its operation, as the philosophers say, the soul, having its operations in God, through the union that it has with God, lives the life of God, and thus its death has been changed into life—which is to say that animal[3] life has been changed into spiritual life. For the understanding, which before this union understood in a natural way with the strength and vigour of its natural light, by means of [4] the bodily senses, is now moved and informed by another and a higher principle, that of the supernatural light of God, and, the senses having been set aside, it has thus[5] been changed into the Divine, for through union its understanding and that of God are now both one. And the will, which aforetime loved after a low manner, that of death,[6] and with its natural affection, has now been changed into the life of Divine love; for it loves after a lofty manner with Divine affection and is moved by the power and strength of the Holy Spirit in Whom it now lives the life of love,[7] since, through this union, its will and His will are now only one. And the memory, which of itself perceived only figures and phantasms of created things, has become changed through this union, so that it has in its mind the eternal years spoken of by David.[8] And the natural desire, which had only capacity and strength to enjoy creature pleasure that works death, is now

---

[1] Romans viii, 13.
[2] Ephesians iv, 22–4.
[3] Bg: 'natural.'
[4] Bg, P: 'through the life of.'
[5] Bg, P: 'it thus understands divinely and has thus.'
[6] Bg, P omit: 'that of death.'
[7] Bg: 'the life of God.'
[8] Psalm lxxvi, 6 [A.V., lxxvii, 5].

changed so that it tastes and enjoys that which is Divine, being now moved and satisfied by another and a more living principle, which is the delight of God; for it is united with Him and thus it is now only the desire of God. And finally, all the movements and operations and inclinations which the soul had aforetime, and which belonged to the principle and strength of its natural life, are now in this union changed into Divine movements, dead to their own operation and inclination and alive in God. For the soul, like the true daughter of God that it now is, is moved wholly by the Spirit of God, even as Saint Paul teaches, saying: 'That they that are moved by the Spirit of God are sons of God Himself.'[1] So, as has been said, the understanding of this soul is now the understanding of God; and its will is the will of God; and its memory is the memory of God; and its delight is the delight of God; and the substance of this soul, although it is not the Substance of God, for into this it cannot be substantially changed, is nevertheless united in Him and absorbed in Him, and is thus God[2] by participation in God, which comes to pass in this perfect state of the spiritual life, although not so perfectly as in the next life. And in this way the soul is dead to all that was in itself, for this was death to it, and alive to that which God is in Himself; wherefore, speaking of itself, the soul well says in this line: 'In slaying, thou hast changed death into life.' Wherefore the soul may here very well say with Saint Paul: 'I live, now not I, but Christ liveth in me.'[3] In this way the death of this soul is changed into the life of God, and there may also be applied to it the saying of the Apostle: *Absorpta est mors in victoria*.[4] And likewise the words of Osee, the prophet, who, in his own person,[5] says as from God: 'O death, I will be thy death.'[6] This is as though he were to say: I am life, being the death of death, and death shall be absorbed in life.

35. In this wise the soul is absorbed in Divine life, being withdrawn from all that is secular and temporal and from natural desire, and brought into the cellars of the King,[7] where it rejoices and is glad in its beloved, and remembers His breasts more than wine, saying: 'Although I am black, I am beautiful, daughters of Jerusalem; for my natural blackness is changed into the beauty of the heavenly King.'[8]

36. In this state of life, perfect as it is, the soul is, as it were,

---

[1] Romans viii, 14.   [2] S: 'and, thus absorbed, has become God.'
[3] Galatians ii, 20.   [4] I Corinthians xv, 54.
[5] Bz: 'in his own presence.'   [6] Osee xiii, 14.
[7] Bz: 'into the halls of the King.' C: 'into the cellar of the King.' Bg, P: 'into the secret mansion (*morada*) of the King.'
[8] Canticles i, 4.

interiorly and exteriorly keeping festival, and has in its mouth,[1] which is its spirit, a great song of joy to God, as it were a song new and ever new, turned into joy and love, having knowledge of its happy state. At times it has rejoicing and fruition, saying within its spirit those words of Job, namely: 'My glory shall be always renewed and as a palm tree shall I multiply my days.'[2] Which is as much as to say: God Who, remaining within Himself unchangeably, makes all things new, as the Wise Man says, being united for ever in my glory,[3] will make my glory ever new—that is to say, He will not suffer it to grow old as it was before; and I shall multiply my days like the palm tree—that is, my merits unto Heaven, even as the palm tree sends out its branches to Heaven. For the merits of the soul that is in this state are ordinarily great in number and quality, and it is accustomed to sing to God in its spirit of all that David says in the Psalm which begins *Exaltabo te, Domine, quoniam suscepisti me*, particularly those last two verses, which say: *Convertisti planctum meum in gaudium mihi, etc., conscidisti saccum meum, et circumdedisti me laetitia.*[4] That my glory may sing to Thee, and I may not be ashamed.[5] O Lord my God, I will praise Thee for ever. And it is no marvel that the soul should experience with such frequency these joys,[6] this jubilation and this fruition, and should make these praises to God, for, apart from the knowledge which it has of the favours that it has received,[7] it now feels God to be so solicitous in granting it favours, and addressing it in such precious and delicate[8] and endearing words, and magnifying it with favour upon favour, that it believes that He has no other soul in the world to favour thus, nor aught else wherewith to occupy Himself, but that He is wholly for itself alone. And, when it feels this, it confesses its feeling like the Bride in the words of the Songs: *Dilectus meus mihi et ego illi.*[9]

STANZA III

Oh, lamps of fire, In whose splendours the deep caverns of sense which were dark and blind With strange brightness Give heat and light together to their Beloved!

[1] [*Lit.*, 'palate.'] [2] Job xxix, 18, 20.
[3] Bz: 'being now thus prevented in my glory.'
[4] Psalm xxix, 12 [A.V., xxx, 11]. [5] C gives these words in Latin only.
[6] Bg, P: 'that with such great faith the soul should be enkindled in these joys.'
[7] S: 'that it has known and received.' [8] Bz: 'and delectable.'
[9] Canticles ii, 16.

EXPOSITION

MAY God be pleased to grant me His favour here, for in truth it is very[1] needful if I am to explain the profound meaning of this stanza: and he that reads it will need to give it his attention, for, if he have no experience of this, it will perhaps be somewhat obscure and prolix to him, though, if he should have such experience, it will perchance be clear and pleasing. In this stanza, the soul magnifies its Spouse and gives Him thanks for the great favours which it receives from the union that it has with Him, by means whereof it says here that it receives abundant and great knowledge of Himself, all full of love, wherewith the faculties and senses, which, before this union, were dark and blind, have been enlightened and enkindled with love, and can now be illumined, as indeed they are, and through the heat of love can give light and love to Him Who illumined and enamoured[2] them. For the true lover is content only when all that he is in himself, and all that he is worth, and all that he has and receives, are employed in the Beloved; and the more of this there is, the greater is the pleasure that he receives in giving it. In this the soul here rejoices, because with the splendours and the love that it receives it will be able to shine resplendently before its Beloved and to love Him. There follows the line:

Oh, lamps of fire,

2. In the first place it must be known that lamps have two properties, which are to give light and heat. In order to understand the nature of these lamps whereof the soul here speaks, and how they give light and burn within it and give it heat, it must be known that God, in His one and simple Being, is all the virtues and grandeurs of His attributes; for He is omnipotent, wise, good, merciful, just, strong and loving,[3] and so forth, and has other infinite attributes and virtues[4] whereof we have no knowledge; and, as He is all these things in His simple Being, when He is united with the soul, at the time when He is pleased to reveal knowledge to it, it is able to see in Him all these virtues and grandeurs distinctly[5]—namely, omnipotence, wisdom and goodness, mercy, and so forth. And, as each of these things is the very Being of God in one sole reality, which is the Father or the Son or the Holy

---

[1] Bg, P omit 'very.'
[2] Bg, P omit: 'and enamoured.'
[3] Bg, P omit: 'and loving.'
[4] S omits: 'and virtues.'
[5] Bz omits: 'distinctly.'

Spirit, each attribute being God Himself and God being infinite light and infinite Divine fire, as we have said above, it follows from this that, in each of these innumerable attributes, He gives light and heat as God,[1] and thus each of these attributes is a lamp which gives the soul light and gives it also the heat of love.

3. And inasmuch as in a single act of this union the soul receives the knowledge of these attributes, God Himself is[2] to the soul as many lamps all together, each of which, in a distinct way, gives light to it in wisdom and gives it heat, for from each lamp the soul has distinct knowledge and by each is enkindled in love. And thus with respect to all these lamps individually the soul loves and is enkindled[3] by each, as also by all of them together, for, as we have said, all these attributes are one being; and thus all these lamps are one lamp, which, according to its virtues and attributes, gives light and heat as many lamps. Wherefore the soul, in a single act of knowledge of these lamps, loves through each one, and herein loves through all of them together, and in that act bears the quality of love through each one, and of each one, and of all together, and through all together. For the splendour given it by this lamp of the Being of God, inasmuch as He is omnipotent, gives it the light and heat of the love of God inasmuch as He is omnipotent. And therefore God is now to the soul a lamp of omnipotence, giving it light and all knowledge[4] according to this attribute. And the splendour given it by this lamp according to the Being of God, inasmuch as He is knowledge, sheds on it the light and heat of the love of God inasmuch as He is wise; and therefore God is now to it a lamp of wisdom. And the splendour given it by this lamp of God inasmuch as He is goodness[5] sheds upon the soul the light and heat of the love of God inasmuch as He is good; and accordingly God is now to it a lamp of goodness. And, in the same way, He is to it a lamp of justice, and of fortitude, and of mercy, and of all the other attributes that in this state are represented to the soul together in God. And the light that the soul receives from them all together is communicated to it by the heat of the love of God wherewith the soul loves God because He is all these things; and thus in this communication and manifestation of Himself that God makes to the soul (which, as I think, is the greatest that He

---

[1] Bg: 'in each of these attributes, which, as we said, are innumerable, and are His virtues, He gives light and heat as God.'

[2] Bg, P: 'He is.'

[3] So C, S.   Bz: 'the soul is enkindled.' Bg, P: 'And thus with respect to all these lamps the soul understands and loves and is enkindled.'

[4] Bg, P: 'light, love and all knowledge.'   [5] Bz: 'truth.'

can make to it in this life), He is to it as innumerable lamps which give it knowledge and love of Him.

4. These lamps were seen by Moses on Mount Sinai, where, when God passed by,[1] he fell prostrate on the ground, and began to cry out and to proclaim some of these attributes, saying: 'Emperor, Lord, God that art merciful, clement, patient, of much compassion, true, that keepest mercy for thousands, that takest away sins[2] and evil deeds and faults, so that there is no man who of himself is innocent before Thee.'[3] Herein it is clear that the majority of the attributes and virtues of God which Moses then learned in God were those of God's omnipotence, dominion, deity, mercy, justice, truth and uprightness; which was a most profound knowledge of God; and since, according to that knowledge,[4] love was likewise communicated to him, the delight of love and the fruition that he experienced therein were most sublime.

5. From this it follows that the delight which the soul receives in the rapture of love communicated by the fire of the light of these lamps is wondrous, and boundless, being as vast as that of many lamps, each of which burns in love, the warmth of one being added to the warmth of another, and the flame of one to the flame of another, as also the light of one to the light of another, so that any attribute is known by any other; and thus all of them become one light and one fire, and each of them becomes one light and one fire. The soul, then, is here completely absorbed in these delicate flames, and wounded subtly by love in each of them, and in all of them together more wounded and deeply alive in the love of the life of God, so that it can see quite clearly that that love belongs to life eternal, which is the union of all blessings. So that the soul in that state in some wise perceives and knows well the truth of those words of the Spouse in the Songs, where He said that the lamps of love were lamps of fire and flames. 'Beauteous art thou in thy footsteps and thy shoes, oh, prince's daughter.'[5] Who can recount the magnificence and rarity of thy delight and majesty in the wondrous splendour and the love of thy lamps?

6. Divine Scripture relates that of old one of these lamps passed before Abraham and caused him the greatest darksome horror, because the lamp was that of the rigorous justice which He was about to work

---

[1] Bg: 'when God passed quickly before him.'
[2] Bg, P: 'the sins of the world.'   [3] Exodus xxxiv, 6–7.
[4] Bg, P add: 'of God.'   [5] Canticles vii, 1.

in the sight of the Chanaanites.[1] Then, oh soul so greatly enriched, shall not all these lamps of the knowledge of God which give thee a pleasant and loving light cause thee more light and joy of love than that single lamp caused horror and darkness in Abraham? And how great and how excellent and how manifold shall be thy joy, since in it all and from it all thou receivest fruition and love, and God communicates Himself to thy faculties according to His attributes and virtues? For, when a man loves another and does him good, he does him good and loves him according to his own attributes and properties. And thus thy Spouse, being as Who He is within thee, grants thee favours; for, since He is omnipotent, He does good to thee and loves thee with omnipotence; and since He is wise, thou perceivest that He does thee good and loves thee with wisdom; and, since He is infinitely good, thou perceivest that He loves thee with goodness; since He is holy, thou perceivest that He loves thee and grants thee favours with holiness; since He is just, thou perceivest that He loves thee and grants thee favours justly; since He is merciful, compassionate and clement, thou perceivest His mercy, compassion and clemency; and, since His Being is strong and sublime and delicate, thou perceivest that He loves thee with strength, sublimity and delicacy; and, since He is clean and pure, thou perceivest that He loves thee with cleanness and purity; and, since He is true, thou perceivest that He loves thee truly; and, since He is liberal, thou knowest that He loves thee and grants thee favours with liberality, without self-interest,[2] solely that He may do thee good; as He is the virtue of the greatest humility, He loves thee with the greatest humility, and with the greatest esteem, making thee His equal, joyfully revealing Himself to thee,[3] in these ways, which are His knowledge, by means of this His countenance full of graces, and saying to thee, in this His union, not without great rejoicing on thy part; I am thine and for thee, and I delight to be such as I am that I may be thine to give Myself to thee.

7. Who, then, can describe that which thou perceivest, oh, blessed soul, when thou knowest thyself to be thus loved and to be exalted with such esteem? Thy belly, which is thy will, is like that of the Bride, and as the heap of wheat which is covered and set about with lilies.[4] For in these grains of the wheat of the bread of life[5] which thou art tasting

[1] Genesis xv, 12–17.
[2] C: 'with liberality, feeling no impediment or self-interest.'
[3] Bz adds: 'in this union.'
[4] Canticles vii, 2.
[5] [Lit., 'grains of bread of life.']

all together, the lilies of the virtues that surround thee are giving thee delight. For these are the King's daughters, of whom David says that they have delighted thee[1] with myrrh and ambar and other aromatic spices, for the communications of knowledge given thee by the Beloved concerning His graces and virtues are His daughters; and thou art so wholly engulfed and absorbed in them that thou art also the well of living waters that run with vehemence from Mount Libanus, which is God,[2] in the which stream thou art become marvellously glad with all the harmony of thy soul and even of thy body, which has become a Paradise watered by springs Divine.[3] Thus may the words of the Psalm be accomplished in thee, namely: 'The vehemence of the river makes glad the city of God.'[4]

8. Oh, wondrous thing! At this time the soul is overflowing with Divine waters, which flow from it as from an abundant source whose Divine waters gush in all directions. For, although it is true that this communication of which we are speaking is light and fire from these lamps of God, yet this fire, as we have said, is here so sweet that, vast as it is, it is like the waters of life which quench the thirst of the spirit with the vehemence that it desires. So these lamps of fire are living waters of the spirit, like those that came upon the Apostles,[5] which, though they were lamps of fire, were also pure and clear water, as the prophet Ezechiel called them when he prophesied that coming of the Holy Spirit, saying: 'I will pour out upon you, saith God, clean water, and will put My spirit in the midst of you.'[6] And thus this fire is likewise water, for this fire is pre-figured in the sacrificial fire that Jeremias hid in the cistern, which was water when it was hidden and fire when they brought it out for the sacrifice.[7] And thus this spirit of God, while hidden in the veins of the soul, is like sweet and delectable water quenching the thirst of the spirit; and, when the soul offers the sacrifice of love to God, it becomes living flames of fire, which are the lamps[8] of the act of love and of the flames to which we referred above as being described by the Spouse in the Songs. For this reason the soul here calls them flames. For not only does it taste them as waters within itself, but it likewise offers them as an act of love to God like flames. And, inasmuch as in the spiritual communication of these lamps the soul is enkindled and set in the exercise of love, in an act of love it

---

[1] Bg, P: 'that they delight thee in thy love.'
[2] Canticles iv, 15.   [3] Bz: 'a paradise of Divine rejoicing.'
[4] Psalm xlv, 5 [A.V., xlvi, 4].   [5] Acts ii, 3.
[6] Ezechiel xxxvi, 25.   [7] 2 Machabees i, 20–22. [Cf. p. 58, n. 2, above.]
[8] Bz: 'flames.'

calls them lamps rather than flames, saying: 'Oh, lamps of fire.' All that can be said in this stanza[1] is less than what there is to be said, for the transformation of the soul in God is indescribable. It can all be expressed in this word—namely, that the soul has become God of God by participation in Him and in His attributes, which are those that are here called lamps of fire.

In whose splendours

9. In order to explain the nature of these splendours of the lamps whereof the soul here speaks and the way wherein the soul shines forth in splendour, we must first make it clear that these splendours are the communications of loving knowledge which the lamps of the attributes of God give forth to the soul, wherein the soul, united according to its faculties, also shines forth like them, being transformed into loving splendours. This brilliance of splendour wherein the soul shines forth with the heat of love is not like that produced by material lamps, which burst into flame and thus illumine the things around them, but is like that of the brilliance within the flames. For the soul is within these splendours, wherefore it says: 'In whose splendours': that is to say, it is 'within' them; and not only so, but, as we have said, it is transformed and turned into splendours. And so we shall say that it is like the air which is within the flame and is enkindled and transformed into flame, for flame is naught else but enkindled air, and the movements made and the splendours produced by this flame are not simply of air, nor simply of the fire, whereof it is composed, but of air and fire together, and the fire causes this union with the air that is enkindled within it.

10. And in this way we shall understand that the soul with its faculties is enlightened within the splendours of God. And the movements of this Divine flame, which are the vibrations and the bursts of flame which we have described above, are not made only by the soul that is transformed in the flames of the Holy Spirit, neither are they made by Him alone; but by the Spirit and the soul together, the Spirit moving the soul, even as the fire moves the air that is enkindled. And thus these movements of God and the soul together are not only splendours, but are also glorifications in the soul. For these movements and bursts of flame are the playing of the fire[2] and the joyful festivals which we said, in the second line of the first stanza, the Holy Spirit

---

[1] Bg, P: 'in this matter.'
[2] Bz: 'are the fires and the playing [of the fires].'

causes within the soul, wherein it seems that He is ever about to grant it eternal life and remove it to His perfect glory, and make it at last to enter truly within Himself. For all the blessings, both the early and the late, the great and the small, that God grants the soul He grants to it always with the motive of bringing it to eternal life,[1] just as all the movements made and the bursts of flame produced by the enkindled air have the purpose of bringing it to the centre of its sphere; and all these movements that it makes are attempts to bring it there. But, because the air is in the sphere proper to it, it cannot bring it; just so, although these movements[2] of the Holy Spirit are most effective in absorbing the soul into great glory, yet this is not perfectly accomplished until the time comes for the soul to leave the sphere of air—which is this life of the flesh—and to enter into the centre of its spirit, which is perfect life in Christ.

11. But it must be understood that these movements[3] are movements of the soul rather than of God; for God moves not. And so these glimpses of glory that are given to the soul are stable, perfect and continuous, with firm serenity[4] in God, as they will also be in the soul hereafter, without any change between greater and lesser, and without any intervening movements; and then the soul will see clearly how, although here below it appeared that God was moving in it, God moves not in Himself, even as the fire moves not in its sphere; and how, since it was not perfect in glory, it had those movements and bursts of flame in a foretaste of glory.[5]

12. From what has been said, and from what we shall now say, it will be more clearly understood how great is the excellence of the splendours of these lamps which we are describing, for these splendours by another name are called overshadowings. To understand this it must be understood that 'overshadowing' signifies 'casting of a shadow,' and for a man to cast his shadow over another signifies that he protects him, befriends him and grants him favours. When the shadow covers the person, this is a sign that he who overshadows him is now near to befriend and protect him. For this reason that great favour which God granted to the Virgin Mary—namely, her conception of the Son of God—was called by the angel Saint Gabriel an overshadowing of the Holy Spirit. 'The Holy Spirit,' he said, 'shall

---

[1] Bz: 'to eternal glory.'   [2] P, S: 'these motives.'
[3] Bg adds: 'of the flame.' P adds: 'of the soul.'
[4] Bg, P have 'sweetness' for 'serenity.' [The first redaction (p. 59, above) has 'not' before 'stable.']
[5] Bg, P add: 'even as the stars twinkle from afar.'

come upon thee and the power of the Most High shall overshadow thee.'[1]

13. For the better understanding of the nature of this casting of a shadow by God, or (which is the same thing) these overshadowings of great splendours, it must be understood that everything has and makes a shadow in conformity with its nature and size. If the thing is opaque and dark[2] it makes a dark shadow,[3] and if it is light and fine[4] it makes a light and fine shadow: and thus the shadow of an object which is dark[5] will be a dark shadow of the size of that dark object, and the shadow of a light object[6] will be a light shadow of the size of that light object.

14. Now, inasmuch as these virtues and attributes of God are enkindled and resplendent lamps, and are near to the soul, as we have said, they will not fail to touch the soul with their shadows, which will be enkindled and resplendent likewise, even as are the lamps by which they are cast, and thus these shadows will be splendours. In this way the shadow cast upon the soul by the lamp of the beauty of God will be other beauty, of the nature and proportions of that beauty of God; and the shadow cast by strength will be other strength of the proportions of the strength of God; and the shadow cast by the wisdom of God will be other wisdom[7] of God, of the proportions of that wisdom of God. And so with the remaining lamps; or, more correctly, it will be the same wisdom and the same beauty and the same strength of God, in shadow, for here on earth the soul cannot perfectly comprehend it,[8] and since this shadow is in such conformity with the nature and proportions of God—that is, with God Himself[9]—the soul has, in shadow, an effective realization of God's excellence.

15. What, then, will be the shadows that the Holy Spirit will cast upon this soul—namely, the shadows of the grandeurs of His virtues and attributes? For He is so near to the soul that He not only touches it in shadows, but is united with it in shadows and splendours, and it understands and experiences God in each of them according to His nature and proportions in each of them? For it understands and experiences Divine power[10] in the shadow of omnipotence; and it understands and experiences Divine wisdom in the shadow of Divine

---

[1] St. Luke i, 35.   [2] Bz: 'small and dark.'
[3] Bz: 'a small and dark shadow.'
[4] Bg, P: 'clear and light.' Bz, C: 'clear, light and fine.'
[5] [Lit., 'of a darkness.']   [6] [Lit., 'of a light.']
[7] Bg, C, P omit: 'of God.'
[8] Bg, P read: 'and, more correctly, it will be the same beauty of God, in shadow, for the soul, although perfect, cannot comprehend it.'
[9] Bg, P omit this parenthetical clause.   [10] Bg: 'Divine omnipotence.'

wisdom; understands and experiences infinite goodness in the shadow of infinite goodness which surrounds it[1]; and so forth. Finally, it experiences the glory of God in the shadow of glory, which causes it to know the nature and proportions of the glory of God when all these pass by in bright and enkindled shadows cast by these bright and enkindled lamps, all of which are in one lamp of one single and simple Being of God, which actually shines forth upon it in all these ways.

16. Oh, what the soul will feel here, when it experiences the knowledge and communication of that figure which Ezechiel saw in that beast with four faces, and in that wheel[2] with four wheels, when he saw that its appearance was as the appearance of kindled coals and as the appearance of lamps![3] The soul will see the wheel, which is the wisdom of God, full of eyes within and without, which are Divine manifestations of knowledge and the splendours of His virtues, and will hear in its spirit that sound made by their passage, which was like the sound of a multitude and of great armies,[4] signifying many grandeurs of God, of which the soul here has distinct knowledge in one single sound of God's passing through it. Finally, it will experience that sound of the beating of wings, which the Prophet says was as the sound of many waters and as the sound of the Most High God[5]; this indicates the vehemence of the Divine waters, which we have described, and which, at the beating of the wings of the Holy Spirit, overwhelm the soul and make it to rejoice in the flame of love, so that it now enjoys the glory of God in His likeness and shadow,[6] even as this Prophet says that the visions of that beast and that wheel were similitudes of the glory of the Lord.[7] And to what a height may this happy soul now find itself raised! How greatly will it know itself to be exalted! How wondrous will it see itself to be in holy beauty! How far beyond all telling! For so copiously does it become assailed by the waters of these Divine splendours that it is able to see that the Eternal Father, with bounteous hand,[8] has granted it the upper and the lower streams that water the earth, even as the father of Axa gave these to her when she longed for them,[9] for these irrigating waters penetrate both soul and body, which are the upper and the nether parts of man.

17. Oh, wondrous excellence of God that these lamps of the Divine

---

[1] C omits: 'in the shadow ... surrounds it.'
[3] C has only: 'was as the appearance of coals.'
[4] P: 'and of servants.'
[6] Bg: 'likeness and the favour of His shadow.'
[7] C: 'of the wheel of the Lord' [cf. Ezechiel i, 28].
[8] Bg, P omit: 'with bounteous hand.'
[9] [Judges i, 15. Cf. p. 62, n. 1, above.]

[2] C: 'that cart.'

[5] [Ezechiel i, 15–25.]

attributes should be one simple being in which alone they are experienced, and yet that they should be distinctly seen,[1] each being as completely enkindled as the other and each being substantially the other! Oh, abyss of delights, that art the more abundant in proportion as thy riches are gathered together in the infinite simplicity and unity of Thy sole Being, so that each one is known and experienced in such a way that the perfect knowledge and absorption of the other is not impeded thereby, but rather each grace and virtue that exists in thee is light that comes from some other of thy grandeurs, so that through thy purity, oh, Divine wisdom, many things are seen in thee when one thing is seen, since thou art the store-house of the treasures of the Father, the splendour of eternal light, a stainless mirror and image of His goodness.[2] For in thy splendours are

The deep caverns of sense

18. These caverns are the faculties of the soul—memory, understanding and will—of which the depth is proportionate to their capacity for great blessings, for they can be filled with nothing less than the infinite. But considering what they suffer when they are empty we can realize in some measure the greatness of their joy and delight when they are filled with God, for one contrary can give light to another.[3] In the first place, it must be noted that these caverns of the faculties, when they are not empty and purged and cleansed from all creature affection, are not conscious of their great emptiness, which is due to their profound capacity. For in this life any trifle that remains within them suffices to keep them so cumbered and fascinated that they are neither conscious of their loss nor do they miss the immense blessings that might be theirs, nor are they aware of their own capacity.[4] And it is a wondrous thing that, despite their capacity for infinite blessing, the least thing suffices to cumber them, so that they cannot receive these blessings until they are completely empty, as we shall say hereafter. But, when they are empty and clean, the hunger and thirst and yearning of their spiritual sense become intolerable; for, as the capacities[5] of these caverns are deep, their pain is deep likewise, as is also the food that they lack, which, as I say, is God. And this great feeling of pain commonly occurs towards the close of the illumination and purification of the soul, ere it attain to union, wherein it[6] has satisfaction. For,

---

1 Bg, P: 'seen and experienced.' Bz: 'seen and enjoyed.'
2 Wisdom vii, 26   3 [Cf. p. 27, l. 1, above.]
4 Bz omits the last clause.   5 [Lit., 'the stomachs.']
6 Bg, P: 'wherein that spiritual appetite.'

when the spiritual appetite is empty and purged from every creature and from every creature affection, and its natural temper is lost and it has become attempered to the Divine, and its emptiness is disposed to be filled, and when the Divine communication of union with God has not yet reached it, then the suffering caused by this emptiness and thirst is worse than death, especially when the soul is vouchsafed some foresight or glimpse of the Divine ray and this is not communicated to it.[1] It is souls in this condition that suffer with impatient love, so that they cannot remain long without either receiving or dying.

19. With respect to the first cavern which we here describe—namely, the understanding—its emptiness is thirst for God, and, when the understanding is made ready for God, this is so great that David compares it to that of the hart, finding no greater thirst wherewith to compare it, for the thirst of the hart is said to be most vehement. 'Even as the hart (says David) desires the fountains of the waters, even so does my soul desire Thee, O God.'[2] This thirst is for the waters of the wisdom of God, which is the object of the understanding.

20. The second cavern is the will, and the emptiness thereof is hunger for God, so great that it causes the soul to swoon,[3] even as David says, in these words: 'My soul desires and faints for the tabernacles of the Lord.'[4] And this hunger is for the perfection of love to which the soul aspires.

21. The third cavern is the memory, whereof the emptiness is the melting away and languishing of the soul for the possession of God, as Jeremias notes in these words: *Memoria memor ero et tabescet in me anima mea.*[5] That is: With remembrance I shall remember, and I shall remember Him well and my soul shall melt away within me; turning over these things in my heart, I shall live in hope of God.

22. The capacity of these caverns, then, is deep; for that which they are capable of containing, which is God, is deep and infinite[6]; and thus in a certain sense their capacity will be infinite, and likewise their thirst will be infinite, and their hunger also will be infinite and deep, and their languishing[7] and pain are infinite death. For, although the soul suffers not so intensely as in the next life, it suffers nevertheless a vivid image of that infinite privation, since it is to a certain extent

---

[1] Bz: 'and the Divine, in union with God, is not communicated to it.' Bg, P: 'and God communicates not Himself to it.'

[2] Psalm xli, 1 [A.V., xlii, 1].

[3] C abbreviates: 'and the emptiness thereof causes the soul to swoon.'

[4] Psalm lxxxiii, 3 [A.V., lxxxiv, 2].   [5] Lamentations iii, 20–1.

[6] S: 'is deep in infinite goodness.'   [7] C: 'their swooning.'

prepared to receive fullness; although this suffering is of another kind, for it dwells in the bosom of the love of the will, and this love does not alleviate the pain; for the greater is the love, the greater is the impatience of the soul for the possession of its God, for Whom it hopes continually with intense desire.

23. But, seeing it is certain that, when the soul desires God with entire[1] truth, it already (as Saint Gregory says in writing of Saint John[2]) possesses Him Whom it loves, how comes it, O God, that it yearns for Him Whom it already possesses? For, in the desire which, as Saint Peter says,[3] the angels have to see the Son of God, there is neither pain nor yearning, since they possess Him already; so it seems that, if the soul possesses God more completely according as it desires Him more earnestly, the possession of God should give delight and satisfaction to the soul. Even so the angels have delight when they are fulfilling their desire in possession, and satisfying their soul continually with desire, yet have none of the weariness that comes from satiety; wherefore, since they have no weariness, they continually desire, and because they have possession they have no pain. Thus, the greater is the desire of the soul in this state, the more satisfaction and desire it should experience, since it has the more of God and has not grief or pain.

24. In this matter, however, it is well to note clearly the difference that exists between the possession of God through grace itself alone and the possession of Him through union; for the one consists in deep mutual love, but in the other there is also communication. There is as great a difference between these states as there is between betrothal and marriage. For in betrothal there is only a consent by agreement, and a unity of will between the two parties, and the jewels and the adornment of the bride-to-be, given her graciously by the bridegroom. But in marriage there is likewise communication between the persons, and union. During the betrothal, although from time to time the bridegroom sees the bride and gives her gifts, as we have said, there is no union between them, for that is the end[4] of betrothal. Even so, when the soul has attained to such purity in itself and in its faculties that the will is well purged[5] of other strange tastes and desires, according to its lower and higher parts, and when it has given its consent to God with respect to all this, and the will of God and of the soul are as one in a

---

[1] Bz: 'intense.'
[3] 1 St. Peter i, 12.
[5] S: 'is very pure and well purged.'
[2] Hom. XXX in Evang.
[4] S reads: 'nor is that the end.'

free consent of their own,[1] then it has attained to the possession of
God through grace of will, in so far as can be by means of will and
grace; and this signifies that God has given it, through its own consent,
His true and entire consent, which comes through His grace.

25. And this is the lofty state of spiritual betrothal of the soul with
the Word,[2] wherein the Spouse grants the soul great favours, and
visits it most lovingly and frequently, wherein the soul receives great
favours and delights. But these have nothing to do with those of
marriage, for the former are all preparations for the union of marriage;
and, though it is true that they come to the soul when it is completely
purged from all creature affection (for spiritual betrothal, as we say,
cannot take place until this happens), nevertheless the soul has need
of other and positive preparations on the part of God, of His visits
and gifts whereby He purifies the soul ever more completely and
beautifies and refines it so that it may be fitly prepared for such high
union. In some souls more time is necessary than in others, for God
works here according to the state of the soul. This is prefigured in
those maidens who were chosen for King Assuerus[3]; although they
had been taken from their own countries and from their fathers'
houses, yet, before they were sent to the king's bed, they were kept
waiting for a year, albeit within the enclosure of the palace. For one
half of the year they were prepared with certain ointments of myrrh
and other spices, and for the other half of the year with other and
choicer ointments, after which they went to the king's bed.[4]

26. During the time, then, of this betrothal and expectation of
marriage in the unctions of the Holy Spirit, when there are choicest
ointments[5] preparing the soul for union with God, the yearnings of the
caverns of the soul are wont to be extreme and delicate. For, as those
ointments are a most proximate preparation for union with God,
because they are nearest to God and for this cause make the soul more
desirous of Him and inspire it with a more delicate affection for Him,
the desire is more delicate and also deeper; for the desire for God is a
preparation for union with God.

27. Oh, how good a place would this be to warn souls whom God is
leading to these delicate anointings[6] to take care what they are doing
and into whose hands they commit themselves, lest they go backward,

---

[1] Bg, P: 'in a consent that is ready and free.'
[2] P: 'with God the Word.' Bg: 'with the Word, God.'
[3] Esther ii, 12.   [4] Bz omits: 'after which . . . bed.
[5] Bg, P: 'when there are now the choicest ointments.'
[6] Bz: 'unions.'

were not this beyond the limits of that whereof we are speaking! But such is the compassion and pity that fills my heart when I see souls going backward, and not only failing to submit themselves to the anointing of the spirit so that they may make progress therein, but even losing the effects of that anointing of God which they have received, that I must not fail to warn them here as to what they should do in order to avoid such loss, even though this should cause us to delay the return to our subject a little. I shall return to it shortly, and indeed all this will help us to understand the properties of these caverns. And since it is very necessary, not only for these souls that prosper on this way but also for all the rest who seek their Beloved, I am anxious to describe it.

28. First, it must be known that, if a soul is seeking God, its Beloved[1] is seeking it much more; and, if it sends after Him its loving desires, which are as fragrant to Him as a pillar of smoke that issues from the aromatic spices of myrrh and incense,[2] He likewise sends after it the fragrance of His ointments, wherewith He attracts the soul and causes it to run after Him. These ointments are His Divine inspirations and touches, which, whenever they are His, are ordered[3] and ruled with respect to the perfection of the law of God and of faith, in which perfection the soul must ever draw nearer and nearer to God. And thus the soul must understand that the desire of God in all the favours that He bestows upon it in the unctions[4] and fragrance of His ointments is to prepare it for other choicer and more delicate ointments which have been made more after the temper of God, until it reaches such a delicate and pure state of preparation that it merits union with God and substantial transformation in all its faculties.[5]

29. When, therefore, the soul reflects that God is the principal agent in this matter, and the guide of its blind self, Who will take it by the hand and lead it where it could not of itself go (namely, to the supernatural things which neither its understanding nor its will nor its memory could know as they are), then its chief care will be to see that it sets no obstacle in the way of Him that guides it upon the road which God has ordained for it, in the perfection of the law of God and faith,[6] as we are saying. And this impediment may come to the soul if it allows itself to be led and guided by another blind guide; and the blind guides that might lead it out of its way are three, namely, the

---

[1] Bg, P: 'its Beloved, God.'   [2] Canticles iii, 6.
[3] Bz: 'are anointed.'   [4] Bz: 'communications.' C: 'unions.'
[5] Bg, P omit: 'in all its faculties.'
[6] Bz: 'of the love of God and of the law and of faith.'

spiritual director, the devil and its own self. And, that the soul may understand how this is, we will treat shortly of each of them.[1]

30. With regard to the first of these, it is of great importance for the soul that desires to make progress in recollection and perfection to consider in whose hands it is placing itself; for, as is the master, so will be the disciple, and, as is the father, so will be the son. And let it be noted there is hardly anyone who in all respects will guide the soul perfectly along the highest stretch of the road, or even along the intermediate stretches, for it is needful that such a guide should be experienced as well as wise and discreet. The fundamental requirement of a guide in spiritual things is knowledge and discretion; yet, if a guide have no experience of the nature of pure and true spirituality, he will be unable to direct[2] the soul therein, when God permits it to attain so far, nor will he even understand it.

31. In this way many spiritual masters[3] do much harm to many souls, for, not themselves understanding the ways and properties of the spirit, they commonly cause souls to lose the unction of these delicate ointments, wherewith the Holy Spirit gradually anoints and prepares them for Himself, and instruct them by other and lower means which they have used and of which they have read here and there, and which are unsuitable save for beginners. They themselves know no more than how to deal with these—please God they may know even so much!—and refuse to allow souls to go beyond these rudimentary acts of meditation and imagination, even though God is seeking to lead them farther, so that they may never exceed or depart from their natural capacity, whereby a soul can achieve very little.

32. And in order that we may better understand the characteristics of beginners, we must know that the state and exercise of beginners is one of meditation and of the making of discursive exercises and acts with the imagination. In this state, it is necessary for the soul to be given material for meditation and reasoning, and it is well for it to make interior acts on its own account, and even in spiritual things to take advantage of the sweetness and pleasure[4] which come from sense; for, if the desire is fed with pleasure in spiritual things, it becomes detached from pleasure in sensual things and wearies of things of the world. But when to some extent the desire has been fed, and in some sense habituated to spiritual things, and has acquired some

---

[1] Bg, P: 'of each of these blind guides.'
[2] Bz: 'to examine' [*examinar* for *encaminar*].
[3] Bg: 'fathers.'   [4] C: 'the fervour, favour and pleasure.'

fortitude and constancy, God then begins, as they say, to wean the soul and bring it into the state of contemplation, which in some persons is wont to happen very quickly, especially in religious, because these, having renounced[1] things of the world, quickly attune their senses and desires to God, and their exercises become spiritual through God's working in them; this happens when the discursive acts and the meditation of the soul itself cease, and the first fervours and sweetness of sense cease likewise, so that the soul cannot meditate as before, or find any help in the senses; for the senses remain in a state of aridity, inasmuch as their treasure is transformed into spirit, and no longer falls within the capacity of sense. And, as all the operations which the soul can perform on its own account naturally depend upon sense only, it follows that God is the agent in this state and the soul is the recipient; for the soul behaves only as one that receives and as one in whom these things are being wrought; and God as One that gives and acts and as One that works these things in the soul, giving it spiritual blessings in contemplation, which is Divine love and knowledge in one—that is, a loving knowledge, wherein the soul has not to use its natural acts and reasonings,[2] for it can no longer enter into them as before.

33. It follows that at this time the soul must be led in a way entirely contrary to the way wherein it was led at first. If formerly it was given material for meditation, and practised meditation, this material must now be taken from it and it must not meditate; for, as I say, it will be unable to do so even though it would, and, instead of becoming recollected, it will become distracted. And if formerly it sought sweetness and love and fervour, and found it, now it must neither seek it nor desire it, for not only will it be unable to find it through its own diligence, but it will rather find aridity, for it turns from the quiet and peaceful blessings which were secretly given to its spirit, to the work that it desires to do with sense; and thus it will lose the one and not obtain the other, since no blessings are now given to it by means of sense as they were formerly. Wherefore in this state the soul must never have meditation imposed upon it, nor must it make any acts, nor strive after sweetness or fervour; for this would be to set an obstacle in the way of the principal agent, who, as I say, is God. For God secretly and quietly[3] infuses into the soul loving knowledge and wisdom without any intervention of specific acts, although sometimes

---

1 S: 'abandoned.'
2 Bz omits: 'and reasonings.'
3 Bz: 'secretly and in a hidden way.'

He specifically produces them in the soul for some length of time. And
the soul has then to walk with loving advertence to God, without
making specific acts, but conducting itself, as we have said, passively,
and making no efforts of its own, but preserving this simple, pure and[1]
loving advertence and determination, like one that opens his eyes with
the advertence of love.

34. Since God, then, as giver, is communing with the soul by means
of loving and simple knowledge, the soul must likewise commune
with Him by receiving with a loving and simple knowledge and
advertence, so that knowledge may be united with knowledge and love
with love. For it is meet that he who receives should behave in conformity with that which he receives, and not in any other manner, in
order to be able to receive and retain it as it is given[2] to him; for, as the
philosophers say, anything that is received is in the recipient according to the manner of acting of the recipient. Wherefore it is clear that
if the soul at this time were not to abandon its natural procedure of
active meditation, it would not receive this blessing in other than a
natural way. It would not, in fact, receive it, but would retain its natural
act alone, for the supernatural cannot be received in a natural way, nor
can it have aught to do with it. And thus, if the soul at this time
desires to work on its own account, and to do aught else than remain,
quite passively and tranquilly, in that passive and loving advertence
whereof we have spoken, making no natural act, save if God should
unite it with Himself in some act, it would set a total and effective impediment in the way of the blessings which God is communicating to
it supernaturally in loving knowledge. This comes to pass first of all in
the exercise of interior purgation wherein, as we have said above, it
suffers, and afterwards in sweetness of love. If, as I say, and as in truth
is the case, the soul receives this loving knowledge passively and after
the supernatural manner of God, and not after the manner of the
natural soul, it follows that, in order to receive them, this soul must be
quite annihilated in its natural operations, disencumbered, at ease,
quiet, peaceful, serene, and adapted to the manner of God; exactly like
the air, which receives the greater clarification and heat from the sun
when it is pure and cleansed from vapours and at rest. Therefore the
soul must be attached to nothing—to no exercise of meditation or
reasoning; to no kind of sweetness, whether it be of sense or of spirit;
and to no other kind of apprehension.[3] For the spirit needs to be so

---

[1] S omits: 'simple, pure and.'   [2] Bz: 'as it was given.'
[3] S: 'of operation.'

free and so completely annihilated that any kind of thought or meditation or pleasure to which the soul in this state may conceive an attachment would impede and disturb it and would introduce noise into the
deep silence which it is meet that the soul should observe, according
both to sense and to spirit, so that it may hear the deep and delicate
voice in which God speaks to the heart in this secret place,[1] as He said
through Osee,[2] in the utmost peace and tranquillity, so that the soul
may listen and hear the words of the Lord God to it, as David says,[3]
when in this secret place He speaks this peace.

35. When, therefore, it comes to pass that the soul is conscious of
being led into silence, and hearkens, it must forget even the practice
of that loving advertence of which I have spoken, so that it may remain
free for that which the Lord then desires of it; for it must practise that
advertence only when it is not conscious of being brought into solitude or interior rest[4] or forgetfulness or attentiveness of the spirit,
which, in order that it may be perceived, is always accompanied by
a certain peaceful tranquillity and interior absorption.

36. Wherefore, whatever be the time or season, when once the soul
has begun to enter into this pure and restful state of contemplation,
which comes to pass when it may no longer meditate and is unable to
do so, it must not seek to gather to itself meditations, neither must it
desire to find help in spiritual sweetness or delight, but it must stand in
complete detachment above all this and its spirit must be completely
freed from it, as Habacuc[5] said that he must needs do in order to hear
what the Lord should say to him. 'I will stand upon my watch,' he says,
'and I will fix my step upon my munition, and I will watch to see that
which will be said to me.' This is as though he had said: I will raise up
my mind above all the operations and all the knowledge that can be
comprehended by my senses, and above that which they can keep and
retain within themselves: all this I will leave below. And I will fix the
step of the munition of my faculties,[6] not allowing them to advance a
step as to their own operation, so that through contemplation I may
receive that which is communicated to me from God. For we have
already said that pure contemplation consists in receiving.

37. It is not possible that this loftiest wisdom and language of God,
such as is contemplation, can be received save in a spirit that is silent
and detached from sweetness and discursive knowledge. For this is

---

[1] S: 'in this important secret place.'　　　　　[2] Osee ii, 14.
[3] Psalm lxxxiv, 9 [A.V., lxxxv, 8].
[4] S: 'into solitude, with all interior rest.'　　　　　[5] Habacuc ii, 1.
[6] Bz: 'of the communication of my faculties.' S omits: 'of my faculties.'

that which is said by Isaias, in these words: 'Whom shall He teach knowledge and whom shall He make to hear its voice?'[1] Them that are weaned from the milk—that is, from sweetness and pleasures—and them that are detached from the breasts—that is, from particular apprehensions and knowledge.

38. Oh, spiritual soul, take away the motes and the hairs and the mists,[2] and cleanse thine eye, and the bright sun shall shine upon thee, and thou shalt see clearly.[3] Set the soul in peace, and draw it away and free it from the yoke and slavery of the weak operation of its own capacity, which is the captivity of Egypt, where all is little more than gathering straw to make bricks; and guide it, oh, spiritual director, to the promised land flowing with milk and honey, remembering that it is to give the soul this freedom and holy rest which belongs to His sons that God calls it into the wilderness. There it journeys adorned with festal robes, and with jewels of silver and of gold, having now left Egypt,[4] by which is meant the sensual part of the soul, and emptied it of its riches. And not only so, but the Egyptians[5] are drowned in the sea of contemplation, where the Egyptian of sense finds no support, or foothold, and thus is drowned, and sets free the child of God—that is, the spirit that has gone forth from the limits[6] and the slavery of the operation of the senses (which is to say from its scant understanding, its lowly perception, and its miserable loving and liking) so that God may give it the sweet manna, which, though the sweetness thereof contains within itself all these sweetnesses and delights for which thou desirest to make the soul work, nevertheless, being so delicious that it melts in the mouth, the soul shall not taste of it if it desire to combine it with any other delight or with aught else. Endeavour, then, when the soul is nearing this state, to detach it from all coveting or spiritual sweetness, pleasure, delight and meditation, and disturb it not with care and solicitude of any kind for higher things, still less for lower things, but bring it into the greatest possible degree of solitude and withdrawal. For the more nearly the soul attains all this, and the sooner it reaches this restful tranquillity, the more abundantly does it become infused with the spirit of Divine wisdom, which is the loving, tranquil, lonely, peaceful, sweet inebriator of the spirit. Hereby the soul feels itself to be gently and tenderly wounded and ravished, knowing not

[1] Isaias xxviii, 9.   [2] Bz, C omit: 'and the mists.'
[3] Bg, P omit: 'and thou shalt see clearly.'
[4] Bg, C, P: 'having now despoiled Egypt.' Bz: 'Christ having now despoiled it' [or 'him'].
[5] S: 'the giants.'   [6] Br, Bz, C: 'the narrow limits.'

by whom, nor whence, nor how. And the reason of this is that the Spirit communicates Himself without any act on the part of the soul.

39. And the smallest part of this that God brings to pass in the soul in holy rest and solitude is an inestimable blessing, greater sometimes than either the soul itself, or he that guides it, can imagine; and, although this may not be very clearly realized at the time, it will in due course become manifest. But the soul has at least been able[1] to attain to a perception of estrangement and withdrawal from all things, sometimes more so than at others, together with an inclination to solitude and a sense of weariness with regard to all worldly creatures and a sweet aspiration of love and life in the spirit. And in this state anything that does not imply such withdrawal is distasteful to it, for, as they say, when a soul tastes of the spirit, it conceives a distaste for the flesh.

40. But the blessings that this silent communication and contemplation leave impressed upon the soul without its perceiving them at the time are, as I say, inestimable; for they are the most secret and therefore the most delicate anointings of the Holy Spirit, which secretly fill the soul with spiritual riches and gifts and graces; for, since it is God Who does all this, He does it not otherwise than as God.

41. These anointings, then, and these touches, are the delicate and sublime acts of the Holy Spirit, which, on account of their delicate and subtle purity, can be understood neither by the soul nor by him that has to do with it, but only by Him Who infuses them, in order to make the soul more pleasing to Himself. These blessings, with the greatest facility, by no more than the slightest act which the soul may desire to make on its own account, with its memory, understanding or will, or by the application of its sense or desire or knowledge or sweetness or pleasure, are disturbed or hindered in the soul, which is a grave evil and a great shame and pity.

42. Oh, how grave a matter is this, and what cause it gives for wonder, that, while the harm done is inconspicuous, and the interference with those holy anointings almost negligible, the harm should be more serious, and a matter for deeper sorrow and regret, than the disquieting and ruining of many souls of a more ordinary nature which have not attained to a state of such supreme fineness and delicacy! It is as though a portrait of supreme and delicate beauty were touched by a clumsy hand, and were daubed with coarse, crude colours. This would be a greater and more crying and pitiful shame than if many more ordinary portraits were besmeared in this way. For

[1] Bg, Bz, C, P add 'now.'

when the work of so delicate a hand as this of the Holy Spirit has been thus roughly treated, who will be able to repair its beauty?

43. Although the gravity and seriousness of this evil cannot be exaggerated, it is so common and frequent that there will hardly be found a single spiritual director who does not inflict it upon souls whom God is beginning to draw nearer to Himself [1] in this kind of contemplation. For, whenever God is anointing the contemplative soul with some most delicate unction of loving knowledge—serene, peaceful, lonely and very far removed from sense and from all that has to do with thought—so that the soul cannot meditate or think of aught soever or find pleasure in aught, whether in higher things or in lower, inasmuch as God is keeping it full of that lonely unction and inclined to rest and solitude,[2] there will come some spiritual director who has no knowledge save of hammering and pounding with the faculties like a blacksmith, and, because his only teaching is of that kind, and he knows of naught save meditation, he will say: 'Come now, leave these periods of inactivity, for you are only living in idleness and wasting your time. Get to work, meditate and make interior acts, for it is right that you should do for yourself that which in you lies, for these other things are the practices of Illuminists and fools.'

44. And thus, since such persons have no understanding of the degrees of prayer or of the ways of the spirit, they cannot see that those acts which they counsel the soul to perform, and those attempts to make it progress along the path of meditation, have been made already, for such a soul as we have been describing has by this time attained to negation and silence of sense and discursive reasoning, and has reached the way of the spirit, which is contemplation,[3] wherein ceases the operation of sense and the soul's own discursive reasoning, and God alone is the agent and it is He that now speaks secretly to the solitary soul, while the soul keeps silence. And if, now that the spirit has achieved spirituality in this way that we are describing, such directors attempt to make the soul continue to walk in sense, it cannot but go backward and become distracted. For if one that has reached his goal begins to set out again for it, he is doing a ridiculous thing, for he can do nothing but walk away from it.[4] When, therefore, through the operation of its faculties, the soul has reached that quiet

---

[1] [Cf. p. 73, n. 3, above.]
[2] S: 'full of that lonely rest and inclined to solitude.
[3] Bg, P: 'the life of the spirit, which is the contemplative life.'
[4] Bg, P: 'but leave it.'

recollection which is the aim of every spiritual person, wherein ceases the operation of these faculties, it would not only be a vain thing for it to begin to make acts with these faculties in order to reach this recollection, but it would be harmful to it, for it would cause it distraction and make it abandon the recollection that it already has.

45. Now these spiritual directors, not understanding, as I say, the nature and properties of the soul's spiritual solitude and recollection, in which solitude God effects these sublime anointings in the soul, superpose or interpose other anointings, which consist in more elementary spiritual exercises,[1] and make the soul work in the way we have described. There is as much difference between this and what the soul previously enjoyed as between any human operation and a Divine operation and between the natural and the supernatural; for in the one case God is working supernaturally in the soul and in the other case the soul alone is working naturally.[2] And the worst result is that, through the exercise of its natural operation, the soul loses its interior recollection and solitude and consequently spoils the wondrous work that God was painting[3] in it. It is thus as if the director were merely striking an anvil; and the soul loses in one respect and gains nothing in the other.

46. Let such guides of the soul as these take heed and remember that the principal agent and guide and mover of souls in this matter is not the director, but the Holy Spirit, Who never loses His care for them; and that they themselves are only instruments to lead souls in the way of perfection by the faith and the law of God, according to the spirit that God is giving to each one. Let them not, therefore, merely aim at guiding these souls according to their own way and the manner suitable to themselves, but let them see if they know the way by which God is leading the soul, and, if they know it not, let them leave the soul in peace and not disturb it. And, in conformity with the way and the spirit by which God is leading these souls, let them ever seek to lead them into greater solitude, tranquillity and liberty of spirit and to give them a certain freedom so that the spiritual and bodily senses may not be bound to any particular thing, either interior or exterior, when God leads the soul by this way of solitude, and let them not worry or grieve, thinking that it is doing nothing; for, though it is

---

[1] Bg, P: 'which consist in more labour and spiritual exercises.'
[2] Bg, P: 'and in the other it is only itself working and its operation is no more than natural.' Bz reads similarly, but omits 'only.' C: 'for in the one case God is working and in the other only the soul itself is working and its operation is no more than natural.'
[3] S: 'was working.'

not working at that time, God is working in it. Let them strive to disencumber the soul and to set it in a state of rest,[1] in such a way that it will not be bound to any particular kind of knowledge, either above or below, or be fettered by covetousness of any sweetness or pleasure or any other apprehension, but that it will be empty in pure negation with respect to every creature and will be established in poverty of spirit. It is this that the soul must do as far as in it lies, as the Son of God counsels, in these words: 'He that renounceth not all the things that he possesseth cannot be My disciple.'[2] This is to be understood, not only of the renunciation of all temporal things[3] with the will, but also of the surrender of spiritual things, wherein is included poverty of spirit, in which, says the Son of God, consists blessedness.[4] When in this way the soul voids itself of all things and achieves emptiness and surrender of them (which, as we have said, is the part that the soul can play), it is impossible, if the soul does as much as in it lies, that God should fail to perform His own part by communicating Himself to the soul, at least secretly and in silence. It is more impossible than that the sun should fail to shine in a serene and unclouded sky; for as the sun, when it rises in the morning, will enter your house if you open the shutter,[5] even so will God, Who sleeps not in keeping Israel, still less slumbers,[6] enter the soul that is empty and fill it with Divine blessings.

47. God, like the sun, is above our souls and ready to communicate Himself to them. Let those who guide them, then, be content with preparing the soul for this according to evangelical perfection, which is detachment and emptiness of sense and of spirit; and let them not seek to go beyond this in the building up of the soul, for that work belongs only to the Father of lights, from Whom comes down every good and perfect boon.[7] For, if the Lord, as David says, builds not the house, in vain does he labour that builds it.[8] And since God is the supernatural artificer, He will build supernaturally[9] in each soul the building that He desires, if you yourself prepare it and strive to annihilate it with respect to its operations and natural affections, which give it no capacity or strength for the erection of the supernatural building, but at this season disturb rather than help. To prepare the soul

---

[1] S: 'of solitude and rest.'
[2] [St. Luke xiv, 33.]
[3] S: 'of all bodily and temporal things.'
[4] St. Matthew v, 3.
[5] S: 'the window.'
[6] Psalm cxx, 4 [A.V., cxxi, 4]. This is the reading of S. The other MSS. repeat 'sleeps.'
[7] St. James i, 17.
[8] Psalm cxxvi, 1 [A.V., cxxvii, 1].
[9] S: 'naturally.'

thus is your office; and the office of God, as the Wise Man says,[1] is to direct the way of the soul—that is to say, to direct it to supernatural blessings, by ways and in manners which neither you nor the soul can understand. Say not, therefore: 'Oh, the soul is making no progress, for it is doing nothing!' For if it is true that it is doing nothing, then, by this very fact that it is doing nothing, I will now prove to you that it is doing a great deal. For, if the understanding is voiding itself of particular kinds of knowledge, both natural and spiritual, it is making progress, and, the more it empties itself of particular knowledge and of the acts of understanding, the greater is the progress of the understanding in its journey to the highest spiritual good.

48. 'Oh,' you will say, 'but it understands nothing distinctly, and so it cannot be making progress.' My reply to you is that it would rather be making no progress if it were to understand anything distinctly. The reason of this is that God, towards Whom the understanding is journeying, transcends the understanding and is therefore incomprehensible and inaccessible to it; and thus, when it is understanding, it is not approaching God, but is rather withdrawing itself from Him. Therefore the understanding must withdraw from itself, and walk in faith, believing and not understanding. And in this way the understanding will reach perfection, for by faith and by no other means comes union with God; and the soul approaches God more nearly by not understanding than by understanding. Grieve not, therefore, at this, for if the understanding goes not backward (which it would be doing if it desired to occupy itself with distinct knowledge and other kinds of reasoning and understanding, and desired not to be at rest) it is making progress, for it is voiding itself of all that it could apprehend, nothing of which could be God; for, as we have said, God cannot be apprehended by the soul.[2] In this matter of perfection not to go backward is to go forward; it signifies the progress of the understanding, and a gradual increase of faith, and thus it is a progress in darkness, for faith is darkness to the understanding. Wherefore, since the understanding cannot know what God is, it must of necessity walk toward Him in submission and not by understanding;[3] and thus, what you are condemning in your penitent is fitting for his good—namely, that he should not occupy himself with distinct kinds of

---

[1] Proverbs xvi, 9.
[2] S: 'by the heart that is occupied.'
[3] S: 'in submission, and therefore walks not by understanding.'

understanding, since by their means he cannot attain to God, but will rather embarrass himself in journeying to Him.

49. 'Oh,' you will say, 'but if the understanding understands not distinctly the will will be idle and will not love, since the will can only love that which is understood by the understanding; and this must always be avoided on the spiritual road.' There is truth in this, especially as regards the natural acts and operations of the soul, wherein the will loves only that which is distinctly understood by the understanding. But in the contemplation of which we are speaking, wherein God, as we have said, infuses Himself into the soul, there is no necessity for distinct knowledge, nor for the soul to perform any acts of the understanding, for God, in one act, is communicating to the soul light and love together, which is loving and supernatural knowledge, and may be said to be like heat-giving light, which gives out heat, for that light also enkindles the soul in love; and this is confused and obscure to the understanding, since it is knowledge of contemplation, which, as Saint Dionysius says, is a ray of darkness to the understanding. Therefore, as is intelligence in the understanding, so also is love in the will. For, as to the understanding this knowledge infused in it by God is general and dark, without distinction of intelligence, so the will also loves in a general way, without any distinction being made as to any particular thing that is understood. Now as God is Divine light and love, in the communication of Himself which He makes to the soul, He informs these two faculties (understanding and will) equally, with intelligence and love. And as He Himself cannot be understood in this life, the understanding is dark, as I say, and after the same fashion is love in the will; although sometimes in this delicate communication God communicates Himself more to the one faculty than to the other, and acts on the one more than on the other, the soul being at times more conscious of understanding than of love, while at other times it is more conscious of love than of understanding; at times, again, all is understanding, without any love,[1] and at times all is love and there is no understanding. Therefore I say that, as far as concerns the soul's performance of natural[2] acts with the understanding, there can be no love without understanding; but in the acts which God performs and infuses in the soul, as in those of which we are treating, it is different, for God can communicate Himself in the one faculty and not in the other. Thus He can enkindle the will by means of a touch of the heat

[1] Bg, P omit: 'at times, again, all is understanding, without any love.'
[2] S: 'interior.'

of His love, although the understanding may have no understanding
thereof, just as a person can be warmed by a fire without seeing the
fire.

50. In this way the will may oftentimes feel itself to be enkindled or
filled with tenderness and love without knowing or understanding
anything more distinctly than before, since God is setting love in order
in it, even as the Bride says in the Songs, in these words: 'The King
made me enter the cellar of wine and set in order charity in me.'[1] There
is no reason, therefore, to fear that the will in this state will be idle;
for, if of itself it leave performing acts of love concerning particular
kinds of knowledge, God performs them within it, inebriating it
secretly in infused love, either by means of the knowledge of contemplation, or without such knowledge, as we have just said[2]; and these
acts are as much more delectable and meritorious than those made by
the soul as the mover and infuser of this love—namely, God—is
better than the soul.

51. This love is infused by God in the will when it is empty and
detached from other pleasures and particular affections, both higher
and lower. The soul, therefore, must see to it that the will is empty and
stripped of its affections; for if it is not going backward by desiring
to experience some sweetness or pleasure, it is going forward, even
though it have no particular perception of this in God, and it is soaring
upward to God above all things, since it takes no pleasure in anything.
It is going toward God, although it may be taking no particular and
distinct delight in Him, nor may be loving Him with any distinct act,
for it is taking greater pleasure in Him secretly, by means of that dark
and general infusion of love, than it does in all things that are distinct,
for it sees clearly in this state that nothing gives it so much pleasure
as that solitary quiet. And it is loving Him above all things that can be
loved, since it has flung from itself all other kinds of sweetness and
pleasure which have become distasteful to it. And there is thus no
reason to be troubled, for, if the will can find no sweetness and pleasure
in particular acts, it is going forward; seeing that to refrain from going
backward and from embracing anything that belongs to sense is to go
forward towards the inaccessible, which is God, and thus there is
no wonder that the soul has no perception thereof. Wherefore, in
order to journey to God, the will has rather to be continually detaching

---

[1] Canticles ii, 4.
[2] Bz: 'infused love, or by means of the knowledge of simple contemplation, as we have just said.'

itself from everything delectable and pleasant than to be conceiving an attachment to it. In this way it completely fulfils the precept of love, which is to love God above all things; and this cannot be unless it have detachment and emptiness[1] with regard to them all.

52. Neither is there any cause for misgivings when the memory is voided of its forms and figures, for, since God has no form or figure, the memory is safe if it be voided of form or figure, and it is approaching God the more nearly; for, the more it leans upon the imagination, the farther it is going from God, and the greater is the peril wherein it walks, since God is incomprehensible and therefore cannot be contained in the imagination.

53. These spiritual directors such as we have been describing fail to understand souls that are now walking in this solitary and quiet contemplation, because they themselves have not arrived so far, nor learned what it means to leave behind the discursive reasoning of meditations, as I have said, and they think that these souls are idle. And therefore they disturb and impede the peace of this quiet and hushed contemplation which God has been giving their penitents by His own power, and they cause them to follow the road of meditation and imaginative reasoning and make them perform interior acts, wherein the aforementioned souls find great repugnance, aridity and distraction, since they would fain remain in their holy rest and their quiet and peaceful state of recollection. But, as sense can perceive in this neither pleasure nor help nor activity, their directors persuade them to strive after sweetness and fervour, though they ought rather to advise them the contrary. The penitents, however, are unable to do as they did previously, and can enter into none of these things, for the time for them has now passed and they belong no more to their proper path; and so they are doubly disturbed and believe that they are going to perdition; and their directors encourage them in this belief and parch their spirits, and take from them the precious unctions wherewith God was anointing them in solitude and tranquillity. This, as I have said, is a great evil; their directors are plunging them into mire and mourning; for they are losing one thing and labouring without profit at the other.

54. Such persons have no knowledge of what is spirituality. They offer a great insult and great irreverence to God, by laying their coarse hands where God is working. For it has cost Him dearly to bring these souls to this place and He greatly esteems having brought them to this solitude and emptiness of their faculties and operations,

[1] Bg, P: 'and spiritual emptiness.'

that He may speak to their hearts, which is what He ever desires. He has Himself taken them by the hand, and He Himself reigns in their souls in abundant peace and quietness, causing the natural acts of their faculties to fail wherewith they toiled all night and wrought nothing. And He has brought peace to their spirits without the work and operations of sense, for neither sense nor any act thereof is capable of receiving spirit.

55. How precious in His sight is this tranquillity and slumbering or withdrawal[1] of sense can be clearly seen in that adjuration,[2] so notable and effective, that He utters in the Songs, where He says: 'I adjure you, daughters of Jerusalem, by the goats and harts of the fields, that ye awaken not my beloved nor cause her to wake until she please.'[3] Herein, by introducing these solitary and retiring animals, He gives us to understand how much He loves that solitary[4] forgetfulness and slumber. But these spiritual directors will not let the soul have repose or quiet, but demand that it shall continually labour and work, that it may leave no room for God to work, and that that which He is working may be undone and wiped out through the operation of the soul. They have become as the little foxes which tear down the flowering vine[5] of the soul[6]; for which reason the Lord complains through Isaias, saying: 'You have devoured My vineyard.'[7]

56. But, it may possibly be said, these directors err with good intent, through insufficiency of knowledge. This, however, does not excuse them for the advice which they are rash enough to give without first learning to understand either the way that the soul is taking or its spirit. Not understanding this, they are laying their coarse hands upon things that they understand not, instead of leaving them for those who are able to understand them; for it is a thing of no small weight, and no slight crime, to cause the soul to lose inestimable blessings and sometimes to leave it completely confused[8] by rash counsel. And thus one who rashly errs, being under an obligation to give reliable advice—as is every man, whatever his office—shall not go unpunished, by reason of the harm that he has done. For the business of God has to be undertaken with great circumspection, and with eyes wide open, most of all in a case[9] of such great importance and a

---

[1] Bg, Bz, P: 'annihilation.'   [2] Bz: 'comparison.' P: 'conjunction.'
[3] Canticles iii, 5.   [4] Bg: 'voluntary.'
[5] S: 'the flower of the vine.'   [6] [Canticles ii, 15.]
[7] Isaias iii, 14.
[8] [The original has a stronger word: 'vitiated,' 'corrupted.' Cf. the energetic metaphor used in the first redaction (p. 79, n. 6, above).]
[9] S: 'in things.'

business so sublime as is the business of these souls, where a man may bring them almost infinite gain if the advice he gives be good and almost infinite loss if it be mistaken.

57. But if you will still maintain that you have some excuse, though for myself I can see none, you will at least be unable to say that there is any excuse for one who, in his treatment of a soul, never allows it to go out of his jurisdiction, for certain vain reasons and intentions which he best knows. Such a person will not go unpunished, for it is certain that, if that soul[1] is to make progress by going forward on the spiritual road, wherein God is ever aiding it, it will have to change the style and method of its prayer, and it will of necessity require instruction of a higher kind and a deeper spirituality than that of such a director. For not all directors have sufficient knowledge to meet all the possibilities and cases which they encounter on the spiritual road, neither is their spirituality so perfect that they know how a soul has to be led and guided and directed in every state of the spiritual life; at least no man should think that he knows everything[2] concerning this, or that God will cease leading a given soul farther onward. Not everyone who can hew a block of wood is able to carve an image; nor is everyone who can carve it able to smooth[3] and polish it; nor is everyone that can polish it able to paint it; nor can everyone that is able to paint it complete it with the final touches. Each one of these, in working upon an image, can do no more than that with which he himself is familiar, and, if he tries to do more, he will only ruin his work.

58. How then, we may ask, if you are only a hewer of wood, which signifies that you can make a soul despise the world and mortify its desires;[4] or, if at best you are a carver, which means that you can lead a soul to holy meditations but can do no more: how, in such a case, will this soul attain to the final perfection of a delicate painting, the art of which consists neither in the hewing of the wood, nor in the carving of it, nor even in the outlining of it, but in the work which God Himself must do in it? It is certain, then, that if your instruction is always of one kind, and you cause the soul to be continually bound to you, it will either go backward, or, at the least, will not go forward. For what, I ask you, will the image be like, if you never do any work upon it save hewing and hammering, which in the language of the soul is exercising the faculties? When will this image be finished? When

---

[1] Bg, P: 'if the soul that has come hither.'
[2] S: 'that he lacks nothing.'
[3] C, S: 'to perfect.'
[4] [*Lit.*, 'appetites.'] Bg, P: 'its passions and appetites.'

or how will it be left for God to paint it? Is it possible that you yourself can perform all these offices, and consider yourself so consummate a master that this soul shall never need any other?

59. And supposing that you have sufficient experience to direct some one soul, which perchance may have no ability to advance beyond your teaching, it is surely impossible for you to have sufficient experience for the direction of all those whom you refuse to allow to go out of your hands; for God leads each soul along a different road and there shall hardly be found a single spirit who can walk even half the way which is suitable for another. Who can be like Saint Paul and have the skill to make himself all things to all men, that he may gain them all? You yourself tyrannize over souls, and take away their liberty, and arrogate to yourself the breadth of evangelical doctrine, so that you not only strive that they may not leave you, but, what is worse, if any one of them should at some time have gone to discuss, with another director, some matter which he could not suitably discuss with you, or if God should lead him in order to teach him something which you have not taught him, you behave to him (I say it not without shame) like a husband who is jealous of his wife; nor is your jealousy even due to desire for the honour of God, or for the profit of that soul (for you must not presume to suppose that in neglecting you in this way he was neglecting God): it is due only to your own pride and presumption, or to some other imperfect motive relating to yourself.

60. Great is the indignation of God with such directors, whom He promises punishment when He speaks through Ezechiel and says: 'Ye drank of the milk of My flock and clothed yourselves with their wool and ye fed not My flock. I will require My flock at your hand.'[1]

61. Spiritual directors, then, ought to give these souls freedom, for, when they would seek to better themselves, their directors have an obligation to put a good face upon it,[2] since they know not by what means God desires such a soul to make progress, especially when the penitent dislikes the instruction that he is receiving, which is a sign that it is of no profit to him, either because God is leading him on farther, or by another way than that by which his director has been leading him, or because the director himself has changed his way of dealing with his penitents. The director, in such a case, should himself

---

[1] Ezechiel xxxiv, 2, 3, 10.
[2] C: 'when, in order to better themselves, they seek another director, their director has an obligation to put a good face upon it.'

advise a change, since any other advice springs from foolish pride and presumption or from some other pretension.

62. Let us now leave this question and speak of another more pestilential habit of such directors as these, which also belongs to others worse than they. For it may come to pass that God will be anointing certain souls with the unctions of holy desires and impulses to leave the world, to change their life and condition, to serve Him and despise the world (it is a great thing in His eyes that He should have succeeded in bringing them thus far, for the things of the world are not according to the will of God), and these directors, using human arguments or putting forward considerations quite contrary to the doctrine of Christ and His way of humility and despising of all things, place obstacles in their path or advise them to delay their decision, from motives of their own interest or pleasure, or because they fear where no fear is; or, what is still worse, they sometimes labour to remove these desires from their penitents' hearts. Such directors show an undevout spirit, and are clad, as it were, in very worldly garb, having little of the tenderness of Christ, since they neither enter themselves by the narrow gate of life, nor allow others to enter. These persons our Saviour threatens,[1] through Saint Luke, saying: 'Woe unto you that have taken away the key of knowledge, and enter not in yourselves nor allow others to enter.'[2] For these persons in truth are placed as barriers and obstacles at the gate of Heaven; they hinder from entering those that ask counsel of them, yet they are aware that God has commanded them, not only to allow and help them to enter, but even to compel them to enter. For God says, through Saint Luke: 'Insist, make them come in, that My house may be filled with guests.'[3] They, on the other hand, are compelling souls not to enter; such are blind guides who can obstruct the life[4] of the soul, which is the Holy Spirit. This comes to pass with spiritual directors in many more ways than have been mentioned here; some do it knowingly, others unconsciously; but neither class shall remain unpunished, since, having assumed their office, they are under an obligation to know and consider what they do.

63. The second blind guide of whom we have spoken, who can hinder the soul in this kind[5] of recollection, is the devil, who, being himself blind, desires the soul to be blind also. When the soul is in these lofty and solitary places wherein are infused the delicate unctions

---

1 Bg: 'admonishes.'   2 St. Luke xi, 52.
3 St. Luke xiv, 23.
4 Thus P, S. The other authorities read: 'the way.'
5 Bz: 'this business.'

of the Holy Spirit (at which he has heavy grief and envy, for he sees that not only is the soul gaining great riches, but is flying beyond him and he can in no wise lay hold on it), inasmuch as the soul is alone, detached and withdrawn from every creature and every trace thereof, the devil tries to cover this withdrawal, as it were, with cataracts of knowledge and mists[1] of sensible sweetness, which are sometimes good, so that he may entice the soul more surely, and thus cause it to return[2] to a different way of life and to the operation of sense, and to look at these delights and this good knowledge which he sets before it, and embrace them, so that it may continue its journey to God in reliance upon them. And herein he very easily distracts it and withdraws it from that solitude and recollection, wherein, as we have said, the Holy Spirit is working those great and secret things. As the soul is of itself inclined to sensible enjoyment, especially if these are the things which it is really desiring and understands not the road that it is taking, it is very easily led to cling to those kinds of knowledge and delights which the devil[3] is giving it, and withdraws itself from the solitude wherein God had placed it. For, it says, as it was doing nothing in that solitude and quiet of the faculties, this other state seems better, for now it is certainly doing something. It is a great pity that it cannot[4] realize how, for the sake of one mouthful—of some one delight or some particular kind of knowledge[5]—it is preventing itself from feeding wholly upon God Himself. This God effects in that solitude wherein He places the soul, for He absorbs it in Himself through these solitary and spiritual unctions.

64. In this way, with hardly any trouble, the devil works the gravest injuries, causing the soul to lose great riches, and dragging it forth like a fish, with the tiniest bait, from the depths of the pure waters of the spirit, where it had no support or foothold, but was engulfed and immersed in God. And hereupon he drags it to the bank, giving it help and support, and showing it something whereon it may lean, so that it may walk upon its own feet with great labour instead of floating in the waters of Siloe, that go with silence, bathed in the unctions of God. And to this the devil attaches such importance that it is a matter for great marvel; and, since a slight injury is more serious to a soul in this condition than is a serious injury to many other souls, as we have said,

---

[1] C: 'and particles.'   [2] Bg, P: 'to turn back.'
[3] Bz: 'the horned devil' [the adjective is depreciatory].
[4] Bz: 'that it thinks it was doing nothing and cannot.'
[5] Bg: 'of one mouthful and a particular delight.' P: 'of one mouthful of no such particular delight.'

there is hardly any soul walking on this road which does not meet with great injuries and suffer great losses. For the evil one takes his stand, with great cunning, on the road which leads from sense to spirit,[1] deceiving and luring the soul by means of sense, and giving it sensual things, as we have said.[2] And the soul thinks not that anything is being lost thereby, and therefore fails to enter into the innermost chamber of the Spouse, but stands at the door to see what is happening outside in the sensual part. The devil, as Job says, beholdeth every high thing[3] —that is to say, the spiritual high places of souls—that he may assault them. Therefore if perchance any soul enters into high recollection, since he cannot distract it in the way we have described, he labours so that he may at least be able to make it advert to sense[4] by means of horrors, fears or pains of the body, or by outward sounds[5] and noises, in order to bring it out and distract it from the interior spirit, until he can do no more and so leaves it. But with such ease does he corrupt these precious souls and squander their great riches, that, although he thinks this of greater importance than to bring about a heavy fall in many others, he esteems it not highly because of the facility with which it is done and the little effort that it costs him. In this sense we may understand that which God said to Job concerning the devil, namely: 'He shall drink up a river and shall not marvel, and he trusteth that the Jordan may run into his mouth—by the Jordan being understood the summit of perfection. In his eyes, as with a hook, shall he take him, and with stakes shall he bore his nostrils.'[6] That is, with the darts of the knowledge wherewith he is piercing the soul, he will disperse its spirituality; for the breath which goes out through his nostrils, when they are pierced, is dispersed in many directions. And later he says: 'The beams of the sun shall be under him and they shall scatter gold under him as mire.'[7] For he causes souls that have been enlightened to lose the marvellous rays of Divine knowledge, and from souls that are rich he takes away and scatters the precious gold of Divine adornment.

65. Oh, souls! Since God is showing you such sovereign mercies as to lead you through this state of solitude and recollection, withdrawing you from your labours of sense, return not to sense again.

---

[1] Bg, P add: 'as is his invariable custom, so that the soul may not pass from sense to spirit.'
[2] Bg follows the first redaction [p. 83, above] in this sentence.
[3] Job xli, 25.
[4] Bz, C: 'to cause it to be diverted to sense.'
[5] Thus Bg, P. The other MSS. [and P. Silverio] read 'senses.'
[6] Job xl, 18–19 [A.V., xl, 23–4].   [7] Job xli, 21 [A.V., xli, 30].

Lay aside your operations, for, though once, when you were beginners, they helped you to deny the world and yourselves, they will now be a great obstacle and hindrance to you, since God is granting you the grace of Himself working within you. If you are careful to set your faculties upon naught soever, withdrawing them from everything and in no way hindering them, which is the proper part for you to play in this state alone, and if you wait upon God with loving and pure attentiveness, as I said above, in the way which I there described (working no violence to the soul,[1] save to detach it from everything and set it free, lest you disturb and spoil its peace and tranquillity), God will feed your soul for you with heavenly food, since you are not hindering Him.

66. The third blind guide of the soul is the soul itself, which, not understanding itself, as we have said, becomes perturbed and does itself harm. For it knows not how to work save by means of sense and reasoning with the mind, and thus, when God is pleased to bring it into that emptiness and solitude where it can neither use its faculties nor make any acts, it sees that it is doing nothing, and strives to do something: in this way it becomes distracted and full of aridity and displeasure, whereas formerly it was rejoicing in the rest of the spiritual silence and peace wherein God was secretly exercising it.[2] And it may come to pass that God persists in keeping the soul in that silent tranquillity, while the soul also persists with its imagination and its understanding in trying to work by itself. In this it is like a child, whom its mother tries to carry in her arms, while it strikes out with its feet and cries out to be allowed to walk, and thus neither makes any progress nor allows its mother to do so. Or it is as when a painter is trying to paint a portrait and his subject keeps moving: either he will be unable to do anything at all or the picture will be spoiled.

67. The soul in this state of quiet must bear in mind that, although it may not be conscious of making any progress or of doing anything, it is making much more progress than if it were walking on its feet; for God is bearing it in His arms, and thus, although it is making progress at the rate willed by God Himself, it is not conscious of such movement. And although it is not working with its own faculties, it is nevertheless accomplishing much more than if it were doing so, since

---

[1] The MSS. show considerable divergences here, adding, as in the first redaction [p. 84, above], 'which must be when you have no desire to be attentive' (Bz). C, P omit 'no.' S [followed by P. Silverio]: 'which must be when you are not unwilling to not be attentive.' Bg reads similarly, but omits the second 'not,' thus reversing the sense.

[2] Bg, G: 'was secretly giving it joy' [*a gusto* for *a gesto*].

God is working within it. And it is not remarkable that the soul should be unable to see this, for sense cannot perceive that which God works in the soul at this time, since it is done in silence; for, as the Wise Man says, the words of wisdom are heard in silence. Let the soul leave itself in the hands of God and entrust itself neither to its own hands nor to those of these two blind guides[1]; for, if it remains thus and occupies not its faculties in anything, it will make sure progress.

68. Now let us return to the matter of these deep caverns of the faculties of the soul wherein we said that the suffering of the soul is wont to be great when God is anointing and preparing it with the most sublime[2] unctions of the Holy Spirit in order that He may unite it with Himself. These unctions are so subtle and so delicate in their anointing that they penetrate the inmost[3] substance of the depth[4] of the soul, preparing it and filling it with sweetness in such a way that its suffering and fainting with desire in the boundless emptiness of these caverns is likewise boundless. Here we must note this: if the unctions that were preparing these caverns of the soul for the union of the spiritual marriage with God are as sublime as we have said, what do we suppose will be the possession of intelligence, love and glory which understanding, will and memory attain in the said union with God? It is certain that, even as was the thirst and hunger which characterized these caverns, so now will be the satisfaction and fullness and delight thereof; and, as was the delicacy of the preparations, even so will be the wonder of the possession of the soul and the fruition of its sense.

69. By the sense of the soul is here understood the virtue and vigour that belong to the substance of the soul that it may perceive and have fruition of the objects of the spiritual faculties by means of which it tastes the wisdom and love and communication of God. Hence in this line the soul calls these three faculties—memory, understanding and will—the deep caverns of sense; for by means of them and in them the soul has a deep perception and experience of the grandeurs of the wisdom and the excellences of God. Wherefore it is with great propriety that the soul here calls them deep caverns, for, as it perceives that they are able to contain the deep intelligences and splendours of the lamps of fire, it realizes that they have capacity and depth as great as are the various things which they receive from the intelligences, the sweetnesses, the fruitions, the delights, and so forth, that come

---

[1] Gg: 'of the two other.'
[3] Bz, S: 'final.' P: 'infinite.'
[2] Bg, P: 'most subtle.'
[4] Bz: 'of the sense.'

from God. All these things are received and established in this sense of
the soul, which, as I say, is the soul's virtue and capacity for perceiving,
possessing and having pleasure in everything, and the caverns of the
faculties minister this to it, even as to the ordinary sense of the fancy
there flock the bodily senses, with the forms of their objects, and this
sense is the receptacle and storehouse for them. This common sense
of the soul, therefore, which has become a receptacle and store-house
for the grandeurs of God, is enlightened and made rich to the extent
that it attains this lofty and glorious possession.

Which were dark and blind

70. That is to say, before God enlightened them and made them
glorious. For the understanding of this it must be known that there
are two reasons for which the sense of sight may be unable to see:
either it may be in darkness or it may be blind. God is the light and the
object of the soul; when this light illumines it not, it is in darkness,
even though its power of vision may be most excellent. When it is in
sin, or when it employs its desires upon aught else, it is then blind;
and even though the light of God may then shine upon it, yet, because
it is blind, the light cannot be seen by the darkness of the soul, which
is the ignorance of the soul. Before God enlightened it through this
transformation, the soul was blind and ignorant concerning many
good things of God, even as the Wise Man says that he was blind
before Wisdom illumined him,[1] using these words: 'He illumined my
ignorance.'[2]

71. Speaking spiritually, it is one thing to be in darkness and another
to be in thick darkness; for to be in thick darkness is to be blind (as
we have said) in sin; but to be in darkness only is something that may
happen when one is not in sin. This may be in two ways: in the natural
sense, when the soul has no light from certain[3] natural things; and in
the supernatural sense, when it has no light from certain[4] supernatural
things; and with regard to both these things the soul here says that
its sense was dark before this precious union.[5] For until the Lord said:
Fiat lux, thick darkness was upon the face of the abyss of the cavern of
sense of the soul; and the deeper is this abyss and the more profound
are its caverns, the more abysmal and profound are the caverns and the
more profound is the thick darkness that is upon it with respect to the

---

[1] Bz: 'before [He] enlightened and illumined him.'
[2] Ecclesiasticus li, 26.   [3] Bg, P omit 'certain.'
[4] Bg, C, P omit 'certain.'   [5] C, S: 'precious unction.'

supernatural, when God, Who is its light, enlightens it not. And thus it is impossible for the soul to raise its eyes to the Divine light, or even to think of such light, for it knows not of what manner is this light, since it has never seen it; wherefore it cannot desire it, but will rather desire thick darkness, knowing what this is like; and it will go from one darkness to another, guided by that darkness, for darkness cannot lead to anything save to fresh darkness. Then, as David says: 'Day unto day uttereth speech, and night unto night showeth knowledge.'[1] And thus one abyss calls to another abyss; namely, an abyss of light calls to another abyss of light, and an abyss of thick darkness to another abyss of thick darkness; each like calls to its like and communicates itself to it. And thus the light of the grace that God had already given to this soul, wherewith He had enlightened the eye of the abyss of its spirit, opened it to the Divine light, and so made it pleasing to Himself, has called to another abyss of grace, which is this Divine transformation of the soul in God, whereby the eye of sense is so greatly enlightened and made pleasing to God that we may say that the light of God and that of the soul are both one, the natural light of the soul is united to the supernatural light of God and the supernatural light alone shines; even as the light created by God was united with that of the sun and the light of the sun alone now shines without the other failing.

72. And the soul was also blind inasmuch as it took pleasure in other things than God; for the blindness of the higher and rational sense is that desire which, like a cataract and a cloud, overlays and covers the eye of reason, so that the soul shall not see the things that are in front of it. And thus, for as long as the soul took any pleasure in sense, it was blind and could not see the great riches and Divine beauty[2] that were behind the cataract. For just as, if a man sets anything before his eyes, however small, this suffices to obstruct his sight so that he cannot see other things that are in front of him, however large they be, just so any small desire or idle act in the soul suffices to obstruct its vision of all these great and Divine things, which come after the pleasures and desires for which the soul longs.

73. Oh, that one might describe here how impossible it is for the soul that has other desires to judge of the things of God as they are! For, in order to judge the things of God,[3] the soul must cast out wholly from itself its own desire and pleasure and must not judge them

---

[1] Psalm xviii, 2 [A.V., xix, 2].
[2] Bg, P: 'the Divine riches and grandeurs.'
[3] Bz abbreviates: 'to obstruct its vision of all these great things of God as they are. For, in order to judge the things of God aright.'

together with Him; else it will infallibly come to consider the things of
God as though they were not of God and those that are not of God as
though they were of God. For, when that cataract and cloud of desire
covers the eye of judgment, the soul sees nothing but the cataract—
sometimes of one colour, sometimes of another, just as it may happen
to be; and the soul thinks that the cataract is God, for, as I say, it can
see nothing beyond the cataract, which covers the senses, and God cannot be apprehended by the senses. And in this way desire and the
pleasures of the senses hinder the soul from a knowledge of lofty
things. This the Wise Man well expresses, in these words, saying:
'The deceit of vanity[1] obscureth good things, and the inconstancy of
concupiscence transformeth the sense devoid of malice'—that is to say,
good judgment.[2]

74. Wherefore those persons who are not spiritual enough to be
purged of their desires and pleasures, but still to some extent follow
their animal nature with respect to these, may think much of the things
that are viler and baser to the spirit, which are those that come nearest
to the sensual condition according to which they still live, and they
will consider them to be of great importance; while those things that
are loftier and more greatly prized by the spirit, which are those that
are farthest withdrawn from sense, they will count of small importance
and will not esteem them, and sometimes will even consider them to be
folly, as Saint Paul well expresses it in these words: 'The animal man
perceiveth not the things of God; they are to him as foolishness and
he cannot understand them.'[3] By the animal man is here understood
the man that still lives according to natural desires and pleasures. For,
although certain pleasures of sense may be born in the spirit, yet, if a
man desires to cling to them with his natural desire, they are no more
than natural desires; it is of small importance that the motive or
object of this desire should be supernatural if the desire proceeds from
nature[4] and has its root and strength in nature; it does not cease to be
a natural desire, for it has the same substance and nature as if it related
to a natural matter and motive.

75. But you will say to me: 'It must follow, then, that, when the
soul desires God, it desires Him not supernaturally and therefore its
desire will not be meritorious in the sight of God.' I reply that it is true
that that desire of the soul for God is not always supernatural, but only

---

[1] C: 'of the will.'   [2] Wisdom iv, 12.
[3] 1 Corinthians ii, 14. S: 'and it is very difficult for him to understand them.'
[4] Bg, P: 'from a natural motive.'

when God infuses it, and Himself gives it its strength, and then it is
a very different thing from natural desire, and, until God infuses it, it
has little or no merit. When you, of your own accord, would fain
desire God, this is no more than a natural desire; nor will it be anything more until God be pleased to inform it supernaturally. And thus
when you, of your own accord, would fain attach your desire to
spiritual things[1], and when you would lay hold upon the pleasure of
them, you exercise your own natural desire, and are spreading a
cataract over your eye, and are an animal being.[2] And you cannot
therefore understand or judge of that which is spiritual, which is
higher than any natural desire and sense. And if you are still doubtful,
I know not what to say to you save to bid you read these words again,
and then perhaps you will understand them, for what I have said is
the substance of the truth, and I cannot possibly enlarge upon it here
any further.

76. This sense of the soul, then, which before was dark, without
this Divine light of God, and was blind, because of its desires and
affections, is now not only enlightened and bright in its deep caverns[3]
through this Divine union[4] with God, but has even become as it were
resplendent light in the caverns, which are its faculties.[5]

With strange brightness   Give heat and light together to their Beloved!

77. For, now that these caverns of the faculties are so wonderful,
and so marvellously[6] infused with the wondrous splendours of those
lamps, which, as we have said, are burning within them, they are sending back to God in God, over and above the surrender of themselves
which they are making to God, since they are illumined and enkindled
in God, those same splendours which the soul has received with loving
glory; they turn to God in God, and become themselves lamps enkindled in the splendours of the Divine lamps, giving to the Beloved
the same light and heat of love that they receive;[7] for in this state,
after the same manner as they receive, they are giving to Him that
receives and has given with the very brightness that He gives to them;
even as glass, when the sun strikes it, sends out splendours likewise;

---

[1] Bg, P: 'attach your desire to spiritual things and taste them.'
[2] S: 'and you do not cease to be an animal being.'
[3] C adds: 'of sense.'
[4] S: 'through this most high and Divine union.'
[5] Bg, P add: 'so much so, that they.'
[6] Bg, P: 'so wonderfully and marvellously.' Bz has 'greatly mortified' for 'wonderful.'
[7] Bg, P add: 'from Him.'

although the former is after a nobler manner, because the exercise of the will intervenes.

78. 'With strange brightness' signifies that the brightness is strange in a way that is far remote from all common thought and all description and every way and manner. For the brightness with which God visits the soul is like to the brightness wherewith the understanding receives Divine wisdom and is made one with the understanding of God; for one cannot give save in the way wherein is given to him. And like to the brightness wherewith the will is united in goodness[1] is the brightness wherewith the soul gives to God in God the same goodness; for the soul receives it only to give it again. In the same way, according to the brightness wherewith the soul has knowledge of the greatness of God, being united therewith, it shines and gives heat of love. According to the brightness of the other Divine attributes which are here communicated to the soul—fortitude, beauty, justice, etc.— are the manners of brightness wherewith the sense, having fruition, is giving to its Beloved, in its Beloved—that is to say, giving that same light and heat that it is receiving from its Beloved; for, since in this state it has been made one and the same thing with Him, it is after a certain manner God by participation; for, although this is not so as perfectly as in the next life, the soul is, as we have said, as it were a shadow of God. And in this way, since the soul, by means of this substantial transformation, is the shadow of God, it does in God and through God that which He does through Himself in the soul, in the same way as He does it; for the will of these two is one and thus the operation of God and that of the soul are one. Therefore, even as God is giving Himself to the soul with free and gracious will, even so likewise the soul, having a will that is the freer and the more generous in proportion as it has a greater degree of union with God, is giving God in God to God Himself, and thus the gift of the soul to God is true and entire. For in this state the soul sees that God truly belongs to it, and that it possesses Him with hereditary possession, with rightful ownership,[2] as an adopted child of God, through the grace that God gave to it, and it sees that, since He belongs to it, it may give and communicate Him to whomsoever it desires of its own will; and thus it gives Him to its Beloved, Who is the very God that gave Himself to it. And herein the soul pays God all that it owes Him; inasmuch as, of its own will, it gives as much as it has received of Him.

[1] C: 'united with the Divine will.'
[2] Bz: 'with rightful ownership and possession.'

79. And since, in making this gift to God, it gives it to the Holy Spirit, with voluntary surrender, as that which is His own, that He may be loved therein as He deserves, the soul has[1] inestimable delight and fruition, for it sees that it is giving to God that which is His own and which becomes Him according to His infinite Being. For, although it is true that the soul cannot give God Himself to Himself anew, since He in Himself is ever Himself, yet, in so far as the soul is itself concerned, it gives perfectly and truly, giving all that He had given to it, to pay the debt of love.[2] And this is to give as has been given to it, and God is repaid by that gift of the soul—yet with less than this He cannot be paid. And this He takes with gratitude, as something belonging to the soul that it gives to Him, and in that same gift He also loves the soul, as it were, anew,[3] and so at this time there is formed between God and the soul a reciprocal love in the agreement of the union and surrender of marriage, wherein the possessions of both, which are the Divine Being, are possessed by each one freely, by reason of the voluntary surrender of the one to the other, and are possessed likewise by both together, wherein each says to the other that which the Son of God said to the Father in Saint John, namely: *Omnia mea tua sunt, et tua mea sunt et clarificatus sum in eis.*[4] That is: All My possessions are Thine, and Thine are Mine, and I am glorified in them. In the next life this happens without any intermission in the perfect fruition thereof. But in this state of union this comes to pass when God brings about[5] this act of transformation in the soul, although not with the same perfection as in the life to come. And it is evident that the soul can make that gift,[6] although it is greater than its capacity and its being; for it is evident that one who possesses many peoples and kingdoms as his own, which are much greater in importance,[7] can give them to whom he desires.

80. This is the great satisfaction and contentment of the soul, to see that it is giving to God more than it is in itself and is in itself worth,[8] with that same Divine light[9] and Divine warmth which He gives to it;

---

1 Bg, P: 'has as it were.'
2 [*Lit.,* 'to pay the love.'] C, S: 'to gain the love.'
3 Bg: 'that it gives to Him, and in that surrender of God the soul also loves as it were anew, and He gives Himself freely to the soul anew and therein loves the soul.'
4 St. John xvii, 10.
5 Bg: 'when God excites.'
6 Bg, P: 'that so great gift.' [This text has *el*, not *al*, like that of the first redaction. Cf. p. 91, n. 8, above.]
7 Bg adds: 'than himself.'
8 Bg adds: 'giving God to Himself with such great liberality, as that which is its own.'
9 C: 'Divine light and brightness.'

this[1] comes to pass in the next life through the light of glory, and, in this life, through most enlightened faith. In this way, the deep caverns of sense, with strange brightness, give heat and light together to their Beloved. The soul says 'together,' because the communication of the Father and of the Son and of the Holy Spirit in the soul are made together, and are the light and fire of love in it.

81. But here we must make a brief observation on the brightness wherewith the soul makes this surrender. Concerning this it must be noted that, as the soul enjoys a certain image of fruition caused by the union of the understanding and the affection with God, being delighted and constrained by this great favour, it makes the surrender, of God and of itself, to God, in wondrous manners. For, with respect to love, the soul presents itself to God with strange brightness; and equally so with respect to this shadow of fruition; and likewise with respect to praise, and, in the same way, with respect to gratitude.

82. With regard to the first of these, the soul has three principal kinds of love which may be called brightnesses. The first is that the soul now loves God, not through itself, but through Himself; which is a wondrous brightness, since it loves through the Holy Spirit, even as the Father and the Son love One Another, as the Son Himself says, in Saint John: 'May the love wherewith Thou hast loved Me be in them and I in them.'[2] The second kind of brightness is to love God in God; for in this vehement union the soul is absorbed in the love of God and God surrenders Himself to the soul with great vehemence. The third kind of love which is brightness is that the soul here loves Him for Who He is; it loves Him not only because He is bountiful, good, glorious,[3] and so forth, with respect to itself, but much more earnestly, because He is all this in Himself essentially.

83. And with regard to this image of fruition there are also three other principal kinds of brightness, no less wonderful.[4] The first is that the soul in this state has fruition of God through God Himself, for, as the soul in this state unites understanding with omnipotence, wisdom, goodness, and so forth, albeit not so clearly as it will do in the next life, it delights greatly in all these things, understood distinctly, as we have said above. The second principal brightness belonging to this delight is that the soul delights itself duly in God alone, without any intermingling of creatures. The third delight is that it enjoys Him for Who He is alone, without any intermingling of its own pleasure.

---

[1] S: 'Divine warmth and solitude; this, etc.'   [2] St. John xvii, 26.
[3] Bg, C, P: 'good, glory.'   [4] S adds: 'and precious.'

84. With respect to the praise which the soul offers to God in this union, there are three kinds of brightness here also. First, the soul praises God as a duty, for it sees that He created it to offer Him praise, as He says through Isaias: 'I have formed this people for Myself; it shall sing My praises.'[1] The second kind of brightness of this praise comes from the blessings which the soul receives and the delight that it has in offering Him praise. The third is that it praises God for that which He is in Himself; even if to do so caused the soul no delight at all, it would still praise Him for Who He is.

85. With respect to gratitude, again, there are three kinds[2] of brightness. First, there is gratitude for the natural and spiritual blessings and the benefits which the soul has received. Secondly, there is the great delight which the soul has in praising[3] God, because it is absorbed with great vehemence in this praise. Thirdly, the soul praises God because of what He is, and this praise is much more profound and delectable.

STANZA IV

How gently and lovingly thou awakenest in my bosom,
    Where thou dwellest secretly and alone!
And in thy sweet breathing, full of blessing and glory, How
    delicately thou inspirest my love!

EXPOSITION

HERE the soul turns to its Spouse with great love, extolling Him and giving Him thanks for two wondrous effects which He sometimes produces within it by means of this union, noting likewise in what way He produces each and also the effect upon itself which in each case is the result thereof.

2. The first effect is the awakening of God in the soul, and the means whereby this is produced are those of gentleness and love. The second effect is the breathing of God in the soul and the means thereof are in the blessing and glory that are communicated to the soul in this breathing. And that which is produced thereby in the soul is a delicate and tender inspiration of love.

3. The stanza, then, has this meaning: Thine awakening, O Word

---

[1] Isaias xliii, 21.
[2] Bg, P: 'three principal kinds.'
[3] S: 'in loving.'

and Spouse, in the centre and depth of my soul, which is its pure and
inmost substance, wherein alone, secretly and in silence, Thou dwellest
as its only Lord, not only as in Thine own house, nor even as in Thine
own bed, but intimately and closely united as in mine own bosom—
how gentle and how loving is this![1] That is, it is exceedingly gentle and
loving; and in this delectable breathing which Thou makest in this
Thine awakening, delectable for me, filled as it is with blessing and
glory, with what delicacy dost Thou inspire me with love and affection
for Thyself! Herein the soul uses a similitude of the breathing of one
that awakens from his sleep; for in truth, the soul in this condition
feels it to be so. There follows the line:

How gently and lovingly thou awakenest in my bosom,

4. There are many ways in which God awakens in the soul: so many
that, if we had to begin to enumerate them, we should never end. But
this awakening of the Son of God which the soul here desires to
describe, is, as I believe, one of the loftiest and one which brings the
greatest good to the soul. For this awakening is a movement of the
Word in the substance of the soul, of such greatness and dominion
and glory, and of such intimate sweetness,[2] that it seems to the soul
that all the balms and perfumed spices and flowers in the world are
mingled and shaken and revolved together to give their sweetness;
and that all the kingdoms and dominions of the world and all the
powers[3] and virtues of Heaven are moved. And not only so, but all the
virtues and substances and perfections and graces of all created things
shine forth and make the same movement together and in unison. For,
as Saint John says,[4] all things in Him are life, and in Him they live and
are and move, as the Apostle says likewise.[5] Hence it comes to pass
that, when this great Emperor moves in the soul, Whose kingdom,
as Isaias says, is borne upon His shoulder[6] (namely, the three spheres,
the celestial, the terrestrial and the infernal, and the things that are in
them; and He sustains them all, as Saint Paul says, with the Word of
His virtue)[7] then all the spheres seem to move together. Just as, when
the earth moves, all material things that are upon it move likewise, as
if they were nothing, even so, when this Prince moves, He carries His
court with Him, and the court carries not Him.

---

[1] Bg, P: 'is this awakening!'
[2] Bz: 'such immense sweetness.' C: 'such great sweetness.'
[3] Bg, P: 'all the creatures, powers.'
[4] St. John i, 3.   [5] Acts xvii, 28.
[6] Isaias ix, 6.   [7] Hebrews i, 3.

5. Yet this comparison is highly unsuitable, for in this latter case not only do all seem to be moving, but they also reveal the beauties of their being, virtue, loveliness and graces, and the root of their duration[1] and life. For there the soul is able to see how all creatures, above and below, have their life and strength and duration in Him, and it sees clearly that which the Book of the Proverbs expresses in these words: 'By Me kings reign, by Me princes rule and the powerful exercise justice and understand it.'[2] And although it is true that the soul is now able to see that these things are distinct from God, inasmuch as they have a created being, and it sees them in Him, with their force, root and strength, it knows equally that God, in His own Being, is all these things, in an infinite and pre-eminent way,[3] to such a point that it understands them better in His Being than in themselves. And this is the great delight of this awakening: to know the creatures through God and not God through the creatures; to know the effects through their cause and not the cause through the effects; for the latter knowledge is secondary and this other is essential.

6. And the manner of this movement[4] in the soul, since God is immovable, is a wondrous thing, for, although in reality God moves not, it seems to the soul that He is indeed moving; for, as it is the soul that is renewed and moved[5] by God that it may behold this super-natural sight, and there is revealed to it in this great renewal that Divine life and the being and harmony of all creatures[6] in it which have their movements in God, it seems to the soul that it is God that is moving, and thus the cause takes the name of the effect which it produces, according to which effect we may say that God is moving, even as the Wise Man says: 'Wisdom is more movable than all movable things.'[7] And this is not because it moves itself, but because it is the beginning and root of all movement; remaining in itself stable, as the passage goes on to say, it renews all things. And thus what is here meant is that wisdom is more active than all active things. And thus we should say here that it is the soul that is moved in this motion, and is awakened from the sleep of its natural vision to a supernatural vision, for which reason it is very properly given the name of an awakening.

7. But God, as the soul is enabled to see, is always moving, ruling

[1] Bz: 'detraction.'   [2] Proverbs viii, 15.
[3] [*Lit.*, 'with infinite eminence.'] S: 'with infinite immensity.'
[4] Bz, C: 'knowledge.'   [5] Bz: 'is moved and guided.'
[6] Bg, P: 'of all things and creatures.'
[7] Wisdom vii, 24. Bz has 'causes' for 'things.'

and giving being and virtue and graces and gifts to all creatures, containing them all in Himself, virtually, presentially and substantially; so that in one single glance the soul sees that which God is in Himself and that which He is in His creatures. Even so, when a palace is thrown open, a man may see at one and the same time the eminence of the person who is within the palace and also what he is doing. And it is this, as I understand it, that happens upon this awakening and glance of the soul. Though the soul is substantially in God, as is every creature, He draws back from before it some of the veils and curtains which are in front of it, so that it may see of what nature He is; and then there is revealed to it, and it is able to see[1] (though somewhat darkly, since not all the veils are drawn back) that face of His that is full of graces. And, since it is moving all things by its power, there appears together with it that which it is doing, and it appears to move in them, and they in it, with continual movement; and for this reason the soul believes that God has moved and awakened, whereas in reality that which has moved and awakened is itself.

8. For such is the lowly nature of this kind of life which we live[2] that we believe others to be as we are ourselves; and we judge others as we are ourselves, so that our judgment proceeds from ourselves and begins with ourselves and not outside ourselves. In this way the thief believes that others steal likewise; and he that lusts, that others also are lustful like himself;[3] and he that bears malice, that others bear malice, his judgment proceeding from his own malice; and the good man thinks well of others, his judgment proceeding from the goodness of his own thoughts; and so likewise he that is negligent and slothful thinks that others are the same. And hence, when we are negligent and slothful in the sight of God, we think that it is God Who is slothful and negligent with us, as we read in the forty-third Psalm, where David says to God:[4] 'Arise, Lord, why sleepest Thou?'[5] He attributes to God qualities that are in man; for though it is they that are asleep and have fallen, yet it is God Whom he bids arise and awaken, though He that keepeth Israel never sleeps.

9. But in truth, though every blessing that comes to man is from God, and man, of his own power, can do naught that is good, it is true to say that our awakening is an awakening of God, and our uprising is an uprising of God. And thus it is as though David had said: Raise

---

[1] Bz: 'to descry.'
[3] S: 'that others are of his condition.'
[4] Bg adds: 'in our name.

[2] Bz: 'of our consideration.'

[5] Psalm xliii, 23 [A.V., xliv, 23].

us up and raise us up again[1] and awaken us, for we are asleep and we have fallen in two ways. Wherefore, since the soul had fallen into a sleep, whence of itself it could never awaken, and it is God alone that has been able to open its eyes and cause this awakening, it very properly describes it as an awakening of God, in these words: 'Thou awakenest in my bosom.' Do Thou awaken us, then, and enlighten us, my Lord, that we may know and love the blessings that Thou hast ever set before us, and we shall know that Thou hast been moved to grant us favours, and that Thou hast been mindful of us.

10. That which the soul knows and feels in this awakening concerning the excellence of God is wholly indescribable, for, since there is a communication of the excellence of God in the substance of the soul, which is that breast of the soul whereof the lines here speak, there is heard in the soul an immense power in the voice of a multitude of excellences, of thousands upon thousands[2] of virtues of God, which can never be numbered. In these the soul is entrenched and remains terribly and firmly arrayed among them like ranks of armies and made sweet and gracious in all the sweetnesses and graces of the creatures.

11. But this question will be raised: How can the soul bear so violent[3] a communication while in the weakness of the flesh, when indeed there is no means and strength in it to suffer so greatly without fainting away, since the mere sight of King Assuerus on his throne, in his royal apparel and adorned with gold and precious stones, caused Queen Esther such great fear when she saw how terrible he was to behold that she fainted away, as she confesses in that place where she says she fainted away by reason of the fear caused by his great glory, since he seemed to her like an angel and his face was full of grace.[4] For glory oppresses him that looks upon it if it glorifies him not. And how much more should the soul faint here, since it is no angel that it sees, but God, Whose face is full of graces of all the creatures and of terrible power and glory and Whose voice is the multitude of His excellences? Concerning this Job enquires, when we have such difficulty in hearing a spark, who shall be able to abide the greatness of His thunder.[5] And elsewhere he says: 'I will not that He contend and treat with me with much strength, lest perchance He oppress me with the weight of His greatness.'[6]

12. But the reason why the soul faints not away and fears not in this

---

[1] [Lit., 'Raise us up twice.']
[2] P, S: 'of thousands.' Bz: 'of millions upon thousands.'
[3] [Lit., 'so strong.']   [4] Esther xv, 16.
[5] Job xxvi, 14. P: 'of His face.'   [6] Job xxiii, 6.

awakening which is so powerful and glorious is twofold. First, being, as it now is, in the state of perfection, wherein its lower part is throughly purged and conformed with the spirit, it feels not the suffering and pain that are wont to be experienced in spiritual communications by spirit and sense when these are not purged and prepared to receive them; although this suffices not to prevent the soul from suffering when it is faced with such greatness and glory; since, although its nature be very pure, yet it will be corrupted because it exceeds nature, even as a physical faculty is corrupted by any sensible thing which exceeds its power, in which sense must be taken that which we quoted from Job. But the second reason is the more relevant: it is that which the soul gave in the first line—namely, that God shows Himself gentle.[1] For, just as God shows the soul greatness[2] and glory in order to comfort and magnify it, just so does He grant it grace so that it receives no suffering, and protect its nature, showing the spirit His greatness, with tenderness and love, without the natural senses perceiving this, so that the soul knows not if it is in the body or out of the body. This may easily be done by that God Who protected Moses with His right hand that he might see His glory. And thus the soul feels the gentleness and lovingness of God proportionately to His power and dominion and greatness, since in God all these things are one and the same. And thus the delight of the soul is strong, and the protection given to it is strong in gentleness and love, so that it may be able to endure the strength of this delight; and thus the soul, far from fainting away, becomes strong and powerful. For, when Esther swooned, this was because the King showed himself to her at first unfavourably; for, as we read in that place, he showed her his burning eyes and the fury of his breast. But when he looked favourably upon her, stretching out his sceptre[3] and touching her with it and embracing her, she returned to herself, for he had said to her that he was her brother and she was not to fear.

13. And thus, when the King of Heaven has shown Himself as a friend to the soul, as its equal and its brother, the soul is no longer afraid; for when, in gentleness and not in wrath, He shows to it the strength of His power and the love of His goodness, He communicates to it the strength and love of His breast, and comes out to it from the throne (which is the soul) even as a spouse from his bridal chamber where he was hidden. He inclines to the soul, touches it with the sceptre

---

[1] Bg adds: 'kind and loving.'   [2] Bg: 'this greatness.'
[3] Bz: 'his wand.'

of His majesty and embraces it as a brother. The soul beholds the royal apparel and perceives its fragrance—namely, the wondrous virtues of God; it observes the splendour of gold, which is charity; it sees the glittering of the precious stones, which are knowledge of created substances, both higher and lower; it looks upon the face of the Word, which is full of graces that strike this queen (which is the soul) and likewise clothe her, so that she may be transformed in these virtues of the King of Heaven and see herself a queen indeed, and thus she may say of herself truly that which David says in the Psalm, namely: 'The queen stood at Thy right hand in apparel of gold and surrounded with variety.'[1] And, since all this comes to pass in the inmost substance of the soul, it adds next:

Where thou dwellest secretly and alone!

14. The soul says that He dwells secretly in its breast, because, as we have said, this sweet embrace is made in the depth of the substance of the soul. That is to say that God dwells secretly in all souls and is hidden in their substance; for, were this not so, they would be unable to exist. But there is a difference between these two manners of dwelling, and a great one. For in some He dwells alone, and in others He dwells not alone; in some He dwells contented and in others He dwells displeased; in some He dwells as in His house, ordering it and ruling everything, while in others He dwells as a stranger in the house of another where He is not allowed to do anything or to give any commands. Where He dwells with the greatest content and most completely alone is in the soul wherein dwell fewest desires and pleasures of its own; here He is in His own house and rules and governs it. And the more completely alone does He dwell in the soul, the more secretly He dwells; and thus in this soul wherein dwells no desire, neither any other image or form or affection of aught that is created, the Beloved dwells most secretly, with more intimate, more interior and closer embrace, according as the soul, as we say, is the more purely and completely withdrawn from all save God. And thus He dwells secretly, since the devil cannot attain to this place and to this embrace, neither can the understanding of any man attain to a knowledge of the manner thereof. But He dwells not secretly with respect to the soul which is in this state of perfection, for it feels[2] this intimate embrace within it. Yet this is not always so, for, when the Beloved causes these awakenings to take place, it seems to the soul that He is

---

[1] Psalm xliv, 10.   [2] Bg: 'which ever feels.'

awakening in its bosom, where aforetime He was, as it were, sleeping; for, although it felt and enjoyed His presence, it experienced it as that of the Beloved asleep in its bosom;[1] and, when one of two persons is asleep, the understanding and love of them both are not mutually communicated, nor can they be until both have awakened.

15. Oh, how happy is this soul that is ever conscious of God resting and reposing within its breast! Oh, how well is it that it should withdraw from all things, flee from business and live in boundless tranquillity, lest anything, however small,[2] or the slightest turmoil, should disturb or turn away[3] the bosom of the Beloved within it. He is there, habitually, as it were, asleep in this embrace with the bride, in the substance of the soul; and of this the soul is quite conscious, and habitually has fruition of Him, for, if He were for ever awake[4] within it, communicating knowledge and love to it, it would be already living in glory. For, if one single awakening of God within the soul, and one glance from His eye, set it in such bliss, as we have said, what would its condition be if He were habitually within it and it were conscious of His being awake?[5]

16. In other souls, that have not attained to this union, He dwells secretly likewise; and He is not displeased, since after all they are in grace, though they are not yet perfectly prepared for union. Such souls are not as a rule conscious of His presence save when He effects certain delectable awakenings within them, but these are not of the same kind or quality as that other awakening, nor have they aught to do with it. This awakening is not so secret from the understanding, or from the devil, as that other,[6] for something can always be understood concerning it by means of the movements of sense, inasmuch as sense is not completely annihilated until the soul attains to union, but still preserves certain actions and movements pertaining to the spiritual element, for it is not yet absolutely and wholly spiritualized. But in this awakening which the Spouse effects in this perfect soul, everything that happens and is done is perfect; for it is He that is its sole cause. Thus it is as if [7] a man awakened and breathed; the soul is conscious of a rare delight in the breathing of the Holy Spirit in God, in Whom it

---

[1] Bz, C, S: 'the Beloved sleeping in slumber.'

[2] [*Lit.*, 'lest the very smallest speck,' a stronger expression than in the first redaction.] Bg, Bz read '[manifestation of] knowledge' [*noticia*] for 'speck' [*motica*]. P reads 'sign.'

[3] Bg: 'or move.'   [4] Bg: 'awakening.'

[5] [*Lit.*, 'within it, for it well awake.'] Bg, Bz: 'for it well prepared.'

[6] Bg, Bz, P have confused renderings of this passage. Bz also reads: 'the understanding of man,' and Bg, P: 'another's understanding.'

[7] Bg: 'And then that aspiration and awakening are as if.'

is glorified and enkindled in love. Therefore it utters the lines following:

And in thy sweet breathing, full of blessing and glory,   How delicately thou inspirest my love!

17. Of that breathing of God, which is full of blessing and glory and of the delicate love of God for the soul, I should not wish to speak, neither do I desire now to speak; for I see clearly that I cannot say aught concerning it, and that, were I to speak of it, it would not appear as great as it is.[1] For it is a breathing of God Himself into the soul, wherein, through that awakening of lofty knowledge of the Deity, the Holy Spirit breathes into the soul according to the understanding and knowledge which it has had of God, wherein He most profoundly absorbs it in the Holy Spirit, Who inspires it with Divine delicacy and glory, according to that which it has seen in God; for, His breathing being full of blessing and glory, the Holy Spirit has filled the soul with blessing and glory, wherein He has inspired it with love for Himself, which transcends all description and all sense, in the deep things of God, to Whom be[2] honour and glory. Amen.[3]

[1] So Bg, P. The other authorities [followed by P. Silverio] read: 'it would appear that it is.'

[2] Bg, P: 'be given.'

[3] So S. Bg, C, P: 'and glory *in sæcula sæculorum.* Amen.' Bz: 'and glory in the ages of the ages. Amen.' Bg, P add: '*Laus Deo.*'

END OF THE LIVING FLAME OF LOVE

CAUTIONS

INTRODUCTION

NONE of St. John of the Cross's admirers would contend that his minor prose writings, of which the *Cautions* is the first in order, have anything approaching the same value as the four great treatises by which he is chiefly remembered. They are but crumbs which have fallen from his table, and yet so well-furnished is that table and so genuine are they—so completely unified, in other words, is his teaching—that even those who are familiar with the great ascetico-mystical commentaries would deeply regret their loss.

The gift of St. John of the Cross for combining synthetic with analytic writing gives his minor prose works a character quite their own. He talked and wrote easily and fluently, it is true, but he evidently had a liking for condensed, maxim-like methods of expression: it will be remembered that St. Teresa dubbed him her 'little Seneca.' Probably a large proportion of these works have disappeared, for most of them were addressed to individuals—penitents of the author—and would naturally suffer the same fate as private letters. Some of the more impersonal, which are of fairly general application to those who lead the religious life, have escaped destruction, and one of the chief of these is that known briefly as *Cautions*.

More exactly, its title is 'Cautions which any who would be a true religious and would quickly attain to perfection must needs bear ever in mind.' It has nine sections, in which the religious is warned against man's three most fearful and deadly enemies—the world, the devil and the flesh. Being brief, they can easily be learned by heart and repeated in moments of leisure, perplexity or temptation. The words in the title 'attain to perfection' should be carefully noticed. Even in a short and purely ascetic treatise, the Saint has always in mind the goal of union with God.

The *Cautions* was one of the first of the Saint's writings to be composed when he retired to El Calvario and became regular confessor to the Discalced Carmelite nuns of Beas. In her depositions for the Beatification process made at Beas in 1618, Ana de Jesús, one of the first nuns of that convent and for some time the Saint's penitent, deposed that 'when he went away (from Beas), he left the nuns some cautions concerning the enemies of the soul and a few sentences for each one; and this witness has all those which he left her, with as many more as she could get, and she considers them to be of great value for her consolation.' Again, early in the seventeenth century, the diligent P. Alonso de la Madre de Dios wrote at the end of a description of the Saint's writings:

Other short spiritual treatises he composed, which have not yet been printed; among these, I have one containing nine cautions with which we may challenge the three enemies of the soul. These he wrote at the request of the Discalced nuns of Beas.[1]

There are other early testimonies to the authenticity of this opuscule, though, with certain others, it passed unmentioned by many witnesses who mention the *Ascent*, the *Dark Night*, the *Canticle* and the *Living Flame*.

Few early copies of the *Cautions* have survived: so slight a document was only too easily lost, though a multitude of copies of it must have been made, in view of that same brevity and the nature of its argument. It may be doubted if there were any Discalced friars and nuns who seriously aimed at spiritual progress and had not at some time handled a copy of this little treatise. But, as the printed editions of the Saint's works multiplied, the necessity for these copies grew less and in mid-eighteenth century P. Andrés discovered only a few, and those chiefly in Andalusia.[2] In them he found a considerable number of textual variants, which he attributes partly to revisions by St. John of the Cross himself, since, as he says, not all of them can very well be copyists' errors and there was less scope for correction in that type of treatise. This is quite possible, as we know that the Saint revised the brief 'Mount of Perfection' as well as the extensive *Spiritual Canticle* and *Living Flame*. Still, into generations of copies made at second, third or fourth hand, it is not surprising if there crept innumerable errors of all kinds and it is impossible to do more than speculate on their origin and nature.

The *Cautions* was not included in the *editio princeps* of 1618, nor, although he certainly knew it and mentioned it in his *History* (Bk. IV, chap. viii), did Fray Jerónimo de San José publish it in his edition of 1630. It first appeared in a Latin translation of St. John of the Cross's

---

[1] MS. 13,460, Bk. II, chap. viii.   [2] MSS. 3,653, 6,296, N.L.M.

works which was published at Cologne in 1639. [The first Spanish edition seems to have been published at Gerona, by P. Jerónimo de la Asunción, in 1650.] In 1667, another edition was published by P. Esteban de San José together with some of the *Maxims*. The first collected Spanish edition in which it appeared was that of Barcelona, 1693; here it bore the title 'Instruction and Caution which any man who would be a true religious and would quickly attain to great perfection must ever bear in mind.'

Of the few early copies of the opuscule which are still extant, the best is certainly MS. 6,296, which comes down to us from P. Andrés de la Encarnación and which we follow in this edition as did P. Gerardo also in that of 1912.[1]

[1] [P. Sobrino, in his *Estudios sobre San Juan de la Cruz*, etc. (see p. 240, n. 1, below), gives a critical edition of the *Cautions* on the basis of the Tardón-Granada MS. (here abbreviated TG), and studying in detail the whole question of transmission. His conclusion is that TG and 6,296 are the most reliable MSS. and should jointly form the basis of any future critical Spanish edition, occasionally corrected by 7,741 and 12,398. In the text which follows, such variants from TG as are not mere slips and can be shown in translation have been given in footnotes.]

CAUTIONS

which any who would be a true religious and would quickly attain to perfection must needs bear ever in mind. Addressed to the Carmelite Nuns of Beas.[1]

THE religious who desires to attain quickly to holy recollection, silence, spiritual detachment and poverty of spirit,[2] wherein is enjoyed the peaceful refreshment of the Holy Spirit and whereby the soul attains to union with God, and frees itself from[3] the hindrances which come from all the creatures of this world, and defends itself from the wiles and deceits of the devil, and is disencumbered of itself,[4] must needs practise the following instructions.

2. With habitual care and with no further labour or other kind of exercise, failing not of his own part to do that which his state enjoins on him, he will very quickly come to great perfection, gaining all the virtues together and attaining to holy peace.[5]

3. To this end it must first be noted that[6] the evils which the soul receives come from the enemies aforementioned[7]—namely, the world, the devil and the flesh. The world is the least difficult enemy. The devil is the hardest to understand. The flesh is the most tenacious of all and its assaults continue for so long as the old man exists.

4. In order to conquer any one of these three enemies, it is necessary to conquer them all three; and, if one is weakened, the other two are weakened: and, when all three are conquered, no more war remains in the soul.

AGAINST THE WORLD

5. In order to free thyself perfectly from the evil which the world can do to thee, thou shalt use three cautions.

---

[1] This title appears in many old editions and we see no reason to change it. The MSS. vary greatly here in form, though they agree in substance. In MS. 7,741 the title reads: 'Spiritual Cautions which must be used by the true religious against the enemies of the soul, by our blessed Father Fray John of the Cross.' [TG reads: 'Nine Cautions to be used against three enemies of the soul, taught by the holy Father Fray John of the Cross.']
[2] [TG: 'and spiritual poverty.']   [3] [TG: 'from all.']
[4] [TG: 'is freed from itself.']
[5] This paragraph is lacking in MS. 7,741, [TG] and a number of other copies.
[6] [TG: 'that all.']   [7] [TG: 'enemies of the soul.']

Caution the First

6. The first caution is that for all persons thou shalt have equal love and equal forgetfulness, whether they be thy relatives or no, withdrawing thy heart from these as much as from those; more so, indeed, in some ways, from thy kinsmen, lest flesh and blood quicken with natural love, which is ever alive among kinsfolk, the which thou must ever mortify for the sake of spiritual perfection. Hold them all as strangers to thee; in this way thou dost serve them better than by setting upon them the affection which thou owest to God. Love not one person better than another or thou shalt go astray, for he whom God loves best is worthy to be loved best, and thou knowest not who it is that God best[1] loveth. But if thou art equally forgetful of them all,[2] as befits thee for holy recollection, thou shalt free thyself from going astray as regards the greater or lesser degree of love due to each. Think not of them at all, be they good things or evil things; flee from them in so far as thou fairly[3] canst. And, if thou observe not this, thou hast not learned to be a religious, neither shalt be able to attain to holy recollection, nor to free thyself from the imperfections that come to thee hereby. And if in this matter thou desire to allow thyself[4] a certain licence, the devil will deceive thee in one way or in another, or thou wilt deceive thyself, under some colour of good or of evil. In doing that which has been described lies security, for in no other way canst thou free thyself from the imperfections and evils which the soul obtains from creatures.

Caution the Second

7. The second caution against the world is with respect to temporal good things. Herein it is needful, if thou wouldst truly free thyself from this kind of evil and moderate the excesses of thine appetite, to abhor all kinds of possession and to have no care for them—neither as to food, nor clothing, nor any other created thing,[5] nor as to the morrow. Thou must direct this care to something higher, namely, to seeking the kingdom of God—that is, to not failing God—and the rest, as His Majesty says, shall be added unto us.[6] For He that cares for

[1] 6,296 [and TG] omit 'best,' which, however, is found in 7,741 and 12,398.
[2] 7,741: 'But, if thou treat them all equally.'
[3] 7,741: 'as thou humanly.'   [4] 7,741: 'to keep for thyself.'
[5] [TG reads: 'any other higher created thing,' and continues 'which is seeking the kingdom, etc.' This would appear to be a scribal error.]
[6] [St. Matthew vi, 33.]

the beasts will not be forgetful of thee. In this way shalt thou attain silence and peace in the senses.

CAUTION THE THIRD

8. The third caution is very necessary if thou art to learn to guard thyself in the convent from all evil with respect to the religious. Many, through not observing it, have not only lost the peace and blessing of their souls, but have fallen, and habitually fall, into many evils and sins. This caution is that thou shouldst keep thyself with all diligence from setting thy thoughts upon what happens in the community, and still more from speaking of it; which may concern, or may have concerned, some religious in particular: thou shalt not speak of his character, or of his manner of life, or of any of his business, however grave it be, either under pretext of zeal or of desire to remedy matters, save to that person to whom it is right that thou shouldst speak of it at the appointed time. Nor shouldst thou ever be shocked or marvel at aught that thou seest or hearest, but shouldst strive to keep thy soul in forgetfulness of it all.

9. For if thou desirest to consider any of these things, even though thou live among angels,[1] many things in them will seem to thee to be amiss, since thou wilt not understand the substance of them. Take thou here for an example Lot's wife, who, because she was troubled at the perdition of the Sodomites and looked backward to see what was happening, was punished by God, who turned her into a statue of salt.[2] By this understand that, even though thou live among devils, God wills thee to live among them in such a way that thou look not back[3] in thy thought at their business, but abandon them wholly,[4] striving to keep thy soul pure and sincere with God, undisturbed by thoughts either of one thing or of another. Thou mayest take it for certain that convents and communities will never be without some occasion of stumbling, since there are never wanting devils who strive to overthrow the saints, and God permits this in order to exercise them and prove them. And if thou keep not thyself, as has been said, as though thou wert not in the house, thou canst never be a religious,[5] however

---

[1] 7,741 omits: 'even . . . angels.'
[2] [Genesis xix, 26. A.V. has: 'pillar of salt.' TG reads: 'by the Lord.']
[3] 7,741: 'God wills that, although thou live among them, thou look not back.' 12,398: 'and looked backward, the Lord punished her by turning her into a statue and stone of salt. By this understand that, etc.'
[4] [TG omits: 'wholly.']
[5] The editions read: 'never truly be a religious.'

much thou doest, nor attain to holy detachment and recollection, nor free thyself from the evils that lie herein. For, if thou do not this, however good may be thy aim and however great thy zeal, the devil will entrap thee either in one place or in another, and thou art already securely entrapped when thou dost permit thy soul to be distracted in any of these ways. Remember that which is said by the apostle Saint James: 'If any man thinketh himself to be religious, bridling not his tongue, this man's religion is vain.'[1] This is to be understood no less of inward speech than of outward.

AGAINST THE DEVIL

10. These three cautions should be used by him that aspires to perfection, in order that he may free himself from the devil, his second enemy. To this end it must be noted[2] that, among the many wiles[3] used by the devil to deceive spiritual persons, the most ordinary is that of deceiving them under an appearance of what is good and not under an appearance of what is evil;[4] for he knows that if they recognize evil they will hardly touch it. And thus thou must ever have misgivings concerning that which seems good, when it is not commanded thee by obedience. Security and success in this matter come[5] from taking proper counsel in it.

CAUTION THE FIRST

11. Let the first caution, then, be that, save when thou art so commanded by obligation, thou be moved to nothing, however good and full of charity it may seem, whether it be for thyself or for anyone within or without the house, without being ordered by obedience. In observing this thou gainest merit and security.[6] Avoid attachment[7] and thou shalt flee[8] from the devil and from evils of which thou knowest not, but whereof God shall call for an account of thee in His time. And if thou observe not this caution, both in little things and in great, however successful thou seem to be, thou canst not fail, either to a small or to a great degree, to be deceived by the devil. And, although thou do no worse than fail to be ruled in all things by

[1] St. James i, 26.   [2] [TG reads: 'thou must note.']
[3] So 12,398. The other authorities [and P. Silverio] read: 'the many cautions.'
[4] 7,741: 'and not of evil.'   [5] 12,398: 'Sanity in this matter comes.'
[6] [TG omits: 'and security.']
[7] [Propiedad: a difficult word to translate without paraphrasing. It means 'proprietorship,' 'sense of ownership,' 'sense of control'—the 'propriety' of Fr. Augustine Baker.]
[8] 7,741, 12,398, [TG]: 'and thou fleest.'

obedience, thou strayest and art to be blamed; for God prefers obedience to sacrifice, and the actions of a religious are not his own but belong to obedience, and if thou withdraw them from obedience, thou wilt have to account them as lost.

Caution the Second

12. Let the second caution be that thou never consider thy superior as less than if he were God, be the superior who he may, for to thee he stands in the place of God. And observe that the devil, the enemy of humility,[1] meddles herein greatly. If thou consider thy superior in the way that has been said,[2] thou gainest and profitest greatly; if otherwise, thy loss and harm are great. Keep thyself, therefore, with great vigilance from considering his character, his ways or his habits or any of his other characteristics, for, if thou do this, thou wilt do thyself the harm of exchanging Divine obedience for human, by being moved, or unmoved, only by the visible characteristics of thy superior, instead of by the invisible God Whom thou servest in his person. And thy obedience will be vain, or will be the more unfruitful, if thou take offence at any unpleasing characteristic in thy superior, or rejoice when thou findest him good and pleasant. For I tell thee the devil has ruined the perfection of a great multitude of religious by causing them to consider these characteristics, and their obedience is of very little worth in the eyes of God, because they have considered these things and not paid sole respect to obedience. If thou strive not until thou come to regard it as indifferent to thee, in so far as thine own feelings are concerned, whether this one or that be thy superior, thou canst in no wise become a spiritual person nor keep thy vows well.

Caution the Third

13. The third caution aimed directly against the devil is that thou strive ever to humble thy heart[3] in word and in deed, rejoicing at the good of others as at thine own, and desiring that others be preferred to thyself in all things, and this with all thy heart. And in this way shalt thou overcome evil with good and shalt cast the devil far from thee and shalt have joy of heart; and strive thou to practise this most with respect to those who least attract thee. And know that, if thou practise

---

[1] 12,398 omits: 'the enemy of humility.'
[2] [TG: 'thy superior thus.']
[3] The editions add 'in thought.'

it not thus, thou shalt not attain to true charity neither shalt make progress therein. And love[1] ever to be taught by all men rather than to desire to teach him that is least of all.

AGAINST THE FLESH

14. Three further cautions should be observed by him that desires to conquer himself and his sensual nature, which is his third enemy.

CAUTION THE FIRST

15. The first caution is that thou shouldst understand that thou hast come to the convent only that all may fashion thee and try thee. And thus, in order to free thyself from the imperfections and disturbances that may arise from the temperaments and habits of the religious, and to pluck advantage from every happening, thou must think that all who are in the convent are workmen who are to try thee, as in truth they are. For some have to fashion thee by word, others by deed and others by their thoughts against thee; and thou must be subject to them in all things, even as an image is subject to him that fashions it and to him that paints it and to him that gilds it. And, if thou observe not this, thou shalt not be able to overcome thy sensual nature and thy feelings, neither shalt thou be able to conduct thyself well in the convent with the religious, nor shalt attain holy peace nor free thyself from many evils and occasions of stumbling.

CAUTION THE SECOND

16. The second caution is that thou never fail to perform any good works because of the lack of pleasure or sweetness that thou findest therein, if it be fitting that they should be done in the service of Our Lord[2]; neither perform thou them only for the sweetness and pleasure that they give thee. It behoves thee equally to perform these and others that are distasteful to thee; otherwise it is impossible for thee to gain constancy and overcome thy weakness.

CAUTION THE THIRD

17. Let the third caution be that the spiritual man must never in his exercises set his eyes upon that which is delectable in them and

---

[1] [TG: 'And contrive to love.']   [2] [TG: 'of God.']

thence derive attachment to them, and perform them for this reason only; neither must he flee from that which is displeasing to him in them, but rather he must seek that which is toilsome and distasteful.[1] In this way he bridles his sensual nature; and if thou do otherwise thou wilt neither lose the love of thyself, nor wilt win and attain the love of God.

[1] Some MSS. and editions add here: 'and embrace it.'

COUNSELS TO A RELIGIOUS FOR THE ATTAINMENT OF PERFECTION

INTRODUCTION

THIS instruction, addressed by St. John of the Cross to a religious of his own Order who had asked him for advice on the attainment of progress in the religious life, is very similar, both in content and in form, to the *Cautions*. We have no information as to who this religious was, except that he was not a priest, since the recipient of the instruction is addressed as 'Your Charity' whereas a priest was styled 'Your Reverence.'

The feature of this opuscule is the Saint's insistence that the religious should take no part in affairs, even in those of the community, unless they concern his office or he is commanded to attend to them under his vow of obedience. The perfect religious lives in the monastery as though he were alone in it. This is the central counsel of the four which St. John of the Cross gives in this instruction. Like St. Teresa, he was clearly quite convinced that the practice made for spiritual efficiency and progress.

These *Counsels* were published for the first time only in the Toledo edition of 1912, but they are undoubtedly genuine. There is an early copy in the Convent of the Discalced Carmelite nuns at Bujalance, which was formerly an heirloom in the family of a Commissary of the Inquisition named Don Miguel de Porcuna. Though it bears an inscription in another hand: 'Maxims of our father Fray John of the Cross and his writing,' it is certainly not an autograph, as P. Andrés de la Encarnación discovered two centuries ago;[1] still, as we doubtless owe its careful preservation to the pious belief to the contrary, we have no cause to regret this.

There is a second copy of the *Counsels* in an early Baeza manuscript of which P. Andrés has left a description.[2]

---

[1] 'Having examined this copy with the greatest attention,' wrote P. Andrés in a brief report that has been preserved with it, 'I say first of all that this opuscule is indisputably by our mystical doctor and father St. John of the Cross . . . and secondly that the hand is not his.'   [2] MS. 6,296: Papeles de Baeza.

COUNSELS TO A RELIGIOUS FOR THE ATTAINMENT OF PERFECTION[1]

IN a few words, your Holy Charity has asked a great deal of me, for which much time and paper would be necessary. As I find myself with neither of these things, I will endeavour to be compendious, and to set down only certain points or maxims which contain much in a small space and will lead anyone who observes them perfectly to achieve great perfection. He that would be a true religious and fulfil the duties of the state to which he has vowed before God to conform, and make progress in the virtues and enjoy the consolations and sweetness of the Holy Spirit, will be unable to do this if he strive not with the greatest care to put into practice the four maxims following, which are: resignation, mortification, the practice of virtues and solitude of body and of spirit.

2. In order to observe the first of these—resignation—he must needs live in the monastery as if no other person lived there; and thus he should never intermeddle, either in word or in thought, with the things that happen in the community, nor with those of individuals, nor must he take note of anything concerning them, be it good or evil, nor of their personal qualities. And, even though the world come to an end, he must neither remark upon them nor intermeddle with them, in order to preserve his tranquillity of soul, remembering Lot's wife, who, because she turned her head on account of the cries and the noise made by those that were perishing, was turned into hard stone.[2] This the religious must observe very straitly, and he will then free himself by its means from many sins and imperfections, and will preserve his tranquillity and quietness of soul, and will make great progress in the sight of God, and in that of men. And let great attention be paid to this, for it is of such importance that many religious, through not observing it, have not only never profited by the other works of virtue and religion that they have performed, but have continually fallen away and gone from bad to worse.

---

[1] This opuscule is published according to the Codex of Bujalance. In reality it has no title, except in the editions. The MS. begins with the words, *Jesus Mariae Filius*, which were undoubtedly not written by the Saint.   [2] [Genesis xix, 26. Cf. p. 201, above.]

3. In order to put into practice the second thing—mortification—and to make progress therein, the religious must very truly set in his heart this truth: that he has come to the convent only that he may be fashioned and tried in virtue, and that he is like the stone which has to be polished and fashioned before it can be set in the building. And so he must realize that all who are in the convent are no more than workmen whom God has set there solely that they may fashion and polish him as regards mortification. Some have to fashion him in word, telling him that which he would fain not hear; others in deed, doing in his despite things which he would fain not endure; others in character, being tiresome and troublesome to him both in themselves and in their behaviour; others in thought, so that he feels or thinks that they esteem him not and love him not; and all these mortifications and annoyances he must endure with inward patience, keeping silence for the love of God and realizing that he entered upon the religious life for no other reason than that he might be thus fashioned and made worthy of Heaven. And, if he entered it not with that intent, there was no reason why he should have done so; he should rather have remained in the world, seeking his own comfort, honour, credit and ease.

4. And this second maxim is absolutely necessary for the religious in order that he may fulfil the duties of his state and find true humility, interior quiet and joy in the Holy Spirit. And if he puts it not into practice, nor learns how to be a religious, or even the reason for which he entered the religious life, neither learns to seek Christ, but seeks only himself, he will neither find peace in his soul nor will he fail to sin and to be oftentimes troubled. For occasions of these failings will never be wanting in the religious life, nor would God have them wanting, for, since He brings souls into this life in order to prove and purify them, as gold is purified with fire and hammer, it is meet that there be not wanting trials and temptations of men and of devils, the fire of troubles and afflictions. In these things must the religious exercise himself, endeavouring always to bear them with patience and conformity with the will of God, and not in such a way that, instead of approving him[1] in his time of trial, God will have to reprove him for not having been willing to bear the cross of Christ with patience. Many religious, not realizing that they have entered the religious life for this purpose, endure others with difficulty, and such, when they come to their account, shall find themselves put to great shame and confusion.

[1] The Bujalance MS. has: 'instead of causing him to profit.'

5. In order to put into practice the third counsel, which is the exercise of virtues, the religious must needs have constancy in practising the acts of his religious life and of obedience, without any respect to the world, but for God's sake alone. In order that he may do so in this way, and without being deceived, let him never consider the pleasure or the displeasure which he finds in the work, in doing it or refraining from doing it, but only the reason which he has for doing it for God's sake. And so he must do all things, whether delectable or distasteful, with this sole aim of serving God thereby.

6. And in order to put this into practice determinedly, and with this constancy, and to bring forth the virtues speedily, let him ever have a care to incline himself rather to that which is difficult than to that which is easy, to that which is rough rather than to that which is smooth, and to the grievous and distasteful part of his work rather than to that which is delectable and pleasant in it. Let him not go about selecting that which is but a light cross, for that is an unworthy burden; and the greater the burden, the lighter is it, if borne for God. Let him ever strive likewise that his brothers be preferred to him in all comforts, and set himself ever in the lowest place, and this with a right good will. For this is the way to become great in spirituality, as God tells us in His Gospel: *Qui se humiliat exaltabitur.*[1]

7. To put into practice the fourth counsel, which is solitude, the religious must needs consider all the things of the world as ended, so that, when against his will he is obliged to engage in them, he may do so with as great detachment as if they were not.

8. And let him take no account of things without, since God has withdrawn him from them and led him to neglect them. Let him not do any business himself that he can do by means of a third person, for it greatly behoves him to desire to see nobody and to be seen of none. And let him carefully consider that if God will exact from any one of the faithful a strict account of any idle word, how much more will He not exact an account of every such word, on the day of reckoning, from a religious, whose whole life and works are consecrated to God?

9. I mean not by this that a religious should fail to perform the office which he holds, or any other that is required of him by his obedience, with all necessary and possible solicitude; he must do this in such a way that none can attach any blame to him, which neither God nor obedience demands. To this end let him endeavour to be instant in prayer, which he must not abandon even amidst the exercises

[1] St. Luke xiv, 11.

of the body. Whether he be eating or drinking or speaking or conversing with persons in the world, or whatsoever else he be doing, let him ever be desiring God and having his heart affectioned to Him, for this is a thing most necessary for interior solitude, which demands that the soul let fall no thought that is not directed toward God and that he forget all things which belong to this short and miserable life and which pass away. In no wise let him seek to know aught, save how he may the better serve God and keep His ordinances the more faithfully.

10. If your Charity observe these four things with care, you will very quickly attain perfection, for they are of such mutual assistance to each other that, if a man come short in one of them, he loses thereby that wherein he was gaining and making progress with respect to the rest.

211   SPIRITUAL SENTENCES AND MAXIMS

SPIRITUAL SENTENCES AND MAXIMS

INTRODUCTION

A S we said in the introduction to our first volume, we know from
the testimony of Ana María de Jesús, a nun of the Convent of
the Incarnation at Ávila and one of the Saint's most beloved
spiritual daughters, that St. John of the Cross was accustomed to give
his penitents manuscript notes or 'papers' containing spiritual maxims
and that M. Ana María had herself received a number of these.[1] Since
his penitents in that Convent were numerous and he acted as director
there for five years, he must have written a very large number of such
'papers' and to them must be added many more written for religious
in Beas, Granada, Segovia and other convents and for persons living in
the world.

Had we the whole of this material, it might well be unique both in
size and in value, but there is no reason to think that any early collection of it was ever attempted, and the persecution of St. John of the
Cross shortly before his death probably led many to whom he had
addressed such 'papers' to destroy them. When, early in the seventeenth century, P. Alonso de la Madre de Dios visited all the Andalusian convents of the Reform previously to the Beatification process,
he found vestiges here and there of the spiritual wealth which the Saint
had bequeathed, as it were, to posterity, especially, as we should
expect, at Beas. P. Alonso himself writes concerning this:

When the man of God left the convent of Beas to return to his own at
El Calvario, he would leave each nun a sentence concerning virtue of the
kind which he knew would be of the greatest profit to her, so that they might
read them and be enkindled with fervour. So much did they esteem these
that, even after many years had passed, I saw they still kept collections of
them. Each time, when he returned to his convent, these nuns would tell him
how much they missed his teaching. 'If I do not come back,' he would
answer, 'imitate the sheep, and ruminate on what I have taught you while I
have been here.' And this they did, meditating on what they had heard and

[1] Vol. I, p. xxix.

reading his sentences from his little papers; and when he came back, he would
ask them to give him an account of the profit they had derived from them.[1]

This testimony of P. Alonso's confirms the slightly earlier evidence
of one of the Saint's Beas penitents, M. Magdalena del Espíritu Santo:[2]

In order to awaken fervour in the nuns, and to instruct them in true
spirituality and the practice of the virtues, he would ask them certain
questions, and discuss their answers to them, so that their time was well
spent and they profited by it, for his words were bathed in light from Heaven.
I contrived to note down some of these (questions and answers) so as to
refresh myself by reading them when he was absent and could not discuss
them. . . . When occasion offered, our venerable father wrote letters to the
nuns of Beas—both sisters and superiors—which contained maxims and
instructions of great importance.

One must not suppose that M. Magdalena was the only one of St.
John of the Cross's penitents to make a collection of his spiritual
maxims and notes of his informal instructions. It was a general custom
to do this, and we know from the beatification and canonization
processes that many collections of the kind were then in circulation.
But there were others made by the Saint himself, one of which is
extant, though in an incomplete form. We refer to the well-known
Andújar MS., of which both P. Gerardo and M. Baruzi have published editions,[3] and which is the most extensive autograph of St. John
of the Cross whose authenticity is not disputed. The other extant
autographs are letters, annotations like that of the Sanlúcar Codex and
official documents. P. Andrés de la Encarnación has left on record two
statements as to the genuineness of this manuscript, dated January 19
and 20, 1760. The case which he puts forward, however, is universally
admitted and there is no need to spend time in proving it, the more so
as specimens of the Saint's hand are readily available for comparison
with the published reproductions, or the original, of the Andújar MS.

THE ANDÚJAR MANUSCRIPT

The history of this important document is somewhat obscure. An
early manuscript belonging to the Discalced Carmelite friars of Burgos

---

[1] MS. 13,460 (N.L.M.), Bk. I, chap. xxxvii.
[2] [Cf. Vol. I, pp. xxx–xxxii.]
[3] *Autógrafos que se conservan del Místico Doctor San Juan de la Cruz;* Edición fototípica
Toledo, 1913. *Aphorismes de Saint Jean de la Croix*, Paris, 1924.

contains a literal copy of the Andújar *Maxims* beginning: 'This treatise was given by our father Fray John of the Cross to M. Francisca de la Madre de Dios, nun of Beas.' The statement may quite possibly be correct. M. Francisca, whose testimony of 1618 we have already quoted,[1] was one of the Saint's penitents at Beas and the testimony continues thus:

... There was in his breast a great love of God; and his words, and even the papers and sentences that he wrote enkindled the souls of his hearers in Divine love and made them the more fervent. And the same effect has been experienced by this witness in herself. When she has found (and still finds) herself lukewarm, she has but to read some of these papers of his to become quite different.

Clearly the 'papers' and 'sentences' may perfectly well be those of the Andújar manuscript.

This came into the possession of the Convent of the Reform at Andújar, which was founded in 1590, and thence, probably as a gift, into that of a noble family, which owned the castle of Andújar, named Piédrola. It was here that P. Andrés saw it in 1760, when he was asked to examine it and pronounce judgment on its authenticity as an autograph. His judgment being favourable, the manuscript was even more carefully preserved than before, until in 1918, after an accident had all but resulted in its being destroyed by fire, it was presented by the family to the church of Santa María la Mayor, Andújar, where it can now be seen.

The manuscript lacks the short preface which we find in the Burgos copy (p. 214, below) and which it undoubtedly also possessed until the single folio containing it became lost. This preface describes the object of these 'sayings of light and love': they will be 'of discretion for the journeyer, of light for the journey and of love for the journeying.' There is no 'worldly rhetoric' in them, no 'loquacity and arid eloquence'; they 'speak words to the heart, bathed in sweetness and love' in which God takes pleasure. This is the precise truth. The maxims are simple and unadorned, and, though they have the link and the unity of the Christian perfection to which they point the reader, they can quite well be disconnected one from another, or their order can be changed without any great violence being done to them. They hold no secret of the spiritual life, and initiate us into no ethical experience, with which the Saint's longer treatises have not familiarized

---

[1] [Cf. Vol. I, p. xxxiii.]

us. Their nature precludes them from developing any idea at length and in any case they are ascetic rather than mystical, and the full meaning of many of them can best be appreciated if we relate them with passages from the mystical treatises with which they have doctrinal affinity.

The twenty-fifth maxim is followed by what the Saint himself terms a 'prayer of the soul enkindled with love,' which, amid the inevitable aridity of the apothegms, forms a kind of literary oasis. In it St. John of the Cross pours out his soul in acts of the sincerest humility and deepest love; after this he returns to the ascetic life and takes up the maxim form again until the end of the opuscule. It is unnecessary here to summarize his teaching, so brief and so easily comprehended are the maxims themselves. Nor need we ask, with M. Baruzi, for whom they are intended. St. John of the Cross is primarily addressing his fellow-Carmelites, but also, in a secondary sense, all Christians who wish to make progress in virtue. In all his works, it may be added, he showed himself to be in sympathy with those who lived in the world: such was Doña Ana de Peñalosa, for example, yet he did not scruple to dedicate to her the most advanced of his treatises.

Other Manuscripts of the 'Maxims'

If we may judge by the scanty references to it which are to be found in early documents relating to the Saint, the Andújar MS. was hardly known at all in the seventeenth century. In all his peregrinations among the houses of the Order, P. Andrés appears to have found no single copy of it. From this we may fairly infer that the autograph was acquired by the Piédrola family at a very early date.

Burgos. The only other important MS. of this opuscule belongs to the Discalced Carmelite friars of Burgos. It contains only the first forty-nine maxims of this edition, which are given in the same order as in the Andújar MS. At the end of these a line is drawn across the page and beneath this there follow, in the same hand, forty-two further maxims which are not in the Andújar MS., no indication being given as to their source, except that at the end the copyist has written: 'This is by our venerable father Fray John of the Cross.' These maxims are also addressed to a Beas nun and were first published in the Barcelona edition of the works of the Saint (1693). They are found in the Barcelona MS. next to be described and both their content and their form appear to us to confirm the external evidence of their authenticity.

On the next folio the same amanuensis has copied some further maxims, preceded by the words: 'Our holy Father, treating of the narrowness of the road which leads to life, says thus: "I would that I could convince spiritual persons. . . ."' There follows an exact copy of the paragraph which in our edition of the *Ascent of Mount Carmel* (Vol. I, p. 86), is the eighth of Book II, chapter vii; after this come fifteen maxims which seem to us to be only extracts from his writings made by another person. The MS. also contains some unimportant documents and a few poems.

Barcelona. The Institut d'Estudis Catalans, Barcelona (Biblioteca de Catalunya), has a manuscript containing maxims by St. John of the Cross preceded by the words: 'This paper was copied by our holy father Fray John of the Cross from another which was found in the convent of Beas.' Like the copy in the Burgos MS., and like the edition of 1693, it begins with the preface 'Moreover, O my God and my delight . . .', copies the forty-nine Andújar maxims, and finally, like these authorities, reproduces further maxims, under the heading 'Points of Love.' As far as No. 42, which describes the characteristics of the solitary bird (p. 230, below), the two manuscripts and the Barcelona edition agree exactly. From that point onward, however, there are few maxims found in both the Barcelona MS. and the Barcelona edition (the Burgos MS. ends at No. 49), the others occurring in the edition alone, which was no doubt prepared from a fuller MS. source than either of those mentioned. The exact divergences will be indicated in footnotes below.

From all this it will be clear that some of the maxims attributed to St. John of the Cross were actually written by him, while others were written by his disciples, whether as notes of his addresses or conversation, or as jottings from, or summaries of, his writings. We have described the Andújar autograph and the two MSS. which seem to us to contain maxims from St. John of the Cross's own hand. There are a large number of collections which probably consist of the work of his disciples. P. José de Jesús María, for example, and after him P. Jerónimo de San José, obtained and published copies of sayings attributed to the Saint. To these activities we owe the hundred maxims with which P. Jerónimo furnished the editor of the Latin edition of St. John of the Cross's writings (Cologne, 1639) and which he proposed to publish in Spanish in the eighth book of his *History of St.*

John of the Cross (Madrid, 1641), which book, however, never appeared.[1]

These hundred maxims were included in the edition of the Saint's works published at Madrid in 1649, and are placed near the beginning of it, following the introductory matter and nine of the Saint's letters. In this form the *Maxims* were reproduced in all the editions which followed, until that of Seville, 1703, which gave 365 sentences, one for each day of the year.

The Barcelona edition of 1693, as we have said, first published forty-nine maxims from the Andújar MS. and others which did not appear in that collection but are probably genuine. The importance of this innovation was completely lost upon the editor's contemporaries nor is it given much weight by the editor himself. The title-page merely says: 'In this latest impression are added cautions against the three enemies of the soul and a few fragments of maxims and sentences by the same author, which contain admirable and superior instruction.' In reality, this edition takes the first step towards the publication of a reliable text of the *Maxims*. The name of the person responsible for it has not come down to us but the publication of the new *Maxims* may be credited to the Discalced Carmelites of Madrid, who must have put him in possession of what they considered the best authenticated MSS. of the General Archives of San Hermenegildo. It would seem that at this time there existed collections of maxims and sentences which were partly based upon the Andújar MS. and it may well be that the Saint himself left collections in his own hand, from which they derived, although only one of these is still known to us.

The path taken by the editor of 1693 was not followed for long, for in 1701 there appeared in Seville a work entitled *Spiritual Sentences and Maxims*, edited by Francisco de Leefdael, who pursued an entirely different plan. He divides his maxims, which include many that he himself has extracted from the Saint's writings (indicating their source), into twenty-five classes, each with a comprehensive title, such as 'Imitation of Christ,' 'Theological virtues,' 'Unruly appetites,' 'Fear of God.' Within each of these classes is summarized the Saint's principal instructions on the subject of it. The collection begins with the preface from the Andújar MS., which, however, the editor alters

---

[1] This we know from P. Andrés (*Memorias Historiales*, A. 39) who saw the MS. of this eighth book, containing 'one hundred sentences of our holy Father and nineteen more maxims, besides others which were crossed out in the manuscript.' [He gives further extracts from the MS., which are reproduced by P. Silverio, Vol. IV, pp. xlviii–xlix, but omitted here, as not affecting the main argument.]

with the object of improving its literary form. The 'Prayer of the soul enkindled with love' is included under the seventh head, but this, too, is considerably altered from the form of the Andújar autograph. Among the maxims are interspersed poems by St. John of the Cross and also some by St. Teresa. This edition was no doubt admirable for the purpose for which its pious author compiled it, but did nothing towards the establishment of an authentic text of the *Maxims*—indeed, it hindered the diffusion of the edition of 1693.

Most of the 365 sentences in the collected edition of the Saint's works published at Seville in 1703 are taken from Leefdael's edition. The new editor, P. Andrés de Jesús, who had played a great part in the preparation of the edition of 1701, mentions the Andújar manuscript ('written in the hand of the holy father himself') and describes the sentences not drawn from this source as 'derived from a few letters and from the four chief treatises which compose his works, for the greater convenience and utility of his readers.' These last are marked by the editor with an asterisk.

The *Maxims* have continued to be printed in this new form in all successive editions until our own. P. Andrés de la Encarnación devised an elaborate scheme for publishing them under five headings, but this was never carried into effect, and little can be said to have been lost by the omission, since it involved the perpetuation of the unscholarly procedure of setting the extracts made from the Saint's works by his disciples on the same level as his own original compositions. The Andújar maxims were not published in their original form till P. Gerardo's edition of 1912; P. Gerardo also reproduced the 365 sentences, the first 75 being taken from the Andújar manuscript and the remainder, with their divisions and classifications, from the Seville edition of 1703.

Our own edition of the *Maxims* is based entirely upon the manuscripts of Andújar, Burgos and Barcelona, with which we have collated the edition of 1693. The few additional sentences which we have included bear a reasonable guarantee of authenticity: ten of them (pp. 234–5) come to us from M. Magdalena del Espíritu Santo and fourteen more (pp. 235–6) from a copy made in 1759 by P. Andrés de la Encarnación from a manuscript belonging to the Discalced Carmelite nuns of Antequera which also copies the maxims of the Andújar autographs. We have endeavoured to sift the Saint's authentic maxims and sentences from the compilations of his followers and to present only what came, beyond reasonable doubt, from his own heart and hand.

SPIRITUAL SENTENCES AND MAXIMS[1]

PROLOGUE

MOREOVER, O my God and my delight, my soul has desired, for love of Thee, to employ itself in these sayings of light and love for Thee, for, although I have the tongue wherewith to utter them, I have neither the deeds nor the virtue which pertain to them, and it is with these, my Lord, that Thou art pleased rather than with the language and the wisdom of them. Let other persons, who may be so impelled by them, perchance make progress in Thy love and service, wherein I am lacking, and let my soul find an occasion of comfort in having been the cause for which Thou findest in others that which is lacking in itself.

Thou, Lord, lovest discretion, lovest light, lovest love above the other operations of the soul. Wherefore these sayings will be of discretion for the journeyer,[2] of light for the journey and of love for the journeying. Far hence be worldly rhetoric; far hence the loquacity and arid eloquence of weak and ingenious[3] human wisdom, wherein Thou hast no pleasure; and let us speak words to the heart, bathed in sweetness and love, wherein Thou hast great pleasure, removing perchance causes of stumbling and offences from many souls that stumble unwittingly, and unwittingly do err, thinking that they are successfully following Thy dearest Son, Our Lord Jesus Christ, and becoming like to Him in their life, character and virtues, and in the form of the detachment and purity[4] of their spirit. But do Thou grant it, Father of mercies, for without Thee, Lord, naught will be accomplished.[5]

---

[1] We do not know if the Saint gave any title to these opuscules; this title, however, which we have taken over from the old editions, is quite a suitable one. In the prologue which stands at the beginning of some of the collections, he describes them, very beautifully and very aptly, as 'sayings of light and love.'

[2] B, Bg and the 1693 edition read: 'for the journeying.' [P. Silverio follows these authorities.] The emendation [adopted in the text] is found in a number of other editions.

[3] Thus B, Bg. The editions have: 'weak and deceitful' [engañosa for ingeniosa].

[4] Thus B, Bg. The 1693 edition reads: 'and poverty' [pobreza for pureza].

[5] This prologue is not found in the autograph MS. of Andújar, but it occurs in B, Bg and 1693 and is indisputably genuine.

218

Maxims and Sentences from the Autograph Manuscript of Andújar

1. The Lord has ever revealed to mortals the treasures of His wisdom and His spirit; but now that wickedness is revealing her face more and more clearly, He reveals them in large measure.

2. O Lord,[1] my God! Who that seeks Thee with simple and pure love will fail to find Thee much to his desire and will, since Thou showest Thyself first of all and goest out to meet them that desire Thee?

3. Though the road is plain and easy for men of good will, he that journeys upon it will not journey far and will find much trial therein if he have not good feet and courage, and the perseverance that comes from courage, directed to the same end.

4. Better is it to be heavy-laden and near one that is strong than relieved of one's load and near one that is weak. When thou art heavy-laden thou art near to God, Who is thy strength and is with them that are in trouble. When thou art relieved, thou art near but to thyself, who art thine own weakness. For the virtue and strength of the soul grows and is confirmed by trials of patience.

5. He that desires to be alone, without the support of a master[2] and guide, will be like the tree that is alone in the field and has no owner. However much fruit it bears, passers-by will pluck it all, and it will not mature.

6. The tree that is cultivated and kept with the favour of its owner gives in due season the fruit that is expected of it.

7. The soul that is alone and without a master, and has virtue,[3] is like the burning coal that is alone. It will grow colder rather than hotter.

8. He that falls alone remains on the ground alone and holds his soul of small account, since he trusts it to himself alone.

9. If thou fearest not to fall alone, how dost thou presume to rise alone? See how much more can be done by two together than by one alone!

10. He that falls heavily laden will have difficulty in rising with his load.

---

[1] B, Bg omit: 'O Lord,' and end the previous maxim: 'the Lord reveals them in much greater measure.'

[2] The Saint first wrote: 'without master.' The amended version given in the text is in his own hand.

[3] B, Bg omit: 'and has virtue.' The Saint added: 'and without a master,' as an after-thought, as the MS. clearly shows, to make his full meaning explicit.

11. And he that falls and is blind will not, in his blindness, rise up alone; and if he rise up alone he will journey whither it is not fitting.

12. More does God desire of thee the least degree of purity of conscience than all the works that thou canst do.

13. More does God desire of thee the least degree of obedience and submission than all those services that thou thinkest to do Him.

14. More does God esteem in thee an inclination towards aridity and suffering for love of Him than all the consolations and spiritual visions and meditations that may be thine.

15. Renounce thy desires and thou shalt find that which thy heart desires. How knowest thou if thy desire[1] is according to God?

16. O sweetest love of God that art so little known! He that has found the veins of this mine[2] has found rest.

17. Since if thou fulfil thy desire thou wilt have a double measure of bitterness, desire not to fulfil it even if thou remain in bitterness.

18. Greater unfitness and impurity has the soul in its journey to God if it has within itself the smallest appetite for things of the world than if it were burdened with all the hideous and persistent temptations and all the darkness describable, provided that its rational will refuses them entrance. For the soul that is in the latter case can with confidence approach God to do the will of His Majesty, Who says: 'Come to Me, all ye that labour and are burdened, and I will refresh you.'[3]

19. More pleasing to God is the soul that in aridity and trial submits to that which is reason than the soul which fails to do this but receives consolations in everything that it does.

20. More pleasing to God is one good work, howsoever small it be, that is done in secret with no desire that it shall be known than a thousand that are done with the desire that they may be known of men. For he that with purest love does such works for God's sake not only cares nothing if men see him, but does them not even that God Himself may know it. Such a man, even though God were never to know it, would not cease to do Him the same services with the same joy and purity of love.

21. A good work performed in purity, and wholly for God's sake, in a breast that is pure, makes a kingdom wholly for its master.[4]

22. Twofold are the difficulties of a bird that is caught by the lime:

---

[1] [*Lit.*, 'thy appetite.']
[2] [*Lit.*, 'found its veins.']
[3] St. Matthew xi, 28.
[4] [The order of the Spanish words is kept here though it would seem that 'in a breast that is pure' should follow 'kingdom.']

first it has to free itself and then to make itself clean. And twofold are the troubles of him that fulfils his desire: first, he must free himself, and, once free, must purify himself from that which has clung to him.

23. He that allows not himself to be carried away by his desires will soar upward with ease according to the spirit, even as the bird that lacks no feathers.

24. The fly that clings to honey impedes its flight; and the soul that would cling to spiritual sweetness impedes its liberty and contemplation.

25. Take thou no heed of the creatures if thou wilt keep the image of God clearly and simply in thy soul, but empty thy spirit of them, and withdraw far from them, and thou shalt walk in the Divine light,[1] for God is not like to the creatures.

A Prayer of the Soul Enkindled with Love

Lord, God, my Beloved! If Thou still rememberest my sins and so doest not that which I am ever beseeching of Thee, do Thou Thy will as concerning them, my God, for it is this that I most desire, and exercise Thy goodness and mercy and Thou shalt be known in them[2]; and if Thou awaitest my works in order to grant me my prayer by means of them, do Thou grant them to me and work them in me, and impose on me the penalties that Thou wilt accept, and let Thy will be done. And if Thou awaitest not my works, for what then dost Thou wait, my most merciful Lord? Wherefore tarriest Thou? For if after all it be grace and mercy which I entreat of Thee in Thy Son, take Thou my mite, since Thou desirest it, and grant me this good thing, since Thou desirest it likewise.

Who can free himself from limitations and base modes of acting, if Thou raise him not up to Thyself, my God, in purity of love?

How will a man that is engendered and nurtured in baseness rise up to Thee, if Thou, O Lord, raise him not up with the hand wherewith Thou didst make him?

Thou wilt not take from me, my God, that which once Thou gavest me in Thine only Son Jesus Christ, in Whom Thou gavest me all that I desire; wherefore I shall rejoice that Thou wilt not tarry if I wait for Thee.

---

[1] [*Lit.*, 'the Divine lights.']
[2] [I.e., in the sins, not in the goodness and mercy, as the gender of the Spanish pronoun shows.]

With what procrastinations[1] dost thou wait, since thou canst even now love God in thy heart?

Mine are the heavens and mine is the earth; mine are the people, the righteous are mine and mine are the sinners; the angels are mine and the Mother of God, and all things, are mine; and God Himself is mine and for me, for Christ is mine and all for me. What, then, dost thou ask for and seek, my soul? Thine is all this, and it is all for thee.

Consider not thyself as mean, neither pay heed to the crumbs which fall from thy Father's table. Go thou forth from them and glory in thy glory. Hide thee therein and rejoice and thou shalt have the desires of thy heart.

26. The spirit that is indeed pure concerns not itself with advertence to exterior things, or with human respects, but inwardly, alone and withdrawn from all forms, and in delectable tranquillity, it communes with God, for the knowledge of Him is in Divine silence.[2]

27. The soul enkindled with love is a soul that is gentle, meek, humble and patient.

28. The soul that is hard becomes harder through love of its own self. If in Thy love, O good Jesus, Thou softenest[3] not the soul, it will persist for ever in its natural hardness.

29. He that loses an opportunity[4] is like one that has let a bird fly out of his hand, for he will not regain it.

30. I knew Thee not, my Lord, because I still desired to know and delight in things.

31. Let everything be changed, and that willingly, Lord God, so that we may find rest in Thee.

32. One single thought of a man is of greater worth than the whole world; wherefore God alone is worthy of it.

33. For that which cannot be felt, that which thou feelest[5] not; for that which can be felt, sense; and for the spirit of God, thought.

34. Consider that thy guardian angel does not always move the desire[6] to act, though he ever illumines the reason. Wherefore stay

---

[1] B, Bg: 'With what discretion.' [The phrase, con qué dilaciones, is an unusual one, and discreción might read more naturally. The sense is apparently: 'Why wait upon God's expected grace when you can love Him now?']

[2] B, Bg, 1693: 'is Divine knowledge.'

[3] B, Bg, 1693: 'Thou sanctifiest.'

[4] B, Bg, 1693: 'He that loses a prayer' [oración for ocasión].

[5] The MS. is imperfect here: the reading 'that which does not feel' is admissible [and certainly preferable]; B, Bg, 1693 read as in the text.

[6] ['Desire,' in this and the next paragraph, is apetito, 'appetite.']

thou not for desire before thou perform a virtuous deed, since reason and understanding suffice thee.

35. The desire gives the angel no occasion to move it when it is set upon aught beside.

36. My spirit has dried up in me, because it forgets to feed upon Thee.

37. This that thou seekest and that thou most desirest thou wilt not find by this way of thine, neither by lofty contemplation, but in deep humility and submissiveness of heart.

38. Weary not thyself, for thou shalt not enter into spiritual delight and sweetness[1] if thou give not thyself to mortification of all that thou desirest.

39. Consider that it is the most delicate flower that soonest withers and loses its fragrance. Wherefore beware thou of seeking to walk in the way of spiritual delight, for thou shalt not be constant. But choose thou for thyself spiritual vigour, and have attachment to naught, and thou shalt find sweetness and peace in abundance; for fruit that is both delicious and lasting is gathered in country that is cold and dry.

40. Remember that thy flesh is weak and that naught belonging to the world can give strength or consolation to thy spirit; for that which is born of the world is worldly, and that which is born of the flesh is fleshly, and true spirituality is born of the spirit of God alone, which is communicated neither through the world nor through the flesh.

41. Enter into account with thy reason to do that which it counsels thee on the road to God, and it will be of greater worth to thee with respect to thy God than all the works that thou doest without this counsel and than all the spiritual delights that thou seekest.[2]

42. Blessed is he that puts aside his pleasure and inclination and regards things according to reason and justice in order to perform them.

43. He that acts according to reason is like one that eats of substantial food, and he that is moved by the desire of his will is like one that eats watery fruit.

44. Thou, Lord, turnest gladly and lovingly to exalt[3] him that offends Thee, and I turn not to exalt and honour him that angers me.

45. O powerful Lord, if a spark of Thy empire of justice has so

---

[1] Bg, 1693: 'into the delight and sweetness of Christ.' B: 'into the delight and wisdom of Christ.'

[2] In Bg this maxim ends with the words: 'road to God.'

[3] [The word here twice translated 'exalt' is *levantar*, 'raise,' 'lift up.' In the first clause it seems to mean 'lift up' in the sense of 'aid,' but in the second clause the conjunction of the verb with 'honour' suggests another sense.]

great an effect in the case of a prince who is mortal and who governs and moves the peoples, what effect will Thy omnipotent justice have upon the righteous man and the sinner?[1]

46. If thou purify thy soul of material[2] possessions and desires, thou shalt understand things in spirit; and if thou deny thy desire with respect to them thou shalt enjoy the truth that is in them, understanding that which is sure in them.

47. My Lord God, Thou art no stranger to him that makes not himself a stranger to Thee. How do they say that Thou dost absent Thyself?

48. Truly a man has conquered all things if the pleasure that they bring moves him not to joy and the insipidity which they leave behind causes him not sorrow.

49. If thou desirest to attain to holy recollection, thou shalt attain it, not by admitting, but by refusing.

50. If I go, my God, everywhere with Thee, it will everywhere go well with me, even as I desire it should go well with Thee.[3]

51. That man will not be able to attain to perfection who endeavours not to be satisfied with nothing, so that his natural and spiritual concupiscence may be content with emptiness; for this is needful if a man would attain to the highest tranquillity and peace of spirit; and in this way the love of God is almost continually in action in the simple and pure soul.

52. Since God is inaccessible, see that thou concern not thyself with how much thy faculties can comprehend and thy senses can perceive, that thou be not satisfied with less and that thy soul lose not the agility that is needful for one that would attain to Him.

53. As one that drags a cart uphill, even so does that soul journey toward God that shakes not off anxiety and quenches not the appetite.

54. It is not the will of God that the soul allow aught to trouble it, or suffer trials; if it suffer them because of the adversities of the world, this comes from the weakness of its virtue; for the soul of the perfect man rejoices in that which causes the imperfect soul affliction.

55. On the road to life there is very little bustle and business, and it requires mortification of the will rather than much knowledge. He

---

[1] This maxim is not found in B, Bg.

[2] [The Spanish has extraño, 'strange': the same word is rendered 'stranger' in the next paragraph.]

[3] In B, Bg, 1693 the maxims which correspond with those of the Andújar MS. end here, and there follow others, under the title 'Points of Love,' which will be found on p. 227, below.

that cumbers himself least with things and pleasures will go farthest along that road.

56. Think not that pleasing God lies so much in performing numerous good works as in performing them with good will, and without attachment[1] and respect to persons.

57. At eventide they will examine thee in love. Learn to love as God desires to be loved and lay aside thine own temperament.

58. See that thou meddle not in the affairs of others, nor even allow them to pass through thy memory, for perchance thou wilt be unable to fulfil thine own task.

59. Think not that, because in yonder man there shine not the virtues which thou hast in mind, he will not be precious in God's sight for that which thou hast not in mind.

60. Man knows not either how to rejoice aright or how to grieve aright, for he understands not the distance that there is between good and evil.

61. See that thou become not of a sudden sorrowful because of the adversities that are in the world, since thou knowest not the blessings that they bring with them, these being ordained in the judgments of God for the everlasting joy of the elect.

62. Rejoice thou not in temporal prosperity, since thou knowest not of a certainty that it assures thee eternal life.

63. In tribulation, draw near to God with confidence and thou shalt be strengthened and illumined and instructed.

64. In joys and pleasures draw near at once to God with fear and truth, and thou shalt neither be deceived nor wrapped up in vanity.

65. Take God for thy Spouse and for a Friend with Whom thou walkest continually, and thou shalt not sin, and shalt learn to love, and the things that are needful shall be wrought prosperously for thee.

66. Without labour thou shalt subject people and things shall serve thee, if thou forget both them and thyself.

67. Betake thyself to rest, putting anxieties far from thee and caring not at all for whatsoever comes to pass, and thou shalt serve God as He wills and take thine ease in Him.

68. Behold, God reigns not save in the disinterested and peaceful soul.

69. Though thou perform many actions, yet thou shalt make no progress in perfection if thou learn not to deny thy will and to submit thyself, losing all anxiety concerning thyself and thine own business.

[1] [Cf. p. 202, n. 7, above.]

70. What profit is it that thou give one thing to God if He asks of thee another? Consider that which will please God and do it; in this way shalt thou better satisfy thy heart than with that to which thou thyself inclinest.

71. How presumest thou to take thine ease so fearlessly since thou must appear before God to give an account of the least of thy words and thoughts?

72. Behold how many are they that are called and how few they that are chosen! And see that, if thou have no care for thyself, thy perdition is more certain than thine amendment, especially since so narrow is the way that leads to eternal life.

73. Rejoice not vainly, for thou knowest how many sins thou hast committed and thou knowest not how thou standest with God; but fear, yet have confidence.

74. Since when thine hour of reckoning comes it will grieve thee that thou hast not employed this time in the service of God, wherefore dost thou not order and employ it now[1] as thou wouldst wish to have done wert thou dying?

75. If thou desirest devotion to be born in thy spirit and the love of God and desire for Divine things to grow, cleanse thy soul of every desire and attachment and pretension, so that thou carest nothing for anything. For just as a sick man, when he has cast out the evil humour, is at once conscious of good health and there comes to him a desire to eat, just so shalt thou recover thy health in God if thou attendest to thyself in this matter; and otherwise, however much thou doest, it shall profit thee nothing.

76. If thou desirest to find peace and consolation for thy soul, and to serve God truly, content not thyself with this that thou hast left behind, for perchance thou wilt still have as many impediments as before, or more than before. But leave all these other things that remain to thee and withdraw thyself to one thing alone which brings everything with it—namely, to holy solitude, together with prayer and with Divine and holy reading, and remain there in forgetfulness of all things. For if these things are not incumbent upon thee of obligation, thou wilt be better pleasing to God in being able to keep thyself and make thyself more perfect than in gaining all other things at once. For what shall it profit a man to gain the whole world if he lose his soul?[2]

---

[1] The word 'now' is the Saint's interlinear addition.
[2] The words 'if he lose his soul' have been crossed out in the autograph by a later hand than St. John of the Cross's.

POINTS OF LOVE[1]

1. Straitly restrain thy tongue and thy thoughts and keep thine affection habitually fixed upon God, and He will grant thy spirit Divine fervour.

2. Feed not thy spirit on aught beside God. Cast away concern for all things and have peace and recollection in thy heart.

3. Have spiritual tranquillity in loving attentiveness to God, and, if it be necessary to speak, let it be with the same tranquillity and peace.

4. Have remembrance habitually of eternal life, and of the truth that they that are lowliest and poorest and count themselves as least shall have fruition of the chiefest dominion and glory in God.

5. Rejoice habitually in God, Who is thy health, and know that it is good to suffer in any way for him that is good.

6. Let us consider how necessary it is for us to be our own enemies, and to journey to perfection on the road of holy severity, and let us understand that every word we speak, save by command and under obedience, is laid to our account by God.

7. An intimate desire that God may grant thee that which His Majesty knows thou dost lack for His honour.

8. Crucified inwardly and outwardly with Christ, a man will live in this life with fullness and satisfaction of soul, possessing his soul in his patience.[2]

9. Have a loving attentiveness to God, with no desire to feel or understand anything in particular concerning Him.

10. Habitual confidence in God, esteeming in oneself and in one's sisters that which God most esteems—namely, spiritual blessings.

11. Enter into thy bosom[3] and labour in the presence of the Spouse, Who is ever present and loves thee[4] well.

---

[1] These are to be found in Bg and (with slight variations) in the edition of 1693 and in the MS. copy in the library of the Institut d'Estudis Catalans, Barcelona. Bg seems the most reliable authority and is accordingly followed in the text above.

[2] [Apparently a reference to St. Luke xxi, 19: *In patientia* vestra *possidebitis animas vestras.*]

[3] For *seno* ['bosom'] B, Bg have *cieno* ['slough,' 'mire']; Bg, however, has the correction *seno* and 1693 also reads *seno*.

[4] [The pronoun is feminine, as one would expect from the reference to 'sisters' in the last maxim. The feminine pronoun recurs in later 'Points.']

12. Be unwilling to admit into thy soul things that have in themselves no spiritual substance, lest they make thee lose the desire for devotion and recollection.

13. Let Christ crucified be sufficient for thee, and with Him do thou suffer and rest; for which cause do thou annihilate thyself with respect to all things, both without and within.

14. Endeavour that things be naught to thee, and that thou be naught to things; forgetting all, dwell thou in thy recollection with the Spouse.

15. Love trials greatly and repute them of small account if thou wilt attain the favour of the Spouse, Who hesitated not to die for thee.

16. Have fortitude of heart against all things that move thee to that which is not God and be thou a lover of the Passion[1] of Christ.

17. Have interior detachment from all things and set not thy pleasure on any temporal thing and thy soul shall find such good things in recollection as it knows not.

18. The soul that walks in love[2] wearies not neither is wearied.

19. The poor man who is naked will be clothed; and the soul that is naked of desires, of willings and of nillings will be clothed by God with His purity, desire and will.

20. There are souls that wallow in the mire even as animals wallow in it, and others that soar like the birds which purify and cleanse themselves in the air.

21. One word spake the Father, which Word was His Son, and this Word He speaks ever in eternal silence, and in silence must it be heard by the soul.

22. We must measure our trials by ourselves, and not ourselves by our trials.[3]

23. He that seeks not the Cross of Christ seeks not the glory of Christ.

24. God conceives not love for the soul by considering its greatness, but by considering the greatness of its humility.[4]

25. He that is ashamed to confess Me before men, says the Lord, him will I also be ashamed to confess before My Father.[5]

26. Hair that is combed with frequency is untangled, and there will

---

[1] 1693: 'of the passions.'

[2] So B, Bg. The 1693 edition has: 'that walks enkindled with love.'

[3] [That is, presumably, we must brace ourselves to the trials that come—i.e. rise up to their measure—and not scale them down to our own measure, by saying that we can only bear trials within certain limits of intensity.]

[4] B: 'of its humility and contempt'; 1693: 'of its contempt and humility.'

[5] 1693 omits this maxim ,which is ,of course, simply a verse from the Gospel.

be no difficulty in combing it as often as one desires; and the soul that with frequency examines its thoughts, words, and deeds, which are like the hair, and that does all things for love of God, will find that its hair is quite free from entanglement. Then the Spouse will look upon the neck of the Bride, and will be captivated by it, and will be wounded by one of her eyes, namely by the purity of intention wherewith she performs all her acts. We begin to comb our hair from the crown of the head if we desire it not to be tangled; all our works must begin from the crown—that is, from the love of God—if we wish them to be without entanglement and pure.

27.[1] The heavens are stable and not subject to generation, and souls which are of heavenly texture are also stable, and are not subject to the generation of desires or to aught else, for after their kind they are like unto God, and are never moved.

28. Eat not of forbidden fruit, which is that of this present life, since blessed are they that do hunger and thirst after justice, for they shall have their fill. That which God seeks to do is to make us gods by participation, as He is God by nature, even as fire converts all things into fire.

29. All the goodness that we have is lent to us and God considers it as His own.[2] It is God that works and His work is God.

30. Wisdom enters through love, silence, and mortification; great wisdom is it to be able to keep silence and to look neither at the words nor at the deeds nor at the lives of others.

31. All for me and naught for Thee.[3]

32. All for Thee and naught for me.

33. Allow thyself to be taught, allow thyself to be commanded, allow thyself to be brought into submission and despised, and thou shalt be perfect.

34. Five evils are caused in the soul by any desire[4]: first, it is made uneasy; second, it is confused; third, it is soiled; fourth, it is weakened; and fifth, it is darkened.

35. Perfection lies not in the virtues which the soul knows itself to have; it consists in those which Our Lord sees in the soul. And this is a closed book[5]; wherefore the soul has no excuse for presumption, but as regards itself must humble itself to the ground.

---

[1] Bg omits this maxim, which is found, however, in B and 1693.
[2] [I have ventured to make a slight correction in P. Silverio's punctuation of this sentence, which greatly improves the sense.]
[3] [For the meaning of this sentence, see p. 232, § 52, below.]
[4] [apetito.]
[5] [Lit., 'closed burden.'] 1693 reads: 'closed letter' [which suggests the phrase used in the text].

36. Love consists not in feeling great things, but in having great detachment and in suffering for the Beloved.

37. The whole world has not the worth of a man's thought, for that thought is due to God alone; and thus whatever thought of ours is not centred upon God is stolen from Him.

38. The faculties and senses must not be employed wholly upon things, but only in so far as is unavoidable. With this exception all must be left free for God.

39. Look not at the imperfections of others, keep silence, and have continual converse with God. These three things will uproot great imperfections from the soul and will make it mistress of great virtues.

40. The signs of interior recollection are three: first, if the soul have no pleasure in transitory things; second, if it have pleasure in solitude and silence and give heed to all that leads to greater perfection; third, if the things which were wont to help it (such as considerations, meditations, and acts) now hinder it and the soul has no other support in prayer than faith and hope and charity.

41. If a soul becomes more patient in suffering and readier to endure lack of consolations, this is a sign that it is making greater progress in virtue.

42. The characteristics of the solitary bird are five. The first is that it soars as high as it is able. The second, that it can endure no companionship, even of its own kind. The third, that it places its beak against the wind.[1] The fourth, that it has no definite colour. The fifth, that it sings sweetly. These characteristics will belong to the contemplative soul. It must soar above transitory things, paying no more heed than if they were not. It must be so fond of solitude and silence that it can endure the companionship of no other creature. Its beak must be placed so as to meet the wind of the Holy Spirit—that is, it must respond to His inspirations, to the end that, by so doing, it may become more worthy of His companionship. It must have no definite colour— that is, it must desire to do no definite thing save that which is the will of God. It must sing sweetly in the contemplation and love of its Spouse.

43. The habits of voluntary imperfections which are never completely conquered not only hinder Divine union, but also prevent a soul from approaching perfection. Such imperfections are: the habit of much speaking, little unconquered attachments, such as for persons,

---

[1] [*Lit.*, 'to the air.']

clothes, cells, books, different kinds of food, and other conversations and preferences in seeking relish in things, in knowing and hearing them, and other matters like to these.[1]

44. If thou desirest to glory, and desirest not to appear stupid and foolish, put away from thee things that are not thine, and thou wilt have glory of that which remains. But, in truth, if thou puttest away all things that are not thine, thou wilt be changed into nothing, for thou must glory in nothing if thou desirest not to fall into vanity. But let us descend now especially to the gifts of those graces which make men full of grace and pleasing in the eyes of God. It is certain that thou shouldst not glory in those gifts since thou knowest not yet if thou hast them.[2]

45. Oh, how sweet will Thy presence be to me, Thou that art the highest Good. I will approach Thee in silence[3] and will uncover Thy feet[4] that Thou mayest be pleased to unite me unto Thee in marriage, and I will not take mine ease until I have fruition of Thyself in Thine arms. And now I entreat Thee, Lord, not to forsake me at any time in my recollection since I am a spendthrift of my soul.

46. If thou be detached from that which is without and dispossessed of that which is within, and without attachment to the things of God, neither will prosperity detain thee nor adversity hinder thee.

47. The soul that is united with God is feared by the devil as though it were God Himself.[5]

48. The purest suffering bears and carries in its train the purest understanding.

49. The soul that desires God to surrender Himself to it wholly must surrender itself to Him wholly and leave nothing for itself.

50. The soul that is in the union of love has not even the first movements of sin.[6]

51. The tried friends of God very rarely fail God, since they are above all that they can lack.[7]

---

[1] Bg adds at this point: 'This is by our venerable father Fray John of the Cross.' This maxim (43) is not found in B or in 1693, both of which authorities go on to give others which are not in Bg and which we now reproduce. The numbering which we have adopted follows on continuously from the maxims already transcribed. Some of the maxims which follow, but not all, are found in B.

[2] This maxim is found in B.   [3] B ends this maxim here.

[4] [The reference is evidently to Ruth iii, 4, 7.]

[5] This maxim and the six which follow it are found in B.

[6] ['Of sin' is not found in the original.]

[7] B: 'that can make them fail.' [There is a slight play here on the words 'fail' (*faltar*) and 'lack' (*hacen falta*). The version of B makes the play explicit in English, but the sense is not so good.]

52. My Beloved, all that is rough and toilsome I desire for myself, and all that is sweet and delectable I desire for Thee.

53. That which we most need in order to make progress is to be silent before this great God, with the desire and with the tongue, for the language that He best hears is that of silent love.

54. Divest thyself of what is human in order to seek God.[1] A man employs a light in his outward life, so that he may not fall, but light acts in the contrary manner in the things of God. Wherefore it is better to be unable to see and the soul has more security.

55. More profit can be obtained from the good things of God in one hour than from our own good things in a whole lifetime.

56. Love to be unknown both by thyself and by others. Never look at the good things or at the evil things of others.

57. Walk in solitude with God; work in the mean; hide the good things of God.

58. To be prepared to lose and see all others gain at our expense belongs to valiant souls, to generous bosoms, and to liberal hearts. One of the qualities of such souls is that they will give rather than receive even till they come to give their very selves, for they consider the possession of themselves to be a great burden, and prefer to be possessed by others and withdrawn from themselves, since we belong rather to that infinite Good than to ourselves.

59. A great evil is it to have an eye rather to the good things of God than to God Himself. Prayer and detachment.

60. Behold that infinite knowledge and that hidden secret. What peace, what love, what silence is in that Divine Bosom! How lofty a science is that which God there teaches—namely, the science of that which we call anagogical acts, which so greatly enkindle the heart!

61. Great damage and harm is done to the secrecy of the conscience whensoever the fruit thereof is manifested to men, for in such case the soul receives as a reward the fruit of transitory fame. (1) Speak little, and meddle not in things where thou art not consulted. (2) Strive ever to have God present in thee and keep within thyself the purity that God teaches. (3) Excuse not thyself, neither refuse to be corrected by all; listen to every reproof with a serene countenance; think that God addresses it to thee. (4) Live in this world as though there were in it but God and thy soul, so that thy heart may be detained by naught that is human. (5) Count it the mercy of God if at times some good

---

1 [P. Gerardo amended this obscure Spanish sentence to read: 'Simple faith in order to seek God.']

word is spoken of thee, for thou deservest none. (6) Never allow thyself to pour out thy heart, even though it be but for a moment. (7) Never hear of the weaknesses of others, and then, if anyone complain to thee of another, thou mayest tell him humbly to say naught of it to thee. (8) Make complaint of none, ask naught soever, or, if it be needful for thee to ask, let it be with few words. (9) Refuse not work, even though it appear to thee that thou canst not perform it. Let all find compassion in thee. (10) Contradict not; and in no way speak thou words that are not simple and clear.[1] (11) Let thy speech be such that none can be offended by it, and speak of things which it troubles thee not that all should know. (12) Deny not aught that thou hast, even though thou have need of it. (13) Be silent concerning that which God may give thee and remember that saying of the Bride: 'My secret for myself.' (14) Strive to keep thy heart in peace, and let naught that comes to pass in this world make thee uneasy—for consider that it must all come to an end. (15) Trouble not thyself either much or little as to who is against thee and who is with thee; and strive ever to please thy God. Pray to Him that His will may be done in thee. Love Him greatly, for this thou owest Him.

62. Twelve means[2] for arriving at the highest perfection: love of God, love of our neighbour, obedience, chastity, poverty, attendance at choir, penance, humility, mortification, prayer, silence, peace.

63. Never take man for an example in that which thou hast to do, howsoever holy he be, for else the devil will set his imperfections before thee. But imitate Christ, Who is the sum of perfection, and the sum of holiness, and thou shalt never go astray.

64. Seek in reading and thou shalt find in meditation; knock in prayer and it shall be opened to thee in contemplation.

65. The venerable and blessed father[3] Fray John of the Cross was once asked how a man went into ecstasy. 'By renouncing his own will,' he replied, 'and doing the will of God. For ecstasy is naught but the going forth of a soul from itself and its being caught up in God, and this is what happens to the soul that is obedient, namely, that it goes forth from itself and from its own desires, and, thus lightened of its load, becomes immersed in God.'

1 [Spanish, *limpias*, 'clean,' but 'clear' seems to be the meaning, and I suspect that *No contradiga* means 'Contradict not *thyself*.']
2 [Spanish, *estrellas*, 'stars,' 'guiding lights.']
3 B has: 'The holy father.'

MAXIMS THAT BELONGED TO MOTHER MAGDALENA DEL ESPÍRITU SANTO[1]

1. He that with pure love works for God not only cares not whether or not men know it, but does not even do these things that God Himself may know it. Such a one, even though it should never be known, would not cease to perform these same services and with the same gladness and love.

2. Another maxim for conquering the desires.[2] Have thou an habitual desire to imitate Jesus Christ in all His works, conforming thyself to His life, whereon thou must meditate in order to be able to imitate it and to behave in all things as He would behave.

3. In order that thou mayest be able to do this it is necessary that every appetite or taste be renounced, if it be not purely for the honour and glory of God, and that thou remain in emptiness for the love of Him Who in this life neither did nor desired to do more than the will of His Father, which He called His meat and drink.

In order that thou mayest mortify the four natural passions, which are joy, sadness, fear, and hope, follow thou this rule:

4. Strive always to prefer, not that which is easiest, but that which is most difficult; not that which is most delectable, but that which is most unpleasing; not that which gives most pleasure, but that which gives no pleasure. To prefer, not that which is restful, but that which is most wearisome; not that which is consolation, but that which is no consolation; not that which is greatest, but that which is least; not that which is loftiest and most precious, but that which is lowest and most despised; not that which is a desire for anything, but that which is a desire for nothing. To go about, seeking not the best things but the worst. And to have detachment and emptiness and poverty, with respect to everything that is in the world, for Jesus Christ's sake.

Against concupiscence:

5. Strive to work in detachment and to desire that others may do so.

6. Strive to speak in thine own despite and to desire that all may do so.

---

[1] The Maxims which we publish under this heading are the only ones which this religious left in her cell. Some of them will also be found in the *Ascent of Mount Carmel* [Vol. I, pp. 58–9] though with slight verbal differences.

[2] ['desires . . . desire'; *apetitos . . . apetito*.]

7. Strive to think humbly of thyself and to desire that others may do so.[1]

Among other things that he wrote, the Venerable Father once wrote down for each of the nuns one saying for their spiritual profit. I transcribed all these, but there have only remained to me these two which follow:

8. Be strong in thy heart against all things that move thee to that which is not God, and for Christ's sake love thou suffering.

9. Readiness in obedience, joy in suffering, mortification of the sight, the desire to know nothing, silence and hope.

10. Straitly restrain thy tongue and thy thought and fix thine affection habitually upon God, and the Divine Spirit shall give it great fervour. Read thou this often.[2]

OTHER MAXIMS[3]

1. The farther thou withdrawest thyself from earthly things, the nearer dost thou approach heavenly things, and the more thou findest in God.

2. He that knows how to die to all things will have life in all things.

3. Withdraw from evil, work good and seek peace.

4. He that complains or murmurs is not perfect, nor is he even a good Christian.

5. Humble is he that hides himself in his own nothingness and knows how to abandon himself to God.

6. Meek is he that knows how to suffer his neighbour and to suffer his own self.

7. If thou wilt be perfect, sell thy will and give it to the poor in spirit; come to Christ through meekness and humility; and follow Him to Calvary and the grave.

8. He that trusts to himself is worse than the devil.

9. He that loves not his neighbour abhors God.

10. He that works lukewarmly is near to falling.

---

[1] [With §§ 4–7 may be compared *Ascent of Mount Carmel*, I, xiii, §§ 6, 9 (Vol. I, pp. 58–9 of this edition).]

[2] This maxim was found on the same page as the sketch of the Mount of Perfection [see Vol. I, p. xxxii, above]. There is good evidence [cited by P. Silverio, Vol. IV, p. 250, n. 1] for its genuineness.

[3] These Maxims, which we owe to the diligence of P. Andrés de la Encarnación, appear to us authentic. Others, which can be gleaned from the documents connected with the Beatification of St. John of the Cross, often express his thought, but are not written in the style with which we are familiar as his. These last, therefore, we have not included.

11. He that flees from prayer flees from all that is good.

12. Better is it to conquer the tongue than to fast on bread and water.

13. Better is it to suffer for God's sake than to work miracles.

14. Oh, what blessings will be those that we shall enjoy with the sight of the Most Holy Trinity!

LETTERS AND DOCUMENTS

INTRODUCTION

ONLY a very small number of the letters of St. John of the Cross have come down to us, by comparison with the not inconsiderable number which he must certainly have written during his life as a Discalced Carmelite. Before his profession his correspondence would probably have been but small, for Medina was so near to Salamanca that during his student days he must have been in close touch with his family. In those days family life was more real than it is now and travellers would often carry news and affectionate messages to distant relatives of persons from their home towns of whom they themselves knew comparatively little.

As soon as he joined the Reform, and particularly during his early days at Duruelo, Mancera, Pastrana and Alcalá, St. John of the Cross must have begun a frequent exchange of letters with St. Teresa. About the year 1579, during a journey from El Calvario to Baeza, Fray Jerónimo de la Cruz saw him burn a bundle of letters which he had received from St. Teresa, as an act of abnegation. There would have been a corresponding bundle somewhere in the possession of the Mother Foundress, had she been accustomed to keep letters; but one who was so continually journeying would have found it hard to make a habit of this, even had she so desired, and further, persecution was always sufficiently near at hand to make it unwise to preserve correspondence. Later, he wrote often to St. Teresa during his life in Andalusia, as well as to PP. Antonio de Jesús, Jerónimo Gracián and Nicolás Doria, on matters concerning the government of the Order.

Both on spiritual matters, too, and on the business of the Order, the Saint must have written many letters to the nearest of his disciples, such as PP. Juan Evangelista and Juan de Santa Ana. Further, we know from contemporary evidence[1] that he wrote to at least one lay person, Doña Ana de Peñalosa. But most of his letters on spiritual matters appear to have been addressed to Discalced Carmelite nuns, to many

---

[1] Deposition of M. Ana de San Alberto, Prioress of Caravaca (MS. 12,738, fol. 565).

of whom he acted as confessor and director. Probably most of these were addressed to the nuns of Beas and Córdoba, rather than to those of Granada and Segovia, where he lived more continuously and therefore had less need to write.

From an early age St. John of the Cross had a genius for the direction of his Carmelite daughters, which St. Teresa, herself so greatly skilled in the knowledge of human nature, observed with great satisfaction. He may be said to have specialized in this particular branch of spiritual work from the age of twenty-nine, or even earlier. The disappearance of almost all the letters that he wrote to his penitents, therefore, is an irreparable loss. It is clear from what we have of them that they are as precious as any fragment of some lost treatise of his would be. Though couched in natural, simple and spontaneous language, they expound the same sublime doctrine of detachment and emptiness of the faculties. They have none of the infinite and marvellous variety of the letters of St. Teresa, none of her wonderful nervous vitality and unaffected, childlike fun. The letters of few men have surpassed those of this unrivalled woman. Yet his epistolary style is not without its merit, or even without its charm. Its prevailing note is seriousness, but not a seriousness that repels. Speaking for ourselves, we find the Saint's letters more than usually attractive.

The maxim-like phrases which are scattered through them are in no way unworthy of his great treatises.

Desolation is a file, and the endurance of darkness is preparation for great light.[1]

The mouth of desire must be opened toward Heaven and must be empty of aught else that might fill it.[2]

Where there is no love, put love and you will find love.[3]

Even so short a selection as this suggests one great characteristic of the Saint—the union, in his life and in his thought, of a singular gentleness with a sobriety and severity of conduct and doctrine that have seldom been equalled. The letters to the Prioress and Discalced nuns of Córdoba and to those spiritual daughters of his who lamented the discredit into which he fell in his last months on earth are full of this twofold quality. Through his stern asceticism we continually catch glimpses of uncreated Beauty.

There are familiar passages, too, in these letters which reveal something of the Saint's personal relations with some of his friends. None

[1] [Letter I.]   [2] [Letter V.]   [3] [Letter XXII.]

has greater charm than that addressed, from Segovia, to Doña Juana de Pedraza, the pious Granada lady, who had reproached him with having forgotten her.[1] It was of the letters of this same lady, with whom he evidently corresponded frequently, that he made the observation, so delightful in its context: 'If they were not so tiny, it would be better.'[2]

Of the twenty-nine extant letters, about one-quarter are fragmentary. It seems improbable that any early collection was made, for in that case more would surely have been preserved. M. Agustina de San José, who had known St. John of the Cross in Granada, related in 1614 how many of his letters to her nuns were given into her keeping and how finally they urged her to burn them during the period of persecution which immediately preceded his death.[3] Similar testimony is borne by P. Jerónimo de San José.[4] Many of the letters, nevertheless, must have survived these years, since various deponents in the processes of beatification and canonization describe themselves as being still in possession of them. 'I had many letters from him,' deposed M. Ana de San Alberto, for example, 'which I esteemed and kept like relics. Since his death I have been giving them to religious who asked me for them out of devotion.'[5] P. Alonso de la Madre de Dios reported having seen many such letters, of which unhappily he did not make copies, though he specifies the recipients of a number of them and mentions the places from which they were written. In particular he speaks of two written by the Saint to his old friend and companion at Duruelo, P. Antonio de Jesús, then Provincial of Andalusia, after he had provisionally fixed upon La Peñuela as the place of his retirement.

Not only had St. John of the Cross no friends like St. Teresa's beloved P. Gracián and María de San José to collect and keep his letters as a labour of love, but little trouble seems to have been taken, in the century after his death, to ensure their preservation. P. Andrés de la Encarnación comments regretfully upon this omission.[6] The first signs of any attention to so important a task are to be found in the *Historia* (1641) of P. Jerónimo de San José, who in his narrative inserts passages from no less than sixteen letters. These have served as bases for successive editions. True, only nine of them found a place in the 1694 edition of the Saint's writings and only in the edition of 1703

---

[1] [Letter XVIII.]　　　　　　　　　　　　　　　[2] [Letter IX.]
[3] MS. 8,568, p. 445; *Memorias Historiales*, A. 35.
[4] *Historia*, Bk. VII, chap. v, § 7.　　　　　[5] *Memorias Historiales*, C. 9.
[6] MS. 3,180, Adiciones E, Nos. 13, 14. [Sobrino, pp. 112–30, 134–5 (see next note), has compiled a list of thirty lost letters, giving such details as are known about them.]

were they all included. P. Gerardo was the first to increase the number, which he brought up to twenty-five, to which there have since been made only a few additions.[1]

We add several documents, written or signed by the Saint when Vicar-Provincial of Andalusia, some of which have not previously been published. On the other hand, we omit a few formal and conventional documents, in no sense *composed* by the Saint, which P. Gerardo included, as well as a prayer to the Blessed Virgin, once thought to be an autograph MS., but now recognized as being in the somewhat similar hand of a nun. Though the Saint might, of course, have been the author of the prayer, there is no evidence for this whatsoever.

[1] [In his 1929–31 edition, P. Silverio added one letter, and in the 1940 edition (Bibliography, No. 31, below) he included also a fragment recently found in an Italian convent (XXVI of this edition). In 1950, P. José Antonio de Sobrino, S.J., published two more letters (XXIV, XXIX) from a manuscript, discovered at Granada, which was written, about 1630, by a Basilian monk at El Tardón (*C.W.S.T.J.*, III, 82). I am indebted to him for permission to translate these, and also to quote from his *Estudios sobre San Juan de la Cruz y nuevos textos de su obra* (Madrid, 1950), which discusses, not only the *Letters*, but also the *Cautions* (of which it gives a new text) and certain points of interest connected with the *Ascent of Mount Carmel* and the *Dark Night of the Soul*.

In the footnotes to the *Letters*, the Tardón-Granada MS. is denoted by the abbreviation TG.]

LETTERS OF
SAINT JOHN OF THE CROSS

LETTER I

To M. Catalina de Jesús

BAEZA, JULY 6, 1581.

Greets the Mother, for whom the Saint has a particular esteem, and tells her that he does not write at greater length because he does not know where she is.[1]

Jesus be in your soul, my daughter Catalina. Although I do not know where you are, I want to write you these lines, trusting that our Mother will send them on to you if you are not with her; and, if you are not with her, be comforted with me, for I am in exile farther away still and am alone down here;[2] for since I was swallowed by that whale[3] and cast up in this strange harbour, I have not been found worthy to see you again, nor the saints that are up yonder.[4] God has done all

[1] The original of this letter, according to P. Andrés de la Encarnación, was venerated in the second half of the eighteenth century at the Convent of Discalced Carmelite nuns in Calatayud. There is a copy in the National Library, Madrid, made by P. Alonso el Asturicense (MS. 12,738), which is here followed.

Mother Catalina de Jesús was a native of Valderas, in the province of León, and professed at the Carmelite Convent of Valladolid on December 13, 1572. In 1580, she went to Palencia, where she was living when St. John of the Cross wrote her this letter. When St. Teresa left Ávila, in January 1582, to found a convent in Burgos, she passed through Palencia and took a number of nuns with her to this new house, including M. Catalina. In the first canonical elections of this new Community, held under the presidency of P. Gracián on April 21, 1582, M. Catalina was elected superior by all the votes except her own (cf. *Biblioteca Mística Carmelitana*, Vol. VI, p. 370). Later she left Burgos for Soria, where she died.

It is difficult to discover from M. Catalina's history the origin of her friendship with St. John of the Cross, to which this letter points. She may perhaps have been at Ávila at some time when the Saint was confessor to the Convent of the Incarnation there. This letter seems to indicate that their relations were those of personal friends, and not merely of correspondents.

[2] ['Down here,' i.e. in Andalusia, where, as we know, the Saint was less happy than in his native Castile.]

[3] The reference is to his imprisonment at Toledo.

[4] This Pauline phrase refers to his fellow-religious in Castile. Though he left his Toledan prison in August 1578, he had not had an opportunity in the meantime to see any of them.

241

things well, for, after all, desolation is a file, and the endurance of darkness is preparation for great light.

God grant that we walk not in darkness. Oh, how many things I should like to say to you! But I am writing in complete darkness, realizing that you may not receive this letter; so I am breaking off without ending it. Commend me to God. I will not say any more about things down here, for I have no desire to do so.

From Baeza, July 6, 1581.

Your servant in Christ,
FRAY JOHN OF THE CROSS.

(Superscription): For Sister Catalina de Jesús, Discalced Carmelite, wherever she may be.

LETTER II

TO M. ANA DE SAN ALBERTO, PRIORESS OF CARAVACA

Date uncertain.

(Fragment.)

Without having been previously informed of it, he tells her of a certain interior affliction that she was suffering, leaving her tranquil.[1]

How long, daughter, do you suppose that you will be carried in the arms of others? I desire to see in you so great a detachment from the creatures and an independence of them that hell itself would not suffice to trouble you. What are these uncalled-for tears that you are shedding nowadays? How much valuable time do you suppose you have wasted on these scruples? If you would communicate your

---

[1] This fragment was published by P. Jerónimo de San José in his *History* of St. John of the Cross, Bk. V, chap. v, § 10. It must have been written very shortly after Letter I. P. Jerónimo says of it: 'By means of these words he removed those fears and she very soon experienced the fulfilment of what he had prophesied. She was thinking of looking for a certain person so as to write to him of the favour which Our Lord had granted her herein, when she received a letter from the venerable Father telling her all that had come to pass in her soul.' This fragment and the next (Letter III) can also be found in a statement (MS. 12,738) taken from M. Ana by P. Juan Evangelista, and signed by her. The text of this statement is followed, with regard to both fragments, in the present edition.

Mother Ana de San Alberto, a much-loved and respected friend of both St. Teresa and St. John of the Cross, was a native of Malagón, where she took the veil in the convent founded there by St. Teresa in 1568. When in 1575 St. Teresa went through Malagón on her way to found the convent at Seville, she took M. Ana with her as far as Beas. From the Andalusian capital she sent her to found a convent at Caravaca, having great trust in her ability and discretion, and for many years she was Prioress of Caravaca. It was here that she came to know St. John of the Cross who was there on various occasions.

trials to me, go to that spotless mirror of the Eternal Father, which is His Son, for in that mirror I behold your soul daily, and I doubt not but that you will come away from it comforted and will have no need to go begging at the doors of poor people.

LETTER III

To M. Ana de San Alberto, Prioress of Caravaca

Date uncertain.

(Fragment.)

Counsels her to journey to perfection without dependence upon any creature and to cast aside unfounded scruples which do harm to her spirit.[1]

. . . Since you say nothing to me, I tell you not to be foolish and harbour fears that make the soul cowardly. Give to God that which He has given you and gives you daily. It seems to me that you are trying to measure God by the measure of your own capacity; but you should not do so. Prepare yourself, for God seeks to do you a great favour.

FRAY JOHN OF THE CROSS.

LETTER IV

To M. Ana de San Alberto, Prioress of Caravaca

SEVILLE, JUNE 1586.

Informs the Mother of the solemnity with which the foundation of Discalced Carmelite friars at Córdoba was inaugurated and describes the transference of the nuns of Seville to their own house. Matters concerning the foundation at Caravaca.[2]

[1] This fragment also was published by P. Jerónimo de San José (*History*, Bk. V, chap v, § 11), who took it from the statement made by M. Ana, and referred to above (p. 242, n. 1). P. Jerónimo tells us that this letter was written by St. John of the Cross when in Granada, and, since he knew M. Ana at least as early as 1581, when he was at Caravaca for the elections there, it may easily have been written at a date very little later. [P. Sobrino points out that in MS. 12,738, Letters II and III are given in the inverse order, and infers from the context that that order is correct.]

[2] The autograph of this letter was venerated at the Duruelo priory until the time of the secularization of the religious houses in Spain in the nineteenth century. It is mentioned by P. Andrés de la Encarnación (*Memorias Historiales*, I, 60) and by P. Manuel de Santa María. On the expulsion of the religious from Duruelo, this letter was sent to some nuns at Arévalo, who presented it to the *corregidor* of that town in gratitude for his help to them in their troubles. It is now the property of the Marquesa de Reinosa. It measures 31 by 22 cms. and consists of two folios, the upper half of the second of which (cf. p. 245, n. 5, below) is missing. The superscription is on the letter.

On another half-sheet are the words: 'I, Fray Juan de San José, Prior of this house of

Jesus be in your soul. When I left Granada for the foundation at Córdoba, I had written to you in haste. And afterwards, when I was in Córdoba, I received your letters and the letters of those persons who were going to Madrid, and who must have thought that they would catch me at the Council. But you must know that it has never met, as we have been waiting for these visitations and foundations to end, and the Lord hastens matters so much in these days that we are unable to do anything. The friars' foundation at Córdoba was concluded with the greatest acclamation and solemnity throughout the city that has ever been known in connection with any religious Order. For all the clergy of Córdoba and all the confraternities gathered together and the Most Holy Sacrament was taken from the Cathedral with great solemnity: all the streets were beautifully hung and the crowds reminded one of Corpus Christi Day. This was on the Sunday after the Ascension; the Bishop came to preach and praised us very much in his sermon. Our house is in the best part of the city—that is to say, in the parish of the Cathedral.[1]

I am now in Seville for the transference of our nuns, who have bought some excellent houses; they cost almost fourteen thousand ducats but are worth more than twenty thousand.[2]

They are already in them and on St. Barnabas' Day the Cardinal is to place the Most Holy Sacrament there with great solemnity. And I mean to leave another house of friars here before I go, so that there will be two houses of our friars at Seville. And between now and Saint John's Day I go to Ecija, where, with God's help, we shall found another, and then to Málaga, and thence to the Council.[3]

Discalced Carmelite friars of Duruelo, added this sheet of paper which was missing from this letter of our father St. John of the Cross. It seems to have contained the date, which is not in the letter as we have it, but we have the signature of the Saint, and also, at the foot of the letter, three lines in his own handwriting. And as a witness of the truth of this I have signed it in the same house, on the 22nd of August, 1680. *Fray Juan de San José*.'

There can be very little missing from the letter as it has come down to us; the missing lines seem to refer to Doña Catalina de Otálora, one of the persons who chiefly contributed to St. Teresa's having founded the Convent of Discalced nuns at Caravaca.

[1] The Carmelites took over the church of San Roque, in the parish of the Cathedral, a central part of the city, on May 18, 1586. St. John of the Cross was at that time Vicar-Provincial of the Discalced in Andalusia.

[2] The Saint had authorized the Discalced nuns of Seville to purchase these houses in a document dated April 12, 1586.

[3] On May 13, 1586, the nuns were transferred from the Calle de la Pajería (now the Calle de Zaragoza) to the house where they still live in the Calle de Santa Teresa, in the parish of Santa Cruz. Neither the second foundation of the Discalced friars in Seville, nor the foundation of Ecija, was carried out at that time. The former, that of El Santo Ángel, dates from 1588; the latter, from 1591. About this time the Saint sickened with a fever in Guadalcázar, so that he could not, as he proposes in the letter, go on to Málaga, where in the preceding year he had founded a Convent of Discalced nuns; there had been

I only wish I had a commission for your foundation as I have for these, and that I were not expecting to have to do so much wandering about. But I hope in God that the foundation will be made and I shall do all that I can in the Council. Tell that to those persons, to whom I am writing.

I have greatly regretted that the contract with the Fathers of the Company has not been drawn up, because, as I see them, they are not people who keep their word; and so I fancy that not only will they deviate partially from it, but they will change their minds altogether if they are so inclined. Note, then, that I advise you, without saying anything, either to them or to anyone else, to discuss with Señor Gonzalo Muñoz[1] the purchase of that other house, which is on the far side, and let the deeds be drawn up, for they can see that they have the whip hand,[2] so they are getting overbearing. And it will very soon be known that we are buying these houses solely in order to make up for our annoyance, and thus they will come to terms without all this breaking of heads, and we shall even make them give us everything we want. Say very little to people about this and do it, for sometimes one cannot take a precaution without at the same time taking another.[3]

I should like you to send me the little book of the *Songs of the Bride*, for Madre de Dios will presumably have copied it by now.[4]

This Council meeting is greatly delayed, and I regret it, because of the entry of Doña Catalina, for I want to give . . .[5]

Your servant,
FRAY JOHN OF THE CROSS.

See that you give my special remembrance to Señor Gonzalo

a house for friars since 1584. As one of the Discalced Definitors he had to assist at the chapter convoked in Madrid, for August 13, 1586, by P. Nicolás Doria, where, among other matters, that of publishing St. Teresa's writings was considered.

[1] D. Gonzalo Muñoz was one of the leading citizens of Caravaca and very well disposed to the Discalced. On May 5, 1583, we find P. Gracián writing from Almodóvar del Campo to the Prioress of Caravaca, authorizing her to receive two of D. Gonzalo's daughters into the community.

[2] [*Lit.*, 'that they have got hold of the rope'—a not dissimilar metaphor.]

[3] This is a long and complicated question of which a full explanation cannot be given here. Briefly, there was a house and garden, the property of Sister Isabel de San Pablo, which adjoined a Jesuit College. The Jesuit Fathers claimed to have a right to this house, possibly because of some verbal agreement with Isabel's mother, and actually took possession of it. This led to some feeling between the two communities. The Rector of the College assured the Prioress that they would arrive at a satisfactory agreement, but St. John of the Cross has evidently no great confidence that this will be so and hence warns the Prioress to take every precaution.

[4] The allusion is to the *Spiritual Canticle*, of which a copy was being made by Francisca de la Madre de Dios, who had been professed in her native town of Caravaca on June 1, 1578.

[5] From an inspection of the manuscript, it would seem that some fifteen lines are missing from this letter.

Muñoz. I do not write to him lest I should weary him, and because your Reverence will say to him what I say here.

(Superscription): To M. Ana de San Alberto, Prioress of the Discalced Carmelite nuns at Caravaca.[1]

LETTER V

To the Discalced Carmelite Nuns of Beas

MÁLAGA, NOVEMBER 18, 1586.

Gives the Discalced nuns admirable instruction concerning emptiness and detachment from creatures.[2]

Jesus be in your souls, my daughters. Are you thinking that, since you see me so silent, I have lost sight of you, and cease from considering how with great ease you may become holy, and how, with great delight and under sure protection, you may go rejoicing in the beloved Spouse? Well, I shall come to you and you will see that I have not been forgetting you, and we shall see what wealth you have gained in pure love and in the paths of eternal life and what excellent progress you are making in Christ, Whose brides are His delight and crown: and a crown deserves not merely to be sent rolling along the floor, but to be taken by the angels and seraphim in their hands and set with reverence and esteem on the head of their Lord.

When the heart is occupied with mean things, the crown rolls along the floor, and each of these mean things gives it, as it were, one kick farther. But when man attains, as David says, to loftiness of heart, then is God magnified with the crown of that lofty heart of His bride, wherewith they crown Him in the day of the joy of His heart,[3] wherein He has His delights when He is with the sons of men. These waters of interior delights have not their source in the earth: the mouth of desire must be opened toward Heaven, and must be empty of aught else that might fill it, so that thus the mouth of desire, neither clogged

---

[1] This superscription forms part of the autograph manuscript.

[2] The autograph of this letter is found in the parish church of Pastrana, which had it, no doubt, from the former Discalced Carmelite convent at Pastrana. It was first published by D. Mariano Pérez y Cuenca in his *Recuerdos Teresianos de Pastrana* and is of particular value as confirming our knowledge of St. John of the Cross's warm regard for the nuns of Beas. There are a number of early copies extant, notably one in the codex of the *Spiritual Canticle* belonging to the Discalced friars of Segovia.

[3] The Segovian copy reads 'of His coronation' [*coronación* for *corazón*]. The reference, despite the mention of David, seems to be to Canticles iii, 11.

nor closed by the taste of aught else, may be completely empty and wide open toward Him Who says: 'Open thy mouth wide and I will fill it for thee.'[1]

He, then, that seeks pleasure in aught else keeps not himself empty that God may fill him with His ineffable joy, and, in the state in which he goes to God, even so does he go out from Him, for his hands are encumbered and he cannot take what God gives him. May God deliver us from such evil encumbrances, which impede such sweet and delectable freedom.[2]

Serve God, my beloved daughters in Christ, following His footsteps of mortification in all patience, in all silence and with all desire to suffer. Become the executioners of your own pleasures, mortifying yourselves if perchance there is still aught left in you that has yet to die and that impedes the interior resurrection of the spirit. May that spirit dwell in your souls! Amen.

From Málaga.

Your servant,
FRAY JOHN OF THE CROSS.
November 18, 1586.

LETTER VI

TO THE DISCALCED CARMELITE NUNS OF BEAS [OR GRANADA][3]

GRANADA, NOVEMBER 22, 1587.

New spiritual instructions for the nuns. What the soul ordinarily needs is not to write and speak but to be silent and act. The best means of preserving one's spirituality is to suffer. Solitude and recollection in God.[4]

Jesus, Mary, Joseph[5] be in your souls, my daughters in Christ. Your letter comforted me greatly: may Our Lord reward you for it! My not having written has not been for lack of willingness, for truly

---

[1] [Psalm lxxx, 11; A.V., lxxxi, 10.]   [2] [*Lit.*, 'liberties.']
[3] [See p. 249, n. 3, below.]
[4] This letter belonged to the Discalced Carmelite friars of Zaragoza and seems to have disappeared in the siege of that city during the War of Independence. There are two almost identical copies in the National Library, Madrid (MS. 12,738, fol. 767, and MS. 13,245, fol. 247). In the text we follow the latter copy, which was made from an earlier copy, at Duruelo, in 1761, by P. Manuel de Santa María. [There is also an excellent copy in the Tardón-Granada MS., agreeing more closely with MS. 13,245 than with 12,738: this copy is discussed in full by P. Sobrino, pp. 84-92.]
[5] [P. Silverio omits this last word, which is found in MS. 13,245, but not in other copies.]

I desire your great good, but because it seems to me that enough has already been said and written for the accomplishment of what is needful; and that what is lacking (if anything be lacking) is not writing or speaking, for of this there is generally too much, but silence and work. And, apart from this, speaking is a distraction, whereas silence and work bring to the spirit recollection and strength. And therefore, when a person once understands what has been said to him for his profit, he needs neither to hear nor to say more, but rather to practise what has been said to him silently and carefully, in humility and charity and self-contempt, and not to go away and seek new things, which serve only to satisfy the appetite in external matters (and even here are unable to satisfy it) and leave the spirit weak and empty, with no interior virtue. Hence such a one profits neither at the beginning nor at the end. He is as one that eats again before he has digested his last meal, who, because his natural heat is divided between both meals, has no strength to convert this food into substance, and becomes indisposed.

It is very needful, my daughters, to be able to withdraw the spirit from the devil and from sensuality,[1] for otherwise, without knowing it, we shall find ourselves completely failing to make progress and very far removed from the virtues of Christ, and afterwards we shall awaken, and find our work and labour inside out. Thinking that our lamp was burning, we shall find it apparently extinguished, for when we blew upon it, and thought thereby to fan its flame, we may rather have put it out. I say, then, that, if this is not to be, and in order to preserve our spirituality (as I have said) there is no other way[2] than to suffer and work and be silent, and to close the senses by the practice of solitude and the inclination to solitude, and forgetfulness of all creatures and all happenings, even though the world perish. Never, for good or for evil, fail to quiet your hearts[3] with tender love,[4] in order that you may suffer in all things that present themselves. For perfection is of such great moment, and spiritual delight is of so rich a price—may God grant that all this may suffice; for it is impossible to continue to make progress save by working and suffering with all virtue, and being completely enwrapped in silence.

---

[1] MS. 12,738: 'from our sensuality.'
[2] [No hay medio. Thus the text of MS. 13,245. P. Silverio, following a marginal note, reads: No hay mejor remedio: 'there is no better remedy.' The other copies also have this.]
[3] MS. 12,738: 'allow your hearts to become disquieted.'
[4] [Lit., 'with the bowels of love.']

I have understood,[1] daughters, that the soul which is easily inclined to talk and converse is but very little inclined towards God; for, when it is inclined toward God, it is at once, as it were, forcibly drawn within itself, that it may be silent and shun all conversation, for God would have the soul enjoy Him more than it enjoys any creature, howsoever excellent and suitable such a creature may be.

I commend myself to the prayers of your Charities; and be certain that, small as my charity is, it is so completely centred in you that I never forget those to whom I owe so much in the Lord. May He be with us all. Amen.

From Granada, on the 22nd of November, 1587.

FRAY JOHN OF THE CROSS.

The greatest necessity we have is to be silent before this great God with the desire[2] and with the tongue, for the language which He alone hears is the language of silent love.

(Superscription): To Ana de Jesús and the other Discalced Carmelite sisters of the Convent of Granada.[3]

LETTER VII

To M. Leonor Bautista, Beas

GRANADA, FEBRUARY 8, 1588.

Commiserates with her on her trials and counsels her to bear them with pleasure, for God's sake.[4]

Jesus be in your Reverence. Think not, daughter in Christ, that I

[1] MS. 12,738: 'I understand.'   [2] MS. 12,738: 'with the spirit.'

[3] [MS. 13,245, from which this superscription is taken, clearly says 'Granada,' and, though it might seem strange that St. John of the Cross should write so long a letter to nuns in the same city, it would not be difficult to find reasons for this. The difficulty resides in the fact that Ana de Jesús, who is mentioned by name, and who had gone from Beas to Granada as Prioress in 1582, left Granada, and went to Madrid as Prioress, in 1586, holding that office for three years. This is pointed out by P. Manuel de Santa María in a manuscript marginal note in MS. 13,245, and is, in any case, a well-known fact. P. Silverio, in the edition here translated, reads 'Granada,' but in his 1940 edition, without giving any reason, he substitutes 'Beas,' presumably in order to resolve the contradiction between superscription and heading. In the heading, 'Beas' occurs in several copies (TG, e.g., begins: 'Letter which the holy father Fray John of the Cross . . . sent to the nuns of his Order in the town of Beas'), but this is even less likely to have been correct than 'Granada.']

[4] The autograph, in a good state of preservation, is venerated in the Convent of Discalced Carmelite nuns of Barcelona. It measures 31 by 23 cm. and is written on one side only. There is a photographic reproduction in P. Gerardo's *Autógrafos*.

The nun to whom the letter was written was born at Alcaraz, in the province of Albacete, and professed at Beas in 1578. She had just laid down her office as prioress; it is to this that the Saint alludes in the last sentence of the second paragraph.

have ceased to grieve for you in your trials or for those that share them with you; yet, when I remember that God has called you to lead an apostolic life, which is a life of contempt, and is leading you by that road, I am comforted. Briefly, God desires that the religious shall live the religious life in such a way that he shall have done with everything, and everything shall be as nothing to him. For He Himself desires to be the only wealth of the soul and its comfort and its delectable glory. A surpassing favour has God granted your Reverence, for now, forgetting all things, your Reverence will be able to rejoice in God alone, and for love of God will care nothing as to what they do with you, since you belong not to yourself but to God.

Let me know if your departure for Madrid is certain, and if the Mother Prioress is coming, and commend me greatly to my daughters Magdalena and Ana,[1] and to them all, for I have no opportunity to write to them.

From Granada, on the 8th of February, (15)88.

FRAY JOHN OF THE CROSS.

LETTER VIII

TO P. AMBROSIO MARIANO DE SAN BENITO, PRIOR OF MADRID

SEGOVIA, NOVEMBER 9, 1588.

Changes of convent by certain religious. The Prior and Sub-prior must get on well together. Nobody must interfere with the novices.[2]

Jesus be in your Reverence. The need for religious, as your Reverence knows, is very great, on account of the large number of existing foundations. Therefore your Reverence must have patience until Fray Miguel leaves you to await the Father Provincial at Pastrana, for he has then to go and complete the foundation of that convent at Molina.[3] The Fathers also thought it would be well to give your

---

[1] These were two of the nuns of Beas, both of whom are mentioned elsewhere in these volumes.

[2] The autograph, well preserved, is in the possession of the Discalced Carmelite nuns of St. Joseph's, Ávila. On P. Ambrosio Mariano, one of the Discalced friars most greatly esteemed by St. Teresa, see her *Foundations*, Chap. xvii [*C.W.S.T.J.*, III, 81–4].

[3] This foundation did not prove a success. The friar here mentioned was P. Miguel de Jesús, Sub-prior of Madrid.

Reverence a sub-prior; and so they have given you Fray Ángel,[1] as
they think he will get on well with his prior, which is the most necessary thing in a convent. Will your Reverence then give to each of
these his letters patent? It will also be well if your Reverence loses no
opportunity of seeing that none, be he priest or no, meddles with the
novices in his dealings with them; for, as your Reverence knows, there
is nothing more harmful than to pass through many hands and for
others to go about interfering with the novices. It is right to help and
relieve Fray Ángel, since he has so many novices, and also to give him
the authority which belongs to a sub-prior, as we have done, so that
he may be the more respected in the house. As to Fray Miguel, it
seems that there is no great need for him to be here just now, and that
he will be able to serve the Order better elsewhere. With regard to
Father Gracián, nothing new has happened, save that Fray Antonio is
now here.[2]

From Segovia, November 9, (15)88.

FRAY JOHN OF THE CROSS.[3]

LETTER IX

TO DOÑA JUANA DE PEDRAZA, GRANADA

SEGOVIA, JANUARY 28, 1589.

*The Saint acknowledges the letters which his spiritual daughter, Doña
Ana, has written him. Spiritual counsels: detachment from everything and
blind obedience to the spiritual director. It is fitting that we should never
be without our cross. He begs her not to write such tiny letters.*[4]

[1] Fr. Ángel de San Gabriel.

[2] The reference is to the troubles of P. Gracián [described briefly in *Studies of the
Spanish Mystics*, Vol. II, pp. 152–9] with his Order. Both St. John of the Cross and P.
Mariano were well disposed to him. Fray Antonio (i.e. de Jesús), as a member of the Con-
sulta (*S.S.M.*, II, p. 156) which now governed the Reform, was obliged by disposition
of the Consulta to reside in Segovia, the only exception to be made being that of P.
Mariano himself, who was to retain the priorate at Madrid.

[3] After the signature is written, in another hand: 'P. Gregorio de San Angelo kisses
your Reverence's hands.'

[4] The autograph is in the Convent of Discalced Carmelite friars at Concesa, in Italy.
A photographic reproduction was published by P. Anastasio de San José in his *Somma di
Mistica Teologia*. Owing to the letter having been long folded, several words are no
longer legible.

Doña Juana de Pedraza was a disciple of the Saint and may well have been sister of
the then Archdeacon of Granada. [Cf. p. 266, n. 2.]

Jesus be in your soul. A few days ago I wrote to you by way of Fray Juan,[1] replying to this your last letter, which, as was to be expected, was greatly valued. In that letter I said that, as far as I can see, I have received all your letters, and have sympathized with your griefs and troubles and times of loneliness, which, even when you have said nothing about them, have always cried out to me to such an extent that even with your pen you could not have said more. All these things are rappings and knockings upon the soul, calling it to greater love, and causing more prayer and sighings of the spirit to God, that He may fulfil that for which the soul begs for His sake. I told you that there was no cause to enter that . . .,[2] but that you must do what you are commanded, and, if you are hindered from doing this, be obedient and tell me about it, and God will provide what is best. God takes care of the affairs of those who love Him truly without their being anxious concerning them.

In matters pertaining to the soul, it is best for you, so as to be on the safe side, to have attachment to nothing and desire for nothing, and to have true and complete attachment and desire for him who is your proper guide, for to do otherwise would be not to desire a guide. And when one guide suffices, and you have one who suits you, all others are either superfluous or harmful. Let your soul cling to nothing; and, if you fail not to pray, God will take care of your affairs, for they belong to no other master than God, nor can they do so. This I find to be true of myself, for, the more things are mine, the more I have my heart and soul in them and the more anxious I am about them; for he that loves becomes one with the object of his love, as does God with him that loves Him. Hence one cannot forget this without forgetting one's own soul; and for the object of one's love one indeed forgets one's own soul, for one lives more in the object of one's love than in oneself.

O great God of love, and Lord, how much of Thine own riches dost Thou not set in him that loves naught and takes pleasure in naught but Thyself, since Thou givest Thyself to him and makest him one thing with Thyself through love! And herein Thou givest him to love and have pleasure in that which the soul most desires in Thee and that which brings it the greatest profit. For we must not be without our cross, even as our Beloved had His cross until He died the death of love. He orders our sufferings in the love of that which we most need, so that we may make the greater sacrifices and be of the greater worth.

[1] P. Juan Evangelista.   [2] Several words which follow are illegible.

But it is all short, for it continues only until the knife is raised, and then Isaac remains alive, with the promise that his children shall be multiplied.

Patience is needful, my daughter, in this poverty, for patience enables us to leave our country,[1] and to enter into life to have full fruition of it all, which is ... of life.[2]

Now I know not when I shall go. I am well, although my soul lags far behind. Commend me to God and give the letters to Fray Juan,[3] or to the nuns, more often, whenever you can, and if they were not so tiny, it would be better.

From Segovia, on January 28, 1589.

FRAY JOHN OF THE CROSS.

LETTER X

To a Girl from the Province of Ávila who wished to become a Discalced Nun

SEGOVIA, FEBRUARY.

He replies to her, telling her how to behave with respect to her sins, to the Passion of the Lord and to everlasting glory.[4]

Jesus be in your soul. The messenger came upon[5] me at a time when I could not reply before he went on his way, and now at this moment he is waiting again. May God ever give you His holy grace, my daughter, so that at all times it may all be employed in His holy love,[6] as is your obligation, for it was for this alone that He created you and

---

[1] [The original adds 'well.']   [2] Here several words are illegible.

[3] P. Juan Evangelista.

[4] This letter was published by P. Jerónimo de San José (*History*, Bk. VI, chap. vii, § 3), who says: 'It was written to a girl from Madrid who wished to be a Discalced nun, and later entered a convent of the Order founded at a place in New Castile called Arenas, which was afterwards transferred to Guadalajara. She was a native of Narros del Castillo, a village in the diocese of Ávila. The venerable Father used to give her Communion when he was confessor at the Incarnation, and she was in the house of Doña Guiomar de Ulloa, in Ávila, and later he was in the habit of writing to her. Out of respect and devotion to him, and as his spiritual daughter, she took the name of Ana de la Cruz.'

The original of the greater part of this letter was formerly to be seen at the Convent of Discalced Carmelite nuns at Alcalá. It was published by D. Vicente de la Fuente in one of the series of autograph letters which he began to edit, and was reproduced in *El Monte Carmelo* in November 1916. It is now no longer to be found in this convent, however, and the nuns seem to have no idea of the manner of its disappearance or of its whereabouts. P. Jerónimo's version is used for the first three sentences and the last three paragraphs. [P. Sobrino suggests the substitution of two emendations from MS. 12,738, which are given in notes below.]

[5] [*Me ha topado*. MS. 12,738 reads *me ha tomado*, 'took (i.e. caught) me,' which sounds rather the more natural of the two.]

[6] [MS. 12,738 adds: 'and service.']

redeemed you.[1] On the three points about which you write to me there would be a great deal to say, more than the present lack of time and the limitations of this letter allow; but I will write to you of three others, so that you may be able to derive a certain amount of profit from them.

With regard to sins, which God so much abhors that they led Him to suffer death, it is well that, in order duly to mourn for them and not to fall into them, you have as few dealings as you can with other people, and shun them, and never say more than is necessary upon any subject; it would be well if you never had any more to do with them than is strictly necessary and reasonable, however holy they may be; and in this way you will keep the law of God with great punctiliousness and love.

With regard to the Passion of the Lord, strive to chasten your body with discretion, abhor and mortify yourself, and desire not to do your own will and pleasure in aught, for this was the cause of His death and passion; and whatever you do, let it all be by the advice of your mother.[2]

Thirdly, with regard to glory: in order to think of it often and to love it, account all the riches of the world and the delights thereof to be mud and vanity and weariness, as indeed they are, and prize naught soever, however great and precious it be, save being right with God, since all that is best here below, compared with those eternal blessings for which we are created, is vile and bitter, and, although its bitterness and vileness be brief, it will abide for ever in the heart of him that prizes them.[3]

I am not forgetting your affairs, but it is impossible to write more now, though I should very much like to do so. Commend them often to God and take Our Lady and Saint Joseph for your advocates in the matter.

I commend myself earnestly to your mother. Ask her to regard this letter as written to her also, and commend me, both of you, to God, and, of your charity, beg your friends to do the same.

God give you His Spirit.

From Segovia, February.

FRAY JOHN OF THE CROSS.

[1] [After this word the Alcalá autograph begins.]
[2] Earlier editions read: 'of your master.' The mother of this girl, however, it would appear, was very devout.
[3] Here the Alcalá autograph ends. The signature below it is that of another autograph document pasted on the paper.

LETTER XI

To a Religious, his Penitent

*Gives him very useful counsels for progress in virtue. Persuades him to
set his will upon God and withdraw all his joy from the creatures.*[1]

The peace of Jesus Christ, son, be ever in your soul. I received your
Reverence's letter, in which you tell me of the great desires that Our
Lord gives you to occupy your will with Him alone, and to love Him
above all things, and in which you ask me to give you a few directions
as to how you may achieve this.

I rejoice that God has given you such holy desires and I shall
rejoice much more at your putting them into execution. To this end
you should notice that all pleasures, joys and affections are ever caused
in the soul by the will and desire for things which appear to you good,
fitting and delectable, since the soul considers these to be pleasing and
precious; and in this way the desires[2] of the will are drawn to them,
and it hopes for them, and rejoices in them when it has them, and fears
to lose them; and thus, through its affections for things and rejoicing
in them, the soul becomes perturbed and unquiet.

So, in order to annihilate and mortify these affections for pleasures
with respect to all that is not God, your Reverence must note that all
that wherein the will can have a distinct joy is that which is sweet and
delectable, since this appears pleasant to it, and no sweet and delectable
thing wherein it can rejoice and delight is God, for, as God cannot
come within the apprehensions of the other faculties, so neither can He
come within the desires and pleasures of the will; for in this life, even
as the soul cannot taste of God essentially, so none of the sweetness
and delight that it tastes, howsoever sublime it be, can be God; for,

---

[1] This letter is found in P. Jerónimo de San José's *History*, etc. [Bk. VI, chap. vii, § 2].
There are also extensive fragments of it in the Pamplona Codex [cf. Vol. I, p. 7 of this
translation] and in another very early manuscript which was to be found at Duruelo and
which P. Andrés copied for the Codex of Alcaudete [Vol. I, pp. 7–8]; the relation
between the subject-matter of the letter and that of the *Ascent of Mount Carmel* is of
course a very close one. [Cf. Vol. I, p. 314, n. 2, and the bracketed note to the 2nd edition
of this translation.] There are many variants between these Codices and P. Jerónimo's
version of the letter, nor do the Codices agree verbally between themselves. The year in
which the letter was written is uncertain; it may well be 1589, when the Saint, we know,
was in Segovia.

[2] [The noun translated 'desire' here and below, to the end of the letter, is *apetito*, and
the verb *apetecer*; earlier in the letter the words used are *deseo* and *querer*.]

further, all that the will can have pleasure in and desire as a distinct thing, it desires in so far as it knows it to be such or such an object. Then, since the will has never tasted God as He is, neither has known Him beneath any apprehension of the desire, and consequently knows not what God is like, it cannot know what it is like to taste Him, nor can its being and desire and experience attain to the knowledge of the desire for God, since He is above all its capacity.

And thus it is clear that no distinct object from among all objects that the will can enjoy is God. Wherefore, in order to become united with Him, a man must empty and strip himself of every inordinate affection of desire and pleasure for all that can be distinctly enjoyed, whether it be high or low, temporal or spiritual, to the end that the soul may be purged and clean from all inordinate desires, joys and pleasures whatsoever and may thus be wholly occupied, with all its affections, in loving God. For, if in any wise the will can comprehend God and become united with Him, it is by no apprehensible means of the desire, but by love; and, as neither delight nor sweetness nor any pleasure that can pertain to the will is love, it follows that none of these delectable feelings can be a proportionate means whereby the will may unite itself with God, but only the operation of the will, for the operation of the will is very different from its feeling; it is through the operation that it becomes united with God, and has its end in Him, Who is love, and not through the feeling and apprehension of its desire, which makes its home in the soul as its end and object. The feelings can only serve as motives for love if the will desires to pass beyond them, and not otherwise; and thus delectable feelings do not of themselves lead the soul to God, but cause it to rest in themselves; but in the operation of the will, which is to love God, the soul sets on Him alone its affection, joy, pleasure, contentment and love, leaving all things behind and loving Him above them all.

Wherefore, if any man be moved to love God otherwise than by the sweetness which he feels, he is already leaving this sweetness behind him and setting his love on God, Whom he feels not; for, if he set it upon the sweetness and pleasure that he feels, dwelling upon this and resting in it, this would be to set it upon creatures or things pertaining thereto and to turn the motive into the object and the end; and consequently the act of the will would become harmful; for, as God is incomprehensible and inaccessible, the will, in order to direct its act of love toward God, has not to set it upon that which it can touch and apprehend with the desire, but upon that which it cannot comprehend or attain thereby. And in this way the will remains loving that which is certain, in very truth, by the light of faith, being empty and in darkness, with respect to its feelings, and transcending above all that it can feel with the understanding, and with its own intelligence, believing and loving beyond all that it can understand.

And thus he would be very ignorant who should think that, because spiritual delight and sweetness are failing him, God is failing him, and should rejoice and be glad if he should have them, and think that for this reason he has been having God. And still more ignorant would he be if he went after God in search of this sweetness, and rejoiced and rested in it; for in this case he would not be seeking God with his will grounded in the emptiness of faith and charity, but spiritual sweetness and pleasure, which is of creature, following his taste and desire; and thus he would not then love God purely, above all things (which means to set the whole strength of the will upon Him), for, if he seizes hold upon that creature and clings to it with the desire, his will rises not above it to God, Who is inaccessible; for it is impossible that the will can rise to the sweetness and delight of Divine union, or embrace God, or experience His sweet and loving embraces, save in detachment and emptying of the desire with respect to every particular pleasure whether from above or from below; for it is this that David meant when he said: *Dilata os tuum, et implebo illud.*[1]

It must be known, then, that the desire is the mouth of the will, which opens wide when it is not impeded or filled with any morsel— that is, with any pleasure; for, when the desire is set upon anything, it becomes constrained, and apart from God everything is constraint. And therefore, in order for the soul to succeed in reaching God and to become united with Him, it must have the mouth of its will opened to God alone, and freed from any morsel of desire, to the end that God may satisfy it and fill it with His love and sweetness, and it may still have that hunger and thirst for God alone and refuse to be satisfied with aught else, since here on earth it cannot taste God as He is; and furthermore, that which it can taste, if it so desire, as I say, impedes it. This was taught by Isaias when he said: 'All you that thirst, come to the waters,' etc.[2] Here he invites those that thirst for God alone to the fullness of the Divine waters of union with God, though they have no money—that is, no desire.

---

[1] ['Open thy mouth wide, and I will fill it.'] Psalm lxxx, 11 [A.V., lxxxi, 10].
[2] Isaias lv, 1.

Very meet is it, then, if your Reverence would enjoy great peace in your soul and achieve perfection, that you should surrender your whole will to God, so that it may thus be united with Him, and that you should not employ it in the vile and base things of earth.

May His Majesty make you as spiritual and holy as I desire.

From Segovia, on the 14th of April.

FRAY JOHN OF THE CROSS.

LETTER XII

TO M. MARÍA DE JESÚS, PRIORESS OF CÓRDOBA

SEGOVIA, JUNE 1589.

Replies to various questions concerning the observance of the Rule on which she had consulted him.[1]

Jesus be in your Reverence and make you as holy and poor in spirit as you desire and as His Majesty will grant me for you.

Here is the licence for the four novices; see that they are good for God's service.

I will now reply briefly (for I have little time) to all your questions, having spoken of them first with these Fathers, for our own is not here, as he is travelling. May God bring him back![2]

1. The discipline with rods is now no longer given even though the rite be ferial, for this expired with the Carmelite rite, which was only at certain times and had few ferias.

2. Secondly, do not as a rule give leave to all the nuns, or to any of them, to take the discipline thrice weekly, in compensation for this or any other penance, and do not, in particular cases, depart from the ordinary routine. You will see what it is best to do in the matter. Keep to the usual practice.[3]

1 The autograph is in the convent of Discalced Carmelite nuns at Brussels. This is the first time that it has been published in an edition of St. John of the Cross's works. It has no superscription, but it is practically certain that it was written to M. María de Jesús, who, having recently been appointed Prioress of the new community, consulted the Saint on several points of government.

2 The Saint means that, before answering his correspondent's questions, he had discussed them with the members of the Consulta, of which he was temporarily Superior, P. Doria ['our own (Father)'] having left for his canonical visit to the convents of Andalusia.

3 An interesting summary of the Carmelite rite can be read in Fr. Zimmerman's *Ordinaire de l'Ordre de Notre-Dame du Mont-Carmel*, pp. v–xxiii. St. Teresa's Reform adopted the Latin rite in 1586. The discipline mentioned is only used at present occasionally during Lent and on canonical visits. It may be added that one of the observances of

3. Let them——that is, the community——not ordinarily rise earlier than the constitution orders.

4. The licences expire when the term of the prelate expires, and therefore with this letter I send you a new licence which will allow the entrance into the convent, in case of need, of confessor, physician, barber and workmen.

5. Fifthly, as you have now plenty of vacant places, when what you say is necessary, we can treat of the question of Sister Aldonza. Commend me to her and commend me to God. And abide with Him, for I cannot write at greater length.

From Segovia, June 7, 1589.

FRAY JOHN OF THE CROSS.[1]

LETTER XIII

TO M. LEONOR DE SAN GABRIEL, CÓRDOBA[2]

SEGOVIA, JULY 8, 1589.

Gives her very wholesome instruction from which to extract much spiritual advantage on her leaving the Discalced Carmelites at Seville for the convent which had just been founded at Córdoba.[3]

Jesus be in your soul, my daughter in Christ. I thank you for your letter and I thank God that He has been pleased to use you in this foundation of yours, for His Majesty has done this in order that He may use you still more; for, the more He is pleased to give, the more He makes us to desire, until He leaves us empty in order to fill us with good things. You will be well recompensed for the good things in Seville that you are now forgoing for the love of the sisters, for,

the Calced which St. Teresa lightened was that of the discipline, which according to her Constitution may only be taken on Fridays, whereas the Calced nuns took it thrice weekly throughout the year.

[1] In a very early hand, that of a woman, is written, beneath this signature: 'This letter is all in the handwriting of our venerable father Fray John of the Cross. Do not give it away, for it is a great relic.' These words are followed by others, now indecipherable.

[2] [The Córdoba convent having been founded ten days before this letter was even written (see n. 3, below), it must clearly have been sent there, and not, as P. Silverio has it, to Seville. MS. 12,738 reproduces the superscription thus: 'To M. Leonor de San Gabriel, Discalced Carmelite, at Córdoba.' Cf. Sobrino, pp. 95–6.]

[3] From P. Jerónimo de San José: *History*, etc., Bk. VI, chap. vii, § 4. Leonor de San Gabriel was a native of Ciudad Real, who had been professed at Malagón in 1571. St. Teresa took her with her, when she passed through Malagón on her way to found the convent at Seville. She became a great favourite of St. Teresa, who calls her 'an angel for her simplicity' and often refers to her in her letters. Cf. particularly Letter 304 [*Letters*, London, 1951, p. 712]. The new foundation at Córdoba, to which M. Leonor went from Seville as Sub-prioress, was made on June 28, 1589.

inasmuch as there is no room for the boundless gifts of God save in a heart that is empty and solitary, and they enter none but such a heart, therefore the Lord, Who loves you greatly, loves you to be quite alone, desiring to be Himself your only companion. And your Reverence will need to set your mind on being contented with Him alone, that you may find all content in Him; for, although the soul be in Heaven, yet, if the will be not prepared to desire it, the soul will not be content; and this is how it is with God (although God is ever with us) if we have our heart affectioned to aught else, and not to Him alone.

I am quite sure that the nuns of Seville will feel lonely there without your Reverence; but perchance your Reverence had already done all that was possible there and it pleases God that you should be used elsewhere, for this new foundation will be an important one; and thus let your Reverence seek to be of great help to the Mother Prioress, and show great conformity and love in everything; although I know quite well that I need not charge you thus, as you have sufficient seniority and experience to know already what usually happens in these foundations; for which reason we have chosen your Reverence; for, as for nuns, there were so many here that there is no room for them.

Give Sister María de la Visitación[1] my particular regards and tell Sister Juana de San Gabriel[2] that I thank her for her message. May God give your Reverence His Spirit.

From Segovia, July 8, 1589.

FRAY JOHN OF THE CROSS.

LETTER XIV

TO M. LEONOR DE SAN GABRIEL, CÓRDOBA

MADRID, JULY ——.

Comforts her in a trial that came to her and tortured her greatly.[3]

Jesus be in your soul, my daughter in Christ. Your letter filled me with sympathy for you in your trouble and I grieve that you have it

[1] This nun, a native of Alcalá de Henares, went with M. Leonor from the Sevilian convent to that of Córdoba.

[2] This was one of the Beas nuns who was sent to the new foundation at Córdoba.

[3] The autograph is to be seen, together with a letter of St. Teresa, in the convent of Discalced Carmelite nuns at Sanlúcar la Mayor. Unfortunately its corners have been cut in order to fit the letter into its oval reliquary and several parts (indicated in the text by dots) are missing. No copy of the complete letter is known.

because of the harm that it may cause your spirit and even your bodily health. But I must tell you that I do not think you have any great reason to feel this trouble as you are doing, since I do not . . . to our Father . . . with no kind of misfortune . . . remembrance of such . . . and even if there were . . . it will be . . . your repentance; and if there were still any (trouble) . . . I . . . given . . . to speak well.[1] Do not be troubled about it, and take no notice of it, for you have no need to do so. For I am certain that it is a temptation which the devil brings to the spirit so that it may occupy in it that which should be occupied in God. Have courage, my daughter, and be given greatly to prayer, forgetting this and that, for after all we have no other blessing nor . . . support, nor comfort (than?) this, and after we have left all for God it is right that we should have no support or comfort in aught save Him. And yet it is a great . . . for us to have Him, so that He may (stay?) with us and that He may give nothing . . . for the soul that . . . comfort and thinking that . . . His Majesty will be . . . when we are not in trouble, for . . . is not . . . I will do it.

From Madrid, July . . .

LETTER XV

To M. Maria de Jesús, Prioress of the Discalced Nuns of Córdoba

Segovia, July 18, 1589.

Gives admirable instruction with respect to poverty, which there is so much opportunity to practise, principally in new foundations. What nuns must be like whom God chooses as the first stones of a foundation.[2]

Jesus be in your soul. You[3] are obliged to make return to the Lord for the cordiality with which they have received you in Córdoba, the

[1] The general meaning of this phrase seems to be that M. Leonor, who was of a very kindly disposition, is afraid that P. Nicolás Doria, with whom she had had a great deal to do in Seville, has been offended with her, and the Saint is reassuring her and offering to intercede with him if necessary.

[2] The original of this letter is venerated in the convent of the Discalced Carmelite nuns at Córdoba and is in excellent preservation. It measures 32 by 22 cm. It was reproduced photographically by P. Gerardo in his *Autógrafos*. P. Jerónimo published the letter in his *History*, etc., Bk. VI, chap. vii.

M. María de Jesús, together with her sister Catalina de Jesús, founded the Convent of the Discalced at Beas. St. Teresa's eulogy of her in chap. xxii of the *Foundations* should be read together with this letter.

[3] [This 'you' is plural throughout the first two paragraphs.]

account of which I have been greatly cheered to read. And that you should have gone into such poor houses and in such great heat has been the ordinance of God, that you may give cause for edification and show forth what you profess, which is to follow Christ in detachment, in order that they that are moved to join you may know in what spirit they must come.

Herewith I send you the whole of the licences; at first you must look carefully at all whom you receive, because the rest will be formed according to their standard. And see that you keep the spirit of poverty and contempt for everything (otherwise you know that you will fall into a thousand spiritual and temporal necessities), desiring to content yourselves with God alone. And know that you will have, and be conscious of, no necessities other than those to which you desire to subject your hearts; for he that is poor in spirit is the more constant and joyful in privation, since he has made nothing and nothingness his all, and thus finds breadth of heart in everything. Blessed is that nothingness and blessed is that secret place of the heart that is of such great price that it possesses everything, yet desires to possess nothing for itself and casts away all care so long as it can burn the more in love.

Greet all the sisters from me in the Lord and tell them that, as Our Lord has taken them for His foundation-stones, they must consider what manner of stones they ought to be, since others will be built up upon those that are strongest; let them profit by this first outpouring of His Spirit that God gives in these beginnings, that they may make an entirely fresh start upon the road of perfection, in all humility and detachment, both within and without, not in a childish spirit, but with a robust will; let them practise mortification and penance, desiring that this Christ should cost them something, and not being like those who seek their own convenience and comfort, whether in God or apart from Him; but rather let them suffer, both in God, and apart from Him, for His sake, in silence and hope and loving remembrance. Say this to Gabriela[1] and to her sisters from Málaga.[2] To the others I am writing. May God give you His Spirit. Amen.

From Segovia, July 18, 1589.

Fray John of the Cross.

Fray Antonio and the Fathers commend themselves to you. Give my greetings to the Father Prior of Guadalcázar.

---

[1] The MS. has 'Grabiela.' [The metathesis is frequent, occurring for example in the letters of St. Teresa, where she speaks of 'la su Grabiela'—i.e. M. Leonor de San Gabriel.]

[2] M. Leonor de San Gabriel and her companions from Malagón are meant.

LETTER XVI

To M. Magdalena del Espíritu Santo, Córdoba

Segovia, July 28, 1589.

Encourages her to endure the trials of the new foundation gladly.
'In these beginnings God wants no slothful souls.'[1]

Jesus be in your soul, my daughter in Christ. I am delighted to see your good resolutions which you set down in your letter. I praise God, Who provides for all things, for there will be ample need of all these resolutions in the beginnings of these foundations, on account of the heat, the straits, the poverty and the labour that there will be throughout, and none must perceive if these things afflict you or no. Take note that in these beginnings God wants no slothful or delicate souls, still less souls that are lovers of themselves; and therefore His Majesty aids souls more in these beginnings, so that with a little diligence they can go forward in all virtue; and it has been a great blessing and a mark of God's favour that He has passed over others and led you to this place. And, even if that which you leave had cost you more, it is nothing, for in any case you would have had to leave it soon; and, to have God in everything, a soul must have nothing in everything; for how can the heart which belongs to one belong in any degree to another?

To Sister Juana[2] I say the same. Let her commend me to God and may He be in your soul. Amen.

From Segovia, July 28, 1589.

FRAY JOHN OF THE CROSS.

LETTER XVII

To P. Nicolás de Jesús María (Doria), Vicar-General
of the Discalced

Segovia, September 21, 1589.

Replies, in the name of the Consulta, to various questions which P.
Nicolás, who was absent from Segovia, had put to him.[3]

[1] Published by P. Jerónimo de San José (*History*, Bk. VI, chap. vii, § 5) and in M. Magdalena's own account of the life of the Saint, who was her only director, from the time he first knew her at Beas (1578) until his death thirteen years later.
[2] Juana de San Gabriel, a nun who went from Beas to Córdoba with M. Magdalena.
[3] A copy of this letter occurs in MS. 12,738, p. 759, together with the note: 'This letter

Jesus, Mary be with your Reverence. We were delighted to hear that your Reverence had arrived safely and that everything is going so well with you and with the Nuncio. I hope in God that He will care for His family; here the poor creatures are well and happy; I shall try to get the work done quickly as your Reverence has commanded, although so far the . . .[1] have not arrived.

With regard to receiving persons in Genoa[2] who know no grammar, the Fathers say that it matters little that they should not know it, if they understand Latin with the sufficiency ordered by the Council, so that they know how to construe; and, if they are ordained in Italy with no more than this, it seems that they can be received. But, if the Ordinaries in Italy are not content with that, it seems that they have not the sufficiency ordered by the Council, and it would be troublesome to have to bring them over here to ordain them or teach them. And actually they would not wish many Italians to come over here.

The letters will go to Fray Nicolás, as your Reverence says. May Our Lord preserve you for us as He sees we have need of you.

From Segovia, September 21, (15)89.[3]

FRAY JOHN OF THE CROSS.

was faithfully and truly copied in Valladolid by Fray Antonio de la Madre de Dios, of the convent of Burgos, from one that was written by our father Fray John of the Cross.'

For the proper understanding of the letter and others which follow, it is essential to know something of the history of P. Nicolás Doria and of the creation of the Consulta (cf. *Studies of the Spanish Mystics*, Vol. II, p. 156). The Consulta was created at the Chapter which met in Madrid on June 19, 1588. After six weeks, on the proposal of St. John of the Cross, its headquarters were transferred to Segovia. P. Mariano, however, for special reasons, continued to hold his office of Prior of the Convent at Madrid. The Consulta was moved to Segovia on August 10, 1588, and, on September 16, P. Nicolás left Segovia to visit some of the newly divided provinces of the Reform, leaving the Saint as first definitor, as president of the Consulta and as superior of the house at Segovia in his absence.

[1] [The word omitted is *avenidas*, conjectured by P. Silverio to be an error for *avenidos*, which is the same word as that translated above as 'happy' (*bien avenidos* : well satisfied, agreed). Its use at all here would seem to be another error: some other word must be meant.]

[2] P. Doria had founded the first Italian Discalced convent at Genoa in 1584. He had now left Segovia to visit the convents of the Reform as Vicar-General. It is clear from the context that a number of young Italians were anxious to take the habit of the Reform.

[3] This is the date on the copy described above, and, although P. Doria returned from his visits to the convents, as described in the first note to this letter, on March 3, 1589, we see no objection to it. For he may perfectly well have set out for a further series of visits in the late summer; there is no evidence to the contrary, and, as the early autumn is a temperate and settled time of the year for travelling, and the difficulties of travelling on foot or on a humble mount were considerable, the supposition that he made a second journey seems a likely one.

LETTER XVIII

To Doña Juana de Pedraza, Granada

Segovia, October 12, 1589.[1]

The Saint courteously and religiously reminds this lady that he has not forgotten her. He assuages certain uneasinesses which she has felt, because of her somewhat scrupulous conscience. Let her live in dark faith, certain hope and complete charity and fear nobody.[2]

May Jesus be in your soul. I thank Him for giving me His grace, so that, as you say, I do not forget the poor. But I do not, as you also say, live a sheltered life, and it hurts me dreadfully[3] to think that, when you say that, you really believe it. That would be too bad after so many marks of kindness, which you have shown me when I least merited them. I have done anything but forget you; just think, how could I forget one who is in my soul, as you are? While you are walking in that darkness and in those empty places of spiritual poverty, you think that everyone and everything are failing you; but that is not surprising, for at those times it seems to you that God is failing you too. But nothing is failing you, nor have you any need to consult me about anything, nor have you any reason to do so, nor do you know one, nor will you find one: all that is merely suspicion without cause. He that seeks naught but God walks not in darkness, in whatever darkness and poverty he may find himself; and he that harbours no presumptuousness and desires not his own satisfaction, either as to God or as to the creatures, and works his own will in any way whatsoever, has no need to stumble or to worry about anything. You are progressing well; remain in quietness and rejoice. Who are you to be anxious about yourself? A fine state you would get into if you did that!

You have never been in a better state than now, for you have never been humbler or more submissive, nor have you ever counted yourself, and everything in the world, as of such little worth; nor have you ever known yourself to be so evil, nor God to be so good, nor have you ever served God so purely and disinterestedly as now, nor do you

---

[1] [Sobrino (pp. 98–9) follows MS. 13,245, which gives the date as 1588.]

[2] Cf. Letter IX, n. 1. This autograph can be seen at the Convent of the Discalced nuns at Valladolid. There are also a number of copies of it.

[3] [The original, *harto me hace rabiar*, a very strong expression, can denote anger ('It makes me absolutely furious') or anguish. In MS. 13,245, the copyist has crossed out the phrase and substituted *harta pena me da*, 'it causes me the greatest grief,' no doubt considering this more in character.]

any longer go, as you may have been apt to do, after the imperfections of your will and your own resolution. What do you desire? What kind of life do you imagine yourself as living in this world? How do you imagine yourself behaving? What do you think is meant by serving God, but abstaining from evil, keeping His commandments and walking in His ways as best we can? If this be done, what need is there of other apprehensions, or of any other illumination or sweetness whether from one source or from another? In these things as a rule the soul is never free from stumbling-blocks and perils, and is deceived and fascinated by the objects of its understanding and desire and its very faculties cause it to stray. And thus God is granting the soul a great favour when He darkens the faculties and impoverishes the soul so that it may not be led astray by them; and how can it walk aright and not stray, save by following the straight road of the law of God and of the Church, and living only in true and dark faith and certain hope and perfect charity, and awaiting its blessings in the life to come, living here below as pilgrims, exiles and orphans, poor and desolate, with no road to follow and with no possessions, expecting to receive everything in Heaven?

Rejoice and put your trust in God, for He has given you signs that you can quite well do so, and indeed that you ought to do so; should you do otherwise, it will not be surprising if He is wroth at seeing you so foolish, when He is leading you by the road that is best for you and has set you in so sure a place. Desire no way of progress but this, and tranquillize your soul, for all is well with it, and communicate as is your wont. Confess, when you have something definite to say; there is no need to talk. When you have anything to say you will write about it to me, and write to me quickly, and more frequently; you can always do that through Doña Ana, when you cannot do it through the nuns.

I have been somewhat indisposed, but am now well again, though Fray Juan Evangelista[1] is ailing. Commend him to God, and me likewise, my daughter in the Lord.

From Segovia, October 12, 1589.

FRAY JOHN OF THE CROSS.[2]

[1] Fray Juan Evangelista was the Saint's (appropriately named) Beloved Disciple. He gave him the habit at Granada and for a long time lived on intimate terms with him. He sent him from Granada, where of course they both knew Doña Juana, to Segovia, and made him procurator of the Segovia priory.

[2] [MS. 13,245 adds the following superscription: 'To Doña Juana de Pedraza, at the house of the Archdeacon of Granada, opposite the College of the Abbots.' Cf. Sobrino, p. 99.]

LETTER XIX

To M. María de Jesús, Prioress of the Discalced Carmelite Nuns of Córdoba

MADRID, JUNE 20, 1590.

He counsels her not to worry overmuch about the temporal business of the house. Convents have to be governed by means of virtues and desires from Heaven rather than by cares and plans for what is temporal and earthly. Let the nuns live in all religion and perfection, united with God and in God.[1]

Jesus be in your soul, my daughter in Christ. The reason why I have not written during all this time, as you say, is rather that I have been in an out-of-the-way place like Segovia than because of any unwillingness, for my will is always constant, and I hope in God that it will continue to be so. I have been very much grieved at your troubles.

With regard to the temporal business of your house, I should not like you to be over-anxious about it, for God will else be forgetting you, and you will all come to have much necessity, both temporal and spiritual, for it is our solicitude that brings us to necessity. Cast your care upon God, daughter, and He will nourish you; for He that gives and is pleased to give the greatest things cannot fail in the least. See that you lack not the desire to lack and to be poor, for in that same hour your spirituality will be lacking and you will begin to grow weaker in the virtues. And if you desired poverty before, now that you bear rule you must desire and love it much more; for you must govern the house and furnish it with living desires and virtues from Heaven rather than with cares and plans for what is temporal and earthly; since the Lord tells us not to take thought for what we shall eat or what we shall put on tomorrow.

What you must do is to try to lead your soul and the souls of your nuns into all perfection and religion, in union with God, forgetting all creatures and all respect for creatures, being wrought wholly in God, and glad in Him alone, and I guarantee you all the rest. I find it difficult to think that the houses will give you anything, now that you are in such a good place as this that you have and are receiving such good nuns. Still, if I see an opening anywhere, I will not fail to do what I can.

[1] The autograph of this letter, in excellent preservation, is to be found in the convent of the Discalced Carmelite nuns at Córdoba.

I wish the Mother Sub-prioress great consolation. I hope in the Lord that He will give it her, so that she may have courage to continue on her pilgrimage and exile in love for His sake. I am writing to her now. To my daughters Magdalena, San Gabriel and María de San Pablo, María de la Visitación, San Francisco and all the rest, my many greetings in our Good. May He be ever in your spirit, my daughter. Amen.

From Madrid, June 20, 1590.

FRAY JOHN OF THE CROSS.

I shall soon return to Segovia, as I believe.

LETTER XX

TO A CARMELITE NUN WHO SUFFERED FROM SCRUPLES

He gives her prudent and wise rules for behaviour when attacked by scruples, so that they may do no harm to her soul.[1]

Jesus, Mary. In these days be employed inwardly in desiring the coming of the Holy Spirit, and both during the festival and afterwards continue in His presence, and let your care and esteem for this be such that nothing else attracts you, neither consider aught else, whether it be trouble or any other disturbing memories; and during the whole of this period, even though there be omissions in the house, pass them over for the love of the Holy Spirit, and for the sake of what is necessary to the peace and quiet of the soul wherein He loves to dwell.

If you can put an end to your scruples, I think it would be better for your quietness if you were not to confess during these days. When you do confess, let it be after this manner: with regard to advertences and thoughts, whether they have respect to judgments or whether to unruly representations of objects or any other movements that come to you without the desire and collaboration of your soul, and without your desiring to pay attention to them, do not confess these or take any notice of them or be anxious about them, for it is better to forget

---

[1] The autograph is to be seen, in a fair state of preservation, at the convent of Discalced nuns of St. Joseph and St. Anne, Madrid. The person to whom it was addressed may have been one of the nuns of that community, which was founded in 1586 by some of the Saint's spiritual daughters. No date or place of writing is given (a rare occurrence with St. John of the Cross), but the context shows that the letter was written just before Pentecost, perhaps in Madrid, between 1589 and 1591.

them, although they trouble your soul the more; at most you might describe in general terms the omission or remissness that you may perchance have noted with respect to the purity and perfection which you should have in the interior faculties—memory, understanding and will. With respect to words, confess any excess and imprudence that you may have committed as regards speaking truly and uprightly, and out of necessity and with purity of intention. With regard to actions, confess the way in which you may have diverged from the path to your true and only goal, which you should follow without respect of persons —namely, God alone.

And, if you confess in this way, you may rest content, without confessing any of these other things in particular, however much interior conflict it may bring you. You will communicate during this festival, as well as at your usual times.

When anything disagreeable and displeasing happens to you, remember Christ crucified and be silent.

Live in faith and hope, though it be in darkness, for in this darkness God protects the soul. Cast your care upon God, for you are His and He will not forget you. Do not think that He is leaving you alone, for that would be to wrong Him.

Read, pray, rejoice in God, your Good and your Health, and may He give you His good things and preserve you wholly, even to the day of eternity. Amen. Amen.

FRAY JOHN OF THE CROSS.

LETTER XXI

TO M. ANA DE JESÚS, SEGOVIA

MADRID, JULY 6, 1591.

Comforts the Mother for the vexation which she had felt when the Chapter of the Reform held in Madrid left the Saint without office. His sublime instruction exhorting her to resignation and conformity with the plans of Providence.[1]

[1] The original of this letter, measuring 26½ by 21½ cm., is preserved by the Discalced Carmelite nuns of the Convent of Corpus Christi at Alcalá de Henares. It was published by P. Jerónimo de San José (*History*, Bk. VII, chap. ii, § 3). For M. Ana de Jesús, cf. St. Teresa's *Foundations*, chap. xxi. [*Complete Works of St. Teresa*, III, 105.] When St. John of the Cross, as a member of the Consulta, went to live at Segovia and became confessor to the Discalced nuns there, M. Ana de Jesús was one of his most devoted and exemplary penitents.

On June 6, 1591, a Chapter General of the Reform at Madrid deprived St. John of the

Jesus be in your soul. I thank you heartily for having written to me, and this puts me under a greater obligation to you than I had before. You must be glad rather than otherwise and give hearty thanks to God because things have not happened as you desired; for, as His Majesty has ordained it thus, it is best so for us all; it only remains for us to apply our wills to it, so that we may see it as it really is. For things that give no pleasure, good and fitting though they may be, seem bad and adverse, and this clearly is not so, either for me or for anyone. For it is very advantageous for me, since, now that I am free and no longer have charge of souls, I can, by Divine favour, if I so desire, enjoy peace, solitude and the delectable fruit of forgetfulness of self and of all things; and, as for the others, it is good for them also to be without me, as they will thus be free from the faults which they would have committed through my unworthiness.

What I beg of you, daughter, is that you beg the Lord to continue His favour to me, for I still fear that they may make me go to Segovia[1] and not leave me wholly free, although I will do what I can to escape from this also; but, if this cannot be, Mother Ana de Jesús will not have escaped from my hands, as she supposes, and thus she will not die with this regret that, as she thinks, the opportunity to be very holy is over. For, whether I go or remain, and wherever or however I may be, I shall not forget her nor take her name from the list[2] of which she speaks, for truly I desire her everlasting good.

Now, till God gives us this in Heaven, let her occupy herself in practising the virtues of mortification and patience, and desire to behave in suffering in some measure as did this our great God, when He was humbled and crucified; for this life is of no use, unless we imitate Him. May His Majesty keep you and increase you in His love, amen, even as His holy and beloved bride.

From Madrid, July 6, 1591.

FRAY JOHN OF THE CROSS.

Cross of office. This evidently came as a great surprise to the Segovia nuns, as this and the next letter show.

[1] According to P. Jerónimo (*History*, Bk. VII, chap. ii, § 2) P. Doria asked the Saint to go as Vicar to Segovia. With complete submission, he answered that his preference would be for the retirement of La Peñuela, the loneliest house which the Reform then possessed, in order to prepare himself to go to New Spain (Mexico) whither he was destined. As we know, he died five months later, at Úbeda.

[2] [Perhaps a list of persons for whom the Saint prayed.]

LETTER XXII

To M. María de la Encarnación, Segovia

MADRID, JULY 6, 1591.

(Fragment.)

Tells her not to grieve at what happened at the Madrid Chapter. 'Think only that God ordains all.'[1]

... As to my affairs, daughter, let them not grieve you, for they cause no grief to me. What I greatly regret is that blame is attributed to him who has none; for these things are not done by men, but by God, Who knows what is meet for us and ordains things for our good. Think only that God ordains all. And where there is no love, put love and you will find love....[2]

LETTER XXIII

To P. Juan de Santa Ana

SEGOVIA.

Believe not him that preaches the doctrine of the broad way, even though he do miracles.[3]

Jesus: If at any time, my brother, any man, whether in authority or no, would persuade you to accept any doctrine of the way that is broad and of the greatest ease, believe him not, neither embrace it, even though it be confirmed with miracles, but seek penance and still

---

[1] Of this letter, written on the same day as No. XXI, we have only this precious fragment, worth a volume on Christian resignation, which was preserved by P. Jerónimo de San José (*History*, Bk. VII, chap. ii, § 4). M. María was Prioress of the Discalced nuns of Segovia when this letter was written. In a canonical deposition made during the process at Segovia (1616), she speaks of the letter and quotes from memory the last two sentences in abbreviated form, describing the occasion of its being written.

[2] [More literally, 'you will draw love out.']

[3] Quoted by P. Jerónimo de San José (*History*, Bk. VII, chap. viii, § 1). The date is probably 1591. [Sobrino (pp. 101–6) comments at length on the letter. Briefly, he believes (i) that it is only a passage from the middle or end of a letter, and that P. Jerónimo should not have prefaced it with the word 'Jesus'; (ii) that the identity of the addressee is probably but not certainly that here given; (iii) that P. Alonso el Asturicense's date of 1590 is more probable than 1591.]

more penance and detachment from all things, and never, if you would attain to the possession of Christ, do you seek Him without the Cross. . . .

LETTER XXIV[1]

To Doña Ana del Mercado y Peñalosa, Segovia

La Peñuela, August 19, 1591.

He reached La Peñuela nine days previously and is very happy there. The vastness of the desert is good for both soul and body. Present occupations and future plans. Spiritual counsels.

Jesus be in your soul. Although I have sent you a letter by way of Baeza describing the events of my journey, I was glad that these two servants of Señor Don Francisco were passing, as I can now write you these lines, which will be more certain of reaching you.

I said in my other letter how anxious I was to remain in this desert[2] of La Peñuela, six leagues from Baeza, where I arrived nine days ago.[3] I am getting on here very well, glory to the Lord, and am in good health, for the vastness of the desert is a great help both to the soul and to the body, though my soul[4] is in a very poor way. It must be the Lord's will that the soul also should have its spiritual desert: let whatever best pleases Him be very welcome, for His Majesty well knows what we are of ourselves. I cannot say how long this state of things will

---

[1] [Letters XXIV–XXIX will be found not to correspond exactly with those in P. Silverio's 1929–31 edition. Letter XXIV was first published by P. Sobrino, in 1950, from TG (Vol. III, p. 240, above), and has not previously appeared in English. The mode of address, the references to Don Luis and Doña Inés, and the similarity of the content with that of Letter XXVIII (in P. Silverio's edition, XXV) make it certain that the recipient was Doña Ana de Peñalosa (on whom see Vol. III, p. 4, above). External evidence of this is provided by Fray Andrés de la Encarnación, who, in describing the letter, says that it was written 'to Señora Doña Ana de Peñalosa. It tells her of his arrival at La Peñuela, sets down many praises of solitude and gives her important counsels for the quiet (*sosiego*) of her soul.' Nothing is known of the other letter sent via Baeza.]

[2] [The MS. has *desierto*, 'desert,' which P. Sobrino writes with a capital letter, as if the reference were to the type of hermitage-priory generally known by its Spanish name of Desierto. The first foundation of this kind was not made till 1592, at Bolarque, on the Tagus (*S.S.M.*, II, 282), but, as the La Peñuela priory was a particularly austere one, St. John of the Cross may have used the word in that sense.]

[3] [This would seem to indicate that St. John of the Cross arrived at La Peñuela on August 10, 1591, a little later than had previously been supposed. It should be noted that the Spanish has *habrá nueve días*, 'it *will be* nine days'—the use of the future tense which often implies approximation or doubt. P. Sobrino, however (p, 49), interprets the phrase as meaning 'exactamente el 10 de agosto.']

[4] [*Lit.*, 'the soul'; but, as the verb is in the indicative, the reference can only be to his own soul. Cf. p. 253, above: 'I am well, although my soul lags far behind.']

last, for Father Fray Antonio de Jesús warns[1] me from Baeza that they will not allow me to stay here for long. Be that as it may: I find I get on very well without news and the desert is an admirable training-ground.[2]

This morning we have just been gathering our chick-peas—we spend our mornings in that way. Some other day we shall thresh them. It is pleasant to handle these dumb creatures—better than being handled ourselves by living ones.[3] May God allow it to continue: pray Him to do so, my daughter. Happy though all this makes me, I shall not fail to go when you[4] wish.

Be careful about your soul, and do not go confessing scruples, or first motions, or mere awareness of things upon which the soul has no wish to dwell; and look after your bodily health; and do not fail to pray whenever you can.

I said in the other letter (though this one will reach you first) that you can write to me by way of Baeza, as there is a courier service, directing your letters to the Discalced Fathers at Baeza; I have notified them about sending them on to me.

My kind regards to Señor Don Luis and to my daughter Doña Inés.[5] May God give you His Spirit, amen, as I desire.

From La Peñuela, August 19, 1591.

FRAY JOHN OF THE CROSS.

[1] [*Lit.*, 'threatens': cf. the reference to Fray Antonio in Letter XXVIII (p. 276, below).]

[2] [*Lit.*, 'the exercise of the desert is admirable,' or, as we might say to-day, 'the desert is splendid training.']

[3] [St. John of the Cross is no doubt referring, somewhat grimly, to the severe handling he had received, first from the friars of the Observance, years before, and then, only a few weeks previously, from his own brethren.]

[4] ['You' is *ella*, which can mean either 'she' or 'you' (fem.). One would have expected *Él* ('He,' i.e. God), but we gather from the first paragraph of Letter XXVIII that Doña Ana was pressing a certain course of action on the Saint, so that the reading may be correct.]

[5] [Don Luis was Doña Ana's brother, and Doña Inés, one of the Saint's penitents, her niece.]

LETTER XXV

To M. Ana de San Alberto, Prioress of Caravaca[1]

La Peñuela, August (?) 1591.

(Fragment.)

Resignation in trials. In silence and hope will be our strength.

My daughter: You will already know of the many trials that we are suffering. God allows this for the glory of His elect. In silence and hope will be our strength. Commend me to God, and may He make you holy.

LETTER XXVI

To an Unknown Person[2]

La Peñuela, August 22, 1591.

If we have right intentions, and refrain from sin, all will go well with us.

May God give us right intentions in all things and may we never knowingly admit sin. If that is so with us, the conflict[3] may be fierce and spread in many directions, but its end will be sure and everything will turn into a crown. Give my greetings to your sister, and my good wishes in the Lord to Isabel de Soria, and tell her I am surprised she is not at Jaén, as there is a priory[4] there. May the Lord be in your soul, daughter in Christ.

From La Peñuela, August 22, 1591.

Fray John of the Cross.

---

[1] This fragment (XXIV in P. Silverio's edition) was quoted by the recipient in the course of depositions made by her in 1616 in connection with St. John of the Cross's beatification. She describes it as having been written to her from La Peñuela.

[2] [This fragment was unknown when P. Silverio's five-volume edition of the Saint's works was published, but he included it in his single-volume edition, published in 1940 (Bibliography, No. 31, below). The autograph is venerated in the convent of Discalced Carmelite nuns at Chiaia, near Naples.]

[3] [The Spanish has *balería*, which means a collection or supply of bullets, and in this context makes little sense. I suggest as an emendation *batería*, which, unlike *balería*, is found in Covarrubias (1611), and one of the meanings of which is 'hail of blows,' 'battering.' The context demands a freer rendering than this.]

[4] [I translate *monasterio* as 'priory,' rather than 'convent' (the more usual meaning at this time), because a priory of the Reform was founded at Jaén in 1588, whereas nothing is known of the existence of a convent there as early as 1591. The Spanish *no está* could be equally well rendered 'you are not' and 'she is not.' If 'you' is correct, the addressee may have been a man.]

LETTER XXVII

To P. Juan de Santa Ana

LA PEÑUELA, 1591.

He reassures him, telling him not to be grieved by the information that was being given against him (the Saint) with the intention of taking his habit from him.[1]

Jesus . . . do not let this worry you, son, for they cannot take the habit from me save for incorrigibility or disobedience, and I am quite prepared to amend my ways in everything in which I have gone astray, and to be obedient, whatever the penance they give me. . . .

LETTER XXVIII

To Doña Ana del Mercado y Peñalosa, Segovia

LA PEÑUELA, SEPTEMBER 21, 1591.

He informs her of his departure for Úbeda in order to cure a slight attack of fever which needed medical aid. Congratulates Don Luis del Mercado, Doña Ana's brother, because from being a Chancery judge he has become a priest of the Lord. His own health.[2]

Jesus be in your soul, daughter. Here at La Peñuela I received the packet of letters which the servant brought me. I greatly appreciate the trouble you have taken. Tomorrow I go to Úbeda[3] to cure a slight

[1] Of this letter we have only the fragment preserved by P. José de Jesús María (*Vida*, Bk. III, chap. xx). P. Juan was one of the Saint's best-loved disciples whom he had come to know at El Calvario on his arrival there from Toledo, and who later accompanied him on his journey to found the convent of Baeza and elsewhere. [P. Silverio numbers this XXVI (*Obras completas*, IV, 291), making it the last of the Saint's extant letters and supposing it to have been written at Úbeda. P. Crisógono, however (*Vida y obras*, etc., p. 439, n. 79), quotes the evidence of the recipient to prove that it was written at La Peñuela. It is here placed in its correct chronological position.]

[2] The autograph, beginning with the words 'I think I shall need . . .', belongs to the Discalced Carmelite nuns of Salamanca, and is reproduced photographically by P. Gerardo (Bibliography, No. 36, below) and Baruzi (No. 35). Fortunately, P. Jerónimo de San José published the letter from the autograph in its original state, and we follow his copy in the first four sentences.

[If Letter XXVIII is compared with Letter XXIV (from TG), also addressed to Doña Ana, it will probably be concluded that the second was written in answer to her reply to the first. The end of the first paragraph is clearly connected with the second and third paragraphs of the earlier letter.]

[3] [He did not, in fact, leave until September 28: cf. P. Crisógono, *Vida y obras*, etc., p. 445, n. 1.]

bout of fever, for I have been having attacks of it daily for over a week, and if it does not go[1] I think I shall need medical aid; but I go with the intention of returning here again, for in truth I am deriving great good from this holy retreat; and thus, concerning your caution to me not to go with Fray Antonio, be assured that, both in this and in all the rest that you ask, I will act with all possible care.

I am delighted that Señor Don Luis is now a priest of the Lord. May this be so for many years and may His Majesty fulfil the desires of his heart! Oh, what a happy state it would be to leave behind one's anxieties and to enrich the soul speedily with Him! Give him my good wishes. I do not venture to ask him to remember me sometimes when he is at the Sacrifice; I myself, as his debtor, shall do this always for him; for although I am forgetful I could never fail to remember him, since he is so near to his sister, whom I have always in my memory.

Give my daughter Doña Inés my many greetings in the Lord and pray both of you that He may be pleased to prepare me to be taken to be with Him.

Now I can think of no more to say, and so, on account of the fever, I stop, though I would gladly go on.

From La Peñuela, September 21, 1591.

FRAY JOHN OF THE CROSS.

You write nothing of the lawsuit, if it continues or is over.

LETTER XXIX

TO A SPIRITUAL DAUGHTER[2]

Worldly and spiritual riches.

You have seen, daughter, what a good thing it is to be without money, for, if we have any, people can rob us of it and disturb our

---

[1] [P. Silverio, apparently by an oversight, omits from the edition here translated the words *y si no me quitan*, 'and if it does not go.']

[2] [This is the second of the unpublished letters edited by P. Sobrino (cf. p. 240, above). Fray Andrés de la Encarnación describes the addressee as 'a spiritual person, apparently a woman under the Saint's direction.' This description is supported by the tone of the letter, the opening words 'You have seen . . .' (presumably referring either to a previous instruction or to some experience of hers which she had recounted to him) and the final paragraph, suggestive of a close acquaintanceship. P. Sobrino makes the further deduction that the recipient lived near the writer, but I do not find his reasons for this convincing. There is really no clue, in the letter as we have it, to its date, to the place in which it was written or to its recipient's identity.]

quiet, and also how the treasures of the soul should be hidden away and left in peace, so that we may not know they are there or even so much as catch a glimpse of them; for there is no worse thief than one who lives in the house.[1] May God preserve us from ourselves; may He give us whatever pleases Him and never reveal it to us until it be His will to do so. After all, he who lays up treasures for love's sake lays them up for another, and it is well that He should keep them for Himself and enjoy them, since they are all for Him, and that we ourselves should neither see them with our eyes nor enjoy them, lest we should rob[2] God of the pleasure which He has in the humility and detachment of our hearts and our contempt of worldly things for His sake. It is a very great treasure, and one that brings great joy, for the soul to discover that it is going[3] to give Him such manifest pleasure,[4] and to pay no heed to the foolish ones of this world, who can keep nothing for the future.

The Masses will be said, and I shall be very glad to go if they do not advise me to the contrary.[5] May God keep you.

FRAY JOHN OF THE CROSS.

TRANSLATOR'S APPENDIX TO THE LETTERS

P. Sobrino (Vol. III, p. 240, n. 1, above) publishes (op. cit., pp. 65–9) three fragments, apparently of letters by St. John of the Cross, which, as we have them at second-hand, it seems most suitable to relegate to an appendix. They are reproduced in MS. (N.L.M.) 13,482, in a chapter headed 'Fragments of our holy Father' (fols. 143r–150r).

[1] [That is to say, if we, who have spiritual treasures, set our affections on them instead of on God, we are robbing Him in the worst possible way because we are members of His own household. This thought, expressed rather cryptically here, is developed and made more explicit in the sentences which follow.]

[2] [The verb used, desflorar, suggests to P. Sobrino (p. 59) that the Saint's intention is to compare humility, detachment and contempt of the world to flowers, and it is true that Covarrubias (1611) gives the literal meaning of the word, quitar la flor, before derived ones, but I suspect that flor here means 'bloom,' 'lustre.']

[3] [Lit., '. . . great joy, to see that the soul is going, etc,' as if the treasure were God's. But I think the logical subject of 'to see' is 'the Christian.']

[4] [There is a play upon words here which cannot be rendered in English. The words '(very great) treasure . . . to discover' are (harto) descubierto tesoro; 'manifest' is al descubierto, 'open,' 'unconcealed.']

[5] [The words 'to the contrary' are not in the Spanish, but I take them to be implied. P. Sobrino (p. 57, n. 1) discusses the possibility that the negative particle crept in by an error, but decides against it, I am sure rightly.]

I

A nun says in her deposition: Coming to the Madrid foundation[1] from Granada, and gathering that a nun needed him, he put himself to very great inconvenience to write this to her: 'Daughter, in emptiness and dryness as regards all things, God will prove those who are valiant soldiers, that they may win His battle, which are they who can drink the water in the air (*sic*), without their breasts' cleaving to the ground, even as did the soldiers of Gedeon, who conquered with dry clay[2] and lamps enkindled within it, signifying dryness of sense, and within it the good and enkindled spirit.'[3]

II

The same nun says: To M. María del Nacimiento, who was Prioress at Madrid, he wrote another letter of such a kind that it astonished her to see how closely he was in touch with her interior life when he was so many leagues distant. I remember a few words of the letter, in which he taught her 'to seek the treasure hidden in the field, although she thought she was not finding it, for, if she found it, it would no longer be hidden, and consequently would not be a treasure.'

III

To a nun of Segovia, he wrote when he was being[4] persecuted, exhorting her to bear opposition well: 'Love deeply those who oppose you and love you not, for in that way love is engendered in a breast where there is none. Even so does God deal with us, loving us in order that we may love Him by means of the love which He has for us.'[5]

---

[1] [*Translator's note:* The Madrid convent of the Reform was founded on September 17, 1586—not, as P. Sobrino says, February 25, 1586, which was the date of the foundation of the Madrid priory. So busy was St. John of the Cross, during 1586, making foundations in the south that he is unlikely to have gone to Madrid before April 1587, when he was in Valladolid for the Chapter held there.]

[2] [*Translator's note:* The 'dark pitchers' of Judges vii, 16, and *Ascent of Mount Carmel*, II, ix (Vol. I, p. 94, above).]

[3] [This fragment was published in *Vida y obras*, etc. (1946: Bibliography No. 34, below), p. 1,233, from a copy on fol. 1,005 of MS. (N.L.M.) 12,738.]

[4] [*Lit.*, 'when he is.']

[5] [This extract is from a deposition made by M. Elvira de San Angelo, Prioress of the Reformed convent of Medina del Campo.]

SUNDRY DOCUMENTS

(Written or Signed by St. John of the Cross)

I

Judgment given by the Blessed Father upon the Spirituality and the Method of Procedure in Prayer of a Nun of our Order.[1]

IN the affective way of prayer followed by this soul there seem to be five defects, if it be judged by the standard of pure spirit. First, it appears that she has a great eagerness for possession,[2] whereas true spirituality is always characterized by great detachment in the desire. Secondly, she has overmuch confidence and too few misgivings lest she stray interiorly; unless a soul have these misgivings the Spirit of God never keeps it from evil, as the Wise Man says. Thirdly, she seems anxious to persuade others to believe that her experiences are good and abundant; this never happens with true spirituality, which, on the contrary, desires men to make little account of their experiences and to depreciate them, as the spiritual soul itself does. Fourthly, and most important, there seem to be no signs of humility in this method of prayer which she follows; now when the favours granted to the soul are genuine, as she says they are in her case, these experiences are not habitually communicated to the soul that is not first humble and annihilated with interior humility; and if she had these signs she would not fail to write something of the matter here, and indeed much, for the first thing that it occurs to the soul to speak of and to prize are the signs of humility, which furthermore are so evident that they cannot be hidden. It is true that they are not equally notable in all apprehensions of God, but these apprehensions, which she here describes as union, are never found apart from them. *Quoniam antequam exaltetur anima*

---

[1] P. Jerónimo, in his *History* of St. John of the Cross (Book VI, chap. vii, § 8), has handed down to us his judgment, written by the Saint at the request of P. Doria. The nun in question had caused great anxiety to the superiors of the Discalced Carmelite Order, and P. Doria, who was Vicar-General at the time, ordered her to prepare a full account of her spiritual life and experiences, which is the basis of the Saint's report here reproduced.

[2] [*Propiedád.* See p. 202, n. 7, above.]

humiliatur,[1] *et*: *Bonum mihi, quia humiliasti me*.[2] Fifthly, the style and language which she here uses do not seem in agreement with the spirituality to which she here lays claim: for spirituality teaches us to write in a simple style without the affections and exaggerations which are found here. All this that she says about what she said to God, and what God said to her, seems to be nonsense.

My advice would be that she should be neither ordered nor permitted to write anything about such things as these, nor should her confessor give any appearance of wishing to hear about them, save in order to deprecate them. Let her be tested in the practice of the virtues alone, and especially in self-contempt, humility and obedience. Such acid tests will result in the purification of her soul, which has received so many favours. But the tests must be severe, for there is no evil spirit that will not undergo some degree of suffering to save his own reputation.

II

FOUNDATION OF THE DISCALCED CARMELITE NUNS OF MÁLAGA[3]

Jesus Mary.

To the honour and glory of the Most Holy Trinity, Father, Son and Holy Spirit, three Persons and one true God alone, and to that of the glorious Virgin Saint Mary of Mount Carmel.

This monastery of Saint Joseph of Málaga, belonging to the Discalced Carmelite nuns, was founded on the seventeenth day of February in the year one thousand five hundred and eighty-five. It was founded with the favour of Señora Doña Ana Pacheco and of Señor Pedro Verdugo, her husband, purveyor to the galleys of His Majesty. For this purpose were rented the houses of Doña Constanza de Ávila. To the foundation came the following nuns: first, M. María de Cristo, native of the city of Ávila, daughter of Francisco de Ávila and of Doña María del Águila, his wife, who in the world was called Doña María de Ávila; M. María de Jesús, as Sub-prioress, a native of the town of Beas, daughter of Sancho Rodríguez de Sandoval Negrete and of

---

[1] Proverbs xviii, 12.
[2] Psalm cxviii, 71 [A.V., cxix, 71].
[3] This short account of the foundation of the Convent of Discalced nuns at Málaga is found on the first folio of the original Book of Professions and Elections of that convent. It is written by Fray Diego de la Concepción and signed by St. John of the Cross.

Doña Catalina Godínez, his wife, who in the world was called Doña María de Sandoval. These brought with them Sister Lucía de San José and Sister Catalina Evangelista and Sister Catalina de Jesús, all choir nuns duly professed.

The foundation was made in poverty, with no temporal aid. May it please God to preserve it in poverty until the consummation of the age, that it may have fruition of eternal riches for ever with Him. Amen.

Given in the said Convent of Saint Joseph, on the first day of July in the year one thousand five hundred and eighty-six. Signed by our names.

FRAY JOHN OF THE CROSS,
Vicar Provincial.

FRAY DIEGO DE LA CONCEPCIÓN,
Scribe.

III

LICENCE WHEREBY THE DISCALCED NUNS OF CARAVACA MAY
EFFECT A CONTRACT ON LEGITIMES AND POSSESSIONS
(DECEMBER 15, 1585)[1]

Jesus Mary.

Fray John of the Cross, Vicar Provincial in this district of Andalusia of the Discalced Carmelites. By these presents I give leave and permission to the Reverend Father Prior and the members of our Convent of Nuestra Señora de los Remedios in Triana of Seville, whereby they may effect the contract and agreement which the said Convent has made on the legitimes and possessions of the father and mother of Fray Juan de Jesús, son of the Licentiate Gaspar de Jaén and of Doña Isabel de Segura, his wife, inhabitants of this city, and may receive the two hundred ducats which, by reason of the profession of the said Fray Juan de Jesús, are given to the said Convent on behalf of his said parents. That which on account hereof may be proved to have been given to the Convent is to be taken into account and allowance may be made and is hereby made for any deeds and articles which are firm and valid, and there may be given letters of payment and settlement,

---

[1] From the Archivo de Protocolos, Seville. The original document, which is in the Saint's writing throughout, was reproduced in the *Boletín Carmelitano*, April 15, 1929.

and there may be renounced any other inheritances and possessions which now and at any other time may belong to the said Convent on behalf of the said Licentiate Gaspar de Jaén and Doña Isabel de Segura, his wife.

Given at Granada, signed by my name and sealed with the seal of my office on the fifteenth day of December, 1585.

FRAY JOHN OF THE CROSS,
Vicar Provincial.

IV

LICENCE WHEREBY THE DISCALCED NUNS OF SEVILLE MAY BUY
AND MOVE INTO A NEW HOUSE (GRANADA, APRIL 12, 1586)[1]

Jesus Mary.

By these presents, I, Fray John of the Cross, Vicar Provincial of both the friars and the nuns of the Discalced in the Order of Our Lady of Carmel in this district of Andalusia, do here license the most noble Señor Pedro de Cerezo, inhabitant and resident of the city of Seville, and the Mother Prioress Isabel de San Francisco, and the Discalced nuns of the Convent of Saint Joseph in the said city, all of them together and each of them *in solidum*, to negotiate and effect the purchase of the houses which belonged to Pedro de Morga, near Santa Cruz, and to draw up and authorize any letters of sale, with their chapters and clauses firm and valid in and out of law. For all this and all that concerns it I give my full authority and permission, in so far as I may and am able to give it by right.

Item, I give leave to the said Mother Prioress and the nuns of the said Convent to transfer their house and present abode to the said house when it seems best to them to do so.

In witness thereof I have set my signature to this licence and sealed it with the seal of my office.

At Granada on the twelfth day of April, 1586.

FRAY JOHN OF THE CROSS,
Vicar Provincial.

[1] The original document, first published by P. Silverio, is in the keeping of the Discalced Carmelite nuns of Seville.

V

Licence of Fray Francisco de la Ascensión and Fray Diego de la Resurrección (1586)[1]

I, Fray John of the Cross, Vicar Provincial of the Discalced Carmelites in the district of Andalusia. By these presents I give leave to the Reverend Father Fray Francisco de la Ascensión, Rector of our College of Our Lady of Carmel at Baeza, to present himself to the Most Reverend Ordinary of the diocese of Jaén, for a licence to confess and preach, since I consider him apt and sufficient for that purpose, in so far as human frailty allows. And likewise I give leave to the Reverend Father Fray Diego de la Resurrección, member of the said College and master of students therein, to present himself likewise for preaching and confession to the said Most Reverend Ordinary.

Given in Granada, signed by my name and sealed with the seal of my office, on the twenty-first day of . . . [2] in the year 1586.

FRAY JOHN OF THE CROSS,
Vicar Provincial.

VI

Licence to the Discalced Carmelite Nuns of Málaga for the purchase of Houses (November 23, 1586)[3]

Fray John of the Cross, Vicar Provincial of the Discalced Carmelites, both of friars and of nuns, in the district of Andalusia. By these presents I give leave to the Mother Prioress and nuns of our Convent of Saint Joseph and Saint Peter, in the city of Málaga, for the purchase of the houses which are in the possession of Doña Úrsula de Guzmán, as guardian of her son and heir, and for the authorizing of any deed or deeds upon the sale of the said houses, which shall be firm and valid in and out of law. And by these presents I declare the said purchase to be good, and in so far as pertains to me I stand security for the price that is given for them and for any other contract which may be made concerning the said purchase. Given in Málaga, signed

---

[1] N.L.M., MS. 12,738, fol. 770.
[2] The month is omitted in the original.
[3] N.L.M., MS. 12,738, fol. 754.

with my name and sealed with the seal of my office on the twenty-third day of November, 1586.

Item, I give leave to the said Mother Prioress and the said nuns to take possession of the said houses, when they have them, at what time and in what manner best suits them. Given *ut supra*.[1]

FRAY JOHN OF THE CROSS,
Vicar Provincial.

VII

ELECTION OF PRIORESS OF THE CARMELITE NUNS OF GRANADA (NOVEMBER 28, 1586)[2]

On the twenty-eighth day of the month of November, 1586, was made the election of the Prioress, Sub-prioress and Treasurer in this Convent of Saint Joseph of Granada. I, Fray John of the Cross, Vicar Provincial, was present at the said election; and testify that Mother Beatriz de San Miguel was canonically elected Prioress, Mother Ana de la Encarnación Sub-prioress and Sister Mariana de Jesús and Sister María de Jesús Treasurers. And in witness of the truth thereof I have signed this with my name upon the day, month and year *ut supra*.

FRAY JOHN OF THE CROSS,
Vicar Provincial.

VIII

LICENCE TO ENGAGE IN LITIGATION GIVEN TO THE DISCALCED NUNS OF CARAVACA (MARCH 2, 1587)[3]

Fray John of the Cross, Vicar Provincial of the Discalced Carmelites in this district of Andalusia. By these presents I give leave to the Prioress and nuns of the Convent of the glorious Saint Joseph, which is that of the Discalced Carmelites, in the town of Caravaca, to lay their case before any lawful tribunal, concerning the houses which the Fathers of the Company have taken from them, and which belong

---

[1] This paragraph and signature are in the hand of the Saint; the remainder is in that of his secretary.

[2] The original is in the Book of Elections at Granada and was published by P. Gerardo in his *Autógrafos*, p. 84.

[3] The original is in the possession of the Carmelite nuns of Caravaca.

to the site of their Convent, which houses belonged to Alonso de Robres, inhabitant of the said town of Caravaca; and to this end they may delegate their power to any attorney or attorneys of any of the chancelleries of his Majesty, as may seem best to them, and they may continue their suit in any lawful manner. For all this and all that concerns it I give them my full authority, as I am lawfully entitled to do.

In faith hereof I have given this document, signed by my name and sealed with the seal of my office.

Dated in our Convent of Our Lady of Carmel, in the town of Caravaca, on the second day of March, 1587.

FRAY JOHN OF THE CROSS,
Vicar Provincial.

IX

FACULTY GRANTED TO THE DISCALCED OF LA FUENSANTA (MARCH 8, 1587)[1]

Fray John of the Cross, Vicar Provincial of the Discalced Carmelites in this district of Andalusia. By these presents I give leave to the Father Prior and members of the house of La Fuensanta[2] to negotiate as seems best to them with Juan Ruiz de Ventaxa upon the demand and application made by his son Fray Francisco de Jesús María to the said Convent of La Fuensanta, and to make any assignment or assignments and renouncements with regard to this matter.

Item, I give them leave to negotiate with Juan Sánchez de Guzmán, brother of Fray Francisco de San José, concerning the property which may come into the possession of the said Convent through the said friar; upon this matter they may draw up any deed or deeds, treaties and agreements, and may receive the instructions of the said Fray Francisco, as also in the case of the said Juan Ruiz de Ventaxa.

Given in our College of Baeza, signed with my name and sealed with the seal of my office, on the eighth day of March, 1587.

FRAY JOHN OF THE CROSS,
Vicar Provincial.

[1] The original belongs to the Ayuntamiento of Úbeda; a photographic reproduction of it was published in the *Boletín Carmelitano*, March 15, 1928. The signature is the Saint's.

[2] La Fuensanta is a shrine near Villanueva del Arzobispo, in the province of Jaén, where, in 1583, P. Gabriel de la Asunción founded a house of the Discalced Reform, afterwards abandoned.

X

FACULTY GIVEN TO THE MOTHER PRIORESS OF BARCELONA FOR THE RECEPTION OF THREE NOVICES (OCTOBER 1588)[1]

Fray John of the Cross, Definitor-in-Chief of the Congregation of Discalced Carmelites and President of the Consulta of the said Congregation, in the absence of our Most Reverend Father Vicar-General, etc. According to the decision of our Consulta, by these presents I give leave to the Mother Prioress of the Discalced Carmelite nuns of our Convent in the city of Barcelona for the reception into our habit and Order of three novices, according to the form and order laid down by our laws with respect to the reception of novices.

In faith hereof I have given this document, signed with my name and sealed with the seal of our Consulta, in this our Convent of Segovia in the month of October of the year 1588.

FRAY JOHN OF THE CROSS,
Definitor-in-Chief.

FRAY GREGORIO DE SAN ANGELO,
Secretary.

XI

CONFIRMATION OF THE PRIORESS OF SAINT JOSEPH'S, VALENCIA (NOVEMBER 4, 1588)[2]

... and Holy Spirit. Amen.

Giving her, as by these presents we do, the cure and administration of the said Convent, and our nuns therein; and, in the virtue of the Holy Spirit, I order all the nuns of the said Convent, by holy obedience and under precept, to obey this Prioress. In faith hereof, I have given this, signed by my name and by the Secretary of the Congregation, and sealed with the seal of our Consulta in this our Convent of Segovia, on the fourth day of November in the year 1588.

FRAY JOHN OF THE CROSS,
Definitor-in-Chief.

FRAY GREGORIO DE SAN ANGELO,
Secretary.

[1] The original is in the possession of the Discalced Carmelite nuns of Barcelona.
[2] The original belongs to the Convent of Discalced nuns in Valencia. The signature is in the hand of St. John of the Cross. The first words are missing.

XII

A Receipt for Articles belonging to the Sacristy
(November 14, 1588)[1]

Fray John of the Cross, Prior in the Convent of Our Lady of
Carmel in the city of Segovia, acknowledges the receipt, from the hand
of Señor Francisco de Castro, of the ornaments and other articles for
the sanctuary, from Señora Doña Ana de Peñalosa, as described in
this schedule. In witness to the truth hereof I have set my name on
the fourteenth day of November, 1588.

FRAY JOHN OF THE CROSS.

[1] These lines were written by St. John of the Cross at the foot of the inventory of the
articles given by Doña Ana de Peñalosa to the church which she had just built for the
Discalced Carmelites at Segovia. A photographic reproduction was published in the
Mensajero de Santa Teresa y de San Juan de la Cruz for January 1930.

SPIRITUAL SAYINGS ATTRIBUTED TO
SAINT JOHN OF THE CROSS[1]

BY virtue of the command which has been given to 'me, says
Father Fray Eliseo de los Mártires,[2] I make the following
declaration: I knew our father Fray John of the Cross and had
to do with him on many and diverse occasions. He was a man of
medium height, with a serious and venerable expression, somewhat
swarthy and with good features; his demeanour and conversation were
tranquil, very spiritual and of great profit to those who heard him and
had to do with him. And in this respect he was so singular and so
effective that those who knew him, whether men or women, left his
presence with greater spirituality, devotion and affection for virtue.
He had a deep knowledge and a keen perception of prayer and communion with God, and all the questions that were put to him concerning these matters he answered with the highest wisdom, leaving those
who consulted him about them entirely satisfied and greatly advan-
taged. He was fond of recollection and given to speaking little; he
seldom laughed and when he did so it was with great restraint. When
he reproved others as their Superior (which happened frequently)
he did so with a gracious severity, exhorting them with brotherly
love, and acting throughout with a wondrous serenity and gravity.

FIRST SAYING.—He greatly objected to imperious commands
being given by superiors to their religious, especially in the Reformed
Orders, and was wont to say that nothing shows a man to be so unworthy of commanding others as the fact that he commands them im-
periously; we should rather endeavour to bring it about that those
under us never leave our presence downcast.

He never spoke with duplicity or artifice, to which he took the
strongest objection, for he said:

---

[1] This document was first published by P. Gerardo, whose version has been collated
with N.L.M. MS. 13,245, fols. 248–51. Another copy, differing slightly from this, is in the
possession of the Carmelite friars of Segovia. Preference is here given to the N.L.M. copy.
[2] Fray Eliseo de los Mártires (1550–1620), an Extremaduran, was professed at Granada
and came into contact with St. John of the Cross on several occasions. Later, he became
one of the principal Fathers of the Reform in Mexico.

SECOND SAYING.—That artifice violated the sincerity and purity of the Order, and that many did it grievous harm by inculcating methods of prudence of a human kind which caused souls spiritual sickness.

THIRD SAYING.—He said concerning the vice of ambition that in reformed communities it is almost incurable, being the most infectious of all vices; it colours and taints the rule and conduct of the Order with appearances of virtue and of the greatest perfection, so that warfare with evil becomes sterner and spiritual sickness more incurable. And he said that this vice is so powerful and pestilent as to make such sinners of those who suffer from it that the devil is able to throw their lives into confusion and entanglement and thus to confound their confessors. He had great perseverance in prayer and in the practice of the presence of God and in anagogical movements and acts and ejaculatory prayers.

FOURTH SAYING.—He said that the entire life of a religious is (or ought to be) a doctrinal sermon, with these words, which should be repeated several times a day, for its text: Die and perish[1] rather than sin. He said that these words, if they spring from the will, cleanse and purify the soul and make it to grow in the love of God, in grief at having offended Him and in firmness of purpose to offend Him no more.

FIFTH SAYING.—He said that there are two ways of resisting vices and acquiring virtues. The one is common and the less perfect, which is when you endeavour to resist some vice, sin or temptation by means of the acts of virtue which conflict with this vice, sin or temptation and destroy it. If, for example, I am conscious of the vice or temptation of impatience or of the spirit of vengeance in my soul because of some harm which I have received or some insulting words, I then resist it by means of some good meditation, such as that on the Passion of the Lord (*qui cum male tractaretur, non aperuit os suum*); or by means of meditation upon the blessings which are acquired by suffering and of the conquest of a man by himself; or by thinking that God commanded that we should suffer, since suffering brings us profit, etc. By means of such meditations I am moved to suffer, accept and desire such insults, affronts or evils as this, to the glory and honour of God. This manner of resisting and fighting such temptation, vice or sin begets the virtue of patience, and it is a good method of resistance, though difficult and less perfect.

[1] [Sp., *morir y reventar*: 'die and burst.']

There is another way of conquering vices and temptations and acquiring and gaining virtues, which is easier, more profitable and more perfect. According to this, by its loving anagogical movements and acts alone, without any other exercises whatsoever, the soul resists and destroys all the temptations of our adversary and attains virtues in the most perfect degree. This, the venerable Father was wont to say, becomes possible after this manner. When we feel the first movement or attack of any vice, such as lust, wrath, impatience or a revengeful spirit when some wrong has been done to us, we should not resist it by making an act of the contrary virtue, in the way that has been described, but, as soon as we are conscious of it, we should meet it with an act or movement of anagogical love directed against this vice, and should raise our affection to union with God, for by this means the soul absents itself from its surroundings and is present with its God and becomes united with Him, and then the vice or the temptation and the enemy are defrauded of their intent, and have nowhere to strike; for the soul, being where it loves rather than where it lives, has met the temptation with Divine aid, and the enemy has found nowhere to strike and nothing whereon to lay hold, for the soul is no longer where the temptation or enemy would have struck and wounded it. And then, oh, marvellous thing! the soul, having forgotten this movement of vice, and being united and made one with its Beloved, no longer feels any movement of this vice wherewith the devil desired to tempt it, and was succeeding in doing so; in the first place, because, as has been said, it has escaped, and is no longer present, so that, if it may be put in this way, the devil is as it were tempting a dead body and doing battle with something that is not, feels not and is for the time being incapable of feeling temptation.

In this way there is begotten in the soul a wondrous and heroic virtue, which the angelic doctor Saint Thomas calls the virtue of a soul that is perfectly purged. This virtue, said the holy Father, is possessed by the soul when God brings it to such a state that it feels not the movements of vice, nor its assaults, attacks or temptations, because of the loftiness of the virtue which dwells in this soul. Hence there arises within it and comes to it a most lofty perfection which takes from it all concern about being praised or exalted or insulted or humbled or about whether men speak well of it or ill. For, as these loving and anagogical movements raise the soul to so high and sublime a state, their truest effect upon the soul is to make it forget all things other than its Beloved, Who is Jesus Christ. Hence, as has been said, when it is united with its God and in converse with Him, it finds that no temptations can wound it, since they cannot rise to that place whither the soul has risen or to which God has raised it: *Non accedet ad te malum.*

Here the venerable Father Fray John of the Cross said that attention must be paid to beginners, whose anagogical or loving acts are not so ready, quick or fervent as to enable them to absent themselves entirely from their surroundings and unite themselves with the Spouse. If, he said, they find that, on making this anagogical act, they do not completely forget the vicious movement of the temptation, they should not fail to take advantage of all possible weapons and considerations in order to resist it, until they vanquish the temptation completely. And the way wherein they must resist and vanquish it will be this. First let them resist it with the most fervent anagogical movements whereof they are capable, and let them perform and practise these many times; and, if these suffice not (for the temptation is strong and they are weak), let them then use all the weapons (namely, good meditations and exercises) that they find necessary for this resistance and victory. And let them believe that this method of resistance is excellent and sure, since it includes within itself all the crafts of war which are both important and necessary.

And he would say that those words of the 118th Psalm, *Memor esto verbi tui servo tuo, in quo mihi spem dedisti,* are so powerful and effective that by their means anything whatsoever may be accomplished with God.

And he assured us that, if we devoutly repeated the words of the Holy Gospel, *Nesciebatis quia in his, quae Patris mei sunt, oportet me esse?* our souls would be filled with a desire to do the will of God in imitation of Christ Our Lord, and with a most ardent desire to suffer for love of Him and for the good of souls.

He also said that when once the Divine Majesty intended to destroy the city of Constantinople completely by means of a most cruel tempest, the angels were heard to repeat these words three times: *Sanctus Deus, Sanctus Fortis, Sanctus Immortalis, miserere nobis.* By means of these supplications God was at once appeased and the storm ceased, having already caused much harm and threatened worse. Thus, he would say, these words have power with God in such individual needs as fire, water, winds, tempests, wars and other necessities of soul and body, honour, possessions, etc.

SIXTH SAYING.—He would also say that love for the good of one's neighbour is born of the spiritual and contemplative life, and that, as this is commanded us by our Rule, we are also clearly commanded and charged to have this zeal for the profit of our neighbour. For the Rule aims at making persons observe the mixed and compounded life so that they may embrace and include within themselves two lives, the active and the contemplative, in one. This mixed life the Lord chose for Himself because it is the most perfect. And the state and method of life of the religious who embraces it is the most perfect of its kind; but, in saying and teaching this, he would say that it should not be repeated publicly because of the few religious that there were, and lest these should become uneasy, but rather we should hint at the contrary until there were a great number of friars.

And, when he expounded the words of Christ Our Lord already quoted: *Nesciebatis quia in his, quae Patris mei sunt, oportet me esse?* he said that that which is of the Eternal Father must here be understood of nothing else than the redemption of the world, and the good of souls, wherein Christ Our Lord uses the means fore-ordained by the Eternal Father. And he would repeat that marvellous phrase written in confirmation of this truth by Saint Dionysius the Areopagite: *Omnium Divinorum Divinissimum est cooperari Deo in salutem animarum.* That is, that the supreme perfection of any souls in their rank and degree is to progress and grow, according to their talent and means, in the imitation of God, and the most wondrous and divine thing is to be a co-operator with Him in the conversion and conquest of souls. For in this there shine the very works of God, and to imitate Him in them is the greatest glory. For this reason Christ Our Lord called them works of His Father and cares of His Father. And it is clearly true that compassion for our neighbour grows the more according as the soul is more closely united with God through love; for the more we love, the more we desire that this same God shall be loved and honoured by all. And the more we desire this, the more we labour for it, both in prayer and in all other possible and necessary exercises.

And such is the fervour and power of God's charity that those of whom He takes possession can never again be limited by their own souls or contented with them. Rather it seems to them a small thing to go to Heaven alone, wherefore they strive with yearnings and celestial affections and the keenest diligence to take many to Heaven with them. This arises from the great love which they have for their God and it is the true fruit and effect of perfect prayer and contemplation.

SEVENTH SAYING.—He was accustomed to say that two things serve the soul as wings whereby it is able to rise to union with God:

these are affective compassion for the death of Christ and for our neighbour; and that, when the soul pauses to have compassion for the Cross and Passion of the Lord, it must remember that herein He was working our redemption all alone, as it is written: *Torcular calcavi solus*. From this thought the soul will receive many other most useful thoughts and meditations.

EIGHTH SAYING.—In a certain address which he gave in the Convent of Almodóvar del Campo he spoke of solitude and repeated the words of Pope Pius II of blessed memory, who said that a restless friar was worse than a devil. And he added that, if religious had to pay visits, they should always go to houses of good repute, where the conversation was restrained and seemly.

NINTH SAYING.—Expounding the words of Saint Paul, *Signa apostolatus nostri facta sunt super vos, in omni patientia, in signis, et prodigiis, et virtutibus*, he pointed out that the Apostle set patience above miracles. Patience, therefore, is a surer sign of the apostolic man than the resuscitation of the dead. I can testify that Fray John of the Cross was an apostolic man with respect to that virtue, for he endured with a singular patience and tolerance all the trials that beset him, which were very great and would have brought down the cedars of Mount Lebanon.

TENTH SAYING.—Speaking of those who had to confess women, as one experienced herein, he would say that they should be somewhat stern with them, for to treat them gently only affected their feelings and they failed to profit thereby. And he said that God had punished him with regard to this, by hiding from him a certain woman's very grave sin; she had deceived him for some time, and she did not trust him because he was gentle with her; and the Lord ordained things so that it should be revealed to him in another way within our own Order, and of this I have full information.

ELEVENTH SAYING.—He once said to me that if we should see urbanity lost in the Order, which was part of Christian and monastic life, and if instead there should enter cruelty and ferocity in superiors (which is a vice proper to barbarians) we should mourn the Order as ruined. For, he said, who has ever seen men persuaded to love the virtues and things of God by harshness and with blows? In this connection he would quote those words from the 34th chapter of Ezechiel: *Cum austeritate imperatis eis, et cum potentia*.

And he said that, when religious are brought up with such irrational severity, they become pusillanimous in undertaking things of great virtue, as if they had been brought up among wild beasts, as Saint Thomas says in the 20th Opuscule of *De Regimine Principium*, Chapter III, in these words: *Naturale est enim, ut homines sub timore nutriti in servilem degenerent animum, et pusillanimes fiant ad omne virile opus et strenuum.* And he also quoted the words of Saint Paul: *Patres, nolite ad iracundiam provocare filios vestros, ne pusillanimes fiant.*

TWELFTH SAYING.—And he said it was to be feared that to train religious in this way was a mark of the devil, for if they are trained by this method of fear, their superiors dare not warn or reprove them when they go astray. And if, by this means or by any other, the Order should reach such a state that those of its members (especially the seniors) who, by the laws of charity and justice, in meetings and chapters and on other occasions, dared not say what they should, either through weakness, pusillanimity or fear lest they should offend their superior and therefore should be given no office (which is a common ambition), the Order would become completely relaxed and ruined.

THIRTEENTH SAYING.—So true is this that the good father Fray John of the Cross would say that he would prefer that such friars should not make their profession in the Order, for if they did so it would be governed by the vice of ambition and not by the virtue of charity and justice. And this (he would say) is clearly seen when nobody raises protests in chapter, but everything is ceded and allowed to pass, because everyone is intent on pressing his own interests. This causes serious harm to the common good and nourishes the vice of ambition.

He said that denunciations should be made without correction, since what has just been described is a pernicious vice opposed to the common good.

And whenever he said these things it was after he had spent long periods in prayer and colloquy with Our Lord.

FOURTEENTH SAYING.—He would say that superiors must often beseech God to give them religious prudence so that they might rule wisely and lead the souls committed to their charge to Heaven. He was accustomed to praise Father Fray Agustín de los Reyes for this virtue, which he had in an excellent degree.

FIFTEENTH SAYING.—I sometimes heard him say that there is no lie so carefully devised and composed that, if we study it carefully, we cannot tell it in one way or in another to be a lie.

Nor, he would say, is there any devil so completely transfigured as an angel of light as not to be recognizable if he be looked at carefully.

Nor is there any hypocrite so artfully concealed and dissimulated that you cannot discover him after a few glances.

SIXTEENTH SAYING.—With regard to a severe punishment imposed by a certain superior, he pronounced a phrase divine in its wisdom: Christians, and especially religious, must always see that they chastise the bodies of delinquents, lest their souls be endangered, but they must not use extraordinary cruelty, as do tyrants and those who rule by cruelty. He said that superiors should often read the words of Isaias, chapter xli, and of Saint Paul (1 Corinthians ix, 10).

SEVENTEENTH SAYING.—On one occasion, when a candidate for the habit was proposed to him, he had several conversations with him, and advised that he should not be received because a bad odour came from his mouth, and this signified that he was unhealthy inwardly; and as a rule, he said, such persons are evilly inclined, cruel, false, fainthearted, murmurers, etc.; for it is a rule of philosophy that the habits of the soul correspond to the temper and humour of the body.

This is all I remember at the moment. If I remember more, I will advise our Father General in fulfilment of his command. Given in Mexico, on the twenty-sixth day of March, 1618.—Fray Eliseo de los Mártires.

APPENDICES TO THE WORKS OF
SAINT JOHN OF THE CROSS

A.—Documents illustrative of the Saint's Life, Works and Virtues[1]

I

A Narrative dealing with the Life of St. John of the Cross by M. Magdalena del Espíritu Santo

Jhs. M[a].

IN the name of Our Lord Jesus Christ I obey the command which has been given me to speak in detail of our venerable father Fray John of the Cross. God knows with what bashfulness and difficulty I do it, not being able to tell if what I write is of any importance. If it is not so, this will be due to my lack of understanding; your Reverence, using the understanding with which God has enlightened you, will judge if any of it is important. If it has already been narrated, and more fittingly narrated, as I expect is the case, I beg Your Reverence, for the love of God, to do the office of a father, and to bear patiently with my defects and ignorances, together with the great delay with which I write this; the reason has been the rheumatism in hands,[2] which has made it impossible for me to write more.

On the first occasion when our venerable father Fray John of the Cross visited Beas, he arrived there a short time after leaving his prison in Toledo. He was weak and weary, but his words and demeanour were such that it was easy to see how intimate was the life which he lived with God. For some days he bore himself with such

---

[1] [This appendix contains the majority of the documents answering to this description published by P. Silverio. Irrelevant documents and passages have been omitted, together with a few documents and passages which repeat almost verbally others which are included. The order of arrangement is approximately chronological; where the date of a document is not given and cannot be conjectured, the document is placed according to its subject. The narrative of M. Magdalena del Espíritu Santo comes first, on account of its length, and the important 'Reply' of Fray Basilio Ponce de León is given a place apart.]

[2] [*Un corrimiento a las manos*. The word *corrimiento*, though archaic in this sense in Spain, is still used for 'rheumatism' in some parts of Spanish America.]

restraint and spoke so few words, that it was wonderful to see him, but in his converse with M. Ana de Jesús he revealed the heavenly treasures possessed by his soul. On certain occasions that presented themselves, our venerable Father said that our holy Mother Teresa of Jesus was 'his beloved daughter' and M. Ana de Jesús replied: 'This father Fray John of the Cross seems a very good man, but he is very young to speak of our Mother Foundress as "my daughter."' And this very thing she wrote to our holy Mother, begging her to pray God to provide them with some person to whom to communicate certain interior matters concerning herself and the sisters of which they needed to speak.

Our holy Mother answered her: 'I assure you that I should be very glad to have my father Fray John of the Cross here; he is indeed very dear to me and one of those with whom it has profited me greatly to have converse. Let my daughters speak to him quite plainly, for I assure them that they may do so as with myself, and it will be of great satisfaction to them, for he is a very spiritual man and has great experience and learning. Those of us here who have been instructed by him miss him very much. Let them give thanks to God, therefore, that He has ordained that they should have him so near. I am writing to him that he is to help you all, and I know that of his great charity he will do so in any case of necessity that may present itself.'

I had myself been afflicted by Our Lord with certain interior trials and a religious who was my confessor had been commanded under obedience to go far away for a long time.[1] I was therefore bidden to make my confession to our venerable Father, who was there just then: I was the first nun to do so on that occasion. When I began my confession, and when he talked to me, as he did at some length, I was filled inwardly with a great light which brought me quiet and peace and a particular love of suffering for God's sake, together with desires to acquire the virtues which are most pleasing to Him; and this inward light, which seemed to penetrate my soul, lasted for some time, a thing I had not previously experienced. The other nuns also learned something of the great power which the holy Father had with God and of the good effects which he produced in their souls; and also (which was still more wonderful) his great humility, combined with his great worth and constant integrity, and his great mortification, and the detachment which he had from all that is not God, as well as his great

---

[1] Fray Pedro de los Ángeles, superior of El Calvario, who was succeeded by St. John of the Cross when he was chosen to go to Rome on the business of the Discalced Reform.

gentleness and kindness. His words were full of light from Heaven, so that even to those who understood not what was contained in them they brought satisfaction and comfort, together with desires and esteem of the virtues.

The words of this holy man concerning faith, hope and charity, and austere conduct, strict obedience, continual prayer, sure confidence in God and supernatural prudence seem to have implanted these virtues in those with whom he had to do. The general profit which they brought, and also the profit in particular cases, it is impossible to deny.

All the nuns grew to have the greatest love and respect for him, for in his holy life there was nothing worthy of reproach, while there were many things most exemplary and edifying to all.

When the holy Father left his prison, he took with him a little book in which he had written, while there, some verses based upon the Gospel *In principio erat Verbum*, and some verses which begin: 'How well I know the fount that freely flows, Although 'tis night,' and the stanzas or *liras* that begin: 'Whither hast vanishèd?' as far as the stanzas beginning 'Daughters of Jewry.' The remainder of them he composed later when he was acting as Rector of the College at Baeza. Some of the expositions were written at Beas, as answers to questions put to him by the nuns; others at Granada.

This little book in which the holy man wrote while in prison, he left in the Convent of Beas and on various occasions I was commanded to copy it. Then someone took it from my cell—who, I never knew. The freshness of the words in this book, together with their beauty and subtlety, caused me great wonder, and one day I asked him if God gave him those words which were so comprehensive and so lovely. And he answered: 'Daughter, sometimes God gave them to me and at other times I sought them.'

He took great care to flee from idleness, and when he had some free time he would use it in writing, or would ask for the key of the garden and go and weed it and do other similar things; and sometimes he busied himself in making certain walls and floors in our convent. If he had a companion, he took him with him so that he might help; if not, he asked for assistance from some of the sisters. He also liked to dress the altars, which he would do with great neatness and delicacy, and in silence.

On occasions when the church was closed to us,[1] and others said

---

[1] [*Lit.*, 'on occasions of interdict'—i.e. when the faithful were forbidden for some reason to attend the Divine offices.]

that it might be opened and we might go in to hear Mass by the privileges of the Order, the holy Father would say to us: 'Daughters, humility and subjection to the Ordinary are more important than the making use of privileges. Do not forget that, for there will always be sufficient people to look after the privileges.'

He also occasionally wrote spiritual things that were very profitable. There, too, he composed the Mount, and drew a copy with his own hand for each of our breviaries. Later, he added to these copies and made some changes in them.

He was greatly inclined to the mortification of the passions and to prayer and the frequenting of the sacraments, and he devised certain proofs by which he could examine the reverence and esteem with which the nuns communicated. He taught that one must go with great resignation to seek permission, not only to communicate, but for anything whatever. We were to say to our superior: Mother, does your Reverence desire that I should communicate? —and similarly with regard to anything else for which we asked permission.

Once when the sisters were talking of certain approaching days on which there would be Communion and on which they desired permission to be given them to communicate, the superior had asked our venerable Father to practise the sisters in mortification just as he practised the friars who were under his charge. He heard Sister Catalina de San Alberto, who was a lay sister, and had great virtue and devotion to the Most Holy Sacrament, say with regard to one of these approaching days in which Communion was obligatory: 'On that day Communion is certain; on these other days that we are speaking of, it will be necessary to ask for permission.' The holy Father took note of that phrase which she used—'I am certain of Communion'—and, without showing that he had taken note of it, remembered the day of which the sister had spoken, although it was some time ahead, and, when Sister Catalina de San Alberto came up to the altar,[1] he kept her a short time without giving her the Host. She rose and other sisters came and were communicated; then she came again to communicate but the holy Father did as he had done before; again she rose and gave place to others. Finally she came back once more to communicate but the holy Father went away without giving her the Host. The sister remained in confusion, not knowing the reason for this; and afterwards, when

[1] [*Lit.*, 'to the little window,' i.e. the opening in the chancel-grille, through which enclosed nuns were communicated.]

they were all together in the presence of the venerable Father, some of the nuns asked him why he had not communicated the sister who was so certain of herself. 'For this reason,' he answered, 'that she may understand that what she imagined is not the case.' Then the sister recalled what she had said and the others remembered it for the future.

At other times, in order to increase the nuns' fervour and to teach them true spirituality and the practice of the virtues, he would ask them certain questions; and would discuss the replies which they gave so that the time passed very profitably and they learned much from him, for his words were bathed in heavenly light. I tried to set down some of these things so as to find refreshment in reading them when he was absent and we could not talk to him, but they took the papers from me without giving me an opportunity to copy them. I can set down here only what they left:

He who works for God with pure love not only cares nothing that men should know it, but does not even do it so that God Himself may know it. Even though it might never be known, such a man would not cease to render the same services with the same joy and love.

Another saying with respect to the conquering of the desires:

Have a general desire to imitate Jesus Christ in all His works, conforming thyself with His life, upon which thou must meditate in order to be able to imitate it and to behave in all things as He would behave.

In order to be able to do this it is necessary to renounce every desire or taste, if it be not purely to the honour and glory of God, and to remain in emptiness for the love of Him who in this life neither did nor desired to do aught save the will of His Father, which He called His meat and food.

In order to mortify the four natural passions, which are joy, sorrow, fear and hope, profit by what follows.

Strive always to prefer, not that which is easiest, but that which is most difficult; not that which is most delectable, but that which is most unpleasing; not that which gives most pleasure, but that which gives no pleasure. Prefer not that which is restful, but that which is most wearisome; not that which gives consolation, but that which gives no consolation; not that which is greatest, but that which is least; not that which is loftiest and most precious, but that which is lowest and most despised; not that which is a desire for anything but that which is a desire for nothing. Strive not to go about seeking the best of things, but the worst; and strive to cultivate detachment and emptiness and poverty, for Jesus Christ's sake, with respect to that which is in the world.

Against concupiscence:

Strive to work in detachment and desire others to do so.
Strive to speak in thine own despite and desire all to do so.
Strive to think humbly of thyself and desire others to do so.

Among other things that he wrote, the venerable Father once wrote a saying for each of the nuns to further their spiritual progress. Although I copied all these, only the two following were left to me:

Have fortitude in thy heart against all things that may move it to that which is not God and love suffering for Christ's sake.

Readiness in obedience, joy in suffering, mortification of the sight, the desire to know nothing, silence and hope.

On such occasions as presented themselves, our venerable Father wrote letters to the nuns of Beas, both sisters and superiors, containing maxims and teaching of great importance. I do not know what they have done with them, for it is more than forty years since I left the convent for the foundation of this convent of Córdoba.

When our venerable Father went to found the College of Baeza, in which M. Ana de Jesús, who was Prioress at Beas, had given him no little help with letters to persons of importance, both ecclesiastical and lay, she also tried to help him, as far as she could, with regard to ornaments of the sacristy and other necessary things. The holy Father received them humbly and gladly, and, though in few words, thanked her warmly for them, and gave proof of his esteem for them. His was a celestial joy, since he was about to labour in rendering that new service to the Divine Majesty.

A few days after this foundation had been made, he went back to Beas with Fray Juan de Santa Ana, whom the Mothers asked if he had been at that foundation. The said Father did not reply and his saintly superior said that the Father had laboured gladly whenever an occasion presented itself, that he was a good worker and helped them and caused them esteem for his virtue, so that he obliged them to strive after virtue anew.

When he was Rector of that College, and his Vice-Rector was Father Fray Gaspar de San Pedro, he sent him several times to preach at Úbeda. On one occasion, among others, they begged him urgently to accept an invitation to return and preach at a solemn festival. He replied that he would do so, but, because he omitted to say that he would do so if permission were given him, his saintly superior refused him permission, and, although they expected him at Úbeda and rang the bells for his sermon, he did not go there on that occasion. The venerable Father having taken him to Beas as his companion, Father Gaspar de San Pedro told the nuns what had happened, as we have described it. 'It is better that a man should not preach at all,' was the holy Father's comment, 'than that he should preach of his own will, for the mortification, though he dislike it, will bring him greater profit. If this Father or any other should speak to them of such things, let him explain that such things are done here below to mortify them, so that we may make easy for one another the practice of true mortification which there should be among us.'

The venerable Father wrote to one of the superiors known to me, advising her not to profess a certain novice. This superior did not take his advice and persuaded herself that the result would not be what the holy man had foretold—namely, that if they professed her she would cause them uneasiness and give them much cause for anxiety. So she made all possible haste and concluded certain things concerning the said profession and then professed her without waiting for the Father to come. In two days' time he arrived. When they told him that that novice had made her profession, he did not repeat his prophecy but went away without saying anything to the superior or to any other person, and went on to other convents on his round of visits, until essential obligations compelled him to return. Before many years had passed there happened to that nun and to the convent precisely what the Father said.

With a view to the foundation of the convent of our Mothers of Granada, at the request of M. Ana de Jesús, the Father went from Beas to Ávila for our Mother Saint Teresa. But her Reverence excused herself, alleging that she had in hand the foundations of Palencia and Burgos.[1] He then entrusted the making of this foundation to M. Ana de Jesús and sent for M. Antonia del Espíritu Santo and M. María de Cristo to help her, and also told them to take M. Beatriz de Jesús from the Toledo convent. They reached Beas some time in December,[2] very weary with so long a journey made at a time of the severest cold. But the greater were the trials which these things brought them in the service of God, the greater was their content, encouragement and joy,

[1] Actually she had only that of Burgos, the Palencia foundation having already been completed.
[2] On December 8.

and their readiness to suffer other new and greater trials for Our Lord's sake.

Some days afterwards, the holy Father accompanied M. Ana de Jesús and the other Mothers who went to Granada. When he was in that city he helped them in every way that he could, and I do not remember the particular things which they said had happened to them.

After some time our Mothers asked that a foundation should be made at Málaga. They suggested for its superiors M. María de Cristo, M. Lucía de San José, who had gone from the convent of Beas to the foundation of Granada, and also M. Catalina de Jesús, who had been professed at Granada. And the venerable Father went to Beas for M. María de Cristo, whence they all went together. Five of them went to Málaga, and for various reasons it seemed well that one of those who had gone from Beas should remain at Granada and return to Beas when occasion offered, as was done after some time.

When the venerable Father had arrived from the Málaga foundation, he went there with them, and on the road the mount of M. María de Cristo took fright and ran away, for what reason nobody knew, and threw M. María de Cristo with considerable force on to a great cliff, and such was the violence of her fall that all who saw her thought it had killed her and dismounted with incredible anxiety and sorrow. For some time the Mother, who had a great wound in her head, was unconscious, until the holy Father arrived and laid his hands on her, and applied his handkerchief to the wound and wiped it, whereupon the Mother came to herself and felt able to go on, so they continued the journey immediately. Some of those who were there affirmed that much of the blood from the wound had remained on the cliff and related what had happened on the journey. The Mothers wrote about this to the convent at Beas and of the marvellous way in which M. María de Cristo grew well enough to finish her journey to Málaga, and was also able to share in the labours and anxieties of the foundation, for which there was no lack of occasion, or of difficulties to offer to God. Among these was the case of a nun who lost her senses and threw herself out of a window and died from the injuries which she sustained : this was a matter which grieved the whole Order and especially those who were nearest to her.

On this occasion the holy Father was at the Chapter which was being held at Lisbon, and, before returning to his own convent, he heard of the matter, and, with his accustomed charity, endeavoured to console the nuns and had two of them brought from the convent of Caravaca so that they might help in the choir and other exercises. One of these, M. Ana de la Encarnación, was elected sub-prioress when she arrived at Granada, and in her place M. Antonia del Espíritu Santo went to Málaga, together with M. María de San Pablo, the other nun who was brought from Caravaca. On account of this and the prayers of the holy Father, it pleased God that very soon there entered novices, persons of importance, for the observances of the Order and the increase of the house; here, as elsewhere, the words, counsels, letters and habits of the holy Father were heavenly lights for the illumination and welfare of their souls.

Our venerable Father likewise accompanied M. Ana de Jesús from Granada to Madrid to found the convent there.[1]

In the year 1589 was made the foundation of this convent of Córdoba, dedicated to the glorious saints Anne and Joseph, and the choice of the nuns who came to this convent was made by our venerable and holy Father. As superior he chose M. María de Jesús, from whose virtues and qualities he derived great satisfaction. She was a native of Beas and the younger of the two sisters who founded the convent there; the holy Father had talked with her and confessed her many times. He had also chosen her to be sub-prioress and novice-mistress of the foundation of Málaga, and in this and all her offices she worked well and always gave a good account of what was commended to her. She was very prudent and strict in her observance of all manners of government. Her mortifications and penances were very great and no less was her charity, while in prayer she was ever ready, persevering and continuous. When her Reverence was superior and I was sacristan or portress, I had several times to go to her with messages; and when she delayed in giving me a reply I would ask her for the love of God to give it me, so that I might give it to the person who was waiting while I went to attend to other necessary occupations. And she would answer me very modestly and gently: 'Wait, sister, for first of all we must needs commend it to God so that we may not go astray.'

She exercised herself in prayer for many years with very great faith and confidence. She was three times elected prioress, and in other convents they desired to have her in the same office, being sure of the satisfaction that would be given by her wise rule in things spiritual and temporal. During the last years, when she was not superior, she was charged by the superior to look after the work, and both this and other

[1] These two lines are interlinear, but the hand is that of M. Magdalena.

things that were given her to do, she did with perfection. What she did with extreme success was to profit by her time; if she were without occupation for a single moment, she would betake herself to a little place which was set apart for the purpose and there she would be habitually found on her knees, or prostrated in prayer, her eyes full of tears which she shed with a joyful and serene countenance.

During the time when she had charge of the novices in the convents of Málaga and Córdoba, the profit and joy and satisfaction which she brought to them became clear. This was due to her great vigilance for the profit of their souls, while neither in this nor in aught else did her great peacefulness, tolerance, serenity and joy ever fail her; she was ever composed in her demeanour and very religious. I lived in her company at Beas for several years, and also in Córdoba during the years that she was there, and I always saw that she esteemed poverty, and strove to be most punctilious in obedience and pious in the extreme, kind to the sick and fond of engaging in humble occupations; all this very sincerely. God tried her patience through adversities and trials which came to her in many ways. During the last years of her life she suffered from several serious and painful illnesses, and as a remedy for these ills and those of her soul she had frequent recourse to the sacraments. She greatly esteemed and loved the sacraments, and frequented them very devoutly all her life; this devotion set its mark upon her and endeared her to many, and much evidence could be given concerning it.

I have described these virtues of M. María de Jesús almost without meaning to do so, in order to show how excellent was the choice which our venerable Father made of her as superior and how solicitous was this Mother about religious observances, both as to herself and as to those under her charge, and the concern which she had about giving a good account of everything to God, Whom she besought fervently for the good of her own soul and of the souls of those who were in her charge. And once, among the many occasions when she prayed thus, Our Lord answered her, saying that none of her daughters would be condemned to eternal punishment. The Mother said nothing of this until her last illness, when she was making her confession on her death-bed, and then she told it to Fray Pedro de Santa María, her confessor, and he related it after her death, which was as exemplary as her life had been.

From the time she came to this foundation she ordered and settled its affairs in such a way that they all proceeded with notable piety and

peace, and acquired a good name which through the goodness of God
has lasted to this day. May He be blessed for it!

To this end great help was found in the counsels of our venerable
Father and the advice that he gave when occasion offered. Only two
letters containing such advice have been kept, which, since the instruction contained in them is most sublime, I shall set down after
describing the other nuns whom he chose for this foundation, all six
of whom were most able, virtuous and exemplary. I was undeservedly
granted the favour by God that the rest were equally good. May it
please my good Jesus that I be not confounded for having failed to
profit as I should.

From the convent of Málaga, together with the said Mother, there
came M. María de San Pablo, who was a native and a professed nun
of the convent of Caravaca. This mother, on account of the unhappy
death of the nun in Málaga who lost her senses, was ordered by our
venerable Father to go to Málaga with another nun a few months after
the foundation. There she showed as great virtue and set as good an
example as she had done in Caravaca, where she had been chosen for
this purpose, by our venerable Father, on account of her good reputation. She was both able and intellectual and had also all the sense and
prudence that could be desired, and was so pleasant and tranquil that,
without failing in the least in her religious observances, she won every
soul. Not only the nuns and the Order, but all those who had to do
with her in connection with her offices—whether as doorkeeper or as
superior—esteemed, loved and obeyed her, and this she merited by
her many and great virtues and in particular by the gift that God gave
her of lightening the trials and difficulties of others and persuading
them to be guided by Him. Although her words were few, the good
results of those words upon the hearers were many. She was the best
in all manual exercises, and, through the strength which God gave her
to perform them and the joy with which she did so, was the inspiration and example of the community. When she had novices under her,
she brought great profit to their souls, making them desirous of acquiring the virtues and increasing in them both joy and mortification,
and thus producing nuns noteworthy in religious observance.

In these exercises she was engaged under obedience for about
twenty-one years, after which God gave her a most happy death. She
made acts of faith and reverence to the sacraments and received them
with reverence so great that it would have edified the very stones and
would have sufficed to convert heretics had there been any present.

His Divine Majesty took her to Himself of a pleurisy at the age of forty-eight years, in the month of September 1610. In all her behaviour she did honour to the noble and Christian example set her by her parents, which was very noteworthy.

Besides these two Mothers who came from the convent of Málaga, there came also a novice whom they had received as a lay sister and who had been there for two years, so that she was able to be professed a short time after coming to Córdoba. She was called Bernardina de San Francisco and was a great servant of Our Lord; out of her continual ill-health she drew great spiritual profit.

From our convent at Seville there came to be sub-prioress of this foundation M. Leonor de San Gabriel, who had been for some years the companion and attendant of our Mother Saint Teresa of Jesus. She had been taken by her Reverence from the house at Malagón to the foundation of Beas, and thence to that of Seville. She was greatly loved by our glorious Mother Saint Teresa of Jesus by reason of her great virtues, which were written in her face; and, together with a notable discretion and prudence, she had an angelic purity and sincerity, being a person of great prayer and divine sentiments, as was shown in her words, which inspired all to love and serve God. Although she had continuous ill-health, she had also great patience and tranquillity, encouraged all and laboured as much as she was able, and, wherever she was, inspired everyone with peace and with outward and inward quietness.

She was in this house for a little more than five years, after which time she had a serious illness, being given up by the doctors and thought to be on the point of death. But Our Lord gave her to understand that He still needed her here to exercise her in other and greater trials, and that she should become superior at Sanlúcar.[1] She discussed this with her spiritual adviser, with all the secrecy that the matter demanded. Soon she began to recover from her illness and God inspired the Mothers of the convent at Sanlúcar to elect her by unanimous agreement as their superior. They sent for her to take over her office, which she did, giving great edification and satisfaction, not only to the nuns and to their superiors, but to everyone who had to do with her. When the period of her office was over, she was brought to Seville, where she was also elected superior for two or three periods of three years—I do not remember exactly for how long—and, while she was there, God took her to Himself, to reward her for all that she had

[1] Sanlúcar la Mayor, a convent founded in 1590.

suffered for love of Him, both as to ill-health and as to other trials, and for the many kinds of mortification which she had endured, not only with great patience but also with joy.

A great part of all this was shared by her companion who came to this foundation from the convent at Seville. Although her age and constitution gave promise that she would have the strength to perform the work which is usually done in foundations, God brought things to pass concerning Sister María de la Visitación (as she was called) according to His own good pleasure. On her journey she stayed at Guadalcázar,[1] where all the nuns met on their way to Córdoba (for it had turned out to be necessary to wait at Guadalcázar for a few days) and were entertained by Don Luis Fernández de Córdoba, a son of the lord of that town, and at that time Dean of Córdoba, afterwards becoming Bishop of Salamanca and of Málaga and Archbishop of Santiago and of Seville, whence God took him from this exile and vale of tears that he might have fruition of Him.

According to the will of God, there came to her at Guadalcázar, though she was the youngest and most high-spirited of the nuns, an indisposition which lasted continuously for seven or eight days, of such a kind that she suffered ceaselessly and was unable to follow the rule of the community. This indisposition developed into a terrible hydropsy, which was a living death to her, and the doctors marvelled at her great patience and joy and eagerness to encourage others, for which she had particular grace and desire and felicity, and great understanding and capacity, and such devotion and virtues so great that I cannot describe or indicate them. Later she was elected sub-prioress, and this office, like others which were given to her under obedience, she performed with great perfection and exactness. She was a native of Alcalá de Henares and had been professed at Seville. The serious and dangerous illness which she suffered compelled doctors and surgeons to apply severe remedies, all of which she endured with great patience and joy; and although our venerable Father knew less of her than of any others who came to this foundation, she certainly was not the one to give least satisfactory and perfect example of her great virtues and devoutnesses.

Our venerable Father entrusted her choice to M. Isabel de San Francisco, who was superior of our foundation of Seville, and she obeyed him, choosing her from among the rest for the occasion of this foundation, since she had experience and illumination from God;

1 About twelve miles from Córdoba, on the road to Seville.

after which time God was pleased to call her to Himself. She received the sacraments and remained in possession of her faculties until the moment of her death, to the general consolation of those who were present, both of the Provincial, Mother Superior and confessors, and of the nuns her companions. She died on December 19, 1595, when she had not yet completed the period of her office as sub-prioress, which office she fulfilled, though with unusual difficulty, until her death.[1]

From the convent of Beas, our venerable Father chose Sister Juana de San Gabriel for the foundation of this convent. This sister had been professed at Beas, and, when our venerable Father was Rector at the College of Baeza (of which town she was a native), he had been her confessor, and had known her, while she was still in the world. The nuns were greatly influenced by what they heard of the satisfaction which the holy Father felt at this sister's vocation, great spirituality and faculty for recollection, and so she was received and given the habit, although she had no dowry with which to help the convent. Our venerable Father confessed her and gave her communion both when she was a novice and after she had been professed. He always esteemed her humility and fervent desires for mortification and penance, for which she had great inclination, and her continual exercise of which obliged her superiors to see to the restraining of her fervour lest her health should suffer. She continually made use of many and most severe disciplines and employed hair shirts and other mortifications which were quite extraordinary.

She had both skill and grace in her practice of all the offices of the community and in aiding the nuns therein with humility and charity, to the profit of her soul and her edification of her companions. She had a most beautiful voice, of which she made use in the Divine office and also at times of recreation, and there was also a natural charm and grace in all her words and sayings. Thus if from time to time she failed to put in an appearance at recreation, on account of necessary occupations, her superiors would endeavour to find somebody else to do her work so that the community should not be deprived of the pleasure and delight which they took in recreation when she was present. This was due to no effort of her own, but to a natural aptitude, quite devoid of artifice or premeditation; and yet the others were not slow to realize that all she said was in conformity with Christianity and

---

[1] [Here the writer adds: 'which was on the twentieth of December in the year 1595: if I remember rightly, it was in the month of December.']

true devotion, which she greatly esteemed and in which she had great fervour and gave great edification. God took her after she had suffered long and borne much illness during her last years, with great patience and courage; she was well prepared for death, having for all this time read and performed the acts and exercises of the manner of holy dying, which she had with her continually. It was on the day of the glorious Saint Augustine, in the year 1621, that His Divine Majesty took her from the pains of this vale of tears to eternal rest and the reward of her good life. Her loss caused very great loneliness, which is felt to this day.

God brought me in her company from the same convent, where I came to receive the habit, from a place thirty leagues away, in La Mancha de Aragón, where I was born, called Belmonte. I was professed in Beas and remained for thirteen years in that holy house. I consider it a particular act of mercy on the part of God that obedience should have brought me where there were so many perfect examples of all the virtues as in these nuns aforementioned, so that they should cover and endure my faults with their great charity, and aid me, in sickness and in health, as they have done, like true mothers and sisters of my soul, both in bodily things and in spiritual, in such a way as cannot be described. This Our Lord Jesus Christ will do on the day when He reveals to the world all the works that have been performed in His holy service, and it will also be revealed how ill I have profited by this good which I might have learned from the other nuns who have been brought to this house by true vocation for a religious life and have worked so truly in His service.

I have said all this so that it may be seen how important it is to make choice of suitable people for the foundations. Because our venerable Father did this so carefully, the result, through the goodness of God, has been due observance, peace, quiet and a good name for this convent, and nothing has happened to its discredit. I believe that this has arisen from the prayers and desires of our venerable Father to the Lord, for which he will have received the rewards of glory. . . .[1]

Although the venerable Father wrote many letters and maxims to the nuns of this convent, due care was not taken to preserve them. At the time of the foundation of this house two miracles happened. In a

---

[1] After a long digression the writer goes on to reproduce three letters written by St. John of the Cross, which will be found elsewhere in this volume and are therefore not given here.

well which had long been dry, and at the hottest period of a year which was particularly dry, so that the majority of the wells in this part of the country had no water, Our Lord provided a very great abundance of water so that the work of adapting the house for conventual purposes could be continued. M. María de Jesús told a man to lower a bucket into the well, for the men were unable to continue their work. He was unwilling to do so, and certainly it seemed foolish to tell him to draw water from a dry well, but when he drew up the bucket it was full of water, which was quite fresh and clear and very abundant, and did not fail until it was necessary to close it up after several years (I believe it must be more than twenty years), because a grave was being dug and the well was in the place where deceased nuns were buried.

It is not known if our venerable Father played any part in this, and thus nothing has been said about it, nor about another very great miracle which Our Lord performed on the eve of the day when we were about to place the Most Holy Sacrament in the convent. The bell was ringing, and the staircase of the bell-tower, which is lofty and narrow, was full of matting from the church. They suggested that he should light some of the matting as there was no illumination, and, without realizing the danger of fire, he did so, and was badly burned and choking for breath. His name was Sebastián de Escavias.

A few hours before, with great ceremony, they had brought us an image of Our Lady, very beautiful and richly adorned, so that we might place it on the high altar. It would be about three-quarters of a metre high or a little more. It was given by a Peruvian who, in his will, had ordered it to be given to this convent, which he knew was about to be founded.

The man commended himself to Our Lady of Light, for thus the image was named, and immediately someone (it is not known who or how) reached through a little window, took it from the flames and placed it on the roof of an apartment near the tower. This was not in front of the window but slightly to one side; and in a most miraculous way a large number of people saw it and came to the fire. Then they marvelled, and gave thanks to God, to Whom nothing is impossible, and the nuns, who were all around the holy image, besought God to help them in this necessity.

On the next day, with great solemnity and devotion, the Lord Bishop, Don Francisco Pacheco, placed the Most Holy Sacrament in the chapel. He was very glad to have this convent in Córdoba, for he had desired and striven for it since leaving Málaga, where he also had a particular affection for the nuns of our convent and was accustomed to give them alms.

What this house received from his Lordship was the church of Saint Anne, which was a shrine of great devotion, and is in the best and healthiest part of the city. This gift was received with general pleasure by all the natives. May He Who can do all things reward him and them.[1] Amen. Amen.

II

LETTER BY FRAY DIEGO DE LA CONCEPCIÓN (BUJALANCE, NOVEMBER 15, 1603)[2]

Jesus.

. . . Our father Fray John of the Cross, who said the first Mass at Duruelo and was the founder of that holy priory, for which reason, and for many more, he is given the title of founder of this holy Order (for that priory, though afterwards abandoned, was the first in our sacred Order) . . . was a very great contemplative and engaged in prayer of a most lofty kind. This I know because, when he was Prior at Granada, I was one of his novices and was under him for a long time; and, when he was Vicar Provincial of these two provinces of Seville and Granada, at a time when they had no provincials, I was his companion and had to do with him for a long time.

This said Father of ours, Fray John of the Cross, was also a holy man, of great patience, and desirous of suffering for God's sake; this I know because, when he was persecuted by certain friars of our holy Order and was sent to La Peñuela, I was at that time in that holy house, and, during the whole period in which we were there together, I never heard him speak ill of any of his persecutors, nor did he murmur or say ill of another in his presence; and, if anyone were imprudent in speech, he would tell him to be silent.

While he was at La Peñuela his fatal illness began and they took him to Úbeda to be cured; here, at that time, the Prior was Fray Francisco Crisóstomo. When they had purged and bled him, his fever subsided, but so much matter gathered in one foot that it swelled up, and after a few days (I was myself present at the time) they made an incision on the arch of his foot. About half a pint of matter must have come out;

[1] P. Jerónimo de San José writes: 'All this paper is in the handwriting of M. Magdalena del Espíritu Santo, a nun of Córdoba.'

[2] An autograph letter. N.L.M., MS. 12,738, fol. 1,037. [The first paragraphs are omitted as being irrelevant to our subject.]

the doctor was astounded at seeing so much. After this they made four more incisions—two at one side of the arch and two more at the other—so that there were five in all. From these wounds our Father derived great spiritual joy and gave thanks for them to Our Lord, saying: 'Greatly do I thank Thee, my Lord Jesus Christ, that Thou hast been pleased to give me in this foot alone five wounds such as Thou hadst in Thy feet, hands, and side. How have I deserved so great a favour?' And, though his pain was as great as can be imagined, he never complained, but bore it all with great patience.

After his death, they buried him in the church, and on one penitential night the Prior commanded that the lamp should be put out, as is the use and custom. And, when it had been quenched, the church was still very bright, and the religious could see that that brightness issued from the grave of the holy Father, Fray John of the Cross.

Further, I have heard that the cloths which were placed on his wounds have wrought many miracles, as will be certified by the religious who were at Úbeda at that time. . . .

Having read this, I ratify what has been said. It is all true *in verbo sacerdotis* and is dated in the convent of Our Lady of Carmel, at Bujalance, on the fifteenth day of November in the year 1603.

FRAY DIEGO DE LA CONCEPCIÓN.

FRAY BERNARDO DE SANTA MARÍA,
Prior.

FRAY JUAN DE SAN PEDRO,
Secretary.

III

REPORT BY FRAY LUCAS DE SAN JOSÉ (SEGOVIA, AUGUST 20, 1604)[1]

Jesus Mary.

In fulfilment of the command of our Father General,[2] in which he orders us to say what we know concerning the virtues and lives of the departed and the wondrous things that God has wrought in them and through them, I say as follows: In this convent of Segovia I knew our father, Fray John of the Cross, when he was Definitor, for the space of

---

[1] N.L.M., M.S. 12,738, fol. 841. The letter is signed by Fray Lucas de San José.

[2] This, like many of the following reports, was written in response to an order issued by the General of the Discalced Order on March 14, 1614, with the object of obtaining as much information as possible concerning the life of St. John of the Cross.

three years. I was a witness of the blamelessness of his life, which was full of many virtues; in particular he lived in the presence of Our Lord, as could be clearly seen by his addresses and his conversations, not only with the religious but also with those of the world with whom he spoke. He would at once lead the conversation to the things of Our Lord, and for this he had a most singular ability; he spoke of Our Lord better than I have ever heard anyone else speak of Him.

He had also a great gift for government, for, without losing any of his meekness and gentleness, which were great, he could when necessary reprove those under him severely and correct their faults. There was one noteworthy case in particular in this convent in which he showed his great ability and also the tranquillity of his heart, which he never lost on such an occasion. It was on one of the days after Easter when a sermon was to be preached and the bell had been rung for it. There were a great many people in the church, both the founders of the convent and other persons. This holy Father was in choir, with the other friars, singing the Mass, and, when it was time for the sermon, he sent for me to notify the Father who was to preach, that the time had come. The Father answered that he could not preach, and, when I had twice given this answer to Fray John of the Cross, he told me a third time, very quietly, to go and deliver the message, and to tell this Father that he was needed, and to say to him, briefly and without making any disturbance, that he was not to fail to do what was required of him. But the Father who was to preach, being very obstinate, would not come, saying that he was not ready. Our blessed Father knew that he did not refuse to come because of indisposition, but from obstinacy, and because he was not in the humour; instead of growing angry, or showing any perturbation, or leaving the choir to speak to him, he took no notice of him and sent to notify the celebrant that the Mass was to go on. He lived with him in perfect peace and tranquillity for about a fortnight without saying anything to him about the matter. But when somebody came one day to enquire for this friar, the holy Father said that he was indisposed and could not come down; and in this way he continued to show his displeasure until the friar confessed his fault in the refectory, when he reproved him in a restrained but very telling way.

He allowed all this time to pass because he knew that, so long as the person concerned was unrepentant, it would be of no use to reprove him, but would only do great harm; whereas by waiting in this way, commending the matter in the meanwhile to God, he was preparing him to receive his correction with humility, and also to do such penance as was fitting, to our edification. And this was one of the things for which that same Father was wont later to praise the holy Father in his eulogies of him.

Among his other great virtues was that of humility; on no account would he allow it to be said that he was the founder of the Reform, or one of the first two founders. If this matter was touched upon, he would at once exclaim: 'Stop saying that!' He was always very willing to allow others to converse with important people, leaving for himself insignificant persons, and the brethren, with whom he conversed with great affability, ever seeking an occasion to speak to them of Our Lord and of the manner in which they should pray.

He had great respect for religious, whoever they were, and for ecclesiastical matters, and he would allow none to speak of them in his presence, save in terms of praise; if anyone did so, he always reproved him. He was greatly addicted to decency in Divine worship, and he himself would often come and help to arrange things that had to be done in church.

He slept very little—about two hours nightly—and he spent a great part of each night writing and busying himself with vigils and prayer. . . .

I heard this same Father say one day, when all the friars were present, that he blushed when he remembered all the mistakes he had made in matters of government. This caused all of us that were present great edification, for he had ever great talent for government, as several of the oldest of the Fathers bore witness.

FRAY LUCAS DE SAN JOSÉ.

IV

LETTER BY ISABEL DE SAN JERÓNIMO AND THE NUNS OF CUERVA CONCERNING THE SAINT'S ESCAPE FROM PRISON[1]

A brief account by a nun of this convent of Discalced Carmelite nuns of Cuerva, named Isabel de San Jerónimo, concerning what she knows of our venerable Father, Fray John of the Cross, whom she knew and with whom she had to do on several occasions.

First, I, Isabel de San Jerónimo, declare that, during the time I knew our Father, Fray John of the Cross, and had to do with him, I

[1] N.L.M., M.S. 12,738, fol. 819.

recognized the very great and admirable virtues which shone in him. He had very great patience in the most severe trials which he had to suffer at the beginning of the Reform of our sacred Order; for the Calced Carmelites of Toledo kept him for many days imprisoned in their convent, where he suffered greatly; so much so that a point was reached when he seemed to be at death's door. Finding himself in this condition, he let himself out of a window in the room where he was imprisoned; this window is so high that merely to look at it from the ground makes the head swim, and thus his escape was miraculous rather than natural. He reached the ground at a place that was surrounded so that there was no way out. Finding himself in difficulties, and not knowing what he could do, he went to sleep for a time, and when he awoke found himself in the street, so that he could reach our convent of Discalced Carmelite nuns in Toledo. On the road from the house whence he escaped to ours there are always many people, and it was in the day-time that he came, so Our Lord set him free in such a way that, as I have said, he was able to reach our convent. It was I who spoke to him at the turn when he arrived;[1] he seemed at the point of death and asked us to help him.

At this time M. Ana de la Madre de Dios, a nun of that convent, was ill; and, hearing that our father Fray John of the Cross was there, she said that she needed to make her confession and asked for him to be brought to her. He went and heard her confession, but he was so worn out and ill that we had to keep him in the convent and church, lest the Calced fathers should re-capture him, from the morning of his arrival until the evening of the same day.

Great as were the trials he had suffered, which had brought him to such an extremity, his patience was no less great, and we never heard from him a word of complaint or murmuring; there shone in him the greatest humility, and both in this virtue and in that of patience he was a wonderful man and set a great example.

The Mother Prioress of that convent, M. Ana de los Ángeles, in view of the great need of the holy Father that we should help and comfort him, sent for Don Pedro González de Mendoza, uncle of the Conde de los Arcos and a Canon of Toledo Cathedral, a great servant of God, well known to us all. She begged him to take the Father into his house, which he did, keeping him there for several days. And, when he was

---

[1] From other accounts we learn that the doorkeeper was one Leonor de Jesús, but that Isabel de San Jerónimo had been temporarily substituted for her as being more discreet and experienced. [Cf. the account on p. 319, below.]

fit to travel, he sent him with a servant from his own house to a priory of the Discalced Fathers of our Order far from Toledo; and when the servant came back he wondered greatly who this holy Father could be who emitted such fragrance.

This is what I can say with all truth concerning this holy man, and, since it is true, I sign it with my name.

ISABEL DE SAN JERÓNIMO.

All that Sister Isabel de San Jerónimo has said concerning our venerable father Fray John of the Cross, almost all of us who are nuns in this convent have heard from her, and from other nuns, in particular from M. Ana de los Ángeles and M. Ana de la Madre de Dios, who have repeated it to us on several occasions. From these we have heard great praises of him, and he has been spoken of as a very holy person, of very great virtues, of which these nuns are well informed, since they have known him and had to do with him. And all the other persons whom we have heard speaking of him have done so in the belief and opinion that he is a saint, which is the common opinion and report. . . . He came to this convent only once, very soon after its foundation, when there were very few nuns here, and we cannot therefore speak of him in detail save from hearsay, but those who spoke of him have always said that his words had great effect and power in their souls and seemed to kindle them with fervour and love of God. This has also been the experience of those of us who did not know him save by his writings, for these produce a great effect and impression on those who read them, and not only upon ourselves, but also, as we have heard, upon other persons outside the Order who read them. This is what we know in common concerning this saint, and in witness of its truth we sign this with some of our names.

MARIANA DE JESÚS.

FRANCISCA DE LA MADRE DE DIOS.

MARIANA DE SAN ÁNGEL.

ISABEL DE JESÚS.

LUISA DEL NACIMIENTO.

FRANCISCA DE SAN ELISEO.

INÉS DE JESÚS.

MARIANA DE SAN ALBERTO

TERESA DE JESÚS MARÍA.

MARÍA DE JESÚS.

V

LETTER BY M. CONSTANZA DE LA CRUZ[1]

Jesus Mary.

In fulfilment of the order which your Reverence gives me, I testify that on the morning when the holy Father left his prison (or, more correctly, when God took him thence) I was a novice at Toledo. I found him so greatly changed that he seemed fitter for the next life than for this. . . .

One morning, when we were at prayer, there was a knock at the door and a message was sent to the Mother Prioress that it was Fray John of the Cross. The Mother, who was very prudent, opened the door to him at once with the justification that he was needed to confess a sick nun. It made us all very sorry to see him in a very old black soutane, and so completely worn out that they dared give him nothing to eat, save a few stewed pears with cinnamon.

While Mass was being said, they took him to the church by the door which at that time we used when we went in to dress it. He showed such fervour when he began to speak of God and to describe the great trials which he had suffered that it was striking to hear him. He told us that he had been imprisoned for nine months and in great affliction of every kind; that he had had no light save what entered through a tiny hole in the wall, by which he could just read the Divine office, but, as the light was so poor, he could not sit down. Each Friday they took him to the refectory, where they gave him a very severe discipline. One Friday they failed to take him there and he said to the person whose business it was to take him: 'Brother, why have I been deprived of my deserts?' He caused such great edification that from that time onward they had a little pity on him.

Among other things he got them to bring him a clean tunic. With regard to this, I am not sure that he did not tell us that he only changed his tunic on that one occasion during all those nine months.

His escape from prison came about in this way, according to his own description. He asked his gaoler, who had given him a clean tunic, to bring him the necessary things for mending his clothes. When he

---

[1] N.L.M., M.S. 12,738, fol. 823. Constanza de la Cruz, professed in the convent of the Discalced nuns at Toledo in 1579, afterwards went to the new foundation of Villanueva de la Jara, where she wrote this letter.

found that he had scissors and thread, as His Majesty had ordained, he took his bedlinen, which must have been very poor, cut it into strips and sewed the strips together, and thus, though he knew not the height of the corridors, he had sufficient material to escape. On the night when he was to escape from prison, his cell was bolted as on every other night. But when they bolted it God inspired him to insert his finger, and thus it was not secured. Everything throughout bore the clear trace of Our Lord's intention to set him free. He commended himself to His Majesty, and, after Matins, when the friars were all at rest, he left his room with the bundle of strips, passing the room wherein was sleeping that very severe superior, Tostado. He had a lighted lamp, but God in His goodness was so favourable to him that nobody woke and perceived it. He knotted the strips of linen, so as to be able to make use of them in his descent, and, when he was at the bottom, he found himself in the greatest difficulty of all, for he discovered that he was in the enclosed courtyard of a convent of nuns. He said afterwards that he was about to throw himself upon their mercy, and could think of no other remedy, for the wall was high and its surface quite smooth. He commended himself very earnestly to the Mother of God, and it seemed to him that she raised him up and gave him strength to get over the wall. When he got down into the street, God helped him further. I do not remember how He did this, but, having done so much for him, He would not fail to do the rest.

Returning to what I said about his entry into our Toledo convent, the Calced friars arrived to ask with all due discretion if a Father of the Order was there called Fray John of the Cross. The portress, who had even more discretion than they, answered them excellently, without lying, but leaving them puzzled as to whether the nuns had seen any religious. This portress was Sister San Jerónimo, whom your Reverence knows well; she was taken to Cuerva to M. Ana de los Ángeles and is a sister of the white veil. All that day the Calced waited around our convent.

The Saint was with us at the grille of the church speaking very sublimely of Our Lord and of a work upon the Most Holy Trinity which he had composed in his prison, so that it was a heavenly joy to hear him. As night was approaching, the good Mother Ana de los Ángeles, being very zealous and prudent in all things concerning honesty of life, said that she thought it not lawful to him to spend the night there, even in the church, and that she would arrange for a trustworthy gentleman to come, from whom all the Calced together would

not take him away. So she sent for Don Pedro González de Mendoza, a
leading Canon of Toledo Cathedral, who also held other high offices;
he was the uncle of Don Pedro Laso, who is still living.

This gentleman brought his carriage and they gave him some
clerical garments, and all went so well that, after a few days, this worthy
gentleman sent him to Almodóvar del Campo.

As I was a novice, I was living apart from the other nuns, and so I
do not repeat many things which others might say about the holy
Father, as I am not sure of them. M. María de Jesús, who was Prioress
at Toledo, and is now here (for we were novices together and came
from Molina), will perhaps be able to remember better than I. Also
Teresa de la Concepción, a sister who has taken the white veil, and
who at that time was the infirmarian and gave the holy Father that
meal which I described, with all the rest who are still living, such as
M. Leonor de Jesús at Beas, and M. Francisca de San Eliseo at Sabiote.
These were older than I and will know more of what happened.

One more thing I have remembered which the holy Father said—
namely, that he had so little to eat that he thought they were trying to
bring his life more quickly to an end and that he felt in himself that his
vitality was leaving him. It has also occurred to me that M. María de los
Mártires was there at the time and, with her great regard for truth, will
be able to give a good account of it.

May Our Lord be held in reverence in all His works, for so He
desires for the good of our souls.

May His Majesty keep your Reverence many years to His greater
honour and glory and for the greater good of our holy Order.

Your Reverence's unworthy subject,

CONSTANZA DE LA CRUZ.

My fingers being as they are, I cannot write this with my own
hand.[1]

VI

LETTER BY V. MARÍA DE JESÚS CONCERNING ST. JOHN OF THE CROSS[2]

This is what I know of the great virtues of our venerable father
Fray John of the Cross, whom I knew and saw many times and in

[1] This line and the signature are in the hand of the author of the letter.
[2] An autograph letter, N.L.M., MS. 12,738, fol. 817. The writer professed at Toledo
in 1578.

whom I always recognized great sanctity and a truly celestial spirit. He taught great self-denial and mortification and detachment from all things, even from the wholly spiritual, and he led souls into great resignation to the Divine will and taught them to aim at the greatest perfection. This is what I knew and saw concerning him.

After the Calced friars had imprisoned him in their Carmel and he had escaped from that imprisonment, he himself related to us the great trials which he had suffered there and the severity with which those holy friars had treated him; he said that they had grieved him greatly and caused him great humiliation and mortification by what they had said to him. Some of this he repeated to us but I cannot remember it in detail, except that they enjoined upon him that he must never return to the Discalced. They took his Discalced habit from him and gave him a habit of the Calced, and they imprisoned him with such rigour that he had no light by which to say the Divine office save a small skylight in the roof of the cell in which he was imprisoned.

The food they gave him was very bad, and on Fridays they took him to the refectory, with bare shoulders, where they recited his faults to him—namely, that he had gone over to the Discalced and had founded new convents according to the Reform and other things of this kind—and they gave him very severe disciplines, in which all the friars took part, and mortified him greatly, giving him bread and water and afterwards sending him back to his prison.

He said that all this made him greatly contented; and that Our Lord showed him many favours during this period, by communicating Himself to him with great consolations; and that he said not a word to these friars, notwithstanding all that they were doing to him. He declared that his great grief was that our holy Mother and the Discalced brethren knew nothing about him, for nobody knew where the Calced friars were keeping him, although our Mother and all the religious were making great efforts to discover this. He was also very anxious and troubled lest the houses of the Discalced should be abolished, as they told him in the prison would happen; but he said to us that he had confidence throughout that nothing of the kind would come to pass.

He told us that he grew so ill and weak that he thought he was dying, and that, while he was in this state, during the octave of Our Lady of the Assumption, she appeared to him and told him to leave the prison, the doors of which were open at night on account of the great heat, but he feared to do so on account of his weak condition, which made it impossible for him to escape save with the greatest difficulty. Never-theless, he said, she returned to him frequently and told him to go, saying that she would aid him. At last, he told us, he could resist no longer, and determined to leave the prison, letting himself down through a very high window by means of his bedclothes which he tied together so as to be able to descend by them. When he was on the ground, he said, he found himself in a courtyard of a convent of nuns; he had fallen on some great stones and was sorely bruised. But Our Lady set him free and he came to no harm, though he said that, when he found himself in such straits, he thought he must be the weariest man in the world. It was impossible for him, by his own natural strength, to get out of the courtyard into which he had come down, for the walls were very high and he was so weak and ill that he felt he was at death's door.

Now he was greatly troubled, he continued, for it would have been a great trial if the friars had found him there on the next morning. So he commended himself often to Our Lord and to His most holy Mother and said he thought it must have been by their aid that he found him-self outside the walls; it seemed to him that Our Lady had helped him to surmount them and that it had been a miracle. He then came here and we brought him into the convent to hear the confession of a nun who was very ill, and in this way the Lord delivered him; for friars and alguaciles came at once to seek him and surrounded the house; but the Superior sent for a Canon of the Cathedral and let him out of the con-vent by the door which we used for going into the church. The Canon was Treasurer of the Cathedral and a very important person, called Don Pedro González de Mendoza; he went into the church and took our Father into his carriage and drove him home secretly, gave him clerical clothes and sent him to Almodóvar, thus garbed, with many precautions. And one of the men who took him there said, when he came back, that he did not know who that cleric could be who emitted the odour of sanctity. . . .

Of this, and no more, I am certain; and because it is the truth I sign it with my name.

MARÍA DE JESÚS.

VII

Letter by Fray Bernardo de los Reyes (Vélez-Málaga, April 10, 1614)[1]

Jesus.

In fulfilment of the command given by our father, Fray Gabriel de Cristo, Provincial of the Province of our father San Angelo, in the Discalced Carmelite Order, which instructs every religious to state what he knows with respect to the life and sanctity of our father, Fray John of the Cross, religious of the said Order, I state that I knew him for a long period, both when I was in the world and since being in religion, and I was under him in the Order. Since that time I have always heard much good spoken by all of his virtue and sanctity, and on all the occasions which presented themselves of speaking about the said Father I never remember having heard aught but praise of his great virtues, which were well known to all, and this both during his life and after his death. . . . For myself, during the whole time I knew him, I saw a simple, sincere, unaffected sanctity; he spoke of spiritual things with such readiness that one would think he had them prepared; and he needed no material for this, but in speaking of any small thing —even of a trifle—he would soar in his discourse so that he carried us away with him and we listened to him with such delight that none of us ventured to speak until he had finished. He often spoke in this way during recreation. In all the time that I knew him I saw nothing in his conduct worthy of reproof nor observed in him any imperfection. He was full of charity, especially with the sick; he was very sympathetic to all; he had a rare prudence and the gentlest way of government; he had also the gift of discernment of spirits. I was with him at Lisbon, for a Chapter General, and observed that all the religious went on one day or another to see the nun who had the famous marks of wounds on her body, and made great efforts, not only to see her but also to obtain relics of her; for she had a great reputation, both among learned men and among spiritual persons. But it was impossible to persuade the said father, Fray John of the Cross, either to go to see her or to approve such conduct in a woman; indeed, I heard him say that the religious in our house did ill in going to see her. I have heard that, at the time of the foundation of our Reform, the Calced fathers persecuted him greatly, and I know that he met with great

[1] An autograph document, N.L.M., MS. 12,738, fol. 1,029.

opposition among ourselves, especially a short time before his death. This is what I know, and I therefore sign it with my name at Vélez, on this tenth day of April, 1614.

FRAY BERNARDO DE LOS REYES.

VIII

LETTER BY V. MARÍA DE JESÚS (LERMA, APRIL 11, 1614)[1]

Jesus Mary.

What I can remember having heard of our father Fray John of the Cross I think I heard from M. Ana de Jesús, now in Flanders, who had a great deal to do with him. When he was quite young, he heard the call to enter the religious life, and he was doubtful about the choice of an Order, because he desired to enter one in which the Rule was very much relaxed, so that he might do his utmost to reform it, for he thought that by so doing he would render a great service to Our Lord. So he went from one religious house to another to see in which the Rule was least severe; and as at that time a Carmelite house had been founded in the village where he was staying, and he must have seen some mismanagement, as the foundation was not yet properly established, this seemed to him the Order which he was seeking, and accordingly he took the habit in it. Later, whether because he saw that he could not endure it, or because Our Lord had not yet revealed to him how it was to be reformed, he was about to go to the Carthusian Order when our holy Mother, Teresa of Jesus, heard of him. He now began a life of great penitence, prayer and strictness in the observance of the Rule, and thus, though he was so young, he was respected by the oldest, who were careful not to commit faults in his presence. If they were talking together at a time when it was forbidden they would say when they caught sight of him in the distance: 'Fray John is coming,' and would go away. He had a cell with a little window overlooking the church, where he spent a great part of the night in prayer. Once when he was looking through this window he observed something which showed him that a grave offence to Our Lord was about to be committed. He went to the friar who knew about this, and, though he was very young and this friar was of mature years and held a post of confidence in the convent, he reproved him with dignity and told him to see to it then and there that this was not done or he would go

---

[1] An autograph letter, N.L.M., MS. 12,738, fol. 911.

and tell the Prior. And the other friar did as he said. Among other trials which the holy Father suffered at the time of the separation of the Discalced province, the Calced fathers imprisoned him for some time (I believe it was eight months) in a very narrow prison, where he suffered severe penalties and was very frequently taken to the refectory to receive discipline—I fancy it was every third day approximately. He was fed badly and treated very severely. A friar had pity on him and arranged for the prison door to be left open one night so that he escaped and began to climb from one roof to another and so reached the street. As it was night he could not see the place into which he was coming down and he entered the courtyard or garden of a convent of nuns. When it began to get light he realized where he was and became greatly afflicted; so he betook himself to prayer, and, without knowing how, found himself in the street.

As he was making a journey by night, he fell from a high precipice, and, as he did so, he felt as if someone was sustaining him in the air so that, by clutching some plants, he was able to save himself. At this same time M. Ana de Jesús was at prayer and it was suddenly represented to her that Fray John of the Cross was in great peril and with great emotion she commended him to God. A few days afterwards, the Father reached the place where she was and she asked him what had happened to him during the journey and if he had found himself in any great trial or peril. 'Why do you ask?' he said. She answered by telling him what had happened to her while she was at prayer and the day and the hour of it. 'Then it was you who were sustaining me?' he said, and told her what had happened to him.

I have also heard (though I cannot remember from whom) that, when the said Father was concerned with the spiritual progress of a nun belonging to another Order, he went several times to confess her, and the devil, anxious to sow his tares, assumed Fray John's figure and habit, and went to the convent to ask for the nun, and they duly sent for her. When he was with her in the confessional or locutory, Fray John came to ask that she should be sent for. 'But it is no time,' said the portress, 'since your Reverence sent for her and she went into the locutory!' He understood what had happened and went and found the devil talking with her, but I have such a bad memory that I cannot properly recall the rest of what happened. I think he ordered the devil to say who he was, because otherwise the nun would not believe what he had said.[1]

[1] This incident is said to have happened in the convent of Augustinian nuns at Ávila.

I also heard that, when he wrote a book expounding several passages from the Songs, he dealt with that subject very reverently, writing it all upon his knees.

In our Segovia convent I heard it said that he had warned the Mother Prioress of that convent to take great care with a certain nun, for she would lose her reason; and so it came to pass, though the prophecy must have been made more than ten years earlier. I do not remember the exact words in which he said this. I also heard that at the end of his life he was very ill, and among other illnesses, had certain wounds; and that the surgeon took off some of the bandages which were covering these and with them cured other sick persons by applying them to them. In general, on almost every occasion that I have heard anything of the Father, it has been in high praise of his great virtue and religious character and I have never heard anything about him that contradicts this.

Thus I sign this letter on this eleventh day of April, 1614, in this convent of the Mother of God at Lerma.

MARÍA DE JESÚS.

IX

LETTER BY FRAY DIEGO DE LA ENCARNACIÓN (SEGOVIA, APRIL 26, 1614)[1]

Jesus Mary.

In fulfilment of the command given by our Father Provincial, Fray Luis de la Madre de Dios, to state what I know with respect to the virtue and sanctity of our father Fray John of the Cross, the first man to take our Discalced habit, I say as follows:

First, in the thirty-six years, approximately speaking, that I have spent in religion, I have always observed that the whole Order has held and esteemed the said Father to be one of the holiest, most exemplary and most virtuous of religious who have belonged to it—I might even say the holiest of them all. He was the most perfect example of every kind of virtue, especially that of charity towards his neighbour, for he succoured others in all the necessities that they presented to him, whether spiritual or bodily, with all solicitude and care, according as their state and profession allowed. He was particularly attentive to

<hr>

[1] An autograph document, N.L.M., MS. 12,738, fol. 889.

the needs of those who were under him, loving them and helping them in every fit manner, so that, at the same time as he corrected and amended their faults, he encouraged and persuaded them to a better observance of the law of God and of their essential vows and of the Rule and Constitutions of the Order. Yet, rigorous and meticulous as he was in this, he was nevertheless greatly loved by those whom he ruled, to such an extent that anyone who had ever experienced his company sought it always.

He was marvellous in his practice of prayer and contemplation—I believe that in this respect he was the loftiest and most fervent religious known to our time, as is witnessed by certain treatises concerning this virtue which he left for our edification and instruction. One of these is called the *Ascent of Mount Carmel* and another the *Dark Night of the Soul*. From these and others may be deduced how this servant of God reached the highest degree of prayer and contemplation which a soul can attain in this life.

From these treatises may also be inferred the severity of the mortification which he practised, both within and without, and the great annihilation and contempt which he had for himself, together with the extreme poverty of spirit which, one would think, could hardly be greater in any soul still living this life.

It may also be inferred what a great spiritual master he was and what deep experience he had in the spiritual life. He had the gift of discernment of spirits and of giving light and guidance to souls walking here below. They came to him from many parts and were ruled and governed by his opinion, holding and esteeming him as a Divine oracle. He was a great penitent: not content with performing the things commanded by our Rule and Constitutions, which are considerable, he added many more to them.

But the virtue which shone most brightly in him was that of patience, for he suffered many of the gravest persecutions innocently, bearing them with great conformity and resignation to the will of God, without defending or excusing himself or complaining of his persecutors; he likewise suffered the gravest illnesses and indispositions of the body. It would be a very long tale to relate his virtues in detail; this I leave to others.

One thing I will not fail to mention, small though it is, since I was an eye-witness of it and was greatly edified by it. One day, at the time when this Father was Definitor of the Order, he arrived at a priory where I was living after Compline had been said; he was very tired and in great need of rest and refreshment, for it was a period of great heat. The religious went out to receive his blessing, since he was the father of them all and their superior in the Order. But the Prior had some scruple about their talking with him after Compline had been said, and, in some agitation, began to point out to them that, whoever the visitor might be, he could not allow it. Our father, Fray John of the Cross, without speaking a word to him or showing any annoyance, either before or afterwards, retired at once, though he was the Prior's superior, being Definitor, and though it was but a little time since the Prior had been a novice under him.

After our Father had been superior in our convent of Segovia, I went as superior to the same convent, and found in his rule there much to imitate. By his example and virtue he had caused great edification in virtue and good living, not only in the convent but also among those in the world who had much to do with him; for all with whom he spoke remained greatly affected by all the good that they saw in him, and enkindled in the love of God and desire to serve him. It is as if this Father were a burning torch who not only enkindled all the hearts of those with whom he had to do but also prepared them to burn with love themselves. . . .

All this is well known and commonly reported, not only within the Order but also among those in the world. This I say in fulfilment of this command and I have signed it on the twenty-sixth day of April, 1614.

FRAY DIEGO DE LA ENCARNACIÓN.

X

LETTER BY MARÍA DE LA ENCARNACIÓN (OCTOBER 30, 1614)[1]

Jesus Mary.

In order to comply with obedience and the command which your Reverence has given us to relate what we know and have heard of the virtues and sanctity of our venerable and holy father Fray John of the Cross, I relate to the honour and glory of Our Lord and in praise of that faithful servant of his, that I, wretched and miserable as I am, had the privilege of knowing him, that I made my confession to him several times and had to do with him here in Madrid, where he came with M. Ana de Jesús to the foundation of our nuns there, where I

---

[1] An autograph letter, N.L.M., MS. 12,738, fol. 827.

afterwards took the habit. Whensoever he confessed and communicated me, I felt a great benefit in my soul, for his words had great
power and he spoke in a most lofty manner of the love of God and of
prayer and contemplation. He could speak of nothing else, and his
words were so gracious that they remained in the souls of the hearers,
and enkindled in them the fire of the love of God. It always seemed that
his soul was at prayer. I can bear witness that Her Majesty the Empress[1]
(whom may God have in His glory) was greatly devoted to him and
honoured and esteemed him as a saint and read his books and treatises
which deal with the loftiest prayer and contemplation and with the love
of God. I repeat that Her Majesty read them with great pleasure and
devotion and said that in all her life she had never read or heard things
so devout or sublime.

I heard the Father himself say that he had written these treatises
on prayer in his prison—the Toledo convent where the Calced fathers
kept him many days, at the beginning of his career, when the reform of
our holy Order had just begun. Here they ill-treated him and persecuted him sorely on account of the reforms which he had made and of
his having left them.

He suffered many trials and much ill-treatment in prison, as my holy
Mother María del Nacimiento can effectively witness. At that time this
Mother was in the Toledo house; later she went to the Madrid foundation, where she became sub-prioress, and had charge of the novices;
I was under her there and often heard her speak of the great trials
which this holy man had suffered. When God set him free from his
prison, he went to the convent of the Toledo nuns, and he was so
emaciated and weak on account of the hunger which he had been forced
to endure in prison, with other kinds of ill-treatment, that they hardly
knew him, nor could he talk to them; it seemed that he was at death's
door.

I heard him tell this same Mother that he had endured these trials,
and others, and the illnesses which he had suffered, with great patience
and joyfulness of soul, for the love of God. When he was in Madrid, he
often came to our convent to hear our confessions, and so, on two or
three occasions, I heard him describe all this; he would say that his
soul had never been more contented nor had he ever rejoiced in the
sweetness and light of Our Lord as during that long period when he
was in that prison. It was very gloomy and dark, he said, so that hardly

---

[1] When she first met the Saint the writer was in the service of María, consort of Maxi-
milian II, Emperor of Germany, Philip II's sister.

sufficient light entered it for reading, but Our Lord provided for him, for through a very small opening there came a ray of sunlight, which consoled him, and by which he was able to write the exposition of those spiritual stanzas which he composed, beginning:

> Upon a darksome night,
> Kindling with love in flame of yearning keen
> —O moment of delight!—
> I went, by all unseen,
> New-hush'd to rest the house where I had been.

This poem treats in a most lofty way of the intimate communication, contemplation and union of the soul with God and of His Divine love.

Often, too, I heard M. Ana de Jesús and M. María del Nacimiento (may God rest her soul!) relate of our holy Mother Teresa of Jesus, that she greatly esteemed and loved this venerable Father and was for a long time his penitent, and said of him that she loved him tenderly, since his soul was most sincere and pure, and he was a man without craft or malice, and practised the loftiest contemplation and lived in the greatest peace. What I can say with great truth is that, whenever I saw him and spoke with him, his expression and demeanour were like those of an angel from Heaven and he seemed to be in prayer and in the presence of the Lord. He had a peaceful and holy joy, and there shone in him charity, humility, meekness and a grave and religious modesty. . . .

Our holy Mother Teresa of Jesus has left much information about this holy man in her *Foundations*, where she describes at length his call to our Order, and relates how he was proposing to become a Carthusian, and also describes his great virtue and religious character. If M. Ana de Jesús is alive, she can say much of this venerable Father, for she knew him for a long time at Beas and he went with her to the foundations at Granada and Madrid; and I understand that she knows much about him, and can go into great detail. At Talavera, too, there is a nun who has taken the white veil, called Ana de Jesús, who is a daughter of the Granada convent and knew and saw much of this holy man both there and in Madrid. When we were together in the Madrid convent, I heard this sister relate many things of the sanctity and virtue of our venerable father Fray John of the Cross. If she is not dead, she will relate these better than I, for I have a poor memory and do not recall things well.

Both from those whom I have here named and from many other persons who knew this holy Father, your Reverence may learn much of his great and heroic virtues and sanctity; and, since all that is here written is the strictest truth, I sign it with my name, on this day of the glorious and holy Father Serapion, the thirtieth day of October of this year 1614, in this convent of our Father Saint Joseph of Consuegra.

MARÍA DE LA ENCARNACIÓN.[1]

XI

LETTER BY ISABEL DE JESÚS MARÍA (CUERVA, NOVEMBER 2, 1614)[2]

Jesus Mary.

The virtues and sanctity of our father Fray John of the Cross were very great and in particular there shone forth in him a marvellous meekness and patience in the great trials which he suffered during his life, especially at the time of the separation of our province in the year 1580. The Calced fathers kept him imprisoned in their Carmel at Toledo, and dealt him the greatest affliction and the harshest treatment, so that he felt himself to be at the point of death and determined to escape. Herein he was miraculously aided by Our Lord and His most holy Mother. He let himself down from his prison by a window, tearing up the sheets from his bed and making ropes of them, and by this means lowering himself from a great height. When he came to the ground he found himself in an enclosed space from which it was impossible for him to escape on account of the great height of the walls; finding himself in such affliction and with no human remedy, he was about to cry out to the friars themselves to have mercy on him and take him back to his prison. But Our Lord came to his help, and, without knowing how, he found himself in the street outside that enclosure.

At dawn he arrived at our convent of Discalced nuns in Toledo. His natural strength and energy were exhausted, what with his perturbation and the trials of his prison, so that he could scarcely speak to the portress. But he begged her with great humility to succour him speedily as he believed they were coming after him.

---

[1] In a long postscript the writer apologizes for the 'bad style' of the letter and begs for a blessing.

[2] An autograph letter, N.L.M., MS. 12,738, fol. 835.

The prioress of that time, M. Ana de los Ángeles, was greatly confused, and could not think what she could do to help him in this peril.
It so pleased Our Lord, however, that a nun who was ill in bed should
say that she needed to make her confession, and ask that this Father
should come and confess her. He did so, and afterwards, with great
secrecy, he went into the convent church, where he hid for some hours,
until the Mother Prioress sent for Don Pedro González de Mendoza,
Canon of the Cathedral of Toledo, and uncle of the Count of
Arcos. He took the Father in his carriage, brought him to a safe
place and afterwards sent him to a convent of Discalced friars of
the Order. The servant who accompanied him, when he returned,
asked the nuns what friar was this, for there came from him a celestial
fragrance.

I remember, too, that at the time when we had him hidden in the
church, he recited some verses which he had composed and had in his
head and a nun wrote them down. There are three of them, all treating
of the Most Holy Trinity, so lofty and devout that they seemed to
kindle fire. We have them in this convent of Cuerva. They begin:

> Far away in the beginning
> Dwelt the Word in God Most High.

This happened when I was a novice at Toledo.

The works and writings of this Father are held in the greatest
honour and esteem; I have heard it said, both of his works and of his
words, that they enkindled with celestial fire, and this I have also myself
experienced. His works are so spiritual and so greatly esteemed that
they are kept and preserved as a precious treasure, and no person's
entreaties can prevail for them to be taken out. The Count of Arcos
has in great esteem some *liras* or lyric poems by this Father, with a
gloss or exposition to each stanza, a most delicate and spiritual work,
beginning: 'Whither hast vanishèd?'

During the time that Our Lord entrusted this holy man with the
duty of government, he exercised his office with great rectitude, charity
and prudence, as may be seen in the letters and the order which he
sent to our Mother Ana de los Ángeles, when she was prioress. I
understand that he acted with equal prudence on all other occasions
and I have never heard anything to the contrary, but always that
in the religious life, in prayer and in patience, he was admirable. . . .

This is what I know of that great religious, at first hand and from
the testimony of persons who had some acquaintance with his life.

But what I have said is nothing compared with what remains to be said about his great sanctity. I hold him as a saint. And in witness to the truth of this I sign it with my name, at Cuerva, on this second day of November in the year 1614.

ISABEL DE JESÚS MARÍA.

XII

LETTER BY MARÍA DEL SACRAMENTO (CARAVACA, NOVEMBER 7, 1614)

Jesus Mary.

In fulfilment of the order given us by your Reverence to say what we know of the virtues of our father Fray John of the Cross, I testify that, since he first came to this part of the country as Rector at Baeza, more than thirty-fours years ago, we have all recognized that he was a man of great holiness and of most sublime spirituality in the things of God, together with a particular gift of prayer, and a great talent for leading souls into the way of prayer.

At that time, I heard him say that he sometimes abstained from saying Mass for some days in order to avoid the burden of devotion, and that the result of this had been different from his expectations, for the mercies which God then showed him were much greater. Speaking wittily of this he said: 'Our Lord is really quite embarrassing'; by which he indicated how great are the favours which His Majesty shows to those to whom He communicates Himself.

All the sufferings which came to him he bore with the patience and perfection of a true saint; he was the first man to pass from the Miti-gated Rule of our Order to the Primitive Rule. When the Calced fathers had him in their power, they ill-treated him greatly, shutting him up in a foul little cell, where he could get only enough light to say the Divine Office by standing on a stone. When they could not bring him to their way of thinking by any other means, they took him from his cell to the refectory to give him disciplines. But the door of the prison was left open and he succeeded in returning to the Discalced, in great peril of his life, passing through gates and over walls. He told us that in that cell he had composed what he wrote about the Book of the Songs, the Most Holy Trinity and the Psalm *Super flumina Babilonis*.

He grieved greatly for the trials suffered by Father Gracián, which was natural, as he also shared them.

A short time before they took away the habit from Father Gracián, he wrote to M. Ana de San Alberto, who lives in this convent, saying: 'Daughter, God has permitted these times to come upon us in order to prove His elect. In silence and hope shall be our strength.' I heard Fray Agustín de los Reyes, who was Provincial of Andalusia and is now dead, say that the persecutions suffered by Fray John of the Cross were worse than those of Father Gracián, for he had himself witnessed them. These were the very words of the said Father.

I heard Fray Gabriel de Cristo, now Provincial of Andalusia, when he held the same office previously, speak of the patience and obedience of our blessed Father. When he was at Úbeda, he said, in the early days of the sickness of which he died, he felt unable to go to the refectory, and sent to ask the Prior to excuse him, which he refused to do, and sent commanding him sternly to go. With all humility he obeyed and went. This Prior had been under the blessed Father and had received the greatest kindness from him. I heard the same Father Provincial say that our father Fray John had proved himself, in one thing that he had said, to have the spirit of prophecy. When he was making a hurried journey he was asked the reason for his haste, and replied that he was going to prevent someone who would upset the Order from making his profession. When he arrived, the profession had already been made and events showed that he had spoken the truth.

I also heard one of our friars (I think it was Fray Cristóbal de San Alberto, at his death Prior of Manzanares), say that our Father was in Portugal at the time when the nun of the Anunciada was held in such great esteem for her supposed sanctity. Some of the religious suggested to him that he should go to see her. He replied that he had no desire to do so. Father Mariano answered: 'Come, go and see her, for her superiors are proposing to enclose her!' The blessed Father answered: 'They ought to have done so already, for God will reveal her impostures.' And this turned out and happened as he had said.

I also heard this same friar say that, on the night of his death, he asked what hour it was, and that, when they told him, he said: 'We will go and say Matins in Heaven.' And in fact he died just before midnight.

When he was Provincial here, and was saying Mass in our church, the said M. Ana de San Alberto saw him surrounded by a great light. Afterwards she asked him why he had spent so long over that Mass, and he answered: 'Why do you ask, my daughter?' In telling her what had happened, he said: 'Our Lord has shown me so great a favour that, if He had not provided for me, I could not have received it. He told me to tell the Prioress to see that a convent of Discalced friars is founded here, and that He would be greatly pleased by this, and would assist it.' And His Majesty fulfilled His promise, for soon afterwards He put it into the heart of a devout cleric to come forward with substantial alms to buy the site; and everything favoured it, and M. Ana de San Alberto, the Prioress, with the other nuns of this convent, gave them two hundred ducats, although we had still a great deal to do ourselves which was very necessary.

When I heard something about its being the will of God that this foundation should be made, I persuaded the said Mother to tell me in detail what had happened, as far as she knew it, and she related to me what I have written. . . .

I now recall a phrase of his teaching which I heard myself and which is worthy always to be kept in remembrance. 'The smallest anxiety of the soul is ill-bestowed if it have not to do with God.'

May His Majesty keep your Reverence many years to do Him such services as these in furthering the honour of His servants, who merit it likewise. At Caravaca, in this convent of Discalced Carmelite nuns, dedicated to the glorious Saint Joseph, on the seventh day of November, 1614.

María del Sacramento.

To our father Fray Alonso de Jesús María, Provincial of the Discalced Carmelites of the Province of the Holy Spirit, whom may Our Lord preserve.

XIII

Account of the Life of the Saint by Fray Juan Evangelista, Prior of Caravaca[1]

In obedience to the command of our Father Definitor-in-chief and of the Fathers Definitors of the Consulta, concerning the enquiry into the virtues and holiness of the deceased religious of our Order, I write as follows:

First, I state that I knew our father Fray John of the Cross and lived and travelled with him for eleven years. He was a native of Fontiveros.

---

[1] An autograph document, N.L.M., MS. 12,738, fol. 559.

He died at Úbeda and his body lies in the convent of Segovia. I recognized the great virtue and religious character of this holy man. I knew him when he was Rector at Baeza, twice Prior of Granada, Vicar Provincial of these two provinces and Definitor-in-chief of the Consulta. These offices, as I observed, he discharged in a most holy and exemplary manner all the time that I had to do with him. He was given to retirement from the world and had very little communication with persons in the world, only such as was necessary. He was greatly opposed to religious having to do with persons in the world; he very seldom entered their houses and that only when it was necessary to do so.

He was a man of great penitence, and, despite his frequent attacks of ill-health, he often did penance and had a great desire for it. Once, when I was walking with him, I saw that, next to his flesh, he was wearing drawers made of knotted rope. I asked him why he was wearing these and begged him to take them off at least during his journey. 'Son,' he answered, 'it is relaxation enough to go on horseback; we must not take our ease all the time.'

I often heard him speak of the persecutions and trials which he had suffered at the beginning of his career and of how the Calced Fathers had kept him in prison for nine months, giving him the discipline every Friday, and, as food, bread and water. I can testify that his shoulders were so sore that on one day he could not bear the serge of his habit and I believe he told me that it was due to this.

He was a man of the deepest prayer, to which, as will be seen from his books, he was greatly affectioned. I saw him write these books and I never saw him open a book in order to write them. He relied upon his communion with God, and it can be clearly seen that they are all the result of experience and practice and that he had personal experience of the subject of his writings. I saw a number of things which have to do with his prayer and communion with God. On one occasion I entered his cell and found him as it were in a trance. 'Father,' I said to him, 'what is the matter with your Reverence?' 'Son,' he answered, 'I must have been asleep.' But it seemed to me that this was no way to sleep and I put the question to him again and urged him to tell me what had happened to him. Then he answered me: 'See that this is never told to anyone' (I was at that time his confessor). This happened in Segovia, when he was Definitor-in-chief. I gave him my word and he then said to me: 'I think I was enraptured; I saw certain friars of ours in a great trial and I cried to them to go away from where

they were, but they would not; then I saw that they had all perished.'
I testify that on several occasions I heard him advise those religious
to do what seemed fitting and they would never listen to him, and a
little while afterwards I saw that what the holy Father said to me had
happened to them.

On another occasion, when he was Vicar Provincial, the Father
Provincial, Fray Nicolás de Jesús María, gave him a piece of work
which we went to perform together. The city opposed this, but he
said that he was bound to do it because it was the express command
of his superior. They insisted that it was not to be done; whereupon,
seeing himself in difficulties, and unable to refrain from doing the
thing because it was a command, he said to me: 'Let us ask the help
of God and we will see what is His will.' He said Mass (it was the day
of Saint Martin, Bishop, to whom he had great devotion) and he
prayed. When he had finished, he said to me: 'We can safely go away,
for that is God's will.' Then I knew that he was acting from obedience.
Similar things happened on many other occasions.

He was extremely fond of solitude and in it consisted his greatest
pleasure. When he had any work to do he always went among the
rocks. One day I said to him: 'Heaven help us! Your Reverence is
always among the rocks!' 'Do not be surprised at that, son,' he replied;
'when I am among the rocks I have less to confess than when I am
among men.'

He was very fond of reading in the Scriptures, and I never once saw
him read any other books than the Bible (almost all of which he knew
by heart), Saint Augustine *Contra Hæreses*, and the *Flos Sanctorum*.
When occasionally he preached (which was seldom), or gave informal addresses, as he more commonly did, he never read from any
book save the Bible. His conversation, whether at recreation or at
other times, was continually of God; and he spoke so delightfully
that, when he discoursed upon the things of God at recreation, he
would make us all laugh, and we used greatly to enjoy going out. On
occasions when we held chapters, at night after supper he would usually
give devotional addresses; and he never failed to give an address
every night. He had a great gift of resignation and had great trust in
God's mercy with regard to the maintenance of his friars, and so he
never wished the friars to go out to beg for alms. He would say as a
rule that we should serve God and do our duty, and in that way we
should oblige God to do what He had promised. He often said that,
once a friar holds himself of no account, he lacks nothing, and that,

if we would only cease to be anxious about ourselves, God would succour us without fail.

It once happened, when I was his procurator, that one day there was nothing in the house to eat but a few herbs, and I went to ask leave of him to go and look for something to eat. 'God help us, son!' he said to me. 'Are we to have no patience when there is no food for a single day, especially if God wishes to prove our virtue? Go, desist from this intention and betake yourself to your cell, where you can commend this need to Our Lord.' I went away, but after a short time returned, reminding him that some of the friars were sick and it would be reasonable to attend to them. He answered me again that I had little confidence in God, and that, if I were a good friar, I could plead with God for these things from my cell. Thereupon I went away in some embarrassment, but, seeing that there was really great necessity and having respect for the feelings of the friars, I returned to him and said: 'Father Prior, this is tempting Our Lord, Whose will it is that we do what we can for ourselves. Give me leave to go and look for food to-day.' Then he smiled and said: 'Go, and take a companion, and you will see how quickly God will confound you because of your little faith.' So I went out, and just outside the door I met a municipal officer called Bravo. 'Where is your Reverence going?' he said to me. I told him that I was going to look for food. 'Wait,' he answered, 'I will give you this money which has been paid to the alcaldes and magistrates as fines.' Then he gave me twelve doubloons or golden crowns—I forget which. I was very glad, on the one hand, as I could now meet our need, but on the other hand, I felt very keenly what the holy Father had said to me. I went back into the house in great embarrassment, and when he saw me, he said: 'How much greater glory you would have had if you had remained in your cell; for God would have sent what was necessary without all that begging to go out. Learn, son, to trust God.' Several other things of this kind happened. On various occasions, when we were in need, certain persons asked him why he did not visit important people, for they would give him alms. He generally answered: 'If they are more likely to give these alms because I visit them, I will not be the occasion of such a base end and motive. If they are likely to give alms for the love of God He will move them to do so.'

This holy man was poor in the extreme. I never knew him have anything of his own—not even a notebook, or anything else, nor an image nor a cross save that which was in his cell. He once had a small and very good portrait of the holy Mother, which he said was an excellent likeness of her, and he gave it away so as to have nothing.

He was most patient in trials, and, however sore they were and however great the pains and sickness which he had to endure, he was never seen to complain. However much he was insulted, he never opened his mouth to say how badly he was being treated; nor did he find fault with anyone; and during the whole period that I knew him I never heard him utter a murmur, though he had a thousand reasons for doing so. He spoke well of all and in particular of his superiors, whom he held in high esteem and excused if ever the occasion offered; as to this I am qualified to witness. He was extremely charitable and full of compassion. He had a keen sense of the necessities and trials of his neighbours and endeavoured to succour them as often as he could.

He was most humble in his words and deeds. Sometimes he said to me: 'Son, pray God He grant me as a favour that I may die in the possession of no office and that in this life He may grant me purgatory.' He said the same to Fray Agustín de San José. Both these things Our Lord granted him, for when he died he held no office and he suffered the most terrible illness and the greatest pains imaginable. The physician told me that he had never attended anyone who had suffered such terrible pains, nor had he ever seen such patience, for no one heard him complain down to the time of his death. During this illness the Provincial, Fray Antonio de Jesús, said to him, 'Let us talk a while, Father Fray John of the Cross, of those trials of yours and the beginning of those persecutions.' 'My Father,' the Saint answered him, 'let me remember my sins, which are many; do not recall these other matters to me.' I think I never heard him speak of anything but poverty of spirit, renunciation and resignation. Practising these as he did, he was unable to speak of anything else.

Once, while he was living at La Peñuela, a large patch of waste ground caught fire. The fire spread as far as the convent and began to attack the twigs forming part of the fence of our grounds.[1] They told him that it might consume the Most Holy Sacrament, for it seemed to them impossible that the whole convent would not be burned. The holy Father prostrated himself in prayer and those who saw him say that he remained thus for some time praying to Our Lord with tears, and they observed that the fire did not spread beyond the fence.

A lady at Granada, called Doña Juana de Pedraza, told me several times that when the holy Father was in Segovia and she was in

[1] [It was a rough fence made of twigs and brushwood. Cf. p. 343, below.]

Granada (he had often confessed her—she is a very holy person) she wrote to him several times telling him of her trials and necessities; and that, on the same day as she wrote to him, he wrote to her also and his letter satisfied all her needs and answered all her questions. I have heard the same thing from M. Ana de San Alberto, who was formerly Prioress of this convent. His soul was like a temple of God supernaturally illumined, wherein were heard Divine oracles concerning the souls with whom he had to do.

On many occasions I observed the holy Father's great gift of discernment of spirits; he had only to talk to a person once and he would be familiar with his spirit and his method of prayer. He also had a great gift for exorcism, as on several occasions I had the opportunity of discovering. On one occasion, I remember that he was going to cast out a devil from the house of an important person, and, when he had gone away, the devil said: 'Alas, that I cannot vanquish this little friar, nor can I find any way of bringing about his fall! For years he has been persecuting me at Ávila, Torafe[1] and here!' I told this to the Father, but his only reply to what the devil had said about his sanctity was: 'Silence, son, and do not believe this devil, for all he says is lies.'

On the night of his death he kept asking very anxiously what hour it was. When they told him that it was eleven o'clock he said: 'Ah! at midnight we shall go and sing Matins in Heaven.' . . .

His life was honest in the extreme. He related to me how greatly a young girl had for some time been soliciting and persecuting him (when he was acting as confessor to the nuns at Ávila), and, seeing that she could do nothing with him, she went one night into the house where he was living through a courtyard which abutted on that of his house. Then she entered his room and urged and entreated him to hear her; but Our Lord helped him so that he persuaded her to leave the house and gained the victory. He often told me that he had never found himself in a more pressing situation, for she was a girl of good appearance and many good qualities, which made matters worse.[2]

This holy man was most restrained in demeanour; merely to look at him inspired spirituality; he seemed always to be at prayer. I observed many other virtues in this holy Father, but, as it is so long since his death, I cannot recall them. . . . This is the truth as to what I know and I have signed it with my name.

FRAY JUAN EVANGELISTA.

[1] Iznatoraf, a little town in the province of Jaén.
[2] [This story is told in greater detail on p. 343, below.]

XIV

DEPOSITIONS OF FRAY JUAN EVANGELISTA CONCERNING THE SAINT[1]

That which Fray Juan Evangelista knows concerning the life of the holy father Fray John of the Cross is as follows:

First, he often heard it said that, both in the world and in general, the said father Fray John of the Cross was most virtuous, composed and recollected.

Further, he heard the holy Father say that, when he was a child, playing with other children, he fell into a deep well full of water, and, after he had sunk several times and risen to the surface again, they drew him out without any injury. He also heard him talk of the prison in which he had been for so long immured and of his many sufferings there; from his description of his escape from the prison it became clear that it was miraculous, though his humility forbade him to assert this, as also to say that Our Lady had helped him on this and other occasions; he was very modest in these things.

With regard to the theological virtues, this witness deposes that on many occasions he noted to what a high degree this holy Father possessed them. In the matter of the virtue of faith, he deposes that he was well practised therein, and this he observed both in actions of his which he noted and also in his words, for what he taught most of all was that we should live in faith and detachment from all created things, so that he would never be influenced by any personal experiences which might possibly have helped him. This is exemplified in the story of the Portuguese nun with the wounds. A Chapter of this Order was being held in Lisbon; this Father, who was then Prior at Granada, attended it, and all the members of the Chapter went to see these wounds. But they could not prevail upon him to go, for he said that he had no need to see them, as he thought it of more value to have faith in the wounds of Jesus Christ than in all created things, and for that reason he had no need to see anyone's wounds.

With regard to the virtue of hope, this witness says that he observed it shining greatly in this holy Father, for, during the eight or nine years that he lived with him, he took continual note that he lived in

[1] N.L.M., MS. 12,738, fol. 981. This document appears to be an incomplete rough draft of a deposition prepared for the Beatification process. Though it repeats some of the testimony given in the last document, we reproduce it for the interest inherent in any statement by so close a companion of St. John of the Cross as P. Juan Evangelista.

hope and that hope sustained him. Of this he saw many examples, in particular when he was procurator of the priory at Granada, where the Saint was Prior. On one occasion among others, there was great need in the house, and when this witness went to the holy Father to ask leave of him to go out and get what was lacking, he said to him: 'Trust in God and have no fear that He will fail us.' Thereupon he desisted; but, after some time, seeing that it was getting late, this witness returned to the holy Father and told him it was late and there were sick persons in great need, and begged him to give leave to get what was necessary. The holy Father answered: 'Go to your cell and ask God to send what is needful, and trust in Him, and you will see that He will send it.' Thereupon he went away, but, seeing that nothing happened, he returned to the holy Father and said: 'Father, this is tempting God. Give me leave and I will go out and do what I can, for it is very late.' Then he said: 'Go, and you will see how God will confound you for your lack of faith and hope.' This witness went, but near the door of the church he found a municipal officer named Bravo, who asked him where he was going, and he answered that he was going out in search of food or of money to buy it. Then the officer said to him: 'I have here a sum of money which the Audiencia has voted.' And he gave him twelve crowns out of it. These he took and bought what was necessary, and when he returned to the holy Father very shamefacedly, he said to him: 'How much better would it have been if you had trusted in God, for He would have sent what you needed to your cell!' This witness saw other things of the same kind, as when the holy Father would enter the refectory and say grace, when there was nothing to eat; but his confidence was justified, for they always received something to eat within a short time. Because of this confidence which he had in God he would not consent that the friars in any convent where he held rule should go out to beg for alms, either of wheat or of aught else.

Further, this witness knows that the holy Father had that which is spoken of in the sixteenth question. He lived with him for many years, all the time in the same house, and shared his journeys and recreations. On these and other occasions he would always speak of God, and this witness listened to many of his spiritual addresses, on the most sublime subjects, all of them given extempore and without preparation. He never saw any books in his cell, save a Bible, a volume of Saint Augustine and a *Flos Sanctorum*, for he was most devoted to reading the lives of the saints.

Further, this witness observed in the holy Father a great purity of soul and body. The following is one example of this among others. He was at one time the confessor of some nuns in a certain place[1] and lived in a little house near their convent. A very handsome girl became attached to him, and, in order to attain her end, she made use of all possible means, none of which was of any avail. She therefore resolved upon a bold attempt against his honour and profession. One night she climbed over the fence into the little courtyard belonging to this house, and thence entered the holy Father's room, where he was alone at supper. When he saw her, he was astonished, and said that he supposed it to be the devil. Then, with his customary patience, he spoke to her about these things and made her realize her wickedness; so that she left the room and went back to her house. This witness heard this story from the mouth of the holy Father himself, who was accustomed to speak of it with great frankness. . . .

Further, when he was ill, he did such penance as he was able. This witness was once journeying with the holy Father and discovered in an inn some drawers of knotted rope which he had hidden. He asked him why he mortified himself so cruelly when he was so ill. 'Silence, son,' was the reply; 'it is luxury enough to go on horseback. We must not take our ease all the time. . . .'

XV

AN ACCOUNT BY FRAY BARTOLOMÉ DE SAN BASILIO[2]

Being at Úbeda in the same year in which Fray John of the Cross died in the convent there, I learned that he was living at the convent of La Peñuela where, so I heard, a miracle had happened. A field of stubble had caught fire and the fire had reached the fence of the convent grounds, which was made of brushwood and branches of evergreen oak. There were many persons in the convent and they all rushed out to quench the fire lest it should reach the house, but in spite of all they did they could not stop it. Then, they say, Fray John of the Cross went

---

[1] As related above (p. 340), this happened when the Saint was confessor to the nuns of the Incarnation at Ávila.

[2] N.L.M., MS. 12,738, fol. 869. An autograph MS. addressed to P. José de Jesús María, who at that time was engaged in historical investigations at Granada.

out and told them to desist; he fell on his knees near the flames and they went no farther.

In the same convent he had an attack of fever, which robbed him of his appetite; the only thing he felt like eating was a little asparagus, which was not procurable, since it was out of season, the time being the end of August. On his way to Úbeda, where he was going for treatment, he reached Guadalimar about midday. Preparing to take a short rest below the new bridge, he saw a bunch of asparagus on a large stone in the middle of the river. He asked the lay brother who was with him to see if it belonged to anyone who had been gathering it, and he answered: 'Father, this is a miracle, for it is not the season for asparagus, and there is none to be found in this part of the country.' Then he told him to take it and leave its value, which was a *cuarto*, in the place where he had found it. I saw this asparagus myself because I prepared it for him.

On that same night a breaking-out appeared in the fleshy part of the thigh and on the next morning there was another on the arch of the right foot. When the physician began his treatment he said the disease was erysipelas and he made three or four incisions in the same leg, some of them as long as a hand's breadth. To complete the treatment they had then only to take off the bandages and they obtained as much matter as they could wish. He looked on at all this, grasping some ropes which were fastened to the roof, to the great wonder of the physician and all who saw him; he seemed to me to have great content at his wounds.

All the time he was in bed he seemed to be sleeping, save that occasionally he was heard to repeat these words: *Haec requies mea in sæculum sæculi*. This he was heard frequently to repeat when his pain was at its greatest.

It was a great consolation to us that he was in the convent at that time, as the Prior was most imprudent in his rule of it. The holy Father taught him to rule and us to obey; several times I saw him leave his cell in tears at what the holy Father had said to him. For my part I think that one of the greatest sacrifices that he had to make in this life was that, in order to complete the purgation of his sins or to win greater glory, he was brought by Our Lord at the end of his days into contact with such a man as this Prior. If I were to begin to talk about him in detail, I should never end. I only say, therefore, that he felt and suffered more in this way than from all the physical pain which he had to endure.

I believe that many days before his death he knew at what hour he would die. This I gather from certain precautions which I saw him take. Among others, two days before his death, he asked for all the letters that were beneath the head of his bed; there were a great number of them and he burned them all. He died on the Friday night, at the first stroke of twelve; at one o'clock that day he had foretold his death, saying that that same night he would go to Heaven for Matins. . . .

While he was ill, we brought him some musicians, thinking he would find them a relief from his great pain. But he told them to keep silence, for they disturbed other and better music which he heard interiorly; but I think he did this lest he should forget his pain.

During his entire illness (and I was with him all the time) I saw him impatient only on three occasions. The first occasion was when a friar told him that the wound on the instep of his foot was that of the nail; he reproved him sternly, though without loss of composure. On the second occasion, Fray Antonio de Jesús was with him and we asked him to tell us about his early days. He answered that we ought not to talk of such things, for there was nothing to tell about them. Then the Provincial wanted to tell us something of them, and this he took very badly. The third occasion was on a day when the Provincial came to tell him that Our Lord was about to reward him for the trials which he had suffered; he could not bear this either. . . .

FRAY BARTOLOMÉ DE SAN BASILIO.

To my father Fray José de Jesús María, Discalced Carmelite, Priory of the Holy Martyrs, Granada.

XVI

AN ACCOUNT BY M. ANA DE SAN ALBERTO[1]

On the twenty-sixth day of the said month I gave an order to M. Ana de San Alberto to testify to her knowledge of Fray John of the Cross. She said that she had known him well and had had much to do with him. He was a native of Ontiveros and died at Úbeda; his body lies at Segovia. He was Rector at Baeza, twice Prior at Granada, Vicar Provincial of these provinces and Definitor-in-chief of the first Consulta. She had always heard that he had filled these offices entirely as

[1] N.L.M., MS. 12,738, fol. 565. This account is in the handwriting of P. Juan Evangelista but is signed by M. Ana, one of the most proficient of the followers of St. John of the Cross, who was her confessor at Caravaca and frequently exchanged letters with her.

becomes a holy man, with great perfection and to the profit of the friars.

The holy Mother Teresa of Jesus used frequently to say that the soul of this holy Father was one of the holiest and purest that God had in His Church, and that His Majesty had inspired him with wisdom from Heaven. He had the gift of discerning and dealing with spirits, together with such living and effective language that he wrought in souls all that he would. There was once a nun in this convent who suffered a great spiritual trial. This witness testifies that she wrote about it to the holy Mother, who answered her: 'My Father, Fray John of the Cross, is now going to visit you; tell him about this trial, and, with his great sanctity and prudence, I trust in Our Lord, he will put things right for you.' And thus it was; she at once felt the benefit of his help and until her death she testified to the good which he had done to her soul.

When he was Rector at Baeza, he came to this part of the country, and this witness (who was then Prioress) testifies that the holy Father said to her: 'Mother Prioress, why do you not see about founding a house for friars here?' This witness smiled, thinking it to be impossible on account of the poor facilities. 'Take courage and see to it,' he replied, 'for it is the will of God and He will be well pleased at it; see, you will bring it to pass without fail. Let there be a commemoration of Our Lady in the choir, daily without exception; and do not expect much temporal help, for God will give that as you go along.' It happened just as he said. He told me that Our Lord had revealed to him that He would be pleased at the foundation of this convent and gave him to understand that it should be done.

This witness testifies that, when the holy Father was saying Mass in the church of the nuns' convent, she saw his face shining like the sun. This was when he had just elevated the Host for the last time. He was a long time consuming the elements; and from above the corporals there came as it were the loveliest rays of light, which caused us great joy. When Mass was over, he sat down on a chair in the confessional and this witness went to him, and asked him what this was. 'What did you see, daughter?' he asked. And then he became absorbed and could not speak. This witness answered: 'I wanted to know what had been given to your Reverence, for what I saw can have been but the least part of it.' He remained for some time as it were in a trance and when he returned to himself he said: 'God has communicated great blessings to this sinner; with such majesty did He communicate Himself to my soul that I could not finish the Mass. For this reason I am sometimes afraid of beginning to say Mass. But since you alone have seen it, see that you say nothing of it to anyone. Let it serve for your profit and see what God does to a poor worm such as I.'

He once said to this witness that God communicated such things to his soul with regard to the mystery of the Most Holy Trinity that if Our Lord did not succour him with special help from Heaven it would be impossible for him to live; and as it was his natural strength was greatly exhausted.

This witness testifies that once, when he was talking with her, he told her things that were happening within her soul, which she had never told him. On another occasion, when he was Prior at Granada, he wrote to her about certain things that were happening to her, in these words: 'Since you say nothing to me, I tell you not to be foolish and harbour fears that make the soul cowardly. Give to God that which He has given you, and gives you daily, for it seems to me that you are trying to measure God by the measure of your own capacity. But you should not do so. Prepare yourself, for God seeks to do you a great favour.'[1] And so it came to pass. When she was anxious, having no one to whom she could write in confidence about the favours which God had shown her, she testifies that he wrote to her better and more clearly than she could explain to him.

This witness once had the greatest scruples which tormented her greatly and it seemed to her that she could only find relief by communicating them to him. The holy Father then wrote her a letter as she desired, saying: 'How long, daughter, do you suppose that you will be carried in the arms of others? I desire to see in you so great a detachment from the creatures, and an independence of them, that hell itself would not suffice to trouble you. What are these uncalled-for tears that you are shedding nowadays? How much valuable time do you suppose you have wasted on these scruples? If you would communicate your trials to me, go to that spotless mirror of the Eternal Father, for in that mirror I behold your soul daily, and I doubt not but that you will come away from it comforted and will have no need to go begging at the doors of poor people.'[2]

When he was Vicar Provincial he came to visit this convent and said that he would remain for a week. Then one morning he came in in great haste saying that he had to leave on the following day. The nuns

---

[1] [Cf. Letter III, p. 243, above.]
[2] [Cf. Letter II, p. 243, above. After 'Father,' the letter adds: 'which is His Son.']

all tried to persuade him to remain for the time for which he had come. He said that his departure was very urgent and he could not do otherwise than go, for they were in great need at Beas; and that he must go even if the snow grew worse (for it was snowing at the time). Seeing that they importuned him greatly, he said to this witness: 'If I stay, daughter, you will see that they will come for me.' On the same day there arrived a messenger, saying that the Mother Prioress at Beas, M. Catalina de Jesús, was dead. Then he said to this witness: 'It was because I knew this that I wanted to go.'

This witness testifies that the holy Father once wrote some letters from here to Doña Ana de Peñalosa, which she saw because he gave them her to seal up. They treated of various matters concerning her soul and offered her consolation. After this there came a messenger from Granada (where Doña Ana was) bringing some letters for the holy Father; and what he had written to her was as it were an answer to all that she had asked him in them; this the present witness can testify since she read both. She then laughed, seeing that he had replied to the letters before receiving them. 'Why are you laughing, foolish one?' he asked. 'Was it not better that I should write those letters last night, for then I was only going without sleep, whereas now we can be speaking of the things of God?' Such was the usual theme of his conversation, for he always spoke of detachment of spirit, mortification and solitude and of how the soul should be united with God; and his words had such power that they seemed to cleave to the soul.

Again, when they imprisoned him in the tiny prison at Toledo, he suffered many trials and ignominies. They gave him many disciplines, fed him on bread and water and ill-treated him in other ways. And on many occasions they tried to bring him to their way of thinking. Thus, he said, they made him many great offers, particularly two most important ones, giving him, among other things, several pieces of gold. Then he answered them: 'He who seeks Christ in detachment has no need of golden trinkets.' This witness knows that he suffered great trials with very special patience.

A certain man at Ávila suspected that the holy Father (who was confessor there) was hindering him from obtaining a certain thing that he desired. One night he waited for him as he came out of the convent where he had been confessing the nuns of the Incarnation and beat him and maltreated him sorely. The holy Father recognized him but would reveal his name to none, and bore this ill-treatment with the greatest joy, saying to this witness that he had never rejoiced so greatly as in suffering this ill-treatment for the love of God.

Again, this holy Father had a particular gift of exorcism. In one of the convents at Ávila, there was a nun possessed by the devil, and, while she was being exorcised, she said that they were not to grow weary, for the devil feared none save a little friar called Fray John of the Cross. Then they called him in to expel the devil and she began to say many evil things and to utter cries; the holy Father said that it seemed to him there were a hundred thousand devils speaking within her, judging from the diversity of their languages; and God was pleased to deliver her. The devils came out at night and dealt the holy Father many blows, such was their wrath and fury.

When he was Vicar Provincial he came to this house for the election of a Prioress. He began the Mass of the Holy Spirit, and a nun saw him through the grille surrounded by a great light which came from the ciborium, and his figure shone brightly. The nun then went to another part of the grille to see if she could see it and she saw it in the same way. When he had finished Mass and was sitting at the grille, giving the address, there came from him rays of light which passed through the grille and seemed to illumine the whole of the choir. After the election was over, he said: 'God reward you, daughters. I am grateful to you, for you have done the will of God.'

ANA DE SAN ALBERTO.

FRAY JUAN EVANGELISTA.

XVII

LETTER FROM P. JUAN EVANGELISTA TO P. JERÓNIMO DE SAN JOSÉ, GIVING INFORMATION ABOUT THE SAINT AND HIS WRITINGS (JANUARY 1, 1630)[1]

Jhs. Mª.

Pax Christi. I greatly value the kindness which your Reverence shows me in your letter. If I were what I ought to be, your Reverence

[1] This friar, as we have already said, was the inseparable companion of St. John of the Cross during the last years of his life. He acted as his confessor for long periods and was his close confidant and the participant of his joys and sufferings. He wrote this letter and those which follow at the request of P. Jerónimo de San José, who was historian of the Discalced Reform, and at this time was preparing his well-known *History* of St. John of the Cross, which appeared in 1640. This correspondence gives some idea of the great

would be right in envying my good fortune in having had to do with our venerable Father for nine years.[1] During this time I was his companion on his journeys and elsewhere, so that, with his instruction and example before me, I ought to be his true disciple and imitator. But your Reverence must have pity on me, for, despite all the help and all the good that I had from him, I am the worst person in this province; and I assure your Reverence that I am full of confusion and shame when I remember the great opportunities that I had to be what I should, and see that I am just the contrary. I beg your Reverence to commend me to Our Lord, that He may make me pleasing in His sight.

With regard to having seen our venerable Father writing his books, I saw him write all of them, for, as I have said, I was ever at his side. The *Ascent of Mount Carmel* and *Dark Night* he wrote here, in this house, at Granada, little by little, for he was able to proceed with his work only with many interruptions. The *Living Flame of Love* he also wrote in this house, when he was Vicar Provincial, at the request of Doña Ana de Peñalosa, and this he wrote in a fortnight, when he was busy with many other things. *Whither hast vanishèd* was the first thing that he wrote, and this he also wrote here, having written the stanzas in his prison at Toledo.

With regard to all these books and many other things that he wrote, and his numerous addresses, given both in public and in chapters, I never saw him open a book, nor had he one in his cell, save a Bible and a *Flos Sanctorum*, for he always read the life of each saint upon his festival. His cell was so poor that he had nothing in it but a very small table, a bench, his bed and a painted crucifix.

In speaking of God, and in expounding Scripture, he had a marvellous gift; he was never asked about any passage that he could not expound in full detail; and at times of recreation the whole period was often spent, and much more than spent, in the exposition of passages about which he was consulted. One could write about this for ever. During his journeys he said very little, for he spent most of the time in prayer and singing psalms, which was what he sang habitually.

With respect to Fray Pedro de los Ángeles, I cannot remember

diligence with which the Saint's biographer sought information about his life. The information contained in these letters is among the most definite and well authenticated that we possess. All three letters are in the writer's own hand, and are to be found in the original in MS. 12,738, fols. 1,431, 1,435 and 1,439.

[1] Elsewhere the writer tells us that he knew St. John of the Cross for eleven years. There is no real contradiction between these two statements; we know that P. Juan had spoken with the Saint at El Calvario about the year 1578 when he was superior there.

exactly when he went to Rome with Fray Pedro de la Encarnación, but I think it was approximately in the year 1585. With regard to the prophecy that he would return from Rome calced, I do not remember having heard anything about it, for in this matter he was most reserved, and I never heard him say anything that would imply his having supernatural gifts and that could redound to his praise. Nor did I ever hear him speak of his imprisonment and trials, although on a number of occasions he was asked about them.

Concerning this matter I will tell your Reverence something which happened to me about him. One night, very late, when he was Prior of this house of Granada, they came to call him to go out to exorcise a girl of good birth, for in exorcism he had a particular gift from God. After he had been some little time with her he prepared to take some rest. I remained there with some other persons, and the devil began to lament the persistence with which our holy Father persecuted him, saying that in Ávila and in many other places he had cast him from his house, and that he had done his utmost to defeat the Saint and had not been successful, and other things of this kind. And the Saint came out of the room where he was resting and reproved me because I had started to speak with the devil, saying that we should not believe him in anything, and that he was telling lie upon lie in order to deceive us. Thus I saw that he was always very loth to listen to anything that tended to his own esteem and praise. And although I confessed him at Segovia, where many things happened to him, he never told me anything of this kind, though I once caught him in the act, when I entered his cell and found him in ecstasy. When he came out of this, I asked him what had happened to him and he said that while he was enraptured he had seen the Vicar General, who at that time was Father Doria, and the five Definitors, embarking on the sea, and that he cried to them not to do so because they would be drowned if they set sail, and they would not desist and were drowned. This was at the time of the business of Father Gracián. He ordered me strictly not to relate it during his lifetime, and, since it was a supernatural occurrence, I have not related it on occasions that have presented themselves; and if I have told it at any time, which I do not remember having done, it was without making any reference to the supernatural.

All the other things about his life and actions I have related many times and so nothing occurs to me that I can say further.

Your Reverence will see if I can be of assistance to you in anything else. In that case, command me, for I will do it gladly, being the son of your Reverence, whom may Our Lord preserve with increase of His Holy Spirit, as I desire.

Granada, January 1. May God give your Reverence many happy new years and joyful festivals of the Epiphany. Our Father Prior sends your Reverence many remembrances and good wishes. Your Reverence's,

FRAY JUAN EVANGELISTA.

(*Superscription*): To my Father Fray Jerónimo de San José, Discalced Carmelite, whom may Our Lord preserve.

XVIII

LETTER FROM P. JUAN EVANGELISTA TO P. JERÓNIMO DE SAN JOSÉ ON THE SAME SUBJECT AS THE FOREGOING (FEBRUARY 18, 1630)

Jhs. Mª.

Pax Christi, etc. I would fain be in your Reverence's holy house and in your company, so that I might serve your Reverence as secretary and spare you the trouble of writing to me; but as Our Lord has ordered it otherwise, it will be a consolation to me to serve our holy Father in anything, and to give your Reverence pleasure, as I desire to do, and as I shall do on any other occasion that offers.

I greatly value the picture which your Reverence has sent me,[1] and which has given all of us in this house much pleasure, and also a great desire to see the books which are not here and which we need. The *Stanzas* have been particularly desired, for some copies have arrived here from Brussels with quite a number of errors, and I desire to have those which have been printed here for your credit and our pleasure. May Our Lord have them sent as quickly as possible.[2]

With regard to our holy Father having written his books in this

---

[1] P. Jerónimo de San José had had some portraits of the Saint engraved in Madrid and had sent some of them to certain of his correspondents who had shown interest in them. They may possibly have been similar to those which he later published in his biography of the Saint.

[2] The reference is to the edition of the Saint's works edited by P. Jerónimo de San José. In speaking of the copies of the *Stanzas* which had arrived from Brussels, he evidently refers to the edition of 1627 published in that city. [See the reference to the errors in this edition, Vol. II, p. 17.]

house, I will set down the facts about which there is no doubt—namely, that the *Stanzas* beginning 'Whither hast vanishèd,' and the *Living Flame of Love,* he wrote here, for he began and ended them in my time. The *Ascent of Mount Carmel* I found already begun when I came to take the habit, which was a year and a half after this house was first founded; he might have brought them here already begun. But what he certainly wrote here is the *Dark Night,* for I saw him write part of it; this is certain, for I saw it.

With respect to Father Pedro de los Ángeles, I will tell you what I saw with my own eyes and remember as if it were happening now. When I took the habit, which was at Christmas in the year 1582, I found Father Pedro de los Ángeles here; I knew him here for about two years. At the end of that period, he persuaded Father Pedro de la Encarnación, who was Procurator here and his beloved son, that they should go to Rome. They decided to do so and went off hurriedly, and after some time the aforementioned Father Pedro de los Ángeles returned here, having joined the Calced. He came to stay in the house of a secular priest, a great friend of his, where I visited him, and soon afterwards he died. His companion remained in our convent at Genoa, where he died with the reputation of being a great servant of God.

Then, in the year following—namely, in 1583—took place the Chapter of Almodóvar, which was attended by our holy Father, who was re-elected for two years, for superiors at that time were elected for no longer, and Father Pedro de los Ángeles was also here; this took place five months after my taking the habit. Now if Father Pedro had gone to Rome on business of the Order before the separation, how could the prophecy have taken place at Almodóvar? For the separation, and consequently the journey to Rome, was much earlier. With regard to this journey, I have no further information save that, when they went off so hurriedly, it was said in the convent that this Father had left one of his shoes in Rome and was going there to get it. I think there is no more to say about the journey; at any rate, I remember nothing. It was more probably at Baeza, where our holy Father was Rector before he went to Granada; and the most probable thing would be that it was at El Calvario, for our holy Father went from Baeza to Beas to confess the nuns, and stayed for some days at El Calvario, which was on the way to the place where Father Pedro was Prior or Vicar. And if there is no certainty about the place, and the fact of the prophecy itself is certain, it is immaterial where it happened. This that I have said is without the least doubt as trustworthy as though your Reverence had seen it.[1] With respect to the lay brother whom your Reverence describes as being Procurator in the time of our Father, there never was such a brother. During the time that I was with him when I took the habit, I heard it said that a lay brother had recently died here; he was called Fray Alberto, and was a great servant of God of whom all spoke well, but I do not remember having heard that he had been Procurator. He might have been so, however, during the year and a half in which our holy Father was Prior before I took the habit. . . .[2]

May Our Lord preserve your Reverence with great increase of His gifts, as I desire.

Granada, February 18, 1630.

P. JUAN EVANGELISTA.

P.S.—If possible, do me the favour of sending me two volumes of the works of our holy Father;[3] I will give the money to our Father Prior. I shall greatly value this kindness.

XIX

LETTER CONCERNING ST. JOHN OF THE CROSS. WRITTEN BY P. JUAN EVANGELISTA TO P. JERÓNIMO DE SAN JOSÉ (MARCH 12, 1630)

Jhs. Mª.

Pax Christi, etc. Your Reverence's letters are of particular comfort to me and so it will never tire me to answer them but will be a pleasure to me. Your Reverence may command me both in this matter and in any others in which I can be of use, and I will respond with all due willingness.

As to what your Reverence says concerning Father Esminda, who

---

[1] Apparently P. Jerónimo de San José had asked P. Juan Evangelista for trustworthy information about the prophecy referred to. P. Juan Evangelista makes a serious mistake in his reply, as he evidently did not remember that the Provincial Chapter had taken place at Almodóvar in 1578; it was then that the Saint had made this remark. P. Juan Evangelista speaks of the Chapter held in the same town in May 1583, a date with which neither the journey nor its result is compatible. As will be seen in the next letter, the writer later discovers his mistake.

[2] [The remainder of this letter enumerates persons who took the habit while St. John of the Cross was Prior.]

[3] [He adds the words *de misas*, probably meaning that he would pay for the books with money he had received as alms for masses.]

died at the Conception, in Baeza, it is certain that this was before the College was founded, as I have heard it said. The reason is given as being this: if there had been a convent at Baeza, he would not have gone to the hospital; and the holy Father was so fond of suffering and holy poverty, that, had there been a convent, however poor it was, he would have chosen to go there rather than elsewhere.

Concerning our holy Father, there is no doubt that he was Prior of this house when he brought the nuns, for, as I said in my last letter, when I took the habit here, our holy Father had been here a year and a half as Prior, and the nuns came here a year and twenty-three days before I took the habit, so that he had then been Prior for more than five months. This I take as certain and your Reverence may consider it as such.

I had not heard of any other Chapter at Almodóvar than that of which I wrote to your Reverence; it was for this reason that I found difficulty in supposing that the prophecy had taken place there. On the assumption that there was another before the division of the Order, things no doubt took place as your Reverence says.

Our Father Prior and Father Fray Gaspar de Santa María are very grateful to your Reverence for sending them your remembrances, and they return them.

I am well, glory be to Our Lord, and may He preserve your Reverence with great increase of His grace, as I desire.

Granada, March 12, 1630.

FRAY JUAN EVANGELISTA.

(*Superscription*): To my Father Fray Jerónimo de San José, Discalced Carmelite, whom may Our Lord preserve.—Madrid. Porterage: half a real.

B.—REPLY OF R. P. M. FRAY BASILIO PONCE DE LEÓN, PRIMA PROFESSOR OF THEOLOGY IN THE UNIVERSITY OF SALAMANCA, TO THE NOTES AND OBJECTIONS WHICH WERE MADE CONCERNING CERTAIN PROPOSITIONS TAKEN FROM THE BOOK OF OUR FATHER FRAY JOHN OF THE CROSS[1] (JULY 11, 1622)

In fulfilment of your command, Most Illustrious Sir, and submitting all that I say to the correction of the Holy Roman Catholic Church,

---

[1] 'This paper must be kept carefully as there is no copy of it,' reads the note which follows the title on the sheet of paper which serves as a title-page to this opuscule.
The sub-title states that the reply in question was made to the Inquisition (see Vol. I

my feeling with regard to the works of the blessed Father Fray John of the Cross, whose book is also known as the *Dark Night*, is that the study of them should not and must not be prohibited by the Holy Office.

1. First, because this book has in its favour the presumption that its doctrine is true, since it was seen and approved by the University of Alcalá, where the Faculty of Theology is so famous; and at that time it was approved by men who were not only among the most learned in the kingdom, but were also very pious and expert in these matters of prayer and rare virtue: such was Dr. Luis de Montesinos. There were also among them two Masters of the Order of Saint Dominic, Fray Juan González and Fray Lorenzo Gutiérrez, who without dispute are among the most learned of their Order. This weighty body of approval makes it essential, before pronouncing an adverse judgment upon this book, to proceed very slowly and carefully, the more so as some of those who examined it at that time were ministers of the Holy Office and the authority of any others who examine it must needs be very great if their findings are to be opposed to the opinions of such distinguished judges.

2. Secondly, because this great man, Fray John of the Cross, was of blameless life and was the first founder of the celebrated Reform of the Discalced Carmelite Fathers, together with the holy Mother Teresa of Jesus; and for the corner-stones of the building of any religious Order or restoration are chosen notable persons whose virtue is sufficient to restore the building if at any time it falls into ruin. Wherefore it is not to be presumed that for the corner-stone of so great a building God would choose a man whose teaching is so evil, so full of error and so prejudicial to the Church, as some think that to be which is contained in this book.

3. Thirdly, because this great man was nurtured at the breasts of the doctrine of the holy Mother Teresa of Jesus, and of her books, and one of the excellences which the most grave and learned persons find in the doctrine of the Holy Mother is that no deluded persons have

pp. lix ff.). Its author was a native of Granada, the son of a Count of Bailén, his mother being a cousin of Luis de León, who was also a Professor at Salamanca University. Fray Basilio entered the Augustinian Order at the age of twenty-one and later held several Chairs successively at Salamanca. He succeeded to the Prima Chair in 1626 and died on August 28, 1629. The text of the document which is here translated belonged to the Discalced Carmelites of Madrid, whence, at the time of the religious persecutions of the early nineteenth century, it passed to the National Library of Spain. Here it still remains, but for a long time it was mislaid and believed to have been stolen; it was thus little known until it appeared in P. Silverio's edition of the Works of St. John of the Cross. [It has not previously appeared in English.]

made use of it. This is the contention of Fray Luis de León in the apologia to which I refer at the end of this judgment. And since that great Father was brought up on that doctrine and learned from it, as we shall see hereafter, what he wrote, to take objection to his book is to take objection to the doctrine of the holy Mother Teresa of Jesus.

4. Fourthly, because the Discalced Carmelite Order is now taking up the beatification of this blessed Father John of the Cross, since his life and miraculous works are such as to make urgent the preferment of this claim. If there now came from the Holy Office any prohibition of, or embargo upon this book, the Church would certainly not beatify him; for since the life and works of a man are in close correspondence with each other, it would be difficult to persuade the Church that the life of a writer was good if his works, by which he had been guided in his life, were bad. This reason makes it essential to go about this business with the greatest care.

5. Fifthly, because the miracle is well known which has reference to the relics of the uncorrupted flesh of this blessed Father, wherein, in divers manners, is seen the figure of Christ Our Lord. Christ crucified was thus in his flesh after his death, but he would not have Him in his doctrine if this were so far contrary to the Church's teaching. The fact that the figure was imprinted in the flesh of the blessed Father could only result from the fact that Christ was imprinted in his fame, and this would not be so if his doctrine were erroneous; for words are the images of ideas, and thoughts which were so prejudicial, impure and corrupt could have no correspondence with light, purity and spiritual progress in Christ our Lord.

6. Sixthly, because justice brings lawsuits to an end lest they should continue for ever, and so that there may be no opportunity for their revival. Upon the whole case of this book judgment was in effect pronounced after the examination made by the Holy Inquisition of the books of the holy Mother Teresa of Jesus, for, as we shall see, their doctrine is hers, and if the arguments which were then put forward, both for the opposition and for the defence, this being in the time of Cardinal Chiroga [sic], are now studied, it will be found that all that is said against these books is there answered.

I have often thought that the devil, enraged at the good that is done, and has been done, in the Church through the writings of a woman, for innumerable persons have been edified thereby, encourages grave and learned men, who are zealous for the public good, to make zealous endeavours for the prohibition of the doctrine of this blessed Father, so that the doctrine of the holy Mother may tacitly and secretly be attacked and blackened, and that the faithful may be prevented from reading books from which they have obtained such great profit.

And an obligation lies upon us to pay great attention to this point, for, as the universal Church has so completely approved the doctrine of Saint Teresa that, in the collect for her festival, it is called celestial (*cælestis ejus doctrinæ*), which is also a title given by the Church to that of Saint Dionysius, as is seen in its lessons, it follows that, since the doctrine of this blessed Father is the same, it can be shown by evidence that it is implicitly approved by the Church together with the other.

What is now happening with regard to this book in connection with the Illuminists of Seville happened also, at the time of the Illuminists of Llerena and Jaén, in connection with the book entitled the *Ascent of Mount Sion*. Those who persecuted and calumniated it tried to prove that it was the textbook of the doctrine of those Illuminists, as we gather from Epistle VI.[1] In the end the book came out victorious; it was held to be free from blame and pronounced good; so much so that the holy Mother Teresa of Jesus says that it was her guide with respect to the prayer of Union. In the book of her life (chapter xxiii), she writes thus: 'Looking through books to see if I could learn how to describe my method of prayer, I found in one, called *The Ascent of the Mount*, which describes the union of the soul with God, all the symptoms I had when I was unable to think of anything.' All the doctrine of the book of Father Fray John of the Cross, or the most important part of it, is in that book. From this it may clearly be deduced that the question at issue has twice been pronounced upon by the Holy Office, wherefore there should be no possibility of its revival.

7. Lastly, because the doctrine of this book is Catholic, good and profitable for those whom God leads by this road and according to this type of prayer; and these are not numerous, but few and perfect. The whole of its doctrine has been set down, taught and expounded by the most learned doctors and holy men who are free from all suspicion, whose books circulate everywhere, and are widely approved. This, with the favour of God, I shall prove when I discuss each of the propositions which have been criticized by the censors, so that complete and clear satisfaction may be given, consistent with brevity, though none must consider as over-long any defence of innocence.

8. Before coming to discuss this, I assume that one thing is certain:

---

[1] [I.e. Letter VI in the small collection of twelve letters printed with the *Ascent of Mount Sion* (cf. Vol. I, p. lx, above).]

namely that, in order to judge the doctrine of a book, or of a proposition which is found in it, it is necessary to look at the preceding and the following pages, and also at the doctrine taught by the same author elsewhere, so that the true sense of the book or the propositions may be gathered. For there are many propositions in the books of saints, and even in the Sacred Scriptures, which, if wrenched from their context, could be made to appear similar to those from the books of heretics; but in their context they have a very different sense, because the antecedents and the consequents are as different as is heaven from earth.

As an example of this, take the words of Saint Paul, *Justificati ex fide*. These words are used erroneously by heretics, whereas Saint Paul used them in the sense of the Catholic faith. From this it is to be inferred that because certain words or propositions in this book are found in the mouths or the writings of the Illuminists they are not to be condemned as though they were their own. For in their true context they have a very different sense and are based upon different principles, as we shall see in due course in the case of nearly all of these propositions.

9. I assume likewise that we must not believe what we have seen in the Illuminists to be the effect of this doctrine, even though they may repeat some part of what is taught in this book; we must not for that reason describe it outright as erroneous. If they had the purity of life and detachment from all earthly affections and from themselves that this book declares to be necessary to attainment of the perfect state of contemplation, they would not have fallen so shamefully. For anyone who would enter this sanctuary without first cleansing his soul of vices may be sure that he will fall into very grievous sins, as is taught expressly by Saint Augustine in the book *De quantitate animæ*, Chapter xxxiii:

Quod qui prius volunt facere, quam mundati fuerint et sanati, ita illa luce reverberantur veritatis ut non solum nihil boni, sed etiam mali plurimum in ea putent esse, atque ab ea nomen veritatis abjudicent et cum quadam libidine et voluptate miserabili in suas tenebras quas eorum morbus pati potest medicinæ maledicentes refugiant; unde divino afflatu et prorsus ordinatissime illud a Profeta dicitur: Cor mundum crea in me Deus, et spiritum rectum innova in visceribus meis.[1]

This is likewise taught by Saint Bernard in his third sermon on the

[1] Migne, *Patr. lat.*, Vol. XXXII, p. 1,076.

Circumcision,[1] and by Albertus Magnus, in his book *De Adhærendo Deo*, Chapter v, and by Gerson in his treatise on contemplation, and by the holy Fray Tomás de Villanueva, in his commentary upon those words of the Songs, *Capite nobis vulpes parvulas* (folio 124), where, after many other admirable words, he writes as follows:

Post serenatam mentem et ab omni labe mundatam, post vernantem animam, et ab omni perturbatione tranquillam, post hæc (inquam) omnia: Surge, propera, amica mea, etc. Tunc intra Dominici pectoris alveum mellis et favi degustare lateat; tunc Spiritus sancti secreta rimari; tunc cælestium sacramentorum absconditum penetrare; et de fontibus Salvatoris aquas in gaudio haurire tempus est.

And the same doctrine is also taught by a man of apostolic zeal, Fray Bartolomé de los Mártires, Archbishop of Braga, a most learned and most holy man, in his *Compendium of Spiritual Doctrine* (Part II, folio 73), where he says:

Ad hanc vero felicitatem nemo pervenire poterit unquam nisi strenue insistat abnegationi, mortificationi et sui ipsius despectioni, ardentibus in Deum desideriis, et frequentissimis orationibus, præhabita rectitudine et integritate et puritate intentionis.

And in the same book (folio 141) he adduces some words of Gerson:

Contemplationis altitudinem inepti sunt homines in fervore passionum detenti quæ nisi graventur non solum inutiliter et arroganter, sed etiam in maximam sui perniciem homo eam quæreret ut ex vitis Patrum aperte constat.

And in the same book (folio 177) he says with Saint Isidore:

Prius (inquit Isidorus) oportet animam purgare a fædibus terrenarum affectionum quam posse simpliciter et pure in Deum tendere. Sicut enim peculiare et proprium est igni, seclusis impedimentis, sursum ascendere et proprium locum petere, ita animæ pravarum affectionum pondere solutæ, in Deum, qui locus est ipsis proprius, elevari solent.

And the same doctrine is taught in the book entitled the *Ascent of Mount Sion*, Book III, Chapters i, iii, and frequently elsewhere; and it is also elegantly expounded by Father Suárez in his *De Religione*, Vol. II, Book II, Chapter xii.

I have made all this quite explicit because it is relevant to what I shall say hereafter in defending some of these propositions, maintaining that it is unduly severe to attribute to the doctrine of a man of

---

[1] Migne, *Patr. lat.*, Vol. CLXXXIII, pp. 137–42.

apostolic virtue the errors of the Illuminists because they laid hands
upon this or that part of his doctrine instead of following it all. How
far were they from attaining the end to which this book would lead
them, since they followed not the methods which it proposes to them,
but adopted methods entirely contrary to these! If they had embraced
that purity of life and engaged in that practice of the virtues which
this book teaches at every step, they would have prepared themselves
for God's communication to them of the spirit of contemplation; but,
endeavouring by bestial means to attain to this mount of dark light
and of illumined darkness, they readily provoke the wrath of God, and,
instead of life, encounter death. The reason for the errors of these
men must be attributed not to this book but to their own perverse
wills; they would not embrace the methods of the Purgative Way
which this book teaches them, but sought to reach the goal which it
sets before them without taking the first step on the way.

    10. I assume, finally, that because these difficulties are raised against
the doctrine of this book, it must not be thought the less of, but much
the more, nor must we proceed in bad faith, with the aim of condemning it, but in good faith. For it is well known that serious contra-
dictions have been proffered against particular points of the doctrine
which God communicates to certain doctors so that they may expound
them. Consider, for example, the doctrine of Saint Augustine concerning predestination and grace: how frequently it was attacked, until
the Church sponsored it after the labours upon it of Saint Prosper and
Saint Hilary. Or consider the writings of Saint Gregory, which men
began to burn, and burned entirely as far as his work on the Penta-
teuch: they would have burned every one of them if a disciple of his
had not cried out that he had seen a dove on the head of Saint Gregory
when he was writing; and to-day the Church sets great store by all
that he wrote. Or consider, again, the doctrine of Saint Thomas
Aquinas, which caused such concern in Paris that his works also would
have been burned had not his doctrine been defended by Egidius
Romanus, a disciple of the Saint and General of my Order; yet at a
later date the Apostolic See described each article as miraculous.

    The height of contemplation is a height most sublime, trodden by
few, and upon the road to it the devil is wont to conceal himself, and
put on a mask, in order to deceive those whom he cannot deceive with
his own countenance. The experiences concerned are acts of our souls,
very much loftier than anything related to sense; they are difficult
to understand, and are frequently uncomprehended by the very person

to whom they belong. Therefore it is not surprising if the doctrine which treats of them appears new, extraordinary and difficult, and if in the past it has been subjected to calumnies like that of the *Ascent of Mount Sion* and that of the holy Mother Teresa of Jesus.

It will be the will of God that this opposition should serve for the refinement of the gold, and that truth should prevail. We must therefore humbly beseech God for His aid so that we may recognize the truth, lest that which is false should be approved and that which is true should be condemned. And if a man, however learned he be, cannot comprehend the delicacies and subtleties of this type of prayer, he should not for that reason desire the condemnation of books which teach it to those who are capable of practising it nor should he strive to have them recalled, for in the field of virtue there is not one single road, but many, and God leads some persons by one road and some by another. Let us here set down the words of the holy Mother in her *Conceptions of the Love of God* (folio 377, p. 2): 'Not like certain learned men, who, not having been led in this way of prayer by the Lord, and not having the beginnings of spirituality, try so hard to reduce everything to reason, and to measure everything by their own understanding, that it looks as if all their learning is going to enable them to succeed in comprehending all the wonders of God. If only they would learn something from the most holy Virgin!'[1]

Let us trust God, for, if the doctrine is true, however difficult it be, He will give us illumination so that we may recognize it as such. This was expressed admirably by the holy Mother in her *Interior Castle* (Fifth Mansions, Chapter i): 'If I am mistaken, I am very ready to give credence to those who have great learning. For even if they have not themselves experienced these things, men of great learning have a certain instinct to prompt them. As God uses them to give light to His Church, He reveals to them anything which is true so that it shall be accepted. . . . In any case, where matters are in question for which there is no explanation, there must be others about which they can read, and they can deduce from their reading that it is possible for these first-named to have happened. Of this I have the fullest experience; and I have also experience of timid, half-learned men whose shortcomings have cost me very dear.'[2]

We shall now begin to discuss the propositions which are the object of criticism.

[1] [*Conceptions*, Chap. vi: *C.W.S.T.J.*, II, 393.]
[2] [*C.W.S.T.J.*, II, 250.]

Proposition I

(Vol. I, p. 29)[1]

'**It is supreme ignorance for the soul to think that it will be able to pass to this high estate of union with God if first it void not the desire of natural and supernatural things which may pertain to it through self-love.**'

11. This doctrine is sure and true, and is repeated by all writers who deal with the spiritual life and the Prayer of Union, and if the Illuminists who are said to have made use of it had practised it truly they would not have had so miserable a fall. No charge is more often laid upon us by spiritual men than this detachment from all things and from love of self in order that we may attain to the Prayer of Union. One of the marks given by Saint Teresa by means of which a person may know if he is approaching the Prayer of Union is that he must be detached from his own interests (*Life*, Chapter xix). In the third book of the *Ascent of Mount Sion*, and in the first and eighth chapters of that book, the same matter is treated at length. Albertus Magnus, in Chapter ii of the third book of *De Adhærendo Deo*, repeats this doctrine continually:

Quicumque talem statum aggredi et ingredi desiderat et satagit, opus est omnino, ut velut clausis oculis et sensibus, de nulla re penitus implicet aut perturbet, solicitus sit, aut curet, sed cuncta tamquam impertinentia et noxia ac perniciosa funditus excutiat.

And in Chapters iii and v he says:

ab omnibus quantum possibile est, teipsum absolvas: mentis oculum semper in puritate et tranquillitate custodias: intellectum a phantasmatibus et formis rerum infirmarum preserves; voluntatis affectum a curis terrenorum penitus absolvas; et summo vero bono amore fervido radicitus inhæreas.

To this he adds many other good sayings. He also treats of this matter in Chapters vi and viii, where he has these notable words:

Devota namque anima sic debet esse cum Deo unita, et suam voluntatem divinæ voluntati tam conformem habere et facere, quod se cum nulla creatura occupet seu adhæreat, sicut dum non erat creata: ac si nihil sit præter solum Deum et ipsam animam.

[1] [The references in the original are given to the *editio princeps*. We append only the appropriate reference to this edition, but quote the text of each proposition according to P. Basilio.]

The same doctrine is set down by Saint Augustine in the twelfth book of *De Genesi ad litteram*, at the end of Chapter xxvii, where he says: *Sed nisi ab hac vita quisque quodammodo moriatur.*[1] And this is the doctrine of Saint Dionysius in the first chapter of his *De Mystica Theologia*:

Tu autem Timothee carissime, maxima mysticorum spectaculorum exercitatione qua vales, prætermitte et sensus et mentis actiones eaque omnia quæ sub sensum cadunt et animo cernuntur et quæ non sunt et quæ sunt omnia.

And Father Suárez, in the second book of his *De Religione* (Chapter xii, No. 19), expounds the matter thus:

Actiones ergo quas relinquere consulit, illæ tantum sunt quæ circa res alias et extra Deum quodammodo versantur.

And the same Saint Dionysius, in Chapter vii of *De Divinis Nominibus*, says:

Illis veraciter lucere Deum qui impura omnia et pura transiliunt omnem omnium Sanctarum sublimitatum ascensumque transcendunt; cunctaque divina lumina et sonos sermonesque cælestes deferentes caliginem subeunt, ubi veraciter ille est supra omnia.

It is evident from this how greatly this proposition differs from that which was laid down by an Illuminist, who said that, because he saw a boy cross his path, he sinned, because he fulfilled his desire therein; and also how different it is from the opinion of those who say they must be detached from their will by submitting to interior movements whereby the door is opened to the commission of gross actions, just as the Lutheran heretics pay heed only to interior movements for the guidance of their lives, and thus at every step plunge into errors. It is also different from the opinion of others who say that works done out of charity are not done for God's sake but for the sake of self-interest.

Nothing of this can be inferred from the proposition of this Father, who demands only that we detach our desire from all save that which is God, or for God's sake, and demands the negation of all self-love; for He says expressly that this love is the cause of the hindrance of the abundance of the Divine Spirit, even as Saint Augustine said in expounding these words of the Psalmist: *Defecit spiritus meus: Impleat me spiritus tuus.*[2]

---

[1] Migne, *Patr. lat.*, Vol. XXXIV, p. 477.
[2] Migne, *Patr. lat.*, Vol. XXXVII, p. 1,852.

Nor do I see in the proposition of this Father a single word which obliges one to understand that he is demanding more here than that perfect self-abnegation which the saints demand for spiritual perfection. There are some admirable words of Fray Bartolomé de los Mártires in folio 44 of his book:

Nihil tenaci corde possideas, nulli creaturæ mente inhæras: nullius viri quantumvis sancti amicitiam et familiaritatem humanitus expetas, nam non solum, quæ mala sunt, sed etiam bona huic sapientiæ officiunt, si inordinate diliguntur, vel quærantur; nam lamina aurea obiecta oculis non minus quam ferrea visum impedire solet. Privatum amorem ex corde extirpatum et propriam voluntatem deponens, Deo te ipsum tradito et te in ipsum perfectæ transfundito. Numquam ore vel corde, habita tui ipsius et proprii commodi ratione, dicas: hoc volo, hoc nolo, hoc eligo, illud respuo; nec unquam aliquid tuum quæras, sed omni prorsus proprietate rejecta, spolia te ipso et tibi ac omnibus hujus mundi rebus ita moriaris ac si nunquam viveres, aut omnino mortuus esses. In omnibus honorem Dei quærito et id enititor ut ejus voluntas in omnibus impleatur.

What clearer words can be desired for the confirmation of this detachment of the will from all self-love which this author requires for attainment to perfect contemplation? The same doctrine can be found in the said book, at folio 79. How different this proposition is from that which was condemned in the Council of Vienne, under Clement V, we shall say hereafter when we are discussing the ninth proposition.

Proposition II

(Vol. I, p. 66)

In treating of the kinds of night through which a soul must pass in order to reach this union with God, he says of the second night: ' And this second night, which is faith, belongs to the higher part of man, which is the rational part, and, in consequence, is more interior and obscure, since it deprives it of the light of reason, or, to speak more clearly, blinds it.'

12. It is not said in this proposition that grace destroys nature, nor that it is blinded, for faith is light which illumines; nor is it said that the light of reason is lost; but the author says, as the saints say, that through faith man sees and sees not, recognizes and recognizes not, knows and knows not. He knows through the testimony of God and

he knows not because he sees not the things which he believes to be in himself; and likewise through natural reason he attains not these things and surrenders himself as a captive, even as Saint Paul says: *Captivantes intellectum in obsequium fidei.* What Saint Paul here terms the taking captive of natural light by means of faith, this author calls the blinding of the reason, because the soul allows itself to be carried onward with its eyes closed and seeing not, but guided by faith. In this sense Saint Dionysius wrote in the seventh chapter of *De Divinis Nominibus*: *Ignoratione acquiri internam conjunctionem cum Deo.* This is not privative ignorance, which would be a journeying to imperfection rather than to perfection; but in this very thing that a man knows of God he knows what He is not rather than what He is; in which sense Saint Dionysius says also: *Ut illi conjungaris qui supra omnem substantiam omnemque scientiam est ignote.* He means *sine cognitione* only in the sense that the very knowledge that we have of God in this life is ignorance of Him as He is. And so elsewhere he calls it *divinæ caliginis radium*, and illustrates this by quoting the words of the Psalmist: *Qui posuit tenebras latibulum suum.* And in the first chapter of the same book he says: *Eo quoque ipso quod nihil cognoscis, supra sensum mentemque cognoscens.* And at the beginning of the second chapter he says: *Ad hanc nos per lucidam limpidissimamque caliginem admitti oramus, et per visus scientiæque privationem videre et scire eum qui omnem aspectuum scientiamque transcendit.* Note here the phrase *per visus scientiæque privationem*, which is the very phrase used by this author, and is used in the same way. And when Saint Dionysius explains the sense of these negations and affirmations as a matter of truth and not as contrary to each other, he adds:

Hoc ipsum non videre et non scire, est veraciter Deum videre et scire, et eum qui substantia superior est, ex omnium quæ sunt ablatione celebrare.

And elsewhere, writing to his disciple Dorotheus, he says:

Divina caligo et lux inaccessibilis in qua Deus inhabitare dicitur hæc propter nimiam æque substantiam supereminet claritatem, inaccessibilis est: atque ipsa propter substantialis luminis copiam ex ea manantis inaccessibilis existit, in ea 'liquaescit,' in ea absorbitur quisquis Deum videre meruit.

Note here the word *liquaescit*, which means not to destroy nature with that supernatural light that is given by grace, but rather describes how natural reason remains buried and absorbed, being, by comparison with that other light, ignorance and blindness. And Albertus Magnus, in the ninth chapter of his aforementioned book, having set down the same doctrine as this of Saint Dionysius, says: *Et hæc caligo est quam Deus inhabitare dicitur, quam Moises intravit.*

From all this it is very clearly to be inferred that, though faith is a light which illumines, it blinds likewise; and that these propositions are not contrary and consequently are not opposed to the doctrine of Scripture and the saints; and this doctrine may be proved by that same passage from the Apostle quoted by the censor, where Saint Peter says of faith: *Lucerna ardenti in caliginoso loco.* If it be shining, how is it dark? If it be dark, how is it shining? Faith illumines and blinds: it illumines, because it communicates to the soul the truth which it knows by Divine testimony; it blinds, because it expresses truth that is dark and it sees not this as it is in itself, and, because the understanding with its natural argument and reasoning cannot attain to it, it remains without seeing, surrendering itself to the teaching of faith which it has as a guide. All this the holy Fray Tomás de Villanueva, in his commentary on these words, *Capite nobis vulpes parvulas (op. cit.,* Chapter xxvii, p. 2), called in an elegant phrase *cancellata visione.* It is as though one were looking through shutters, so that one partly sees and partly sees not, because the slats of the shutters hinder one.

Proposition III

(Vol. I, pp. 108–9)

In Chapter XIII, the title of which is ' The signs which the spiritual person may recognize in himself, in order that he may begin to strip the understanding of the imaginary forms and reasonings of meditation,' continuing the same matter, he says: ' The first sign is his realization that he can no longer meditate or work with his imagination, neither can take pleasure therein as he was wont to do aforetime; he rather finds aridity in that which aforetime was wont to captivate his senses and to bring him sweetness.'

13. The doctrine of this proposition is all true and very sure: in order to expound it, I divide it into three parts. The first part concerns the stripping of the understanding of imaginary forms; the second, in stripping it of the reasonings of meditation; the third concerns the sign which is set as marking the soul's arrival at this point, which

comes when it cannot meditate or work with the imagination or take pleasure therein. And, in order that the truth of all this may become clear, I first lay down that it is not in the power of man, neither does it fall within the scope of human industry, to reach so high a point of contemplation and the prayer of union as this; it is all the special mercy of God, Who leads into this state such a soul as He wills; the part of the soul itself is to prepare itself by the practice of virtues and to make itself neither unworthy of this blessing nor incapable of receiving it by setting an obstacle before Divine grace. This is the teaching of Father Suárez, in the aforementioned *De Oratione* (Book II, Chapter xiv, No. 6), and of the holy Fray Tomás de Villanueva, in his exposition of the *Song of Songs*, on the words: *Introduxit me Rex in cellam vinariam* (folio 122, p. 1). Here he says:

Habet Rex cellaria multa hic, sicut in cælo varias mansiones; sed ad nullam illarum aliqua intrare præsumat nisi manu Regis fuerit introducta. Et vide an de eis Profeta loquatur: quia cognovi litteraturam tuam introibo in potentias Domini; nam sicut nemo novit quæ sunt hominis, nisi spiritus hominis, qui in ipso est, ita quæ sunt Dei nemo novit, nisi spiritus Dei, et cui spiritus voluerit revelare; ad temporalia eximus, ad spiritualia intramus, sed cum Regi placuerit quemquam intromittere. Sunt cellaria panis, olei, vini, butyri, mellis, aliorumque licorum varia; ad vini cellaria rarus est ingressus nec conceditur nisi illi quæ in umbra fidei requievit, et contemplationis fructibus saturata est.

The same thing is affirmed by Saint Teresa in her *Life* (Chapter xii), and this is noted by Father-Master Fray Luis de León, whose words I shall quote later.

14. This being laid down, we pass to the first part of our argument. That the understanding may attain to working in contemplation, when stripped of imaginary forms and making use only of intellectual images, and that this frequently happens, is proved at length by Father Suárez in the said book (Book II, Chapter x, No. 12; Chapters xiv–xvii) and it is the express doctrine of Saint Augustine in Book XII of *De Genesi ad litteram* (Chapters vi, vii).[1] Here Saint Augustine is distinguishing between corporeal, spiritual and intellectual visions, and these are two things which enter not through the senses. And in Chapter xxvi he says:

Porro autem si quemadmodum raptus est a sensibus corporis ut esset in istis similitudinibus corporum quæ spiritu videntur, ita et ab ipsis rapiatur ut in illam quasi regionem intellectualium vel intelligibilium subvehatur, ubi

[1] Migne, *Patr. lat.*, Vol. XXXIV, pp. 458–9.

sine ulla corporis similitudine perspicua veritas cernitur; nullis opinionum falsarum nebulis obfuscatur; ibi virtutes animæ non sunt operosæ ac laboriosæ. Et infra: una ibi et tota virtus est amare quod videas, et summa felicitas habere quod amas.[1]

This I pointed out in some notes which I wrote on the *Confessions* of B. Alonso de Orozco, Nos. 22 and 23, and it had previously been pointed out by Father-Master Fray Luis de León in a note written by him on the *Interior Castle* of the holy Mother (Seventh Mansions, Chapter i) where he says: 'Though man in this life, if so raised by God, may lose the use of his senses and have a fleeting glimpse of the Divine Essence, as was probably the case with Saint Paul and Moses and certain others, the Mother is not speaking here of this kind of vision, which, though fleeting, is intuitive and clear, but of a knowledge of this mystery which God gives to certain souls, through a most powerful light which He infuses into them, not without created species. But, as this species is not corporeal, nor figured in the imagination, the Mother says that this vision is intellectual and not imaginary.'[2] This was likewise the doctrine of Albertus Magnus, in the book which we have been citing, in Chapter iv of which he says:

Felix ergo qui per abstersionem continuam phantasmatum et imaginum, ac per introversionem et inibi per sursum ductionem mentis in Deum, tandem aliquando obliviscitur phantasmatum quodammodo, ac per hoc consequentes operatur interius nudo ac simplici ac puro intellectu et affectu circa objectum simplicissimum Deum: Omnia igitur phantasmata, species, imagines ac formas rerum omnium citra Deum a mente rejicias ut in solo nudo intellectu et affectu a voluntate tuum pendeat exercitium circa Deum intra te.

This same matter he continues to treat at length in the same chapter. Agreement with this doctrine is shown by Fray Bartolomé de los Mártires, in the second part of his compendium (folio 89, p. 2). After quoting several passages from Saint Dionysius, he says:

O vere beata anima quæ propria omni operatione seposita in vi memorativa nudatur omnibus imaginibus; in intellectu sentit et fovet præfulgidas illuminationes Solis justitiæ.

And the same doctrine is taught in the *Ascent of Mount Sion*, Book III, Chapter iv.

15. The second part of my argument—that the soul strips itself

[1] Migne, *Patr. lat.*, Vol. XXXIV, p. 476.
[2] [For the context, see *C.W.S.T.J.*, II, 331.]

in contemplation and that the understanding reasons not therein but works by means of a simple intelligence alone—is generally received doctrine. It is taught by Father Suárez in Book II, Chapter x of the work aforementioned, and it is the doctrine of Saint Thomas (2ª 2ᵃᵉ, Q. 180, A. 6) where he says that it is a simple act without reasoning, and in this way he expounds the words of Saint Dionysius: *Necessaria est omnis convolutio intellectualium virtutum ipsius*. And Saint Thomas adds: *Ut scilicet cessante discursu figatur ejus intuitus in contemplatione unius simplicis veritatis*; so that, although the soul may previously have been reasoning, there is no reasoning in what the theologian describes as pure contemplation.

The same doctrine is supported by the definition of contemplation given by Saint Bernard in his book *De Scala Claustrali*, viz.: *Contemplatio est mentis in Deum suspensa elevatio*; and also in the second book *De Consideratione ad Eugenium: Est verus certusque intuitus animi de quacumque re, sive apprehensio veri non dubia*. Here should be noted the words *intuitus* and *apprehensio*, which do not mean reasonings. And the same doctrine is supported by Saint Augustine, in Chapter xxxiii of his book *De Quantitate animæ*, where he calls the seventh step of the soul (which is contemplation) *quædam mansio . . . serenitatis et æternitatis afflatus*.[1] These words describe this very thing. And in this prayer of union there is a suspension of the soul and no reasoning whatsoever.

This is taken as being true by Father-Master Fray Luis de León in an apologia which is contained in his compendium of the degrees of prayer (folio 18, p. 1): 'God, applying (to the soul) His light and His strength, draws it near to Himself, suspends the reasoning of the understanding and enkindles the will with unitive love.' And in a note which he wrote to the book of Saint Teresa he called mystical theology

the presentation (to the soul) of a number of things supernatural and divine and the infusion into it of a great abundance of light so that it may see this with simple regard, and without reasoning, consideration or labour, and with such force that it can understand naught else, neither can have pleasure therein. And this does not stop at seeing and wondering, but the light passes to the will, and, becoming fire within it, enkindles it in love. Whosoever suffers this, for so long as he suffers it, has his understanding fixed upon that which he sees, and marvelling at it, and his will burns in love for it, while his memory is completely idle; for the soul that is occupied with present joy

[1] Migne, *Patr. lat.*, Vol. XXXII, p. 1,076.

admits no other occupation of the memory. Of this raising up or suspension of the soul it is said that it is supernatural: that is, that the soul more properly suffers therein than works. And it is said that nobody must presume to raise himself up, before he be raised up: for one reason, because this transcends all our industry and thus would be in vain; for another, because it would show a lack of humility, and the holy Mother warns us of this with good reason, because there are books of prayer which counsel those who pray to suspend thought and to allow nothing to figure in the imagination, with the result that they remain cold and undevout.

The foregoing are the words of Father-Master Fray Luis de León. The same thing is said by Father-Master Gracián in the notes which he wrote on the holy Mother's *Conceptions of the Love of God*; and these are to be found in the aforementioned compendium of the degrees of prayer, folio 381. He says concerning this kind of prayer:

It is true that the soul works not by means of reasoning or meditation, searching for reasons and deducing from them other reasons, but is attentively understanding, and it is for this reason that the Holy Mother and other spiritual persons say that the understanding is bound and works not. By this they mean that it neither reasons nor meditates nor works as it is wont to do when there is no rapture.

And farther on he says:

There is no better example of this than a child asleep. Its mother gives it the breast, and it sucks, swallows and absorbs the milk, though, being asleep, it is unaware that it is doing so.

And the same doctrine is continued at length on folios 384 ff.

Fray Bartolomé de los Mártires, in the book aforementioned (folio 139, p. 2), uses this comparison of the soul with a child asleep to expound the same truth:

Similes namque fiunt parvulo matrem amplexanti, ubera sugenti, qui plerumque nihil videt, aut audit, aut saltem se videre et audire non judicat, experimentali solum delectatione et lætitia occupatus: par est affectualis cognito Theologorum misticorum deliciis affluentium super dilectum suum.

This is also the doctrine of the *Ascent of Mount Sion*. The places in which the holy Mother teaches this same doctrine are innumerable. I shall quote a few: *Life* (ed. Madrid, 1607, p. 105); *Interior Castle*, IV; *Way of Perfection*, Chapters xxviii, xxxi. Note that which she says in great detail (folio 124) where she makes the comparison of the soul with the child; also in *Interior Castle*, IV, i, ii, and V, ii, which is a chapter well worthy of note; and in her *Life*, Chapter xxvii. In this last place she writes as follows:

In this colloquy God makes the understanding attentive, even against its will, so that it understands what is said to it, for the soul now seems to have other ears with which it hears and He makes it listen and prevents it from becoming distracted. It is like a person with good hearing, who is forbidden to stop his ears when people near him are talking in a loud voice: even if he were unwilling to hear them, he could not help doing so. As a matter of fact, he does play a part in the process, because he is attending to what they are saying. But in this experience the soul does nothing, for even the mere insignificant ability to listen, which it has possessed until now, is taken from it. It finds all its food cooked and eaten: it has nothing to do but enjoy it. It is like one who, without having learned anything, or having taken the slightest trouble in order to learn to read, or even ever having studied, finds himself in possession of all existing knowledge; he has no idea how or whence it has come, since he has never done any work, even so much as was necessary for the learning of the alphabet.

This last comparison, I think, furnishes some sort of explanation of this heavenly gift, for the soul suddenly finds itself learned, and the mystery of the Most Holy Trinity, together with other lofty things, is so clearly explained to it that there is no theologian with whom it would not have the boldness to contend in defence of the truth of these marvels.[1]

16. Hence it comes to pass that to some contemplatives it seems as if neither the understanding nor the will is working, not because they are not working, as the holy Mother confesses in many places, as does this same author in many parts of his writings which I shall afterwards note down, but because there is no discursive operation and no labour, but the soul enjoys complete quiet. And, as Saint Augustine admirably says in his book *De Quantitate animæ*, Chapter xxxiii, treating of the same works of the soul according to the seven degrees which he had distinguished: *Fieri potest ut hæc omnia simul agat anima sed id solum sibi agere videatur quod agit cum difficultate aut agit cum timore, agit enim multo quam ceteræ attentior.* And in this degree of prayer the soul works without any labour, as Saint Augustine himself says in the twelfth book of his *De Genesi ad litteram* and the holy Fray Tomás de Villanueva says in the place already cited (folio 22, p. 2): *Intus sine labore videntur.* Furthermore, as Father Gracián opines in the passages aforementioned, if the contemplative continues in the same act, which is not repellent to him, though difficult, he does not seem to be perceiving that he is working, as Father Suárez says in the same book

[1] [*C.W.S.T.J.*, I, 173.]

(Book II, Chapter x, No. 13). His opinion is supported by a passage from Fray Bartolomé de los Mártires, in folio 123 of the said book. He relates that Saint Antony said: *Eum qui perfecte orat non intelligere se aliquid petere*, and adds:

Non enim orans super se reflectitur, non componit aut dividit, sed puro simplicique amoris actu soporatur cum Propheta dicens: In pace in idipsum dormiam et requiescam, etc.

17. From this point follows the second—namely, that many others say that the soul should conduct itself passively herein, because in almost everything it is the Holy Spirit Who now works; but it appears that the soul suffers, and that it works, as was said by Father-Master Fray Luis de León in the words which I quoted above (§ 15) and also Father Suárez in the said book (Book II, Chapter xii, No. 18) where he says:

Est ergo vitalis illa passio, unde non est sine intellectus et voluntatis efficientia. Denominatur autem potius actio quam passio quia principalis motor ibi est spiritus, quia tunc agit per specialissimum auxilium internum, per dona sua, et non tantum per ordinarium modum operandi virtutibus accomodatum.

And in No. 19 he has a passage which is in agreement with what is contained in the number following.

This is also admirably explained by Fray Bartolomé de los Mártires in the book aforementioned (folio 96):

Et ut facilius intelligas quid sit unio animæ cum Deo, scias velim duplicem esse animæ cum Deo unionem per amorem: quædam enim est habitualis, altera actualis: hæc vero duplex: altera activa, quando quilibet nititur Deo semper adesse in intellectu voluntatemque suam semper ad ejus amorem inclinat, aut saltem ardentissimis ad id desideriis abundat; altera passiva, de qua dicit Bernardus, rara hora et brevis mora. Aug. 10 'Confessionum,' cap. 40, aliquando (ait) intromittis me in affectum multum inusitatum introrsus, ad nescio quam dulcedinem quæ si perficiatur in me nescio quid erit quod vita ista non erit, sed recido in hæc ærumnosis ponderibus et resorbeor solitis et teneor et multum fleo sed multum teneor . . . hic esse valeo, nec volo; illic volo nec valeo,[1] sed quamvis hæc fervens dilectio eliciatur a voluntate, dicitur tamen passiva, quia ad illam non excitat voluntas seipsam, velut ad primam, sed inmediate excitatur a Deo fortiter fitque regulariter ac placide cum excessu quodam ac suspensione sensuum, estque mirum in modum dulcis et paucis conferre solet.

[1] Migne, *Patr. lat.*, Vol. XXXII, p. 807.

18. Finally, there follows from this the judgment of the same mystical theologians that the soul at this time must allow itself to be guided by the spirit without carrying on any further reasonings, without resisting the spirit and without intermingling any operations of its own. The holy Mother says this in many places which have been quoted and the famous theologian Francisco Suárez (*op. cit.*, Book II, Chapter xii, No. 19), expounding those words of Saint Dionysius: *Ut prætermittat sensus et mentis actiones*, says as follows:

Vel certe etiam intelligit omnem actionem aliquo modo propriam ipsius hominis, a proprio sensu profectam, et quasi propria inquisitione inchoatam: nam cum anima in altissima contemplatione a Spiritu Sancto movetur, non debet aliquid propriæ actionis miscere, sed Spiritus Sancti ductum sequi, quamvis id efficiat sine vera efficientia, et cooperatione, ut dixi. Et in hoc sensu intelligendus est Dionysius quoties agit de illo gradu perfectionis in quo anima sancta potius patitur quam agit.

This doctrine is very different from that of the Illuminists, who say that in this state of resignation the soul must allow itself to be guided and must itself do nothing. In the first place, what they call resignation and union is a knavery, illusion and imagination of their own and has nothing to do with this other union, wherein there is no deception, as will be said in discussing the sixth proposition. Secondly, the Illuminists do not exclude from their rule any works whatsoever; but advise those who are in that state of resignation to abstain even from works which are good and of obligation, so that that state is nothing but a form of idleness and a training-ground for their gross habits. The mystics exclude operations which belong to reasoning and operations which the subject performs of his own accord, as is explained by Father Suárez, and these they exclude only during the period of perfect contemplation, wherein the soul receives such great illumination from God that it knows with certainty that it is not being deceived.

19. The third part of the proposition is that, when it has reached this point of sublime contemplation, the soul takes no pleasure in discursive reasoning or meditation, but desires only to enjoy that quiet which it possesses and to engage neither in discursive reasoning nor in meditation. This is the express doctrine of the holy Mother in the *Book of her Life* (Chapter vii) where she says that, however much it desire to do so, the understanding cannot speak, save with great difficulty; and in the *Interior Castle* (VI, vii),

There are some people (and a great many have spoken to me about this) on whom Our Lord bestows perfect contemplation and who would like to remain in possession of it for ever. That is impossible; but they retain something of this Divine favour, with the result that they can no longer meditate upon the mysteries of the Passion and the life of Christ, as they could before. I do not know the reason for this, but it is quite a common experience in such cases for the understanding to be less apt for meditation. I think the reason must be that the whole aim of meditation is to seek God, and once He is found, and the soul grows accustomed to seeking Him again by means of the will, it has no desire to fatigue itself with intellectual labour.[1]

Similarly, she writes in the same chapter:

Here the reply may be made that the soul could not meditate even if it would, and, if we understand by meditation what generally goes by that name, this may perhaps be very true. If we were to take any one of the stations of the Passion—let us say the arrest of Our Lord—and meditate upon this mystery, thinking upon all that is contained in it, this is an admirable and most meritorious prayer; but I think those who have attained to perfect contemplation could not do this, though why, I do not know.[2]

The same doctrine is taught by Father-Master Fray Luis de León in the note reproduced above (§ 15), and also by Father Suárez (*op. cit.*, Book II, Chapters xvi ff.) where he recognizes the difficulty experienced by the soul in practising other operations and in allowing itself to be diverted to others when it is enjoying the contemplation aforementioned. With regard to this, let us consider the words of the holy Fray Tomás de Villanueva, in his commentary on the *Songs* (folio 124, p. 1): *Cum sic spiritus loquitur omnis littera fastiditur*. Let this word *fastiditur* be carefully considered; this author says that, when the soul is engaged in that contemplation, and fully occupied with it, and takes no delight in reading and meditation, it is no longer necessary that it should do so, for reading and meditation were a preparation for that which it is now enjoying. The same doctrine is taught by Fray Bartolomé de los Mártires (*op. cit.*, folio 120) where he says:

Amor enim unit, rapit, satisfacit. Est autem raptus vehemens elevatio, fortisque actuatio superioris potentiæ; tunc enim cessant operationes inferiorum potentiarum, vel saltem ita debilitantur, et arescunt, ut superiorem potentiam in suis actionibus nequaquam impediant, aut remorentur. Extasis autem quæ proprie ad solum pertinet intellectum, fit quando intellectus in sui ipsius actu suspenditur, ut potentiæ inferiores etiam eadem ratione penitus

---

[1] [*C.W.S.T.J.*, II, 305.]

[2] [This passage is not an exact quotation, but a summarized version of a paragraph from *Interior Castle*, VI, vii, which will be found in full in *C.W.S.T.J.*, II, 306–7.]

ab actionibus suis cessent; evenit raptus tam in potentiis cognoscitivis quam
in affectiva. Nam rapit aliquando vis imaginativa super omnes vires sensitivas
et exteriores, ut ipsæ nihil curare videantur, et reipsa non curent, propria
objecta ab illis præsentata: ut patet in melancolicis et vehementibus et in
amantibus: et regulariter vehemens aliquis amor, aut alia animi perturbatio
raptus hujus debet esse causa. Ratio etiam quandoque rapitur super omnes
sensus, quod fit quando aliquis ex vehementi affectu seu appetitu vacat
perscrutationibus quidditatum aut veritatum abstrahentium a motu et materia,
et conatur ex notis ignota ratiocinari. Evenit enim sapissime, ut is, qui rapitur
si solum cesset ab operationibus sensuum exteriorum, ita ut omnino ignoret
quid extra fiat, sed etiam virtuti phantasticæ ac imaginativæ actio sua penitus
denegetur: adeo ut phantasma nullum irruere valeat, aut si irruat, non
rationis voluntatisque superioris virtute prematur. Fit enim raptus in simplici intelligentia non solum supra omnes vires sensitivas, sed etiam super
omnem ratiocinationem, quod contigit, cum apex mentis ita fortiter actuatur
in simplici intuitu alicujus intelligibilis spiritualis, præsertim Dei, ut omnem
aliam cognitionem extinguat ac sopiat: dicitur hæc anagogica ductio, et
mentis excessus, mors animæ vivente spiritu, mors Rachelis in partu
Benjamin, et hujusmodi raptus fit solum erga Deum, ex raptu affectus ad
eundem.

20. From what has been said it will now be evident that the doctrine
of this proposition is not that which is taught by the Illuminists—
namely, that thoughts must be set aside in this state, even though they
be good ones. Our author does not say this, but only that the soul takes
no pleasure in meditating and working with the imagination, for
meditation is no longer necessary to it, and may indeed rather be a
hindrance, as the holy Mother says in Chapter iii of her Fourth
Mansions, and in Chapter xxxi of the *Way of Perfection*. She says here
that, during a period of this kind of prayer, meditation is like a heap
of logs placed indiscriminately on the fire in order to quench the spark
of contemplation.

Nor is the doctrine contained in this proposition the doctrine of
the Illuminists that the soul must resign itself into the hands of God,
because if it desires to engage in any work it will become incapable of
the works of this love. In the first place, the restriction imposed by
this love when the soul has reached this point of perfect prayer and
contemplation and union, the Illuminists wish to apply to anyone
who gives himself to prayer. In the second place, it is clear which are
the works that, according to our author, have to be avoided in this
state of contemplation. Furthermore, the Illuminists exclude good
works and works of obligation while they remain in that state of

sloth which they call prayer and resignation and which is quite remote
from the doctrine of this author.

Finally, this author does not exclude good and holy works, or the
affections of virtues, nor does he speak of these, but only of meditation and discursive reasoning during the time of perfect contemplation,
and this only as applied to those who are quite accustomed to it and
who are commonly wont to remain incapable of meditation and discourse, as described in the passage which I quoted from the holy
Mother. Nor do they always cease from making use of meditation in
order to awaken their souls to a new enkindling, according to the
words of David: *Et in meditatione mea exardescet ignis.* And because
meditation serves to awaken the soul when it is cold or asleep or lukewarm, it cannot be inferred that, when the affections have been excited
and the understanding is moved by God through simple knowledge
and love of the will, meditation is of any importance, any more than
the framework of an arch is of importance when the arch is completed. To say this is not to depreciate meditation, but to describe the
time and the season at which it performs its office, and to state when
it is not necessary, since all things, however good they be, have their
reason and their time.

21. I add, furthermore, so that it may be perfectly well understood
how we are to judge those who say that other good thoughts which
may present themselves within this type of prayer are hindrances to
contemplation, an admirable doctrinal passage from that apostolic
teacher Fray Bartolomé de los Mártires (*op. cit.,* folio 97):

Multorum sententiæ fuit, hanc unionem quamvis pura esset, a quibuscum-
que imaginibus posse impedire, licet essent imagines ipsæ utiles, quæ animam
ipsam disposuerant; ut imagines misteriorum humanitatis Christi, et etiam
divinorum attributorum: hoc tamen caute intelligendum est, ne erroris
existat occasio. Si enim intelligamus has imagines, dum se offerunt intellectui
animæ immediate quiescentis, ac fruentis unione divina pura, non esse
tenaciter recipiendas, nec morose eo temporis articulo illis vacandum, aut
rebus quæ illæ repræsentant, sed revera claudendos esse ad eas mentis oculos,
regulariter loquendo, verum hoc fateamur necesse est; divertere enim ad eas
morose impedit progressum immediate unionis cum Deo. Si autem intelligamus has imagines quotiescumque occurrunt pure contemplanti, atque
amanti Deum, impedire hebetareque vigorem ac perfectionem unionis,
credo esse falsum; experientia enim constat hoc sæpe evenire, dum homo in
solum Deum toto mentis actu fertur; fit enim, ut eo tempore raptim occurrat
intellectui hæc imago, videlicet, hic Deus pro me homo factus est, aut
crucifixus; hæ namque imagines non solum non impediunt, verum etiam

promovere et augere solent unionem amoris atque admirationis suspensive;
immo neque imago peccatorum raptim transiens, officiet, videlicet: hic Deus
tot crimina pro sua benignitate condonavit . . . etc. Sæpe etiam contingit
quod dum unio tepescit, rursum sponte ignoscat, si mentem applices ad media
salutifera scilicet ad Christi passionem.

This single passage gives the true sense in which this doctrine is to be
understood and removes all doubt concerning it, and in the blessed
Father Fray John of the Cross no argument will be found that verges
upon that false interpretation, which, as we have said, must be set aside.

I have gone into this proposition at such length because the majority
of those that are to be examined hereafter may be reduced to it, and by
what has been said the objections to the fourth and fifth propositions
are answered.

Propositions IV, V, VI
(Vol. I, p. 206)

**In treating of the formal and substantial locutions which God
grants to certain souls, the author writes as follows: ' The soul
should itself do nothing and desire nothing at the time, but
conduct itself with resignation and humility, giving its free
consent to God; neither should it reject anything nor fear anything. It should not labour in executing what these words express, for by these substantial words God is working in it and
with it, wherein they differ from formal and successive words.
It should not reject them, since the effect of these words remains
substantially within it and is full of the good which comes from
God. As the soul receives this good passively, its action is at no
time of any importance. Nor should it fear any deception, for
neither the understanding nor the devil can intervene herein.'**

22. All this doctrine is certain and true, and that this may be clearly
seen I divide it into four parts. The first part says that there exist these
interior and substantial locutions of God, which are so called by the
mystics, not because they are produced immediately in the substance of
the soul, without any labour of the understanding, but because God
produces them immediately, without the mediation of any creature,
and because of the profound impression of the effects which they
produce. That these locutions come to spiritual persons to whom God
is pleased to grant His favour, there is no doubt. This is the express
doctrine of Saint Gregory (*Morals*, Book V, Chapter ccxix) and of

Saint Bernard's commentary on the *Songs* (Sermon 54). These testimonies I shall quote shortly.

23. The second part of this proposition says that the soul must not work at this time, but must allow itself to be guided by God, giving its free consent to Him with all humility. The following considerations may be urged against those who condemn this teaching, the sense of which, as will be seen, they have not fathomed. According to this author the soul in this state does in fact work, for to give its consent and to humble itself is nothing less than to work with the will. Besides this he says that it hears these locutions of God, and to hear is a work of the understanding. Let it also be observed what this author affirms in Proposition XXVIII, where he says that the soul in this state has merit, and in Proposition XXIX, which says that the soul sees the beauty and the gifts of God, and also that the soul at this time has love for God and praises Him, none of which things can come to pass apart from the operation of the soul. And let these words from the same proposition also be noted: the soul's action consists in looking at God's beauty in everything, and therefore there is such action.

This author, then, does not deny that there are some kinds of work performed by the soul, but only that it reasons and meditates and labours (of which we have already spoken under Proposition III), which operations may cause hindrance in this supreme state of quiet, as is said by Fray Bartolomé de los Mártires (*op. cit.*, folio 90, p. 2) even of good images:

Immo tempore unionis inter Deum et animam, quæcumque (licet bonæ) imagines sunt procul expellendæ, quia sunt media inter utrumque; ideo athleta huc pervenire cupiens, Deo ipsum trahente atque vocante, cum primum senserit se divino amore vehementer inflammari, ac sursum trahi, propere rescindat quaslibet imagines, festinetque ad sancta sanctorum, et ad internum illud silentium in quæ non humana sed divina dumtaxat est operatio, ibi enim Deus ipse est agens, homo vero patiens. Nam dum vires animæ silent, et a propria actione quiescunt, atque ab omni denique externa imagine liberæ sunt, Deus ipse loquitur: easque mentis vires pro libito disponit, et afficit nobilissimum opus in ea peragens.

This makes it clear in what sense this author says that the soul must behave passively, and the same language is used by this Father in words already quoted, which have been expounded in our discussion of Proposition III (§ 17).

And Father Suárez (*op. cit.*, Book XX, Chapter xii) explains how the mystical doctors are to be understood when they declare that these locutions are not produced without the soul's activity, and that the soul works not in them (cf. §§ 21, 22). In that silence which takes place in the soul at that time, the passions and operations of sense, described by Saint Gregory and Saint Bernard, are not called works, as the holy Mother says likewise in the *Book of her Life*, Chapter xx. And thus it is impossible to deduce from this doctrine the conclusion reached by one who objects that the soul is justified without acts, since in reality the soul is working here, as this author says. It is true that certain Catholic doctors are of the opinion that in this state of contemplation the soul is not working freely, and that the soul might therefore not have merit; but in my own view the contrary opinion is the more credible—namely, that the will is free in this state and that the soul has merit. This may be deduced from the words of Saint Augustine in Book XII of his *De Genesi ad litteram* (at the end of Chapter xv)[1] and it is the doctrine of the holy Mother in Chapter xxvi of the *Way of Perfection*, and in folio 377 of the *Conceptions of the Love of God*, and of our author in the proposition here noted.

24. The third part of the proposition says that when these locutions take place the soul must not labour, because God is working in it by means of these substantial words, so that, if He were to say to the soul 'Love Me,' the soul would at once love Him. Here God is uttering truths, the first of which is that these locutions of His are practical and efficacious. This is the doctrine of Saint Bernard, in his commentary on the *Songs* (Sermon 55): *Verbo q.º dicere anima pulchra est et appellare animam infundere est unde amet et se præsumat amari.*[2] This clearly agrees with our author and with the holy Fray Tomás de Villanueva in his commentary on the *Songs* (folio 124): *Quod etiam in hac vita in sanctis impleri existimo, quando non jam per scripturas, sed per se ipsum loquitur eos, et impletur quod scriptum est: erunt omnes docibiles Dei. Cum sic spiritus loquitur, omnis littera fastiditur.* This is likewise the teaching of the holy Mother in Chapter xxv of the *Book of her Life*, and in the third chapter of the Sixth Mansions, where she says: 'The first and surest sign (that a locution is of God) is the power and authority that it bears with it, both in themselves and in the actions which follow them.'[3] . . . And the same doctrine is put forward by Fray Alonso de Orozco in his book entitled *Mount of Contemplation* (folio 138, p. 1). From this it follows, first, that, as our author says, the soul

---

[1] Migne, *Patr. lat.*, Vol. XXXIV, p. 466.
[2] [This quotation comes from Sermon 45, and should read: 'Verbo igitur dicere animæ, *pulchra es*, et appellare *amicam*, infundere, etc.']
[3] [*C.W.S.T.J.*, II, 280.]

must not labour when it is in that state, because, as God is the chief
agent, it works without the least difficulty or labour, but with great
pleasure, as I proved from the teaching of the saints in discussing
Proposition III (§ 16). From this, too, it is evident how true is the
teaching of this author that the effect[1] of these words becomes sub-
stantiated, and thus it must not be cast aside, as is affirmed by the
saints whom we have quoted and by the holy Mother in the Sixth
Mansions (Chapter ix).

25. The fourth part of the proposition is that the soul in this state
must fear no deception because the devil cannot meddle with it. Two
things are said with respect to this, the first of which is that these
locutions of God give the soul great security. This security, I find, is
often described by the saints. Consider the holy Fray Tomás de Villanueva in his commentary on the *Songs* (folio 123, p. 1): *Secura dormire
potest, quæ tale meruit reperire cervical.* And in the next column he says:

Læva capiti superponitur ne collidatur; dextera totum hominem amplexatur ne vel leviter moveatur; optima dextera, bona sinistra; inter has manus,
secura dormit, testimonium habens a Spiritu Sancto quia vel amplexata
non cadet, vel lapsa non peribit; non hominum est hoc testimonium, sed ejus
qui charitate languerat: charitatem languor languorem securitas sequitur.

And again (folio 123): *Est cellarium securitatis, pacis, de quo Apostolus*:
Pax Dei quæ exuperat omnem sensum. This is also the teaching of Fray
Bartolomé de los Mártires (folio 176, p. 1): *Hos effectus prædictos
sequuntur alii duo, scilicet, securitas qua nihil anima timet pati propter
Deum, et qua certissime confidit, se nunquam ab eo separandam.* And
again (folio 180, p. 1): *Experitur insuper in se ipsa quoddam strictis-
simum divinæ amicitiæ vinculum, adeo firmum, ut separari nunquam ab
eo se posse existimet.* This teaching is also found in the Fifth Mansions
of the holy Mother (Chapter i) and Fray Luis de León expounds this
in one of his glosses. The second point is that the soul must not fear
the devil, who cannot intervene in that sublime state of contemplation,
neither can he enter the soul and deceive it in intellectual visions,
although he can do so in corporeal visions. This is the express doctrine
of Saint Augustine (*De Genesi ad litteram*, Book XXII, Chapters iii,
xiii–xiv, xxxi) and the same thing is taught by Saint Thomas (2ª 2ᵃᵉ,
Q. 180, A. 6), in these words:

Et in hac operatione animæ non est error; sicut patet quod circa intellectum
primorum principiorum non erratur, quæ simplici intuitu cognoscimus.

---

[1] [The Spanish has *afecto*, 'affection,' an obvious error for *efecto*.]

And this is expounded by Father Suárez (*op. cit.*, Book II, Chapter x, No. 6). It is also the doctrine of the holy Mother (*Interior Castle*, VI, Chapters ix–x; *Life*, Chapter xxviii). And it is also affirmed by Fray Bartolomé de los Mártires (folio 93, p. 1), where he says:

Ne vero quid suspectum habeat dum luce cælesti consolationeque interna plenius affluit, certe sciat, lumen illud quod in animæ centro lucet, et quo quis Dei bonitatem et propriam sui vilitatem cognoscens in vera proficit humilitate, non a spiritu maligno sed a Deo mirifice infundi. Diabolus namque solet vanos superbosque homines decipere, confictum lumen et falsam ingerens dulcedinem, sed assentiam animæ solus Deus ingredi potest.

From all these places we may deduce the reason for this truth, which is expounded by a number of authors—namely, that contemplation is simple apprehension and that thus there can be no deception in it, which is the reason followed by Saint Augustine and Saint Thomas. Others attribute this to the fact that the devil cannot work immediately in the soul but only by means of bodily or imaginary images, and thus intellectual images must be free from his deceptions.

PROPOSITIONS VII, VIII

(Vol. I, p. 207)

In treating of the various feelings which the soul may have, this author says: 'The soul may have certain most sublime spiritual feelings, which neither the soul nor he that treats with it can know, nor can they understand the cause whence they proceed, or what are the acts whereby God may grant it these favours; for they depend not upon any works performed by the soul, nor upon its meditations.'

26. It is most certain that this most lofty degree of contemplation depends not upon human diligence as upon due or infallible merits. This is what our author says, as I proved above (§ 13), and it is the express doctrine of the holy Mother in Chapter xiii of the *Book of her Life*. It is also that of Fray Bartolomé de los Mártires (*op. cit.*, folio 107, p. 2; folio 130, p. 1):

Habeto ergo pro certo in sola charitate esse regnum Dei, gratiam autem contemplationis inter cæteras gratias gratis datas computato.

And thus this author does not deny the good works whereby the soul makes itself meet for the favours of God, for throughout his book he teaches the practice of the virtues and the purification of the earthly affections and of self-love. Nor is it possible to father upon him the proposition of the Illuminists, who say that, when we are in contemplation, we are not to do good works, even though they be commanded us, for this has no connection with the teaching of our author. For as the feelings of which we have spoken may come to pass in the soul passively without its doing anything effectively on its own part to receive them, so the knowledge of them is received passively in the understanding, and the soul must do nothing on its own part, lest it go astray, but must conduct itself passively.

27. The whole of this proposition is expounded in our discussion of Proposition III (§ 17); where it is defended and explained by means of the doctrine of Catholic doctors and saints, who show in what manner it is to be understood that the soul must conduct itself passively and not work. And here should be noted this phrase of our author 'on its own part,' which shows clearly that he is speaking according to the exposition given by Father Suárez (*op. cit.*, Book II, Chapter ii), which I have discussed above (§§ 17–18).

Proposition IX

(Vol. I, pp. 212–13)[1]

'It is necessary that, in each of these books, the reader should bear in mind the purpose of which we are speaking. . . . For, seeing how we annihilate the faculties with respect to their operations, it may perhaps seem to him that we are destroying the road of spiritual practice rather than constructing it. This would be true if we were seeking here only to instruct beginners, who are best prepared through these apprehensible and discursive operations. But, since we are here giving instruction to those who would progress farther in contemplation, even to union with God, to which end all these means and exercises of sense concerning the faculties must recede into the background, since God Himself is working Divine union in the soul, it is necessary to proceed by this method of disencumbering and emptying the soul, and causing it to reject the natural jurisdiction and operations of the faculties, so that they may become capable of infusion and illumination from supernatural sources.'

[1] [In several places this passage is incorrectly quoted from the *editio princeps*.]

28. The whole of the teaching in this proposition has already been discussed under Proposition III (§ 19). Since discursive meditation, *maxime in ipso tempore contemplationis*, is of no use to the most perfect souls that engage in contemplation, we make a distinction between two parts of this proposition, to the end that this may become more evident. The first part says that contemplation is the work of those that are perfect, which is asserted by Father Suárez (*op. cit.*, Book II, Chapter xi) and is repeated by spiritual persons so frequently that it is unnecessary to quote examples. The second part says that discursive meditation is needless in this state, and this I proved at length in discussing Proposition III (§ 19), quoting the doctrine of saints and doctors upon it. It is therefore a notable injustice to seek to father upon our author, in this and similar propositions, opinions which were condemned in the Council of Vienne, on the subject of the imperfect who practise works of virtue; or the saying of the Illuminists that it is all the same whether one prays or prays not; or the opinion, condemned by Father Gracián, that the soul must not perform works of virtue. There is not a word in our author denying works of virtue to the contemplative; he only denies him discursive meditation when he is in that state of contemplation, *et tempore unionis et meditationis cum Deo*. This is as if he had said that reading must be laid aside when the soul attains to contemplation and love, because reading was only a means to awaken the soul that it might attain that end.

PROPOSITIONS X, XI

(Vol. I, p. 248)

In maintaining that the soul must not rejoice in temporal blessings, this author says: ' It is also a vain thing for men to desire to have children, as do some who trouble and disturb everyone with their desire for them, for they know not if such children will be good or if the satisfaction for which they hope from them will be turned into pain.'

29. These propositions have been expounded and defended in treating of Proposition III. No truth is more frequently repeated by the saints than this: that temporal blessings must not be desired with particular affection, but that all things must be left to the will of God, and to this class belong children born of marriage. Thus this author

does not here condemn or belittle marriage, but only undue affection. This is likewise the teaching of the holy Mother in the first chapter of the *Way of Perfection*, where, after treating of this matter, she ends by saying 'that, were it not necessary to consider human frailty . . . I should like it to be understood that it is not for things like these that God should be importuned with such anxiety.'[1] The gloss of Father-Master Fray Luis de León on this passage gives its meaning as being that if we ask for temporal things, especially in times of greatest necessity, we must be careful to do so only as accessories.

Proposition XII

(Vol. I, p. 292)

In describing the use of images by the spiritual man this author says: 'The devout person sets his devotion principally upon that which is invisible. He needs few images, and uses few, and chooses those that harmonize with the Divine rather than with the human, clothing them, and with them himself, in the garments of the world to come, and following its fashions rather than those of this world. For not only does an image belonging to this world in no way influence his desire; it does not even lead him to think of this world.'

30. It is not possible to father the doctrine of the Illuminists on this author, for in this same chapter, by means of Catholic doctrine, he clearly teaches the respect which we owe to images and the part they play in the Church. He merely says that images are not necessary to the contemplative for his practice of contemplation; previously he has expressly admitted them, but he says that, at the time of contemplation, the affections are already enkindled, and therefore images are then of no use to him since he has truth itself. This is not condemning the use of images, but merely pointing out that they are of little use at that particular time. This is similar to the teaching of Gerson, in his opuscule *De Mystica Theologia*, Chapter iv, where he asks: *An perturbet devotionem internam excessumque mentalem vocalis cantus ecclesiasticus?* And he answers: *Quod re ipsa verum esse videtur et experientia testatur.* And this is confirmed and proved and expounded by Fray Bartolomé

---

[1] *Way of Perfection*, chap. i (*C.W.S.T.J.*, II, 5).

de los Mártires (*op. cit.*, folio 127, p. 2). Furthermore, in this proposition our author condemns the secular clothing with which images are adorned—a thing which has been rebuked in many councils.

Propositions XIII, XIV

Here we have also a defence of Proposition XIII, in which is condemned, besides the things aforementioned, carnal affection for the possession of images, in the sense wherein one might condemn the same kind of affection for the possession of anything. This is referred to in the teaching of Fray Bartolomé de los Mártires (*op. cit.*, folio 74, p. 1): *Nihil tenaci corde possideas, nulli creaturæ mente inhæreas*, and in the other passage which I have quoted above (§ 12). Together with these it is well that the spiritual man should also study the words used by the aforementioned Father (*op. cit.*, folio 32): *Non habeas curiosa et superflua, quia distrahunt et occupant cor; quare nolim affectes habere imagines tabulas curiose depictas.*

By the same argument may be defended Proposition XIV, where this author condemns the grossness of the sentiments of those who set their trust in images, saying that they should rather set it in the Divine efficacy which works through such or such an image, considered as an instrument, more than through another, all of which is Catholic doctrine and is that taught by this author. And thus this author condemns not the devotion to particular sanctuaries, but explains how and by whom this devotion must be expressed so that it may be effective. Here, in my view, he takes his stand upon the doctrine that an image and prototype is not capable of receiving respect, adoration or invocation, which is the doctrine of Father Gabriel Vázquez in his book *De Adoratione Imaginum*, and is followed by other learned men in Spain.

This is the clear meaning of this author, as is seen in the words which follow, to which this proposition refers. He says that when God sometimes grants more favours by means of one image than by means of another of the same kind, the reason, although there may in fact be a great difference in the workmanship of the two images, is that those who use them may have their devotion awakened by means of one rather than by means of another. Wherefore the reason why God works miracles and grants favours by means of certain images rather than by means of others is that this practice awakens the sleeping devotion and affection of the faithful, and, when devotion is enkindled and prayer is persevered in by means of an image, this is a means by which God hears the prayer and grants that which is besought of Him. And by the instrumentality of that image, through the soul's prayer and affection, God continues to grant favours and miracles, for the soul that has devotion to the image has it also to the Saint which that image represents. This is also the sense of Propositions XV and XVI.

Propositions XV, XVI, XVII

(Vol. I, p. 331)

'The loving mother is like the grace of God, for, as soon as the soul is regenerated by its new fervour for the service of God, He treats it in the same way; He makes it to find spiritual milk, sweet and delectable, in all the things of God, without any labour of its own, and also great pleasure in spiritual exercises, for here God is giving it the breast of His tender love, even as to a tender child. Therefore, such a soul has its delight in spending long periods—perchance whole nights—in prayer. Penances are its pleasures, fasts its joys, and its consolations are to make use of the sacraments and to occupy itself in Divine things. In the which things spiritual persons (though taking part in them with great efficacy and persistence and using and treating them with great care) often find themselves, spiritually speaking, very weak and imperfect. For they are moved to these spiritual exercises by the consolation and pleasure that they find in them.'

31. This author does not condemn good works done because of the spiritual pleasure which the soul takes in them, and from devotion, but merely says that to work from that motive is imperfection. This is not to condemn the thing as bad, for there are good things and better things, and Divine providence, in order to move the affections of beginners, is wont at first to communicate such pleasures to them; and this is the common teaching of spiritual men and saints. I know not, therefore, what this proposition can have to do with the saying of the Illuminists that works done for charity are not done for love of God. To say that to do works because of that pleasure and consolation is to work imperfectly is not to say that it is bad, for, even though it be not done expressly from the love of God, it is done for that reason remotely,

inasmuch as the particular good is ordered according to the universal good. By saying that a work is imperfect, or is not as perfect as others, one does not condemn it as bad, just as it is not a condemnation of marriage as bad if we say that it is not as perfect as celibacy, nor is it a condemnation of acting *propter retributionem* if we say that perfection consists in working for God alone without looking at the reward.

And that this is the clear meaning of this author is shown by the words which follow the passage quoted from Fray Bartolomé de los Mártires (*op. cit.*, folio 53, p. 2). He says that God sometimes denies the soul these comforts *ut probemur an stipendio consolationum solum ducti Domino serviamus*. It is therefore not perfection to serve God for the sake of these pleasures and consolations; such works are the works of children, or of weak and imperfect people, who engage in exercises of prayer and in the sacraments from motives of devotion, pleasures and comforts of sense, and who nearly forsake God when aridity comes to their souls. It is of these that God says in the Gospel: *Qui cum gaudio suscipiunt verbum Dei et in tempore tentationis recedunt.* Cf. Fray Bartolomé de los Mártires (*op. cit.*, folios 84, 124, 183). Nor does this proposition reject outward practice of the virtues, though it says that contemplation is better. I give the words of Fray Bartolomé de los Mártires (folio 82, p. 2):

Exercitia enim externa quamvis bona ac pia sint, tamen multo majoris momenti censenda est exercitatio interna, qua homo ardentissime ad Deum non per sensus aut imagines, sed modo quodam supernaturali ita consurgit, ut illi uniatur.

PROPOSITION XVIII

(Vol. I, pp. 338–9)

'It often comes to pass that in their very spiritual exercises, when they are powerless to prevent it, there arise and are felt in the sensual part of the soul unclean motions, and sometimes this happens even when the spirit is deep in prayer, or engaged in the Sacrament of Penance or in the Eucharist. These things are not, as I say, in their power; they proceed from one of three things. The first cause from which they occasionally proceed (albeit rarely and in weak natures) is the pleasure which nature takes in spiritual things. For when the spirit and the sense are pleased, every part of a man is moved by that pleasure to delight

according to its proportion and nature. For then the spirit, which is the higher part, is moved to pleasure and delight in God, and the sensual nature, which is the lower part, is moved to pleasure and delight of the senses.'

32. This proposition requires more detailed consideration than others, as it is very subtle; truth or error may result from a single word expressed in one way or in another. In the first place, I assume that it is a sound doctrine agreed upon among spiritual men that the spirit in which sensual movements have their birth is not a good spirit, nor is any other that incites to evil, as the holy Mother teaches in her book, giving this as a sign of the evil spirit in the seventh of her *Maxims* which are included in the compendium of the degrees of prayer. This is a truth so certain and so generally agreed upon that nobody who possesses the light of reason can assert the contrary, still less a spiritual man of so miraculous a life. In the second place, I assume that it sometimes happens that when the soul is enjoying the most sublime contemplation, other than ecstasy, there arise certain sensual motions in the flesh, and, in order that that state of prayer be not forthwith condemned and denounced as evil, it is well that this doctrine should be set down and understood so that it may be known that prayer and contemplation may be quite good and may come from God, and that at the same time such accidental occurrences may come to pass in the inferior part of the soul. Just so there was light on the summit of Mount Sinai, where Moses was, and at the foot of the mount there were smoke, darkness and quakings of the earth. Let not the spiritual man, then, be forthwith discouraged and afflicted and let him not suppose that his state of prayer is of the devil. It may be of God and yet this may happen, either because of some natural effect that is caused *ex accidenti* in the body, through weakness or heat or dilatation of the pores, or through the inspiration of the devil, who, since he cannot enter the loftiest place of contemplation, is anxious to cause such disturbances as he can. And sometimes these things will come to pass not only without any desire on the part of the contemplative, but even without his perception or knowledge, as happens in dreams, because the force with which the spiritual man is bound closely to his contemplation will not permit him to have knowledge of these movements or of any other exterior actions. And at other times when these things come to pass he will be conscious of them and will grieve greatly at them, as this author says, yet he will be unable to cure his affections

because of the weakness of the natural state of his body, although his soul gives no kind of consent to these things.

The saints whom we have as guides in the Church teach us this doctrine, especially Saint Gregory (*Morals*, Book X, Chapter x), where he expounds this text from Job: *Si subverterit omnia vel in unum coarctaverit quis contradicet ei?*

Sed tamen hanc importunis caro tentationibus impugnet. Cumque ad contemplanda cælestia animus ducitur objectis actionis illicitæ imaginibus reverberatur, nam carnis repente hunc stimulus sauciat quem extra carnem contemplatio sancta rapiebat; cælum ergo simul infernusque coarctatur cum unam eandemque mentem et sublevatio contemplationis illuminat, et importunitas tentationis obscurat, ut et videat intendendo quod appetat et succumbendo in cogitatione toleret quod erubescat; de cælo quippe lux oritur; infernus autem tenebris possidetur. In unum ergo cælum infernusque redigitur cum mens quæ jam lucem patriæ supernæ considerat, etiam de carnis bello occultæ tentationis portat.[1]

And Saint John Climacus, in his fifteenth chapter, which is of chastity, says these notable words:

Let us diligently scrutinize and examine ourselves when we are singing psalms and assisting at the Divine offices, as to the sweetness and pleasure which we sometimes feel on those occasions, whether it is of the spirit of God or of the evil spirit, who sometimes intermeddles in these occupations. Desire not, O youth, to be ignorant, for the better knowledge of thyself and of thy business. For I once knew a case where certain people were praying for their friends and acquaintances, and the thought of them awakened a spark of impure love in their souls, without their being aware of the fact; they rather thought that they had been fulfilling the law of charity.

Of Saint Catherine of Siena it is written in her Life that she suffered such things even at the time of Communion, and, when the Saint was afflicted by this, God said to her: 'Wherefore art thou afflicted? If these things trouble thee, I am with thee.'

By this will be understood the teaching of this proposition. Our author does not say that these sensual motions arise immediately or *per se* from the spirit of the contemplation of God. He says that, at the time when the soul is conscious of the pleasure of contemplation, some sensual delight is wont to be felt in weak natures, and that this delight has its natural explanation in philosophy and medicine. For overmuch joy heats the body and dilates the pores, just as fear makes

[1] Migne, *Patr. lat.*, Vol. LXXV, p. 931.

the body cold and closes the pores. And thus what this author postulates is an effect of the weakness of the body and not of the grace and spirit of contemplation. And he says that this happens seldom and against the will of the person who experiences it, and indeed that it causes him displeasure. And he says that whoever experiences it at any time must take heed and not be unnecessarily afflicted or think that what was the result of a weak nature is due to an evil spirit. I do not know how this can be compared with what has been said and is said by the Illuminists concerning voluntary, not natural, motions; nor how it can be classed with the encouragement given by the advisers of the Illuminists to those who were their carnal rather than their spiritual children, for they would tell them that these gross things were overflowings from the spirit. In this author, however, I find them described as sensual motions not caused by the spirit, whereas in the Illuminists I find grossness described as being an effect of the spirit. In this author I find the motions attributed to the weakness of human nature; in the Illuminists they arise from the malice of the will. In this author I find them described as causing displeasure and pain to those who experience them; in the Illuminists I find that they are brought about by their own knavery. Let it be considered what possible similarity there can be between the one kind of teaching and the other.

PROPOSITIONS XIX, XX, XXI, XXII, XXIII

Propositions XIX and XX have already been expounded under the head of Proposition III. Proposition XXI will be treated under the head of Proposition XXVII. Propositions XXII and XXIII come under Proposition III. There is thus no more to add concerning these.

PROPOSITION XXIV

(Vol. I, p. 421)

This author says that in the dark night of the soul the desires, both sensual and spiritual, ' are put to sleep and mortified, so that they can experience nothing, either Divine or human; the affections of the soul are oppressed and constrained, so that they can neither move nor find support in anything; the imagination is bound, and can make no useful reflection; the memory is

gone, the understanding is in darkness, and hence the will likewise is arid and constrained and all the faculties are void; and in addition to all this a thick and heavy cloud is upon the soul, keeping it in affliction, and, as it were, far away from God.'

33. So that the censors may not think this an exaggeration of the aridities suffered by the soul, let them hear what Saint Bernard says in his third Sermon, *De Resurrectione. Sunt quæ nondum spirituali consolatione recepta, sed nisi breviati fuissent dies quis posset sustinere?* The venerable Fray Alonso de Orozco (*Confessions*, Book II), treating of this same matter, says that the trials of the body are as it were blows upon the wall of the city, which come as it were from without, but the temptations of the spirit strike and wound the interior part of the soul from within and are more deeply felt. And the holy Mother says in the *Interior Castle* that there are many things in this state of prayer which combat the soul with interior affliction, and are felt so keenly and intolerably that she knows not to what she can compare it save to the sufferings of those that are in hell, for in this tempest comes no consolation.

Proposition XXV

Part of this proposition, which deals with the cessation of the soul from working and with its passive conduct, has already been expounded under Proposition III (§§ 17, 18). As regards the part describing the possible entrance of the deception of the devil, this will be expounded under Proposition XXVI.

Propositions XXVI, XXVII

(Vol. I, p. 454)

This author says that 'the two portions of the soul—the spiritual and the sensual—before they can go forth to the Divine union of love, must needs first be reformed, ordered and tranquillized with respect to the sensual and to the spiritual, according to the nature of the state of innocence which was Adam's, notwithstanding the fact that the soul is not free from the state of temptation which belongs to its lower part.'

34. This author here demands the purity which is necessary if the soul is to reach this contemplation and perfect union, whereof we have

spoken in § 9, proving our contention with the doctrine of the saints. This agrees with the doctrine of Fray Tomás de Villanueva (*op. cit.*, folio 122, p. 1): *Dextera totum hominem amplexatur ne vel leviter moveatur.* And also his words *post serenatam mentem et ab omni labe mundatam* (folio 124, p. 2). There is also a description of the purity which is necessary for this contemplation in Fray Bartolomé de los Mártires (Book II, folio 90, p. 2):

Modicus enim amor, tenuisque affectus, quo quis mortali creaturæ adhæret, verbulum otiose prolatum aut bucella panis, aliter quam oportet sumpta, et aliæ hujusmodi, licet minutulæ paleæ efficiunt, ut Deus, qui summæ puritatis est, non intimæ animæ uniatur, donec hæ ordinationes expientur.

The demands put forward by this author are even less than this; and, because he requires such purity in the higher part of the soul, he does not assume that the soul is now free from venial and mortal sins, since the lower part of the soul is left subject to temptations at the time of contemplation. And, apart from this, the powerful grace of God, as I said in my notes to the *Confessions* of Fray Alonso de Orozco (at the end of § 25), is able to preserve the purity of certain souls, so that, if they cannot free themselves of venial sins into which they fall through inadvertence, they nevertheless pass some part of their lives without venial sins which arise deliberately from the will. These are the express words of Father Suárez (*De Gratia*, Vol. II, Book VIII, Chapter ix, § 25):

Loquendo autem de solis peccatis venialibus, credi potest sanctos aliquantulum vel aliquoties interdum pervenire pro aliquo tempore vitæ ad tam perfectum gradum perfectionis, ut raro vel numquam illa committant.

And thus, if this author were to say that those whom God admits to so perfect a degree of contemplation are at that time and for a short time afterwards free from deliberate venial sins, he would be saying nothing against true Catholic doctrine.

This is quite different, then, from the doctrines and propositions of the Illuminists of Seville, who claimed to be free from mortal and venial sins, and to be confirmed in grace, though their lives were evil. This author says not that contemplatives are confirmed in grace nor that they are free from sin; but he rather subjects them to sin, since he affirms that the sensual part of the soul is subjected to the temptations of the devil. He affirms, then, that the soul will not reach this union so long as it commits such sins and has such vicious habits; but, as that union is neither durable nor perpetual in this life, it follows not that the soul will not afterwards be subject to falls; in this way he demonstrates what purity it needs in order to reach this union with God.

PROPOSITION XXVIII

(Vol. III, p. 18)

This author says that ' the acts of love that the soul performs in this union with God are most precious, and even one of them is of greater merit than many more that the soul may have done apart from this transformation.'

35. The teaching of this proposition is most certain and is confirmed by the words of the holy Fray Alonso de Orozco in the *Mount of Contemplation* (folio 136, p. 1). It even seems that one hour of so perfect an exercise, brief time though it be, is of greater worth than others spent in the contemplation of other things. And the words of Albertus Magnus (*De Adhærendo Deo*, Chapter v) are no less definite:

Quapropter si incipisti nudare et purificare a phantasmatibus et imaginibus, et simplificare et tranquillare fiducialiter in Domino Deo cor tuum et mentem tuam, ut haurias et sentias fontem divini beneplaciti in omnibus interioribus tuis et per bonam voluntatem sis Deo unitus in intellectu, sufficit tibi hoc pro omni studio et lectione sacræ scripturæ, et ad dilectionem Dei et proximi ut unctio docet.

The reason of this is clear, for in this perfect contemplation the affection of love grows and is more intense, and is thus more meritorious. And although the habit of grace is most necessary for the acquisition of merit, yet it is held by theologians to be a more probable doctrine that the increase of merit corresponds not to the intensity of this habit, but to the intensity of the act. And if this author says that there is greater merit from this love than there can be without this union, he does not thereby reduce the meritorious principle to union, or exclude charity, for it is clear that the soul cannot reach this union without grace and charity. Our author says that, in that state, through the loftiness of contemplation, the love of the soul grows and is increased, and its merit grows correspondingly; thus he assumes that the soul in this state has both charity and grace. He who begs for it cleanses his soul even of the slightest sins. Nor is it legitimate to infer from this proposition the teaching of the Illuminists of Medo—namely, that the soul that is in this state of relaxation has no need of prayer, recollection or anything else whatsoever.

Proposition XXIX

(Vol. III, p. 32)

This author says that ' in this state of union God permits the soul to see His beauty and entrusts it with the gifts and virtues that He has given it, and all this turns into love and praise, since there is no leaven to corrupt the mass.'

36. This proposition has been defended and expounded under the head of Proposition XXVII. As I said, it does not admit impeccability or freedom to commit venial sins. It only demands the purity which is necessary for such union and this it calls freedom or the absence of corrupting leaven; but this neither signifies impeccability nor affirms it. Saint Paul demanded that we should be impeccable, like babes, when he said: *Expurgate vetus fermentum*; and when he added: *Sicut estis azyma*.[1] But he exhorted us only to greater purity.

To say that God grants the contemplative to see His beauty is not to say clearly that He permits him to see His Essence, as is objected by the censor, for He can reveal His beauty to the soul without allowing it to see His Essence, as we learn from that rapture described by Saint Augustine (*Confessions*, Book IX, Chapter x)[2] and from other authors. The majority of doctors will not admit that this was a clear vision of the Divine Essence, as I observed in my notes to the *Confessions* of Fray Alonso de Orozco, No. 25. Our author's affirmation is the same as that of Gerson, as reproduced by Fray Bartolomé de los Mártires (*op. cit.*, folio 140):

Datur tamen nihilominus aliquando illis ad quandam puram et lucidam divinæ veritatis inspectionem pervenire, quod raro contigit, etc.

This doctrine is also accepted by the school of Scotus—namely, that there may be an abstractive species of the Divine Essence as It is, and that this, when communicated to the soul, will not cause an intuitive vision.

---

[1] [1 Corinthians v, 7.]
[2] Migne, *Patr. lat.*, Vol. XXXII, p. 774.

PROPOSITION XXX

(Vol. III, p. 39)

This author says that ' it will come to pass that the holy soul in this life may be assailed by a seraph armed with a dart of most enkindled love, which will pierce that enkindled coal of fire, the soul.' And later he says: ' If the effect of the wound should sometimes be permitted to pass outward to the bodily senses, to an extent corresponding to the interior wound, the effect of the impact and the wound will be felt without, as came to pass when the seraph wounded Saint Francis. He wounded him with love in his soul and in that way the effect of those wounds became outwardly visible.'

37. This is a very true doctrine founded upon the saying of the Bride *Vulnerata caritate ego sum*, from which Saint Augustine drew those words: *Sagitta vexas tu domine cor meum caritate tua*. This doctrine was expounded by Fray Alonso de Orozco in the *Mount of Contemplation* (folio 138, p. 1). The fifth degree that is experienced by the soul in contemplation consists in its total alienation from itself by reason of its great love for its Beloved, Jesus Christ; for which reason it says with Saint Paul: I live, yet not I, but my Saviour, Jesus Christ, liveth in me.

This is a death most sweet and sacred, preceded by the wound and the sickness whereof we have spoken, and which he had described in writing of the third degree of contemplation. It is also the express doctrine of the holy Mother, in the *Book of her Life*, Chapter xxix, where she relates that which happened to her in the vision of the seraph with the dart, wherewith he enkindled and wounded her heart.

In his hands I saw a long golden spear, and at the end of the iron tip I seemed to see a point of fire. With this he seemed to pierce my heart several times, so that it penetrated to my entrails. When he drew it out, I thought he was drawing them out with it and he left me completely afire with a great love for God. The pain was so sharp that it made me utter several moans; and so excessive was the sweetness caused me by this intense pain that one can never wish to lose it, nor will one's soul be content with anything less than God. It is not bodily pain, but spiritual, though the body has a share in it—indeed, a great share.[1]

It may be noted that Saint Francis was wounded in his soul before

[1] [*C.W.S.T.J.*, I, 192–3.]

being wounded in his body. The effects, then, that Christ Our Lord caused in the bodies of the saints were first caused in their souls; and the wound which Saint Augustine said that his heart experienced through the love of God appeared as a wound in his body. This is affirmed by several weighty authors, among them Fray Juan de los Ángeles in the book entitled *The Triumphs of Love,* where he quotes from Saint Bonaventura concerning this opinion.

The fact that the Illuminists have taken upon their lips the language of the love which wounds the soul does not make that language suspect, for they are traitors who have clad their thoughts in the words of spiritual persons that they may the better deceive. If in addition to the language of the spiritual persons whom they quote they had had their spirituality and lived their lives, they would never have uttered such nonsense.

Proposition XXXI

(Vol. III, p. 44)

This author says: ' This touch is most substantial and the Substance of God touches the substance of the soul. To this state many holy men have attained in this life.'

38. With respect to the matter of the suspension of the soul so that it cannot work, this has been already expounded under Proposition III, in the words of the same author, a fact which the censors fail to notice in examining the very propositions in which these words are stated so clearly. With regard to the most substantial nature of this touch, and its touching the substance of the soul, this is not so un-intelligible[1] as it seems to certain persons, for it is not a theologically improbable opinion that postulates an intimate ecstatic relation with the soul, and its probability is demonstrated by a weighty author of our own time. In order to expound and defend our author, however, we need not have recourse to that doctrine. Our author describes this touch as most substantial because it is immediate and comes to pass without mediation of any creature. It is God Who of Himself speaks and works and awakens the soul so that it may work quite clearly. The saints have described the union of the body of Christ with our bodies, in the Sacrament, as real, natural and substantial, in order to show the truth of this union and conjunction, and to indicate that it comes from no created quality, such as the quality produced in the

---

[1] [The Spanish has 'intelligible,' evidently an error.]

soul by grace. And thus the mystics describe this touch and union
as most substantial, for it comes directly from God, *sine media creatura*,
an opinion which is not deserving of censure.

PROPOSITION XXXII

(Vol. III, p. 67)

**In treating of the impediments which the soul may experience
so that it cannot reach perfect union with God, our author
describes the first as being the spiritual master. ' It is of great
importance for the soul that desires to profit, and not to fall
back, to consider in whose hands it is placing itself. . . for there
is hardly anyone who in all respects will guide the soul perfectly
along the highest stretch of the road, or even along the intermediate stretches.'**

39. In this proposition our author demands certain characteristics
of the master who guides and teaches the soul so that it may make
progress upon this road of perfect prayer; he says that there are few
who can guide the soul on this road. Consider here what I have
quoted above (§ 20) from the holy Mother, and these words of Fray
Bartolomé de los Mártires (*op. cit.*, folio 118, p. 1), where he is quoting
Saint Bernard:

Multi fuere perfecti in theologia mystica absque speculativa, nunquam
tamen theologus aliquis speculativus tantum culmen perfectionis est adeptus,
immo nec perfectus extitit in ipsa acquisita theologia sine mystica.

Here he adds many good words. And in the same book (folio 138,
p. 1) he says:

Hæc mystica sapientia quam Dionysius proprie Christianorum vocat,
citius ac sublimius idiotis simplicibusque, qui nihil aliud quam salutem in
timore et tremore curant, quam eruditis theologis conferre solet, nisi ipsi
toto mentis affectu humilitati studeant.

On folio 140, he quotes an admirable passage from Gerson on the
same matter.

Because this author demands a master who is skilled in this matter
he must not be classed with the Illuminists, who said that there were no
masters save their own, who shared their grossness. This author
denies not that mystical theology may be examined by means of speculative theology, although not all speculative theologians are fitted

to examine it, as is very clearly affirmed by Fray Bartolomé de los Mártires in the passage already quoted. This explanation will serve also as an exposition of Proposition XXXIII.

PROPOSITION XXXIII

What trials the holy Mother endured from the masters into whose hands she fell, until she found one who understood her spiritual nature, is evident from what I related in the first paragraph, and from what the holy Mother says in her books continually. As for the attribution to this author of the denial of works of virtue to the contemplative, this has been expounded in Proposition III, from the discussion of which there also follows the defence of Propositions XXXIV, XXXV and XXXVI.

PROPOSITIONS XXXIV, XXXV, XXXVI, XXXVII
(Vol. III, p. 71)

This author says: ' Set the soul in the liberty of serene peace, and draw it away from the yoke and slavery of its operations, which is the captivity of Egypt, for all this is little more than gathering straw to make bricks; and to lead the soul to the promised land flowing with milk and honey.'

40. From Proposition III we have already seen what are these operations from which it is said that God draws the contemplative away; they are the operations of the inward and the outward senses and of discursive reasonings. These he calls slavery, for they are an imperfect kind of operation, as the saints and spiritual men continually affirm, and as is clear from many of the passages cited above, and the soul at that time is enjoying serene peace. I know not why this should be madness, temerity, error, blasphemy, abuse or heresy. So grave and severe a censure would require very clear demonstration, for that state in which for a time there dwells serenity and peace and some kind of security is witnessed to by the saints and doctors whom I quoted under Proposition VI (§ 25); from which we infer that, for the whole of its life and for as long as it remains in the world, the soul enjoys the highest peace. And that it should enjoy this for some time is not contrary to truth, nor to the saints, but is in close conformity with their

doctrine, as may also be gathered from what is said under Proposition
XXVII (§ 34).

Propositions XXXVIII, XXXIX

Proposition XXXVIII is expounded and defended under the heads
of Propositions III and XVII. The same may be said of Proposition
XXXIX, where it is clear what are the works which are said to impede
and hinder perfect contemplation.

Proposition XL

**This author says that, as this transformation and union cannot
be comprehended by human ability or sense, the soul must void
itself completely and voluntarily, in so far as it is able, from all
such affection and desire as it can contain; for who will take
from God the power to do that which He wills in a soul that is
resigned and stripped and annihilated?**

41. In this proposition the author is not treating of the suspension
of discursive reasoning and the operations of the outward senses,
which are discussed in other propositions, but of the soul's need to
void and annihilate itself with respect to all its particular desires and
affections of love, so that it may comply with the saying of Christ
Abneget semetipsum, and so that it may be prepared for the favours of
God, as is taught by saints and doctors, and as I have related above
(§ 9).

42. If we assume what has been said above, and proved by the
doctrine and testimony of saints and doctors and spiritual men, and if
we assume likewise that all this doctrine is sound, good and in conformity with the Fathers of the Church, there appears to be no fit
reason for the prohibition of this book. There are raised three principal
objections to it: that it is of little utility, that its teaching is difficult,
and that harm has come from such books having been placed in the
hands of women. All these objections were raised to the books of the
holy Mother, which contain the same doctrine as the books of this
author, and to all these objections Father-Master Fray Luis de León
replied in his apologia. I propose to set down here his own words,
which will also serve as a reply.

43. With regard to the question of utility, he writes as follows:
'In order to show that this is calumny, I presuppose that the Prayer of
Union is a suspension of the soul with God, which comes to pass when
the soul is at prayer and is reasoning with its understanding. God,
applying to the soul His light and His power, draws it to Himself and
suspends the reasoning of its understanding, enkindling its will by
means of unitive love. This presupposed, I assert that this writer speaks
truly of union in these books, explaining what it is, wherein it consists, the good effects which it produces and the way wherein it may
be known if it is true or false. If this is to teach union, these books
certainly teach it. But, I ask, what harm can be caused by such teaching,
or how is it unseemly? For if it be said that there is no such kind of
prayer, this is a most false assertion and contrary to what the saints
write about it and to the truth of the faith. For it is clear from Holy
Scripture that there is a prayer of rapture or ecstasy, and if this be so
there is also a prayer which we call that of union. And if it be said, as
no doubt it will be said, that there is such a prayer, it cannot be said
that it is evil, since it is God Who gives it. And if there is such a prayer
and it is good, how can it be wrong to treat of it, to describe its
qualities, and to warn the soul of the errors which it is possible for
persons to commit on this road lest they should commit them? And if
it be said that this kind of prayer cannot be acquired by rules or
precepts, that is profoundly true, and it is the first thing which these
books point out; for they give no rules or precepts, but only admonish
those who are concerned with prayer that, if they would reach this
degree of prayer, they must live with great purity of conscience and
that their hearts must always be detached from earthly things, and that
they must always aspire to that which is most perfect—namely, the
precepts and counsels of the Gospel.

'If, then, this road to union is good and perfect, it is good and
necessary that there should be books which treat of it and describe
its nature and the steps of its progress. How is it reasonable to condemn
a book as evil if it is a guide to a road which is good? For, if it ought
not to be written, this can only be because the road ought not to be
known; and if this be so, it must be because it ought not to be trodden,
which none will be so foolish and ignorant as to dare to assert. On the
contrary, it is useful to tread this road, and therefore a knowledge of
it is necessary, and, for the same reason, it is advantageous to write of
it. Let the critics tell me who receives harm from a knowledge of
union. Not those that have aught to do with it, for they obtain light

so that they may have a better knowledge of that wherewith they have to do. Those that have naught to do with it will of necessity conceive one of two things as a result of what they read here: either wonder at the gifts which God makes to His own children or the desire to follow this road and to leave all things that they may find God, Who is so great a Friend. Both these things are everywhere acknowledged to be useful. It seems that those who object to this have seen no other books on the same subject and are unaware that others have written of it. What an injustice it is to have misgivings about these writings and to fear their going into a thousand places? Let them see Saint Bonaventura, Richard of Saint Victor and John Gerson; and, if they desire to read in the vulgar tongue, let them see the third part of the books called the *Alphabets*.[1] There they will see that what the holy Mother says about this is little by comparison with what these authors say and write about it.'

To this defence, which may very appositely be applied to our author, I add that, in his first book, he treats in most learned fashion the subject of self-abnegation undertaken to the end that the soul may reach this kind of contemplation and union. Other authors, it is true, have treated of exterior abnegation, but none has described abnegation of an interior kind like this blessed Father, or given surer instruction, for the avoidance of error with regard to revelations, a matter which so preoccupies spiritual men and masters in spiritual things. To this day no book has been written comparable with this, as will be seen in practice by anyone who reads the second and third chapters of the first part. Since these two points are so essential in the spiritual life, and since this author treats them so minutely, he may be called the first writer in all Spain on this subject, and I know not how there can be any doubt concerning the utility of these books.

44. As to the second point, Fray Luis de León writes as follows: 'If this is an argument for the prohibition of these books, all books ought to be prohibited, for there are many places in which even those who lecture upon them cannot understand them. How many theologians, I may ask, understand the whole of Saint Augustine? And who is he that understands Saint Dionysius? And what I say of these writers I say of almost all the saints, who in many parts of their works speak, as it were, in Arabic, not only to those who know Latin and Greek, but even to those who profess theology and the Schoolmen. And not only the saints, but these same scholastic doctors are not completely

---

[1] [I.e., the *Third Spiritual Alphabet* of Francisco de Osuna.]

understood by their very disciples, who labour to expound them. Saint
Thomas is not understood in many parts of his writings, still less is
Scotus; the same also applies to Alexander, to Durango and to Henrico
de Grandabo. Apart from this, the little that is written in these books
harms nobody and profits many, for those who understand it profit by
it and those who understand it not are neither harmed nor profited.
Indeed it may be said that even those who understand them not profit
by them, for their obscurity lies, not in their language, but in the nature
of some of the things they say, which cannot be understood by those
who have no experience of them. Yet, even without understanding
them, such persons generally admire them and desire to share the
experiences which they describe, and this is of great profit.'

45. As to the third matter—the harm which it is said these books
have caused when they have fallen into the hands of some of these
Illuminists—I assert, in the first place, that it is well known who are
the persons that have expressly taught this evil doctrine and in whose
teaching it has frequently been condemned—namely, in that of Fray
Alonso de Mello, who deceived the town of Durango. Thus there was
no need for them to seek this doctrine here, where they could not find
it. If they wished to dissemble and authorize it by means of the doctrine
of this book, maliciously understood, in this very fact there can be
found an argument proving how good the book is, since men as evil
as these Illuminists could find no better cloak to throw over their
wickedness than the writings of a man of so pure and miraculous a
life; with a less excellent cloak they would be unable to hide such great
sins as their own and hypocrites are apt to cloak the greatest sins with
the noblest virtues. Here I am adapting the words of Father-Master
Fray Luis de León, in the apologia already quoted, where he replies
to the calumniators of the books of the holy Mother, by referring to
certain revelations which caused women to write about them, to
desire them and to suffer illusions. He says as follows:

'But they say that in women, who are credulous, the desire for
such things opens the door to the entrance of the devil, who is enabled
to deceive them by means of illusions. The unruly desire for revelations may do this, but not reading about revelations which are good
and true, and these books do nothing but take away such desires, as is
clear from the books themselves. From reading, it is said, comes
desire. If this is so, let the sacred books be censored, let ecclesiastical
histories be burned and let the lives of the saints, the Dialogues of
Saint Gregory and the revelations of those who founded religious

Orders and caused them to grow be torn in pieces. In such a case the Church has been deceived and all this time has written and recommended for reading that which opens the door to the devil. So that one who is a friend of himself or of his own excellence may have no occasion to be deceived, let the glory of God be hidden, let not His marvels be known and let this road be closed by which many have been encouraged to love and serve Him. How many have been moved by the honour which is paid to the saints to aim at becoming saints themselves? Let there, then, be no virtue; let not the virtuous acts of many persons be known and celebrated, lest hypocrites find occasion for sin in them. More hypocrites have fallen through such occasion than those who have been deluded by the devil through reading the revelations of God. In these things we must not consider the evil use made of them by a few, but the advantage of all. And the advantage of these writings, if prayer does not make it clear, can be demonstrated by experience, which is a faithful witness to them. Consider the friars and nuns of the Discalced Carmelite Order who have been nurtured in the doctrine of these books and know it by heart: consider if they are mad or deluded, or if there are any who excel them in the purity of true religion and sanctity of the love of God.'

I conclude this judgment by saying that to prohibit this book would be a very serious thing and that, by such an act, the reputation of the Holy Inquisition of Spain might well be greatly impaired. For, as the Discalced Carmelite Order is now treating of the beatification of this blessed Father, a matter which depends entirely upon the purity of his doctrine together with the purity of his life, if the Holy Office in Spain caused this book to be recalled the Order might well appeal to Rome and to the Holy Apostolic See: and, if this book were approved there, as it has been approved here by the University of Alcalá, and would be approved by many other Universities of good standing, it would be a great blow to the reputation of the Holy Inquisition in Spain that what it had done should be undone in Rome, and it would even prepare the way for further appeals to Rome in such matters, which would be a matter of common talk. All this makes it necessary to walk with great circumspection in this business. This I hold, and I have signed this document in Madrid, in the convent of Saint Philip, on the eleventh day of July, 1622.

FR. BASILIO PONCE DE LEÓN.
Prima Professor in Salamanca.

SELECT BIBLIOGRAPHY

The translator here appends details of the principal editions of the works of St. John of the Cross, together with a selected list of books and articles which deal with his life and writings. Such books of reference as encyclopædias and histories of literature are omitted, as are also purely ephemeral articles, of which a large number appeared at the time of the quatercentenary (1942).

Descriptions of many of the editions will be found in the General Introduction to Vol. I of this translation and in the introductions to the individual works.

Long titles have been shortened, except where a work is of exceptional importance or of particular interest to English readers. Where several works have the same, or substantially the same, title, they are given in chronological order.

The Bibliography is divided into thirteen sections:

   I. Bibliographies.
  II. Spanish Editions of Collected Works (in chronological order).
 III. Spanish Editions of Single Works (in alphabetical order of titles).
  IV. Selected Translations into English.[1]
   V. Selected Translations into French.[1]
  VI. Selected Translations into German.[1]
 VII. Selected Translations into Italian.[1]
VIII. Selected Translations into Dutch or Flemish.[1]
  IX. Selected Translations into Portuguese.[1]
   X. Selected Translations into Latin.[1]
  XI. Note on Translations into other languages.
 XII. Abridgements, Anthologies, etc. (arranged in the above order of languages, and, in each division, in alphabetical order).
XIII. Commentaries.

In Section XIII both authors and their works are named in alphabetical order, except that a major work is occasionally given precedence over others. Long though this section is, no subdivisions have been made in it, because so many works would come into more than one of them. For the guidance

[1] In each of these sections editions of the Complete Works come first, followed by editions of individual works in alphabetical order of titles.

of those studying one particular aspect of the subject, however, the following marks are prefixed to the appropriate entries:

* Mainly biographical.
** Includes considerable biographical material.
† Mainly literary.
†† Has reference to the disputed authenticity of some parts of St. John of the Cross's works.

The following abbreviations are used (principally, though not exclusively in Section XIII), to denote periodicals referred to in this Bibliography:

A-A.   *Al-Andalus.* Madrid-Granada.

A.C.   *Archivo Carmelitano.* Madrid.

B.H.S.   *Bulletin of Hispanic Studies.* Liverpool.

B. Hisp.   *Bulletin Hispanique.* Bordeaux.

B.S.S.   *Bulletin of Spanish Studies.* Liverpool.

B.U.G.   *Boletín de la Universidad de Granada.*

Bol. R. Ac. Esp.   *Boletín de la Real Academia Española.* Madrid.

C.D.   *Ciudad de Dios.* Valladolid.

C. y R.   *Cruz y Raya.* Madrid.

C.T.   *Ciencia Tomista.* Salamanca.

E.C.   *Etudes Carmélitaines.* Paris.

Eph. C.   *Ephemerides Carmeliticæ.* Florence.

Esc.   *Escorial.* Madrid.

Est. F.   *Estudis Franciscans.* Barcelona.

Et. F.   *Etudes Franciscaines.* Paris.

H.R.   *Hispanic Review.* Philadelphia.

J.T.S.   *Journal of Theological Studies.* Oxford.

M.C.   *El Monte Carmelo.* Burgos.

M.S.T.   *Mensajero de Santa Teresa y de San Juan de la Cruz.* Madrid.

Man.   *Manresa.* Bilbao.

N.R.T.   *Nouvelle Revue Théologique.* Tournai-Louvain.

R.A.M.   *Revue d'Ascétique et de Mystique.* Toulouse.

R.E.T.   *Revista Española de Teología.* Madrid.

R. Esp.   *Revista de Espiritualidad.* San Sebastián (Nos. 1–5), Madrid.

R.F.   *Razón y Fe.* Madrid.

R.F.E.   *Revista de Filología Española.* Madrid.

R.F.H.   *Revista de Filología Hispánica.* Buenos Aires.

R.V.S.   *Rivista di Vita Spirituale.* Rome.

R. y C.   *Religión y Cultura.* El Escorial.

V. Car.   *Vita Carmelitana.* Rome.

V. Sob.   *Vida Sobrenatural.* Salamanca.

V. Sp.   *Vie Spirituelle.* Paris.

V.V.   *Verdad y Vida.* Madrid.

Z.A.M.   *Zeitschrift für Ascese und Mystik.* Innsbruck.

I. BIBLIOGRAPHIES

(1) Baruzi, Jean: 'Esquisse d'une étude bibliographique,' in *Saint Jean de la Croix et le problème de l'expérience mystique*. Paris, 1924, pp. 713–49.

(2) Benno a S. Joseph, C.D.: 'Bibliographiæ S. Joannis a Cruce, O.C.D., specimen (1891–1940).' In *Eph. C.*, 1947, I, 163–210, 367–81; 1948, II, 584–602; 1949, III, 405–24. (Cf. also I, 393–416.)

(3) Bilbao Aristegui, P.: *Índice de bibliografía sobre San Juan de la Cruz*. Bilbao, 1946.

(4) Carbonero y Sol, León: *Homenaje a San Juan de la Cruz, etc.* Madrid, 1891.

(5) Matías del Niño Jesús, C.D.: 'La bibliografía de San Juan de la Cruz en la Exposición de la Biblioteca Nacional.' In *R. Esp.*, 1943, II, 51–74, 283–321.

(6) Peers, E. Allison: Bibliography in *Studies of the Spanish Mystics*. London, 1927, I, 442–8; 2nd ed., 1951, I, 361–6; 1930, II, 399–400. (A representative selection only.)

(7) Soler, Luis María: 'Estudio crítico: San Juan de la Cruz y su bibliografiá.' In *Homenaje a San Juan de la Cruz en el IV centenario de su nacimiento*. Barcelona, 1945, pp. 1–40.

II. SPANISH EDITIONS OF COLLECTED WORKS
(in chronological order)

(8) *Obras espirituales que encaminan a una alma a la perfecta unión con Dios*. Por el Venerable P. F. Juan de la Cruz.... Con una resunta de la vida del autor y unos discursos por el P. F. Diego de Jesús. Alcalá de Henares, 1618. (This is the *editio princeps*, abbreviated 'e.p.' throughout this translation. It contains: *Subida del Monte Carmelo*, *Noche oscura* and *Llama de amor viva*.)

(9) *Obras espirituales que encaminan a una alma a la perfecta unión con Dios*. Por el Venerable P. F. Juan de la Cruz, primer Descalzo de la Reforma de Nuestra Señora del Carmen. Barcelona, Sebastián de Cormellas, 1619. (A corrected reprint of No. 8.)

(10) *Obras del Venerable y místico Doctor Fray Juan de la Cruz*. Madrid, Viuda de Madrigal, 1630. (This edition contains the author's biography by its editor, Fr. Jerónimo de San José. The *Cántico espiritual* appears in the Works for the first time in Spain.)

(11) *Obras, etc.* Barcelona, Sebastián de Cormellas, 1635. (Substantially a reprint of No. 10.)

(12) *Obras del Venerable y místico Doctor Fray Juan de la Cruz.* Madrid, Gregorio Rodríguez, 1649. (Enlarged edition, including nine letters, one hundred sentences and some poems. Cf. Vol. I, p. lxii, of this translation.) This edition was reprinted:

(13) Madrid, Bernardo de Villa-Diego, 1672.

(14) Madrid, 1679.

(15) Barcelona, Vicente Suria, 1693. (Adds the *Cautelas.*)

(16) Madrid, Julián de Paredes, 1694, 2 vols.

(17) *Obras, etc.* Madrid, Barcelona, 1700.

(18) *Obras, etc.* Seville, 1701. (A compendium rather than a complete edition.) Reprinted, Barcelona, 1724.

(19) *Obras espirituales que encaminan a un alma a la más perfecta unión con Dios con transformación de amor.* Seville, Francisco de Leefdael, 1703. (Includes an outline Life of St. John of the Cross, by the editor, Andrés de Jesús María.)

(20) *Obras, etc.* Pamplona, Pascual Ibáñez, 1774. (A reprint of No. 19.)

(21) *Obras escogidas.* Paris, 1847. (In *Tesoro de escritores místicos españoles,* ed. Eugenio de Ochoa. Contains various works, together with selections from Alejo Venegas, Juan de Ávila and Luis de Granada.)

(22) *Obras, etc.* Madrid, 1853. (Vol. XXVII of the series 'Biblioteca de Autores Españoles,' pp. 1–273. Contains all the works of St. John of the Cross found in the 1703 edition, which it reproduces, and a 'Vida y juicio crítico del V. P. San Juan de la Cruz,' together with works by Malón de Chaide and Hernando de Zárate. Reprinted in 1886, 1908 and 1926. Vol. XXXV, *Romancero y cancionero sagrados,* ed. Justo de Sancha, pp. 67–70, contains some further *romances.* Reprinted in 1872.)

(23) *Obras, etc.* Nueva edición precedida de un prólogo por D. Juan Manuel Ortí y Lara. Madrid, Aurial, 1872, 2 vols.

(24) *Obras, etc.* Barcelona, Viuda de J. Subirana, 1883, 4 vols. (Reproduces No. 19 and adds 100 more *Avisos.*)

(25) *Obras, etc.* Madrid, Asilo de la Santísima Trinidad, 1906, 2 vols. (Reproduces No. 19 and the treatise of the 'Espinas del espíritu,' now first included in an edition of the Saint's works.)

(26) (*Obras.*) *Subida. Noche oscura. Cautelas.* Ed. Francisco Besalú. Madrid, Apostolado de la Prensa, 1906. (On this ed. v. Benno (No. 2), *Eph. C.,* III, 408.)

(27) *Obras del místico doctor San Juan de la Cruz.* Edición crítica y la más correcta y completa de las publicadas hasta hoy, con introducciones y notas del P. Gerardo de San Juan de la Cruz, C.D. Toledo, 1912–14, 3 vols. (Contains much new material, including letters and *Avisos* by the Saint,

various apocryphal works, and numerous documents. Both redactions of the *Cántico espiritual* and of the *Llama de amor viva* are included.)

(**28**) *Obras de San Juan de la Cruz*. Edición popular. Ed. P. Eduardo de Santa Teresa. Burgos, 1925. (Follows text of No. 27, but gives only the second redactions of *Cántico* and *Llama*.)

(**29**) *Obras de San Juan de la Cruz*. Madrid, Apostolado de la Prensa, 1926. (Another popular edition, the text following that of No. 27. 2nd ed., Madrid, 1933. 3rd ed., Madrid, 1941. 4th ed., Madrid, 1943. 5th ed., Madrid, 1948.)

(**30**) *Obras de San Juan de la Cruz, Doctor de la Iglesia*. Editadas y anotadas por el P. Silverio de Santa Teresa, C.D. Burgos, 1929–31, 5 vols. (The edition here translated.)

(**31**) *Obras*. Ed. y notas de P. Silverio de Santa Teresa, C.D. Burgos, 1931. (Popular edition, the text following No. 30, but giving only the second redactions of *Cántico* and *Llama*. 2nd ed., Burgos, 1940. 3rd ed., Burgos, 1948.)

(**32**) *Obras*. Ed. J. M. Gallegos Rocafull. Mexico, Editorial Séneca, 1942.

(**33**) *Obras*. Ed. conmemorativa del cuarto centenario del nacimiento del místico autor. Intr. del P. Bernardo de la Virgen del Carmen, C.D. Notas del P. Silverio de Santa Teresa, C.D. Buenos Aires, 1942. (Text follows that of No. 31.) 2 vols.

(**34**) *(Vida y) Obras*. Ed. P. Lucinio del Santísimo Sacramento, C.D. Madrid, Editorial Católica ('Biblioteca de Autores Cristianos'), 1946. (2nd ed., revised, 1950.)

III. SPANISH EDITIONS OF SINGLE WORKS
(in alphabetical order of titles)

AVISOS, ETC.

(**35**) (SPANISH AND FRENCH TEXTS) *Aphorismes de Saint Jean de la Croix*. Texte établi et traduit d'après le manuscrit autographe, et précédé d'une introduction, par Jean Baruzi. Bordeaux, 1924.

(**36**) *Autógrafos que se conservan del místico doctor San Juan de la Cruz, (Los)*. Edición fototipográfica por el P. Gerardo de San Juan de la Cruz, C.D. Toledo, 1913.

(**37**) (SPANISH AND FRENCH TEXTS) *Les Avis, Sentences et Maximes de Saint Jean de la Croix, Docteur de l'Eglise*. Ed. Dom Ph. Chevallier, O.S.B. (Paris, Bruges), 1933. (See review in *B. Hisp.*, 1934, XXXVI, 110–15.)

(**38**) *Avisos y sentencias espirituales que encaminan a una alma a la más perfecta unión con Dios*. Seville, 1701.

(39) *Avisos y sentencias espirituales del B. P. Juan de la Cruz*. Madrid, 1705. (Appended to *Exclamaciones, o Meditaciones de Santa Teresa, con algunos otros tratadillos de la Santa*, etc.)

(40) *Avisos y sentencias espirituales que encaminan*, etc. Barcelona, 1724.

(41) *Avisos y sentencias espirituales que encaminan a un alma a la más perfecta unión con Dios en transformación de amor*. Barcelona, Padres Carmelitas Descalzos. Undated (?1724).

(42) *Avisos y sentencias espirituales*. Madrid, Patronato social de buenas lecturas, 1914. (Biblioteca de Cultura Popular, Tomo XII. Also contains letters and poems.)

(43) *Avisos y sentencias espirituales*. Buenos Aires, 1932.

(44) *Camino breve para la perfección, o Avisos y cautelas*. Vich, 1892.

(45) *Cautelas de nuestro extático padre y doctor místico San Juan de la Cruz*, etc. Valencia, 1687.

(46) *Cautelas . . . para el espiritual aprovechamiento y perfección de las almas*. Burgos, 1911.

(47) *Cautelas, avisos y sentencias. . . .* Ed. PP. CC. DD., Segovia. Segovia, 1929. (Includes also the *Avisos de Santa Teresa de Jesús*.) 2nd ed., Madrid, 1942.

(48) *Cautelas, avisos, sentencias y poesías*. Ed. P. Silverio de Santa Teresa, C.D. Burgos, 1933. (Text follows that of No. 30.)

(49) *Instrucción y cautelas que ha menester traer siempre delante de sí el que quisiere ser verdadero religioso y llegar en breve a mucha perfección*. Barcelona, 1908.

(50) *Máximas*. Segovia, 1924.

(51) *(Suma espiritual) . . . Avisos y sentencias*, etc. Burgos, 1904. (See No. 176.)

CÁNTICO ESPIRITUAL

(52) *Declaración de las Canciones que tratan del ejercicio de amor entre el alma y el esposo Cristo, en la cual se tocan, y declaran, algunos puntos y efectos de oración*. Por el V. P. Fray Juan de la Cruz, etc. Brussels, Godefredo Schoevarts, 1627.

(53) *Cántico espiritual entre el alma y Cristo su Esposo, en que se declaran varios y tiernos afectos de oración y contemplación, en la interior comunicación con Dios*. Por el V. P. Fray Juan de la Cruz. Madrid, 1629.

(54) *Cántico espiritual*. Paris, Michaud, n.d. (?1912).

(55) *Cántico espiritual entre el alma y Cristo su esposo*. Madrid, Biblioteca Corona, 1916.

(56) (SPANISH AND GERMAN TEXTS) *Cántico Espiritual*. Munich, 1924.

(57) *Cántico Espiritual (El), según el MS. de las Madres Carmelitas de Jaén.* Ed. y notas de M. Martínez, Burgos. Madrid, 1924 ('Clásicos Castellanos.'). 2nd ed., 1936.

(58) *Cántico Espiritual y Poesías de San Juan de la Cruz, según el códice de Sanlúcar de Barrameda.* Ed. y notas del P. Silverio de Santa Teresa, C.D. Burgos, 1928, 2 vols.

(59) (SPANISH AND FRENCH TEXTS) *Cantique Spirituel, Le.* Notes historiques. Texte critique. Version française, par Dom Ph. Chevallier. Paris, Bruges, 1930. (See review in *B. Hisp.,* 1931, XXXIII, 164–70.) 2nd ed., Paris, Bruges, 1933.

(60) *Cántico espiritual.* Buenos Aires, 1942. (Coleccion 'Los Místicos.')

(61) *Cantique spirituel, Le Texte définitif du.* Ed. Philippe Chevallier, O.S.B. Solesmes, 1951. (Spanish text and commentary.)

LLAMA DE AMOR VIVA

(62) *Llama de amor viva.* Ed. PP. CC. DD. de Segovia (P. Valentín de San José, C.D.). Segovia, 1930.

NOCHE OSCURA

(63) *Noche escura del alma y Declaración de las canciones que encierran el camino de la perfecta unión de amor con Dios, cual se puede en esta vida, y las propiedades admirables del alma que a ella ha llegado.* Por el Venerable P. F. Juan de la Cruz. Barcelona, 1619.

POESÍAS

(64) 'Canciones místicas.' In M. J. Quintana: *Poesías selectas castellanas,* Vol. I, 1830, pp. 265–73. ('Noche oscura' and 'Cántico espiritual' only.)

(65) *Poesías de San Juan de la Cruz y de Santa Teresa de Jesús (Todas las), recogidas y publicadas por W. Storck.* Münster, 1854.

(66) *Poesías.* (In Biblioteca Universal, Tomo V, with poems by Luis de León.) Madrid, 1873.

(67) *Poesías de San Juan de la Cruz.* Ed. Ángel María de Santa Teresa, C.D. Burgos, 1904.

(68) *Poesías.* Recopilación y prólogo del P. Gerardo de San Juan de la Cruz. Madrid, 1921. ('Letras españolas.')

(69) (SPANISH AND FRENCH TEXTS) *Poèmes mystiques de Saint Jean de la Croix (Les).* Ed. par un Frère des Ecoles Chrétiennes. Paris, 1922.

(70) *Poesías escogidas.* Madrid, 1927. (Biblioteca Alma, Vol. III.)

(71) *Poesías, etc.* Segovia, PP. Carmelitas Descalzos, 1929.

(72) *Poesías.* Ed. E. Allison Peers. Liverpool, 1933.

(73) *Poesías completas, versos comentados, avisos y sentencias, cartas.* Ed., prólogo y notas de Pedro Salinas. Madrid, 1936. (Contains the complete poems, selections from the prose commentaries to the *Cántico espiritual* and *Llama de amor viva,* and selected maxims and letters. Text follows that of No. 30.)

(74) *Poesías completas.* Ed. Luis Guarner. Valencia, 1941.

(75) *Obra poética seguida de fragmentos de sus Declaraciones.* Prólogo de M. Manent. Barcelona, 1942.

(76) *Poesías completas de San Juan de la Cruz.* Prólogo y revisión de A. Valbuena Prat. Barcelona, 1942.

(77) *Poesías.* Ed. de gran lujo. Barcelona, 1943. (Limited edition, with illustrations.)

(78) *Poesías.* Buenos Aires, 1943.

(79) *Poesías completas y otras páginas.* Selección, estudio y notas por José Manuel Blecua. Zaragoza, 1946. (Clásicos Ebro.)

(80) (SPANISH AND ENGLISH TEXTS) *Poems of Saint John of the Cross.* With English translations by E. Allison Peers. London, 1947.

(81) (SPANISH AND FRENCH TEXTS) *Trois poèmes majeurs de Saint Jean de la Croix.* Ed. P. Darmangeat. Paris, 1947.

(82) (SPANISH AND FRENCH TEXTS) *Poèmes mystiques.* Texte espagnol et version française de Benoît Lavaud. Neuchâtel, 1948.

(83) (SPANISH AND ENGLISH TEXTS) *The Poems of St. John of the Cross.* The Spanish text with a translation by Roy Campbell. London, 1951.

(See also No. 511.)

IV. SELECTED TRANSLATIONS INTO ENGLISH
(See also Nos. 80, 83)

(84) *The Complete Works of St. John of the Cross.* Translated from the original Spanish by D. Lewis. Edited by the Oblate Fathers of S. Charles. With a preface by Cardinal Wiseman. London, 1864, 2 vols. (2nd ed., with biographical introduction, 1889.)

(According to P. Benno a S. Joseph (*Eph. C.,* 1947, I, 190–1), a similar edition was published in 1891, which he has seen and described. It is not in the British Museum. Presumably it was a reprint of the above.)

(85) *Complete Works of St. John of the Cross, Doctor of the Church.* Translated from the critical edition of P. Silverio de Santa Teresa, C.D., by E. Allison Peers. London, 1934–35, 3 vols.

(86) *Ascent of Mount Carmel.* Translated by David Lewis. With corrections, and a prefatory essay on the development of mysticism in the Carmelite

Order, by Benedict Zimmermann. London, 1906. (Other editions: London, 1914; London, 1918; London, 1922; London, 1928.)

(**87**) *Dark Night of the Soul.* Translated by Gabriela Cunninghame-Graham. London, 1905. (2nd ed., London, 1922.)

(**88**) *Dark Night of the Soul.* Translated by David Lewis. With corrections, and introductory essay by Benedict Zimmermann. London, 1908. (Other editions: London, 1916 (revised); London, 1924 (revised 'conformably to the best critical Spanish edition'); London, 1936.

(**89**) *Instructions and precautions of St. John of the Cross, preceded by a short sketch of his life and followed by some spiritual letters to the nuns of his Order, etc.* Wheeling, W. Virginia, 1918.

(**90**) *Living Flame of Love. Letters, Poems and Minor Writings.* Translated by David Lewis. With an essay by Cardinal Wiseman, and additions and an introduction by Benedict Zimmermann. London, 1912. (Other editions: London, 1919; London, 1934.)

(**91**) *Poems of St. John of the Cross.* Text and translation by E. Allison Peers. (See No. 80.)

(**92**) *Poems of St. John of the Cross, The.* Text and translation by Roy Campbell. (See No. 83.)

(**93**) *Song of the Soul.* Translated by John O'Connor. Abergavenny, 1927.

(**94**) *Spiritual Canticle of the Soul.* Translated by David Lewis. With corrections and an introduction by Benedict Zimmermann. London, 1909. (Another edition: London, 1919.)

V. SELECTED TRANSLATIONS INTO FRENCH
(See also Nos. 35, 37, 59, 69, 81, 82)

(**95**) *Œuvres spirituelles pour acheminer les âmes à la parfaite union avec Dieu*, traduites d'espagnol en français par M. R. Gaultier. Paris, 1621.

(**96**) *Œuvres spirituelles . . . Nouvellement revues par le R. P. Cyprien de la Nativité de la Vierge.* Paris, 1641, 2 vols. (No. 122 is a reprint of this text.)

(**97**) *Œuvres spirituelles . . .* traduites par Cyprien de la Nativité. Augmentées d'un traité théologique de l'âme avec Dieu par L. de Sainte Thérèse, et d'un éclaircissement des phrases de la théologie mystique du P. Jean de la Croix par Nicolas de Jésus-Marie. Paris, 1665. (See No. 96.)

(**98**) *Œuvres du bienheureux Jean de la Croix.* Traduction nouvelle par le père Jean Maillard, S.J. Paris, 1694. (Reprinted: Paris, 1695.)

(**99**) *Œuvres spirituelles.* Nouvelle édition augmentée des Lettres du P. Berthier sur la doctrine spirituelle de Saint Jean de la Croix, etc. Avignon, 1828, 3 vols. (Other editions: Avignon, 1834; Paris, 1846; Paris, 1849; Paris, 1862; Paris, 1864.)

(**100**) *Œuvres complètes* (Vol. III, Paris, 1845, pp. 363–760, of *Œuvres très-complètes de Sainte Thérèse . . . suivies . . . des œuvres complètes de . . . Saint Jean de la Croix, etc.* Paris, 1840–45, 4 vols.) (The translation is that of Jean Maillard.)

(**101**) *Œuvres spirituelles. . . . Traduites par le Père Maillard.* Paris, 1864.

(**102**) *Œuvres complètes (Les) et la vie de Saint Jean de la Croix, premier Carme déchaussé et directeur de sainte Thérèse. Par Mgr. Gilly, évêque de Nîmes.* Paris, 1866–94, 4 vols.

(**103**) *Œuvres de Saint Jean de la Croix.* Traduites par Charles-Marie du Sacré Cœur, C.D. Toulouse, 1876.

(**104**) *Vie (par le P. Jérome de S. Joseph) et Œuvres spirituelles de l'admirable docteur mystique le bienheureux père Saint Jean de la Croix.* Traduction nouvelle, faite sur l'édition de Séville, 1702, publiée par les soins des Carmélites de Paris. Paris, Poitiers, 1876, 4 vols. (2nd ed., Paris, Poitiers, 1890 ; 3rd ed., Paris, Poitiers, 1892–4 ; 4th ed., Paris, Poitiers, 1903 ; 5th ed., Paris, Poitiers, 1910 ; 6th ed., Paris, 1922 ; 7th ed., Tours, 1928 ; 8th ed., Tours, 1936.)

(**105**) *Œuvres spirituelles de St. Jean de la Croix.* Trad. H(ector) Hoornaert. Lille, Desclée de Brouwer, 1915–18, 3 vols. (The title-page of each volume begins with the title of the individual work, the general title following it.) (2nd ed., Lille, 1922–3, 4 vols ; 3rd ed., Bruges, Paris, 1927–8, 3 vols., with general title at head of title-page.)

(**106**) *Œuvres spirituelles.* Trad. P. Grégoire de S. Joseph, C.D. Monte Carlo, 1932–45, 7 vols. (2nd ed., Paris, 1947.)

(**107**) *Œuvres de saint Jean de la Croix, Docteur de l'Eglise et Père du Carmel réformé.* Trad. nouvelle par la mère Marie du Saint-Sacrement, C.D. Bar-le-Duc, 1933–7, 4 vols.

(**108**) *Œuvres spirituelles du bienheureux père Jean de la Croix, premier Carme déchaussé . . .* et coadjuteur de la sainte mère Thérèse de Jésus. Traduites d'espagnol en français por le R. P. Cyprien de la Nativité de la Vierge, C.D. Ed. nouvelle par le P. Lucien-Marie de S. Joseph, C.D. Bruges, Desclée de Brouwer, 1942, 2 vols. (Uses P. Silverio's critical ed. in the revision.) 2nd ed., Bruges, 1947. 3rd ed., Paris, 1949.

(**109**) *(Œuvres.) La Montée du Carmel. La Nuit obscure et la Vive Flamme d'amour.* Trad. H(ector) Hoornaert. Ed. revue et complétée. Buenos Aires, Montreal, 1944, 3 vols.

(**110**) *Avis et maximes sur la vie spirituelle. . . .* Trad. publiée par les soins des Carmélites d'Aire sur l'Adour. Tarbes, 1895.

(**111**) *Avis, sentences et maximes.* Trad. Dom Philippe Chevallier. Paris, Bruges, 1933. (See No. 127.)

(112) *Canciones, nouvellement traduits par René-Louis Doyon, avec une étude sur la poésie de l'amour mystique.* Paris, 1920.

(113) *Cantique d'amour divin entre Jésus-Christ et l'âme dévote.* Composé en espagnol par le B. Père Jean de la Croix, etc. Traduit par M. René Gaultier, Conseiller d'Etat. Paris, Taupinart, 1622.

(114) *Cantique spirituel (Le) et la Vive Flamme d'amour.* Trad. nouvelle faite sur l'édition de Séville, 1702. Ed. augmentée des lettres du P. Berthier sur la doctrine spirituelle de Saint Jean de la Croix et d'une analyse de ses œuvres en deux sermons, par Mgr. Landriot. Paris, 1875, 2 vols.

(115) *Cantique spirituel de St. Jean de la Croix (Le).* Ed. Dom Ph. Chevallier. (See No. 61.)

(116) *Cantique spirituel (Le), ode d'amour divin entre Jésus-Christ et l'âme dévote,* trad. et présenté par Jean Descola. Paris, n.d. (1932).

(117) *Cantique spirituel.* Traduction du texte espagnol. Bruges, Desclée de Brouwer, 1933. (Republication of part of No. 61.)

(118) *Cantique d'amour divin entre Jésus-Christ et l'âme dévote.* Paris, Eds. du Raisin (1944).

(119) *Cantique spirituel.* Chansons entre l'âme et l'époux. Traduction de Rolland Simon. Algiers, 1945.

(120) *Cantique spirituel entre l'âme et Jésus-Christ son époux, composé par S. Jean de la Croix.* Traduit par le R. P. Cyprien. Paris, 1947.

(121) *Cantique spirituel.* Texte du MS. de Jaén. Traduit par G. Lévis-Mano. Paris, 1947.

(122) *Cantiques spirituels de Saint Jean de la Croix.* Nouvellement revus et corrigés sur l'original, par le R. P. Cyprien de la Nativité de la Vierge, et traduits en vers français par le même. Paris, 1917.

(123) *Cantiques spirituels.* Avec la traduction en vers français du R. P. Cyprien de la Nativité de la Sainte Vierge, recueillis et présentés par Rafael Tasis. Paris, 1946.

(124) *Maximes spirituelles.* Paris, 1850. (Appended to F. de Lamennais' translation of Louis de Blois: *Le Guide spirituel, ou le Miroir des âmes religieuses.* Reprinted, Paris, 1860. New ed., Paris, 1927.)

(125) *Maximes et avis spirituels, etc.* Traduits pour la première fois en français sur l'édition espagnole de 1702 par un père de la Compagnie de Jésus. Paris, 1875.

(126) *Maximes et avis spirituels.* Publié par les Carmélites de Paris. Paris-Poitiers, 1895.

(127) *Mots d'ordre de Saint Jean de la Croix, docteur de l'Eglise (Les),* ed. Dom Ph. Chevallier. Paris, 1933. (Described as complementary to the *Avis, sentences et maximes* (Bruges, 1933). 'Offre logiquement groupées

toutes les pensées venues des cahiers, des réponses et des billets du Saint.'
(2nd ed., Solesmes, 1947.)

(**128**) *Poèmes mystiques de St. Jean de la Croix.* Prologue de Maurice
Brillant. Paris, 1922.

(**129**) *Poèmes mystiques* (*Les*) . . . trad. Lucien-Marie de Saint-Joseph,
C.D. Paris, Bruges, 1943.

(**130**) *Trois Poèmes de Saint Jean de la Croix adaptés en français.* Trad.
Armand Godoy. Paris, 1937.

(**131**) *Précautions spirituelles, avis et maximes.* Trad. P. Grégoire de
Saint-Joseph, C.D. Rennes, 1919.

(**132**) *Vive Flamme d'amour* (*La*) *et la déclaration des cantiques qui
traitent de la plus intime union et transformation de l'âme en Dieu.* . . . Trad.
par le R. P. Cyprien de la Nativité de la Vierge. Paris, Chevallier, 1641.

VI. SELECTED TRANSLATIONS INTO GERMAN
(See also No. 56)

(**133**) *Die Sämmtliche Schriften des heiligen Johann vom Kreuz.* Prague,
1697.

(**134**) *Die Sämmtliche Schriften, etc.* herausgegeben von Gallus Schwab.
Sulzbach, 1830, 2 vols.

(**135**) *Leben und Werke des heiligen Johannes vom Kreuz, ersten Barfüssen-
Karmeliten zum ersten Male vollständig aus dem spanischen.* Originale übersetzt von Peter Lechner. Regensburg, 1858-9, 3 vols.

(**136**) *Des heiligen Johannes vom Kreuz Sämmtliche Werke.* Neue deutsche
Ausgabe von P. Aloysius ab Immac. Conceptione und P. Ambrosius a S.
Theresia, C.D. München, 1924-9, 5 vols.

(**137**) *Aufstieg zum Berge Karmel, oder der Weg zur vollkommenen
Vereinigung der Seele mit Gott.* (Trans. L. Stocker, O.S.B.) Graz, 1891.

(**138**) *Sämmtliche Gedichte des heiligen Johannes vom Kreuz und der heiligen
Theresia von Jesus.* Gesämmelt und übersetzt von W. Storck. Münster, 1854.

VII. SELECTED TRANSLATIONS INTO ITALIAN

(**139**) *Opere spirituali che conducono l'anima alla perfetta unione con Dio,*
composte dal ven. P. F. Giovanni della Croce, etc. Tradotte dalla spagnuola
in questa nostra lingua italiana dal P. Fr. Alessandro di S. Francesco,
Definitore Generale della Congregatione d'Italia. Rome, 1627.

(140) *Opere spirituali* . . ., *nelle quali s'insegna la vera strada, che conduce anima alla perfetta e soave unione con Dio, etc.* Venice, 1643.

(141) *Opere spirituali, etc.* Venice, 1658. (Reproduces No. 140.)

(142) *Opere spirituali, etc.* Venice, 1680.

(143) *Opere spirituali, etc.* Venice, 1682. (Reproduces No. 140.)

(144) *Opere spirituali, etc.* Venice, 1683. (Reproduces No. 140.)

(145) *Opere spirituali, etc.* Venice, Poletti, 1707. (Reproduces No. 140.)

(146) *Opere spirituali, etc.* Venice, 1729. (Reproduces No. 140).

(147) *Opere di San Giovanni della Croce, etc.* Trad. P. Marcos di San Francesco. Venice, 1747.

(148) *Opere di San Giovanni della Croce, etc.* Venice, Angelo Geremia, 1748, 2 vols. (Reproduces No. 147.)

(149) *Opere di San Giovanni della Croce.* Trad. dal P. F. Marco de San Francesco. Genoa, 1858–9, 2 vols.

(150) *Opere spirituali.* Trad. Paolo de Töth. Milan, 1912, 2 vols. (2nd ed., Acquapendente, 1927, 2 vols.)

(151) *Opere tradotte a cura dell'ordine dei carmelitani scalzi* (dal R. P. Nazareno dell'Addolorata, C.D.). Milan, 1927–9, 3 vols. (2nd ed., Rome, 1940, 1 vol.)

(152) *Opere complete di S. Giovanni della Croce.* Trad. R. P. Nazareno dell' Addolorata, O.C.D. Firenze, 1948.

(153) *Aforismi e poesie.* Testo spagnuolo con introduzione e versione a cura di Giuseppe de Luca. Brescia, 1933.

(154) *Avvisi e massime.* Milan, 1924.

(155) *Cantico spirituale (Il)*, a cura di Guido Manacorda. Florence, n.d (?1946).

(156) *Cantico spirituale*, a cura del R. P. Nazareno dell' Addolorata. Torino, 1947.

(157) *Cantico spirituale.* Introduzione e versione a cura del P. Gabriele di S. Maria Maddalena. Florence, 1948.

(158) *Cautele, avvisi e massime spirituali.* Rome, 1940.

(159) (*Disciplina claustrale* . . . *con.* . . . .) *Cautele e sentenze spirituali.* Firenze, 1893.

VIII. SELECTED TRANSLATIONS INTO DUTCH OR FLEMISH

(160) *Geestelijke Werken, etc.* Antwerp, 1637.

(161) *Verhole Wercken van den Salighenende verlichten heeræn Johannes van den Cruyce*, overgheset door Servatius van den H. Petrus, O. Carm. Ghent, 1693–1703.

(**162**) *Geestelijke Werken van den H. Johannes a Cruce* ... uit her spaansch vertaald ... door P. Fr. Henricus a S. Familia, C.D. Ghent, 1916–19, 3 vols. (2nd ed., Brussels, 1931–2, 3 vols.)

(**163**) *Geestelijke raadgevingen en leerspreuken van den heiligen Johannes a Cruce* ... vertaald door P. Fr. Henricus a S. Familia, C.D. Ghent, 1917. (From the translation in No. 162.)

(**164**) *Voorzorgen tegen wereld, duivel, vleesch, door sint Jan van het Kruis.* Ghent, 1924. Trans. by P. Coelestinus a S. Joseph, C.D.

IX. SELECTED TRANSLATIONS INTO PORTUGUESE

(**165**) *Obras de são João da Cruz, doutor da Igreja,* trad. pelas carmelitas descalças do ... Rio de Janeiro. Rio de Janeiro, 1946.

(**166**) *Obras espirituais.* (Trans. by the Discalced Carmelite nuns of Fatima.) Fatima, 1947.

(**167**) 'Avisos e sentenças espirituais. Quatro avisos a um religioso para alcançar a perfeição. Cautelas.' In *Doutrina de Sta. Teresa e S. João da Cruz.* Oporto, 1943.

X. SELECTED TRANSLATIONS INTO LATIN

(**168**) *Opera mystica.* .... ex Hispanico idiomate in latinum nunc primum translata per R. P. Fr. Andrean a Jesu, Polonum eiusdem Ordinis Religiosum. Elucidatio phrasium mysticæ theologiæ auctore Nicolas a Jesu Maria. Cologne, 1622. (Reprinted Cologne, 1639 ; Cologne, 1710.)

XI. NOTE ON TRANSLATIONS INTO OTHER LANGUAGES

Other versions given by P. Benno (No. 2) are :

(**169**) Bohemian (22 : I, 198).

(**170**) Hungarian (38 : I, 370 ; 88–90 : III, 421–2).

(**171**) Polish (46–7 : I, 380–1 ; 69 : III, 416 ; 97 : III, 423–4).

XII. ABRIDGEMENTS, ANTHOLOGIES, ETC.

SPANISH

(**172**) *Antología literaria.* Salamanca, 1927.

(**173**) *Antología de San Juan de la Cruz.* Ed. J. Domínguez Berrueta. Madrid, 1941.

(174) *Páginas escogidas.* Ed. F. Gutiérrez. Barcelona, 1940.

(175) *Selección y nota de Ramón Sijé.* In *C. y R.*, 1933, No. 9, pp. 86–100.

(176) *Suma espiritual de San Juan de la Cruz.* Ed. Ángel María de Santa Teresa. Burgos, 1904.

ENGLISH

(177) *The Mystical Doctrine of St. John of the Cross.* An Abridgement made by C(harles) H(enrion). London, 1934. (Reprinted, 1946.) (Trans. from No. 181.)

(178) *A Retreat under the guidance of St. John of the Cross.* By M. Mary of the Blessed Sacrament. London, 1930.

(179) *The Spirit of St. John of the Cross.* Consisting of his maxims, sayings and spiritual advice on various subjects. Trans. Canon Dalton. London, 1863.

(180) *Thoughts of St. John of the Cross for every day.* Compiled by Kathleen Mary Balfe. London, 1924.

FRENCH

(181) *Abrégé de toute la doctrine mystique de Saint Jean de la Croix.* Ed. Charles Henrion. St. Maximin (Var), 1925.

(182) *Abrégé de la doctrine de Saint Jean de la Croix.* Ed. Charles Henrion. Paris, 1947.

(183) *Selections.* In M. de Wasmer: *Huit mystiques espagnols.* Paris, 1940.

(184) *Sentences spirituelles choisies des œuvres de . . . sainte Thérèse de Jésus et du . . . Père Saint Jean de la Croix.* Par le R. P. Ange de S. Joseph. N.p., 1846.

ITALIAN

(185) *Compendio della mistica teologia di S. Giovanni della Croce.* Opera inedita di un padre Carmelitano scalzo. Siena, 1886.

XIII. COMMENTARIES

(186) *Anon: *Life of Saint John of the Cross of the Order of Our Lady o Mount Carmel.* London, 1873.

(187) *Anon: *Vita del mistico dottore S. Giovanni dalla Croce, primo Carmelitano Scalzo.* Treviso, 1837.

(188) *Anon: *Vida de San Juan de la Cruz,* por un socio del Apostolado. Madrid, 1913. (Contains also some poems.)

(189) A.: 'En torno al misticismo poético de San Juan de la Cruz.' In *Basílica Teresiana,* 1916, pp. 228–47.

(190) A.M.: 'San Juan en Francia.' In *Esc.*, 1942, IX, 366–8.

(191) *A. de la P.: *San Juan de la Cruz.* Madrid, 1928. (Contains also the poems.)

(192) Adolfo de la Madre de Dios, C.D.: 'Estado y acto de contemplación. La contemplación adquirida según San Juan de la Cruz.' In *R. Esp.*, 1949, VIII, 96–126.

(193) Alaejos, Abilio, C.M.F.: 'Hispanidad de la mística de San Juan de la Cruz.' In *R. Esp.*, 1948, VII, 281–324.

(194) *Alessandro di Santa Teresa, C.D.: *Terzo Centenario di San Giovanni della Croce. . . . Vita dello stesso.* Rome, 1891.

(195) †Alonso, Dámaso: 'La caza de amor es de altanería. Sobre los precedentes de una poesía de San Juan de la Cruz.' In *Bol. R. Ac. Esp.*, 1947, XXVI, 63–79.

(196) †Alonso, Dámaso: 'El misterio técnico en la poesía de San Juan de la Cruz.' In *Poesía española.* Madrid, 1950, pp. 227–321.

(197) †Alonso, Dámaso: *La Poesía de San Juan de la Cruz (Desde esta ladera).* Madrid, 1942. 2nd éd., Madrid, 1946. (Contains also the text of the poems and selections from the prose commentaries upon them. See reviews in *B. Hisp.*, 1944, XLVI, 95–101; *R.F.H.*, 1943, V, 377–95.)

(198) †Alonso, Dámaso: 'Sobre el texto "Aunque es de noche."' In *R.F.E.*, 1942, XXVI, 490–4.

(199) Alonso, Joaquín María, C.M.F.: 'Biblia y mística en San Juan de la Cruz.' In *R. Esp.*, 1950, IX, 330–57.

(200) Alphonse de la Mère des Douleurs: *Pratique de l'oraison mentale et de la perfection d'après Sainte Térèse et Saint Jean de la Croix.* Paris, Lille, Bruges, 1909–14, 8 vols. (Sp. trans. of Vol. I, Barcelona, 1911.)

(201) Anastasio María de San José, C.D.: *Somma di mistica teologia* compilata cogli scritti del Santo tradotti dallo spagnuolo ed annotati da Fr., etc. Parma, 1904.

(202) Andrés de Jesús María, C.D.: *Compendio de la vida de San Juan de la Cruz.* First published in the edition of 1703 (No. 19), and in P. Gerardo's edition (No. 27), I, 7–154.

(203) Aniceto del D. Redentor, C.D.: 'La inhabitación de la Santísima Trinidad en el alma, según San Juan de la Cruz.' In *R. Esp.*, 1943, II, 37–49.

(204) Antonio, Nicolás: In *Bibliotheca Hispana.* Roma, 1672, I, 517–18.

(205) Arbiol, Antonio: *Mística fundamental de Cristo Señor nuestro.* Explicado por el glorioso y beato Padre San Juan de la Cruz. Zaragoza, 1723. (Other editions: Barcelona, 1748; Madrid, 1761.)

(**206**) Ariceta, Lucas, O.F.M.: 'El hábito infuso de contemplación en San Juan de la Cruz.' In *V.V.*, 1949, VII, 501–51.

(**207**) Arintero, Juan G., O.P.: 'Influencia de Santo Tomás en la mística de San Juan de la Cruz y Santa Teresa.' In *V. Sob.*, 1924, VIII, 21–42.

(**208**) Asín Palacios, Miguel: 'Un precurso hispano-musulmán de San Juan de la Cruz.' (Ibn 'Abbād de Ronda, 1332–89.) In *A.A.*, 1933, I, 7–79. Also in *Huellas de Islam*, Madrid, 1941, pp. 235–304, and in *Obras escogidas*, Madrid, 1946, I, 243–326. (Fr. tr. in *E.C.*, 1932, XVII (i), 113–67.)

(**209**) Athanase de l'Immaculée-Conception: *Traité des épines de l'esprit de Saint Jean de la Croix*. Trad. de l'espagnol. Paris, 1896.

(**210**) Azorín (José Martínez Ruiz): 'Un sensitivo.' In *Los Valores literarios*. Madrid, 1913, pp. 55–9.

(**211**) **Baruzi, Jean: *Saint Jean de la Croix et le problème de l'expérience mystique*. Paris, 1924. (2nd ed., with fresh preface, Paris, 1931.)

(**212**) Baruzi, Jean: 'Le problème des citations scripturaires en langue latine dans l'œuvre de Saint Jean de la Croix.' In *B. Hisp.*, 1922, XXIV, 18–40.

(**213**) Baruzi, Jean: 'Saint Jean de la Croix.' In M. Gorce and R. Mortier: *Histoire générale des religions*. Paris, 1947.

(**214**) †Bataillon, Marcel: 'Sur la genèse poétique du *Cantique spirituel* de Saint Jean de la Croix.' In *Estudios de filología e historia literaria* (Homenaje al R. P. Félix Restrepo, S.J.). Bogotá, 1950, pp. 251–63.

(**215**) †Bayo, Marcial José: 'Aspecto lírico de San Juan de la Cruz.' In *R. Esp.*, 1942, I, 300–8.

(**216**) Behn, J.: 'San Juan de la Cruz.' In *Stimmen der Zeit*, 1938, CXXXIII, 216–36.

(**217**) Bell, A. F. G.: 'Saint John of the Cross, a portrait.' In *B.S.S.*, 1930, VII, 13–21.

(**218**) Benjamin de la Trinité, C.D.: 'Education sanjuaniste.' In *Sanjuanística* (No. 509), pp. 305–66.

(**219**) ††Bernadot, M-V., O.P.: 'Le texte authentique du *Cantique spirituel* de Saint Jean de la Croix.' In *V. Sp.*, 1923, Supplément, VII, 154–61.

(**220**) Bernhardt, W.: 'Der Urquell, ein Gesang des hl. Johannes vom Kreuze.' In *Z.A.M.*, 1933, VIII, 322–9.

(**221**) Besse, Ludovic de: *Eclaircissements sur les œuvres mystiques de Saint Jean de la Croix*. Paris, 1893. (Reprinted, Paris, 1928.)

(**222**) †Blecua, José Manuel: 'Notas sobre poemas del siglo XVI: I, Los antecedentes del poema del "Pastorcico" de San Juan de la Cruz.' In *R.F.E.*, 1949, XXXIII, 378–80.

(223) Boine, G.: 'S. Giovanni della Croce.' In *Ferita non chiussa*, Modena, 1939, pp. 209–62.

(224) Bonnard, M.: 'Les influences réciproques entre Sainte Thérèse de Jésus et Saint Jean de la Croix.' In *B. Hisp.*, 1935, XXXVII, 129–48.

(225) Boudon, H. M.: *La Vive flamme d'amour dans le Bienheureux Jean de la Croix, etc.* Paris, 1778.

(226) Brice (*pseud.*) (Rev. Fr.), C.P.: *Spirit in darkness: a companion to Book Two of the 'Ascent of Mount Carmel.'* New York, 1946.

(227) Brice (*pseud.*) (Rev. Fr.), C.P.: *Teresa, John and Thérèse: a family portrait of three great Carmelites.* New York, 1946.

(228) **Bruno de Jésus-Marie, C.D.: *Saint Jean de la Croix* (with preface by J. Maritain). Paris, 1929. (2nd ed., 1932.) (English translation: (229) *Saint John of the Cross.* London, 1932. Spanish translations: (230) Madrid, 1943; (231) Buenos Aires, 1947.)

(232) Bruno de Jésus-Marie, C.D.: 'Du Mont Carmel aux mystiques français.' In *E. C.*, 1947, XXVI, 363–77.

(233) Bruno de Jésus-Marie, C.D.: *L'Espagne mystique. Sainte Thérèse d'Ávila, Saint Jean de la Croix, Le Greco.* Paris, 1946. (234) English ed. *Three Mystics.* New York, 1949.

(235) *Bruno de Jésus-Marie, C.D.: 'La mort de Saint Jean de la Croix.' In *V. Sp.*, 1930, XXI, 160–9.

(236) Bruno de Jésus-Marie, C.D.: 'Saint Jean de la Croix, maître de sagesse.' In *Eph. C.*, 1949, III, 427–41.

(237) *Bruno de Jésus-Marie, C.D.: *Vie d'amour de Saint Jean de la Croix.* Paris, 1936. (An abridgement of the larger Life.)

(238) Butler, Cuthbert, O.S.B.: *Western Mysticism.* London, 1922.

(239) Cabassut, A., O.S.B.: 'L'impeccabilité dans l'état d'union transformante, d'après Saint Jean de la Croix.' In *V. Sp.*, 1930, XXI., Supplément, pp. 57–75.

(240) Calaber (Abbé): *La Terminologie de Saint Jean de la Croix dans la 'Montée du Carmel' et la 'Nuit obscure.'* Suivie d'un abrégé de ces deux ouvrages. Paris, Angers, 1904.

(241) †Campo, Agustín: 'Poesía y estilo de la *Noche oscura.*' In *Revista de Ideas estéticas.* Madrid, 1943, III, 33–58.

(242) Capánaga de San Agustín, Victorino, O.S.A.: 'La interioridad católica de San Juan de la Cruz.' In *R. Esp.*, 1946, V, 206–21.

(243) Capánaga de San Agustín, Victorino, O.S.A.: *San Juan de la Cruz. Valor psicológico de su doctrina.* Madrid, 1950.

(244) Carbonero y Sol, León: *Homenaje a San Juan de la Cruz . . . en el tercer centenario de su (muerte).* Madrid, 1891.

(245) Carmona Nenclares, F.: 'San Francisco de Asís y San Juan de la Cruz.' In *Est. F.*, 1931, XXV, 313–37.

(**246**) †Carré-Chataignier, A.: *Essai sur les images dans l'œuvre de Saint Jean de la Croix.* Thèmes directeurs et classes d'images. Paris, 1923.

(**247**) Castro Albarrán, A.: *El Espiritualismo en la mística de San Juan de la Cruz.* Salamanca, 1929.

(**248**) *Certamen literario en honor de San Juan de la Cruz.* Segovia, 1892.

(**249**) **Chandebois, Enrique (Henri): *La lección de Fray Juan de la Cruz.* Trad. esp. de G. Fernández Shaw. Barcelona, 1942.

(**250**) †Chandebois, Henri: 'Lexique, grammaire et style chez St. Jean de la Croix. (Notes d'un traducteur.)' In *Eph. C.,* 1949, III, 543–7.

(**251**) **Chandebois, Henri: *Portrait de Saint Jean de la Croix. La Flûte de roseau.* Paris, 1947.

(**252**) Chandebois, Henri: *Propos de lumière et d'amour de Saint Jean de la Croix.* Paris, 1947. (On the *Maxims.*)

(**253**) ††Chevallier, Philippe, O.S.B.: 'Le Cantique spirituel de Saint Jean de la Croix a-t-il été interpolé?' In *B. Hisp.,* 1922, XXIV, 307–42.

(**254**) ††Chevallier, Philippe, O.S.B.: 'Le Cantique spirituel interpolé.' In *V. Sp.* Suppléments, 1926, XIV, 109–62; 1927, XV, 69–109; 1930, XXII, 1–11, 80–9; 1931, XXIII, 29–50.

(**255**) ††Chevallier, Philippe: 'Deux textes du *Cantique spirituel.*' In *V. Sp.,* 1932, XXV, 274–86.

(**256**) Chevallier, Philippe, O.S.B.: 'La doctrine ascétique de Saint Jean de la Croix.' In *V. Sp.,* 1927, XVI, 175–96.

(**257**) Chevallier, Philippe, O.S.B.: 'La vie du "Cantique spirituel" et l'esprit scientifique.' In *E.C.,* 1938, XXIII, (i), 215–36.

(**258**) Chevallier, Philippe, O.S.B.: 'La pauvreté de l'âme qui chante le "Cantique spirituel."' In *E.C.,* 1939, XXIV (i), 226–47.

(**259**) Chevallier, Philippe, O.S.B.: *Saint Jean de la Croix. Le texte définitif du Cantique spirituel.* Solesmes, 1951. (The same work as No. 61.)

(**260**) Claire de Jésús, C.D.: *Saint Jean de la Croix. Sa Liturgie commentée.* Ghent, 1926.

(**261**) Claire de Jésús, C.D.: *Saint Jean de la Croix intime, ou Etude sur le cœur de Saint Jean de la Croix.* Ghent, 1923.

(**262**) Claudio de Jesús Crucificado, C.D.: 'Concepto de la vida espiritual, perfección cristiana y sus estados según San Juan de la Cruz.' In *M.C.,* 1942, XLIII, 355–80.

(**263**) Claudio de Jesús Crucificado, C.D.: 'Influencia y desarrollo de la autoridad y doctrina de San Juan de la Cruz hasta las controversias antiquietistas.' In *Homenaje de devoción y amor a San Juan de la Cruz.* Segovia, 1928 (No. 365), pp. 240–80.

(264) Claudio de Jesús Crucificado, C.D.: *Normas de perfección cristiana y religiosa.* Burgos, 1933.

(265) Clovis de Provins, O.F.M. Cap.: 'Les nuits mystiques d'après S. Jean de la Croix.' In *Est. F.*, 1933, XLV, 154-68, 411-38, 530-52.

(266) *Collet, M.: *La Vie de Saint Jean de la Croix.* Turin, Paris, 1769. Reprinted (267) Paris, 1796 ; (268) Paris, 1837.

(269) *Compendium vitæ, virtutum et miraculorum, necnon actorum in causa Canonizationis B. Joannis a Cruce.* Rome, 1726.

(270) †'Corona poética de San Juan de la Cruz.' In *Esc.*, 1942, IX, 339-50. (Includes: Manuel Machado: 'Juan de la Cruz, poeta'; Gerardo Diego: 'Palabras proféticas'; Adriano del Valle: 'Poesía incompleta'; Leopoldo Panero: 'Las manos ciegas'; Luis Felipe Vivanco: 'Éxtasis de la luz'; Alfonso Moreno: 'Las dos ciudades'; Luis Rosales: 'El bosque de miel.')

(271) Correa de la Cerda, Fernando: *Historia da vida*, etc. Lisbon, 1680.

(272) Corte, Manuel de: 'L'expérience mystique chez Plotin et Saint Jean de la Croix.' In *E. C.*, 1935, XX (ii), 164-215.

(273) Corts Grau, José: 'San Juan de la Cruz y la personalidad humana.' In *Esc.*, 1942, IX, 187-203.

(274) Cossío, José María de: 'Rasgos renacentistas y populares en el "Cántico espiritual" de San Juan de la Cruz.' In *Esc.*, 1942, IX, 205-28.

(275) *Crisógono de Jesús Sacramentado, C.D.: 'Biografía inédita.' In *Vida y obras, etc.* No. 34, pp. 1-488. (2nd ed., pp. 1-509.)

(276) Crisógono de Jesús Sacramentado, C.D.: 'Introducción al estudio de la filosofía en el misticismo de San Juan de la Cruz.' In *R. Esp.*, 1942, I (b), 231-40.

(277) Crisógono de Jesús Sacramentado, C.D.: 'Relaciones de la mística con la filosofía y la estética en la doctrina de San Juan de la Cruz.' In *Esc.*, 1942, IX, 353-65.

(278) Crisógono de Jesús Sacramentado, C.D.: *San Juan de la Cruz. El Hombre, el Doctor, el Poeta.* Barcelona, Labor, 1935.

(279) Crisógono de Jesús Sacramentado, C.D.: *San Juan de la Cruz, su obra científica y su obra literaria.* Madrid, 1929, 2 vols.

(280) Crisógono de Jesús Sacramentado, C.D.: 'San Juan de la Cruz, místico completo.' In *Ecclesia*, 1942, XXXI, 13-22.

(281) Crisógono de Jesús Sacramentado, C.D.: 'Valor del sistema místico de San Juan de la Cruz.' In *Revista de la Universidad de Oviedo*, 1942.

(282) Crisógono de Jesús Sacramentado, C.D.: *Vida de San Juan de la Cruz.* San Sebastián, 1941.

(283) Dalbiez, R.: 'Une récente interprétation de Saint Jean de la Croix.' In *V. Sp.*, 1929, XIX, Supplément, 1–28, 49–79.

(284) Delacroix, Henri: In *Etudes d'Histoire et de Psychologie du mysticisme*. Paris, 1908, pp. 248–62.

(285) Delgado, P., O.S.A.: 'Las claridades de la *Noche oscura*.' In *Homenaje de devoción y amor a San Juan de la Cruz*. Segovia, 1928, pp. 121–36.

(286) *Demimuid, Maurice: *Saint Jean de la Croix*, 1542–91. Paris, 1916. (Collection 'Les Saints.')

(287) †Diego, Gerardo: 'Música y ritmo en la poesía de San Juan de la Cruz.' In *Esc.*, 1942, IX, 163–86.

(288) †Diego, Gerardo: 'San Juan de la Cruz, poeta lírico.' In *Esc.*, 1942, IX, 13–22.

(289) Diego de Jesús, C.D.: 'Apuntamientos . . . para más fácil inteligencia de . . . las Obras espirituales de . . . San Juan de la Cruz.' Published in *Obras*, Alcalá, 1618 (No. 8), pp. 615–82, in many other of the early editions and in Gerardo: *Obras, etc.* (No. 27), III, 465–502.

(290) Domínguez Berrueta, Juan: *Un Cántico a lo divino. Vida y pensamiento de San Juan de la Cruz*. Barcelona, 1930.

(291) Domínguez Berrueta, Juan: *Santa Teresa de Jesús y San Juan de la Cruz. Bocetos psicológicos*. Madrid, 1915.

(292) †Domínguez Berrueta, M.: *El Misticismo de San Juan de la Cruz en sus poesías. Ensayo de crítica literaria*. Madrid, 1894.

(293) †Domínguez Berrueta, M.: *El Misticismo en la poesía. Estudio de crítica literaria. San Juan de la Cruz*. Salamanca, 1897.

(294) Doroteo de la Sagrada Familia, C.D.: *Diálogos místicos sobre la 'Subida del Monte Carmelo.'* Barcelona, 1942.

(295) Doroteo de la Sagrada Familia, C.D.: *Escuela de oración mental según el método de San Juan de la Cruz y de los grandes místicos de la Orden Carmelitana*. San Sebastián, 1943.

(296) Doroteo de la Sagrada Familia, C.D.: *Guía espiritual de la contemplación adquirida según la doctrina del Místico Doctor de la Iglesia San Juan de la Cruz y sus discípulos*. Madrid, 1942.

(297) Dosithée de Saint Alexis, C.D.: 'Dissertazione sopra la Theologia Mistica in cui si fa vedere, che la doctrina di S. Giovanni della Croce è opposta a quella de' falsi Mistici, etc.' In *Opere*, Venice, 1748 (No. 148), pp. 541–74.

(298) *Dosithée de Saint Alexis, C.D.: *Vie de Saint Jean de la Croix*, Paris, 1727, 2 vols. (Later editions: (299) Paris, 1782 ; (300) Paris, Tours, 1872, 3 vols.)

(301) Edmondo-M. della Passione, C.D.: 'Il "Monte" de S. Giovanni della Croce.' In *Sanjuanistica* (No. 509), pp. 3–24.

(302) Eduardo de Santa Teresita, C.D.: *Un Nuevo Autógrafo de San Juan de la Cruz.* Vitoria, 1948.

(303) Efrén de la Madre de Dios, C.D.: 'La esperanza según San Juan de la Cruz.' In *R. Esp.*, 1942, I (b), 255–81.

(304) **Efrén de la Madre de Dios, C.D.: *San Juan de la Cruz y el misterio de la Santísima Trinidad en la vida espiritual.* Zaragoza, 1947. (Has a bibliography on St. John of the Cross, St. Teresa and the literature of the Trinity.)

(305) Efrén de la Madre de Dios, C.D.: 'En torno a mi obra sobre San Juan de la Cruz.' In *M.C.*, 1948, XLIX, 43–55.

(306) Elorduy, E., S.J.: 'El concepto de teología mística en San Juan de la Cruz.' In *Man.*, 1942, XIV, 226–46.

(307) †Emeterio de Jesús María, C.D.: 'Ensayo sobre la lírica carmelitana hasta el siglo XIX.' In *M.C.*, 1949, LIII, 5–173.

(308) Emeterio de Jesús María, C.D.: 'La poesía sanjuanista en la evolución del sentimiento cósmico.' In *M.C.*, 1942, XLIII, 477–520.

(309) †Emeterio de Jesús María, C.D.: *Las Raíces de la poesía sanjuanista y Dámaso Alonso.* Burgos, 1950. (Chiefly a critique of No. 197.)

(310) †Encinas y López de Espinosa, R.: *La Poesía de San Juan de la Cruz.* Valencia, 1905.

(311) Enrico di S. Teresa, O.C:D.: 'Il contenuto oggettivo della conoscenza ascetico-mistica di Dio.' In *Sanjuanistica* (No. 509), pp. 259–302.

(312) Enrique del Sagrado Corazón, C.D.: 'Influencias de San Juan de la Cruz en el P. Fr. Miguel de la Fuente, Carmelita Observante.' In *R. Esp.*, 1949, VIII, 346–60.

(313) Enrique del Sagrado Corazón, C.D.: 'Jan van Ruusbroec, como fuente de influencia posible en San Juan de la Cruz.' In *R. Esp.*, 1950, IX, 288–309, 422–42.

(314) *Escorial (Esc.).* The issue for November 1942 is a 'número extraordinario dedicado a San Juan de la Cruz.' The most important articles in this issue are listed separately.

(315) Esparza, Eladio: 'Un códice sanjuanista en Pamplona.' In *Príncipe de Viana*, Pamplona, 1943, pp. 106–9.

(316) ††Eugenio de San José, C.D.: 'Algunos reparos a un artículo de Fr. Ph. Chevallier, O.S.B., sobre el *Cántico espiritual* de San Juan de la Cruz.' In *M.S.T.*, 1927, V, 103–13, 142–6.

(317) ††Eugenio de San José, C.D.: 'El *Cántico espiritual.* Ed. novísima por Dom Chevallier, O.S.B.' In *M.C.*, 1931, XXXV, 301–9, 353–61, 387–412.

(**318**) Eugenio de San José, C.D.: 'El Desposorio espiritual en la mística de San Juan de la Cruz.' In *M.S.T.*, 1929, VII, 309–20.

(**319**) ††Eugenio de San José, C.D.: 'La nueva edición del *Cántico espiritual* por Dom Chevallier.' In *A.C.*, 1931, I, 105–23.

(**320**) Eugenio de San José (Eugenius a Sto. Joseph), C.D.: 'Pro Doctoratu Sancti Joannis a Cruce.' In *Analecta Ordinis Carmelitarum Excalceatorum*, 1926–9.

(**321**) Eulogio de San José, C.D.: *Doctorado de Santa Teresa de Jesús y de San Juan de la Cruz*. Córdoba, 1896.

(**322**) *Evaristo de la Virgen del Carmen, C.D.: *El Nuevo Doctor de la Iglesia San Juan de la Cruz*. Toledo, 1927.

(**323**) Ezequiel del Sagrado Corazón de Jesús, C.D.: *Método de oración y contemplación según San Juan de la Cruz*. Bilbao, 1935.

(**324**) Felicia, Sister: In *Seven Spanish Mystics*, Cambridge, Mass., U.S.A., 1947, pp. 23–33.

(**325**) *Felipe Maria de San Pablo, C.D.: *Vita del B. Giovanni della Croce*, etc. . . . Rome, Naples, 1675.

(**326**) *Francisco di S. Geltrude: *Vita della serafica vergine S. Teresa di Gesù*. . . . Con un cenno della vita di S. Giovanni della Croce. Con l'aggiunta del Sentenziario spirituale. Terza ed. Naples, 1855.

(**327**) **Francisco de Santa María, C.D.: *Reforma de los Descalzos, etc.*, Vol. II. Madrid, 1655. (Various other editions and translations. Contains thirty-seven chapters on St. John of the Cross.)

(**328**) **François de Sainte Marie, C.D.: *Initiation à Saint Jean de la Croix*. Paris, 1944. (2nd ed., Paris, 1946.)

(**329**) Frost, Bede: *Saint John of the Cross*. . . . *An introduction to his philosophy, theology and spirituality*. London, 1937.

(**330**) Gabriel of Bl. Denis, C.D.: 'The three signs of initial contemplation. A comparative study.' (Based on St. John of the Cross.) In *Eph. C.*, 1949, III, 97–129.

(**331**) ††Gabriel de Sainte Marie-Madeleine, C.D.: 'Autour du "Cantique spirituel."' In *E.C.*, 1934, XIX (i), pp. 197–210.

(**332**) Gabriel de Sainte Marie-Madeleine, C.D.: 'Le Cantique de l'amour.' In *Sanjuanistica* (No. 509), pp. 87–132.

(**333**) Gabriel de Sainte Marie-Madeleine, C.D.: 'Le problème de la contemplation unitive.' In *Eph. C.*, 1947, I, 5–53, 245–77.

(**334**) Gabriel de Sainte Marie-Madeleine, C.D.: *San Giovanni della Croce, dottore dell' amore divino*. Florence, 1937. (2nd ed. (**335**), Florence, 1943. English tr. (**336**), London, 1940. See also No. 338. French tr. (**337**), Paris, 1947.

(338) Gabriel de Sainte Marie-Madeleine, C.D.: *St. John of the Cross, Doctor of divine love and contemplation.* Cork, 1946. Combines No. 336 and *Acquired Contemplation,* a translation of *La Contemplazione acquisita.* Florence, 1938.

(339) Gallego Morell, Antonio: *San Juan de la Cruz en Granada.* Granada, 1946. (Reprinted from *B.U.G.,* 1946, XVII, 145–57.)

(340) García, Félix, O.S.A.: 'San Juan de la Cruz y la Biblia.' In *R. Esp.,* 1942, I (b), 372–88.

(341) †García Blanco, M.: 'San Juan de la Cruz y el lenguaje del Siglo XVI.' In *Castilla,* Valladolid, 1941–3, II, 139–59.

(342) García Morente, Manuel: 'La idea filosófica de la personalidad de San Juan de la Cruz.' In *M.C.,* 1943, XLIV, 135–43, 193–9.

(343) García Rodríguez, Buenaventura, C.M.F.: 'Taulero y San Juan de la Cruz.' In *V. Sob.,* 1949, I, 349–62, 423–36.

(344) Garrigou-Lagrange, R., O.P.: *L'Amour de Dieu et la croix de Jésus.* Etude de théologie mystique . . . d'après . . . les principes de saint Thomas d'Aquin et la doctrine de Saint Jean de la Croix. Juvisy (1929).

(345) Garrigou-Lagrange, R., O.P.: 'Les grandes épreuves des saints et la doctrine de S. Jean de la Croix.' In *V. Sp.,* 1942, julio-agosto.

(346) Garrigou-Lagrange, R., O.P.: *Perfection chrétienne et contemplation selon S. Thomas d'Aquin et S. Jean de la Croix.* Saint-Maximin, 1924. (English tr. (347), Saint-Louis, London, 1937.)

(348) *Gaspar de la Anunciación, C.D.: *Representación de la vida del B. P. Fr. Juan de la Cruz.* Brussels, 1677.

(349) Genevois, Marie-Albert, O.P.: 'Introduction à Saint Jean de la Croix.' In *V. Sp.,* 1947 (ii), LXXVII, 426–45.

(350) Gerardo de San Juan de la Cruz, C.D.: *Los Autógrafos, etc.* (See No. 36.)

(351) Gesualdo dello Spirito Santo, O.C.: *San Juan de la Cruz.* Bilbao, 1947. (Translated from the 2nd Italian ed.)

(352) ††Giovanni di Gesù Maria, C.D.: 'Il "Cantico spirituale" e la critica.' In *R.V.S.,* 1949, III, 207–13. (On the work of Jean Krynen, No. 406.)

(353) Gómez, A. del P.: 'San Juan de la Cruz, director espiritual.' In *R. Esp.,* 1942, I, 389–410.

(354) González López, Luis: *San Juan de la Cruz en la provincia de Jaén.* Jaén, 1951.

(355) Gorostiaga, Juan: 'San Juan de la Cruz escriturista.' In *Cuba y San Juan de la Cruz,* Habana, 1944, pp. 21–36.

(356) Gotti, Cardenal, C.D.: *Compendio della vita de San Giovanni della Croce.* Savona, 1857.

(357) Groult, Pierre: 'St. Jean de la Croix, Docteur de l'Eglise. Sa doctrine mystique.' In *N.R.T.*, 1927, LIX, 561–91.

(358) †Guillén, José: 'La poética en el *Cántico espiritual.*' In *R. Esp.*, 1942, I, 438–47.

(359) Hapig, B.: 'Die Theologie der Mystik nach dem Hl. Joannes vom Kreuz.' In *Scholastik*, 1938, XII, 481–97.

(360) Hausherr, Irénée, S.J.: 'Les Orientaux connaissent-ils les "nuits" de Saint Jean de la Croix?' In *Orientalia Christiana Periodica*, Rome, 1946, XII, 5–46.

(361) *Heriz, Paschasius, C.D.: *Saint John of the Cross.* Washington, 1919. See also No. 426.

(362) Hernández, E., S.J.: 'La contemplación adquirida según San Juan de la Cruz.' In *Man.*, 1942, XV, 202–25 ; 1947, XIX, 97–121.

(363) Hernández, E., S.J.: 'El número de los místicos según San Juan de la Cruz.' In *R.F.*, 1930, XC, 41–50, 341–60.

(364) †Herrero García, M.: *San Juan de la Cruz. Ensayo literario.* Madrid, 1942.

(365) *Homenaje de devoción y amor a San Juan de la Cruz.* Crónica y conferencias místicas del segundo centenario de su canonización celebrada en Segovia en octubre de 1927. Segovia, 1928.

(366) *Homenaje de Úbeda a su compatrono San Juan de la Cruz.* Úbeda, 1935.

(367) Hoornaert, R.: *L'Ame ardente de Saint Jean de la Croix.* Bruges, 1928. 2nd ed. (368), Tournai, 1947. (English translation by A. Thorold (369): *The Burning Soul of St. John of the Cross.* London, 1931.)

(370) †Hornedo, R. M. de, S.J.: 'Boscán y la célebre Estrofa XI del "Cántico espiritual."' In *R.F.*, 1943, CXXVIII, 270–86.

(371) †Hornedo, R. M. de, S.J.: 'Fisonomía poética de San Juan de la Cruz.' In *R.F.*, 1943, CXXVII, 320–42.

(372) †Hornedo, R. M. de, S.J.: 'El Humanismo de San Juan de la Cruz.' In *R.F.*, 1944, CXXIX, 133–50.

(373) †Hornedo, R. M. de, S.J.: 'El Renacimiento y San Juan de la Cruz.' In *R.F.*, 1943, CXXVII, 513–28.

(374) Huijben, J., O.S.B.: 'Ruysbroeck et Saint Jean de la Croix.' In *E.C.*, 1932, XVII, (ii), 232–47.

(375) *Hutchings, W. H.: *Exterior and Interior Life of St. John of the Cross.* Oxford, 1881.

(376) Iriarte, M., S.J.: 'Una gran preocupación de S. Juan de la Cruz: La formación de los directores espirituales.' In *Man.*, 1942, LII, 302–18.

(377) J. S.: 'La noche activa del sentido.' In *Man.*, 1942, LII, 270–301.

(378) Jacques de Jésus, C.D.: 'Notes sur les livres de Saint Jean de la Croix.' In *E.C.*, 1911, I, 352–7; 1912, II, 264–9.

(379) *Jerónimo de San José, C.D.: *Compendio de la vida de . . . San Juan de la Cruz*. Barcelona, 1891.

(380) *Jerónimo de San José, C.D.: *Dibujo del venerable varón Fray Juan de la Cruz*. Madrid, 1629. (Another ed., Barcelona, 1883.)

(381) *Jerónimo de San José, C.D.: *Historia del Venerable Padre Fr. Juan de la Cruz, Primer Descalzo Carmelita, etc*. Madrid, 1641.

(382) Jesús García, Buenaventura de: 'La meditación en San Juan de la Cruz.' In *V. Sob.*, 1943, XLIV, 276–86.

(383) Jesús García, Buenaventura de: 'La mística en San Juan de la Cruz.' In *V. Sob.*, 1944, XLV, 99–112, 275–83.

(384) Jesús García, Buenaventura de: 'Para quiénes escribió S. Juan de la Cruz?' In *V. Sob.*, 1943, XLIII, 340–53.

(385) Jiménez Duque, Baldomero: 'Una interpretación moderna de San Juan de la Cruz.' In *R.E.T.*, 1944, IV, 315–44.

(386) Jiménez (Duque), Baldomero: 'Noches del alma. La Noche obscura de la fe.' In *R. Esp.*, 1945, IV, 151–68.

(387) Jiménez Duque, Baldomero: 'La pedagogía de San Juan de la Cruz.' In *R. Esp.*, 1942, I (b), 309–31.

(388) Jiménez Duque, Baldomero: 'La perfección cristiana y San Juan de la Cruz.' In *R.E.T.*, 1949, IX, 413–44.

(389) Jiménez Duque, Baldomero: 'Problemas místicos en torno a la figura de San Juan de la Cruz.' In *R.E.T.*, 1940–1, I, 963–83.

(390) †José de Jesús Crucificado, C.D.: 'Aspecto cultural de S. Juan de la Cruz.' In *Sanjuanistica* (No. 509), pp. 369–409.

(391) José de Jesús Crucificado, C.D.: 'El P. Tomás de Jesús, escritor místico.' In *Eph. C.*, 1949, III, 305–49.

(392) José de Jesús María (Quiroga), C.D.: 'Don que tuvo San Juan de la Cruz para guiar las almas a Dios.' In Gerardo (No. 27), III, 511–70.

(393) *José de Jesús María (Quiroga), C.D.: *Historia de la vida y virtudes del Venerable Padre Fray Juan de la Cruz, etc*. Brussels, 1628. (Reprinted, Brussels, 1632. 2nd ed., Málaga, 1717. 3rd ed., Burgos, 1927. Italian trans., Brescia, 1638. Reproduced by Gerardo (No. 27), III, 511–76.

(394) José de Jesús Nazareno, O.SS.T.: 'Conocimiento y amor en la contemplación según San Juan de la Cruz.' In *R. Esp.*, 1949, VIII, 72–95.

(395) *José de Santa Teresa, C.D.: *Resunta de la Vida de . . . San Juan de la Cruz, etc*. Madrid, 1675. (Reprinted (396), Murcia, 1779.)

(397) *José de Santa Teresa, C.D.: 'Vida de Nuestro Padre San Juan de la Cruz, etc.' In *Flores del Carmelo*, Madrid, 1678, pp. 557–607.

(398) Juan de la Asunción, C.D.: *Pastor de Monte Carmelo, San Juan de la Cruz . . . en sus Cautelas religiosas*. Madrid, 1729.

(399) Juan de Jesús María, C.D.: 'El díptico Subida-Noche.' In *San-juanística* (No. 509), pp. 27–83.

(400) Juan de Jesús María, C.D.: '¿Las anotaciones del Códice de San-lúcar son de S. Juan de la Cruz?' In *Eph. C.*, 1947, I, 154–62. Cf. I, 313–66.

(401) ††Juan de Jesús María, C.D.: 'El "Cántico espiritual" de San Juan de la Cruz y "Amores de Dios y el alma" de A. Antolínez. (Con ocasión de la obra de M. Jean Krynen.)' In *Eph. C.*, 1949, III, 443–542; 1950, IV, 3–70.

(A briefer study of Krynen's work, by the same author, will be found in *M.C.*, 1949, LIII, 13–37.)

(402) Juan José de la I(nmaculada) C(oncepción), C.D.: 'Acción hipostática del Espíritu Santo en la santificación del alma.' In *R. Esp.*, 1945, XVII, 440–5.

(403) Juan José de la I. C., C.D.: *La Psicología de San Juan de la Cruz*. Santiago de Chile, 1944.

(404) Juan José de la Inmaculada Concepción, C.D.: *El Último Grado del amor*. Ensayo sobre la 'Llama de Amor Viva' de San Juan de la Cruz. Santiago de Chile, 1941.

(405) ††Krynen, Jean: 'Un aspect nouveau des annotations marginales du borrador du "Cantique spirituel" de Saint Jean de la Croix.' In *B. Hisp.*, 1947, XLIX, 332–421.

(406) ††Krynen, Jean: *Le Cantique Spirituel de Saint Jean de la Croix commenté et refondu au XVIIᵉ siècle*. Salamanca, 1948.

(See reviews in *B. Hisp.*, 1949, LI, 188–94 (cf. 1951, LIII, 393–412); *R. Esp.*, 1950, IX, 88–98; *V. Sp.*, 1948 (ii), LXXIX, 526–33. Also Nos. 352, 401.)

(407) Labourdette, M., O.P.: 'La foi théologale et la connaissance mystique d'après Saint Jean de la Croix.' In *Revue Thomiste*, 1936–7, XIX, 593–629; XX, 16–57, 191–229.

(408) Lajeunie, E., O.P.: 'Les "feux" du "Cantique spirituel."' In *V. Sp.*, 1932, XXVI, 276–85.

(409) Landrieux, Mgr.: *Sur les pas de Saint Jean de la Croix dans le désert et dans la nuit*. Paris, 1924. (Several times reprinted.)

(410) Lebreton, J.: 'La nuit obscure d'après Saint Jean de la Croix. Les sources et caractère de sa doctrine.' In *R.A.M.*, 1928, IX, 3–24.

(411) Ledrus, M., S.J.: 'Sur quelques pages inédites de Saint Jean de la Croix.' In *Gregorianum*, Rome, 1949, XXX, 347–92; 1951, XXXII, 247–80.

(412) *Lewis, David: *Life of St. John of the Cross*. London, 1897.

(413) †Lida, María Rosa: 'Transmisión y recreación de temas greco-latinos en la poesía lírica española.' In *R.F.H.*, 1939, I, 20–79, *passim*.

(414) *Light on Mount Carmel*. A guide to the works of St. John of the Cross. London, 1926. (An English version of No. 221.)

(415) Longpré, A.: 'La théologie mystique de Saint Jean de la Croix.' In *Revue de l'Université d'Ottawa*, VI, 91–8.

(416) López Estrada, F.: 'Una posible fuente de San Juan de la Cruz.' In *R.F.E.*, 1944, XXVIII, 473–7.

(417) ††Louis de la Trinité, C.D.: 'Autour du "Cantique spirituel."' In *E.C.*, 1931, XVI (ii), 1–42 ; 1932, XVII (i), 168–76, XVII (ii), 125–56.

(418) Louis de la Trinité, C.D.: *Le Docteur mystique.* Paris, 1927.

(419) Louis de la Trinité, C.D.: 'L'obscure nuit du feu d'amour.' In *E.C.*, 1938, XXIII (ii), 7–32.

(420) Louis de la Trinité, C.D.: 'Le procès de béatification de S. Jean de la Croix et le "Cantique Spirituel."' In *Revue des sciences philosophiques et théologiques*, 1927, 39–50, 165–87.

(421) Louis de la Trinité, C.D.: 'Saint Jean de la Croix, directeur d'âmes.' In *V. Sp.*, 1927, XVI, 302–9.

(422) Louis de la Trinité, C.D.: 'Sèche et obscure nuit de contemplation.' In *E.C.*, 1937, XXII (ii), 206–29.

(423) Lucas de San José, C.D.: *La Santidad en el claustro, o Cautelas del seráfico doctor místico San Juan de la Cruz*, comentadas por——. Barcelona, 1920. 2nd ed. (424), Barcelona, 1923. 3rd ed., enlarged (425), Tarragona-Barcelona, 1929. 4th ed. (426), Barcelona, 1946. English trans. by Paschasius Heriz, C.D., as *Holiness in the Cloister*, Chicago, 1920.

(427) Lucien-Marie de St. Joseph: 'A la recherche d'une structure essentielle de la nuit de l'esprit.' In *E.C.*, 1939, XXIII (ii), 254–81.

(428) Lucinio del S.S., C.D.: 'La doctrina del cuerpo místico en San Juan de la Cruz.' In *R. Esp.*, 1944, III, 181–211 ; 1945, IV, 77–104, 251–75.

(429) Luis de San José, C.D.: *Concordancias de las obras y escritos de . . . San Juan de la Cruz.* Burgos, 1948.

(430) ††Macdonald, Inez Isabel: 'The two versions of the *Cántico Espiritual.*' In *Modern Language Review*, Cambridge, 1930, XXV, 165–84.

(431) *Magdalena del Espíritu Santo: 'Relación de la vida de San Juan de la Cruz (1630).' In Silverio: *Obras* (No. 30), I, 323–39.

(432) Maldonado, Francisco: 'La estrofa 24 del "Cántico espiritual."' In *Revista de ideas estéticas*, Madrid, 1943, III, 3–16, 19–49.

(433) Marasso, Arturo: 'Aspectos del lirismo de San Juan de la Cruz.' In *Boletín de la Academia Argentina de Letras*, 1945, XIV, 582 ff.

(434) Marcelo del Niño Jesús, C.D.: 'Las noches sanjuanistas y las *Moradas* teresianas.' In *M.C.*, 1942, XLIII, 288–354.

(435) Marcelo del Niño Jesús, C.D.: *El Tomismo de San Juan de la Cruz.* Burgos, 1930.

(436) *Marcos di San Francesco, C.D.: 'Vita di San Giovanni della Croce.' In *Opere*, etc., Venice, 1747, 1748 (Nos. 147–8, above. Previously published in Flemish, Louvain, 1675).

(437) **Marie-Eugène de l'Enfant Jésus: 'Saint Jean de la Croix, vie extérieure. Son portrait.' In *V. Sp.*, 1927, XVI, 141–74.

(438) Marie-Joseph du Sacré-Cœur, C.D.: 'La contemplation acquise est enseignée à leurs disciples par saint Jean de la Croix et sainte Thérèse: nouveaux témoignages qui le confirment.' In *E.C.*, 1925, X, 109–32.

(439) Marie-Joseph du Sacré-Cœur, C.D.: 'Saint Jean de la Croix mieux connu.' In *E.C.*, 1926, XI, 1–27.

(440) Maritain, Jacques: 'Saint Jean de la Croix, praticien de la contemplation.' In *E.C.*, 1931, XVI, 61–109.

(441) Maritain, Jacques: 'Sur "l'égalité d'amour" entre Dieu et l'âme d'après Saint Jean de la Croix.' In *E.C.*, 1932, XVII (i), 1–18.

(442) Martín de Jesús María: *San Juan de la Cruz al alcance de todos*. Barcelona, 1943.

(443) Mascall, E. L.: *A Guide to Mount Carmel*. London, 1939. (An analytical summary of *Subida*.)

(444) *Maza, Josefina de la, and Jiménez Salas, María: *Vida de San Juan de la Cruz*. Madrid, 1947. (A popular biography.)

(445) Melo, Antonio, O.F.M.: 'San Juan de la Cruz escriturista.' In *Cuba y San Juan de la Cruz*, Habana, 1944, pp. 3–20.

(446) Menéndez-Reigada, Ignacio G., O.P.: 'Santo Tomás y San Juan de la Cruz.' In *V. Sob.*, 1942, XLII, 161–9 ; XLIII, 13–21 ; 105–14.

(447) Mesnard, Pierre: 'La place de Saint Jean de la Croix dans la tradition mystique.' In *Bulletin de l'Enseignement public du Maroc*, 1942, pp. 191–233.

(448) Milner, Max: *Poésie et vie mystique chez Saint Jean de la Croix*. Paris, 1951.

(449) ††Mogenet, Henri, S.J.: 'L'ordre primitif du Cántico.' In *R.A.M.*, 1937, XVIII, 280–91.

(450) Montalvillo, Juan José: 'Concepto general de contemplación en San Juan de la Cruz.' In *R. Esp.*, 1949, VIII, 49–71.

(451) *Monte Carmelo, El (M.C.)*. Número extraordinario con motivo del IV Centenario natal de San Juan de la Cruz, 1942, XLIII, pp. 251–541. (Contains eight special articles on St. John of the Cross.)

(452) Muñoz, Jesús, S.J.: 'Los apetitos según San Juan de la Cruz.' In *Man.*, 1942, LII, 328–39.

(453) Muñoz Garnica, M.: *San Juan de la Cruz*. Ensayo histórico. Jaén, 1875. (Ital. trans. by A. Piantoni, Rome, 1881.)

(454) Muñoz Sendino, José: 'Los Cantares del Rey Salomón en versos líricos por Fray Luis de León. Paralelo con el *Cántico espiritual* de San Juan de la Cruz.' In *Bol. R. Ac. Esp.*, 1948, XXVIII, 411–61; 1949, XXIX, 31–98.

(455) Nicolás de Jesús María, C.D.: *Phrasium mysticae theologiae V. P. F. Joannis a Cruce . . . Elucidatio.* Alcalá, 1631. (Various translations.)

(456) Nigg, Walter: In *Grosse Heilige*, Zürich, 1946, pp. 221–63.

(457) Nilo di S. Brocardo, C.D.: 'Demonio e vita spirituale.' In *Sanjuanistica* (No. 509), pp. 135–223.

(458) *Notre Dame, Liverpool, Sisters of: *Life of Saint John of the Cross, Mystical Doctor.* London, 1927.

(459) Olphe-Galliard, Michel, S.J.: 'Le Père Surin et Saint Jean de la Croix.' In *Mélanges . . . F. Cavallera,* Toulouse, 1948, pp. 425–39.

(460) †Orozco Díaz, E.: 'Mística y plástica. (Comentarios a un dibujo de San Juan de la Cruz.)' In *B.U.G.,* 1939, XI, 273–95.

(461) †Orozco Díaz, E.: 'La palabra, espíritu y materia en la poesía de San Juan de la Cruz.' In *Esc.,* 1942, IX, 315–35.

(462) Ors, Eugenio d': 'Estilo del pensamiento de San Juan de la Cruz.' In *R. Esp.,* 1942, I (b), 241–54. (See also *Estilos del pensar,* Madrid, 1945.)

(463) Ortega, A. A., C.M.F.: *Razón teológica y experiencia mística. En torno a la mística de San Juan de la Cruz.* Madrid, 1944.

(464) Osende, V., O.P.: 'La mística en las poesías de San Juan de la Cruz.' In *V. Sob.,* 1948, XLIX, 341–7.

(465) *Otilio del Niño Jesús, C.D.: *San Juan de la Cruz.* Barcelona, 1940.

(466) **Pascal du Saint-Sacrement, C.D.: 'Saint Jean de la Croix.' In *Dictionnaire de Théologie Catholique,* Paris, 1924, VIII, cols. 767–87. (Contains a bibliography.)

(467) Pastorale, A.: 'Sul *no saber* de S. Giovanni della Croce.' In *Scritti di varia filosofia,* Milan, 1940, pp. 323–44.

(468) Pastourel, Dom: 'La doctrine de Saint Jean de la Croix.' In *Annales de Philosophie chrétienne,* Octobre, 1912.

(469) *Pedro de San Andrés: *Vie de Saint Jean de la Croix.* Aix, 1675.

(470) Peers, E. Allison: 'Saint John of the Cross.' In *The Mystics of Spain,* London, 1951, pp. 23–4, and (extracts) 112–30.

(471) Peers, E. Allison: *Saint John of the Cross.* Cambridge, 1932.

(472) Peers, E. Allison: 'St. John of the Cross.' In *St. John of the Cross, and other lectures and addresses,* London, 1946, pp. 11–53. Reprints No. 471, with additions.

(473) Peers, E. Allison: 'St. John of the Cross. An appreciation for his fourth centenary.' In *The Tablet,* July 4, 1942.

(474) Peers, E. Allison: 'St. John of the Cross.' In *Spanish Mysticism, a Preliminary Survey*, London, 1924, pp. 26–29, and (extracts) 108–18, 220–8. Similar material in *El Misticismo español*, Buenos Aires, 1947, pp. 40–3, 143–54.

(475) **Peers, E. Allison: *Spirit of Flame*. A study of St. John of the Cross. London, 1943. (Reprinted New York, 1944.)

(476) Peers, E. Allison: 'St. John of the Cross.' In *Studies of the Spanish Mystics*. London, 1927, Vol. I, pp. 227–88 ; 2nd ed., 1951, pp. 183–233.

(477) Peers, E. Allison: 'Two Newly Discovered Letters by St. John of the Cross.' In *The Tablet*, October 13, 1951.

(478) Peers, E. Allison: 'The Source and the Technique of San Juan de la Cruz's poem "Un pastorcico. . . ."' In *H.R.*, 1952, XX.

(479) Peers, E. Allison: 'The Alleged Debts of San Juan de la Cruz to Boscán and Garcilaso de la Vega.' In *H.R.*, 1953, XX.

(480) Peláez, J.: *Autógrafos del místico doctor San Juan de la Cruz*. Toledo, 1913.

(481) †Pérez Embid, Florentino: 'El tema del aire en la poesía de San Juan de la Cruz.' In *Arbor*, Madrid, 1946, V, 93–8.

(482) Piazza, A. G. (and others): *San Giovanni della Croce : L'uomo, la dottrina, l'influsso*. Florence, 1942.

(483) Pierluigi di S. Cristina, C.D.: 'Il ritorno alla giustizia originale.' In *Sanjuanistica* (No. 509), pp. 227–55.

(484) Pino Gómez, Aurelio del: 'San Juan de la Cruz, director espiritual.' In *R. Esp.*, 1942, IV, 389–410.

(485) Ponce de León, Basilio, O.S.A.: see Vol. III, pp. 355–404, above.

(486) Poulain, A.: *La Mystique de Saint Jean de la Croix*. Paris, 1892.

(487) Probst, J. H.: 'El Beato Ramón Lull y San Juan de la Cruz.' In *Est. F.*, 1951, LII, 200–4.

(488) Razi, Ernest: *St. Jean de la Croix. Sa vie et sa doctrine*. Paris, 1861.

(489) Remuñán García, M.: 'San Juan de la Cruz, figura de la raza.' In *Boletín de la Universidad de Santiago de Compostela*, 1942, 27–43.

(490) *Revista de Espiritualidad*. (*R. Esp.*) Julio-Diciembre, 1942. Quatercentenary number: 'A San Juan de la Cruz.' (The principal articles only are entered separately.)

(491) Reypens, L.: 'Ruusbroec en Juan de la Cruz. Hun overeenstemming omtrent het toppunt der beschouwing.' In *Ons geestelijke erf*, Antwerp, 1931, V, 143–85.

(492) Rodríguez, Conrado, O.S.A.: 'Las dos noches de San Juan de la Cruz.' In *C.D.*, 1927, CLXI.

(493) †Rodríguez, Conrado: 'La lección de Fray Luis (de León) y de San Juan de la Cruz.' In *R. y C.*, 1928, II, 544–58.

(494) Rojo, Casiano, O.S.B.: *La Oración mental según San Juan de la Cruz y Santa Teresa de Jesús*. Burgos (Silos), 1921.

(495) Román de la Inmaculada, C.D.: '¿Es quietista la contemplación enseñada por San Juan de la Cruz?' In *R. Esp.*, 1949, VIII, 127–55.

(496) Romero de Torres, E.: 'Una escritura de San Juan de la Cruz.' In *Boletín de la Real Academia de la Historia*, Madrid, 1916, XIX, 65–70.

(497) Rosenbaum, Sidonia C.: 'The revival of St. John of the Cross.' In *Modern Language Quarterly*, Seattle, 1946, VII, 145–52.

(498) *Rossell, Pedro: *Epítome de la vida de San Juan de la Cruz*. Barcelona, 1675.

(499) Rousselot, P.: In *Les Mystiques Espagnols*, Paris, 1867, pp. 379–408.

(500) Rubí, Basilio de, O.F.M. Cap.: 'Mística sanjuanista y sus relaciones en la Escuela franciscana.' In *Est. F.*, 1951, LI, 77–95.

(501) Rubio, David, O.S.A.: *San Juan de la Cruz. La Fonte*. La Habana, 1946. (Also as *La Fonte de San Juan de la Cruz y Otros Ensayos*, Madrid, 1948.)

(502) †Sabino de Jesús, C.D.: *San Juan de la Cruz y la crítica literaria*. Santiago de Chile, 1942.

(503) San José, L. de: *La Santidad en el claustro o cautelas del seráfico doctor místico San Juan de la Cruz*. Barcelona, 1920.

(504) *San Juan de la Cruz*, *Revista de*: Carmelitano-teresiana dirigida por los PP. Carmelitas Descalzos. Segovia, Vols. I–III, 1890–2 ; Córdoba, Vols. IV–V, 1893–4.

(505) †Sánchez Cantón, F. J.: '¿Cabe hablar de San Juan de la Cruz y las artes?' In *Esc.*, 1942, IX, 301–14.

(506) Sánchez Castañer, Francisco: 'La *Llama de amor viva*, cima de la mística y de la poesía del Doctor Extático.' In *Boletín de la Universidad de Santiago de Compostela*, 1942, 3–26.

(507) †Sánchez Moguel, A.: *El Lenguaje de Santa Teresa de Jesús. Juicio comparativo de sus escritos con los de San Juan de la Cruz*, etc. Madrid, 1915.

(508) Sandoval, A. de: *San Juan de la Cruz*. Madrid, n.d. (1942).

(509) *Sanjuanistica*. Studia a professoribus facultatis theologicae Ordinis Carmelitarum discalceatorum . . . edita. Rome, 1943. (The principal articles are entered separately.)

(510) Scaramelli, G. B.: *Dottrina di San Giovanni della Croce, compresa con metodo chiaro in tre trattati*. . . . *E Discernimento degli spiriti*, etc. Rome, 1946.

(511) **Sencourt, Robert: *Carmelite and Poet*. A framed portrait of St. John of the Cross. With his poems in Spanish. London, 1943.

(512) **Sepich, J. R.: *San Juan de la Cruz, místico y poeta*. Buenos Aires, 1942.

(513) Silverio de Santa Teresa, C.D.: *Historia del Carmen Descalzo en España, Portugal y America*. Vol. V: San Juan de la Cruz. Burgos, 1936.

(514) Silverio de Santa Teresa, C.D.: 'Fray Juan de la Cruz, Doctor providencial.' In *R. Esp.*, 1942, I (b), 332–71.

(515) Simeón de la Sagrada Familia, C.D.: 'La doctrina de la gracia como fundamento teológico con la doctrina sanjuanista.' In *M.C.*, 1942, XLIII, 521–41.

(516) Simeón de la Sagrada Familia, C.D.: 'Un nuevo códice manuscrito de las Obras de San Juan de la Cruz, usado y anotado por el P. Tomás de Jesús.' In *Eph. C.*, 1950, IV, 95–148.

(517) Simeón de la Sagrada Familia, C.D.: 'El principio teológico previo y fundamental de toda la obra sanjuanista.' In *R. Esp.*, 1944, III, 225–37.

(518) Simeón de la Sagrada Familia, C.D.: 'San Juan de la Cruz y el Purgatorio.' In *R. Esp.*, 1945, IV, 19–30.

(519) Sobrino, José Antonio de, S.J.: *Estudios sobre San Juan de la Cruz y nuevos textos de su obra*. Madrid, 1950. (See review in *B.H.S.*, 1951, XXVIII, 188–92.)

(520) Soler, Luis M. (ed.): *Homenaje a San Juan de la Cruz en el IV Centenario de su nacimiento*. Barcelona, 1945.

(521) *Stanislao de Santa Teresa, C.D.: *S. Giovanni della Croce*. Milan, 1926.

(522) *Summa de la vida y milagros de San Juan de la Cruz*. Antwerp, 1625.

(523) Sumner, M. O.: *St. John of the Cross and Modern Psychology*. London, 1948. (A lecture.)

(524) Surgy, P. de: 'La source (les degrés) de l'èchelle d'amour de Saint Jean de la Croix.' In *R.A.M.*, 1951, XXVII, 18–40 (source); 237–59, 327–46 (degrés).

(525) Symons, Arthur: 'The Poetry of Santa Teresa and San Juan de la Cruz.' In *Contemporary Review*, 1899, LXXV, 524–51.

(526) Taylor, A. E.: 'Saint John of the Cross and John Wesley.' In *J.T.S.*, 1945, XLVI, 30–8.

(527) *Théodore de S. Joseph, C.D.: *Vie iconologique de S. Jean de la Croix*. Courtrai, 1926.

(528) Thibon, Gustave: 'Nietzsche et Saint Jean de la Croix.' In *E.C.*, 1934, XIX (ii), 17–86.

(529) Thomas de Saint-Laurent, R. de: *Saint Jean de la Croix*. Avignon, 1926.

(530) Torró, Antonio, O.F.M.: 'La relación entre la actividad natural y la divina en la vida mística según la doctrina de San Juan de la Cruz.' In *Homenaje de devoción y amor a San Juan de la Cruz*, Segovia, 1928, pp. 213–39.

(531) *Trenor Palavicino, Leopoldo: *Juan de Yepes. Medio Fraile y Doctor de la Iglesia*. Una peregrinación por los paisajes de San Juan de la Cruz. Madrid, Valencia, 1927.

(532) Truc, G.: *Les mystiques espagnols: Sainte Thérèse et Saint Jean de la Croix*. Paris, 1921.

(533) Vaca, César, O.S.A.: 'San Juan de la Cruz y algunos aspectos del problema espiritual moderno.' In *R. Esp.*, 1942, I (b), 282–99.

(534) Valentí, José Ignacio: *Examen crítico de las obras de San Juan de la Cruz*. Madrid, 1892.

(535) Valentín de la Sagrada Familia, C.D.: 'Apuntes sobre la prosa carmelitana hasta el siglo XIX.' In *M.C.*, 1949, LIII, 3–109.

(536) Valentín de San José, C.D., and Berenguer, Isidro Albert: 'Sobre el retrato de San Juan de la Cruz.' In *R. Esp.*, 1942, I, 411–27.

(537) Vallée (R. P.), O.P.: *Saint Jean de la Croix: sa vie, sa doctrine*. Paris, Lille, 1892.

(538) Vega, Angel Custodio: 'San Juan de la Cruz y Fray Luis de León. Tres poesías inéditas.' In *C.D.*, 1944, p. 317–41.

(539) †Verschaeve, E. H. C.: *De Dichter Joannes a Cruce*. Bruges, 1926.

(540) Victor de Jesús María, C.D.: 'Un conflicto de jurisdicción.' In *Sanjuanistica* (No. 509), pp. 413–528.

(541) Victor de San José, C.D.: '¿Influencias de San Juan de la Cruz en *El Condenado por desconfiado*?' In *M.C.*, 1942, XLIII, 425–50.

(542) *Vie Spirituelle, La. (V. Sp.)* The special number for 1926, devoted to St. John of the Cross, contains several important articles, by Dom Philippe Chevallier, P. Garrigou-Lagrange, O.P., and P. Gabriel de Ste. Marie-Madeleine, C.D. Vol. LXVII, No. 1 (July–August 1942) is a quatercentenary number devoted to St. John of the Cross.

(543) Villacorta, Juan Carlos: 'San Juan de la Cruz. Al vuelo de su pensamiento y de su vida.' In *V.V.*, II, 437–42.

(544) *Villiers, Cosmas de: In *Bibliotheca carmelitana*, Orléans, 1752, Vol. I, cols. 829 ff.

(545) Vilnet, Jean: *Bible et mystique chez Saint Jean de la Croix*. Paris, 1949.

(546) *Vita Carmelitana (V. Car.)*, No. 4, November 1942, is a St. John of the Cross quatercentenary number, containing five short articles on the man and five on his work.

(547) Vossler, Karl: 'San Juan de la Cruz.' In *La Poesía de la soledad en España*, Buenos Aires, 1946, pp. 247–54. (Trans. of *Poesie der Einsamkeit in Spanien*. Munich, 1935–8, 3 vols. 2nd ed., Munich, 1941.)

(548) Waxman, S. M.: 'Three Spanish saints (St. Ignatius of Loyola, St. Teresa of Jesus, St. John of the Cross).' In *Hispania*, Stanford University, 1936, XIX, 177–90.

(549) Wenceslao del S. Sacramento, C.D.: *Fisonomía de un Doctor. Ensayo crítico.* Salamanca, 1913, 2 vols.

(550) Wessely, F.: *Johannes vom Kreuz, der Lehrer des vollkommenen Lebens.* Vienna, 1938.

(551) Wild, K.: 'Das Höchstziel des mystischen Gnadenlebens. Unter dem Gesichtspunkt der Seelenführung nach dem hl. Johannes vom Kreuz.' In *Z.A.M.*, 1933, VIII, 97–116.

(552) Wild, K.: 'Das Wesen der mystischen Beschauung nach dem hl. Johannes vom Kreuz.' In *Z.A.M.*, 1934, IX, 107–24.

(553) Winklhofer, Alois: *Die Gnadenlehre in der Mystik des hl. Johannes vom Kreuz.* Freiburg-im-Breisgau, 1936.

(554) Winklhofer, Alois: 'Die Gnadenlehre in der Mystik des hl. Johannes vom Kreuz. Eine Selbstbesprechung.' In *Z.A.M.*, 1937, XII, 72–8.

(555) Winklhofer, Alois: 'Querschnitt durch die Johannes-v-Kreuz-Literatur.' In *Z.A.M.*, 1936, XI, 153–9.

(556) Yela Utrilla, J. F.: 'San Juan de la Cruz y la aventura mística.' In *Revista de la Universidad de Madrid*, II, 94–121.

(557) Zimmerman, B., C.D.: 'The problems of the "Spiritual Canticle."' In *Dublin Review*, 1934, Vol. 194, pp. 258–66.

(558) Zöckler, O.: *Petrus von Alcantara, Theresa von Avila und Johannes vom Kreuz.* Leipzig, 1864–5.

INDICES

I. SUBJECT-INDEX TO THE WORKS OF ST. JOHN
OF THE CROSS

[*Note.*—This index and those which follow have been made by the editor of the present edition and cover the whole of the text (with the exception of the pages (II, 385–408) showing the Granada variants from the Sanlúcar Codex of the *Spiritual Canticle* and those (II, 417–25) giving in verse form the poems indexed elsewhere), together with the introductions and notes where stated. In the subject-index anything approaching exhaustiveness is of course impossible to attain within small compass, since such themes as Night, Purgation, Union, Virtues occur on many hundreds of pages. For this reason the cross-references given in italics after numerous headings should be used freely.

Readers desiring a fuller subject-index should consult Luis de San José, C.D.: *Concordancias de las obras y escritos de . . . San Juan de la Cruz* (Burgos, 1948), which can be used with this edition, since the chapter and paragraph numberings in both follow P. Silverio.]

Abandonment of the soul in the Dark Night of the Spirit (*Night, Purgation*), I, 385–6
Absence of God from the soul (*Aridity, Night, Purgation*), II, 31–7, 187–98. God is in reality never absent from the soul, I, 190
Active life (*Virtues, Works*), II, 328; III, 292
Activity and passivity(*Passivity*), I, 114, 236–7
Aloofness of the contemplative soul (*Quiet, Solitude, Tranquillity*), II, 114–15, 329–30
Ambition in religious(*Religious*), III, 289
Aminadab(*Devil*)
Anagogical acts, III, 232, 289, 290, 291
Angel, Guardian, III, 222
Angels, Good, I, 449–53; II, 263
Annihilation(*Desire, Detachment, Mortification*), I, 83 ff., 378–9, 397–8; II, 100; III, 69 ff., 161 ff., 228, 255
Apprehensions of the understanding (*Favours, Locutions, Rapture, Revelations, Visions*), I, 95–294, *passim.* Natural imaginary apprehensions, I, 103–8. Supernatural imaginary apprehensions, I, 122–9. Spiritual apprehensions, I, 173–81
Aridity(*Darkness, Detachment, Night, Purgation, Temptation, Trials*), I, 350 ff.; II, 112, 127, 281–2, 334; III, 25–6, 69, 85, 115, 160, 178, 220. Aridity no proof of God's absence from the soul, II, 32, 188; III, 257, 265. Aridity striving with love, III, 25–8, 115–18. How it may be known if aridity is the result of purgation, I, 351–6
Articles of the faith (*Faith*), I, 192–3; II, 64, 236
Artifice, III, 289
Ascetic practices, Asceticism (*Detachment, Mortification, Penance, Purgation*), I, 131, 275
Assimilation of the soul to God (*Deification, Equality, Fruition, Marriage, Participation, Transformation, Union*), I, 441
Attachment, Nature of (*Desire, Detachment*), I, 255–6. Religious must avoid attachment, III, 201–2, 250
Attentiveness to God(*Passivity, Quiet*)
Attributes, Divine (*God*), II, 163, 367; III, 54–7, 146–8
Avarice, Spiritual, I, 336–8
Awakening of God in the soul, III, 94–100, 188–93
Awareness of God, Loving (*Passivity, Quiet, Tranquillity*)

Beauty and ugliness, I, 25–6; III, 25, 114–15. Beauty of God, II, 157, 229–33, 360, 361. Beauty, visible and invisible, II, 212
Beginners (*Love, Lovers, Meditation, Night, Purgation*), III, 68, 159–60, 291

361; II, 126, 152, 266–7, 357; III, 200–5, 225, 231, 234–5, 242–3, 252, 267, 279. Detachment of the understanding, I, 82–92. Detachment from things of the spirit as well as from things of sense, I, 83, 84, 422–3. Benefits of detachment, I, 254–7, 263–4, 270–2, 279–81, 287–9, 293, 362–71.

Devil, II, 337–8; III, 199, 202–4, 290. Nature and limitations of his knowledge, I, 153 ff. Limitations of his power, I, 447–53; II, 88, 141–2, 301; III, 100, 193. Deceptions of the Devil in supernatural apprehensions (*Apprehensions, Locutions, Revelations, Visions*), I, 188, 189, 190, 192, 199–204, 227 ff., 284–5, 377. The Devil tempts souls to pride, I, 332, 333; to impurity, I, 339–40. The Devil and the Dark Night of the Spirit, I, 447–53. He is the blind guide of the progressive, III, 82–4, 175–8. He distracts the soul during the Spiritual Betrothal(*Betrothal, Illuminative Way*), II, 124, 262–3, 264–5, 285–6; but is conquered by the proficient, II, 173–6, 381–4. He fears the soul united with God (*Marriage, Union*), III, 231. The Devil represented as Aminadab, II, 173–6, 265, 381–3. Methods of fighting the Devil, III, 202–4.

Difficulty of writing on mystical experience, I, 182; II, 24, 96, 178, 312; III, 13, 53, 103, 145

Directors (*Confessors*)

Discernment of spirits, I, 185–6

Discipline for religious, Use of, III, 258

Dryness(*Aridity*)

Ecstasy (*Rapture*)

Eloquence, Use and abuse of, I, 312–14

Emptiness of the faculties(*Aridity, Detachment, Faculties, Passivity, Quiet, Tranquillity*)

Enemies of the soul(*Devil, Flesh, Trials, World*),III, 199

Envy, Spiritual, I, 347–9, 369

Equality of the soul with God (*Deification, Fruition, Marriage,Participation, Transformation, Union*), II, 88, 120, 164–5, 301, 346, 369; III, 99, 192–3

Essence, Divine (*God, Marriage, Union*), II, 31–3, 187–9, 229, 374–5 ; III, 44–5, 135–6

Essential glory (*Fruition*), II, 370–1

Estimation, Love of, I, 415

Eucharist, Holy (*Communion*), I, 197, 269, 338; II, 428, 432; III, 19, 108

Evil spirits(*Devil, Enemies, Night, Purgation, Trials*)

Evils, Privative and positive, I, 54–5, 249–54

Exercises, Spiritual, I, 331; II, 92, 202, 269, 306, 328

Faculties of the soul (*Contemplation, Passivity, Quiet, Tranquillity*), I, 79–82, 211; II, 39, 40, 98, 104, 106, 126, 139, 140–1, 146, 154, 267, 278, 282, 284, 322, 324–5, 356–7; III, 23–4, 50–1, 61–4, 85–6, 114, 142–3, 154–7, 179, 230, 269. Union of the faculties, II, 165, 369–70

Faculty, Concupiscible, II, 139–40, 283–4

Faith (*Contemplation, Darkness, Illumination, Illuminative Way, Night, Understanding*), I, 63–210, *passim* (especially I, 65–70), 443; II, 63, 117, 191–2, 235–6, 342–3. Faith teaches us about God, I, 232–3; II, 454. By faith the soul journeys to God, II, 192. Faith and understanding (*Understanding*), I, 68; II, 80, 314. Faith as dark night (*Night*), I, 67–74. Faith as proximate means to union with God, I, 93–5

Fancy(*Imagination*), I, 104, 122 ff.; II, 138–9, 282

Favours granted by God to the soul (*Apprehensions,Consolations, Locutions, Revelations, Sweetness,Visions*),II, 66–9, 91–6, 141–2, 240–2, 284–6, 305–6; III, 45–6, 146–7, 279

Fear, Spirit of, II, 96–7, 312–13

Fervour of the soul in contemplation (*Contemplation, Favours, Sweetness*), I, 435–6

Festivals, Ways of keeping (*Ceremonies, Eucharist*),I, 299–301

Flesh as enemy of the soul (*Enemies*),III, 199. Methods of combating the flesh,III, 204–5.

Forgetfulness(*Detachment,Passivity, Tranquillity*)

Fornication, Spirit of, I, 372

Fortitude of the soul (*Boldness,Virtues*),I, 368;II, 43–4, 87–8, 116, 135, 295, 340–1; III, 228, 235

Friendships, Spiritual, I, 341–2

Fruition (*Transformation, Union, Vision of God*),II, 54, 80–1, 88, 145, 175, 192, 217; III, 92, 100–1, 185–6, 194, 231

II. INDEX TO THE PRINCIPAL FIGURES OF SPEECH USED BY ST. JOHN OF THE CROSS

[*Note.*—Scriptural figures are not included in this index except where, besides being introduced as references or quotations, they are developed by the Saint in his argument.]

III. INDEX TO THE SCRIPTURAL QUOTATIONS AND REFERENCES MADE BY ST. JOHN OF THE CROSS

[*Note.*—References are to the Douai Version of the Bible. Where the Authorized Version differs from this, the corresponding chapter and verse references will be found in the footnotes on the pages indicated.]

GENESIS

1: II, 46, 208
2, 24: II, 133, 293
12, 8: I, 306
15, 12–17: III, 56, 148
19, 26: III, 201, 207
21, 13: I, 309
28, 12: I, 434
30, 1: I, 416, 438; II, 53, 216
46, 3–4: I, 141

1, 3: III, 87
8, 9: II, 246
13, 4: I, 306
16, 13: I, 306
21, 8: I, 362
22, 2: I, 307
28, 13–19: I, 306
31, 34–7: I, 292
49, 4: I, 47

1, 31: II, 48, 211
8, 11: II, 151
15, 7: I, 140
17, 1: I, 205
21, 10: I, 27
27, 22: I, 196
29, 20: I, 436
35, 2: I, 31

EXODUS

3–4: I, 203
4, 10: I, 429
8, 7: I, 450
18, 21–2: I, 169, 251
24, 12: I, 306
32, 31–2: I, 439
33, 19: II, 161, 366

33, 22–3: II, 149, 279

34, 30: II, 129, 271

3, 6: I, 364
4, 14–15: I, 167
14, 20: I, 69; II, 426
20, 19: I, 176
27, 8: I, 32
33, 5: I, 362
33, 20: I, 90, 176, 233;
II, 230

34, 2–3: I, 31

34, 40: II, 136

3, 7–8: II, 38, 199
7, 11–22: I, 450
16, 3: I, 397
23, 8: I, 250
32, 7–28: I. 300
33, 12–13: II, 230, 350
33, 22: I, 177;
II, 191;
III, 29, 99, 120
34, 6–7: I, 183; III, 55,
147

LEVITICUS

10, 1–2: I, 32, 300

NUMBERS

11, 4: I, 30
17, 10: I, 32
22, 32: I, 156

11, 5–6: I, 353
22, 7: I, 253

12, 6–8: I, 126
22, 22–3: I, 284

DEUTERONOMY

4, 12, 15: I, 125
30, 20: II, 200
32, 15: I, 250, 251, 252, 253

4, 24: II, 380; III, 36, 127
31, 21: II, 199
32, 33: II, 40, 201

6, 5: I, 243, 408
31, 26: I, 32

JOSUE

6, 21: I, 53

9, 14: I, 162

452

PSALMS

PROVERBS

ECCLESIASTES

CANTICLE OF CANTICLES (A.V., SONG OF SOLOMON)

WISDOM

APOCALYPSE (A.V., REVELATION)

IV. INDEX TO THE PRINCIPAL PERSONS REFERRED TO IN THE INTRODUCTIONS, TEXT AND NOTES OF THIS EDITION

[*Note.*—Twentieth-century writers are not included, nor, with a few exceptions, are religious of the sixteenth and seventeenth centuries except those whose writings or depositions are quoted, mentioned or reproduced. References are not given to the Bibliography. Religious of the Carmelite Order and all saints are indexed under their Christian names; other persons under their surnames.]